W9-BXL-288

MAGILL'S LITERARY ANNUAL

1995

MAGILL'S LITERARY ANNUAL 1995

Essay-Reviews of 200 Outstanding Books Published in the United States during 1994

With an Annotated Categories List

Volume One
A-Mo

Edited by
FRANK N. MAGILL

SALEM PRESS
Pasadena, California   Englewood Cliffs, New Jersey

∞ The paper used in these volumes conforms to the American National Standard for Permanence of Paper for Printed Library Materials, Z39.48_1984.

LIBRARY OF CONGRESS CATALOG CARD NO. 77-99209

ISBN 0-89356-295-5

FIRST PRINTING

PRINTED IN THE UNITED STATES OF AMERICA

PUBLISHER'S NOTE

Magill's Literary Annual, 1995, is the fortieth publication in a series that began in 1954. The philosophy behind the annual has been to evaluate critically each year a given number of major examples of serious literature published during the previous year. Our continuous effort is to provide coverage for works that are likely to be of more than passing general interest and that will stand up to the test of time. Individual critical articles for the first twenty-two years were collected and published in *Survey of Contemporary Literature* in 1977.

For the reader new to the Magill reference format, the following brief explanation should serve to facilitate the research process. The two hundred works represented in this year's annual are drawn from the following categories: fiction; poetry; literary criticism, literary history, and literary theory; essays; literary biography; autobiography, memoirs, diaries, and letters; biography; history; current affairs; science, history of science, and technology; education; ethics and law; fine arts and film; medicine; nature, natural history, and environment; philosophy and religion; psychology; and women's issues. The articles are arranged alphabetically by book title in the two-volume set; a complete list of the titles included can be found at the beginning of volume 1. Following a list of titles are the titles arranged by category in an annotated listing. This list provides the reader with the title, author, page number, and a brief description of the particular work. The names of all contributing reviewers for the literary annual are listed alphabetically in the front of the book as well as at the end of their reviews. At the end of volume 2, there are four cumulative indexes covering works from the years 1977 to 1995: an index of Biographical Works by Subject, the Category Index, the Title Index, and the Author Index. The index of biographical works is arranged by subject rather than by author or title. Thus, readers will be able to locate easily a review of any biographical work published in the Magill annuals since 1977 (including memoirs, diaries, and letters—as well as biographies and autobiographies) by looking up the name of the person. Two new indexes added to this year's Annual are the Category Index and the Title Index. Following the Title Index is the Author Index. Beneath each author's name appear the titles of all of his or her works reviewed in the Magill annuals since 1977. Next to each title, in parentheses, is the year of the annual in which the review appeared, followed by the page number. In all four indexes, titles which appeared in *Magill's History Annual*, 1983, and *Magill's Literary Annual, History and Biography*, 1984 and 1985, are indicated parenthetically by an "H" followed by the year of the Annual in which the review appeared.

Each article begins with a block of top matter that indicates the title, author, publisher, and price of the work. When possible, the year of the author's birth is also provided. The top matter also includes the number of pages of the book, the type of work, and, when appropriate, the time period and locale represented in the text. Next, there is the same capsulized description of the work that appears in the annotated list of titles by category. When pertinent, a list of principal characters or of personages introduces the review.

The articles themselves are approximately two thousand words in length. They are original essay-reviews that analyze and present the focus, intent, and relative success of the author, as well as the makeup and point of view of the work under discussion. To assist the reader further, the articles are supplemented by a list of additional reviews for further study in a bibliographic format.

LIST OF TITLES

LIST OF TITLES

LIST OF TITLES

LIST OF TITLES

TITLES BY CATEGORY

ANNOTATED

TITLES BY CATEGORY

FICTION page

page

TITLES BY CATEGORY

TITLES BY CATEGORY

TITLES BY CATEGORY

POETRY page

LITERARY CRITICISM
LITERARY HISTORY
LITERARY THEORY

TITLES BY CATEGORY

ESSAYS

page

LITERARY BIOGRAPHY

AUTOBIOGRAPHY
MEMOIRS
DIARIES
LETTERS

TITLES BY CATEGORY

BIOGRAPHY

HISTORY

TITLES BY CATEGORY

CURRENT AFFAIRS

SCIENCE
HISTORY OF SCIENCE
TECHNOLOGY

FINE ARTS
FILM

MEDICINE

NATURE
NATURAL HISTORY
ENVIRONMENT

PHILOSOPHY
RELIGION

PSYCHOLOGY

WOMEN'S ISSUES

CONTRIBUTING REVIEWERS FOR 1995 ANNUAL

Michael Adams
Fairleigh Dickinson University

Andrew J. Angyal
Elon College

Stanley Archer
Texas A&M University

Jean W. Ashton
Columbia University

Bryan Aubrey
Maharishi International University

Dean Baldwin
Pennsylvania State University, Erie, Behrend College

Dan Barnett
Butte College

Richard P. Benton
Trinity College, Hartford

Charles Merrell Berg
University of Kansas

Gordon N. Bergquist
Creighton University

Harold Branam
Savannah State College

Gerhard Brand
California State University, Los Angeles

Cynthia K. Breckenridge
Independent Scholar

Peter Brier
California State University, Los Angeles

Jean R. Brink
Arizona State University

David J. Buehrer
Valdosta State University

Jeffrey L. Buller
Georgia Southern University

John Carpenter
University of Michigan

Ethan Casey
Independent Scholar

Thomas J. Cassidy
South Carolina State University

Balance Chow
San Jose State University

C. L. Chua
California State University, Fresno

John J. Conlon
University of Massachusetts at Boston

Peter Crawford
Independent Scholar

Mary Virginia Davis
California State University, Sacramento

Frank Day
Clemson University

Bill Delaney
Independent Scholar

Francine Dempsey
The College of Saint Rose

J. R. Donath
California State University, Sacramento

Michael Duncan
Independent Scholar

William U. Eiland
University of Georgia

Robert P. Ellis
Worcester State College

Robert Faggen
Claremont McKenna College

Rebecca Hendrick Flannagan
Southern Illinois University at Carbondale

Roy C. Flannagan III
Southern Illinois University at Carbondale

Robert J. Forman
St. John's University, New York

Raymond Frey
Centenary College, New Jersey

Ann D. Garbett
Averett College

Leslie E. Gerber
Appalachian State University

Richard Glatzer
Independent Scholar

Louise Grieco
Independent Scholar

Daniel L. Guillory
Millikin University

Donald E. Hall
California State University, Northridge

Terry Heller
Coe College

William L. Howard
Chicago State University

Theodore C. Humphrey
California State Polytechnic University, Pomona

Philip K. Jason
United States Naval Academy

Shakuntala Jayaswal
University of New Haven

Jane Anderson Jones
Manatee Community College

Steven G. Kellman
University of Texas at San Antonio

W. P. Kenney
Manhattan College

Karen A. Kildahl
South Dakota State University

James B. Lane
Indiana University Northwest

Eugene Larson
Los Angeles Pierce College

Leon Lewis
Appalachian State University

Elizabeth Johnston Lipscomb
Randolph-Macon Woman's College

Liesel Litzenburger
Independent Scholar

Janet Lorenz
Independent Scholar

R. C. Lutz
University of the Pacific

Joanne McCarthy
Tacoma Community College

Mark McCloskey
Independent Scholar

Philip McDermott
Independent Scholar

David W. Madden
California State University, Sacramento

Paul Madden
Hardin-Simmons University

Paul D. Mageli
Independent Scholar

Maria Theresa Maggi
University of Idaho

Edward A. Malone
University of Missouri, Rolla

Lois A. Marchino
University of Texas at El Paso

Peter Markus
Independent Scholar

Charles E. May
California State University, Long Beach

Laurence W. Mazzeno
Ursuline College

Kenneth W. Meadwell
University of Winnipeg, Manitoba, Canada

Leslie B. Mittleman
California State University, Long Beach

Robert A. Morace
Daemen College

Robert E. Morsberger
California State Polytechnic University, Pomona

Edwin Moses
Bloomsburg University

Daniel P. Murphy
Hanover College

John M. Muste
Ohio State University

Stella Nesanovich
McNeese State University

George T. Novotny
University of South Florida

Lawrence J. Oliver
Texas A&M University

Lisa Paddock
Independent Scholar

Robert J. Paradowski
Rochester Institute of Technology

David B. Parsell
Furman University

Thomas R. Peake
King College

David Peck
California State University, Long Beach

Cliff Prewencki
Independent Scholar

Elwood Reid
Independent Scholar

Rosemary M. Canfield Reisman
Independent Scholar

Claire J. Robinson
Independent Scholar

Jaclyn Rodriguez
Occidental College

Carl Rollyson
Baruch College of the City University of New York

Joseph Rosenblum
University of North Carolina at Greensboro

Robert L. Ross
University of Texas at Austin

John K. Roth
Claremont McKenna College

Marc Rothenberg
Smithsonian Institution

Edward St. John
Loyola Law School

Barbara Elman Schiffman
Independent Scholar

Barbara Kitt Seidman
Linfield College

R. Baird Shuman
University of Illinois at Urbana-Champaign

Thomas J. Sienkewicz
Monmouth College, Illinois

Marjorie Smelstor
University of Wisconsin—Eau Claire

Harold L. Smith
University of Houston, Victoria

Ira Smolensky
Monmouth College, Illinois

Gerald H. Strauss
Bloomsburg University

James Sullivan
California State University, Los Angeles

Ronald G. Walker
Western Illinois University

Bruce Wiebe
Independent Scholar

John Wilson
Independent Scholar

James A. Winders
Appalachian State University

Michael Witkoski
Independent Scholar

Shawn Woodyard
Independent Scholar

Robert Yahnke
University of Minnesota

MAGILL'S
LITERARY ANNUAL
1995

ACHILLES IN VIETNAM
Combat Trauma and the Undoing of Character

Author: Jonathan Shay (1941-   )
Publisher: Atheneum (New York). 246 pp. $20.00
Type of work: Psychology

While brilliantly sustaining a dialogue between Homer's epic and the testimony of disturbed Vietnam War veterans, Shay aims to persuade people to meet their moral obligations toward those they send to war

Sometimes the most remarkable books come from scholars working at the intersection of two seemingly unrelated fields. Unfettered by a single methodology or disciplinary mind-set, such thinkers can make the kind of discoveries that newly illuminate the human condition and newly perceive its constants and variables. Such a book is Jonathan Shay's *Achilles in Vietnam: Combat Trauma and the Undoing of Character*, a brilliant discussion of the American way of dealing with war's losses that holds in a most provocative tension a reading of Homer's *The Iliad* (c. 800 B.C.) and a clinical familiarity with combat veterans of the Vietnam War suffering from post-traumatic stress disorder (PTSD).

Shay argues that Homer's representation of the combat experiences of his hero (and other characters) includes important insights that have been overlooked by mental health professionals. Clues to the dynamics of combat trauma applicable to veterans of recent wars can be gleaned from the travails of Achilles. Conversely, the testimony of Vietnam War combat soldiers can inform interpretation of *The Iliad*. Above and beyond the symbiosis of these fields of investigation, Shay is concerned with character itself—not character as the consequence of an author's art of characterization, but the essence of personality and personhood. It is not only what is called "sanity" that is at stake, but something more profound.

Shay's chapters lay out essential issues one by one. In "Betrayal of 'What's Right,'" he finds parallel causes of disorientation and despair in his paired texts. Construing an army as "a social construction defined by shared expectations and values," Shay observes the effects on subordinates when leaders betray that moral order. Agamemnon betrays Achilles by commandeering the prize of honor (Briseis) voted to him by the troops. His outrage and disorientation parallel that of many Vietnam veterans who found their sense of "what's right" betrayed by the institution to which they offered their loyalty. That betrayal took many forms, from faulty equipment to supply shortages to a system of rotating officers that kept soldiers in the situation of being led by relative novices. Equipment failure, as Shay points out, is frequent in *The Iliad*, but the Homeric soldier usually supplies his own equipment, so that its failure cannot be felt as a betrayal of trust.

Indeed, throughout his study Shay manages a fine balance of attention between the similarities and contrasts in the lives of warriors separated by twenty-seven centuries. One similarity, a consequence of the "betrayal of *thémis*" (what's right), is the constriction of the soldier's social and moral space. The "us-against-them" outlook creates unusually strong bonds among members of the fighting unit, while it dilutes or destroys all other attachments to the human community. At the far end of this process, the soldier can become an isolated world and law unto himself. Desertion and unusual cruelty to prisoners are typical behaviors that follow from the creation of this shrunken moral sphere. Men of good character, men like Achilles, behave like criminals. The anticredo of the Vietnam War soldier, "Don't mean nothin'," signals the collapse of value in the soldier's inner world and the consequent collapse of good character.

In his discussion of the grieving soldier, Shay drives home essential differences between the Homeric world and the condition of the American soldier in Vietnam. After underscoring once again the special affections that develop among men who share the experience of war, Shay investigates the special relationship between Achilles and Patroklos, counterpointing this analysis with references to the testimony of Vietnam veterans.

The differences that Shay urgently uncovers have to do with the process of grieving. For the Homeric soldier, tears were a natural sign of grief, and exhibitions of grief were not considered unmanly. In American culture, however, these emotions cannot be acted out. Weeping and wailing are signs of losing control that are not tolerated in American military culture and hardly accepted in the culture at large. Bottled up, grief becomes a poison that unbalances and distorts character. *The Iliad* shows a healthy, restorative communalization of grief. Shay points out the significance of the two funerary truces in *The Iliad* as cultural indications of respect for the mourning process. He also reminds readers of how the fallen soldier's comrades retrieved the body and engaged together in the mourning process. Not so in Vietnam, where there was no time to grieve, no ceremonial process, and no prestige in lamentation. Unlike in Homer's world, strangers cared for the dead, and the unit went on as if nothing had happened. Yet something *had* happened, and "thwarted, uncommunalized grief," Shay insists, "is a major reason why there are so many severe, longterm psychological injuries from the Vietnam War." Chief among these injuries is survivor's guilt.

In spite of the opportunity for communal mourning, Achilles' sense of betrayal, grief, and guilt is so strong that he enters into the berserk state. In this state he no longer acts the hero but has stepped over the line that separates valorous action from savage cruelty. Often triggered by "unexpected deliverance from certain death," the berserk state as described by Homer has its direct parallels in the behavior of Vietnam combat veterans who have also experienced betrayal, grief, and guilt. Shay provides several passages of testimony from his patients to underscore the characteristics of this state. Whether the men felt themselves to be godlike or bestial, there is no doubt that they lost their humanity. Fearless, reckless, insensible to pain, they become capable of the worst atrocities. Disconnected from the human community, these men, if they survive, will have a difficult time finding their way back and forgiving themselves.

The berserk rages in *The Iliad*, Shay argues, were of briefer duration than those among Vietnam combat veterans. Furthermore, grief-stricken Homeric soldiers were not urged on by their superiors with the equivalent of "Don't get sad. Get even!" In any case, for Shay the berserk state leads to lifelong psychological injury. Once someone enters this state, that person is changed forever. The episodic recurrence of the berserk state in civilian life is the most extreme consequence of combat trauma.

After finishing his exploration of the sequential phases of combat trauma, Shay attends to a series of associated themes. Principal among these is "dishonoring the enemy" (chapter 6). In *The Iliad*, Shay observes, the enemy is considered worthy of respect. Unlike the "demonized adversary" American soldiers confronted in Vietnam, Achilles and his men faced a foe that they considered valiant. In fact, when Achilles does show a loss of respect for the enemy, Homer points to this as a sign of Achilles' moral disintegration. Only modern habits of mind, Shay asserts, maintain a good-guy-versus-bad-guy response to the Greeks and Trojans. This difference in attitude toward the human worth of the enemy did not change the vehemence with which combat was waged. In Shay's view, however, the demonizing of the enemy contributed to the prolonged post-combat suffering of the Vietnam War veteran: "Restoring honor to the enemy is an essential step in recovery from combat PTSD."

Shay is not blind to the essential differences between combat as represented by Achilles and the experience by American troops in Vietnam. All features cannot be treated by parallel or inversion. The differences, though, only bring further risk to the mental health of modern warriors. In his chapter "What Homer Left Out," Shay summarizes several themes in the testimony of Vietnam War veterans that have no echoes or very weak ones in Homer's portrayal of combat and its consequences. These include shortages and deprivation, friendly fire (accidental exposure to the weapons of one's own forces), fragging (assassination of a superior), prolonged suffering of the wounded, and civilian suffering. Several of these items add to the veteran's sense of betrayal of "what's right," while fragging is a clear instance of reacting to this sense of betrayal. The consequences for the perpetrator of such wartime crimes as gang rape include a later life lacking in intimacy and healthy sexual experience.

In a curious chapter called "Soldier's Luck and God's Will," Shay compares the ways in which the soldiers in Homer's world accounted for actions seemingly beyond their control with the Vietnam veterans' interpretations of similar happenings. He concludes that the Homeric soldiers had an advantage in being able to blame the gods for their hardships and to see the flow of fortune in part as the consequence of the gods' own contests or shifting favoritism. Judeo-Christian culture, on the other hand, posits a loving God: "When war shattered this assumption, American soldiers in Vietnam lost a sustaining idea." With God either absent or without compassion, the possibility of human virtue is diminished. In the following chapter, Shay elaborates his notion that the gods of *The Iliad* may be viewed as a metaphor of social power. The attitudes Vietnam combat veterans had toward military and civilian authorities—those who exercised power at a safe distance from the battlefield—parallel those that Homeric soldiers had toward the gods. Indeed, in the battlefields described by Homer, the leaders experienced the risks and terrors of war. In these chapters, Shay's comparisons provide new perspectives on *The Iliad*, especially when he discusses Homer's ironic treatment of Zeus's supposed concern for humankind.

In his closing chapters, Shay attends most closely to the short- and long-term consequences of combat. Quoting the wife of William Shakespeare's valiant Hotspur, Shay outlines the symptoms of PTSD. He is less concerned with inventorying symptoms, however, than with convincing readers that "prolonged combat can wreck the personality." Nevertheless, Shay reviews such traits as untrustworthiness of perception, amnesia, irrational combat vigilance, depression, and suicidality. Finding no meaning in life, the unhealed veteran becomes unfit for participation in American civic and political enterprises that depend on values, trust, and the democratic struggle for the shape of the future.

Shay offers no easy reassurance about the possibility of healing for the sufferer of combat trauma. Though the betrayed trust and innocence of the veteran cannot be restored, other symptoms can be ameliorated, and many veterans can recover to the point of living lives of personal satisfaction and value to others. Shay insists that healing is done *by* survivors and not *to* survivors. Narrative such as *The Iliad* can make a positive contribution to the healing process, but only if listeners are ready to respect and be changed by the narrator while refraining from passing judgment. Narrative projects, under the proper circumstances, contribute to the beneficial communalization of the trauma.

Shay's burden is to persuade Americans to meet their moral obligations toward those they send to war. That obligation includes caring about "how soldiers are trained, equipped, led, and welcomed home." The costly, devastating character changes associated with PTSD can be prevented or reduced if Americans demand that their military take a number of steps. These include protecting unit cohesion, valuing griefwork, avoiding the encouragement of berserking, eliminating intentional injustice as a motivational technique, respecting the enemy's humanity, and acknowledging (rather than denying) psychiatric casualties.

Short of ending warfare as a way of solving problems, Shay calls upon readers to assert their own humanity in ways that lessen the damage Americans do to their own people. He is asking us to refuse complicity in the kind of betrayal that robs individuals and society of physical and moral well-being. Shay's voice is informed and impassioned. *Achilles in Vietnam* should be required reading for all present and future government and military leaders. It is a valuable and inspirational text for all citizens.

Philip K. Jason

Sources for Further Study

Booklist. XC, April 1, 1994, p. 1415.
Choice. XXXII, November, 1994, p. 508.
Kirkus Reviews. LXII, March 15, 1994, p. 382.
Library Journal. CXIX, April 1, 1994, p. 120.

The New York Times. June 13, 1994, p. C15.
The New Yorker. LXX, September 26, 1994, p. 114.
Publishers Weekly. CCXLI, March 7, 1994, p. 58.
The Virginia Quarterly Review. LXX, Autumn, 1994, p. 770.
The Wall Street Journal. May 16, 1994, p. A16.
The Washington Post Book World. XXIV, June 5, 1994, p. 17.

THE AFTERLIFE AND OTHER STORIES

Author: John Updike (1932-)
Publisher: Alfred A. Knopf (New York). 316 pp. $24.00
Type of work: Short stories

John Updike's eleventh short-story collection, his first in seven years, contains twenty-two stories, most of which originally appeared in The New Yorker

No other living writer is so unmistakably identified with that well-known brand of modern fiction called *The New Yorker* story as John Updike is. A master of lyrical prose style, minimalist plot, and ennuied character, Updike seems to have always been there waiting for readers in the thickly textured and inconspicuously placed columns of *The New Yorker*'s slick, cartoon-populated pages. Thus, it was inevitable, although it is still disconcerting to discover, that this former "whiz kid" of the smooth and subtle prose style has grown old. It was only a matter of time after the death of his best-known character creation, Rabbit Angstrom, that Updike would infuse the short-story form—of which he has always been a consummate master—with his own experience of middle age.

The title of this collection of short fictions, also the title of the first story, reflects a typical Updike irony: Instead of alluding to some metaphysical realm, Updike's "afterlife" is that ambiguous human condition just past middle age. In fact, midlife is such a pervasive theme of these stories that the primary Library of Congress search key for the book is "Middle-aged persons—United States—Fiction." Updike, in his sixties, has written here about men mostly in their fifties and sixties, who have entered such a state with, if not joy, at least graceful acceptance.

Carter Billings, the fiftyish hero of the title story, is startled to discover that many of his friends are doing sudden, surprising things in their middle age. When he and his wife go to visit one such couple who have moved to England, Billings has an incidental encounter with his own mortality that unsettles his settled ways. Waking up one night to go to the bathroom in the strange house, he tumbles down the stairs until the oval knob of a banister post strikes him a solid blow in the center of his chest. The ache all the next day makes him feel delicate, alert, and excited. As is typical of the modern short story, although the incident is minor and domestic, it is symbolic of something more serious. As a result, Billings thinks of his life as merely going through the motions and realizes with chagrin that there are vast areas of the world about which he no longer cares.

His impulsive purchase of an expensive eighteenth century bureau made of elm burl is also a simple domestic act, but it signifies his shift to flirting with the surprising and the unpredictable. As Billings and his wife make their way back to the home of their friends after some sightseeing, a fierce Atlantic storm strikes. Billings perceives a "miraculous lacquer" over each roadside twig, each reed of thatch in the roofs, each tiny daisy in the grass, and thinks of the sensitive center of his chest as being the seal of a nocturnal pact, a passport to this particular day. Thus, when the Billingses arrive home to find his friend worried about them, Billings, having had his epiphany, muses that they are all beyond that now. "The Afterlife" is a typical delicate Updike story, lyrical, low-key, and resonant with realization.

"A Sandstone Farmhouse," the longest story in the collection and first-place winner of the 1991 O. Henry Award, is also understated, lyrical, and elegiac. The structure of the piece is simple and predictable: Joey, fifty-four, must "deal with" his mother's possessions that have accumulated in the old farmhouse where she was born and has recently died—a plot premise that presages a nostalgic focus on the past. As Joey goes through his mother's effects, she comes alive to him as a young woman with a life of hope and desire of her own. Comparing his own transitory life in Manhattan to the solidity of the stone building where his mother lived, Joey discovers that although he had always wanted to be where the action was, it turned out that what action there was had been there in the farmhouse.

Although these stories reflect quiet recognition and acceptance, some of them convey a sad sense of having irrevocably passed important milestones. In "Conjunctions," Geoffrey Parrish, approaching sixty, finds through his new telescope a "small comfortable place in the spangled void" of the winter sky, where Jupiter and Mars seem to trace some movement of "titanic gears." The relationship of the planets is a metaphor for the mystery of his relationship with his wife, which began with romance under the stars but which, inevitably, seems now to be like a wound that has nearly healed. In "Short Easter," Fogel is sixty-two; aware that retirement is drawing close, he finds all sorts of reasons for irritation. The increasing failures of his body anger him; he is becoming more and more absent-minded; he wishes that he had a younger wife. Nothing "happens" in the story except that on Easter—the traditional holiday of rebirth—he sneaks into his son's old room to take a nap. When he awakens alone and disoriented, he looks around the room to find everything in its place, yet something also "immensely missing."

Yet discontent is not the theme most heard in these stories; rather, it is a sense of security, nostalgia, and comfort. In "Falling Asleep Up North," a middle-aged man getting over a bout of sleeplessness recalls a trip with his family to Expo 67. He ponders that as humans age, the distinctions between being asleep and being awake fade; furthermore, he is comfortably reconciled to the fact that as humans age their drift becomes southerly, because going north is unnecessary effort. In "The Brown Chest," a man charts the various moves of an old wooden chest until it finally comes to rest, along with other old pieces of furniture, in a barn that he owns. Less a story than a sort of metaphoric meditation, the piece closes when his grown son wants to look at some of the furniture with a young woman he plans to marry. When the man's future daughter-in-law inevitably asks to open the chest, out sweeps the smell of family, "family without end."

Updike also likes to play in these short stories, to create a new spin on an old myth. For example, "Tristan and Iseult" is like a finger exercise, a simple description of a man having his teeth cleaned by a hygienist. The story playfully explores the threat of pain that is the "mystical spice to these liaisons," the fact that no one knows his hidden shame as well as the hygienist does, and the basic principle that lies between them like a sword—that she is always a stranger. "Brother Grasshopper" is a variant on the old fable of the ant and the grasshopper, ending with the protagonist scattering the ashes of his grasshopper friend. Rather than teaching the lesson of storing up food for the winter, however, Updike's fable ends with the more prudent friend recalling the grasshopper's focus on his family as priceless—"treasure, stored up against the winter that had arrived."

In "The Journey to the Dead," a variant on the Greek myth of Persephone, a dying woman makes a man realize that "the dead hate us and we hate the dead." She so frightens him with the reality of death that he flees her as he might the Gorgon's head from Hades. In "Cruise," a man meets a modern-day Calypso on a voyage through the Mediterranean that purports to follow Ulysses' famous journey home in Homer's *The Odyssey* (c. 800 B.C.). In what she claims is the last gasp of his youth, Calypso tells the middle-aged protagonist to stay with her and he will never die. Since, being a mere mortal, he cannot stand the monotony of eternity, he rejects her siren call, but he is unable to be sure that he has made the right decision.

"Farrell's Caddie" is a playful, satiric game in which an American man plays golf at the Royal Caledonian Links in Scotland attended by a most unusual caddie, who gives him advice not only about what club to use but also about his marriage, his financial investments, and a female subordinate who has been flattering him. Peppered with thick Scottish brogue and wry humor, the story is little more than fluff, but as always with Updike, it is shrewd fluff. "The Man Who Became a Soprano" is a geometrically precise treatment of a small group of suburbanites who form a recorder group and find a momentary sense of transcendent meaning in the music they create.

Also relatively light are the two stories "Aperto, Chiuso" and "Bluebeard in Ireland"—travel stories about a couple named George and Vivian, who, approaching the irrevocable turning points of age sixty and forty respectively, are showing their nerves. Anyone who has traveled to a foreign country with a spouse will recognize the irritability that overtakes those who are at the mercy of an unfamiliar culture. Near the end of "Bluebird in Ireland," when Vivian accuses George one more time of getting them lost and declares that she will not move another step, he wryly imagines her body weakening and dying there, her skin and bones being washed away by the weather until they blend into the earth. As they laboriously trudge through the Irish landscape in search of their car, the thought of death for either of them feels exalting to George in this biblical wilderness of a land emptied by famine and English savagery. The story ends in a comic/serious scene: Vivian has to urinate alongside the roadside, and the scent of ammonia rising from the turf makes George momentarily think, "Let's have a baby," only to admit to himself that they are too old.

Practically all the stories here echo some new Updike realization about the inevitability of growing older. In one, a character experiences the return of the childhood phenomenon of the mutability of things—the transformation of a chair into an animal with long legs, or the sense that a totally dark room is full of teeming presences about to bite him. In another, a man watches another man sleep and is struck by the tragic dignity of the supine male form, like that of a stone knight eroding on a tomb. In still another story, a man is obsessed with eating as the only way he has left to intersect with the world; fearing that his life is too small, he tries to fill the sense of emptiness within him.

It is inevitable that the last story in this collection about the grace and joy of growing older would be entitled "Grandparenting." Given the nature of divorce and the reconstituted family in the modern era, however, the joys of becoming a grandparent are not so simple as they once were. There is a kind of comic nostalgia and tenderness in this story about two divorced parents coming together to witness the birth of their first grandchild. Such an event not only mandates memories of the past, when they were parents of their own child, but also points toward the future, when the grandchild will once more unite them in a way that is perhaps sounder than their marriage had been. New husbands, old wives, new sons-in-law, old memories meet in hospital waiting rooms and motels, waiting and watching for a new birth that unites them in spite of the pain of the past. The last line of the story, and the book, is an appropriate coda to this collection of the elder Updike at his finest. As the grandfather holds the child to his chest more weakly than the infants he called his own, he knows, "Nobody belongs to us, except in memory."

Charles E. May

Sources for Further Study

Booklist. XCI, September 15, 1994, p. 84.
Chicago Tribune. November 20, 1994, XIV, p. 3.
Los Angeles Times. November 14, 1994, p. E5.
National Review. XLVI, December 31, 1994, p. 64.
The New York Review of Books. XLII, January 12, 1995, p. 20.
The New York Times Book Review. XCIX, November 6, 1994, p. 7.
Publishers Weekly. CCXLI, September 5, 1994, p. 88.
Time. CXLIV, November 14, 1994, p. 96.
USA Today. November 17, 1994, p. D5.
The Washington Post. October 26, 1994, p. C2.

AGAINST THE EVIDENCE
Selected Poems, 1934-1994

Author: David Ignatow (1914-   )
Publisher: Wesleyan University Press/University Press of New England (Hanover, New Hampshire). 178 pp. $30.00; paperback $14.95
Type of work: Poetry

Sixty years of biting and poignant urban lyricism from David Ignatow, arranged chronologically, challenge readers with a distinctive aesthetic integrity as relevant today as it was when he began writing

A small volume of David Ignatow's poems not included in this collection, *The Animal in the Bush: Poem on Poetry*, opens with the following lines: "I dig black hunks out of myself, making way for light and air./ I admire the ugliness of the pieces, bulky and shapeless, and set them/ on a mantlepiece for study." This odd little metapoem is as much a precise statement of Ignatow's aesthetic and poetic objective as it is an inaccurate one. One could also say that the effect of reading his collected poetry is much like being stuck in an Edward Hopper painting, hunched over a bleak counter, resigned to no coffee and a flat, two-dimensional existence. Such a self-conscious and unromantic sensibility is strikingly postmodern at the same time that it is elegiac of a period of American life and sensibility gone by. It is also unpredictable, in that just when readers might think they know what is coming, they get a strong, hard curveball. The certainty of the surprise curve is actually a defining feature of this collection, spanning seven decades of poetic achievement. Ignatow writes in a voice that chases its tail and watches itself do so vigilantly, fiercely, a characteristic that has prompted critics to praise and criticize him for decades.

Those who have heard the stories of their grandparents or great-grandparents who immigrated from Europe to work in the cities and factories of the eastern United States in the first two decades of the twentieth century have a link to the sensibility about industrial work and the alienation it can cause which fuels Ignatow's poetry. It is this version or channel of history, no matter what decade of this century the poems have been written in, that informs his vision. What then, have younger poets and readers of poetry to learn from him, in a society running at breakneck technological speed down the information superhighway, reinventing the concept of history itself as human beings race through their lives? Surprisingly, or perhaps predictably enough (depending on one's point of view), there is plenty to learn. Robert Bly commented twenty years before this collection that of his generation of poets (Theodore Roethke, Robert Lowell, John Berryman, Karl Shapiro), Ignatow "is the only [one] to whom the young have rallied." He bases his contention on another fascinating observation that seems to illuminate a driving force in Ignatow's sensibility: "Ignatow notices human emotions are not becoming less insistent, but more insistent, and they have a greater influence on events. As western man sinks nearer to his instincts, his emotions become more demanding." Twenty years after Bly made this remark, the phenomenon he articulated has become, if anything, even more insistent, and it is the rising pitch of this phenomenon that makes Ignatow's poetry riveting and keeps it as far away as imaginable from being obsolete. However "unpleasant" or "raw" it may make readers feel at times, it is always honest about feeling the pulse of this elemental reaction forced on Westerners by the living conditions of their culture.

Ignatow's poems are tightly knitted together. His "confessional explorations of the private self" travel the length of the instinctual scale in such a way that pulling one line out seems to ensure that its strangeness or humor or haunting image will deflate once outside the powerful context of juxtaposition in which it thrives. Discussing the personal voice and vision of existence driving these poems seems especially important, since they do not offer themselves up willingly to line-by-line explication. In spite of the fact that the poet makes much in his preface of the reorganization of his work by decade as opposed to the thematic and less chronological nature of earlier collections, the dynamic of mood and voice is what unifies more than sixty years of poetic craft.

The best way to describe this ingenious roller coaster, which is simultaneously minimal and convoluted, is to look at some poems that break the back of any other attempt to impose a scheme on them. Ultimately, David Ignatow does not "soften with age" or "harden with age" or move away from one subject and back toward another. He has one subject: the opaque inevitability of death and the dances people do around it. These urban "dances" celebrate the rare sense of connectedness that meaningful, creative labor brings while being astutely aware that meaningless, life-sucking toil robs human beings of the life force even before death can get around to it. The poems, early, middle, or late, are always insistent, and alternately haunting, violent, amusing, and terse in their mirroring of people's attempts to delay or welcome or dread what is unavoidable for breathing, mortal creatures.

Sometimes such a dance takes the form of surreal narrative, as in "The Briefcases," a poem written during the 1960's. The poem begins with the narrative dislocation "It was then that," which is repeated when women, as well as men, are "prohibited" from "carrying briefcases . . . in public as a mark of impotence." The strangest turn of the narrative comes with the revelation that the women's briefcases hold "tiny men/ packed neatly in small cartons/ to be opened in private homes." Inside this vivid image of sexual politics is the same concern for death that is revealed more blatantly and openly in other poems. Loving is an act of surrender on frighteningly intimate terms with impotence, as death is, and is imaged powerfully in the lines that follow: "Oh the little men danced on the tables/ and kissed the lips of the women/ who gave their lips to be kissed, and the tall men who carried the briefcases/ withdrew into the dark rooms of the houses." The strange attractors of birth and death are "married" in the end of the poem, when the speaker tells us he could not say for sure how this all ended, but he did "hear/ that the women chose to live/ and the once little men and/ those withdrawn into the dark/ gave birth." If such an ending seems unexpected, it is important to note that such surprising disjunction is Ignatow's signature way of ending his poems.

Such images as the tiny men are memorable because they are delivered in a stark, colloquial reporting style. Thirty years later, Ignatow's characteristic brand of black humor, which seeks to heighten this "realistic" style of diction until it and the scenes it describes become absurd, is seen in the short prose poem "Here I Am with Mike," dedicated to Dan Rather. The speaker is evidently a persona of the famous newscaster:

> Here I am, with mike in hand, shooting down the rapids in my business suit, broadcasting to the world my sensations as I near my death. Occasionally you hear me blubber, a wave having knocked against my mouth. But it all gets said, though when I plunge over the falls the force of it will knock the mike out of my hand. In the meantime, I keep my head, reporting myself in fear, fright and elation at the experience I could have only by shortening my life. I'm enjoying it all.

Ignatow named the collection for a poem from the 1960's with a similar combination of death's grim inevitability and the individual artistic stand in the face of it. "Against the Evidence" is perhaps less strange and more straightforward, though it is an equally voyeuristic look at an idiosyncratic, self-contained sense of isolation that attempts to claim universal sway over human existence—in effect, it is human existence, according to Ignatow. Though some postmodern critics wish not to concern themselves with the author's intention at all, Ignatow's poems scream insistence on such individual proclamation. While his narrative style and accompanying images may startle with their apparently postmodern disconnectedness, the sum of such images is not to assert or proclaim disconnectedness as a state of being. "Against the Evidence" is an important case in point. It begins with a somewhat surreal image that might appear to indicate the absolute autonomy of the text: "As I reach up to close each book/ lying on my desk it/ leaps up to snap at my fingers." Inside the narrative of the "biting book," he muses that he "believe[s] [he] often thinks their thoughts for them (the books)" and that he never knows where "theirs leave off and [his own] begin." Yet the poem does not end with a vindication of this disclaimer, which might seem further enforced by the odd and beautifully syllogistic lines that echo each other by claiming, "Nothing must be said of estrangement/ among the human race and yet/ nothing is said at all/ because of that." Instead, the poem ends with an unadorned, even raw attempt to vitiate such abstract complexities, and it is this very rawness that identifies an Ignatow ending. Since no book will help, despite his love and awe for them, the speaker of the poem declares:

> I stroke my desk,
> its wood so smooth, so patient and still.
> I set a typewriter on its surface
> and begin to type
> to tell myself my troubles.
> Against the evidence, I live by choice.

In the *Contemporary Authors New Revision Series*, volume 31 (1990), Ignatow reiterates the intention voiced in "Against the Evidence," showing the poem to be another articulation of the vision that shapes this late collection of his life's work: "My avocation is to stay alive; my vocation is to write about it; my motivation embraces both intentions and my viewpoint is gained from a study and activity in both ambitions."

If such a statement might not be considered explicitly hopeful, it is certainly a compelling embrace of existence, despite its elemental and sharply tuned delivery. Throughout his long career, Ignatow has been noticed for such bald statements of intention or fact, characteristically placed at the end of his poems. Often they are not as "hopeful" as this one, but always they seem determined to brandish the opaque quality of flat, personal statement, which either closes down or invites connection to the reader independently of its own intent, or even more strangely, because of it.

Within this aesthetic consistency, there is an interesting range of suitable subjects, as well as a range of treatment of those subjects. In the second poem by the title "In a Dream," the poet describes himself at the age of fifty meeting his eighteen-year-old self on the steps of his father's house, longing for deliverance "into his own life." The fifty-year-old self tries to tell the eighteen-year-old that "nothing will turn out right," that he will want to "avenge [himself] on those close to [him] especially," and that he will become a "passionate stranger," even to himself. The response? "My eighteen year old self stands up/ from the concrete steps and says,/ Go to hell/ and I walk off." That the poem allows no reconciliation between the young and the old because it would not be "natural" or "authentic," even in a dream, is perhaps one reason that Ignatow's voice seems hauntingly relevant to younger readers. Yet the process of how one's experience of authenticity changes almost nightmarishly as one ages is powerfully expressed. The wisdom, the sadness, the acceptance of the wild ride "down the rapids" (with or without Dan Rather) is visited yet again.

Perhaps the poems that veer furthest away from such stark exactitude or naturalistic determinism are the ones about trees, leaves, and human hair. These natural objects seem to possess a magical quality for Ignatow, evoking a brand of shameless paganism wherein death is not feared but accepted peacefully, at least by those without human self-reflexivity, such as the trees. In these poems it seems that the best of humankind can be found in people's willingness to imitate other living things. Noteworthy examples include "Their Mouths Full," "Behind His Eyes," and "One Leaf," though these are certainly not the only ones worth mentioning. The "pagan," somewhat Heraclitean philosophy espoused in this set of mostly later poems (from the 1980's and beyond) is definitively expressed in the prose poem "Of That Fire," though it has no trees in it. It begins: "Inside I am on fire. Imagine, though, coming up to City Hall and asking if there is a Department of Burning Need, ready for emergency, I am the emergency." Later in the poem he imagines that "the cops will ask [him] sarcastically 'Where is the fire?'" The speaker pleads guilty, admitting publicly that he has "no evidence but [his] spoken word, and all the while . . . the cop, the judge and jury, too, are burning within, with not a shred of evidence either." Though they laugh and think him "crazy" and themselves "sane," the speaker ends by claiming that they do not know "they are dying in the fire that was lit in them, born of that fire." This beautiful and consuming image of the life force works masterfully to combine humor and poetic vision seamlessly, a rare accomplishment in contemporary poetry.

For readers who may believe that reading these poems by decade does not necessarily augment understanding of Ignatow's evolution as a poet, there remains a curveball to be thrown as a closing comment. In the "Poems of the Eighties" section there is a small gem titled "Above Everything," which, placed where it is in this volume, becomes a comment that readers would not understand so powerfully other than in chronological order. It begins: "I wished for death often/ but now that I am at its door/ I have changed my mind about the world./ It should go on; it is beautiful,/ even as a dream, filled with water and seed." Such an exquisite retraction of the dominant preoccupation with death as an absolute in many of the poems, especially the earlier ones, is breathtaking evidence that Ignatow refuses to fall prey to the limits of his own sensibility. He promises that should he remember this life in the next, he will "praise it above everything." This willingness to reflect and embrace comes mostly in the later poems and punctuates the very end of the book with a poem titled "The Life." Although human beings are still in a quirky aesthetic world in which resting after love is like being a water bug, the poet is no longer in a hurry to "catch at [his] prey, the poem that like the victim of the water bug would affirm [his] life." Instead, he prefers to lose his "sense of self in this watery support," declaring, with yet another surprising ending to nearly seven decades of poetry, "Let this be the life of love."

Nobody can throw a curve like that and not be remembered with the kind of coded admiration that writers give one another as they examine one another's words. *Against the Evidence: Selected Poems, 1934-1994* both evokes and deserves the thoughtful attention that constitutes the highest respect one author can give another.

Maria Theresa Maggi

Sources for Further Study

Booklist. XC, February 1, 1994, p. 990.

Library Journal. CXIX, March 15, 1994, p. 75.

Poetry. CLXV, January, 1995, p. 219.

The Virginia Quarterly Review. LXX, Summer, 1994, p. 99.

AIR AND FIRE

Author: Rupert Thomson (1955-   )
First published: 1993, in Great Britain
Publisher: Alfred A. Knopf (New York). 310 pp. $23.00
Type of work: Novel
Time: The 1890's
Locale: Baja, Mexico

A chronicle of a French couple's sojourn in a frontier landscape

Principal characters:
SUZANNE VALENCE, a young Frenchwoman
THÉOPHILE VALENCE, her husband, an engineer
WILSON PHARAOH, an American prospector
CAPTAIN FÉLIX MONTOYA, a Mexican aristocrat

Of Rupert Thomson's novels, *Dreams of Leaving* (1988) and *Five Gates of Hell* (1991), the latter best foreshadows the highly literary characters and style of Rupert Thomson's *Air and Fire*. The structure of this novel, moreover, proceeds in the framework of a three-month period and through a balance of obsessions.

The focal protagonist of *Air and Fire* is Suzanne Valence, for it is through her that one is meant to judge the rationalism of her husband, Théophile, as a failure, and it is because of her that the characters Wilson Pharaoh and Félix Montoya round out the male obsessions in the novel.

Air and Fire reminds one of Gustave Flaubert's *Madame Bovary* (1857; English translation, 1886), for Emma Bovary and Suzanne Valence have genteel if provincial French backgrounds, both are restless, both marry men of science (Emma a doctor, Suzanne an engineer) who are blind to their wives' needs, and both women ignite the passions of aristocrats and follow their own passions to the threshold of death.

Beyond these, Suzanne Valence has the chance for the kind of travel that Emma Bovary does not. A protégé of Gustave Eiffel, Théophile Valence is sent by him to construct an iron church in Santa Sofía, an impromptu town in Baja, Mexico, on the Sea of Cortez. With the "two thousand, three hundred and forty-eight component parts" of this church stowed on the steamer S.S. *Korrigan*, Théo, having let Suzanne accompany him, sets out on this journey, which for him is a task of measurable difficulties and for Suzanne is a wondrous adventure. She even relishes the perilous detour of the ship around Cape Horn.

In its rawness and heat, the environment into which Suzanne disembarks fills her with interest in it, its people, and sex. By this time, however, Théo, fifteen years older than she and obsessed with erecting his church, cannot relieve her, and she is drawn to Wilson Pharaoh, an American drifter, and even to Félix Montoya, a Mexican aristocrat. Of these two, Wilson is an idealist and Montoya a tyrant. These traits govern their love for Suzanne. It is during April that she journeys to and begins to settle in Santa Sofía, adjusting to Calle Francesca in the French quarter of town, and Suzanne also conducts Wilson and Montoya to the center of the plot in this month, because they fall in love with her.

May, the second time frame of the novel, begins as Montoya invites the Valences to tea (meaning Suzanne, to whom he gives the invitation) and ends as Théo asks Wilson to look after his wife in the name of his "friendship" with her. The June section begins with Montoya's love letter to Suzanne and ends with Wilson's return from the desert into which Suzanne has fled and from which Théo has begged him to rescue her.

The news of Montoya's death by mutilation and lynching, brought on by his tyrannical nature, and Wilson's preparation to sail north to San Diego, which his idealistic nature anticipates, are important features of the July—or concluding—part of the novel. The use of Wilson and Montoya to help bracket, and at the end bolster, the time line of *Air and Fire* shows how critical they are to the plot, just as their desire for Suzanne is critical to revealing their true natures.

Although he is a prospector, Wilson cannot "imagine being rich." "The idea of gold . . . the looking for it" defines him, not its possession. Suzanne is the human form of gold to him, continually to be moved toward rather than obtained. Suzanne fails to see how awful it is for him to translate Montoya's love letter for her, so he drinks himself into a raving melancholy and vanishes into the desert. Nevertheless, he cannot shake his love for Suzanne. When she herself retreats into the desert, thinking that this will save Montoya from being killed, as she dreams he will be, Wilson follows her. He does not rescue her so much, in fact, as play out his sense of her, not only seeing her head on the ground in a nimbus (or saintly halo) of crystals he mistakes for gold but also burying what he thinks is her corpse in the lake at Mission San Ignacio.

Montoya, on the other hand, wants Suzanne so badly that he is willing to kill to get her. She is flattered by his attention and curious about its intensity. With Théo too absorbed by his work to protect her, she lets herself be driven alone to Montoya's house for tea. He has, however, "prepared a feast for her . . . She felt almost crushed by the weight of the food." Later, he demands that she desert Théo: "We could go now. My carriage is waiting behind the rocks." When she refuses, he shoots his horse. Even later, his invitation to go for a ride with him on the submarine he has had renovated for his use has all the subtlety of a subpoena. Suzanne is enchanted by the underside of the Sea of Cortez, though, until Montoya all but rapes her. Her anger saves her from him, but not from his cruel self-assurance: "He's old," he says of Théo. "Soon he'll be dead . . . And then . . . I'll be waiting."

Suzanne's love itself is pure. Unlike her literary forebear, Emma Bovary, she genuinely loves her husband. Because of this, she can neither give in to Montoya's siege of her body and heart nor understand Wilson Pharaoh's need for her desire. Still, since Théo has failed her own desire, she masturbates, entertains Montoya's advances, and overindulges Wilson's friendship, for she has him play the piano for her in the afternoons, cooks for him, paints a rose on the cast of his broken foot, and goes on a fishing trip with him.

Suzanne's nature is more complex, however, than her need for love and adventure.

She has dreams that prophesy death. She has the first of these when she is a child; she dreams her doll falls down a slope. Shortly after this, she and her friend Claire sneak aboard a barge loaded with apples, on top of which Claire loses her footing and dies sliding to the bottom. Suzanne has many other dreams that give her a glimpse of the future in general, but after she marries Théo and has sex with him, the dreams disappear—that is, until sex itself disappears from her life in Santa Sofía. Then her prophetic dreams come back, notably the one she has about Montoya, which at first shows two Indian women dancing in his uniform and later shows Montoya being crucified by Indians who have gone on a rampage.

So Suzanne is a mysterious character who shimmers between the greedy love of Félix Montoya and the generous love of Wilson Pharaoh. She stands for an extreme romanticism balancing the extreme rationalism that her husband represents.

Symbols, indeed, are basic to the style of *Air and Fire*, and they are always associated with its characters. For example, La Huesuda ("the Bony One") is a whore whom Wilson Pharaoh sleeps with early in the novel. Her balcony is a symbol of her, for it is rickety; it collapses under Wilson's weight, proving as dangerous as La Huesuda proves to be later in the story. When Wilson rebuilds her balcony at the end, he is rebuilding his relationship with her—with the town, really—unlike Théo, whose iron church remains a shambles after an Indian uprising wrecks it following an accident in one of the French mines.

The church itself is a symbol of the rationalism embedded in Théo's character, useless to his wife and to the Indians, whose sense of life is rooted in chance and nature. In Suzanne's case, water symbolizes her need to be fluid, pure, submerged, and fulfilled.

For Wilson, gold and Suzanne herself (including her red-blond hair, reminding him of Saffron, a woman he has carried a love for since he was sixteen) symbolize the beauty toward which his life must move in order to mean anything. In a way, gold and Suzanne are interchangeable for Wilson; he sees "her skin like gold lifted dripping from a river" and "her head crowned in gold, which was the way he had always imagined her."

Often such symbols incorporate extremes, such as Montoya's uniform, which shows his conceit, and his submarine, which shows his perversion of the rational. One symbol, however, in the story is fitted to moderation, and it is Dr. Emile Bardou's waistcoats. They are gorgeous; one, for example, is "cream silk brocade . . . overlaid with a tracery of ferns in palest green and gold"; another is "raspberry, peppermint and gold"; yet another "resembled a garden in summer: pale-gold roses planted in a field of green." The Indians in the uprising loot the doctor's waistcoats, thinking that they will magically protect them from harm. They are wrong, for the waistcoats are not supernatural but symbolize the beauty of nature brought into balance with art and the useful logic that Bardou represents as a doctor.

Thomson's less structural tropes are pleasant surprises in themselves. Of La Huesuda's anger at Wilson Pharaoh, for example, Thomson writes, "His clothes flew from the dark hole of her room like dirt scratched by a cat." He says of Suzanne, "She could see a section of the coastline. It looked like a biscuit; if she reached out and touched it, it would crumble." Of Théo's mother he says, "She resembled an engine of war that could be wheeled onto any battlefield and would always find the weakest point."

Air and Fire does not limit its audience. It has romance, adventure, and exotic locales for those who wish to be entertained, and characters and a style saturated with significance for those who wish to be enriched. The wide aim of such a novel is hard to achieve, but Rupert Thomson has done it.

Mark McCloskey

Sources for Further Study

Booklist. XC, December 15, 1993, p. 739.
The Christian Science Monitor. February 10, 1994, p. 13.
Kirkus Reviews. LXI, November 1, 1993, p. 1352.
Library Journal. CXVIII, November 15, 1993, p. 101.
London Review of Books. XV, July 8, 1993, p. 19.
The New York Times Book Review. XCIX, March 13, 1994, p. 18.
The New Yorker. LXX, March 28, 1994, p. 115.
Publishers Weekly. CCXL, November 29, 1993, p. 54.
The Times Literary Supplement. April 9, 1994, p. 21.
The Washington Post. XXIV, January 21, 1994, p. G2.

THE AKHMATOVA JOURNALS
Volume I, 1938-41

Author: Lydia Chukovskaya (1907-)
First published: Zapiski ob Anne Akhmatovoy (1938-1941), Vol. 1, 1989, in Russia
Translated from the Russian by Milena Michalski and Sylva Rubashova
Poetry translated by Peter Norman
Publisher: Farrar Straus Giroux (New York). 310 pp. $27.50
Type of work: Literary memoir
Time: 1938-1941
Locale: Russia

Lydia Chukovskaya's work tells the story of the great poet Anna Akhmatova's struggle to survive and write during one of the most difficult periods of Russian history

Principal personages:
ANNA AKHMATOVA, one of the great poets of the twentieth century
LYDIA CHUKOVSKAYA, her close friend and supporter
LEV GUMILYOV, the son of Anna Akhmatova and Nikolay Gumilyov
OSIP MANDELSTAM, a poet and friend of Akhmatova who died in a camp after his arrest on political charges
MARINA TSVETAEVA, a poet and Akhmatova's contemporary
BORIS PASTERNAK, a poet, novelist, and memoirist who aided Akhmatova at great risk to himself

In Russia, poets enjoy the kind of popularity that Western cultures reserve for film and rock stars. Like many other Russian children, Lydia Chukovskaya read and memorized poetry from an early age, and her favorite poet was Anna Akhmatova. Lydia's father, Korney Chukovsky, a well-known writer of children's stories and a literary critic, took his thirteen-year-old daughter to meet Akhmatova, and Lydia was overwhelmed that she was meeting her idol in person. In 1938, Chukovskaya met Akhmatova once again, in Leningrad, and she was to become Akhmatova's close friend and confidante. Chukovskaya's *The Akhmatova Journals* begin with that meeting and go on to describe the way Akhmatova and other Russians struggled to survive during the Stalinist era, a time of wholesale persecution and mass murder during which no Russian was safe.

Students of Akhmatova's life and work are fortunate that Chukovskaya's diaries were written and survived. Chukovskaya was accepted by Akhmatova both because of her loyal support and because she had a vast knowledge and intuitive grasp of Russian literature. As their friendship developed, Akhmatova came to rely on Chukovskaya's help not only with the difficulties of daily life in one of the darkest eras of Russian history, but also with advice regarding the poet's work. Chukovskaya helped Akhmatova organize her works for publication, check and correct proofs of her works, and determine how the works should be punctuated. Ultimately, however, Chukovskaya provided the most important service to Akhmatova and her readers by memorizing Akhmatova's works, thereby ensuring their survival in an era when many of the poet's greatest works could not be committed to paper because of the political persecution that would be sure to follow. In a ritual that recurs throughout the journals, Chukovskaya would study a poem until she had memorized it, after which Akhmatova would light a match and burn the manuscript.

Anna Akhmatova's life had not always been one of suffering and deprivation. Born in 1889 into the aristocratic Gorenko family, Akhmatova fell in love with poetry early on, and she never considered being anything except a poet. She took the name Akhmatova when her father told her that her poetry would bring shame to the Gorenko name. She selected the name because her family traced its history back to Khan Akhmat, the last of the Tatar rulers to control Russia. By selecting the name Akhmatova, the young poet both rejected her father's attitude toward poetry and paid tribute to her family's history.

Akhmatova began to publish her verses in her early twenties; her first verse collection, *Vecher* (evening), came out in 1912, and her second, *Chetki* (rosary), was published in 1914. Almost immediately, she achieved the kind of success that most writers dream about all their lives. It was clear to everyone who had any understanding of literature that Akhmatova was a powerful force in Russian poetry. Like many other writers of her time, she wrote most often about love, and particularly about unrequited love; unlike all but a handful of poets, however, she wrote in a new way. Because of her tremendous knowledge and understanding of Russian literature, she was able to assimilate the techniques of the past. For this reason, Akhmatova's work can be seen as falling squarely within the tradition of Russian poetry. At the same time, however, she found new ways to convey meaning.

When Akhmatova began her writing career, the work of the Symbolists held sway in Russia. She respected the Symbolists—especially Aleksandr Blok—but, along with Osip Mandelstam, Nikolay Gumilyov (who became her first husband in 1910), and a few others, she founded a school of poetry called Acmeism, which declared symbolic writing passé. The Acmeists rejected the techniques of Symbolism in order to create works that focused on the details of daily life. Akhmatova's writing used concrete images to portray the psychological states experienced by the people about whom she wrote, and it did so in a way that was acclaimed not only by critics, but also by the reading public.

Akhmatova became a kind of icon of Russian literature in the tremendously creative era that literary critics call the Silver Age of Russian literature and art. In the years before the Russian Revolution broke out, Akhmatova came to symbolize all that was best in Russian literature. In addition, she was a beautiful woman who seemed to have an innate gift for attracting attention. Many of her contemporaries have mentioned that when Akhmatova entered a room, usually wearing her trademark shawl, everyone else was eclipsed. She became a superstar, and the public watched her every move. She was often seen reading in public, especially in the famous Stray Dog cabaret in St. Petersburg, where well-known writers, actors, and musicians of the day gathered to socialize and perform.

Akhmatova's fame worked against her when the Bolsheviks seized power. The Communist Party set about to tear down the old society and build a new one, and the old values no longer held. For the Communists, Akhmatova was a symbol of the old regime. Love poetry was a relic of the bourgeois past—something to be discarded. All art had to promote the good of the state. It did not help that Akhmatova had spent much of her youth living in Tsarskoye Selo ("czar's village"), the town in which the czar had maintained a residence. The place was a symbol of aristocratic decadence. Akhmatova's life, like her work, was anathema to the Communist view of life and society.

After the revolution, Akhmatova's life became tremendously difficult. She was rarely able to publish her work, and when she did manage to publish a new collection of verse, most of her best work could not be included. In spite of these problems, however, Akhmatova continued to write. She wrote about the difficulties of life in the new Soviet state, and ultimately she came to symbolize persistence and survival in the face of tremendous suffering.

Chukovskaya's journal about Akhmatova begins in 1938, a year of unbelievable horror for the Russian people. In 1937, Nikolay Ezhov took over the directorship of the NKVD, the People's Commissariat of Internal Affairs, and unleashed a reign of terror that has no parallel in Russian history. The era of the Ezhov Terror was a time when no one was safe. The NKVD had orders to arrest a certain percentage of the Russian population, and it has been estimated that some eight million people were spirited away by the secret police during that era. Ultimately, Ezhov and his henchmen, after losing power in July of 1938, were themselves executed.

The lives of Akhmatova and innumerable other Russians were torn apart by the political purges of the Stalinist era, which lasted from 1924 to 1953. Nikolay Gumilyov, Akhmatova's first husband, was executed in 1921 because he had allegedly conspired against the state. In 1935, their son, Lev Gumilyov, was arrested and released. He was arrested again in 1938 and was held by the authorities for seventeen months. Chu-kovskaya's journals record Akhmatova's efforts to intercede with the authorities on her son's behalf. They also mention Akhmatova's attempts to send letters and packages to her son, and to other incarcerated individuals about whom she cared deeply. It was also during the time period covered by the journals that Akhmatova wrote much of her great work *Rekviem* (1963; *Requiem*, 1964), which focuses on the suffering of those whose loved ones had been imprisoned or killed by the secret police.

Chukovskaya shows the many facets of Akhmatova. Her diary witnesses the poet's bravery in the face of both political persecution and her own irrational fears. This woman, who was able to help her friends and neighbors at tremendous risk to herself, was sometimes afraid to walk upstairs or cross the street. Courage was important to her. In one entry, discussing a friend's refusal to have a necessary operation, Akhmatova says, "Death—that's what will happen. That's the punishment for cowardice!" The book also records many conversations between Chukovskaya and Akhmatova on the subject of literature. One of many interesting topics of conversation was the revulsion Akhmatova held for Leo Tolstoy, the great novelist. Akhmatova was particularly incensed by Tolstoy's treatment of his fictional character Anna Karenina. According to her, "The entire novel is based on a false physiological and psychological premise. . . . Tolstoy wanted to prove that a woman who leaves her lawful husband is a prostitute. And his attitude towards her is vile."

Chukovskaya's remarkable work is invaluable for the light that it sheds on Akhmatova's life and views, and it provides many remarkable vignettes that give the reader the flavor of life under Stalin. It will be particularly enlightening for those who already know something about both Akhmatova and Russian history. For various reasons, however, the book is not a good place to begin a study of Akhmatova. Because of the danger of keeping such a journal, many of Chukovskaya's entries are written in a sort of code. She sometimes uses key words to refer to works or incidents that are not mentioned in the text itself. In some cases, the author explains these entries in footnotes, but in others, even Chukovskaya has forgotten what she meant at the time. Throughout the book, Chukovskaya and Akhmatova refer to friends and acquaintances by using only their names and patronymics, which often makes it difficult to keep track of the people who are being discussed. The book does include a list of personages that makes it possible to look up individuals by first names and patronymics, but going back and forth is a time-consuming and distracting process. It would be wise for anyone who wishes to read Chukovskaya's journals first to read a biography of Akhmatova, such as Roberta Reeder's *Anna Akhmatova: Poet and Prophet* (1994).

One of the most useful features of *The Akhmatova Journals* is the inclusion of translations of some of Akhmatova's poems. As Chukovskaya says, they are "Those without which my entries would be hard to understand." It is unfortunate, however, that the edition does not include an introduction dealing with Akhmatova's life and placing Chukovskaya's work in historical perspective. The book does include a workable index that makes it a useful tool for the student of literary history and biography.

Shawn Woodyard

Sources for Further Study

Belles Lettres. IX, Summer, 1994, p. 79.
Chicago Tribune. July 31, 1994, XIV, p. 4.
Library Journal. CXIX, April 15, 1994, p. 73.
Los Angeles Times Book Review. May 1, 1994, p. 3.
New Statesman and Society. VII, June 10, 1994, p. 40.
The New York Times Book Review. XCIX, July 10, 1994, p. 24.
Publishers Weekly. CCXLI, January 24, 1994, p. 44.
The Times Literary Supplement. August 5, 1994, p. 21.
The Wall Street Journal. VII, May 25, 1994, p. A14.
The Washington Post Book World. XXIV, April 24, 1994, p. 2.

ALAN PATON
A Life

Author: Peter F. Alexander
Publisher: Oxford University Press (New York). 510 pp. $35.00
Type of work: Biography
Time: 1903-1988
Locale: South Africa

A thorough and competent biography of an important novelist and opponent of the apartheid regimes in South Africa

Principal personages:
ALAN PATON, a South African novelist
JAMES PATON, his father
EUNICE PATON, his mother
ATHOLL PATON, his younger brother
DORIS "DORRIE" PATON, his younger sister
DORIS FRANCIS PATON, his first wife
ANNE PATON, his second wife
RAILTON DENT, one of his earliest and closest friends
JAN HENDRICK HOFMEYR, his friend, a South African politician
JOAN MONTGOMERY, one of his lovers
MARY BENSON, a lover who remained a close friend
PETER BROWN, his close associate in the Liberal Party

Alan Paton is best known for his novel *Cry, the Beloved Country* (1948), a searing account of the inhumanity of apartheid that is marked by a lyrical love for his native South Africa. Published in New York by Scribner's without advance publicity, it became an instant best-seller—the first edition was sold out on the first day of publication. Reviews were laudatory, praising not only the novel's human message but also its beautiful language. Paton was hailed as a major new novelist and as a political voice of extraordinary moral authority. His novel would eventually be translated into twenty languages and sell more than fifteen million copies.

As Paton's biographer, Peter F. Alexander, demonstrates, Paton's novel came at precisely the moment when the world was becoming aware of the injustice of apartheid. In the late 1940's, the Afrikaner-dominated National Party had taken power in South Africa and was determined to enforce a rigid separation of the races and to promulgate policies that ensured white dominance of the political and economic system. Paton's biography parallels the twentieth century history of his country. His moral growth and politics—which seemed, for much of his life, out of kilter with his surroundings—have come to appear, since the election of Nelson Mandela as South Africa's president, prophetic of his country's potential for reform.

Paton was born in 1903 in Natal province. His father, James, had emigrated from Scotland and found a position as a court stenographer. James Paton seems to have been a man of frustrated ambitions. He wrote competent but pedestrian poetry and never rose above his first job. He was bitter and took his anger out on his children. He beat all of them. He sometimes beat his wife. He was jealous of his children's accomplishments, never attending their prize ceremonies or sports matches. He was mean and greedy, always eating the best things at the table while his children looked at him with envy and hatred. He was prudish about sex, although he was clearly attracted to young women and may have had assignations with some of them. He belonged to a small Christian sect, the Christadelphians, pacifists strictly focused on Christ's second coming.

As the oldest child, Alan often bore the brunt of his father's rages. Yet something in James's Christianity appealed to Alan, and he seemed able to forgive, if not love, his father. His younger brother Atholl rebelled, beating up and ridiculing their father as soon as he became old enough to exert his strength. Alan's sister, Dorrie, remained a Christadelphian, and later a coolness developed between her and Alan when he renounced the creed in favor of the Anglican Church. Alan and Atholl were also estranged, for the younger but stronger Atholl also beat up Alan, an incident that neither brother was ever able to forget.

An able student, Alan early gave promise of surpassing his father's position in life. A keenly sensitive young man, he may have had some sympathy for his stymied father—although Alexander's biography presents no evidence of it. Paton pursued a teaching career, but he also wanted to write and to achieve political success. He was a proponent of what was often called in the late nineteenth century "muscular Christianity." Paton was much influenced by an older friend, Railton Dent, a kind of father figure who helped him to see Christianity as an active religion, vitally committed to improving this world as a way of keeping faith with the eternal world of salvation to which every Christian aspires.

Paton liked to think of himself as an inspiring and well-liked teacher. This is how he presents himself in his autobiographies. His biographer ably demonstrates, however, that many of James Paton's unfortunate traits manifested themselves in his son. Alan Paton beat students mercilessly. A group of them were so incensed at his whippings that they conspired to waylay him. He escaped their retribution by accident.

Given the painful experiences with his father, what was Paton thinking when he beat boys? It was not unusual at this time to believe that beating instilled discipline. Did Paton think, however, that his father's beatings had disciplined him? They certainly had not had that kind of influence on his brother Atholl. Alexander is strangely incurious about this apparent mean streak in Paton. The biographer is perhaps hindered from speculating because Paton himself did not question why he beat students. Indeed, Paton minimized this aspect of his teaching, even though it was foremost in the minds of the Paton students whom Alexander interviewed. It is possible, as Alexander suggests, that the students were exaggerating the beatings. Yet Paton's own childhood and the vehemence of the students' memories suggest a darker side to Paton's character than the biographer seems willing to explore. Alexander does not avoid the issue, but he disposes of it by noting that the beatings seem to have diminished as Paton grew more experienced and confident.

Paton gradually tired of teaching and sought a post that would challenge his administrative skills, show off his political skills, and demonstrate that he could make a contribution to the national scene. He got his chance at Diepkloof, a reformatory for African boys. In fact, it was run like a prison—almost a concentration camp, with barbed wire, inmates sleeping practically on top of one another, overflowing and reeking latrine buckets, and no opportunities for exercise or rehabilitation. Over more than a decade, Paton gradually transformed the camp into a reform school, removing most of the prison rules and routines and even pioneering a furlough system.

Paton took great risks and suffered failures. Boys ran away, committed crimes, and abused the trust he placed in them. His success rate improved, however, as he developed rituals and ceremonies that bound boys to the system, giving them opportunities to learn and to display their talents. One escapee who voluntarily gave himself up and returned to Diepkloof said that he did so because he had given his word to abide by its rules and was ashamed of having broken them.

Paton expected to parlay his success at Diepkloof into an important political post. He believed that he had a patron in Jan Hendrick Hofmeyr, an official in the United Party government—a group of Englishmen and Afrikaners whom Paton believed to be dedicated to reforming South Africa and avoiding the excesses of Afrikaner nationalism, which opposed British influence and belittled black and colored (mixed-race) South Africans. To Paton—and to most whites—reform did not mean anything like power sharing, let alone equality, with the black population. Not until the late 1940's, with the triumph of the Afrikaner Nationalist Party, did Paton realize that his own sense of humanity required acknowledging that of blacks.

Hofmeyr proved to be a huge disappointment to Paton, although Paton never stopped trying to impress him or to hint that he expected a post from his powerful friend. Even when Hofmeyr became a member of the United Party cabinet during World War II, he did not reward Paton with a post. Hofmeyr claimed that he could do nothing for his ambitious friend. This seems unlikely. Although Alexander has carefully studied the correspondence between Hofmeyr and Paton, he says little about what Hofmeyr really thought of Paton. Once again, the biographer's silence seems the result of lack of evidence. Yet enough is known of Hofmeyr to analyze what went wrong with Paton's career. Paton was surely too earnest for Hofmeyr, who was not as liberal as Paton supposed—or not willing to act on his putative progressive principles. This much can be made out from Alexander's narrative, but it is frustrating that the biographer does not try to explore this important relationship more carefully, because it clearly had an impact on Paton's politics after World War II.

The success of *Cry, the Beloved Country* was what eventually liberated Paton from Diepkloof. He could not have stayed much longer, because the Nationalist regime was undoing his reforms and was institutionalizing apartheid, disfranchising the colored population, and shifting huge black populations into separate settlements. Paton protested these developments, becoming a full-time journalist and activist in the antiapartheid cause.

At first, Paton's politics seemed courageous and morally unassailable. He was one of the earliest and most powerful voices against apartheid, establishing the Liberal

Party, a coalition of whites and blacks that worked for black and colored enfranchisement and equal rights. Yet the Liberal Party never appealed to more than a tiny minority of whites and blacks, and it never won a parliamentary seat. Paton began to be heavily criticized when he would not endorse calls for the violent overthrow of the Nationalist government. He earned more enmity when he opposed sanctions against his country, arguing that boycotts would hurt blacks more than others. Paton was no revolutionary. He despised the Communist Party, which allied itself with the African National Congress. He found himself isolated when South Africa, aroused in the 1960's and 1970's with calls for black power, seemed destined for revolution.

Paton rarely wavered in his political principles. Alexander makes a good case for his steadfast and ultimately wise vision of the future, in which not violence but love would triumph and make a multiracial society possible. Still, certain puzzling aspects of Paton's politics are not clear. Why, for example, did he not join the Progressive Party? It had only one representative in Parliament, Helen Suzman, but it proved a much more effective force than Paton's small band of liberals. Alexander says that Paton was on good terms with Suzman, yet he did not make common cause with her. Why not?

On Paton's private life, Alexander is compassionate. Paton's first wife never gave him the full affection he craved. She seems to have been especially niggardly when it came to sex, warming up to her husband only at those times when he strayed to other women. Paton's lapses in fidelity were apparently rare, for he took his marriage vows quite seriously and felt guilty at breaking them. His second wife, Anne, gave him a new lease on life, stimulating him in his last fifteen years to write another novel and to complete a second volume of his autobiography. Paton's sons, interviewed for this biography, were ambivalent about him. In some respects, he treated them as his father had treated him. They found him aloof, although he did not subject them to the relentless beatings that James had administered to him.

Not all readers will agree with Alexander's assessment of Paton's importance as a writer. To be sure, *Cry, the Beloved Country* has earned its place as a classic. Paton's other two novels, Alexander admits, have not had nearly the impact of his first success, although the second, *Too Late the Phalarope* (1953), may actually be his best fiction. Alexander seems to think that Paton has been somewhat neglected as a poet. Yet if one judges by the examples he quotes (and he quotes too many of them), Paton's verse does not merit much reevaluation.

Carl Rollyson

Sources for Further Study

Booklist. XCI, September 15, 1994, p. 100.
Kirkus Reviews. LXII, August 1, 1994, p. 1033.
New Statesman and Society. VII, August 12, 1994, p. 40.

Publishers Weekly. CCXLI, August 8, 1994, p. 406.
The Spectator. CCLXXIII, August 13, 1994, p. 21.
The Times Literary Supplement. September 2, 1994, p. 22.
The Washington Post Book World. XXIV, November 27, 1994, p. 4.

THE AMERICAN PRESIDENCY
An Intellectual History

Author: Forrest McDonald (1927-)
Publisher: University Press of Kansas (Lawrence). 516 pp. $29.95
Type of work: History
Time: 1789-1992
Locale: The United States

This book provides a history of the American presidency, from its origins and implementation through its modern metamorphoses

Principal personages:

ALEXANDER HAMILTON, who advocated a strong presidency and was the most powerful cabinet officer in the Washington Administration
JAMES MADISON, not only the fourth president but also one of the most influential voices in the framing of the chief executive's role as set forth in the Constitution
GOUVERNEUR MORRIS, another framer of the Constitution, who sought a strong executive and suggested that the legislative and executive functions be separate branches of government
GEORGE WASHINGTON, the first to mold the presidency by his own personality
THOMAS JEFFERSON, whose activism changed the direction of the office
FRANKLIN DELANO ROOSEVELT, whose effective sponsoring of legislation expanded the role of government
RONALD REAGAN, who sought to reverse the expansion of government

The American people have had high expectations for their president, but rarely has he been able to fulfill them. Pledging to downsize government after two decades of enormous expansion, Ronald Reagan entered and left office barely able to slow its growth. Refractory foreign problems such as Vietnam and the Iran hostage situation haunted and drove out of office Presidents Lyndon B. Johnson and Jimmy Carter. Government scandals such as Watergate and Whitewater plagued the presidencies of Richard Nixon and Bill Clinton. Part of the problem may be that lesser men occupy the office than in its early days. Part may be the increasing complexity of government, the country, and the world. As Forrest McDonald points out in *The American Presidency: An Intellectual History*, another part of the problem is the Constitution of the United States itself. In some measure, it was purposely designed to hamper the president (as well as the other branches of government), so that no person or group could wield excessive power and thus threaten liberty. McDonald's book provides a history not only of the American presidency but also of the ideas about power and governance that influenced its creation.

McDonald divides his study into three parts: "Roots," "Establishment," and "Evolution." The first traces the ideas and assumptions with which the Founding Fathers were familiar and which underlay their conceptions of the presidency. For example, an obvious model was the English form of limited monarchy, a "mixed" form of government combining monarchy, oligarchy, and democracy. Since many of the framers were trained in the English law, they were aware of the distinguished legal commentaries written through the centuries by such men as Henry Bracton (thirteenth century), Sir John Fortescue (sixteenth century), Sir Edward Coke and Sir Matthew Hale (seventeenth century), and Sir William Blackstone (eighteenth century). From each of these men, the American founders gained some justification for declaring their independence and, later, common ground on which they could debate their own constitution.

Bracton, for example, expounded on the dual nature of the king of England's power. The power of governance was by divine right and absolute, but the power of jurisdiction (the power to decide legal issues) bound the king to laws enshrined in custom. This qualification of absolute power was a crucial precedent for the colonists, for in the Declaration of Independence they could not have listed the various violations of law committed by King George III if they had not thought a king bound by law. Another concept that provided justification for the colonists' declaration of independence was that of the ancient constitution, articulated by Fortescue: that is, the notion that England, even through various conquests, revolutions, and abuses, was ultimately governed by a set of customs that traced their lineage as far back as Rome. This powerful myth gave the Americans another pretext for revolution, for they believed that they were called upon to restore that ancient and valid constitution rather than continue to serve the one corrupted by George III. Coke also invoked the mysterious and sacred power of the ancient constitution to defend the judiciary from kingly encroachment, and Blackstone articulated the notion that the English constitution balanced and checked the interests of king, lords, and commoners, a clear precedent for the system of checks and balances adopted by the framers of the U.S. Constitution.

Many of these same questions of power and governance were expounded by political theorists as well. Eighteenth century Americans were the beneficiaries of the vast literature written in the preceding century in response to the English Civil War. The "commonwealthmen" who seized control from the monarchy in the mid-seventeenth century wrote of the desirability of a mixed government, of separation of powers, and of checks and balances. On the other side of that debate were monarchists such as Sir Thomas Hobbes, who argued that the only reliable solution to individual clashes of will was a compact with a sovereign in which each individual's will was absolutely subject to the will of the sovereign, and Sir Robert Filmer, who argued that patriarchy—authority and the duty to obey it—preexisted government and that there had never been an egalitarian golden age. John Locke's "Two Treatises of Government," which refuted Filmer and glorified the English revolution, was very popular among the colonists, because it justified a people's declaring independence if the compact of government was broken.

After treating the roots of the presidency, McDonald devotes part 2 of his study to the establishment of the office. This section includes discussion of the constitutional conventions, the ratification, and the presidencies of George Washington and Thomas

Jefferson, which had as much impact on subsequent thinking about the office as had the Constitution itself.

Limiting the president but still allowing for an effective executive was a central problem the Founding Fathers faced as they framed the Constitution. The very notion of a chief executive is ambiguous. The phrase implies that the president merely executes the will of others (Congress), but the Framers knew from history that discretionary powers were needed to allow the executive to rule situations over which no law governs, even to rise above the law should an emergency occur. Their fear of executive tyranny is epitomized in the difficulty they had deciding on a name and a form of address for their chief executive. During the eighteenth century, McDonald points out, "president" was a particularly innocuous term, and perhaps this is why it was chosen. Although "his excellency" was settled upon as the form of address used for the president, this provision was removed by the drafting committee because it might be offensive to a ratifying populace stirred by the antimonarchical rhetoric of Thomas Paine.

Among those who favored a strong executive were men who had been frustrated during the revolutionary war by the ineptitude of the Continental Congress. Alexander Hamilton, a military aide to George Washington, was one of them. Others, such as Gouverneur Morris and James Madison, sought a strong executive because they feared legislative tyranny. Morris sought to separate the executive and the legislative into two independent branches of government. Ultimately, however, although the convention aimed to follow the doctrine of the separation of powers, it did not do so precisely. It created separate branches of government, but their powers were intermingled. For example, the president's right to recommend legislation, the vice president's role as president of the Senate, and the presidential veto gave the executive branch a hand in the legislative process. Similarly, although the president was charged with executing war, only Congress had the power to declare it. This mixing of powers was justified in *The Federalist* by Madison as necessary checks and balances.

The Constitution as written was not as explicit in its designation of the duties of the president as in its enumeration of the duties of Congress. McDonald maintains that this silence on the powers of the presidency was a result of both the framers' ambivalence about investing power in a single person and the universal expectation that Washington would be the first president and that he could be trusted to fill the gaps left in the description of the office. Indeed, McDonald stresses an adjective used by other historians in discussing Washington's role in creating the new country: "indispensable." His selflessness and honorable conduct during the revolution and after it made the office of president "thinkable" and relieved many of the anxieties about possible abuse of power.

As important as Washington in the shaping of the office was Thomas Jefferson. One of the leaders of the first opposition party in the new republic, Jefferson opposed Hamilton, Washington's secretary of the treasury, and what he believed were monarchical tendencies in the Washington and Adams administrations. A man of the people, he downplayed the ceremonial aspects of the office (which Washington had stressed), and he also took a more activist role in directing the legislative agenda in Congress than his predecessors had.

McDonald notes that the balance of power between the three branches of government has shifted over the years. Sometimes Congress has been stronger, sometimes the president, sometimes the courts. Part 3 of *The American Presidency* traces the evolution of the office from Andrew Jackson to the late twentieth century. Rather than organizing by individual presidents, McDonald divides this section into subjects: the president and the law, the president and administration, the president and Congress, and the president as symbol and myth.

Historically, the plan that Congress makes the laws, the president enforces them, and the courts interpret them has never been neatly realized in practice. Reagan believed that the judiciary was effectively overstepping its bounds and making laws rather than interpreting them; thus he sought to restrain it by selecting judges interested in the original intent of the Constitution who would exercise judicial restraint. Robert Bork was such a candidate, but his nomination was refused by Congress. Gerald Ford was convinced that Congress was enacting laws with excessively expensive price tags, so he simply refused to spend the money appropriated. In response to this practice of impoundment, Congress made expenditures mandatory, a factor contributing to the runaway budget deficits of the 1980's and early 1990's.

One of the radical changes in government since Washington's day has been its enormous increase in size and complexity. Civil service, once welcomed as a reform of the spoils system, has in fact created a nightmare, effectively a fourth branch of government, known as the bureaucracy, which is not responsible to an electorate. The regulatory function of government, which the bureaucracy controls, has expanded enormously. From 175 bureaus and agencies in 1923, there were 767 in 1992. By 1991, the Code of Federal Regulations consisted of nearly 200 volumes and more than 100,000 pages. One of the central tasks of the twentieth century president has been managing the massive bureaucracy that controls these regulations. Nixon's response was to surround himself with a counterbureaucracy in the White House of some 4,000 staffers.

The president, with the help of his staff, has become the "legislator in chief," primarily responsible for introducing legislation. Just as regulatory agencies have increased in size and complexity, so has Congress. A congressional staff of 4,300 in the 1950's grew to 32,000 in 1990. In 1861, when Lincoln complained to Congress about the size and redundancy of the bills the legislature had passed during its seventy-two-year history, he was talking about fewer than one hundred bills and resolutions a year, averaging less than one page each. As McDonald ironically notes in contrast, a 1986 tax code simplification act passed by Congress consisted of 925 pages and was only one of 424 bills passed that year. As many as ten thousand bills are introduced yearly. The result is that elected legislators cannot begin to read the bills on which they vote, and apparently they do not even try. More concerned with constituent services and getting reelected, modern legislators have simply abdicated their legislative duties to their staffs.

The president has some power over bad legislation. He can veto it. Yet this is an all-or-nothing approach that can create what was called "gridlock" in the Bush Administration. Denied the line-item veto, which was proposed as early as the Grant Administration, the president has not been able to trim bills of wasteful riders. The result has been a bloated, inefficient, and expensive government.

McDonald notes that in addition to his executive duties, the president is the symbolic leader of his country. Although image has always been an essential aspect of the presidency—witness the importance of Washington's—creating images in the popular mind in order to sway an election did not begin until the standoff between John Quincy Adams and Andrew Jackson in the controversial elections of 1828. Prior to that time, the president was largely chosen through congressional caucuses, that is, by insiders. The concept of negative campaigning, when neither candidate explained what he would do in office but chose only to denigrate the opposition, seems to have begun in 1828.

In the twentieth century, mass media became critical to purveying the presidential image. Theodore Roosevelt was the first to use the press fully. Disliked by reporters and editors from the major newspaper chains, his cousin Franklin Delano Roosevelt gained and retained popularity through his effective use of radio "fireside chats." Since 1960, television's role in creating or destroying the presidential image has become critical. From John F. Kennedy's strong image in the debates with Richard Nixon, to the picture of a nuclear explosion to frighten voters from Barry Goldwater, to Ross Perot's "infomercials," which helped him draw 19 percent of the popular vote, television has had an increasingly powerful influence. McDonald notes that although image creation has become a necessary means to election and retention of office, it consumes too much time and often trivializes the office. Like the bureaucracy, which was once designed to aid in the process of governance, it has become an end in itself.

Although the job is nearly impossible and is complicated by the public's election of often poorly qualified individuals, and despite its inefficiencies and the extraordinary number of presidents who have not been reelected, the presidency has remained stable for more than two hundred years. As McDonald asserts both at the outset and at the end of his remarkably detailed book, the American presidency may be the most powerful secular institution in the world, and it has done much more good than harm.

William L. Howard

Sources for Further Study

America. CLXX, March 19, 1994, p. 25.
The New York Times Book Review. XCIX, February 20, 1994, p. 28.
Presidential Studies Quarterly. XXIV, Summer, 1994, p. 619.
The Times Literary Supplement. June 10, 1994, p. 6.
The Washington Post Book World. XXIV, April 10, 1994, p. 9.
The Wilson Quarterly. XVIII, Autumn, 1994, p. 97.

THE ANGEL OF HISTORY

Author: Carolyn Forché (1950-)
Publisher: HarperCollins (New York). 84 pp. $20.00
Type of work: Poetry

Carolyn Forché compiles the fragments of twentieth century history—including the horrors of war, genocide, the Holocaust, and the atomic bomb—to meditate on the survival of memory in a postapocalyptic age and to give utterance to the unutterable events of our time

Combining the political with the personal—or, as the poet herself contends, creating work that addresses "public concerns, the public self in the world"—has always been Carolyn Forché's forte. While her first volume of verse, *Gathering the Tribes* (1975), chronicles the author's experiences and epiphanies, both private and public, as an adolescent and young adult, her second book, *The Country Between Us* (1981), powerfully demonstrates Forché's evolving political consciousness and connection to the larger external world around her. It is in this latter collection, marked by her experience as a journalist and human rights advocate in El Salvador, that Forché first confronts unflinchingly the atrocities of civil war, political corruption, and violations against life and liberty to attempt, through her "utterance" or language, to transform through sensibility the otherwise purely barbaric. Such a poetic stance or strategy is no small feat at a time when much contemporary poetry has been marked by a retreat from the sociopolitical into an ephemeral realm of personal loss and longing. By addressing head-on the pain and suffering of recent public history—that is, by placing her individual self at the service of political dissent, even outrage—Forché has moved into the company of Pablo Neruda, Octavio Paz, Philip Levine, and Denise Levertov. She has joined that select company of contemporary poets who have managed to wed their personal feelings with an impassioned commitment to the exterior world, however cruel and painful its events may be.

Yet the moral and political depths of Forché's earlier collections may be overmatched by *The Angel of History*, a volume ambitious and comprehensive in its historical vision. This book-length poem, composed in numbered sections and taking in the compiled degradations of twentieth century history, reminds one of T. S. Eliot's "The Waste Land" (1922) in its "shoring up" of the fragments that constitute modern life and culture. The poet's springboard for considering and recording, in sparse, imagistic fashion, past obscenities such as the Holocaust, Hiroshima, and Latin American genocide is Walter Benjamin's "angel of history," which Forché defines in an epigraph: "His face is turned toward the past. Where we perceive a chain of events, he sees one single catastrophe which keeps piling wreckage and hurls it in front of his feet. The angel would like to . . . make whole what has been smashed. But a storm . . . irresistibly propels him into the future to which his back is turned, while the pile of debris before him grows skyward." The apocalyptic strain evidenced in Benjamin's view of the historical process is supported by Forché's own explanation of her book's purpose, which she appends as an epilogue: "These utterances issue from my own encounter with the events of this century but do not represent 'it.' The first-person, free-verse, lyric-narrative poem of my earlier years has given way to a work which [is] . . . polyphonic, broken, haunted, and in ruins, with no possibility of restoration." That is, Forché recognizes the impossibility of trying to explain or transcend the chaos of twentieth century history through art; instead, she is content to record the events of "a world emptying of human belief," to capture, if not valorize, "a memory barely retrieved from a fire . . . (the past) in its hiding place," as the shadowy narrator of part 2 of the volume, entitled "The Notebook of Uprising," cryptically puts it.

Like Forché's previous collections, this volume is elegiac in its tone, portraying, as critic Carole Stone describes, how "history functions as part of the mourning process as [poets] bear witness to the tragedies of a people . . . In doing so they pass through individual grief to collective grief." Given *The Angel of History*'s fragmented form, disjointed images, and apocalyptic lines taken from Elie Wiesel, Franz Kafka, and Paul Valéry, however, it is difficult to conclude here that Forché uses elegy as "a form that at once witnesses history and tries to change it" (as Stone proposes). That is, the poet muses self-reflexively toward the end of part 1, "The Angel of History," if all art is the result of one's having been in danger, of having gone through an experience all the way to the end," such artistic expression cannot hope to expiate the terrors of the past (such as, in this section, the deportation and extermination of French Jews by the Nazis) but can merely witness and chronicle them. Thus, an indeterminate narrator closes "The Angel of History" with another question, since no answer seems possible to explain the atrocities of our recent, collective history:

> As if someone not alive were watching:
> *Bonsoir. Est-ce que je vous dérange?*
>
> Night terrors. A city with all its windows blank.
> A memory through which one hasn't lived.
>
> You see, I told Madame about my life.
> I told her everything.
> *And what did she say?*

Yet even if memory and the poetic recording of it can give no adequate or determinate response to the disastrous events of the twentieth century, Forché implies there is value, even comfort, in confronting public and private griefs. It may be naïve, in a now postapocalyptic world where "the open country of death" is "worse than memory," to "confuse that much destruction with one woman's painful life." Still, Forché seems to contend that only by addressing personal loss and mourning can one both grieve for and protest against a troubled collective history. Again, only by conflating the public and private worlds of the past century can the poet relive history and make its fresh chain of horrors somehow palpable to the reader.

Just how we are to live in such terminal times, and how it is possible for the poet/writer to record and memorialize the travesties of a past that seems beyond comprehension, becomes the focus of part 2 of *The Angel of History*, "The Notebook of Uprising," and the principal focus of the remainder of Forché's volume. Self-reflexively, the poet claims that "the hand moves across the page of its own accord," compelled to chronicle "a time unknown to us" in spite of the warning of Anna, Forché's Czechoslovakian paternal grandmother: "*They didn't want you to know the past. They were hoping in this way you could escape it.*" Such a desire, as Forché sadly recognizes, is only wishful thinking, since the evidence and fragments of history's apocalyptic march are only too visible. "A field of bone chips," "petrochemical plants spewing black smoke," "zones of refuse," "the white-eyed, walking dead," and even, to bring the cataclysm up to date (with reference to the Chernobyl nuclear accident), "a wind from Byelorussia [bringing] . . . blue roses" all announce "a world in decline . . . emptying of human belief."

How can one conjure up hope or even a sense of human survival or continuation, given such conditions, Forché seems to wonder, especially when suffering and decimation seem to be the only common denominators of the past and present historical moment? There is no simple answer to such an ominous question, but perhaps, as Forché writes in part 3, "The Recording Angel," the rebirth of both natural and human life from a "past [that]/ Is circular, like consequence" will come only through the record, in language, that is left behind:

> The earth is a school. It is a waiting room, a foyer giving onto emptiness
> It is for desires, small but beautifully done
> The earth is wrapped in weather, and the weather in risen words

Or, if the earth that human beings have scarred and ravaged, often with the waste of their own bodies, is not eternal or transcendent, the voice that speaks, utters, or writes of it has the potential to be, as well as to keep memory, "a wind passing through the blood trees within us," alive, even when hope seems tenuous at best.

"We revolt against silence with a bit of speaking," Forché pronounces in "Elegy," the poem that opens part 4 of the volume and that encapsulates in fragmented form the poet's devotion to discourse (here, writing) as the means to the survival of memory. Yet in avoiding silence and attempting to utter the seemingly unutterable, those catastrophic events of twentieth century human history, one faces the danger of failing to communicate altogether, as a Hiroshima survivor and the speaker of "The Garden Shukkei-en" admits: "Perhaps my language is too precise, and therefore difficult to understand?" That is, the vivid, all-too-real and all-too-recent details of nuclear holocaust—resulting in skin falling from fingers, brains crushed—may be more gruesome than many can bear or are willing to bear; hence, a collective retreat, as this speaker concludes, into "the silence surrounding what happened to us." The Recording Angel of history, harbinger of its cyclical process, cannot be so selective, nor dismiss such an atrocity to the status of a "dream where the world had been" ("The Testimony of Light"). The present as well as future course of history is likely, Forché reminds the reader again, to repeat the past doggedly, so there is scant consolation in either trying to learn from a Hiroshima (a comfortable cliché used by "new world order" statesmen even today) or to forget it. As the poet prophetically assesses the situation, "The worst is over./ The worst is yet to come"—a fitting epigraph to an age in which the only thing people do seem to learn from history is that humankind never learns anything from history. Yet within such a sparse, nihilistic credo may lie Forché's own revolt against forgetting and her outrage at those who would reduce such unspeakable crimes against humanity to mere political "events" or, worse still, historical footnotes that can be casually passed over.

If the shattered world of twentieth century ruin and decay is Forché's subject throughout *The Angel of History*, then the volume's last section, "Book Codes," stands as a fragmented, concluding reminder of where humankind has been during the past decades and where it is most likely going. Epigrammatic, citational texts borrowed in part from Ludwig Wittgenstein, these poems, like much of the collection, attest, without attempting to account for, what in fact "can be said," finally, about a troubled past whose spokesman is an anonymous voice commanding, "Bear the unbearable." While there seems little consolation to the future in such a somber message, Forché still performs unshakingly the task of any good poet of conscience: to assemble the fragments, ruins, and shards of civilization in order not only to condemn this century's horrors but also to preserve and transform them—to quote Nobel laureate Derek Walcott—through "the ironic serenity of beauty."

If the fragments of this century, like the pages of *The Angel of History*, do not always coalesce into a discernible whole, the poet's action of collecting them, of uttering their very real presence, still serves a necessary moral purpose. Forché compels readers to remember, to record, and to endure, both individually and collectively, as a testament to the past that will continue to haunt the present and future. "How incomplete a moment is human life," Forché writes in "Book Codes: II," the penultimate poem in this volume. Yet it is just such incompletion—the individual's small part within or connection to larger historical forces—that suggests, however darkly, the possibility of restoration or continuation, the belief that humankind can go on, even in a postapocalyptic world that insidiously denies humanity. At the very least, Forché forces her readers to ask what they can bear; at the most and her best, she places them face to face with the Angel of History and asks them to recognize, as Paul Valéry puts it on the book's last page, that "it [can] no longer be distinguished from this world that is about us."

Forché is ultimately telling us that we are and must be as much part of history's devastations as the victims of holocaust and genocide because of our complicity in living in and surviving the twentieth century. It is a message worth preserving, as *The Angel of History* does with stark beauty, since to forget it makes us not only less politically and socially engaged but also, finally, less human.

David J. Buehrer

Sources for Further Study

Bloomsbury Review. XIV, September, 1994, p. 19.
The Nation. CCLIX, October 24, 1994, p. 464.

Publishers Weekly. CCXLI, January 31, 1994, p. 77.
The Threepenny Review. XV, Summer, 1994, p. 18.
The Virginia Quarterly Review. LXX, Autumn, 1994, p. 136.
The Women's Review of Books. XI, July, 1994, p. 31.

ANNA AKHMATOVA
Poet and Prophet

Author: Roberta Reeder (1941-)
Publisher: St Martin's Press (New York). Illustrated. 619 pp. $35.00
Type of work: Literary biography
Time: 1889-1966
Locale: Russia

An ambitious and comprehensive English-language biography of the great Russian poet

Principal personages:

ANNA AKHMATOVA, one of the great poets of the twentieth century
NIKOLAY GUMILYOV, her first husband, a scholar and poet
VLADIMIR SHILEIKO, her second husband, an Assyriologist
LEV GUMILYOV, the son of Nikolay Gumilyov and Akhmatova
NIKOLAY PUNIN, her third husband, an art historian and critic
OSIP MANDELSTAM, her close friend, a major poet
BORIS PASTERNAK, a great poet and novelist who came to her aid in difficult times
JOSEPH BRODSKY, her protégé, a poet who won the 1987 Nobel Prize in Literature

From an early age, Anna Akhmatova seemed destined to live a remarkable life. Born Anna Andreyevna Gorenko on June 23, 1889, she was fascinated by poetry and began to write at the age of seven. Most of her childhood was spent in Tsarskoye Selo (czar's village), which later became a symbol of the aristocratic lifestyle of the prerevolutionary era. She was brought up to prize education and aesthetics, to be a proper child of the aristocracy, but even as a child she learned to keep her own counsel, never hesitating to flout convention when she believed it was in her own best interest to do so. Once when she was out walking, she found a pin in the shape of a lyre. Her governess told her that the find meant that she would someday become a poet.

Young Anna's father did not share his daughter's enthusiasm for poetry, and he told her that her penchant for verse would bring shame to the Gorenko name. Anna never considered giving up poetry. Instead, she adopted the name Akhmatova, which she selected because one of her maternal ancestors was Khan Akhmat, the last of the Tatar rulers to exact tribute from Russia. Akhmat was also a descendant of Genghis Khan, and Akhmatova was proud that the blood of Tatar royalty flowed in her veins. In her celebration of her Asian heritage, Akhmatova was truly Russian. For centuries, Russians have prided themselves on the fact that their country, which is located between Asia and Europe, has been the beneficiary of both Western and Eastern influences in every area of culture, a true melting pot of disparate elements.

Akhmatova's first collection of poetry, *Vecher* (evening), was published in 1912, and the second, *Chetki* (rosary), was published in 1914. Akhmatova was a success with both critics and the public. Her verses, which often dealt with unrequited love, tended to express psychological reality indirectly, by means of precise, evocative imagery.

Her work, which never indulged in the flaccid sentimentalism of most love poetry, electrified the Russian reading public. In addition, Akhmatova was beautiful and charismatic, and she soon became an icon of romantic verse, a true celebrity.

In 1912, along with Nikolay Gumilyov, the poet and critic whom Akhmatova had married in 1910, the poet and prose writer Osip Mandelstam, and several others, Akhmatova founded a new school of poetry called Acmeism. There were few tenets that truly bound the Acmeists together; their primary goal was to move away from the techniques of Symbolism, whose foremost exponent was Aleksandr Blok, and to work with specific, realistic imagery rather than the more mystical, flowery imagery that was the specialty of earlier writers. Among the Acmeists, only Akhmatova and Mandelstam achieved lasting renown, and their success was the result of their own innate poetic gifts, not of the ideas of Acmeism.

Akhmatova's life, like that of all Russians, was disrupted in 1914, when World War I broke out. Gumilyov volunteered for military service and was soon sent to the front. In 1915, Akhmatova's father died and she contracted tuberculosis. In 1917, she and Gumilyov separated, and they were divorced the following year. Also in 1917, the Russian Revolution began and the Bolsheviks seized power. Akhmatova had entered a period of difficulty and deprivation that would last the rest of her life. In 1918, Akhmatova married the Assyriologist Vladimir Shileiko, but the relationship was a failure, and she left him in 1921 to live with friends.

Akhmatova published a third collection of verse, *Belaya staya* (white flock), in Petrograd in 1917. It was not long, however, before the new government banned publication of her works, holding her up as an example of writers who wrote for their own selfish interests rather than for the good of the state. In 1921, Gumilyov was executed by the government on charges of conspiring against the state. It became dangerous for anyone to be associated with or to praise Akhmatova. The poet Vladimir Mayakovsky, whose talent Akhmatova admired, was one of many to denounce her as a relic of a dead era. She continued to produce great work, although she was able to publish her works only sporadically. Much of her best work survived only because it was memorized by those who loved it. Often, Akhmatova's friend Lydia Chukovskaya would sit with her, memorizing a poem from the written version, after which the two would burn the manuscript. They had good reason to be careful. Osip Mandelstam died in a camp after being arrested for writing a poem in which he likened Joseph Stalin's mustache to a cockroach. In spite of government repression, however, there was always an underground audience for Akhmatova's verse.

Akhmatova came to symbolize endurance in the face of the horrors of the Stalinist era. She refused to leave her beloved homeland, and she resolved to survive and write, no matter how difficult the times. In 1934, Akhmatova's son, Lev Gumilyov, was arrested for the first of many times; the next year, Nikolay Punin, Akhmatova's third husband, was also arrested. Akhmatova suffered, along with many other women who had lost husbands and sons to imprisonment, through long waits at the prison in the bitter Russian cold, attempting to get letters and packages through to her loved ones. Later, she was to write the great work *Rekviem* (1963; *Requiem*, 1964), which dealt with the nightmarish experiences through which she and many other women had lived. During World War II, Akhmatova wrote patriotic verse supporting the Russian cause, and she made a radio broadcast urging Russian women to stand fast. In spite of her efforts on behalf of her country, however, Akhmatova was still a pariah in the Soviet state.

After the death of Stalin in 1953, the same year in which Punin died in a Siberian prison camp, life became somewhat easier for Akhmatova. It became possible for her to publish—though in heavily censored editions—some of her work. In 1964, she was allowed to travel to Italy to accept the Taormina prize, and in 1965, she was able to travel to England to accept an honorary degree from Oxford University. Because she was not able to make a living by writing poetry during her later years, Akhmatova supported herself by translating the works of many poets. She also became known as an expert on the life and works of Alexander Pushkin, who is generally considered to be the greatest Russian poet and who was one of her favorites. After surviving to see much of her work published, Akhmatova died in a sanatorium at Domodedovo, near Moscow, on March 5, 1966.

Roberta Reeder, the editor of *The Complete Poems of Anna Akhmatova*, a two-volume dual-language edition published in 1990 by Zephyr Press, is to be congratulated for having produced the first comprehensive biography of Akhmatova to be published in English. She has provided, in a single large work, information about Akhmatova that she has culled from numerous sources, particularly the many works of Akhmatova scholarship that appeared in 1989, the centenary of the poet's birth. Reeder's work is hardly without flaws, but it is certainly the best place for any English speaker to begin a study of Akhmatova's life.

Reeder has opted to present Akhmatova's story in chronological fashion. The ten chapters that form the heart of the biographical work typically begin with Reeder attempting to place Akhmatova's life in the context of the time before moving on to discuss Akhmatova's own history. Naturally, much history is discussed elsewhere as well, but the fact that Reeder makes an attempt to separate historical background from the body of the biography sometimes has the effect of distracting the reader from the chronological flow of the narrative.

The book is, like too many publications in these times, marred by sloppiness. Reeder's writing is sometimes awkward, and the work is riddled with errors in punctuation, grammar, and usage that could have been corrected by an attentive editor. In addition, the first half of the book contains many instances of repetition. Statements about specific works or events, for example, are repeated, sometimes almost verbatim, one or more times. Repetition is not necessarily a flaw, particularly in a long work such as this one, but the way in which it is used here makes it appear to be unwitting rather than a conscious choice. It is too noticeable to be effective.

One has the feeling that Reeder did not have an absolutely precise idea of what the final shape of her work would be. Chapter 9, "The Thaw: 1953-1958," is followed by "Pasternak: The Nobel Prize and Death, 1958-1960," "The Gay Little Sinner Repents: *Poem Without a Hero*," and "Joseph Brodsky: Arrest and Exile, 1963-1965." Clearly,

Reeder has attempted to fit these digressions from the biographical narrative into the overall chronological structure of her book, but the gambit does not work. The flow of the biography is obstructed for the duration of these three chapters, which are followed by the book's final chapter, "The Last Years: The 1960s." The information in the three chapters is interesting and useful, but it would have been more effective either to provide that information piecemeal, throughout the book, or to use the chapters as appendices. It would seem that Reeder succumbed to the understandable desire to fill her work with as much information about her subject as possible, viewing it as a receptacle for the results of her scholarship rather than as a cohesive work.

The book contains a useful index (too many indexes these days are an utter waste of time), endnotes, and a good bibliography. An alphabetical set of capsule biographies of important personages would have been a helpful addition to the volume, and a chronology such as the one that appeared in *The Complete Poems of Anna Akhmatova*, which Reeder edited, would have been more useful still.

In spite of its flaws, however, *Anna Akhmatova: Poet and Prophet* is a fine addition to Akhmatova scholarship. For those readers who are beginning to study Akhmatova, Reeder's book provides a massive amount of biographical information coupled with much discussion of the poet's work; for old Akhmatova hands, the work is a compendium of information drawn from many publications about the great poet. No doubt Reeder's work will be superseded in due course, but for now her trailblazing biography stands alone.

Shawn Woodyard

Sources for Further Study

Library Journal. CXIX, November 15, 1994, p. 66.
The New York Times Book Review. C, January 1, 1995, p. 11.
Publishers Weekly. CCXLI, October 31, 1994, p. 47.
San Francisco Chronicle. January 8, 1995, p. REV1.

ANNUNCIATION

Author: David Plante (1940-   )
Publisher: Ticknor & Fields (New York). 346 pp. $21.95
Type of work: Novel
Time: The 1990's
Locale: England, New York, Italy, and Russia

A search for a missing painting—a Renaissance Annunciation—becomes a symbolic quest for an art historian, her pregnant daughter, and two male friends

Principal characters:
CLAIRE O'CONNEL, an art historian
RACHEL O'CONNEL, her teenage daughter
CLAUDE RICARD, an editor of art books
MAURICE KURAGIN, an elderly Russian expatriate living in London
SIR ROGER LECLERC, a world-renowned art historian

David Plante is interested in the concrete details of daily life but also in the unknowable darkness that surrounds them. Brought up Catholic in Rhode Island by a Quebeçois family, he has, in thirteen novels, detailed a consciousness more than a world. A sense of detachment and dislocation permeates every tale he tells. His first novel was entitled *The Ghost of Henry James* (1970), and he labored under that writer's influence for his first five books. Then, in the Francoeur Trilogy, Plante turned his eye toward his family and found his own spare, dark, abstract voice. That trilogy—*The Family* (1978), *The Country* (1981), and *The Woods* (1982)—in its vivid sense both of the distance that separates family members and of the disquieting mystery of the mundane, bears comparison with Henry Roth's *Call It Sleep* (1934).

Plante has since written *Annunciation*, a novel that by its very title asks to be seen as a Christian allegory. Unlike his previous novels, which are short and autobiographically inspired, *Annunciation* is long and heavily plotted. It depicts a modern world rife with despair, rootlessness, anomie, and suicide. Ultimately, its characters embrace the Catholic faith, enacting a contemporary version of the Annunciation.

The complex plot of *Annunciation* consists of two threads that are eventually twined together. The first concerns Claire O'Connel, an American art historian living in London with her sixteen-year-old daughter Rachel. As the book opens, Claire is spending a rare weekend away from Rachel with her bland English lover George. The afternoon of Claire's return to London, Rachel, returning home from school, is raped. The trauma of the event reverberates throughout the novel.

As readers soon discover, Rachel's father, an atheist, committed suicide several years earlier. Claire, seeking to protect her daughter, has managed to make his death appear accidental. Now, Claire's foremost anxiety is that Rachel will, like her father, take her own life.

After the rape and resulting pregnancy, Rachel is brooding, incommunicative. Claire hovers nervously, yielding to Rachel's desire to keep her plight secret. Ultimately, Rachel decides to have the child rather than undergo an abortion and to drop out of school for a year. A lapsed Catholic, Claire actively encourages her daughter's willfulness; she does not have any other sustenance to offer her.

Meanwhile, in New York, young Claude Ricard, an editor of art books, leads a busy but fundamentally aimless life. Half French-Canadian, half Russian, Claude feels cut off from both his ethnic and his religious heritage. One day, he meets Penelope Madge, an English journalist, at a gallery opening. The two begin an off-again, on-again affair that seems to have little effect on the inscrutably casual Penelope but inspires obsessive feelings in Claude.

Trying to connect with his past, Claude occasionally visits Lidia Rivers, an elderly Russian émigré. Lidia introduces Claude to Marie Clark, a young niece who is about to visit Russia for the first time. Marie is a dutiful, depressive girl who fills her life caring for Lidia. Her trip to Russia only increases her vague disillusionment. Afterwards, she and Claude meet occasionally. They seem to have something in common—a shared heritage, perhaps, and a shared inability to find meaning in that heritage. Mutely, indirectly, Marie seems to appeal to Claude for help.

After Penelope inexplicably rejects him, Claude finds himself overwhelmed by frighteningly violent fantasies about her. Then Marie kills herself. He tries to comfort the devastated Lidia, offering to travel to Russia with her someday, but she is old and frail, and soon she dies. Penelope moves back to England. Claude is left trying to piece together the pieces of his shattered psyche.

The narrative returns to Claire, whose main link with Claude is her ambivalence toward her Catholic past. As a girl, Claire was devoutly religious; now, however, she studies religious iconography with the detached perspective of the art historian. Yet Claire feels no particular devotion to her vocation. She does not know if she will ever complete her dissertation, about the suicidal Renaissance painter Pietro Testa.

Then, perusing an obscure eighteenth century book in the library, Claire reads about a painting by Testa that she has never seen or seen mentioned. It is an annunciation painted for a church in Lucca, Testa's hometown. With Rachel, she travels to Lucca to see what they can discover about the Testa annunciation.

There Claire runs into Henrietta Ridge, a fellow graduate student whose uncle is Sir Roger Leclerc, a renowned art historian who lives outside Lucca. A commanding, self-centered man, Leclerc takes an immediate interest in Rachel; he jokes grotesquely with the girl about the secrets she must have. He takes a cursory interest in the missing Testa annunciation but surmises that it was sold long ago by the Lucca church. Leclerc discusses Testa with Claire; as a fervent Catholic, he finds the painter's suicide not only sinful but also uninteresting. He nevertheless offers Claire a clue to the painting's whereabouts, remembering that an art historian mentioned having seen it before the Revolution in the collection of a Russian prince. He encourages her to contact a Russian friend of his in London, Maurice Kuragin.

Maurice proves to be the pivot on which the plot of *Annunciation* turns. Having accepted a work assignment in London, Claude Ricard meets Maurice at a party. He is drawn to the old man by his youthful energy, his social ease, and his background.

Maurice dotes on Claude, inviting him back to his modest apartment and introducing him to some Russian friends.

Meanwhile, Claire contacts Maurice, who invites her and her daughter to tea. At Maurice's apartment, Rachel senses intuitively that Claude and Maurice will find the picture. Another day, Claude goes for a walk in a park with Rachel. She tells him about the rape—the first time she has mentioned it to anyone other than her mother. Claude finds that he is immensely attracted to her, yet he is unable to reassure her. When they return from their walk, they find that Maurice and Claire have agreed to go to Russia in search of the Testa annunciation. Claude and Rachel agree to join them.

The final section of the novel begins as Claude and Maurice arrive in Moscow ahead of the O'Connels. Immediately Claude begins to feel feverish, and Russia seems to make the old man feeble. Maurice does not recognize anything from his youth. Claude and the old man travel to a rundown apartment complex to meet Sasha and Vera Poliakoff. Vera is distantly related to the Volkanskys, who may have owned the Testa annunciation. The Poliakoffs receive their guests awkwardly but graciously; they have a young son, Alyosha, who fascinates Maurice. As for the Testa painting, Vera and Sasha are completely ignorant. A visiting friend, Katya Platonova, starts to mention someone who might help them find it, but Sasha silences her with a look.

As time passes with no trace of the painting, Claude feels immensely let down, thinking of how Claire and Rachel will arrive in Russia only to be disappointed. Back at the hotel, Maurice, whose health seems shaky, feels compelled to go out and buy a bicycle for Alyosha Poliakoff. On the way back with this present, Maurice suddenly collapses and dies on the street.

The next day, Claude, devastated, finds himself walking in the snow to a nearby bridge. He contemplates jumping off it, but instead he continues walking. Soon he meets a familiar-looking woman: Katya, whom he had met at the Poliakoffs'. She takes him to meet a shady-looking friend named Viktor. Viktor leads them from one decrepit apartment to another. While Viktor and Katya have inscrutable meetings with friends, Claude becomes feverish, hallucinatory.

Claire and Rachel arrive at the Moscow hotel to find no trace of Maurice or Claude. After they check into their rooms, Sasha Poliakoff telephones for Claude. He comes to fetch Rachel and Claire and tells them of Maurice's death. Together, they discuss what could have happened to Claude. That night, back at the hotel, Rachel is on the verge of despair; Claire for the first time urges her to have faith. The next morning, they wander the streets. Frustrated with Rachel, Claire finally tells her that her father died by his own hand. Rachel rushes off, and Claire loses sight of her.

Torn by fear, Claire returns to her hotel, where Sasha is waiting for her. Claude has turned up at his apartment and has found the painting. Claire asks to be taken to it. Claude leads her to a rundown apartment, the home of the Princess Volkanskaya. On a wall behind a sofa, torn and dark, the Testa annunciation is hanging. Claire kneels before it, crying. Soon she hears the sound of Rachel coming up the stairs. Somehow, on her own, the girl has found her way to the painting.

Together, Claude, Claire, and the pregnant Rachel stand awestruck in front of the legendary painting. This mysterious work of art, of only aesthetic interest at first, has become the means by which all three characters have found faith. The novel ends the next day, when Claude takes the girl he loves and her mother to lay flowers on Maurice's grave.

Throughout his career, Plante has had several recurring subjects: family, Catholicism, and homosexuality. Never one to embrace gay liberation, Plante has always insisted on a more complex identity for himself than that of a gay writer. After *The Catholic* (1986), a hothouse novel of homosexual obsession, the homosexual theme begins phasing itself out of his writing as his Catholicism became more emphatic. *The Accident* (1991), his excellent novel prior to *Annunciation*, deals with two very different Americans studying at a Catholic university in Louvain. One is brooding, agnostic, unfocused; the other, extroverted, generous, and a believer, cannot help but alienate his friend with his puppylike attentions. The novel ultimately becomes a depiction of the need for faith, but its power derives from the three-dimensionality of the two students' friendship. Never does Plante violate his characters' psychology to make his metaphysical point.

Annunciation seeks once more to show that only religious faith can make life bearable. Time and again, Claire urges her daughter to rely on her will. Time and again, Claude attempts to confront the darkness within and without him through reason. Ultimately, however, they both come to realize that the strongest element of existence is the irrational, that only by embracing Catholic mystery can they find some comfort.

The novel begins well, rendering both characters' extreme anxiety with great vividness. As Claire and Claude start to travel, though, as their destinies become entwined and various subsidiary characters accumulate around the margins, *Annunciation* begins to strain one's credulity. Suicide follows suicide; despair engenders more despair. Literary devices—the increasingly symbolic use of Russia, for example, or the inexplicable fevers and swoons characters experience when contemplating religion—start to become obtrusive. The novel's themes begin to seem reductive, its outcome predictable.

One cannot excuse these flaws by citing the novel's allegorical intentions. When *Annunciation* works, as it does in depicting Claire's weakness in the aftermath of Rachel's rape or Leclerc's simultaneously sadistic and compassionate treatment of Rachel, it succeeds because of its psychological roundedness, its awareness of human ambiguity. When it fails to convince, it does so because allegorical intent begins to override plausibility, because its plot has become repetitious and unwieldy.

Surely, the morbidity of *Annunciation* must be, at least in part, Plante's reaction to the AIDS epidemic. Abstracted from that context, however, the endless string of deaths becomes overly emphatic, even self-indulgent. Furthermore, the supercharged bleakness of the bulk of the novel renders its final revelation simultaneously obvious and implausible. A novel that takes as its subject darkness and mystery ends up all too programmatic.

Richard Glatzer

Sources for Further Study

Booklist. XC, March 15, 1994, p. 1303.
Chicago Tribune. July 25, 1994, V, p. 2.
Commonweal. CXXI, August 19, 1994, p. 23.
Kirkus Reviews. LXII, March 15, 1994, p. 331.
Library Journal. CXIX, May 1, 1994, p. 139.
Los Angeles Times Book Review. August 7, 1994, p. 15.
The New York Times Book Review. XCIX, May 15, 1994, p. 14.
The New Yorker. LXX, June 27, 1994, p. 195.
Publishers Weekly. CCXLI, March 28, 1994, p. 83.
The Washington Post Book World. XXIV, May 22, 1994, p. 6.

THE ART OF THE PERSONAL ESSAY
An Anthology from the Classical Era to the Present

Editor: Phillip Lopate (1943-)
Publisher: Anchor Books/Doubleday (New York). 777 pp. $30.00
Type of work: Essays

From Seneca to Michel de Montaigne to William Hazlitt to Jorge Luis Borges to E. B. White to Virginia Woolf, this comprehensive essay anthology features some of the best examples of the personal essay as it has evolved over the last two thousand years, written by men and women from diverse cultures

The Art of the Personal Essay: An Anthology from the Classical Era to the Present is an extensive collection of essays compiled by Phillip Lopate, an English professor at Hofstra University in New York City and himself the author of two essay collections. Here, Lopate has selected some seventy-five essays written by fifty authors—including himself—spanning the last two thousand years and representing cultures from all over the globe.

Lopate's thirty-two-page introduction provides a detailed analysis of the personal essay as a literary form. According to Lopate, the personal essay is noted for "its friendly, conversational tone, its drive toward candor and confession, and its often quirky first-person voice." The reader becomes privy to the essayist's most private thoughts, written in a conversational manner, avoiding big words and complicated ideas. Honest, heartfelt, and confessional in tone, the personal essay points up the universality of human experience. According to Michel de Montaigne, the patron saint of the personal essay, "Every man has within himself the entire human condition." Yet at the same time, the personal essay serves as a constant reminder of the sheer solitude involved in the very act of writing.

The anthology is divided into five sections. Section 1, "Forerunners," is dedicated to five early writers whose work is akin to the personal essay: the classical Seneca and Plutarch (Montaigne's favorites), Japanese Sei Shonagon and Kenko, and Chinese Ou-yang Hsiu. Section 2, "Fountainhead," consists entirely of three essays by Montaigne.

Section 3, "The Rise of the English Essay," focusing on the essay's golden age, is deservedly one of the longest sections of the book. Beginning in the seventeenth century with Abraham Cowley's "Of Greatness," this section moves through the centuries with selections by such celebrated authors as William Hazlitt, Robert Louis Stevenson, and Virginia Woolf, ending with George Orwell's "Such, Such Were the Joys. . . ." Section 4, "Other Cultures, Other Continents," features such nineteenth and twentieth century greats as Russian Ivan Turgenev, Chinese Lu Hsun, Japanese Junichiro Tanizaki, Argentinean Jorge Luis Borges, French Roland Barthes, and Nigerian Wole Soyinka.

The fifth and final section, "The American Scene," which is by far the largest section in the collection, begins in the nineteenth century with Henry David Thoreau and features examples of such fine essayists as James Thurber, E. B. White, Gore Vidal, Joan Didion, and Lopate himself. Although this section is overly large, part of it is devoted to essays by such relative newcomers as Scott Russell Sanders, Gayle Pemberton, and Richard Rodriguez.

Besides the standard table of contents, the essays are listed by theme and by form. The themes are as varied as the talent pool, tending toward the familiar and the domestic, with such subjects as friendship, solitude, city versus country life, walking, leisure, writing, food, and death. The essays also take many forms—from humor to meditations to diaries to letters to newspaper columns to mere lists.

Acknowledging the fact that many writers have written personal essays, Lopate states that he tended to choose those who were specifically dedicated to the form. Furthermore, as he does not believe in using excerpts, Lopate had to pass on some excellent examples, such as Virginia Woolf's *A Room of One's Own* (1930) and James Baldwin's *The Fire Next Time* (1963), simply because of their length. Lopate further acknowledges the dearth of women writers in the collection, attributing this to the fact that few wrote in this genre prior to the twentieth century. The same goes for the underrepresentation of certain cultures—not all cultures have been drawn to the personal essay as a form of expression.

That said, this anthology is one of the first to celebrate the personal essay as a distinct literary genre, and it is evident that Lopate's personal preferences are well represented. Each writer is introduced by a brief biography, in which Lopate's eloquent turns of phrases add to the reader's enjoyment of the essays themselves. Regarding William Hazlitt, Lopate writes, "Hazlitt's very irritableness, which goaded him on like sand in an oyster, led in the end to beautifully formed pearls." As for E. M. Cioran, Lopate hits the nail on the head with this description of Cioran's work: "First he isolates and cauterizes the wounds of history with his corrosive intellect, then he cuts away all mental flab, false hopes, and shallow promises to expose the pus underneath."

A further example of Lopate's shrewd analysis can be found in the introduction to Junichiro Tanizaki's essay "In Praise of Shadows." In this essay, Tanizaki begins with a discussion of his building a house, and via his descriptions of woodwork, toilets, plumbing, and lighting, he segues into a lament on the intrusion of Western technology and values on Japanese culture. In the biography of Tanizaki that precedes the essay, Lopate notes, "The essay's structure keeps opening out like a series of rooms; indeed, reading it is like experiencing a piece of wonderfully complex domestic architecture." How much more meaningful becomes the essay with this vivid image planted in the reader's mind.

The Art of the Personal Essay is a volume dense with imagery and insight, a veritable treasure trove of good writing and human idiosyncrasy. After all, personal essayists do not necessarily take the common road; they often play devil's advocate, coming across as curmudgeonly or even mean-spirited. Yet the personal essays included are ripe with universal words of wisdom, from Montaigne, who writes, "And on the loftiest throne in the world we are still sitting only on our own rump," to Carlos Fuentes' "I need, therefore I imagine," to Samuel Johnson's "Greatness is nothing where it is not seen, and power nothing where it cannot be felt." No one recognizes the validity of these people's work more than their fellow essayists, who, according to one reviewer, "quote classical authors when it suits them and quote themselves when it doesn't." Thus Abraham Cowley refers to Montaigne, Hazlitt to Charles Lamb, Adrienne Rich to James Baldwin, and so on.

Despite the span of time evidenced in this anthology, there is a certain timelessness to the themes. When Seneca, writing in the first century A.D., describes the noises he must contend with living as he does above a public bathhouse, he could just as easily have been writing of living in any large city in the 1990's:

> Now imagine to yourself every kind of sound that can make one weary of one's years . . . someone starting up a brawl, and someone else caught thieving, and the man who likes the sound of his voice in the bath, and the people who leap into the pool with a tremendous splash. . . . Then think of the various cries of the man selling drinks, and the one selling sausages and the other selling pastries, and all the ones hawking for the catering shops, each publicizing his wares with a distinctive cry of his own.

These words, written almost two thousand years ago, retain their familiar ring. Similarly, these words of Sei Shonagon, a court lady writing from tenth century Japan, describe one of her many "hateful things": "One has been foolish enough to invite a man to spend the night in an unsuitable place—and then he starts snoring." Richard Steele, writing in the eighteenth century, describes a phenomenon yet familiar to a twentieth century sensibility: "We, that are very old, are better able to remember things which befell us in our distant youth, than the passages of later days." James Baldwin's writing about the Harlem race riots of 1943 calls to mind the Los Angeles riots of 1992. Thus have these writers reached out and latched onto essential truths and passing fancies, pointing up the old adage, "The more things change, the more they stay the same."

Lopate concludes the anthology with a selected bibliography, including works about the personal essay as a literary form, books by authors featured in the anthology, and essays by writers who were not included in the anthology for various reasons. *The Art of the Personal Essay* is a thorough reference source that will appeal to either the student or the general reader. Ironically, because the personal essay proliferated with the growth in the number of periodicals and was written primarily to entertain, it has traditionally been given short shrift as a literary genre. As a scholarly study of this often ignored or overlooked form, this anthology should not only validate the personal essay as a legitimate literary expression by acknowledging and paying homage to its vast heritage but also promote further study of and contributions to this uniquely personal and intimate writing form.

Cynthia K. Breckenridge

Sources for Further Study

Booklist. XXV, April, 1994, p. 376.
Chicago Tribune. March 13, 1994, XIV, p. 4.
Choice. XXXII, October, 1994, p. 276.
The Christian Science Monitor. March 25, 1994, p. 19.
Library Journal. CXIX, February 1, 1994, p. 46.
Los Angeles Times Book Review. February 27, 1994, p. 4.
The New York Times. March 2, 1994, p. C20.
Publishers Weekly. CCXLI, January 10, 1994, p. 56.
The Wall Street Journal. January 31, 1994, p. A10.
The Washington Post Book World. XXIV, April 17, 1994, p. 15.

AS MAX SAW IT

Author: Louis Begley (1933-)
Publisher: Alfred A. Knopf (New York). 146 pp. $21.00
Type of work: Novel
Time: 1974-1990
Locale: Massachusetts, Italy, China, Pennsylvania, and New York

A wealthy middle-aged law professor reflects on his friendship with a famous architect and the architect's young male lover, who dies of an agonizing, inexorable disease

Principal characters:

MAXIMILIAN "MAX" HAFTER STRONG, the narrator, a professor of law at Harvard University
CHARLIE SWAN, his college friend, a famous architect
TOBY, Charlie's young protégé and lover
CAMILLA, Max's first wife, a museum curator from England
LAURA, Max's second wife, the proprietor of a gallery in Milan
ARTHUR, a businessman, Max's college friend
ROLAND CARTWRIGHT, a documentary filmmaker
EDWINA and RICKY HOWE, English aristocrats, Max's part-time neighbors in the Berkshires
EMMA HAFTER STORROW, Max's wealthy elderly cousin
WANG JUN JUN, Max's interpreter-guide in Beijing
EDNA and RODNEY JOYCE, Max's American hosts at La Rumorosa, a sumptuous villa in northern Italy

"I am curious about obligations," declares Maximilian Hafter Strong, by way of explaining why he teaches contract law at Harvard University. A curiosity about obligations is obligatory for any reader who would profit from *As Max Saw It*, his fictional memoir of an unlikely friendship. Yet Max, who writes an acclaimed treatise on contracts, demonstrates his curiosity through distance, through strategies of evasion. Though he admits that "relationships did not stick to me," *As Max Saw It* is a meditation on relationships and obligations that the law professor has, willy-nilly, accumulated over the course of sixteen years and more. They continue to cling, regardless of whether Max acknowledges their claims on his memory and imagination. In his third novel, Louis Begley, an accomplished international lawyer who did not begin publishing fiction until 1991, with *Wartime Lies*, offers an elegant study in emotional insulation. It is unlikely that readers will view the experience that his narrator recounts quite as Max saw it.

As Max Saw It begins on the day that the narrator and Arthur, an old college chum, arrive at La Rumorosa, a sumptuous villa on the shores of Lake Como owned by Edna Joyce, an acquaintance from their days as Harvard undergraduates. Arthur is an opportunistic businessman who has cultivated the art of sponging off the rich, and Max, an obscure professor accustomed to living as and with a graduate student, is touring Europe by tagging along. The reader can deduce the date, August 9, 1974, from the fact that Max listens to Richard Nixon's resignation speech that night on the radio in his room. The novel concentrates closely on the private lives of privileged characters, men and women with enough assets to indulge sumptuous tastes in dining, housing, and travel. Like Begley's previous book *The Man Who Was Late* (1993), it shows a fine eye for the ranks and perquisites of wealth. Yet brief allusions to public events—the Tiananmen Square massacre, John Hinckley's assault on Ronald Reagan, the death of baseball commissioner Bart Giamatti, the fall of the Berlin Wall—calibrate the time frame and remind the reader that no one—neither Nixon nor Max—can extricate himself entirely from history. Withdrawal into the merely personal is as futile as expecting immunity from a plague, especially during the age of AIDS.

At La Rumorosa, Max is immediately implicated in the life of Charlie Swan, another Harvard classmate though four years Max's senior. In Cambridge, tall, brash Charlie was "noted for his prowess in a single scull and with a martini shaker," but he has since become an internationally renowned architect. Though they have not seen each other for more than ten years, Charlie greets Max bluntly, favoring him with intimate confidences, as though recognizing in the reserved professor some mystic link to his own effusive self. While Charlie and all the other house guests spend the morning touring the region around La Rumorosa, Max stays behind and encounters by the poolside an extraordinarily attractive sixteen-year-old youth whom he describes as "Eros himself, longhaired and dimpled, his skin the color of pale amber." He is Toby, Charlie's protégé and an apprentice in his Geneva office. A few years later, while in Beijing to advise the Chinese government on legal matters, Max meets Charlie and Toby again and discovers that they are lovers.

In passing, Max, who comes of undistinguished Rhode Island stock, reveals a few details about his own life. He inherits great wealth from a cousin in Pennsylvania, and he marries an Englishwoman, Camilla, who works at Harvard's Fogg Museum. Yet the narrator's own fortunes are made to seem incidental to the story of Charlie and Toby and how their story intersects with Max's. The professor's newly acquired riches enable him to purchase a rural retreat in the Berkshires of western Massachusetts, near one built by Charlie. Max and Camilla spend long weekends and vacations away from Cambridge in the company of Charlie and Toby as well as other unusual figures. These include Edwina and Ricky Howe, dotty English aristocrats who rotate residences to avoid taxes, and Roland Cartwright, a raffish English documentarian whom Max suspects of sleeping with Camilla. When Camilla announces that she is returning alone to London to accept a position at the National Gallery, Max is too detached from his own relationships to react in any way except to fall sleep.

More notable to Max than the disintegration of his marriage is the relationship between Charlie and Toby, which, despite disparities of age and social status, endures to Charlie's sixtieth birthday. On the evening of the celebration, held at Charlie's Berkshire house, it becomes indubitably clear that Toby, who has developed sores on his face, hands, and forearms, is gravely ill. A few months later, he dies in severe pain in Charlie's bed.

Out of what he characterizes as "a mixture of respect for Toby's dignity, squeamishness about illness, and fear of reaching that point where pity intersects with contempt," Max restrains his curiosity about his friend's dire condition. The death itself occurs as if off-stage; the reader jumps abruptly from a sickbed conversation between Toby and Max to Toby's snowy funeral. It is only later, indirectly, that one learns something of Toby's final moments, when Max recounts a memory that Charlie shared.

It is apparent from his symptoms that Toby probably dies of AIDS, the lethal, epidemic disorder that has disproportionately afflicted homosexual men. Yet *As Max Saw It* is an AIDS novel that never once mentions the dreaded acronym. At least two of its three chief characters are gay, but though in conversations with Max, Charlie delights in flouting prim conventions, the narrator is remarkably reticent about men's love for other men. At one point, Charlie teases Max with the suggestion that he himself might not mind being seduced by Toby. Though later admitting, "I was moved by his beauty," Max never responds explicitly to Charlie's suggestion. Is he merely repressing his homosexual inclinations? If so, is such repression a manifestation of anxiety and obsession? Max professes all-consuming love for Laura, the Italian art dealer who becomes his second wife after lawyerly, long-distance correspondence, yet his text is much more attentive to Toby than to Laura. In its final pages, his joy in Laura's pregnancy is overshadowed by shock at Toby's death. While Max does not explicitly subscribe to Charlie's blatantly misogynous definition of women—"a hole filled with juice that starts to smell like fish upon contact with air"—his memoir is partial to its male characters.

After divorcing Camilla, Max learns that his first wife has indeed been unfaithful to him, though not with Roland but with Toby. The implications of that fact are astounding, but aside from a temporary pique over betrayed friendship, Max, ever the judicious, prudent scholar and scholar of jurisprudence, never acknowledges astonishment or even any awareness of the implications. As the AIDS virus is most commonly transmitted through sexual contact, it is quite possible that Toby has infected Camilla, who in turn has infected Max. Readers are left to ponder the possibility that their narrator is dying of the same harrowing disease that killed Toby; Max does no such pondering himself.

He does announce that he donated blood for a transfusion during Toby's final days. "I am glad that they are going to fill me up with your blood," says Toby. "Charlie also has the same type, so our three bloods are getting all mixed up together." Max records the proclamation of fraternity without any commentary other than an eavesdropping nurse's observation: "We're all related like that . . . only people don't take time to think about it." Preoccupied with abstract concepts of contract law, Max either does not take the time to think about his fellowship with Charlie and Toby or else refuses to concede it to the reader, or himself.

Max's most dramatic act of denial occurs in the concluding paragraphs of the novel, which record Charlie's account of the architect's final moments with Toby. Charlie recalls how, distraught over the agony and impending death of his lover, he rushed into the bathroom and cut up his own cheeks and gums until the blood flowed freely. He then returned to Toby in bed and brought him to orgasm. Since the most efficient way of transmitting the aids virus is sexually and through an open, bloody wound, Charlie's action cannot but be seen as a kind of desperate *Liebestod*, a romantic suicide. Max gives no indication that this is the way he sees it, or that he realizes that infected through Camilla with Toby's AIDS, his blood flows with the same fatal virus that inhabits both Charlie and Toby.

Max visits China as a coddled official guest twice during the sixteen years covered by the novel. He is more comfortable as an outsider in Beijing, behaving according to a formal code of manners, than as an intimate in Massachusetts, where the etiquette seems more confused. He revels in his role of benefactor to Wang Jun Jun, an attractive Chinese guide, but after she comes to study at Harvard, he detaches himself from her when their relationship threatens to undermine his defensive routines.

After publishing a masterly treatise on contract law, Max is appointed Elijah Wooden Professor of Jurisprudence at Harvard—a title that, Camilla teases, "fits him to a T." Charlie Swan, whose parents christened him in sly tribute to Charles Swann, the Proustian character who wastes his life in quest of an unattainable and unworthy love, asks Max, "Do you believe in the fatal irony of names?" Maximilian Hafter Strong lacks the strength of character to confront the multiple ironies in his story that are readily evident to a reader. A wooden, prudent scholar, he is an incongruous choice to narrate a tale of fatal passion that defies convention.

The prose of the narration is exquisitely spare and scrupulously controlled. Reviewers have likened Begley's style to the fastidious finesse of Henry James, but a more obvious precedent for *As Max Saw It* might be *The Good Soldier*, the 1915 novel that Ford Madox Ford subtitled *A Tale of Passion*, though Dowell, its narrator, an emotional eunuch oblivious to the lurid events he is reporting, is ill-equipped to talk of passion. Read obliquely, across what Max concedes having seen, Begley's text admits a rich range of emotions and experiences. Beyond Max's measured cadences the reader can hear a wilder strain, that macabre music of the spheres that Charlie identifies as "the upgathered howl of pain, rising from every corner of the earth. Like a toilet bowl that has overflowed and yet some idiot keeps flushing."

According to Charlie's sanitational simile, *As Max Saw It* is veritably Shakespearean in its intimations of a cosmic void. For all Max's bonhomie, it is a tale told by an idiot.

Steven G. Kellman

Sources for Further Study

Chicago Tribune. May 23, 1994, V, p. 3.
Library Journal. CXIX, April 1, 1994, p. 128.
Los Angeles Times. April 28, 1994, p. E9.
The New York Times Book Review. XCIX, April 24, 1994, p. 13.
The New Yorker. LXX, May 30, 1994, p. 38.

Publishers Weekly. CCXLI, May 2, 1994, p. 276.
Time. CXLIII, April 18, 1994, p. 80.
USA Today. June 17, 1994, p. D3.
The Virginia Quarterly Review. LXX, Autumn, 1994, p. SS128.
The Washington Post Book World. XXIV, April 24, 1994, p. 4.

AUTOBIOGRAPHY OF A FACE

Author: Lucy Grealy
Publisher: Houghton Mifflin (New York). 223 pp. $19.95
Type of work: Autobiography
Time: The 1970's to the 1990's
Locale: New York

A moving account of the author's coming to terms with the disfiguring effects of childhood cancer surgery

Principal personages:
LUCY GREALY, an American poet, who as a child suffered from cancer
HER MOTHER AND FATHER, Irish immigrants to the United States

Autobiography of a Face is the brilliant prose debut of award-winning poet Lucy Grealy. Grealy spent five years of her childhood being treated for cancer. The surgery left her face badly disfigured, and she spent the next fifteen years, as she says, being treated for nothing else than looking different from everyone else. It took more than thirty reconstructive procedures before she could come to terms with her appearance. Until that time, she had to live with the daily torture of peer rejection and the growing fear of never being loved. Feeling ugly, she says, seemed the greatest tragedy of her life: The fact that she had cancer seemed minor by comparison.

The book opens several years after the cancer surgery, with an account of an adolescent Grealy helping a local stable with a pony party in an affluent suburb. She is by then adept at avoiding the curious or hostile gaze of other children by hiding her disfigured jaw behind a curtain of long hair. Anyone who has any lingering doubts that children (to be specific, in this case, boys) can be routinely and systematically cruel beyond adult comprehension will be disabused by this book.

Grealy enjoys working with horses because she gains from them an unconditional acceptance that she does not gain from people. She gets a job at a stable and takes comfort in taking care of the basic needs of the horses. In such work, all extraneous grievances are shed. There is a deeply moving episode in which her parents, through considerable sacrifice, buy her a horse. She has a few months of comparative bliss with the horse before he suddenly dies. Oddly, this happens also with a second horse that replaced the first. Although Grealy's life contains more than its fair share of suffering, she never lapses into self-pity. On the contrary, this is a joyous book, full of humor and lucid insights of the heart and mind that lift readers beyond pain to a realm of compassion and self-knowledge.

The narrative then goes back in time to the chance knock on Grealy's jaw that led to the doctors' discovery that she had cancer. (Her own realization came years later; nobody had actually spoken the word to her to describe her condition.) That discovery leads to the surgery that was to cut away part of her jaw and change her self-image forever. Some years pass, however, before she gains enough self-consciousness to realize that to other people she is ugly. This reality dawns on her with a slow shock.

From then on, her life is an attempt not to be defined by the sneers and contempt of boys at school and men in the street, the unwonted politeness of girlfriends, and the clumsy pity of adults.

A case in point is when she is daily confronted by the mockery of the boys at high school over lunch. In her response to this torture, Grealy shows a precocious maturity. She is aware, even then, that their comments have nothing to do with her, that they are about enabling the boys to appear cool to their friends. Her guidance counselor arranges for her to eat lunch in his office, and every lunchtime from then onward is spent in merciful isolation.

Other cruelty is less premeditated. She recounts a game where one of the girls at the stable asks each of her companions in turn whether, if a certain boy asked her out, she would go. Grealy waits with trepidation for the girl to ask her; she cannot leave her out without seeming to inflict an obvious insult. When Grealy is asked, someone counters by asking why he would want to go out with her. At this moment, Grealy says, she is sure that she will never have a boyfriend.

In comparison to the psychological pain of events such as this, the physical agonies of cancer treatment seem easy and manageable, almost a vacation. Grealy's level gaze never wavers from presenting the rigors of chemotherapy in all of their horror. Yet she rapidly learns to manage this physical suffering, knowing that on the third day after the dreaded injection the vomiting will stop and her strength will return. In fact, chemotherapy becomes for her an arena in which she can prove herself worthy of love—she can be brave and not cry, just as her mother expects. In fact, she does not cry until the very last injection, when all the pent-up tears of the preceding two years well up and demand release.

As the world, with its constant reminders of her "abnormality," becomes ever more threatening, so the hospital becomes ever more comforting—the only place on earth where she does not feel self-conscious. There, her face is her battle scar, her badge of honor. Everyone there is sick, so everyone respects others' deficiencies. Also, as Grealy remarks with her characteristic insight, operations and treatments become more bearable with time and repetition, whereas taunts grow more painful with each one.

This intensely moving and beautifully written memoir constitutes a powerful challenge to a society obsessed with physical perfection. A memorable example is the occasion where Grealy revels in the liberation of walking the streets dressed in a Halloween mask. She wonders how other people can fail to feel the joy of walking down the street without the threat of being ridiculed. In winter, too, she has an excuse to cover the lower part of her face with a scarf and expose the conventionally beautiful upper part to the world. Thus disguised, she says, she talks confidently to people who have no idea that her beauty is a lie. If they think that she is beautiful, they may even love her as a person.

A conscious irony of Grealy's book is that many women who are not disfigured by cancer surgery subject themselves to the same torture. Grealy recounts a telling episode where she is put in a ward full of cosmetic surgery patients who hated their gorgeously hooked noses, their wise lines, their exquisitely thin lips. Beauty, Grealy observes, seems to be only about who is best at looking like everyone else. If she had their faces, any undamaged face, she thinks, she would learn to see the beauty of it.

Yet Grealy adds a further ironic twist against herself. Each time she undergoes yet another reconstructive procedure, she thinks that at last she will start her life, just as soon as she wakes up from this operation. Each time she wakes up, she is disappointed again, but she knows that there will always be another operation, another chance for her life to begin at last, just as soon as she has the face she was "supposed" to have. Here, as elsewhere in this courageous book, Grealy fearlessly faces the psychological temptations of her condition, aware of the fact that she habitually blamed her face for everything that was wrong in her life.

Grealy's world is full of subtle ironies and guilty pleasures. She tells of a boy in a nearby hospital bed, permanently paralyzed from a stupid stunt. Grealy observes that he is like the boys who taunt her at school, but here she is protected by their common circumstances: They are both in pain, both handicapped in different ways, and so he would never dream of saying anything mean to her. With engaging honesty, Grealy confesses that she feels faintly triumphant. Someone from the "other world" of so-called normal people has come over to hers.

Her progressive internalization of the fear and scorn of the world is painful to behold. She goes to extraordinary lengths to hide herself from people's gaze. Sometimes, however, she cannot escape it. At horse shows, etiquette requires that she put her hair up. She leaves it to the very last minute, trying to act casually as she reaches for the rubber band and hairnet. Grealy identifies this simple act as among the hardest things she ever has to do—harder even than chemotherapy and operations. She is certain that no one at the horse shows would ever make fun of her. There is irony, though, in her recognition that although the threat of mockery from others has receded, she is perfectly capable of doing it to herself.

At university, she discovers sex and sees it as her salvation, believing (as many young women do) that if she can get someone to have sex with her, it will mean that she is attractive, that someone will love her. At graduate school studying poetry, she finds a lover, the first of many. Although the relationship does not succeed, at his prompting she begins to dress more like "a woman," exchanging her androgynous clothes for miniskirts and garter belts. She recognizes this as an attempt to use her body to distract people from her face.

Meanwhile, Grealy goes through one reconstructive procedure after another to try to regain her lost beauty. Each time she hopes to wake up from the operation to the perfect new face of her imagination, only to watch one graft after another become reabsorbed into her body and disappear.

Travel becomes an escape from the isolation she frequently experiences in familiar surroundings. In West Berlin, where she does not speak the language, she deliberately develops the art of getting lost. With only her own wits and the help of strangers to get her back home, she discovers a reassuring chaos. She cultivates aloneness in order to put off her loneliness. Yet not all cities offer the safe refuge of anonymity. In London, in an upsetting echo of the high school trauma, she is pursued along the streets by catcalling young men. Initially attracted by her figure, when they get close enough to see her face, they call her ugly and gain amusement from challenging each other to ask her on a date.

Prompted by one of these episodes, Grealy undergoes a revolutionary type of reconstructive operation. Bone is taken from her hip, ground up, and then fashioned into a jaw. For the first time in memory, she looks forward to seeing a face that she likes in the mirror.

The operation is a success. Yet she still does not feel attractive, in spite of what her friends tell her. Instead, she is plagued with self-doubt. Her new face does not look like her. Furthermore, was not her fear supposed to fall away, was not someone supposed to fall in love with her, was not her life supposed to work now that she was beautiful again?

Grealy's story is heart-rending not primarily because of its uniqueness but because of its unexpected universality. There is a message here for all people who postpone their happiness until some mythical date in the future: when they land a job they enjoy, when they lose those twenty pounds, when the right partner turns up, when they have enough money.

The author's life before her final reconstructive surgery consisted of many minor escapes: the curtain of hair, the safe zone of the hospital, horses, sex, travel. Her new face prompts a revelation of the greatest escape of all: her lifelong habit of ascribing to physical beauty the qualities she most desired, attractiveness and lovableness. It was easier to think, she says, that she was still not beautiful or lovable enough than to admit that perhaps these qualities did not belong to this thing she thought was called beauty after all.

At the book's end, Grealy is sitting in a café talking to a man who evidently finds her beautiful. She looks with curiosity at the window behind him in an attempt to recognize herself. This is the final and most delicious irony of *Autobiography of a Face*: So intimate have readers become with Grealy's always strong and ever-growing sense of self that they embrace her final realization that the self is not locatable in the many metamorphoses of the face, that society lies when it says that humans can be most themselves by looking like someone else.

Claire J. Robinson

Sources for Further Study

Ms. V, November, 1994, p. 74.
The New York Times Book Review. XCIX, September 25, 1994, p. 11.
Ploughshares. XX, Fall, 1994, p. 242.
San Francisco Chronicle. December 3, 1994, p. E1.
The Times Literary Supplement. June 17, 1994, p. 31.
The Washington Post. November 29, 1994, p. D2.

BALZAC
A Life

Author: Graham Robb (1958-   )
Publisher: W. W. Norton (New York). Illustrated. 521 pp. $35.00
Type of work: Literary biography
Time: 1799-1850
Locale: France, Switzerland, and Russia

This biography offers a meticulous psychological and philosophical portrait of the literary genius whose extraordinary work laid the foundation for the modern novel

Principal personages:
HONORÉ DE BALZAC, a French writer
BERNARD-FRANÇOIS DE BALZAC, his father
ANNE-CHARLOTTE-LAURE SALLAMBIER DE BALZAC, his mother
HYACINTHE DE LATOUCHE, his friend, agent, and editor
LAURE DE BERNY, one of his mistresses
COUNTESS EVELINE HANSKA, another of his mistresses, whom he married shortly before his death

Honoré de Balzac, one of the great European writers and founder of the modern novel, is the embodiment of nineteenth century France. His monumental work *La Comédie humaine* (1829-1848; *The Human Comedy*, 1885-1893), comprising more than one hundred novels, short stories, and studies, along with several unfinished works, chronicles the transition from a feudal society to an industrialized economy. The prolific creator of more than two thousand characters, linked by family relations or coincidence, Balzac offers a scientific and unified vision of society and the human condition, from the trivial anecdote to the sweeping depiction of the machinations of power. Country life, the bourgeoisie, politics, the military, philosophy: All aspects of French society would eventually find themselves the object of his scrutiny.

Balzac's father, born Bernard-François Balssa into an uninterrupted line of peasants in the south of France, changed his name to Balzac, that of an ancient noble family, and eventually added the supposedly aristocratic *de*. He became a clerk in a lawyer's office, moved to Paris before his twentieth birthday, and rose to occupy such lofty positions as secretary to the King's Council. At the age of fifty, this rather eccentric man accepted an arranged marriage to Anne-Charlotte-Laure Sallambier, eighteen years of age, who came from an ambitious family of haberdashers in Paris. Two years later, in 1799, Honoré was born in Tours. Hours after his birth, he was sent to live with a wet nurse; later, he would see this as his mother's desertion.

At the age of eight, Balzac was sent to the ancient Collège de Vendôme, which would be his home for the next six years. During this time, he would see his mother twice. Even before entering the school, Balzac was an avid reader of adventure stories such as *Robinson Crusoe* (1719), *The Iliad* (c. 800 B.C.), accounts of Napoléon's victories, and the Bible. His solitary time was spent reading and inventing small amusing gadgets, such as the three-nib pen, a time-saver for students required to write lines.

Establishing a rather mediocre record in Latin, geography, history, physics, chemistry, fencing, music, and mathematics, Balzac was sent in 1815 to the Collège Charlemagne in Paris, where the concierge supplied him with forbidden books and coffee—a status symbol because it was a product from the far-off colonies, and later in his life, the fuel of his fictional world. From 1816 to 1818, he studied law at the École de Droit in addition to history, philosophy, and literature at the Sorbonne. Balzac's intellectual development was nurtured by a limitless curiosity, which he hoped to satisfy by following a list he had drawn up of 164 items of future research from gastronomy, acoustics, zoology, and cosmography to differential calculus, cereal-growing, and Presbyterianism. By this time, his will to achieve greatness was clearly established. Despite being offered a full-time position in a Paris law firm, with the chance to take it over after a short apprenticeship, in 1819 Balzac was allowed by his parents to dedicate the following two years to his dream of becoming a writer—with the condition, however, that he live an invisible and disciplined life in Paris, pretending to be visiting relatives in the south of France.

During this time, Balzac, when not immersed in Descartes and Spinoza at the Bibliothèque de l'Arsenal, discovered the novel, then considered to be the type of book read by servants to idle women. To an educated person, such works lacked subtlety and philosophical importance. Tales of the supernatural and gothic novels, for example, were in demand. Balzac became spellbound by this new literary genre, which did not bear the rigor of rhymes but which, with the spread of literacy, could well be his road to glory. Balzac's earliest unfinished novels—*Sténie*, *Falthurne*, and *Corsino*—date from this period.

In 1821, Balzac and Auguste de l'Égreville, a twenty-eight-year-old writer, entered into a professional relationship whereby Balzac would write some novels under single authorship (under his name or a pseudonym) and some in collaboration with l'Égreville, all of which the latter would sell to publishers. In 1822, five such novels were published. Thus began Balzac's first commercial literary enterprises. Living on his own and practically a kept man, deeply in debt to his lover, Laure de Berny, a married woman, Balzac set up shop as a printer seven years after embarking on a literary career. Although monetary rewards were scarce, he came to know the writers Victor Hugo and Alfred de Vigny. Balzac's life as a printer came to an end in 1828, when his business collapsed.

Published in 1829, *Le dernier chouan* (renamed *Les Chouans*; translated as *The Chouans*, 1890), the first building block in the construction of *The Human Comedy*, depicts a monarchist Brittany in rebellion against the revolutionary national government of 1799. This work heralded the creation of a new type of historical novel in which the writer reveals historical trends by using representative characters or "types" in the place of known historical figures. Personally, this period was difficult for Balzac because of a painful collaboration with Hyacinthe de Latouche, his intimate friend, agent, and editor. His relationship with Latouche provides the first glimpses of his versatile sexuality. Balzac's tendencies can be best described not as homosexual nor heterosexual, but simply as sexual. Because of its connotation of sexual deviance in the mid-nineteenth century, male homosexuality was merely touched on in stories of hermaphrodites, such as Henride Latouche's *Fragoletta* (1829), Théophile Gautier's *Mademoiselle de Maupin* (1835; English translation, 1897), and—obliquely—Balzac's *Séraphita* (1835; English translation, 1889). Yet Balzac's introduction of homosexual heroes—Vautrin, Lucien de Rubempré, and Eugène de Rastignac—through subtle and ambiguous descriptions created literary models in the same way that French literature abounded in misers, jealous lovers, and hypochondriacs.

Balzac's rebirth as a writer coincided in 1829 with the death of his father. He regretted enormously that his father had not lived to see him become famous under his own name, but he took heed of his father's warning that his mother would be the strongest and most cunning enemy he would ever meet. It was she, scandalized by her son's unending string of debts, who now controlled the family purse strings.

In 1832, when his mental health had become an object of concern and amusement to other people, Balzac left Paris for Saché in Touraine, where he wished to compose a rebuttal to the gossips. This work would evolve into the novel *Louis Lambert* (1832; English translation, 1889), the story of a genius who transcends the normal plane of reality and goes insane. Balzac's self-diagnosis of aphasia would now seem accurate, for verbal and visual hallucinations, probably attributable to a congenital weakness, recurred throughout his life. During the month spent at Saché, Balzac began to live in his own illusions, convincing himself that he had completed novels barely sketched out. This period was quite short; although it was troublesome for publishers who were taken in by Balzac's delusions, it suggested to Balzac the possibility of combining reality and dream in a fictional world.

Through his correspondence with the Russian countess Eveline Hanska, begun in 1832, Balzac returned to reality. Signing herself "The Stranger" in an anonymous letter mailed from Russia, she chastised Balzac for portraying women as evil monsters in *La Peau de chagrin* (1831; *The Wild Ass's Skin*). In 1833, the two finally met, in Neuchâtel. Until the end of his life, the countess would remain a figure of adoration and inspiration. Following their rapturous meeting, Balzac was hit by a flood of creativity, and he returned to Paris to work on *Eugénie Grandet* (1833; English translation, 1859), which some critics have called his greatest novel.

By the 1830's, Balzac was aging rapidly and, once again, found himself in very deep debt. In mid-1836, he suffered a mild stroke and began having chronic medical problems such as backaches, chest pains, and bronchitis. He felt himself to be suffering from a physical melancholy, with his mind becoming dull from isolation. Overwork became a necessity to stave off bankruptcy but did little to improve his health. In 1836 and 1837 he wrote four novels—*L'interdiction* (1836; *Interdiction*, 1895), *La Vieille Fille* (1836; *The Old Maid*, 1898), *Les Employés* (1837; *The Civil Service*, 1896), and *Histoire de la grandeur et de la décadence de César Birroteau* (1837; *The Rise and Fall of César Birotteau*, 1860)—as well as four short stories, and, among other pieces, the end of *Le Lys dans la vallée* (1834; *The Lily in the Valley*, 1896). He reentered the world of journalism, drafted plays, and for two months worked from midnight to six o'clock in the morning. The revenues from these works enabled him to pay off a substantial portion of his debts. Yet his wish to achieve stylistic perfection forced him to pay for the correction of proofs out of his own pocket, often with advances received from publishers. This endless cycle of debt continued until his death.

In 1842, the preface to *The Human Comedy* appeared. It reveals a comparison of human types to animal species, a theory that all creation proceeded from a single, primordial entity and diversified under the influence of environment, the destructive power of passion, and the perfecting power of society as guiding principles of Balzac's panoramic thought. Rather than a direct and complete reflection of the entire work, the preface is an attempt to marry science and art in the nineteenth century, as well as being Balzac's intellectual biography. By the time the preface was written, Balzac had received word that Eveline Hanska's husband had died. Almost seven years after they had last seen each other, Balzac was prepared to leave for Russia, where he would apply for Russian citizenship and launch a European magazine in St. Petersburg. His romantic pilgrimage to this city in 1843 was heralded by fellow writers, Aleksandr Pushkin and Fyodor Dostoevski among them, as a visit by France's greatest novelist.

Despite further separations owing to the Russian government's unwillingness to allow the countess to leave the country, the couple's love did not waver. In 1846, the future Madame de Balzac suffered a miscarriage; the couple would have had a daughter. In August of 1848, six months after the February Revolution, which saw the fall of the French monarchy, Balzac received extraordinary authorization from the czar to enter Russia, necessary because of social unrest spreading through Europe at that time. At Wierzchownia, the estate of Countess Hanska, Balzac was welcomed into a warm, supportive atmosphere and was revered by servants and peasants. His intention to complete many works proved impossible, however, because of ill health. He was successful in partially correcting the seventeenth volume of *The Human Comedy* but was unable to bring any other project to fruition. Although the other partially corrected versions survived, and, known as the Furne corrigé, provide the basis for most modern editions, the seventeenth volume did not.

The last year and a half of Balzac's life was marked by varied afflictions—bronchitis, gastric fever, ophthalmia, peritonitis, and cardiac hypertrophy. Five months before his death in Paris in 1850 at the age of fifty-one, he and Hanska were married. For Balzac, it was the happy conclusion to a great and noble romance that had lasted sixteen years.

Balzac: A Life is a spellbinding account of the man, literary genius, philosopher, and observer of the human condition. Graham Robb's meticulous and rich anecdotal retelling of Balzac's ideals, passions, and failures reveals his dichotomous nature, driven by his love for Countess Hanska—partially in compensation, perhaps, for the erratic behavior of his clearly nonmaternal mother—and his boundless intellectual curiosity. Intertwined with probing comments that evoke the richness and complexities of *The Human Comedy*, this biography is a beautifully told and supremely sensitive rendering of the life of one of France's most influential writers.

Kenneth W. Meadwell

Sources for Further Study

Booklist. XCI, September 1, 1994, p. 19.
The Christian Science Monitor. September 29, 1994, p. 13.
Kirkus Reviews. LXII, June 1, 1994, p. 760.
Library Journal. CXIX, July, 1994, p. 94.
London Review of Books. XVI, July 7, 1994, p. 14.
Los Angeles Times Book Review. September 11, 1994, p. 2.
The New York Times Book Review. XCIX, September 11, 1994, p. 14.
Publishers Weekly. CCXLI, June 27, 1994, p. 62.
The Times Literary Supplement. June 17, 1994, p. 8.
The Washington Post Book World. XXIV, August 28, 1994, p. 1.

THE BEAK OF THE FINCH
A Story of Evolution in Our Time

Author: Jonathan Weiner (1943-)
Publisher: Alfred A. Knopf (New York). Illustrated. 332 pp. $25.00
Type of work: Science
Time: 1973-1993
Locale: The Galápagos Islands

Through an account of scientific research with Galápagos finches, Jonathan Weiner illustrates natural selection at work

Principal personages:
PETER R. GRANT, a biologist at Princeton University
ROSEMARY GRANT, a biologist and Princeton University faculty member

Volcanic islands represent ideal laboratories for the study of ecology and living forms, for they permit flora and fauna to develop in almost complete isolation. From their origin as sterile masses of lava, over millennia they gradually develop topsoil; then seeds—borne by sea birds, by floating debris, or by humans on brief stops—begin to grow and develop. Once plant communities have been established, they form the basis for animal populations of marine mammals, pelagic birds, or insects and passerine birds blown off migratory courses by storms. A few small land vertebrates, depending on ocean currents, may arrive on floating rafts of vegetation. Once animal life has secured a foothold, it must cope with a climate, terrain, and ecology very different from those of its original habitat. In response, it adapts to the new conditions, over time developing into new and hitherto unknown species. Among the numerous volcanic islands of the world, the most famous are the Galápagos chain off the coast of Ecuador, which Charles Darwin visited in 1835 as a naturalist aboard HMS *Beagle*.

During his stops among the islands, Darwin collected specimens of flora and fauna for further study in England, as he had done in other locations on the voyage. The collected species included several finches of a kind he had never seen; all were similar in color but variable in size and behavior. Most striking to Darwin were the varying sizes of their beaks, suggesting different feeding patterns, though at first he saw little scientific significance in that fact. After returning to England, he posted their skins to the ornithologist John Gould in London and was surprised by his verdict that the finches belonged to previously unknown species. In time, the fourteen species of finches inhabiting the islands became the most studied group of birds in the world. Once it had been determined that they were all descended from a single species, numerous scientists have attempted to explain how this differentiation occurred. Since Darwin's time, one of the native Galápagos species, the largest and the weakest flyer among them, has become extinct, but thirteen species remain on the islands.

Jonathan Weiner's book is primarily an account of one such study of Galápagos finches. Despite its extensive scientific bibliography, it is not a scientific report but rather a narrative of the project of Peter and Rosemary Grant, who have led an ongoing study from Princeton University for the past twenty-one years. They have centered their study upon the ground-feeding finches indigenous to one small uninhabited island, Daphne Major, near the center of the Galápagos chain. While the ground feeders comprise six species, Daphne Major has only three or four species in any numbers. Lacking a freshwater source, the island offers researchers only primitive, stark living conditions. Its forbidding nature, however, ensures that life there has developed without human interference, a fact no longer true of the larger neighboring islands.

Hardly more hospitable to birds than to humankind, Daphne Major's climate consists of a wet and a dry season. If seasonal rains are adequate, the finch population reaches two thousand or somewhat over that, but during the subsequent dry season, the population declines drastically to as few as three hundred during a severe drought. Because of the limited population of finches on Daphne Major and their relative tameness, the Grants have been able to capture and band every bird. Since nests are easily located amid the rather sparse vegetation, unfledged chicks are banded while they are still in the nest. The bands are designed so that individuals within the population can be identified by sight. Rarely, outside a confined area, could a researcher find a limited and easily accessible avian population for a study of this kind.

Unlike earlier researchers, the Grants have taken care to do as little harm to the finches as possible during their long period of study. Mist nets have long since replaced shooting as a means of capturing birds for study (during the early twentieth century thousands of Galápagos finches were shot for scientific study). The procedures used today enable researchers to compile adequate data while interfering little with the daily life of the birds.

Data obtained by the Grants include measurements of beak size, body weight, and wing span as well as records on reproduction and longevity of each bird. In addition, blood samples from individual birds are preserved for further study of alterations in DNA. As is usual in such studies, diets are determined through examination of the intestinal contents of dead birds. Over the twenty-one-year period, the Grants have accumulated data on eighteen thousand individuals. The sheer volume of data is manageable only through computers, and much of their time back at Princeton is spent analyzing the amassed data.

Their project is one of thousands based upon the theory of evolution, which Darwin formulated largely on the strength of observations suggesting that changes in living forms had occurred in the distant past. From an overwhelming body of information—fossil records, the distribution of species over the earth, hybridization, stages of embryo development in higher mammals, the presence of vestigial organs, mutations, the development of domestic breeds through selective breeding—one could infer that evolution of life had occurred. Yet no one in Darwin's time observed one species changing into another, and Darwin thought that such change might require thousands, perhaps millions, of years.

What most interested Darwin was the driving mechanism behind the alterations. From careful study of the breeding of domestic animals, especially pigeons, he observed that breeders deliberately selected those qualities that they wished to be passed down and bred successfully for them. Breeders of bulldogs reported a similar procedure. It was, on the whole, a simple form of what is now known as genetic engineering. Darwin concluded that in nature something similar occurs. In the competition for life, individuals best adapted to their environment have the best chance of passing their genes on to descendants, a pattern he called natural selection.

The occurrence of natural selection has been documented repeatedly by a succession of studies, the most famous example being cited by Weiner. From the 1930's through the early 1960's, northern European cities saw a striking increase in the black mutant form of the peppered moth. The explanation was neither far to seek nor difficult to understand. On city walls and buildings grimed with coal dust and other pollutants, black afforded camouflage from predators. As a result, a higher percentage of mutants survived to reproduce, so that eventually they came to be more populous than the previously dominant lighter form. Following the enactment of environmental laws limiting emissions and promoting the use of natural gas energy, however, the environments became clean and bright once again. Among the moths a decided reversal occurred, so that the lighter form became dominant once again. As with the changes documented by the Grants, decades had to pass before the import of this incidence of natural selection became clear.

The Grants' extensive study, as yet incomplete, has produced mixed and unexpected findings. The Grants have not witnessed the origin of a new avian species. Thus far, studies of new species have been limited either to those created in laboratories through alteration of DNA or to insect or microscopic life, where reproduction is much more rapid than the once-yearly rate normal for small birds. Nevertheless, the Grants have been able to measure significant changes. Their early assumption that large beaks represent an advantage was dramatically confirmed following drought years in the mid-1970's. For their diet the birds are dependent upon cactus seeds, and only large, powerful beaks can crack the largest and toughest seeds. In time of scarcity, large beaks proved advantageous, and following a population decline during one severe drought a higher percentage of large-beaked birds survived to breed. When the beaks of their offspring were measured, the result showed a significant increase in average beak size for the entire population.

It was reasonable to assume that in subsequent generations the finches would become ever larger, with ever larger beaks. Yet contrary to expectations, the population reverted toward the previous norm in subsequent years. With the return of above-normal rainfall, an abundance of seeds worked to the competitive advantage of smaller birds with smaller beaks, for they need less food to reach their ideal metabolic level. The larger birds grew too fast for their strength and died off during the droughts that followed. The study established that changing environments alter the demands for successful competition and thus alter the gene pool of a species more rapidly than is commonly thought. During extreme alterations of the environment, the data appear to show, genetic changes in a species can occur quickly.

Through careful observation, the Grants also discovered that hybridization in nature occurs more commonly than has been thought. It has long been believed that hybridization in nature is rare, though it was well understood that animals such as the large felines hybridize rather freely in captivity. Further, it has generally been assumed that hybrid offspring rarely breed successfully themselves. As Weiner demonstrates, the Grants' project has disproved these assumptions. Not only did the hybrid finches reproduce freely in their natural setting, but the Grants have also concluded that under some conditions hybrids hold a reproductive advantage over nonhybrids. Yet established species do have certain staying powers. The Grants observed the tendency for later generations of hybrids to breed back to nonhybrids and thus to reduce the degree of change while adding to the complexity of the gene pool. Thus there is a kind of regression toward the mean, observable in other wild populations as well.

It is clear that the Grants' research project, even after more than two decades, is far from complete. Much remains to be done with the mass of data and the DNA analysis. The examination of DNA may finally reveal the still-unknown original progenitor of the finches, if it still exists either on the South American mainland or on some Pacific island.

The research conducted on Daphne Major establishes that natural selection works in the way that Darwin thought but is probably more complicated than he realized. As with domestic breeding governed by deliberate decisions, nature selects traits that endow an individual with an advantage in the struggle for life and passes them on to another generation. Yet the environment, or habitat, is also changing, and the species cannot foresee changes that will occur. In a situation that is drastically altered, new and previously disadvantageous traits may serve to promote survival. The Grants have tentatively concluded that drastic changes in habitat can accelerate the process of species formation, though their observations have not established this as fact.

Weiner's account of this extensive project illustrates the principle that nature relinquishes its secrets slowly, to only the most committed. It may well be that in the future, long-term studies will be most productive, even as they are the most demanding. The Grants' project, like Jane Goodall's study of chimpanzees, represents a lifetime effort that promises to produce more conclusions than the dramatic ones reached thus far. Weiner places it well within the context of evolutionary biology, and he makes the import of such studies clear.

Weiner's challenges are to make the book interesting to nonscientists, to explain the significance of the subject without becoming too technical or exaggerating that significance. Throughout, for purposes of clarification, he makes comparisons with numerous similar studies. In addition, he injects humor into the narrative, describes characters and their idiosyncrasies, and exploits local-color possibilities of the setting.

Stanley Archer

Sources for Further Study

Chicago Tribune. June 26, 1994, XIV, p. 7.
Choice. XXXII, November, 1994, p. 483.

The Economist. CCCXXXII, August 13, 1994, p. 80.
Los Angeles Times Book Review. June 19, 1994, p. 2.
Nature. XXXVII, September 1, 1994, p. 27.
New Statesman and Society. VII, September 23, 1994, p. 35.
The New York Times Book Review. XCIX, May 22, 1994, p. 7
Publishers Weekly. CCXLI, April 18, 1994, p. 56.
The Sciences. XXXIV, September, 1994, p. 46.
The Washington Post Book World. XXIV, July 24, 1994, p. 6.

THE BELL CURVE
Intelligence and Class Structure in American Life

Authors: Richard J. Herrnstein (1930-1994) and Charles Murray (1943-)
Publisher: Free Press (New York). 773 pp. $30.00
Type of work: Psychology

The authors argue that intelligence is an inherited and dominant force in the lives of human beings, that it is unequally endowed across groups and individuals, and that it is significantly related to social mobility and social problems

The Bell Curve: Intelligence and Class Structure in American Life is the latest in an intermittent series of works that have emerged in psychology since the turn of the century which argue for a strong relationship between genetics and intelligence. The book tries to demonstrate that intelligence is unequally distributed among ethnic groups and that genetic-based group differences in intelligence rather than environmental influences are responsible for the country's class structure. While the book offers little in the way of new ideas (no social scholar refutes the idea that intelligence has some genetic base or that ethnic groups score differently on intelligence tests), it stands out as the most elaborate discussion of the relationship between intelligence and social class to date. The authors go further than any of their predecessors in arguing that social consequences—upward mobility as well as social pathologies—are directly linked to "cognitive ability." The book is controversial because these ideas, put together, argue for an inherent racial inferiority and an overrepresentation of social pathology among African Americans and Latinos. The book comprises an introduction and four distinct but related parts, with the first three providing the foundation for the policy recommendations proposed in the final section.

Herrnstein and Murray's introduction offers several important premises to their thesis that intelligence is an inherited and dominant force in the lives of human beings. It begins with an essential but brief and incomplete discussion of the conceptualization and measurement of intelligence. The authors' preference for a classical model of intelligence is itself controversial. Classicists presume that intelligence represents a "general intellectual ability" whose structural components can be measured by short paper-pencil tests and reflected in a single score. This may be the most serious flaw in the book. Intelligence scholars have yet to agree on what intelligence is, let alone how it is most effectively measured. Robert Sternberg's 1986 study of intelligence, for example, emphasizes the cognitive processes inherent in problem solving and creativity. In his 1983 study, Howard Gardner proposes seven intelligences or "ways of viewing the world," including linguistic, logical-math, spatial, musical, body-kinesthetic, interpersonal, and intrapersonal. Different cultures may require and therefore emphasize different abilities, resulting in some forms of intelligence having greater value than others. Sternberg's and Gardner's models of intelligence differ from those presented by the classicists and necessitate more complex and individualistic methods of measurement. While Herrnstein and Murray do briefly describe competing schools of thought in the field of intelligence and examples of particular models, they do so far too casually and incompletely, given their thesis. Their focus on the IQ score then, as the best measure of intelligence, directly contradicts more than "popular" or "fashionable" opinion. It is also significantly at odds with the ideas of eminent scholars in the field.

Part 1 of the book, "The Emergence of a Cognitive Elite" (chapters 1 through 4), establishes support for the relationship between intelligence and social mobility by describing the formation of a new class: the "cognitive elite." According to the authors, one consequence of the social policies that began in the 1950's was substantial growth in the college population. Increasingly efficient ability testing widened the pool of prospective students so that intelligence became a more significant screening mechanism than social class. Thus, with the advent of group ability testing, college became a reality for members of the working class and middle class. As the brightest (top-scoring) students were attracted to and concentrated at a handful of elite schools, they began the experience of cognitive stratification, an isolation of the most intelligent individuals in society from the less intelligent, which would continue and intensify in the occupational world. Why should this pattern of isolation continue into the job market? Because, the authors argue, intelligence operates as a screening mechanism here as well. The most elite occupations require higher education, which is limited to the most elite minds. The authors attempt to attribute cognitive success almost exclusively to raw intelligence rather than training, but do so ineffectively, often times inferring, speculating, and offering inappropriate initial assumptions about educational experiences in the United States. Indeed, they virtually equate early educational experiences across social classes and ethnic groups, dismissing the effects of private education, advanced placement classes in select high schools, and other social differences that have been documented as important prerequisites to high scores on aptitude and ability tests.

Since the authors believe that intelligence is largely inherited (rather than simply partly inherited), they predict that economic pressures will only intensify cognitive stratification and segregation, resulting in greater opportunities for a narrower segment of the population: the cognitive elite. They also introduce the reader to their political agenda when they criticize existing prohibitions against hiring based on intelligence testing. Arguing that intelligence is related to efficiency and productivity at all occupational levels, they propose that America and its citizens would be better served if employers were allowed to hire primarily from among the brightest applicants. In short, *The Bell Curve* is a political response to social policies the authors find objectionable. They end this section of the book by suggesting that it may be undesirable to have the cognitive elite continue to form the social policies by which the rest of society must live because less bright people may neither understand nor be capable of adhering to them. This may strike some as a contradiction, for if the brightest cannot establish social policy because they are incapable of anticipating a range of responses from various social and cognitive groups (despite their high cognitive functioning), who is best suited for the task?

If part 1 contains the "good news" about intelligence, parts 2, 3, and 4 contain the "bad." Part 2 of the book, "Cognitive Classes and Social Behavior" (chapters 5-12), offers data about the predictive relationships of intelligence and social class to a range of social problems. In an effort to appear unbiased and scientific, the authors limit the data in these chapters to white subjects. The authors conclude that higher intelligence is associated with socially desirable behavior, and low intelligence with social problems including poverty, high school dropout rates, unemployment, idleness, injury in the workplace, divorce, illegitimacy, welfare dependency, poorer parenting skills, physical, social, and behavioral problems in one's offspring, criminal behavior, and lesser capacity for "civility" and adherence to "middle-class values."

Readers may become overwhelmed by this section of the book, which includes some discussion of statistical procedures and a lengthy series of graphs and tables. The following points should facilitate readers' interpretation of these chapters. Although the statistical methods used by Herrnstein and Murray are appropriate to their task, their emphasis on the statistical significance of the relationships detracts from three important points. First, causality cannot be inferred from correlational analyses. The authors sometimes use statements that directly contradict the statistical interpretations that can be drawn from regression analyses. The use of the word "cause" on page 189 serves as an example: "Our main purpose has been to demonstrate that low intelligence is an important independent cause of illegitimacy." Second, statistical significance is sometimes different from practical significance. For example, some of the group differences presented distinguish between IQ scores within three and six points of one another. What functional difference in intelligence could three points make? Finally, by illustrating only the regression curve, the researchers fail to demonstrate the strength and form of the relationships, implying deceptively that a stronger, more uniform relationship exists. Thus, despite the fact that intelligence explains only a small percentage of the variance among people in any of the analyses presented (often between 2 and 10 percent), the authors' discussion and presentation of the data suggest a more powerful and direct relationship. Although the authors hint at each of these points, the hints are easily subordinated to an overwhelming series of graphs and data, and they are sometimes only included in the appendix. Readers are encouraged to refer to the tables presented in appendix 4 so that they can draw more precise conclusions.

The most controversial section of *The Bell Curve* is found in the third part of the book, "The National Context" (chapters 13-16). It is here that Herrnstein and Murray extend their analyses of cognitive ability and social problems to nonwhite ethnic groups. The authors, to their credit, caution readers that differences within groups are greater than differences between groups, a concept that is difficult to grasp. They also go on to assert, however, that "there are differences between races, and they are the rule, not the exception." What differences do the data suggest? Nothing new. Japanese, Chinese, and Koreans as groups score between three and ten points higher than whites on tests of cognitive ability, while whites score between ten and fifteen points more than blacks. Although the gap between whites and blacks has narrowed in recent years, the authors argue strenuously, in keeping with their previous position about the strong heritability of intelligence, in favor of a genetic basis for intelligence and against any environmental basis. They do so in opposition to data that offer evidence of cultural bias in testing, variation in sibling scores, and the purported impact of transracial adoption.

How are ethnicity and cognitive ability related to social mobility and social problems? With respect to social mobility Herrnstein and Murray suggest that blacks are more likely than their cognitively matched white peers to experience educational and occupational success. For example, some data suggest that blacks are overrepresented in almost all occupations, but most of all in the high-status occupations. With respect to social problems, many of the differences between blacks and whites are reduced or equalized when intelligence is included in the analysis, including annual family income, unemployment, labor force participation, illegitimacy, child development indicators, crime, and adherence to middle-class values. Much of this discussion suggests that America's racial problems are merely sensationalized and that intelligence, rather than race, accounts for social mobility and social problems. Indeed, if intelligent blacks are overrepresented in elite jobs, is not America responding effectively to race?

Their conclusion to this section, the suggestion that "large proportions of the people who exhibit the behaviors and problems that dominate the nation's social policy agenda have limited cognitive ability" is disconcerting. Given the authors' line of reasoning, it is difficult not to conclude that because groups differ and black (and to a lesser extent Latino) IQ scores are lower on average than white IQ scores, and because cognitive ability is primarily inherited and associated with social problems, that blacks as a group are doomed to a life of intellectual inferiority and social pathology.

Having prepared the readers for the inevitability and relative permanence of intellectual inequality, Herrnstein and Murray discuss social policy in part 4 of *The Bell Curve*, "Living Together." The authors' political agenda is most evident in this section of the book.

Their initial concern is with the "dumbing of America," and their recommendations are to shift educational emphasis to the brighter students and offer individuals greater choice in their educational opportunities, particularly through the use of tax credits and vouchers. Evidence is provided for some decline in high school standards (relaxed course requirements in math and science, fewer Advanced Placement courses, lower SAT scores), which they attribute to an inappropriate focus on cognitively disadvantaged students at the expense of cognitively gifted ones. While the causes they offer for the decline (multiculturalism, fostering self-esteem, reducing racial differences in performance) are questionable, it is difficult to argue against increased intellectual standards across the board. Yet, the authors do not do this. Insisting that cognitive ability is difficult to raise, they essentially state that Americans should leave well enough alone and, in contradictory fashion, encourage the development of the cognitive elite. Would that not serve to isolate them further from the population at large?

Educational experiences in the United States are and have always been discrepant, making it difficult to generalize about the role of environment in forming intelligence. Moreover, when there have been opportunities to raise the educational standards for all, the courts have chosen instead to impose a lower limit. Equalizing education is one manner in which the authors' thesis about the relative permanence of ability could be tested. Permitting those with the resources to buy their education is not significantly different from the cognitive and social stratification that presently characterizes American society in the 1990's.

The authors' political agenda is clearest in the two chapters dedicated to a discussion of affirmative action. Chapter 19 is an attack on educational affirmative action; chapter 20, an attack on occupational affirmative action. In the former, the authors argue for class-based affirmative action, although it is clear that they prefer individualism and equal treatment for college applicants (despite favoring differential treatment in education prior to college). It is difficult not to assume that the recommended class-based affirmative action policy is a response to race, especially in the light of the disingenuous concern the authors express about minority self-esteem, the confirmation of minority stereotypes held by whites, and increasingly tense race relations. Their appeal for a "fair" society casts affirmative action as a zero-sum situation which unfairly and unreasonably disadvantages poor whites.

The authors also criticize affirmative action in the workplace. They argue that since the early 1960's, blacks have been overrepresented in white collar and professional jobs, given their intelligence scores, while discrepancies in job performance continue to run along ethnic lines. They find the resulting economic inefficiencies to be unacceptable and propose that affirmative action in the workplace be reconsidered.

Scholars in the area of intergroup relations have recognized for years that ethnocentrism and stereotyping increase during times of economic crisis, because they ease the fears of groups whose status is seen to be in jeopardy. On the one hand, *The Bell Curve* does a good job of alleviating the fears of the "cognitive elite" by justifying the social hierarchy, illustrating social differentiation between groups, and attributing cause for the different social patterns to something inherent and unchangeable in the targeted groups: intelligence. On the other hand, the book is replete with stereotypes of the poor, women, Latinos, Asian Americans, and especially African Americans. By interpreting the differences as they have, Richard J. Herrnstein and Charles Murray are essentially proposing a caste system in which the best society can do is to learn to value and respect the "appropriate places" individuals from the various cognitive classes will occupy.

Jaclyn Rodriguez

Sources for Further Study

America. CLXXI, November 12, 1994, p. 3.

The Economist. CCCXXXIII, October 22, 1994, p. 29.

The Nation. CCLIX, November 7, 1994, p. 516.
Nature. CCCLXXII, December 1, 1994, p. 417.
The New Republic. CCXI, October 31, 1994, p. 4.
The New York Review of Books. XLI, November 17, 1994, p. 7.
The New York Times Book Review. XCIX, October 16, 1994, p. 3.
Newsweek. CXXIV, October 24, 1994, p. 52.
Time. CXLIV, October 24, 1994, p. 66.
The Times Literary Supplement. December 2, 1994, p. 5.

THE BINGO PALACE

Author: Louise Erdrich (1954-   )
Publisher: HarperCollins (New York). 274 pp. $23.00
Type of work: Novel
Time: About 1990
Locale: North Dakota

Lipsha Morrissey answers a mysterious call to return to his home on the Chippewa reservation, where he falls in love with and pursues Shawnee Toose

Principal characters:

LIPSHA MORRISSEY, a well-meaning Chippewa ne'er-do-well who seems destined to become the reservation's traditional medicine man
LYMAN LAMARTINE, his half-uncle, the one successful and ambitious businessman on the reservation
SHAWNEE RAY TOOSE, a talented tribal dancer and clothing designer, and the mother of a son, Redford, supposedly by Lyman
ZELDA KASHPAW JOHNSON, a woman of near fifty who has taken in Shawnee and Redford
LULU NANAPUSH, Lipsha's paternal grandmother and Lyman's mother, a tribal leader
MARIE KASHPAW, Zelda's mother and the sister of Lipsha's maternal grandmother
FLEUR PILLAGER, Lipsha's paternal great-grandmother, a powerful medicine woman

Though the center of *The Bingo Palace* is Lipsha Morrissey's pursuit of Shawnee Toose, this novel is much more than a love story. Lipsha makes essentially the same discoveries about love that several of Louise Erdrich's characters make in the novel that precedes it chronologically, *Love Medicine* (1984; expanded edition, 1993). He discovers that love is the essential medicine, the power that binds humanity together in the face of death. When, at the end of the novel, Lipsha faces death as an adult for the first time, he realizes fully that the human response is to hold on to others, to comfort and protect and receive comfort and protection. On his journey to this realization, when he comprehends the finality of death, he is urgently impelled to love the world, all of creation, without qualification or hesitation. In this novel, however, Erdrich's main efforts go into creating the rich and complex context within which Lipsha's courtship and learning take place. The meanings of the novel emerge from the interactions of Lipsha's self-discovery and lessons in love with his and the reader's growing understanding of the tribal and familial web within which he lives.

Though *The Bingo Palace* is not significantly more difficult than *Love Medicine*, Erdrich takes chances and makes demands on the reader that caused problems for early reviewers, most of whom found the novel lacking in unity. Slow, patient reading and rereading make the novel's problems fairly clear and reveal why Erdrich took chances that would force readers to make extra effort. A main problem is that the novel appears unresolved, as if it demanded a sequel. Several important questions seem unanswered at the novel's close.

One unresolved question is the meaning of the message that brings Lipsha home to the reservation. The book opens with Lipsha's grandmother, Lulu Nanapush, stealing an out-of-date wanted poster for her son, Gerry, who is in prison, and mailing a copy to Lipsha, who—in disgrace—is living outside the reservation in Fargo, shoveling beet sugar at a processing mill. The book then proceeds through twenty-seven chapters, narrated alternately by Lipsha, a tribal voice, and a more general narrative voice. Lipsha and the tribe interpret Lulu's mailing as a message, but no one is quite sure what it means. Lipsha sees it as a call to return home and to change his life. It may be that Lulu wants to rescue Shawnee from the manipulative Zelda Kashpaw. Or it may be that as a tribal leader, she wants Lipsha to move seriously toward succeeding Fleur Pillager in traditional medicine. It turns out that Lipsha is positioned well to help his father when he escapes from prison. This escape and Lulu's response to authorities who come to question her help to further her political aims for the tribe. Lipsha's adventures with his father lead to advances toward all these other possibilities. Perhaps Lulu's intentions included all of them, or perhaps she simply wanted her grandson back with the tribe, free of the empty materialism that threatens him in the "white" world, but she does not say.

This question is resolved in part when one notices the parallels between Lipsha and his great-grandmother, Fleur. Each has miraculously escaped death by drowning; each has lived with some success outside the reservation and brought back something of value; each is noted for and thought to be connected with catastrophes that occur when they are near—though as Lipsha remarks, people tend not to notice the positive events that might be attributed to Fleur. Lipsha has a healing touch, though it deserts him when he is driven to try to profit by it.

Though he is young and seemingly maladroit, Lipsha is a person to whom things happen. Often these things are ridiculous and humiliating, as when—on a vision quest—his vision takes the form of a skunk that sprays him after speaking to him. Whatever Lulu is thinking when she calls him home, she understands that Lipsha, like Fleur, is a center of power. If he returns home, things will happen, and strange as they may appear, she believes that they will be good for Lipsha and for the Chippewa. She has learned in the past what Gerry realizes when the airplane transporting him between prisons crashes, setting him free: What looks like chance and disorder in human life is always part of a pattern too large to be comprehended.

Another unresolved question concerns the new Bingo Palace. Lipsha's half-uncle Lyman Lamartine has developed a plan to bring wealth and comfort to the tribe. Though he is unscrupulous in accumulating money, he seems truly to have the tribe's welfare at heart. Lipsha finally characterizes him as having a gift for seeing the whole picture and making it come true, but as being blind to the personal, unable to understand clearly how his plans will affect the people he uses or the people he wants to benefit. Lyman's most successful business venture has been the current Bingo Palace, a Quonset hut providing food, drink, and general entertainment, which includes gambling and features bingo. He envisions building an elaborate multi-purpose resort on Matchimanito Lake. This complex will attract visitors from all over the region, bringing outside money to the reservation and improving life for the Chippewa. The problem is that the ideal site is sacred tribal land, an important portion of which is owned by Fleur.

The main thing Lipsha learns from the skunk he meets on his vision quest is that this scheme can never work as Lyman envisions it, that it will lead to the destruction rather than the true enrichment of the tribe. The last chapter indicates that Lyman does complete the resort, but it suggests as well that thoughts about its last resident, Fleur, haunt all the Chippewa who frequent the resort, calling their lives into question. Though Erdrich does not show the building of the resort, she makes clear that it is built and that the tribe remains uneasy about its existence.

Perhaps the main seemingly unresolved question of the novel concerns Lipsha's fate. The last chapter he narrates ends with him huddling in a white car, stuck far out in a snow-covered field, as a blizzard buries him. With him is a baby, the unintended passenger in the car that he and Gerry have stolen to get away from Fargo, where he had gone to help Gerry evade the police. Hardly a word is said about Lipsha after this scene. Does he die in the blizzard? Does he ever marry Shawnee? Does he succeed Fleur? None of these questions is answered as directly as is the one about the building of the new resort. Like the question of Lulu's purpose, these questions require the reader to absorb and believe in the cultural values of Erdrich's Chippewa. Erdrich provides hints and requires the reader to construct the answers that fit this world and these people.

That Lipsha survives is suggested by several events that occur on the morning after the blizzard. Now at college studying art and preparing for a career in clothing design, Shawnee dreams that Lipsha kisses her, and she decides that she probably will marry him. She continues making him a ceremonial shirt. Perhaps on the same morning, though no one is sure of this, Fleur goes out to die, to place her own bones in the secret burial cave of her ancestors on an island in the lake. The tribal voice that narrates the last chapter says that she went out thinking of Lipsha, to take his place. In the context of the novel's world, this means that she gives herself to death in place of Lipsha, to save him. By implication, Lipsha is still alive, since this substitution would not be conceived had it not actually taken place. Such a belief would be supported as well by the many traditional stories about the powers of the "four souled"—of whom Fleur is one—to choose substitutes for themselves and, presumably, to offer themselves as substitutes for others.

The reader cannot be certain that Lipsha has in fact survived, that he will marry Shawnee and become the new medicine man, but Erdrich has given the hints and the context in which to interpret them that lead to this conclusion as probable, and she has taken the risk of leaving it to the reader to imagine and to consider such a resolution.

Other unresolved questions may have similar answers or remain mysteries. Lipsha's father is last seen driving across the fields in the blizzard with June Morrissey, Lipsha's dead mother. What becomes of him? Other questions are resolved satisfactorily. Zelda's considerable power and need to love has distorted into a drive to control people's lives for their own good, and this leads to her often harming them. Her daughter Albertine reminds Zelda that she has never really gotten over her first love, whom she rejected because she did not want to live the sort of life her mother lived. As a result, Zelda has a vision of her own and is healed. She decides to let Shawnee go her way, while she takes up with the man she loves, who still resides on the reservation.

Looking at the questions Erdrich raises in her story and how they are resolved or not, considering her mode of narration, with the three main alternating voices, noticing how she draws the reader into a world that is in fundamental ways alien to the mainstream of American culture—these observations suggest why Erdrich has risked writing a difficult novel. To take in the book requires slow, patient reading and rereading. To solve the problems it poses and to be content with solutions that are imagined and not verified requires attuning oneself to the magical worldview that is the central thread of Chippewa tribal life and that is endangered by the new Bingo Palace on the sacred lakeshore. By requiring the reader to enter imaginatively into her world, Erdrich ensures a high degree of identification with her Chippewa. The reader thus comes to share the tribal conviction that Fleur Pillager's medicinal knowledge must be transferred to Lipsha; this thread of continuity must be preserved if the tribe is not to disappear back into its origins, as Lipsha dreams it may during his vision quest. If Fleur's spiritual power does not continue in Lipsha or someone of his ability, then the new resort threatens to absorb the Chippewa into the dominant materialistic culture, and so to make extinct another rich and beautiful, even though imperfect, way of negotiating humanity's relationship with the cosmos.

Terry Heller

Sources for Further Study

The Antioch Review. LII, Spring, 1994, p. 366.
Chicago Tribune. January 9, 1994, XIV, p. 1.
The Christian Science Monitor. January 11, 1994, p. 13.
Los Angeles Times Book Review. February 6, 1994, p. 1.
Ms. IV, January, 1994, p. 72.
The New York Times Book Review. XCIX, January 16, 1994, p. 7.
Publishers Weekly. CCXL, November 15, 1993, p. 72.
Time. CXLIII, February 7, 1994, p. 71.
The Times Literary Supplement. June 17, 1994, p. 23.
The Washington Post Book World. XXIV, February 6, 1994, p. 5.

BLACK BETTY

Author: Walter Mosley (1952-)
Publisher: W. W. Norton (New York). 255 pp. $19.95
Type of work: Novel
Time: 1961
Locale: Los Angeles, California

Easy Rawlins, a black private eye, searches for a wealthy family's missing maid and uncovers a dangerous web of lies and murder

Principal characters:

EZEKIEL "EASY" RAWLINS, a private investigator working within Los Angeles' black community
SAUL LYNX, a white private eye who hires Rawlins
SARAH CAIN, the missing woman's wealthy employer
ODELL JONES, Rawlins' longtime friend, with whom he has had a falling out
MAUDRIA "MAUDE" JONES, Odell's wife
JESUS RAWLINS, Rawlins' adopted teenage son
FEATHER RAWLINS, Rawlins' adopted daughter
RAYMOND "MOUSE" ALEXANDER, a cold-blooded killer and one of Rawlins' oldest friends
ELIZABETH "BLACK BETTY" EADY, the missing woman, an old acquaintance of Rawlins

Since the 1990 publication of his first Easy Rawlins mystery, *Devil in a Blue Dress*, Walter Mosley has become one of the most acclaimed writers of modern detective fiction. Although he now lives in New York City, Mosley, the son of an African American father and a white Jewish mother, spent his early years in Los Angeles, and it is there that he has set his ambitious series of novels. Drawing on an aspect of the city's complex history that has been largely ignored—the changing character of the black community in the years since World War II—Mosley has found a setting and a context for his books that is both utterly original and steeped in the traditions of classic crime fiction.

Mosley's black detective operates within a world that is far removed from the familiar "mean streets" traveled by Raymond Chandler's private eye Philip Marlowe, although the communities themselves are separated by only a few miles. The series begins in 1948 with Rawlins, newly unemployed, falling almost casually into detective work when he is asked to use his connections within the black community to find a missing white girl who sometimes spent time in Watts. Although he never officially or legally becomes a private investigator, his reputation as a reliable man with a talent for detective work soon leads him to other cases. The second book, *A Red Death* (1991), finds Rawlins blackmailed by the Federal Bureau of Investigation into investigating a Jewish union organizer and suspected Communist who is working with a local black church. In *White Butterfly* (1992), Rawlins aids the police with a complicated case that begins with the serial murders of three black women and ends with a white man murdering his daughter for giving birth to a black child.

Black Betty is the fourth book in the series, and it brings Easy Rawlins up to the early 1960's. Since the series began, he has married, fathered a child, lost his wife and daughter to a friend, and unofficially adopted two more children, Jesus and Feather, both of whom he rescued from desperate circumstances during the course of his investigations. As the book opens, Rawlins and his two children are living in an integrated neighborhood in West Los Angeles, having moved out of the South Central area at the close of *White Butterfly*.

Rawlins' new case is set in motion by a visit from a white private eye named Saul Lynx. Lynx has been hired by attorney Calvin Hodge to find Elizabeth Eady, a wealthy white family's maid who is better known as Black Betty. Rawlins had known Betty in Houston twenty-five years earlier, when she was a local beauty with a string of lovers and he was a lovestruck teenager. She had come to Los Angeles with her brother Marlon and found work in Beverly Hills as a maid.

Rawlins begins his search for Betty by tracing Marlon to the desert town of Mecca, where, after a violent encounter with a bigoted store clerk, he finds evidence that Marlon may be dead and an uncashed check that leads him to the Cain mansion in Beverly Hills. There he meets Hodge and Sarah Cain, Betty's employer, as well as Betty's son Arthur and the family's second maid, Gwendolyn, with whom he will later begin a tentative romance. As he is leaving the house, he is arrested, and later he is beaten during a police interrogation by a policeman named Commander Styles. Betty's trail also leads Rawlins to the home of a young boxer named Terry Tyler; he finds Tyler dead and is stabbed in the back with an ice pick by someone hiding in the house. He later learns that it is Betty who has stabbed him, believing him to be Terry's killer, and that Marlon has been beaten to death by two white men searching for Betty.

Rawlins at last finds Betty hiding at a friend's house and learns that both Terry and Gwendolyn are actually her children, fathered by Sarah Cain's abusive father, who was suffocated just prior to Betty's disappearance. A brutal and tyrannical man, Albert Cain had altered his will to leave everything to Betty or her next-of-kin, and someone has been tracking the Eadys down and murdering them. Rawlins suspects Sarah Cain or her son and does indeed learn that Arthur is implicated in his grandfather's death, along with Marlon Eady and Terry. While Rawlins and Lynx are questioning the Cains, Gwendolyn is called away and is later found dead in the garden. Arthur flees the house, and Rawlins and Lynx track him to the home of Odell and Maude Jones, longtime friends of both Rawlins and Betty. There Rawlins finds Arthur's father, Ron Hawkes—the store clerk from Mecca.

Hawkes is still legally married to Sarah Cain and had persuaded Arthur, Marlon, and Terry to murder Albert Cain in the hope of gaining access to his wife's inheritance. After learning the contents of Cain's will, Hawkes murdered both men with the assistance of his friend Commander Styles, and he is also responsible for Gwendolyn's death. Hawkes shoots Saul and escapes, but is later shot by Styles to prevent his own part in the murders from being revealed. At the hospital where Saul is recovering from his wounds, Rawlins meets Mrs. Lynx and discovers to his surprise that she is black.

As in his previous three books, Mosley uses the framework of his plot to explore the realities of black life. In even his most casual contacts with white society, Easy Rawlins is a frequent target for condescension, hatred, and violence. White men refer to him as "boy" although Rawlins is forty-one, and his presence in a white neighborhood is enough to arouse suspicion and hostility. When he is arrested without cause by the Beverly Hills police and subjected to a beating by Styles, Rawlins knows that he has no recourse beyond attempting to placate the corrupt officer and hoping that he can survive the encounter. The treatment he receives is no more than he has come to expect after a lifetime of brutality and disrespect at the hands of white society.

Yet *Black Betty* also offers a portrait of a society on the brink of change. Rawlins now lives in a neighborhood that would have been closed to him in 1948, the year in which *Devil in a Blue Dress* is set, and the civil rights work of Martin Luther King, Jr., is much in his mind. As he comments near the beginning of the book, "The world was changing and a black man in America had the chance to be a man for the first time in hundreds of years." Rawlins views these changes with both hope and caution, well aware that a black man who reaches for too much can still be beaten down without mercy.

This beating need not always take a physical form; financial discrimination is also a potent weapon. One of the book's many subplots involves Rawlins' clashes with a woman named Clovis who has seized control of an investment company from her lover, Rawlins' friend Mofass. The company had been planning—at Rawlins' suggestion—to build a black-owned shopping center in South Central Los Angeles, using primarily Rawlins' property and money. Clovis, however, has sold her investors out to a group of white politicians and businessmen, who have denied the building permits and plan to seize the property from its owners for a city sewage treatment plant, then declare the land unsuitable for a plant and resell it to a white store chain. With the help of Mofass, Rawlins recoups some of his losses, but the land is requisitioned by the city and he sees his investment and his plan for a shopping center taken over by white businessmen. In the book's conclusion, however, he reveals that he later signed on to the construction crew and sabotaged the building's foundations, engineering its eventual collapse. Unable to find justice within the law, he has no qualms about taking his revenge outside its boundaries.

One of the most striking points to emerge in each of Mosley's books is the degree of separation that exists between the black community and the rest of society. In Rawlins' old South Central neighborhood, white faces are an infrequent sight, and the community exists largely outside the awareness—and sometimes the reach—of the white world that surrounds it. Rawlins' children, Feather and Jesus, are not legally his, but he has taken them in knowing that society cares little for their fate and will not look too closely at the details of a black man's life. Jesus, a Hispanic boy whom he saved from a life of child prostitution, has been so severely traumatized by his past that he has never spoken, although he is now in high school. During the course of the book, however, Rawlins discovers that Jesus does speak to Feather, his adored younger sister, and when Rawlins is stabbed, the event becomes the catalyst for the boy's first words to his father. Rawlins' love for his children is one of the book's most engaging features, adding a dimension to his life that helps the character emerge as a fully developed figure living a life filled with ties and obligations.

Mosley's portrayal of the world in which Rawlins moves is also one of *Black Betty*'s strongest features. As his detective tracks the missing woman, Mosley offers the reader vivid miniportraits of a wide variety of individuals: a woman financing her front-yard day-care center by taking gambling bets; an older man dying slowly of cancer; a cowardly bookie and the vicious man who protects him; Odell and Maude Jones, an elderly churchgoing couple who befriended Rawlins in his youth and now hold him responsible for their pastor's death; and Rawlins' old friend Raymond "Mouse" Alexander, recently out of prison and determined to kill whoever turned him in to the police on a murder charge.

One of the book's most illuminating portraits is that of Black Betty herself. Described by Rawlins from his youthful memories as "a great shark of a woman. Men died in her wake," she is seen in her Houston days as a great beauty, a woman with an almost irresistible allure for men. Strong, confident, and unafraid to follow her passions, she leaves an impression on the teenage Rawlins that will last for more than two decades. Upon her arrival in Los Angeles, however, her status as a black woman limits her to domestic work, while her beauty earns for her the unwanted attentions of the master of the house. Betty at first resists Albert Cain's advances, until he sets her brother up in a criminal scheme and uses the evidence to blackmail her into submission. Unable to claim the children she bears as her own, Betty is forced to submit to her employer until his death, when she flees in an attempt to draw blame for his murder to herself. When Rawlins encounters her again after twenty-five years, she is a bitter, grief-stricken, and ultimately defeated woman who has been robbed of everyone she loves by the greed of Cain's family and associates. Her story is unique, but it contains echoes of the lives of many black men and women of her generation who were gradually broken down by a life with too many hardships and no recourse against the injustices of a society that regarded them as second-class citizens.

Walter Mosley's popularity was given a high-profile boost when Bill Clinton listed him as one of his favorite writers after discovering Mosley's work in the wake of the 1992 Los Angeles riots. That the President of the United States should turn to a mystery writer for insights into the city's racial problems is a measure of how skillfully Mosley has used the genre to explore critical social issues and focus attention on a long-neglected aspect of social history.

Janet Lorenz

Sources for Further Study

Booklist. XC, May 1, 1994, p. 1563.

Chicago Tribune. June 26, 1994, XIV, p. 3.

The Christian Science Monitor. July 1, 1994, p. 10.
Fortune. CXXX, August 8, 1994, p. 107.
Library Journal. CXIX, May 1, 1994, p. 141.
Los Angeles Times Book Review. June 5, 1994, p. 3.
The New York Times Book Review. XCIX, June 5, 1994, p. 13.
Newsweek. CXXIV, July 4, 1994, p. 66.
Publishers Weekly. CCXLI, April 25, 1994, p. 60.
The Washington Post. June 20, 1994, p. C2.

BLACKER THAN A THOUSAND MIDNIGHTS

Author: Susan Straight (1961-   )
Publisher: Hyperion (New York). 388 pp. $21.95
Type of work: Novel
Time: The 1990's
Locale: Rio Seco, a fictional Southern California city

This story of a young black man and his family and friends in a California ghetto explores the current situation of the urban black male

Principal characters:
DARNELL TUCKER, a young black man who loves firefighting
BRENDA BATISTE, his girlfriend, whom he gets pregnant and marries
CHAROLETTE TUCKER, their daughter
LOUIS "BIRDMAN" WILEY, their friend, killed in a drive-by shooting
JOHN "RED MAN" and MARY TUCKER, Darnell's parents
ZELENE MARIE "GRANALENE" DUPREE, Darnell's grandmother, now deceased
MR. and MRS. ETIENNE BATISTE, Brenda's parents
ROSCOE WILEY, Louis' father and Mr. Tucker's business partner
DONNIE, Darnell's friend, a security guard
VICTOR and RONNIE, Darnell's friends, sometimes homeless
LEON, Darnell's friend, the local drug dealer
VERNON, Leon's gun-slinging sidekick
GASANOVA, Darnell's friend and Leon's brother
TRENT KING, Darnell's friend, a landscape architect
JUAN and JOSÉ, Darnell's Mexican workers
JOSH FRICKE, a white man who heads the firefighting unit

Aquaboogie: A Novel in Stories (1990), winner of the Milkweed National Fiction Prize, introduced readers to Rio Seco's Westside, a ghetto whose residents speak a black patois as redolent as barbecue and gumbo. *I Been in Sorrow's Kitchen and Licked Out All the Pots* (1992), a much-praised novel spiced with other varieties of the patois, took a Gullah woman from South Carolina's Lowcountry to the Westside. *Blacker than a Thousand Midnights*, featuring more of the rich patois, resumes the Westside saga (including previous characters) by examining the situation of the black male.

Susan Straight, author of these three books, sounds like a new star in the galaxy of black female writers, along the lines of Toni Morrison, Alice Walker, Gloria Naylor, or Ntozake Shange. The books' dust jackets, however, picture a youngish smiling white woman. She should smile, because the literary feat she pulls off is even more impressive than singers' crossing over: She portrays the black community in a totally convincing fashion, right down to the last word of dialect.

Straight's model for Rio Seco (dry river) is Riverside, California, where she was born and grew up in a section resembling the Westside. Apparently she, her husband, and two daughters still live there, close to other relatives and friends. In an afterword to *Aquaboogie*, she noted, "I've been in the community so long, no one remembers any more that I'm not black." She studied at the University of California, Los Angeles and the University of Massachusetts at Amherst, where her instructors included James Baldwin and Julius Lester.

Straight's background helps explain her ability to portray black life and speech, but crossing over into this turf also takes some daring. In *Blacker than a Thousand Midnights*, she is even more daring, crossing over not only racial but also sexual barriers: She explores the mind and life of a young black man, Darnell Tucker, who struggles against racism and ghetto conditions while all around him peers succumb to defeat, drugs, and death.

Straight's subject is certainly on the cutting edge of social concerns. The question, as the media pose it, is whether the black male is an endangered species. While the media themselves—with their discourses of violence, hype, and ignorance—are part of the problem, it is safe to say that the main cause goes back much further. Basically, after centuries of being denied manhood, how will the black male now define it? This is a tough job to give a boy, especially one facing such other disadvantages as racism, poverty, poor education, negative peer pressure, and lack of one or both parents.

The extent of residual racism is underlined in *Blacker than a Thousand Midnights*. Police helicopters with spotlights patrol the Westside at night as if it were some futuristic war zone. Young black men driving around are repeatedly stopped by police, who sometimes flatten them out on the ground and frisk them. While working as security guards, Darnell and his friend Donnie (also black) are mistaken for "perpetrators"; the police turn a dog loose on Darnell and shoot Donnie.

Racial prejudice also pervades the job market. Black men working in the suburbs are viewed with suspicion, and Darnell has to pretend to be Asian to start his own business, Tuan's Oriental Landscape Maintenance Service. They are lucky, though, to have jobs at all. Before starting his own business, Darnell spends considerable time working at temporary jobs, filling out applications, helping his father, and taking care of the baby while his wife works.

An alternative form of "business" that offers quick money is the drug trade. Even Darnell gets his grubstake by making a drug run to Tahoe and Portland. The well-known occupational hazards of this trade are illustrated, however, by Louis' prison term and death in a drive-by shooting. Then there is the kind of company one keeps, exemplified by the rich white "consultant" who runs the operation, the nervous drug dealers such as Leon, and the gun-happy Vernon. Finally, there is the devastating effect of the "product" on people. As various characters make clear, drug dealing is not a morally acceptable business on the Westside.

Otherwise, with unemployment widespread and business opportunities limited, the young men in the novel spend quite a bit of time waiting—waiting for a job, serving time, simply "hanging out" (which seems to be the black version of waiting for Godot). With waiting so endemic in their lives, it is not surprising that they are ready for a little excitement.

Some, in fact, seem to be waiting around to die. Among these are the drug addicts, whom the patois describes either as "sprung" (high) or as "zombies." Equal opportunity operates here: Two of the most pathetic "zombies" are young women, one from

Portland who is willing to lick Darnell's wounds for a ride to Los Angeles and one from Rio Seco who is adept at oral sex because her front teeth have been knocked out. Also showing a death wish are the drug dealers, who appear uncaring and fatalistic.

Then there is Darnell, who has an attraction to fire. Growing up, he would run to see fires and even take along his girlfriend Brenda. Now his ambition is to be a firefighter—an ambition fed by a season in the Conservation Corps and another in a unit fighting forest fires in the mountains. Darnell gets his high from the roaring flames, binding the relationship with a ritual burn across his hand.

His firefighting job in the mountains, however, is only temporary, and besides, the Rio Seco homefront requires his attention. Brenda is pregnant, they are still unmarried, and her daddy is mighty unhappy. Darnell finally works up nerve to face him, Brenda, marriage, and fatherhood.

Thereafter the story becomes a contest between Darnell's marriage to Brenda and his marriage to fires, between domesticity and danger, between life and death. It is not too hard to guess which side wins, as Darnell learns his lesson both symbolically and literally. Bending down to pick up his daughter's fallen Barbie doll saves his life in the drive-by shooting. Then he jeopardizes his daughter's life by chasing a forest fire with Charolette and getting caught in it. They escape, but the experience cures Darnell.

Family values win the day not only in Darnell's relationships with Brenda and Charolette but also in his relationships with his mother-in-law and father. Both support his efforts, and each at a crucial time has a heart-to-heart chat with him. In contrast, Louis' father cuts him off, refuses to acknowledge his existence, and is left holding his ashes.

For the problems facing the black male, then, Straight finds solutions within the family. She does an excellent job of making the reader realize the nature and extent of those problems, and her solutions seem valid. Everyone needs family support, particularly when facing an unfriendly environment and society, and one should assume one's own family responsibilities to help the next generation make it. Clearly, the generational links are important.

The definition of manhood implied by the novel might not seem as satisfactory, as if man were created to be tamed, domesticated, and put out to work by woman. The dichotomy between domesticity and danger in the novel also rings false (even marriage should have some excitement). The way Brenda keeps putting the choice to Darnell—either her or the fires—is enough to drive any man away. She appears irrational, even hysterical, not to mention selfish. One might agree with Darnell's friends that just as Mrs. Batiste has tamed the proud Etienne, Darnell is "pussy-whupped."

One could, however, look at it this way: The black male is up against so much in this society that simply earning a decent living provides plenty of excitement and tests of his manhood. Darnell must dodge the bullets of a cross-town gang during one commute. At any time he could be shot by one of his own customers. Believe it, his dog bites are more than merely ritual wounds.

Harold Branam

Sources for Further Study

The Atlantic. CCLXXIV, July, 1994, p. 107.
Booklist. XC, June 1, 1994, p. 1774.
Boston Globe. June 12, 1994, p. 19.
Chicago Tribune. June 26, 1994, XIV, p. 1.
The Christian Science Monitor. July 1, 1994, p. 10.
Los Angeles Times. June 27, 1994, p. E2.
The New York Times Book Review. XCIX, December 11, 1994, p. 27.
Publishers Weekly. CCXLI, July 4, 1994, p. 41.
San Francisco Chronicle. June 19, 1994, p. REV3.
The Washington Post. June 7, 1994, p. B2.

BLOOD AND BELONGING
Journeys into the New Nationalism

Author: Michael Ignatieff (1947-   )
Publisher: Farrar Straus Giroux (New York). Illustrated. 263 pp. $21.00
Type of work: Current affairs
Time: The early 1990's
Locale: Croatia and Serbia, Germany, the Ukraine, Quebec, Kurdistan, Northern Ireland

An insightful and deeply felt exploration of the tide of nationalism transforming the post-Cold War world

Michael Ignatieff's *Blood and Belonging: Journeys into the New Nationalism* is a useful and deeply felt addition to a growing literature on nationalism. The companion volume to a BBC documentary series, *Blood and Belonging* is intentionally a period piece, a book that could only have been written in the first half of the 1990's, as the great wave of Western optimism engendered by the end of the Cold War and the collapse of the Soviet Union ebbed bitterly away. It is also the work of a disillusioned man. Michael Ignatieff, willing, indeed eager, to hope for the best, concedes finally his bewilderment in the face of the inexplicable obduracy of nationalism. Like the Western statesmen of 1993-1994, Ignatieff respects the immense power and appeal of nationalist movements. More honest than these leaders, he cannot bring himself to say that this renascent nationalism is a good thing, or even something that can be endured.

Ignatieff is spiritually as well as politically and ethnically a stranger to the nationalisms he explores. He calls himself a cosmopolitan. He is a creature of the teeming multiethnic metropolises of the West. Like his fellow cosmopolitans, Ignatieff is indifferent to the passport status of the people with whom he lives and works. National cuisines, arts, and customs are treasures to be shared in common and valued at will. For the cosmopolitan, cultural chauvinism is the epitome of bad form. Ignatieff embodies the cosmopolitanism he admires. His father was an aristocrat exiled by the Russian Revolution. His mother was English. Born in Canada and educated in the United States, Ignatieff has spent most of his adult life in Great Britain and France. He is candid enough to admit, however, that cosmopolitanism and the postnationalist consciousness it inspires are frail blossoms in a hostile world. Cosmopolitanism flourishes only in the cities of the wealthiest Western states. Even there, he observes, it survives only because of the general respect for the law and the efficiency of the policy. Racial and ethnic disturbances in many Western cities, most notably in Los Angeles in 1992, demonstrate the fragility of cosmopolitanism and the propensity of even Western societies to lapse into ethnic warfare.

Like many, Ignatieff had confidently expected that the closing of the Cold War era would usher in a period of peace and ever-ramifying liberty. He thought that the world would come to accept the tolerant, democratic, and market-oriented cosmopolitan ethos. Instead, as old empires broke down, satraps were replaced by warlords, men armed not only with the arsenals of their former masters but also with ideologies based on fealty to blood and tribe. For a man of Ignatieff's sensibilities, this could be seen only as a fall, a return to a more primitive and barbarous level of existence. Ignatieff is too sophisticated a man of the world and too imbued with contemporary social theory to assert in print that people in the throes of nationalist enthusiasm have actually regressed to a more savage estate. Instead, he falls back on Freudian metaphor, envisioning nationalism as a part of humanity long repressed by modern civilization and now suddenly bursting loose from constraint. For the time being at least, humanity's id seems to be mastering its superego.

Ignatieff is uncomfortable with nationalism in any form. Nevertheless, he does distinguish among different types of nationalism through a brief discussion of the concept of nationalism, defined as a belief that the natural division of the world's peoples is into nations. Underlying this conviction are two assumptions. First, the nation provides people with their primary form of identity and belonging. Second, and because of this, defending the nation against external threats is both righteous and necessary. Ignatieff finds all these assertions debatable but generally accepted by his contemporaries. Yet, Ignatieff notes, there are real differences in the world over defining exactly what constitutes a people or nation. Here he makes the distinction between civic nationalism and ethnic nationalism.

Civic nationalism holds that a nation is composed of all the individuals who subscribe to the laws and ideals of a state, regardless of their race, ethnicity, or gender. The nation is conceived of as an association of free and equal citizens who have voluntarily joined themselves to one another for their mutual benefit. This understanding of nationalism is rooted in the seventeenth century political philosophies of thinkers such as Thomas Hobbes and John Locke. It is the incarnation of their theory of a social compact as the origin of a state's sovereignty and legitimacy. Civic nationalism emerged gradually in Great Britain. By the eighteenth century, four nations, the English, Welsh, Scots, and Irish, were united by the British Crown, Parliament, and common law. The American and French revolutions, with their written constitutions and their aggressive and missionary appeal to universal principles, established civic nationalism as the dominant ideal in the West in the nineteenth and twentieth centuries.

The great exception to this pattern of civic nationalism in the West was Germany. Long split into a welter of small principalities, Germany lagged behind states such as Great Britain and France in the development of a nationalist consciousness. This abruptly changed in 1806, with Napoléon Bonaparte's invasion and occupation of Germany. The humiliation of defeat and the tyranny of the French inspired German Romantics to create a new vision of nation. Lacking a single German state, the Romantics argued that nationality lay beyond the confines of government, in the religion, customs and, above all, the language of a people. The nation was the *Volk*. Thus, for the Germans, ethnicity became the foundation of nationalism.

Unlike civic nationalism, which regards an individual's voluntary adherence to shared ideals as essential to nationality, ethnic nationalism emphasizes a passive conception of the nation. A person is simply born into his or her nation. He or she belongs because of language, religion, or some other heritable quality. It is ethnic nationalism that is on the rise in the contemporary world, and that Ignatieff finds the most dangerous. As he points out, ethnic nationalism is not confined to Eastern Europe or the Third World. It is flourishing even in bastions of civic nationalism, in countries such as Great Britain, France, Italy, and Canada.

Ignatieff set out to explore the allure of ethnic nationalism by visiting six disparate lands wracked by national unrest. He chose places with which he had some sort of personal connection or interest, but which also would illuminate the new face of nationalism. His travels thus became a private voyage of discovery as well as a journalistic enterprise. As a cosmopolitan, he wrestled with the dark political forces stirring the earth; as a man, he grappled with the shadows of his past.

Ignatieff spent two peaceful years in Yugoslavia as a boy, while his father served there as a Canadian diplomat. He had noticed some tensions there among the various ethnic groups living in the federation, but nothing that later seemed to presage the breakup of the country. He was impressed by the way people seemed to embrace a unitary Yugoslav identity. Symbolic of the ethnic harmony enforced by the Yugoslavian dictator Tito was the Highway of Brotherhood and Unity, built to link Serbia and Croatia. This road eventually became a highway to nowhere, littered with the debris of battle and broken along an improvised border.

The savagery of the fighting in Croatia and Bosnia shocked Ignatieff. The Serbian destruction of the Croatian town of Vukovar, once famed for its beautiful architecture, seemed to symbolize the insanity of the conflict. The Serbs literally destroyed Vukovar in order to save it. What was once a civilized land became dominated by upstart warlords, enforcing their will through gangs of heavily armed bravos. Ignatieff and his companions were threatened by bands of these gun-toting youths. The swift collapse of Yugoslavia into a Hobbesian morass, in which each ethnic group's hand was raised against the other, and the extraordinary bitterness of the hostility between peoples separated, in Ignatieff's opinion, only by labels suggested to him deeper and darker roots of the nationalist malaise. Vukovar was destroyed because it was pleasing to destroy it. The warlords and their young men brandished their guns and bullied their neighbors because it was satisfying to do so. Looking on the ruins of Yugoslavia, Ignatieff decided that nationalism is merely a blind for humanity's ugliest passions.

Germany and the Ukraine posed different questions for Ignatieff. Germany is the birthplace of ethnic nationalism. Even today, German citizenship is based on blood rather than civic assimilation. Refugees from the Slavic East, descendants of German settlers who left the fatherland hundreds of years before, are readily granted citizenship and the benefits of the German social welfare state, while people of Turkish descent, resident in Germany for decades, find naturalization all but impossible. This nationalist tradition, as well as the memory of the horrors it inspired during the National Socialist period, is becoming a subject of controversy among Germans as they wrestle with the unification of East and West Germany and an influx of refugees from the troubles in eastern and southern Europe. The activities of neo-Nazi skinheads have inspired much apprehension. Ignatieff sees modern Germans as being trapped between their guilt over the National Socialist past and their concern about the tide of foreigners, distaste for the old ethnic nationalism and fear of a genuinely multicultural Germany. The Germans have yet to evolve a modern national identity.

The Ukraine has the difficulty of separating from a Russia with which it was unified politically and culturally for centuries. Ignatieff's own family were Russian aristocrats who owned a large estate in the now independent republic. A trip to his ancestral home, where his family is still remembered, demonstrated vividly to Ignatieff the living force of old ties. In many ways the new Ukraine seemed to him an echo of the old Soviet state, with imperial forms in uniforms, protocol, and the like still cherished by the departed rulers' successors. Ignatieff departed the Ukraine impressed with the tenuousness of nationalist rhetoric when compared with the quotidian reality of displacing memories and creating institutions.

The linguistic nationalism of Francophone Quebec threatens to break up Ignatieff's Canadian homeland. The irony of this for Ignatieff is the living reality of Quebeçois success and independence. French-speaking Canadians are no longer a poor and scorned community. Their language and cultural identity are protected by Canadian law. For many Quebeçois, however, this is not enough, Whether Quebec will ever formally leave the Canadian federation is an open question. Ignatieff was disconcerted to find that emotionally most Quebeçois identify with their province rather than with Canada. The intractability of Quebec nationalism even against the languid backdrop of Canadian civility raised frightening questions for Ignatieff about the willingness of people to accommodate the Other.

The plight of the Kurds had a sobering effect on Ignatieff, convincing him that sometimes the nationalist agitation for a state is both just and necessary. The Kurds are victims of mapmaking. Their mountainous homeland was once part of the Ottoman Empire. In the wake of World War I, it was broken up and divided among various states. Today Kurdistan stretches across the borders of Iraq, Turkey, Syria, Iran, and Armenia. Seen as an internal threat by the majority populations of these states, the Kurds have been hounded and oppressed for decades. Nowhere did they suffer more than in Saddam Hussein's Iraq, where whole villages were massacred in gas attacks. Moved by the Kurdish struggle to maintain a national existence in the face of fierce repression, Ignatieff gained new insight into the sense of belonging that is integral to the nationalist mystique—in this case the fundamental need for cultural and physical security.

In Northern Ireland, Ignatieff revisited the sort of madness he had encountered in Yugoslavia. Here two communities, holding more in common than they would care to admit, are locked in bitter enmity because of the power of memory and prejudices. Ignatieff studied the Protestant Loyalists with fascination, for they live in the exquisitely anomalous situation of professing loyalty to a nation that would just as soon abandon them. Ignatieff sees the perfervid Britishness of the Ulster Loyalists as a sort of cargo cult, all the more pathetic because of the language, tastes, and customs they share with their Irish Catholic neighbors.

Ignatieff comes to no general conclusions about nationalism, except to denounce its ethnic variant. He hazards a few psychological explanations for the phenomenon. The real strength of his book, however, lies in his sharp and empathic reporting. Ignatieff ultimately cannot explain nationalism, but he can record its consequences. Therein lies the real value of *Blood and Belonging*.

Daniel P. Murphy

Sources for Further Study

Booklist. XC, March 15, 1994, p. 1308.
Books in Canada. XXIII, March, 1994, p. 41.
The Canadian Forum. LXXII, January, 1994, p. 5.
Library Journal. CXIX, March 1, 1994, p. 104.
Los Angeles Times. April 7, 1994, p. E3.
The New York Review of Books. XLI, May 26, 1994, p. 44.
The New York Times Book Review. XCIX, April 10, 1994, p. 7.
Publishers Weekly. CCXLI, February 21, 1994, p. 242.
The Times Literary Supplement. February 11, 1994, p. 3.
The Washington Post Book World. XXIV, April 10, 1994, p. 5.

THE BODY FARM

Author: Patricia Cornwell (1956-   )
Publisher: Charles Scribner's Sons (New York). 287 pp. $23.00
Type of work: Mystery novel
Time: The 1990's
Locale: North Carolina and Virginia

When a child is kidnapped and murdered, an elusive serial killer is suspected, but forensic pathologist Kay Scarpetta's investigations lead to an unexpected solution

Principal characters:

DR. KAY SCARPETTA, a forensic pathologist, the chief medical examiner of Virginia
LUCY, her niece, an intern at the Federal Bureau of Investigation Engineering Research Facility
PETE MARINO, a Richmond homicide detective
BENTON WESLEY, chief of the FBI Investigative Support Unit
CARRIE GRETHEN, a research project aide at the FBI Academy
DENESA STEINER, the mother of the murdered girl

The Body Farm is Patricia Cornwell's fifth crime novel since her auspicious 1990 debut with *Postmortem*, which won the top genre awards in three countries. Dr. Kay Scarpetta, forensic pathologist and lawyer, returns as the featured player in this book, and some venues and devices also are familiar, but Cornwell is not a formula writer and once again challenges the limitations of the genre. Though the book's setting links it to the police procedural and its rough-and-tumble realism echoes hard-boiled crime fiction, it transcends both types. At its core, *The Body Farm* is a carefully plotted study of vulnerability as exemplified by victims, perpetrators, and law enforcement officials, including the central character. By focusing on how Scarpetta's dual roles of woman and aunt impinge upon and conflict with her professional responsibilities, Cornwell eschews stereotyping and presents a multidimensional detective.

The novel begins at the Federal Bureau of Investigation (FBI) Academy in Quantico, Virginia, where Scarpetta and others of the FBI's Investigative Support Unit are consulting about the murder of eleven-year-old Emily Steiner, who, according to her mother, was abducted at night from their rural North Carolina home. Five days later, the girl's nude body, with pieces of its flesh cut out, was found at a nearby lake; she had been gagged, bound, sexually assaulted, and killed with a single shot in the head. The modus operandi resembles that of Temple Brooks Gault, one of the FBI's ten most wanted, presumed to have carried out serial killings in Richmond two years earlier. Scarpetta remains obsessed with her failure to have apprehended Gault, who had once been within her reach. She is unable "to shake the chill of doubt . . . and had not stopped wondering what more [she] could have done."

Though everyone considers Gault the prime suspect, Scarpetta raises questions that suggest uncertainty, mainly because of the condition of Emily's body and Denesa Steiner's apparently atypical behavior the night of the alleged abduction. The former leads Scarpetta to the University of Tennessee's Decay Research Facility, dubbed the Body Farm, where forensic scientist Thomas Kats studies corpses in different stages of decomposition. Information she gleans from this grisly place provides her with vital leads.

Scarpetta is distracted from the case, however, by her niece Lucy's presence at the FBI Academy. The daughter of Scarpetta's irresponsible sister, Lucy is an intern in the academy's classified research facility, with the prospect of a regular position after college. A loner whom Scarpetta shelters and nurtures, Lucy becomes involved in a lesbian relationship with an older woman in her unit, later is charged with espionage and dismissed, and then is seriously injured in a staged automobile accident that was intended to kill her aunt. Though the Steiner and Lucy story lines parallel each other, and there indeed is an intersecting link, the Lucy plot seems largely peripheral and sometimes even distracting. Yet it is useful and relevant, for it increases the complexity of the case with what prove to be mainly false leads and adds a personal, feminine dimension to the character of Scarpetta, a woman in a male-dominated profession. In addition to being Lucy's surrogate mother, Scarpetta becomes involved in an affair, which becomes as frustrating as her relationship with Lucy. These elements make Scarpetta a clear counterpoint to the other major female character, Denesa Steiner, a mother and lover. The connection is significant because it gives Scarpetta an edge on her colleagues when it comes to understanding Steiner's motivations and the pathology of her actions.

The progress of *The Body Farm* follows a typical crime-fiction format: After a murder, the authorities quickly settle upon a prime suspect, but events soon overtake the satisfaction that comes with their certainty. In a surprising twist, one of the detectives—Max Ferguson of the State Bureau of Investigation in North Carolina—is found dead in his bedroom, wearing women's undergarments and apparently a victim of accidental hanging while engaged in autoeroticism. Further, frozen pieces of Emily's flesh are found in his refrigerator. Ferguson inevitably becomes a new prime suspect, although Scarpetta suggests a possible setup, a prescient notion to which she returns when learning that Denesa Steiner was one of the last people to have seen him alive. Other suspects briefly surface, including Wren Maxwell, a school friend on whom Emily had a crush, and Creed Lindsey, a black janitor at her school, but they chiefly serve to provide details that enable Scarpetta to place matters into perspective and reconstruct the crime. Typically in crime fiction, the more information gathered, the more complex and confusing a case eventually becomes. In this regard, Scarpetta's sidekick Pete Marino vents his frustration by complaining, "Just when pieces start to fall in place you shake the hell out of them like a damn puzzle in a box."

Marino, Scarpetta's longtime colleague, is her antithesis, as reckless and undisciplined as she is careful and deliberate. At the start, he is a member of the investigative team, as in earlier books, but by the end he is an outsider and almost one of the murderer's victims. Reeling from the breakup of his marriage after thirty-two years, he is attracted to Scarpetta, but when she demurs and becomes involved with Benton Wesley, Marino becomes insanely jealous and susceptible to Denesa Steiner's overtures to his bruised male ego. The obsessive affair with her destroys his objectivity, rendering him useless in the case and even dangerous, as an inadvertent conduit of confidential information. He is, however, only one of many characters with failed relationships. Scarpetta, her sister Dorothy, and Ferguson are divorced; Wesley is unhappily married; Lucy falls for Carrie Grethen's phony offers of love. Only Scarpetta retains her professional equilibrium.

The book is a veritable catalog of her widespread knowledge and perceptive intuition at work. Because of her scientific expertise, she approaches a case largely by studying evidence, and this novel, like its predecessors, shows the pathologist in the laboratory and at the coroner's examining table. (The pervasive verisimilitude characteristic of Cornwall's novels is attributable to her research and the review of her manuscripts by Virginia medical examiners.) Scarpetta also does her legwork, questioning witnesses and potential suspects, visiting sites connected with the case, and taking risks. As she closes in on her prey, she even courts danger, knowingly jeopardizing her life to confirm her conclusions: "I had to see what was there. Nothing was going to stop me, not even fear of her finding me." Marino is correct when he says that she shakes pieces of the puzzle, but Scarpetta knows when some are missing, is aware of what she needs, and realizes when she has them all. Though many help her along the way, she assembles the complete picture mostly by herself.

She is the first to express doubt about Denesa Steiner's credibility, initially by framing random questions and comments, but eventually developing a more carefully formulated suspicion. Because Scarpetta is narrator, the reader is privy to all of her thoughts. This increases veracity and a sense of total participation but also means that the identity of the murderer becomes apparent to the reader long before it is to the police. What remains are the how and why of Emily Steiner's murder, and herein is the centerpiece of the story, because Cornwell shines in her explication of the nuances of the sad, bewildering case, particularly in her development of Denesa Steiner.

Emily's mother is in her mid-thirties, the widow of a teacher at a Christian school. The family had come east from California, where another daughter was said to have died of SIDS (sudden infant death syndrome, or crib death). The first information Cornwell gives about Denesa is that the "little girl decor" of her pillow-filled bedroom "was pastel prints of tiny bouquets of violets and loose flying balloons." Scarpetta describes her as a "rather peculiarly put together woman" who dresses in mourning black and resembles "a spinster missionary." This "puritanical grooming" fails to obscure her beauty: a voluptuous body, patrician nose, high cheekbones, "smooth pale skin and a generous mouth, and curly hair the color of honey." Men are attracted by her beauty and vulnerability, and women's hearts instinctively ache for her. A local officer marvels that Steiner has "this whole area thinking about this case and feeling for her . . . like nothing I've ever seen in my twenty-two years of police work."

Scarpetta discerns a peculiar pattern in Steiner's behavior: From the very start of the case, she has focused attention upon herself, not only by acts of community generosity but also by frequently telephoning the authorities to get information and by alerting journalists to the exhumation of Emily's body. Events and evidence lead

Scarpetta to suspect that Steiner tried to kill Scarpetta and continues to stalk her, because the detective is getting too close to the truth. When Scarpetta recalls that Emily was a frail eleven-year-old who could have passed for eight or nine, she reviews her facts and posits a diagnosis: Denesa Steiner suffered from Munchausen's by proxy, a syndrome in which mothers and other primary care givers "secretly and cleverly abuse their children to get attention. They cut their flesh and break their bones, poison and smother them almost to death. Then these women rush to doctors' offices and emergency rooms and tell teary tales of how their little one got sick or hurt, and the staff feels so sorry for Mother. She gets so much attention." Since such women psychopaths poison and smother defenseless people of any age, Steiner's new lover, Marino, is at risk.

The climax of the novel takes place on a pleasant Sunday when Scarpetta goes home with Steiner after church. Confident of her conclusions, the detective now finds the woman "as cold as the day" and wonders how she "ever could have felt sympathy for her or believed her pain." When Steiner goes upstairs where Marino is sleeping, Scarpetta goes to the basement in search of confirming evidence, which she finds. Before she returns upstairs, Steiner locks the door on her, but Scarpetta escapes through another door, gets Marino's shotgun from his car, breaks open the front door of the house, and runs upstairs. Steiner is "sitting placidly on the edge of the bed where Marino lay, a plastic trash bag over his head and taped around his neck." Steiner grabs Marino's pistol from the nightstand as Scarpetta releases the safety and racks the shotgun, but Scarpetta fires first, kills her nemesis, and revives Marino.

The Body Farm has all the qualities that typify an exemplary police or forensic procedural, but it has more. Cornwell's delineation of characters, with sensitive portraits of even such minor figures as Wren Maxwell and Creed Lindsey, adds substance to the novel, whose theme Scarpetta expresses in this comment: "It seems this is all about people loving people who don't love them back. It's about hurt being passed on." The sensitivity she reveals in the statement may be why readers find her so appealing. There is another reason, which Cornwell identified in a 1992 interview: "There is a fearful symmetry of having this humane, civilized physician, who is sworn by the Hippocratic Oath to do no harm, be the one who is going to these scenes and dealing with the spoils of this hideous irrationality and cruelty."

Gerald H. Strauss

Sources for Further Study

Booklist. XC, July, 1994, p. 1813.
Chicago Tribune. October 2, 1994, XIV, p. 9.
Kirkus Reviews. LXII, July 1, 1994, p. 886.
Library Journal. CXIX, September 1, 1994, p. 213.
Los Angeles Times Book Review. September 11, 1994, p. 18.

The New York Times Book Review. XCIX, October 16, 1994, p. 38.
Publishers Weekly. CCXLI, July 18, 1994, p. 237.
Time. CXLIV, October 3, 1994, p. 84.
The Times Literary Supplement. October 21, 1994, p. 20.
The Washington Post Book World. XXIV, September 11, 1994, p. 8.

BRAZIL

Author: John Updike (1932-)
Publisher: Alfred A. Knopf (New York). 260 pp. $23.00
Type of work: Novel
Time: 1966-1988
Locale: Rio de Janeiro, São Paulo, Brasília, Serra do Buraco, and Mato Grosso, Brazil

An exotic retelling of the legendary romance of Tristan and Iseult against the culturally diverse background of contemporary Brazil

Principal characters:

TRISTÃO RAPOSO, a nineteen-year-old black slum product and petty thief with dreams of prosperity
ISABEL LEME, an eighteen-year-old white girl from an aristocratic family who is attracted to Tristão
SALAMÃO LEME, her remote father, a career diplomat
UNCLE DONACIANO, her sympathetic uncle and surrogate father from Rio de Janeiro
URSULA RAPOSO, Tristão's mother, a prostitute dwelling in a Rio de Janeiro shanty
EUCLIDES RAPOSO, Tristão's half-brother and partner in crime
CHIQUINHO RAPOSO, Tristão's married brother living in São Paulo
CÉSAR, a gunman hired by Isabel's father to separate her from Tristão
AZOR,
CORDELIA,
SALOMÃO,
BARTOLOMEU,
ALUÍSIO, and
AFRODÉSIA, Isabel's children, all sired by men other than Tristão
ANTONIO PEIXOTE, the leader of a jungle band of religious zealots known as the Paulistas
IANOPAMOKO, one of Peixote's consorts, a friend and lover of Isabel
TEJUCUPAPO, a native shaman

John Updike's sixteenth novel is in many ways a new departure for him. Known principally for his lyrical and generally realistic portraits of Pennsylvania and New England suburban lives meticulously situated in their defining period and social locale, Updike literally embarks upon a new fictional territory in *Brazil*. Not only is it his first novel located in Latin America, but it is also his first without a single North American character. The closest there is to a predecessor in his canon is *The Coup* (1978), set chiefly in the mythical African nation of Kush, whose protagonist and narrator was educated in the United States before returning to rule his native land. That novel, a political and ideological satire, concerned American culture as much as it did that of the postcolonial African nation. In contrast, *Brazil* is fully immersed in the sights, sounds, and textures of the beaches of Rio de Janeiro, the shanties of its *favelas*, the industrial wasteland of São Paulo, the geometrical abstraction of the inland capital of Brasília, and—most of all—the vast jungle known as Mato Grosso.

The novel concerns the enduring if much-beleaguered romance between a beach rat and petty thief named Tristão and Isabel, the bored daughter of a diplomat. Their striking differences in race (Tristão being black, Isabel white) and class are only somewhat less of an obstacle in Rio, where "all colors merge into one joyous, sun-tanned flesh-color," than they would be nearly anywhere else. Opposition to the match is immediate and persistent. Both families present obstacles of various kinds; Isabel's father even resorts finally to hiring gunmen to separate the lovers by force. Though separated for years, they are nevertheless reunited and run away to try their luck in the gold mines of Serra do Buraco. After years of toil, during which Isabel bears two children (sired by other men) and Tristão discovers and then loses the nugget that would make their fortune, they are forced to flee once more to escape her father's minions. Again they move west, through the immense jungle of the Mato Grosso, where they come close to starvation and are attacked by Indians, until they are finally rescued by a roving band of religious zealots led by a pair of brothers, Antonio and José Peixote. They remain unhappily separated while in this company for several more years, Isabel as third wife to the elder brother (with whom she bears a retarded son) and Tristão as a virtual slave.

At this point, about two-thirds of the way through the novel, the story suddenly veers into the realm of magical realism, a hybrid form often associated with Latin American fiction but not, heretofore, with Updike's. To ensure their escape from captivity, Isabel visits a native shaman, whom she induces to enact a magical transformation. As a result, she and Tristão, with their racial identities now transposed, escape and make the difficult journey back to the east, there facing renewed encounters with their abandoned relatives, first in Brasília and then in São Paulo. Their last dozen years together are spent in a superficial kind of peace, as Isabel's family bestows on the (literally) transformed Tristão a lucrative job as manager in a textile mill near São Paulo, while Isabel rears three more children (like her other three, all secretly sired by men other than Tristão) in ostensibly respectable bourgeois fashion. Ultimately the elongated circle is completed by the couple's return to the same beach in Rio where they had first met twenty-two years earlier. This return proves tragic when Tristão, ironically, is stabbed to death by beach rats and petty thieves closely resembling his former self.

As usual in Updike's novels, the locale is vividly described. While the new inland capital, Brasília, is rendered as a sort of glass and concrete rectilinear diagram, like a municipal "statue still waiting for life to be breathed into it," and Rio de Janeiro is "pinched between the sea and the mountains," the huge industrial city of São Paulo "had no limits . . . It was part of the vast *planalto*, a port on its edge. Cattle and coffee from the hinterland had funnelled through this place and made it rich, heartless, and enormous." It is the focal point of Brazil's economic transformation into a modern nation and as such the site of "cement-gray people-sprawl, eating up the planet" and polluting it. In contrast, the vast jungle of the Mato Grosso seems limitless, varied, and fecund; despite the dangers of travel there, Tristão and Isabel feel hopeful, as if they were "moving backward in time, away from the furies that excessive population has brought their century, into a chaste space." Here Updike taps a dichotomy familiar in American literature, the contrast between the urban eastern seaboard and the uncharted western territory where new life putatively awaits a worthy claimant. The spiritual and amorous rejuvenation experienced by Tristão and Isabel during their westward sojourn thus has a traditional basis, even as the exotic Brazilian particulars—depicted in convincing particularlity—lend a sense of novelty no longer so readily available in the modern North American landscape.

In an afterword to the novel, Updike states that in addition to other literary sources he names, he derived his "tone and basic situation" from Joseph Bédier's *Roman de Tristan et Iseult* (1900), translated by Hilaire Belloc and Paul Rosenfeld as *The Romance of Tristan and Iseult* (1945). The "basic situation" is that of tragically doomed love. Parallels are numerous. Like his legendary namesake, Updike's Tristão is described as a "knight errant," whose chivalrous gestures toward his beloved include the bestowing of a precious gift (a stolen ring inscribed with the letters DAR, which he interprets as the Portuguese verb "to give") and a solemn vow (not to harm Isabel but to love her). There are omens (a chalice-shaped bloodstain appears after Isabel loses her virginity to Tristão), battles against quasi-monstrous foes (Tristão kills the professional gunman hired by Isabel's possessive father), and dramatic rescues (Tristão "saves" Isabel from imprisonment in her uncle's apartment, from her entrapment in the mining village, and from her brutish bondage to Antonio Peixote and their idiot son). Racial and social class differences are the paramount worldly obstacles to the joining of the lovers, promoting familial opposition just as the legendary lovers were opposed by King Mark of Cornwall and Iseult's jealous attendant Brangwain. Isabel bears six children by other men (and has none with Tristão), just as the legendary Iseult was actually married to King Mark and Tristan to another Iseult (of the White Hands), yet despite these dalliances both couples remained essentially loyal to their "fated" lovers. There is no magic love potion per se in the novel, but Updike's numerous detailed depictions of erotic activity may perhaps provide a sort of modern parallel to the compulsive passion produced by the potion. The Brazilian shaman's magic is an even more direct parallel, though the transformation it brings about is far more complicated and disturbing. Finally, on two occasions Isabel reflects on the "timeless" stories of legendary lovers. She does not identify them by name but thinks of them, suggestively, as stories always involving the same basic events: "Love, pregnancy, infidelity, vengeance, parting. Death—always death in these stories." When Isabel finds Tristão's dead body on the beach at the end of the novel, she again recalls the story "of a woman, long ago, who, her lover dead, lay down beside him and willed herself to die, and did"; Isabel herself attempts to do the same, unsuccessfully as it turns out.

Updike has made use of the Tristan legend previously in his work, most notably in *Couples* (1968). Indeed, in 1963 he wrote a lengthy review of perhaps the best-known modern interpretation of the legend, Denis de Rougement's *L'Amour et l'occident* (1956; *Love in the Western World*, 1983). According to de Rougement, the legend embodies an archetypal pattern of fatal love in which the romance quest disguises a secret death-wish. The object of love is always in some sense unattainable. In fact, that is the true source of the lovers' passion—its deferral and ultimate loss, which only intensify the longing—not any real hope of satisfaction through love's realization. Romantic love is essentially an illusion, a form of narcissism. Tristan and Iseult do not truly love each other so much as the dream of love each represents to the other, or projects onto the other. The lovers secretly seek not a fulfilling relationship represented by marriage and the bearing of offspring but the "sweet suffering" brought about by separation and, ultimately, by death. Thus the love of death (Thanatos) is sublimated into Eros, the passionate longing for an ideal love, the protracted pursuit of which results in death, either literal or spiritual.

This modern, psychological reading of the legend clearly influenced Updike's treatment of his material in *Brazil*. Both Tristão and Isabel believe that their love is "fated." "You were my destiny, and I yours," he tells her; "you and I were brought together not to feed children into the world's maw, but to prove love—to make for the world an example of love." On another occasion he adds, "We hardly exist outside our love, we are just animals without it, with a birth and a death and constant fear between. Our love has lifted us up, out of the dreadfulness of merely living." When they are separated, as they frequently are, they are described as moving about in a kind of trance; and when they become erotically involved with others, as both do, they nevertheless remain "chaste in [their] soul, that spiritual organ where [their] life cried out for its eternal shape." Indeed, such separation only intensifies their dream of "eternal" union. Moreover, revealingly, the proximity of death—as during their dangerous trek through the Mato Grosso—only exacerbates their sexual desire for each other.

Yet it is Isabel's recourse to the shaman's magic that brings about a kind of fulfillment she had not envisioned. Although the transformation helps to free both from bondage to the loathsome Peixote brothers, it also delivers them eventually to a condition that seems closer to "the dreadfulness of merely living" than to an eternal consummation. The story's concluding phase, in which Tristão and Isabel live for years as respectable bourgeois husband and wife and parents in the mechanistic wasteland of São Paulo is, as the author concedes, unredeemably banal. (Updike's readers will smile in recognition of the fact that he has made a major reputation by exploring and celebrating precisely that mode of living in such works as the Rabbit tetralogy.)

Even as he approaches his ironic death, Tristão cannot deny the unwelcome realization that "there was more of [Isabel] than he ever could possess. And the realization . . . that his attempt to possess her had twisted his life into a shape there was no changing, ever—a guilty shape, somehow, stained with murder and desertion." It is longing for his old "innocence" that impels Tristão to his fatal encounter with the beach rats who represent his former self. Isabel's inability to follow him to death ("There would be no miracle today. . . . Tristão [had become] a piece of litter. . . . The spirit is strong, but blind matter is stronger") only testifies to her permanent entrapment in the fatal romantic illusion. She too is dead, in spirit if not in "blind matter."

Whether this grim denouement will succeed with most readers is doubtful. To date the novel has received largely hostile reviews, most of which do not seem to recognize the function of the Tristan myth in expressing the subtle dangers of romantic passion. Several reviewers are put off by Updike's almost gleeful uttering of politically incorrect notions of race and gender. His transposition of a northern European myth onto a postcolonial, polyglot culture raises additional questions for some. What cannot be doubted, however, is the audacity of Updike's foray into new and unknown territory.

Ronald G. Walker

Sources for Further Study

America. CLXXI, August 13, 1994, p. 20.
Commonweal. CXXI, April 8, 1994, p. 18.
Los Angeles Times Book Review. February 6, 1994, p. 3.
The New York Review of Books. XLI, May 12, 1994, p. 23.
The New York Times Book Review. XCIX, February 6, 1994, p. 1.
Publishers Weekly. CCXL, November 22, 1993, p. 48.
Time. CXLIII, February 14, 1994, p. 73.
The Times Literary Supplement. April 1, 1994, p. 21.
The Washington Post Book World. XXIV, February 13, 1994, p. 1.
The Yale Review. LXXXII, July, 1994, p. 165.

THE CATCHER WAS A SPY
The Mysterious Life of Moe Berg

Author: Nicholas Dawidoff
Publisher: Pantheon Books (New York). Illustrated. 453 pp. $24.00
Type of work: Biography
Time: 1902-1972
Locale: Newark, New Jersey; many other locations in the United States; Japan; Panama; South America; Europe; and North Africa

The life of an original and elusive man—baseball player, intelligence agent, and vagabond—is painstakingly reassembled and interpreted

Principal personages:
MORRIS "MOE" BERG, the catcher who became a spy
BERNARD BERG, his father, a druggist
ROSE BERG, his mother, a housewife
SAMUEL BERG, his elder brother, a physician
ETHEL BERG, his elder sister, a schoolteacher
EARL BRODIE, an agent of the Office of Strategic Services (OSS)
HOWARD DIX, Berg's superior in the OSS
WILLIAM DONOVAN, the creator of the OSS
ROBERT FURMAN, an Army engineer and expert in atomic intelligence
SAM GOUDSMIT, a dutch-born physicist
LESLIE GROVES, the military director of the Manhattan Project
WERNER HEISENBERG, a leading German atomic scientist
JOHN KIERAN, a writer
PAUL SCHERRER, a Swiss physicist

When first issued a pistol as an intelligence agent, Morris "Moe" Berg could not keep it from slipping out of his pocket into the lap of the man next to him on an airplane. Seven months later he was assigned the job of killing Werner Heisenberg, the premier German atomic scientist. Berg was a major-league baseball player turned spy for the Office of Strategic Services (OSS), the World War II forerunner of the Central Intelligence Agency (CIA).

Berg's life story has been written before, by a trio of writers with the cooperation of Berg's brother Sam, and again by his sister Ethel. Since Ethel threatened to sue Sam if her name appeared in the former, and since she refused to mention Sam in her book, however, these earlier biographies are incomplete and distorted. Moe lived with Sam for fourteen years and with Ethel for at least six, and Moe's brother and sister had nothing to do with each other—despite living a few blocks apart in Newark, New Jersey. Furthermore, Moe Berg lived a large chunk of his life apart from his siblings. He had hundreds of acquaintances but no close friends. He never married and never stayed in close touch with any one person for an extended period. It has taken an assiduous researcher named Nicholas Dawidoff to piece his life together.

Berg earned a reputation early as one of the most unusual of major-league baseball players and, despite a mediocre career, one of the most celebrated, for he was a bona fide intellectual in a sport that harbored few such in the 1920's and 1930's. A mystery man to his teammates, he nurtured the mystique that grew up around him as a result of the efforts of the various sportswriters whom he charmed, especially the polymath John Kieran of *Information, Please* fame. Berg had been graduated from Princeton University, achieved a law degree in the off-season, and was reputed to speak a dozen languages.

He began his baseball career as a shortstop but lacked mobility and was shifted to catcher, where his flat feet and slowness did not handicap him. He had an excellent throwing arm, seldom made an error, and won the confidence of the pitchers whom he handled. Although an injury suffered in 1929, when he was twenty-seven, turned him into a perennial second- or third-string catcher, it seems that Berg was destined to be such and wished to be no more. He loved to be around baseball parks, but unlike most bench warmers, he did not burn with the desire to play regularly. Instead he entertained relief pitchers in the bullpen with his tales and cultivated sportswriters, who made him famous as "Professor Berg." The legend of Moe Berg had been created long before he bowed out as a player in 1939.

Though Berg was much better equipped than most athletes of his day to live a successful life after his retirement from the sport, he seemed to neglect his most obvious opportunities. Despite his law degree, Berg never practiced law formally, though he occasionally gave legal advice to friends. Early in 1942, he accepted a position monitoring health and fitness in Central and South American republics for the Office of Inter-American Affairs, an agency that was attempting to counter any Nazi influence south of the border. After a year and a half, he resigned for a greater challenge: service with the OSS, the predecessor of the CIA. Indeed, Berg possessed many of the qualities a good intelligence officer needed. He could mix in any crowd, he was linguistically gifted, and he had cultivated a habit of disappearing under people's noses. At any given time, hardly anyone knew where Moe Berg was.

There were times in the next two years when even his new employers did not know where Berg was, but he performed valuable service for the OSS. Under the leadership of William "Wild Bill" Donovan, the OSS numbered among its paramount concerns the determination of the state of the German atomic energy program. The head of the OSS technical section, Colonel Howard Dix, ordered Berg to Italy to try to learn what Italian scientists knew of the matter. The evidence that Berg and others gathered suggested that the Nazis were not close to the development of an atomic bomb, but no one was comfortable relying on educated guesses about the matter. Still, Berg's superiors considered the information that he sent back important.

Meanwhile, Colonel Leslie Groves, the military director of the American bomb program, and Major Robert Furman, his subordinate, were concocting a plan to murder Werner Heisenberg, the German scientist most likely to produce a feasible bomb. Two European scientists, Paul Scherrer and Sam Goudsmit, serving as go-betweens, contacted Berg in Italy. Having learned that Heisenberg, no Nazi but a decidedly patriotic German, was going to lecture in Zurich in December of 1944, Goudsmit briefed Berg. The latter, posing variously as an Arab businessman, a French merchant, and a Swiss physics student, then went to Zurich. In his guise as student he heard Heisenberg's lecture, though German was not one of his better languages and physics hardly his best subject. Nevertheless, he was expected to kill Heisenberg if it seemed necessary. Later, Berg, gun in pocket, was actually able to accompany the otherwise unattended Heisenberg along a Zurich street. He could have killed him, but, probably convinced that Heisenberg could not possibly be close to the realization of the feared bomb, he did not.

Berg's two years as an intelligence agent were not all cloak-and-dagger adventures. He had time in Italy to visit tourist attractions and teach the children of one of his contacts to play baseball. Duty itself could turn comic. After the Russians had occupied Czechoslovakia, it became necessary for Berg to go to Prague. Motoring through the Czech countryside, Berg and three other agents were stopped by Russian soldiers. The resourceful Berg dug into his pocket and held up a document decorated with a large red star at the top. The soldiers never knew that what they respectfully saluted was a piece of Texaco oil company stationery.

Berg's personality did not fit the requirements of the highly professionalized CIA after the war, and thus began the third and longest stage of his adult life, which was either a long anticlimax or a fulfillment, depending on how conventionally one assesses a life. He never again held a regular job, and in most years his income was precisely zero. Yet he lived reasonably well, for not only did his friends support him, but they considered themselves well repaid for doing so. They shared Berg's own conviction that his companionship was worth a dole or a bed for the night—or for a few weeks, if he chose to stay that long. Few could resist his charm, his wide-ranging fund of often-arcane knowledge, and his skill at relating, and often embroidering, his adventures. He had the knack of entrancing his audience without giving himself away. Berg always maintained a certain veil of secrecy which his listeners understood they must not penetrate.

Dawidoff chooses to abandon the chronological approach he has used for Berg's first forty-three years in favor of a long chapter called "A Life Without Calendar," an assortment of anecdotal vignettes representing the last twenty-seven years of a life that the author calls, without much fear of contradiction, "original." Though Berg was often seen with beautiful women and lived with one of them for a while in the early 1940's, he never married. He never learned to drive a car, and he never owned a home or rented anything more permanent than a hotel room. He was devoid of religious beliefs, in this respect resembling his father, who, though not lacking pride in his Jewish heritage, was indifferent to Judaism. He devoured newspapers and books and absorbed random facts like a sponge. A curious, perpetually wandering man, he cultivated hundreds—doubtless thousands—of acquaintances ranging from Albert Einstein to Nelson Rockefeller to Joe Cronin, his onetime teammate and then manager. Kieran and Berg both related versions of the latter's meeting with Einstein. According to Berg's version, the great physicist offered to teach him relativity if Berg would teach him baseball, but then reneged, deciding that Berg would "learn relativity faster." A few of Berg's acquaintances labeled him a charlatan whose encyclopedic knowledge never went deep, but the great majority found him an amazingly well-informed man whose learning was never oppressive and usually entertaining.

The biographer's final chapter, "The Secret Life of Moe Berg," while not revealing any startling secrets hitherto undisclosed, attempts to interpret a life ultimately mysterious, for none of Berg's numerous relationships seems to have been truly intimate. People who listened to his stories for hours came away knowing very little about him. No one knew where he was once he left, and he often left so abruptly as to preclude a good-bye. As Dawidoff sees it, the key to Berg's personality, if indeed there is a key, is his father's insensitivity. Bernard Berg was an Old World man who could see no point in baseball. He could tolerate Moe's playing while in college, as long as Moe kept his grades up, which he did, but he had not worked seven days a week so that the most gifted of his three children might play a boys' game into his adulthood. Despite Moe's pleas, Bernard refused to watch him play. Having failed to gain recognition from his father when it meant most, Moe Berg spent his life trying to gain it from others; afraid that he would be found lacking, he developed his lifelong technique of trying to impress people but retreating before anyone could validly suspect him of being less than he appeared to be.

To some Moe Berg might seem a pathetic individual who missed out on most of what makes life worthwhile, but Dawidoff judges otherwise. "Berg molded himself into a character of fantastic complication who brought pleasure and fascination to nearly everyone he brushed against during his fitful movements around the world."

To piece together the life of this peripatetic man required extraordinary diligence. Dawidoff interviewed hundreds of people in person and by telephone, corresponded with scores more, and spent months picking through uncataloged OSS papers in the National Archives. His "Note on the Sources" runs to ten pages, and his "Selected Bibliography" to six more. The notes themselves fill nearly sixty pages. All this material has been placed unobtrusively at the end of a highly readable and well-paced text. In his documentation Dawidoff omitted the dates of the many interviews, but they surely were concentrated between 1992 and the completion of the manuscript, for Sam Berg died in 1992, before Dawidoff began writing his brother's life. No writer is likely to do better by this most unusual man.

Robert P. Ellis

Sources for Further Study

Booklist. XC, May 15, 1994, p. 1661.
Library Journal. CXIX, May 15, 1994, p. 78.
Los Angeles Times Book Review. October 16, 1994, p. 13.
The New Leader. LXXVII, August 15, 1994, p. 17.
The New York Times Book Review. XCIX, July 24, 1994, p. 1.
Publishers Weekly. CCXLI, June 27, 1994, p. 65.

Sporting News. CCXVIII, October 3, 1994, p. 8.
Time. CXLIV, August 15, 1994, p. 59.
The Wall Street Journal. August 24, 1994, p. A6.
The Washington Post Book World. XXIV, July 3, 1994, p. 3.

THE CAVEMAN'S VALENTINE

Author: George Dawes Green
Publisher: Warner Books (New York). 323 pp. $19.95
Type of work: Novel
Time: The 1990's
Locale: Mainly New York City

In this hybrid mystery, a delusional streetperson takes on the art world as well as his personal demons to solve the murder of a gay model

Principal characters:
ROMULUS (ROM) LEDBETTER, the novel's would-be detective, a homeless, paranoid schizophrenic
LULU LEDBETTER, his daughter
STUYVESANT, his imaginary foe
DAVID LEPPENRAUB, a famous photographer who is dying of AIDS
MOIRA LEPPENRAUB, David's sister, also an artist
SCOTTY GATES, David's favorite model, who is found murdered
MATTHEW, Scotty's would-be lover
DETECTIVE JOHN CORK, lead investigator in the murder of Scotty Gates
VLAD, David Leppenraub's creepy chauffeur, who may or may not be involved in the murder of Scotty Gates

The valentine in George Dawes Green's first novel, *The Caveman's Valentine*, is a body dropped on Valentine's Day in front of a cave inhabited by the novel's would-be sleuth and unwilling hero, Romulus Ledbetter. Known to his fellow homeless as Rom the Caveman, Romulus inhabits a cave in New York City's Inwood Park. The novel opens with an enraged Romulus incoherently ranting and raving as he attempts to fend off the goodwill of an overly zealous social worker. Not only is Romulus homeless by choice, but he also is a paranoid eccentric given to wild fits of inchoate rambling that make him seem like a lost soul one might encounter on the subway or street corner. Yet Romulus is not without charm. When pressed, Romulus becomes a not-half-bad detective, lover, father, or musician. In Romulus Ledbetter, George Dawes Green has created the first conveniently crazy crime solver, in this odd mix of murder, mystery, and madness.

Romulus lets us know that his situation is the direct result of his mortal, but imaginary, enemy, Stuyvesant, who from his perch in the Chrysler Building zaps the unwitting residents of New York City with y-rays and z-rays. The narrative is sprinkled with Romulus' descants on Stuyvesant's zombification campaign. The author uses the y-rays as a device to trigger Romulus' rants whenever logic seems to threaten the narrative with mundane storytelling.

The arrival of the body on Valentine's Day convinces Romulus that strange things are afoot. After watching the news on an unplugged television where "all the news is lies," Romulus stirs from his couch to witness the dumping of a body in a clump of bushes bordering his cave. The police arrive to investigate the murder scene and find

Romulus in midrant. Officer Lulu Ledbetter, Romulus' daughter, attempts impatiently to get the whole story, only to be thwarted by her father's jumbled sense of events. While under questioning by Detective John Cork, Romulus reveals his paranoid belief that Stuyvesant is responsible for the murder, that is, the machinations of the city. Lulu apologizes for her father's behavior, dismissing his account of the car dropping the body as yet another of his myriad hallucinations. Romulus is undeterred even when Cork tells him that there was no murder, and that Scotty Gates died from the cold. Romulus lets forth:

> "Sounds very reasonable. Except that when he was tossed at my doorstep, he was already *dead*. He was *murdered*. . . . You think you can snake this one over on me? But see, I know you! You're Stuyvesant's a—— licker!"

Cork leaves Romulus to his cave, considering the case closed, the car a hallucination, and the body an unfortunate victim of the cold. Several days later Scotty's would-be lover, Matthew, stumbles into Romulus' cave strung out on heroin, and mentions to Romulus how Scotty had been modeling for an extremely famous photographer, who has just announced publicly that he has AIDS and is dying. Matthew tells Romulus that Scotty was forced into many of the poses by the photographer, David Leppenraub, and that he had been abused on several occasions. Matthew's story fuels Romulus' belief that the valentine dumped at his doorstep died from more than the cold. Matthew urges Romulus to find the real killers, awakening the detective in Romulus, who seems all too willing to take up what will prove to be a daunting case. What follows is the soft-boiled, genre-blending search for Scotty's killers.

Matthew tells Romulus the story of how Scotty Gates came to be the model for Leppenraub's most famous series of photographs. He describes Scotty's love/hate relationship with the photographer, and how seemingly harmless photo shoots turned into warped games of sadomasochism that would shock the art world and surely devalue Leppenraub's photographs. Matthew soon convinces Romulus that he must visit Leppenraub and confront him with the charges of murder. With some goading, Romulus makes a promise to find the real killers. Operating on a hunch and a strong sense of conspiracy, Romulus sets off to find the murderer of Scotty Gates.

What follows is one of the book's strongest segments, lifting Romulus out of his dreary, fit-addled existence, into social circles where his paranoia and eccentricities give him the advantage. For three whole days, Romulus manages to stuff his personal demons down into their dungeon as he goes about solving the murder. He showers and manages to cop a suit and tie from a good-hearted businessman who is won over by Romulus' story and his claim to have been a once-promising composer. Through several fairly unbelievable plot twists, Romulus manages to lie his way to an invitation to Leppenraub's farm, posing as a composer who is working on a musical ode to the works of the photographer. It is during this transformation that we get our first glimpse of Romulus' considerable talents. Romulus, who eats his dinner out of dumpsters and wears a Teflon pot lined with squirrel fur to keep the y-rays at bay, makes the perfect guest at Leppenraub's table of pretentious art world wannabes and hangers-on. After several fairly esoteric musical references and some mumbling about his opus, he is immediately accepted at the farm.

While at the farm, Romulus meets Leppenraub's less famous sister, who is also an artist. Moira Leppenraub, beautiful and artistically underappreciated, is drawn to Romulus' troubled mind and past. Along with Moira there is Vlad, Leppenraub's creepy Romanian chauffeur, who Romulus is convinced had a hand in the murder.

Romulus makes his way through the dinner party, set up to honor Leppenraub's release from the hospital after a bout of pneumonia. Romulus drops dated cultural references and stumbles through pretentious conversations about Leppenraub's art. Full of wine and insipid conversation, Romulus relents to the pleas of his fellow guests and plays the piano for the party. Midway through his piece, Romulus begins chanting out the word "murderer," before stopping altogether to continue his rant on Stuyvesant, y-rays, and the conspiracy to murder Scotty Gates. Romulus is properly bounced from the party, only to end up being smuggled back onto the farm by Leppenraub's sister. Moira has her doubts about the death of Scotty Gates, although she assures Romulus that her brother is by and large a benign person, wanting nothing more than to die with his artistic reputation intact.

Romulus and Moira become unlikely lovers. Moira tells Romulus more of Scotty's sometimes sick relationship with her brother. She slips and tell Romulus about a video showing Scotty being tortured before he was allowed to pose for a photograph. She stops short of telling him just who she thinks is responsible. Armed with this new piece of evidence, Romulus starts back to the city. En route, he is chased and nearly run over by the very same car that left the body of Scotty Gates at his cave on Valentine's Day.

Back in the city, Romulus is questioned a second time by his daughter and Detective Cork. Romulus mentions the video tape and describes being chased by the very same car that dumped the body. Detective Cork argues with Romulus over the details and possible motives for Leppenraub to want to murder Scotty. Romulus finally breaks and resorts to his paranoid rant on Stuyvesant until Cork leaves.

Satisfied that the police are now involved in the conspiracy, Romulus searches out Matthew to learn more about the supposed tape. Romulus learns from a couple of junkies that Matthew has been abducted by a pair of men wearing masks, and has not been heard from since. Romulus combs the derelict underground searching for Matthew, only to find him beaten beyond recognition. Matthew manages to warn Romulus about the men before he is taken to the hospital.

With his paranoid fears confirmed, Romulus sets out in earnest to hunt down the tape, hoping to uncover the murderer before they get to him first. When follows is standard gumshoe fare, with Romulus sleuthing about for clues while trying to quell his "Moth Seraphs" of madness, as well as avoiding the imaginary evil, y-rays zapped his way by Stuyvesant, who is sure to have a hand in the conspiracy somewhere.

In plot-driven fare of this nature, one reads to find out what will happen next. With *The Caveman's Valentine*, Green has devised not only a murder mystery, but a complex character study. Much of the book is written from Romulus Ledbetter's point of view, which lends the book a touch of paranoid whimsy, where nothing is as it seems. Enemies, both real and unreal, haunt Romulus through his investigation. Half of the fun in the book is rooting for Romulus to subdue his constant fits of paranoia and interact with the "normal" world long enough for him to solve the crime.

Romulus is the type of character who invokes a sense that a certain perverse logic is at work even in his delusional rants. His conspiracy-laden diatribes against society are the words of a true outsider. Romulus, although semicrazy and most certainly paranoid, speaks the elemental truth of one whose distance from society allows him a unique and sometimes dead-on perception of the functioning of humanity. Throwing aside the conventional, tough-talking detective who has seen it all, Green gives us Romulus in all of his unstable glory. Watching Romulus walking that guy wire of insanity is half of the novel's fun. Will he hold it together long enough to solve the crime? Will he slide further into his delusions? At the heart of this story there is a second mystery—Romulus.

Getting to the bottom of who killed Scotty Gates is only half of the book. Where most mysteries rely on solving the crime for impetus, *The Caveman's Valentine* asks readers to root for its unlikely sleuth, Romulus Ledbetter. Bits and pieces of Romulus' past are sprinkled throughout the search for the killer. Readers learn that he was at one time considered to be a gifted young composer, but few clues other then artistic burnout are given as to why this once-promising composer has forsaken family, career, and society for the comfort of a cave. Several times during the course of the novel Romulus demonstrates flashes of his musical brilliance, only to stop because of the "pain and memories" that playing induces. As his playing scampers off into insane rants and incoherent dissonance, so does the prose:

> "IS IT THE WAY YOU DUMPED HIM IN FRONT OF MY CAVE, LEPPENRAUB? *SPECIAL DELIVERY*, SO I'D KNOW YOU KILL WHENEVER YOU PLEASE, SO I'D COME AND LICK YOUR SHOES AND BEG YOUR BOSS STUYVESANT FOR A POINT-BLANK SHOT OF Y-RAYS INTO MY BRAIN? . . . AND THE HEART HAS . . . *VAMOOSED* FROM THIS CULTURE LONG TIME AGO, AND ANYBODY GETS WIND OF *THAT*, YOU'LL TORTURE HIM AND KILL HIM AND MAKE A VIDEO OF IT AND CALL IT *ART*! AND YOU'LL THROW HIM IN THE SNOW AND *TEACH THE CAVEMAN A LESSON*! AND BURN OUT THE CAVEMAN'S EYES WITH BLUE SKY AND GREEN DUCKS AND BROWN EYES . . ."

What makes the book work both as a character study and a page-turner is Green's grasp of the mystery genre, which lurks on every page. Having the detective be as original and quirky as Romulus Ledbetter is an added delight, giving the book a sense of the surreal with no real forebears or signposts. One can only hope that Green continues in his quest to turn the genre upside down with characters as original and weird as Rom the Caveman.

Elwood Reid

Sources for Further Study

Boston Globe. January 30, 1994, p. 16.
Chicago Tribune. February 13, 1994, XIV, p. 1.
Kirkus Reviews. LXI, November 15, 1993, p. 1410.
Library Journal. CXVIII, December, 1993, p. 174.
Los Angeles Times Book Review. February 20, 1994, p. 5.
The New York Times Book Review. XCIX, January 30, 1994, p. 12.
Publishers Weekly. CCXL, November 1, 1993, p. 65.
San Francisco Chronicle. April 19, 1994, p. E5.

CERTAIN TRUMPETS
The Call of Leaders

Author: Garry Wills (1934-)
Publisher: Simon & Schuster (New York). 336 pp. $23.00
Type of work: Current affairs

Defining a leader as one who mobilizes others toward a shared goal, this biographical study of sixteen leadership types concentrates on the special bond that holds leaders and followers together

While critics decry a lack of leadership, public opinion polls confirm that many Americans distrust those who are entrusted to lead them. Meanwhile, universities and colleges promote their students as leaders in the making, and, especially in politics, there is no lack of people who claim that they can provide the needed direction. Thus, leadership is a American buzzword.

What is leadership, and what, in particular, is good leadership in a democracy like the United States? Such questions are crucial because the idea of good leadership contains an important ambiguity. Good leadership frequently gets equated with effective leadership. Effective leadership, however, may or may not be good—as least insofar as the term "good" contains ethical meanings that make one evaluate goals and the means used to achieve them.

Promising to create more effective leaders, though not necessarily good ones in a moral sense, various how-to books accumulate every year. While leadership is also its concern, Garry Wills's *Certain Trumpets: The Call of Leaders* does not belong to that genre. No simplistic leadership manual, this book meditates deeply on the qualities of intelligence and character that good and effective leadership requires.

Not all of Wills's book is about leadership in the United States, but it clearly focuses on the American scene. For that reason, Wills resists a typical American desire for quick-fix recipes and shows instead the importance of study about the conditions that make leadership possible and necessary. Such study attends to historical circumstances, factors of timing and opportunity, and relationships among people, places, and powers.

Wills has long had a knack for writing prize-winning books about American life. In previous works such as *Lincoln at Gettysburg* (1992), *Nixon Agonistes* (1970), and *Inventing America* (1978), he deployed a masterful combination of disciplined scholarship, philosophical reflection, and irresistible story telling. *Certain Trumpets* employs those resources again, adding to them insightful spins of imagination that ask unconventional questions. What, for example, do Eleanor Roosevelt and George Washington have in common? How might they differ from two other examples—Adlai Stevenson and Madonna—who have some striking, if heretofore unnoticed, similarities?

Certain Trumpets raises such questions because Wills turns his book into a gallery. With metaphorical trumpet calls providing background, Wills's gallery contains thirty-two biographical sketches. These sketches are paired by type and "antitype," the latter category containing people who clarify a leadership type by illustrating flaws and failures. Thus, Wills takes George Washington's antitype to be Oliver Cromwell, a less successful revolutionary. Eleanor Roosevelt's is Nancy Reagan. Madonna, on the other hand, plays antitype to artistic leader Martha Graham, while Adlai Stevenson appears in contrast to Franklin Delano Roosevelt.

Wills's pairings illustrate sixteen kinds of leadership. They range from what he calls the charismatic (the biblical King David) and diplomatic (Andrew Young) to the rhetorical (Martin Luther King, Jr.) and intellectual (Socrates). In each case, Wills fortifies his analyses with insights from theorists such as Niccolò Machiavelli, Max Weber, and Carl von Clausewitz—three individuals judged by Wills to be "the most original and influential in their writings on leadership."

Many things happen in Wills's book, but far from exhausting the possibilities, his eclectic collection suggests that the list of leaders in the book's table of contents could go on and on. Styled impressionistically, each biographical miniature includes fascinating, little-known details that enrich Wills's interpretations of the leading lives he depicts. The result is a historical and ethical understanding of major themes contained in what his subtitle identifies as "the call of leaders."

Wills's well-crafted choice of a title focuses the book's perspective in a few words, especially when one notes the epigraph that follows the title page. This epigraph raises a question asked by St. Paul in one of the New Testament's letters to the Corinthians: "For if the trumpet give an uncertain sound, who shall prepare himself to the battle?"

In Wills's use of trumpet imagery, multiple meanings can be heard. Uncertain sounds—confusion, ambiguity, conflict, dissonance—are all around. They leave people puzzled, perplexed, even paralyzed. Such uncertainty makes us wonder what to do; it even makes us wonder whether anything can be done to improve our circumstances decisively. By contrast, leadership depends, first, on hearing *certain* trumpets.

To be a leader, a person has to discern something akin to a trumpet's call. A stirring is felt, an idea forms, that something important needs to be done. Awareness dawns that what needs doing will not get done unless the person who hears a certain trumpet also follows its call. In this way, a leader is a follower, and what is followed is the beckoning of a possibility that can direct a person's life and make that life one of direction, too. By hearing "certain trumpets," then, leaders concentrate their attention, focus their vision, and strive to find paths of action that cut through bewilderment and bedlam to achieve a desired aim.

The trumpets that call leaders have to sound certain in another important manner as well. Leadership always happens in particular times and places where specific needs exist and definite actions are required. In addition to far-seeing and inclusive vision, leadership involves specificity and even specialization. Thus, since no one can do everything, there must be leaders plural. Leaders, moreover, will be ineffective unless they discern that certain trumpets call them to define the limits of what one can and cannot do. Failure to hear certain trumpets in that way produces the disasters that result from reaching too far by focusing too little, or the disappointments that occur from achieving too little by not reaching far enough.

"Determination, focus, a clear goal, a sense of priorities"—Wills contends that individuals must embody all those qualities for leadership to exist. Yet, necessary though they are, such characteristics are not sufficient to make one a leader. "We easily forget the first and all-encompassing need," Wills reminds his readers. "The leader most needs followers. When those are lacking, the best ideas, the strongest will, the most wonderful smile have no effect."

While effective leadership depends on careful listening to certain trumpets, it hinges no less on the ability to sound a call so that others will also hear the trumpet and respond. A leader's personal agenda, for example, is not enough to create the bond that holds leaders and followers together. The agenda must be one with which others can identify. It must fire the imagination, inspire loyalty, speak to one's sense of what is right, and extend meaning in a group. Thus, Wills explains, the call of leaders requires not only an articulated vision that others can share but also an understanding that the vision will not be shared unless the leader discerns consistently that everything the leader wants to do depends on followers.

In Wills's judgment, for example, presidential candidate Adlai Stevenson fell short as a leader because "he considered it below him, or wrong, to scramble out among the people and ask what *they* wanted. Roosevelt grappled voters to him. Stevenson shied off from them." As a result, the White House eluded Stevenson. Madonna, on the other hand, has never shied off from anything or anybody. Nevertheless, Wills finds her related to Stevenson as a leadership antitype. Enjoying a following for a time, Stevenson campaigned and Madonna entertains, but their celebrity seems destined to leave no enduring legacy.

Eleanor Roosevelt never campaigned for herself, though she did for many others, including her presidential husband. No one would have mistaken her for an entertainer. Yet, unlike her antitype, Nancy Reagan, a whole nation came to see and admire Eleanor Roosevelt as a reformer, and the causes she served—education, civil rights, greater freedom for women—live on. "Many," Wills notes, "succumbed to the spell of her earnestness and joined her in the work that always seemed to multiply around her." Eleanor Roosevelt heard, embodied, and amplified the call of leadership. So did George Washington. He forged a national vision that people wanted to rally around, insisted persuasively that the future of the United States depended on public virtue, and then, when the time was right, he stepped aside to make good his belief that the responsibilities of leadership must be shared for democracy to be healthy.

Two more important themes emerge from Wills's analysis. First, leadership and influence are not the same. Many people exert influence but are not necessarily leaders. The difference is that a leader's work requires a team of people to complete it. Influence, however, can be exerted by an individual who labors more or less alone and who does not depend on followers to achieve a shared goal. Next, when Wills stresses that leadership cannot exist outside of a leader-follower linkage, he identifies what he takes to be the most time-consuming part of leadership, especially in a democracy:

While the follower needs to understand the leader, it is even more imperative that the leader understand the follower, for "followers 'have a say' in what they are being led to." Leaders ignore this reality at everyone's peril and especially their own, because without the loyalty of followers, leaders will be leaders no more. Instead, they will eventually find themselves stripped of their authority.

"To sound a certain trumpet," Wills says, "does not mean just trumpeting one's own certitudes. It means sounding a specific call to specific people capable of response." No part of Wills's book is more important than the emphasis he places on the relationship between leaders and followers. On the one hand, Wills argues, it will no longer do to accept a traditional view that identifies a leader simply as "a superior person, to whom inferiors should submit." Especially in a democracy, that understanding of leadership is a mistake because it obscures the dynamic give-and-take between leaders and followers. On the other hand, Wills recognizes that such give-and-take can produce "leaders" undeserving of the name because they become little more than weather vanes whose points of direction are determined by the fickle winds of popular opinion.

At least in a democracy, trumpets that dictate or coerce will sound an illusory certainty. Such trumpets are unlikely to sustain good leaders for long because of the dissonance and cacophony their sounds eventually produce. Yet vacillating trumpets sound no better. Attuned to fad and fashion, their notes lack direction. They stray off key and drift away from the score. Leadership moving in any of those directions ends up unworthy of the name.

Pursuit of a goal in common is the bond that links leaders and followers together. Take that sharing away and followers dwindle as leadership dissolves. Yet with so much depending on the sharing of goals, how does that bonding occur? Again, Wills offers no simple formula because none exists. Instead, his sound response amplifies and nuances his understanding of how leadership works. Wills stresses, for example, that leadership often is not the result of an individual's focusing vision alone. As his interpretation of Martin Luther King, Jr., illustrates, leaders can be called by the very persons and communities who become their followers. In these cases, would-be followers create leaders by luring them from their midst and thrusting opportunity upon them, by conferring responsibility even when the person who becomes a leader might not have anticipated or desired such authority. Nor do groups and communities always do this consciously. There are situations in which time, circumstance, and fortune conspire with group needs and personal ambitions to move a person to the center of the stage where leaders and followers interact.

Leaders are called by circumstances, by those who become their followers, by their own vision. At the same time, those who lead must also call. They must call for their followers' dedication, loyalty, courage. Specifically, Wills emphasizes that leaders must give a call that is answerable, which in human affairs is not necessarily the most noble call. As the leadership of Adolf Hitler and Joseph Stalin illustrates, such calls can be disastrous. Wills does not say as much as he could or should about destructive leaders, especially those who inflict massive suffering and death. Overall, however, his message is unmistakably ethical. Succinctly defining the leader as "one who mobilizes others toward a goal shared by leader and followers," Wills recognizes that unachievable perfection must not become the enemy of achievable good. Lest tragedy and misery get chances they do not deserve, ways must be found to achieve the good that can be done. That standard measures whether a leader's moral stature rises or falls.

John K. Roth

Sources for Further Study

Chicago Tribune. May 8, 1994, XIV, p. 3.
Choice. XXXII, September, 1994, p. 160.
The Economist. CCCXXXII, July 2, 1994, p. 84.
Foreign Affairs. LXXIII, September, 1994, p. 142.
Los Angeles Times Book Review. August 7, 1994, p. 8.
The New York Times Book Review. XCIX, April 24, 1994, p. 14.
Newsweek. CXXIII, April 25, 1994, p. 67.
Publishers Weekly. CCXLI, March 21, 1994, p. 60.
Time. CXLIII, May 9, 1994, p. 80.
The Washington Post Book World. XXIV, April 24, 1994, p. 3.

CHUCK JONES
A Flurry of Drawings

Author: Hugh Kenner (1923-   )
Publisher: University of California Press (Berkeley). Illustrated. 114 pp. $16.00
Type of work: Film history

A review and critical appreciation of the work of Chuck Jones, one of the premier artists in cinematic animation and the creator of Wile E. Coyote, the Road Runner, and countless other characters

"Steamboat Willie," the third cartoon featuring Mickey Mouse, was the first cartoon produced with sound, and its theatrical release in 1928 transformed motion-picture theater patrons from readers of captions into true audiences, listening to characters speak, hearing background music and sounds. The short animated feature also launched the success of Walt Disney, Mickey's creator. Within a decade, the Disney Studio had developed and perfected the technology to produce *Snow White and the Seven Dwarfs* (1937), one of the most detailed and "realistic" animated films ever made.

Disney's success set the style and established the generally accepted guidelines for the animated film: realistic drawings, well-constructed story lines with a heavy underlacing of sentiment, even sentimentality, and a close relationship between the soundtrack—especially the music—and the action. For much of the rest of the two decades that followed, other studios sought to imitate the Disney formula, only to discover that they lacked the financial and artistic resources needed, not to mention Walt Disney's unique artistic vision; the novelist John Gardner once noted that Disney was one of the true geniuses of American art.

The Warner Bros. studio had its own animation department, and in its earlier days it tried to follow the Disney formula and even was staffed by former Disney artists. Eventually, however, a canny entrepreneur, Leon Schlesinger, brokered a contract with the Warner studio to provide it with cartoons under the generic title "Looney Tunes," and later added the companion series "Merrie Melodies." (Walt Disney had "Silly Symphonies"; the resemblance was not accidental.) Schlesinger, who was no artist himself and who is remembered as a hard and humorless boss, somehow managed to assemble the most remarkable collection of artistic talent ever present in the animated film—and arguably equal to the talent found anywhere in the entire motion-picture industry.

These included voice expert Mel Blanc, music director Carl Stalling, and directors Fred "Tex" Avery, Frank Tashlin, Bob Clampett, Friz Freleng, and Charles "Chuck" Jones. Ensconced in a rickety, isolated bungalow, nicknamed Termite Terrace, on the Warner Bros. lot, this aggregation of individuals (they were too idiosyncratic and quirky to be properly labeled a team) redefined the animated cartoon and established a defiantly different set of conventions and expectations for viewers. As noted literary and cultural observer Hugh Kenner points out in his short but brilliant study *Chuck*

Jones: A Flurry of Drawings, almost certainly the key figure of this group, and perhaps of modern American animation, was Chuck Jones.

The central realization made by the members of this group was that since animated cartoons were not bound by the laws of the physical world, there was no reason that they should be conceived, created, and produced as if so bound. As a matter of fact, there were excellent reasons not to allow the everyday, physical world to intrude into the realm of the animated cartoon. In coming to this realization and then acting upon it, these artists set animation free. Of this group it was the directors, especially Avery, Clampett, and Jones, who both understood and articulated that an animated cartoon had no other laws it was bound to obey than those which it and the medium created. "The world of the transcendent Jones Cartoons," Kenner remarks, "has no firm connections with any world outside of itself."

Rightly so, the residents of Termite Terrace would agree. They wanted no part of the "illusion of life" that ruled at the Disney studios, and Kenner correctly points out that it became a central tenet of Warner Bros. that "what can easily be done in live action, such as human behavior, is specifically *not* the domain of animation."

That was the breakthrough that, in the hands of these artists, created the celebrated cartoons at Warner Bros. They differed from the cartoons of Disney and other animating studios in content, character, and style.

In content, they were, at their best, "about" only themselves. There were, it is true, the fake newsreel shorts, just as there were the wartime propaganda and morale-building cartoons; these, however, were seldom among the better efforts of the Warner studio. The true classics from Termite Terrace are divorced from external reality, and their content is, to a greater or lesser extent, purely internal. The acme, so to speak, is reached with Jones's own "Road Runner" series, which has one basic situation extended, eventually, over four hours, and that situation refers only to itself and the two characters that establish and sustain it: Wile E. Coyote, self-proclaimed genius, and the unflappable, uncatchable Road Runner he pursues with such determined futility.

The characters of the Warner cartoons are unique in animation. They are highly individualistic, immediately recognizable personalities. In most cartoons, even in full-length animated features, the characters are stock figures who seldom achieve for the viewer a definable identity. The Prince in *Snow White and the Seven Dwarfs*, for example, is the "illusion of reality" only in his physical movement; his personality does not exist beyond the level of plot requirements. Donald Duck is characterized by his clothes (sailor suit—actually the jacket alone) and one trait (irascibility). Tom and Jerry cartoons, as Kenner aptly remarks, call "simply for a cat who'd eat a mouse if only he could manage to catch it; but the mouse, being smaller, hence smarter, can always outmaneuver him."

Warner cartoons, however, offer actual characters, such as Bugs Bunny, Daffy Duck, Elmer Fudd, and all the rest, who seem to exist in their own right, and that because they have a distinct and innate personality that defines what they would or would not do in any situation, however unfamiliar. It is not that they will always act the same way; they will not. The particular actions of Daffy Duck in a given situation, for example, vary widely, from explosions of outrage to subtle scheming. What gives him unity of character is difficult to define. Kenner, who raises this key point, admits that " 'neurotic' is a forceless word to set against Daffy's id-like reserves of energy."

What is true of Daffy Duck is true of the other Warner cartoon characters: They may have a dominating attribute, but it is alloyed with other traits that influence, even determine, how it can be applied. In this sense, Kenner shrewdly observes, the viewer can watch Elmer Fudd allowing himself to be befuddled by Bugs Bunny during "Rabbit Seasoning" and can then remark, "That's just like him," in reference to the particular Elmer Fudd and not merely a cartoon hunter chasing a cartoon rabbit. Such a situation can be appreciated much more easily than explained, although Kenner's work is an excellent start.

It is also an excellent start for understanding the Warner Bros. cartoon style, the third key element that unites their content and character. Their style, Kenner maintains—and he is certainly correct regarding those productions directed by Jones—was an odd but effective mixture of cost-conscious economy and obsessive attention to the details that, when honored, made a cartoon hilarious and that, when neglected, created a dud.

To restrain costs, Jones and his fellows developed techniques that used what Kenner terms "selective re-drawing"—that is, using subtle changes (a change of expression, even an eye blink, a wiggling eyebrow) which were overlaid on a base drawing of the character to establish reaction or provide emphasis. Jones and the other directors also restricted the number of characters visible in a single shot, usually to no more than two, and often one of those characters was active while the other was still. According to Jones, this emphasized "the power of a strongly-drawn non-talker as a foil for the voluble. It became what I call Motivated Camera. Having established the rhythm of the relationship between two characters, I could go to one for something to say, go to the other for the reaction." All of this, in its own fashion and through the particular genius of Termite Terrace, translated into a new kind of animation.

The obsession with details shows most obviously in Jones's concern with establishing and maintaining the appropriate gait for each of his characters and for the particular situation in which they find themselves. As Jones points out, while there can be an individual fashion of running, there is still a difference between running when you are the pursued and when you are the pursuer.

There is even a characteristic way of falling—at least, if you want to evoke laughs. Jones's attention to detail in timing in the cartoons was, according to Kenner, exacting. "When the Coyote dropped off the cliff, as he did repeatedly, it would take, says Jones, 'Eighteen frames for him to fall into the distance and disappear, then fourteen frames later he would hit. It seemed to me that thirteen frames didn't work in terms of humor, and neither did fifteen frames. Fourteen frames got a laugh.' "

Of such details did Chuck Jones and the others at Warner Bros. create the films that now appear casually on television every afternoon as well as in honored retrospectives at major museums. These are the fundamental principles of once-routine, six-minute productions that were used to settle and seat audiences before a feature film. These few minutes of animation could not only create characters but also—both within themselves and over a period of time, as viewers saw the same characters over and over in different situations—establish an entire world.

Such animation, as both Chuck Jones and Hugh Kenner are all too aware, has largely passed, at least in its traditional form. In the late 1950's, when cartoons moved from the motion-picture theater to the television, economic and time constraints brought about a product called "limited animation," a cheaper, faster, and much less varied way of making a cartoon. Kenner quotes film critic Leonard Maltin as defining limited animation as "the Muzak of animation," and Maltin is correct. Yet limited animation is already passing; computers can be programmed to do the tedious, repetitive work.

The real problem is not economic, but cultural. Where is the place for the short animated feature? The denizens of Termite Terrace ground out their daily, weekly, yearly quota because cartoons were needed audience fodder in theaters owned by the major film studios. While production time was relatively limited, production values had to be kept to an acceptable minimum—after all, on a large screen, details, or the lack of them, tend to show. Whether they realized it or not, audiences came to expect a certain level of quality. With the advent of television, that changed. Time was drastically reduced, quality declined, creativity was replaced by productivity. Limited screen size and the ease of other distractions compensated. A generation grew up almost not knowing how to watch cartoons such as those starring Bugs Bunny, Daffy Duck, or Wile E. Coyote—or they recognized them as cartoons, but few viewers could tell the difference between full animation and limited animation, between real characters and stock figures. Fewer, probably, cared. It was not until the 1970's that some perceptive film critics began to bring relatively widespread public recognition to Chuck Jones and his contributions. Now, with Hugh Kenner's *Chuck Jones: A Flurry of Drawings*, readers have a witty, insightful examination of this peculiarly American genius and his art.

Michael Witkoski

Sources for Further Study

Booklist. XC, August, 1994, p. 2012.
Kirkus Reviews. LXII, July 1, 1994, p. 926.
National Review. XLVI, October 24, 1994, p. 68.
The New York Times Book Review. XCIX, October 30, 1994, p. 38.
Sight and Sound. IV, December, 1994, p. 38.
The Washington Post Book World. XXIV, October 2, 1994, p. 13.

THE CLIFF

Author: David R. Slavitt (1935-)
Publisher: Louisiana State University Press (Baton Rouge). 154 pp. $21.95
Type of work: Novel
Time: 1989
Locale: Italy

Jack Smith, adjunct assistant professor and failed novelist, assumes a fellowship intended for another Jack Smith and discovers redemption while pillorying academe, publishing, and pretensions of all sorts at a villa in Italy

Principal characters:
JACK SMITH, a failed novelist and adjunct professor of literature (Richard Roe)
LAURA SMITH, his daughter
HARRY BEAMISH, his literary agent
DAPHNE PINCUS, a California poet (Dahlia Levine)
MARK LOWNDES, a publisher of art books (Peter Oliphant)
CLARISSE BETHUNE, Lowndes's "significant other," an art historian (Charlotte Breedlove)
KIRK HOGGEBOOM, a professor of Dutch history (Professor Jan Kinderhook)
HOPE HOGGEBOOM, the wife of Hoggeboom (Fleur Kinderhook)
DR. DAVID GLICKSTEIN, a medical historian
DR. SHELIA GLICKSTEIN, a medical historian
CHARLES MARKS, an antitrust lawyer (Fred Engels)
MOLLY MARKS, the wife of Marks (Emily Engels)
IBRAHIM, a Nigerian economist (Denis Umfalozi)
SANTHA, Ibrahim's wife (Zenana)
ROBERTO, the resident manager of Villa Sfondrata (Roberto Malatesta)
GIANNA, Roberto's wife (Gianna Malatesta)
PAOLO, SERGIO, and NATALE, servants at the Villa Sfondrata
SIGISMUNDO COLANGELO, chair of the Department of English

The Cliff, David R. Slavitt's fiftieth book, is a satiric look at the cosseted world of creative and scholarly retreats financed by foundations. In the case of Jack Smith's stay at the Villa Sfondrata in Bellagio, Italy, the foundation in question is the Westchester Foundation, funded by "Baptist billionaires," "their vast wealth . . . an outward sign of their spiritual good fortune, their heavenly election." Headquartered in New York City in opulent digs, the foundation engages "in various programs throughout the world, some large and some small," involving "the ecologies and economies of whole countries, as well as the psyches of scholars and artists." Villa Sfondrata, where artists and scholars may reside for short periods of time insulated from the world, stands on a cliff above Lake Como. One would think that such an institution as this foundation, whose sponsorship is widely sought, might be immune from the satirist's attack, especially given that Slavitt wrote the book under the auspices of just such a foundation at just such a location. Yet this small novel barely avoids being churlish, nibbling rather than biting the hand that feeds its author.

Indeed, the novel manages a wide array of satiric sorties, attacking the "arrogance" of the foundation's founders and benefactors, their desire to find "talented youngsters . . . turning them into zombies," the cooks, servants, and keepers of the Villa Sfondrata for their penury, poor larder, and poorer wine cellar, and the scholars, artists, and poets who are the recipients of the foundation's largess. Jack Smith, the central figure in the novel, a failed novelist and Prufrockian figure of an "adjunct assistant professor," does not escape either.

Here, exactly, is the hinge of the plot, for this Jack Smith is not "*the* Jack Smith," a world-class historian whose letter from the foundation offering a stay at Villa Sfondrata is casually misdirected by campus mail into the possession of the wrong Jack Smith. To avoid his former wife's attorney's requests for late alimony, Smith decides to accept the invitation. In due course he is snugly ensconced, imposturing his way through days of writing either in his "studio in the woods" or "often in the library, where I can be observed at my labors," which are not, however, an account of the death of Benito Mussolini, the stated project of Jack Smith the historian. Instead, Jack Smith the failed-everything writes "long and all but insane letters to various former friends, my former agent, the people I love and have hurt . . . and the manager of the villa." Among the people he has loved and hurt is his estranged daughter, and the subplot of his engagement or reengagement with her provides one of the few tender elements of the novel. The essential intellectual posture of the novel is, however, provided by his being an impostor, "an outsider who is also inside and is therefore privileged to witness things without being taken in by them."

What, beside foundations and their staffs, does Slavitt satirize? If one looks at his cast of characters (his "ship of fools"), one might be excused for thinking that his targets include all manner of artists and scholars. "So here we are, a Korean agronomist and his wife; a Nigerian economist and his wife . . . ; a lady poet from California . . . ; an antitrust lawyer from Washington, D.C., and his clothes-horse wife; a book designer and his free-spirited 'significant other,' an art historian specializing in garden follies . . . ; and a couple of medical historians, the Drs. Glickstein," and, to be sure, Jack Smith himself.

Each of the temporary residents at Villa Sfondrata is an easy target for the satirist's pen. Yet Slavitt is successful in portraying Smith as attacking more out of a desire to hide his own imposture than out of a moral certainty of his own superiority. Morally, Smith is suspect. Professionally, he cannot get his writing career back on track except, ironically, as a result of the leisure provided through his appropriation of the foundation's grant. His teaching as an "adjunct assistant professor," one of academe's legion of cannon fodder for whom security and pride of place are equally foreign, is not in any way distinguished. He is estranged from his teenage daughter, a situation that is also being rectified as a direct result of the introspection he is forced to undertake as a resident of the villa. Other residents of the villa (and readers of the novel) do not find Smith an easy conversationalist, a respectful friend, or anything but a defensive, if deft, duelist with words.

Yet Slavitt's satiric vehicle yields a measure of growth and redemption. Smith's writing, it turns out, will be published by LSU (Louisiana State University Press, the publisher of *The Cliff*), having been vetted by his agent to an editor who owes him a favor. That neither the agent nor the editor has read the manuscript—a commentary on the state of modern publishing—does not detract from the sense that this publication will serve as part of Smith's redemption.

> So, suddenly, there I was, a writer again, legitimated, working to finish a manuscript for which there was an actual publisher. . . . I wasn't the John Smith they [the Foundation] thought they were inviting, but I wasn't a total fraud. And even if they hadn't intended it, their benefaction had been of greater effect with me and had changed my life more than it could possibly have done with the other Smith.

After learning from his agent, Harry Beamish, that his work has been accepted for publication, Smith is forced to face the kind of fundamental question every writer, every scholar, indeed every person must face: Is it our own experience and our reading of that experience that matter most, or is it the validation or lack thereof that determines who and what we are? "The question was, in simplest form, whether I believed my own experience—which was mostly of failure—or the villa's grandiose version of it? Was I no longer a poseur but, at least for my time here, an important artist and scholar whose views were valuable and wise? Doesn't all art begin with some such arrogance?"

The book thus turns—as all good books do, one supposes—on the old conundrum of appearance versus reality. It is the satirist's task to illuminate the differences between the two, to play the clear light of ironic vision upon the world and by doing so to correct it. Slavitt shows Smith doing this and in doing so finding both professional and personal salvation, forging (the play on words is deliberate) his new identity out of the shards of memory and present distress—and opportunity. Smith writes his daughter, Laura, from whom he has been seriously estranged, that he is writing again and will be published again. As a result, he says, "I am less depressed, able to pick my head up a little, able perhaps even to behave better toward the people I love and who love me. Your name stands high on that very short list, and I hope we can pick up the frayed threads and reknit some kind of comfortable relationship." "Who knows," he writes in a journal entry, "but the terrible discipline of this place may yet set me back on my feet as a writer?"

A major portion of the novel is taken up with Smith's novel, whose first chapter and detailed outline have been submitted to Beamish. As Smith writes in a subsequent letter to Beamish (in which he asks him not to submit it to anyone), "loutish life has once again played the sedulous clerk to art: What I wrote in all innocence has come terribly true." The poet Daphne Pincus (in the novel-within-the-novel named Dahlia Levine) has disappeared, and Smith is afraid that a police investigation will ensue, at the very least exposing him to be the impostor he is, and at the very worst creating suspicion that he has murdered Pincus. If someone were to read his first chapter and his outline, that someone might take them the wrong way. "Literary criticism is in such a mess these days that I'd be lucky not to wind up serving time in a deconstructionist's dungeon for failure to fictionalize enough, for sticking too close to the truth. That, at any rate, might be the 'strong misreading' that could prove to be worse than the total absence of reading to which I had begun to grow accustomed." Slavitt thus attacks both contemporary publishing habits and the fads of literary criticism in a couple of sentences, and leads the cheers at the same time.

In Smith's letters (all but the last one written or composed but not sent), readers get a fuller, unguarded view of the man behind the ironist, the poseur, the impostor. This side of Smith is created with a deft sensitivity that makes Slavitt's slashing satiric attacks elsewhere in the novel all the more delightful and credible. In one such letter, Smith is apologizing to Laura for the pain he has caused her by divorcing her mother. "Like Rigoletto, I wanted to protect you against the beastliness of my gender, and I constructed elaborate fictions for myself about how the wariness children of divorce are made to learn might protect you, serving you well in the turbulence and treachery of the world. But this is not true, I fear, or even plausible." As a novelist—or a former novelist—he admits that he "likes to impose connections and to see order where, in the real world, none exists." This is surely one of the more interesting dilemmas of the artist, who must see, impose, and create order—the very nature of plot, of form, of meaning—out of the chaos of randomness that is (or may be) the nature of the "real world."

The novel-within-the-novel provides a clever contrapuntal movement within which the larger epistemological questions are worked out. As Smith says in his proposal, the narrator is unreliable—but then, narrators are always unreliable. If they seem otherwise, it is only the rage for order, the reader's desire for coherence, that forces the issue so. As Smith says in his heartfelt but unsent letter to Laura, the entire convention of the novel as a form requires writer and reader to "suspend their horse sense for the sake of the story and to allow that . . . good characters can come to good ends and be rewarded with 'happiness ever after' or a stasis that can suggest at least a kind of tranquillity."

True to the form, Slavitt provides just such a resolution for *The Cliff*, so that Smith is redeemed, is published, and will be, one believes, reunited with his daughter, made whole in fact in ways that one may expect, perhaps, only in fiction, a "syntactical Eden . . . where my real residence is." Yet the metanarrative—the machinery of foundation within foundation and the arbitrariness of publishing—suggests that life is never so neat as fiction and that the archangel yet guards the entrance to such an Eden with his flaming sword, prohibiting human entry therein.

Theodore C. Humphrey

Sources for Further Study

Kirkus Reviews. LXII, July 1, 1994, p. 881.
Library Journal. CXIX, August, 1994, p. 133.

Los Angeles Times. November 8, 1994, p. E4.
The New York Times Book Review. XCIX, October 30, 1994, p. 48.
Publishers Weekly. CCXLI, July 25, 1994, p. 34.
The Washington Post Book World. XXIV, September 25, 1994, p. 4.

CLOSING TIME

Author: Joseph Heller (1923-)
Publisher: Simon & Schuster (New York). 448 pp. $24.00
Type of work: Novel
Time: The 1930's to the 1990's
Locale: New York City; Washington, D.C.; Columbia, South Carolina; Pianosa, Italy; Dresden, Germany; Fort Dix, New Jersey; Chicago; and Kenosha, Wisconsin

Three veterans of World War II reflect on their lives and the sad chaos of contemporary America

Principal characters:
JOHN YOSSARIAN, a semiretired consultant and failed writer
SAMMY SINGER, a retired copywriter and failed writer
LEW RABINOWITZ, a retired businessman
MICHAEL YOSSARIAN, Yossarian's artist son
ALBERT TAPPMAN, a minister
MILO MINDERBINDER, a billionaire, Yossarian's sometime employer
MILO "M2" MINDERBINDER, Minderbinder's son
G. NOODLES COOK, a presidential consultant
MELISSA MACINTOSH, a nurse who has a relationship with Yossarian
LITTLE PRICK, president of the United States

Catch-22 (1961), Joseph Heller's first novel, was a true publishing phenomenon—a serious work of fiction discovered by the reading public rather than the literary establishment. There is a myth that the novel was harshly attacked and misunderstood by all its reviewers; actually, the now-classic absurdist account of American airmen during World War II was appreciated in some publications, but not enough to help it sell well outside New York City until it was published in paperback. Released in softcover, *Catch-22* soon found an increasingly enthusiastic public, particularly among young readers, who responded to its antiestablishment theme, especially as the war in Vietnam escalated in an insane way that seemed to mirror Heller's black comedy.

Catch-22 ends as Yossarian, its protagonist, becomes fed up with his commanding officers, who continually raise the number of bombing missions he must fly. He sets out to escape the war and its pervasive absurdity by running from death, representing the individual's hopeless yet admirable protest against the mindless forces conspiring to control his life. That gesture seems a perfectly apt way of ending Yossarian's saga. Yet Heller has chosen to continue, in *Closing Time*, the account of Yossarian and some of his friends from the war. While Heller's sixth novel is described by its publisher as a sequel to *Catch-22*, it has little in common with its predecessor. The earlier work was a hilarious work of passionate anger at the modern world; in contrast, *Closing Time*, while admirable in certain parts, is a fitfully amusing novel of resigned disgust at an even more unfathomable universe.

Closing Time represents the reflections of Yossarian and two other veterans on their old age. Heller has made Yossarian sixty-eight, trimming a decade from his *Catch-22* age to make him believably energetic. Yossarian has allowed himself to drift with the times, focusing his resources on trying to survive, as in the earlier book, to live forever or die in the attempt. Separated from his second wife for a year, this "semi-retired semi-consultant" performs occasional duties for Milo Minderbinder, the most absurd of the *Catch-22* characters, whose M & M Enterprises occupies what was once the Time-Life Building in Manhattan.

As Yossarian tells his son Michael, an occasional artist, his postwar dissatisfaction results in part from never having done what he wanted with his life. Dreaming of being a writer, Yossarian works off and on over the years on a play about Charles Dickens and a comic novel about the composer Adrian Leverkuhn from Thomas Mann's *Doktor Faustus* (1947; *Doctor Faustus*, 1948). Instead of writing, Yossarian has abandoned teaching twice for investment banking, public relations, and advertising, "succeeding . . . as a jack-of-all-trades except any encompassing a product that could be seen, touched, utilized, or consumed, a product that occupied space and for which there was need." He helps Milo try to sell the government a bomber that Milo claims does not work and does not even exist. Yossarian hates himself for never being able to despise the cold, manipulative Minderbinder.

This elderly Yossarian is more easygoing than his younger self but just as alienated. He often compares himself with Gustav Aschenbach, the protagonist of Mann's *Der Tod in Venedig* (1912; *Death in Venice*, 1925). Though younger than Yossarian, Aschenbach has "run out of interests. . . . He did not know that his true creative life was over and that he and his era were coming to a close, whether he liked it or not." Yossarian finds himself in a similar dilemma—hence his willingness to work for Milo—and is angry that he seems to be running out of life as well: "I used to wake up each day with a brain full of plans I couldn't wait to get started on. Now I wake up listless and wonder what I can find to keep me entertained. It happened overnight. One day I was old, just like that. I've run out of youth, and I'm barely sixty-nine." The pregnancy of his much younger girlfriend, Melissa MacIntosh, is his only source of hope.

Sammy Singer, who appears as a minor, unnamed character in *Catch-22* (the airman who faints at the sight of the dying Snowden's wounds) has many parallels with Yossarian, including thwarted ambitions, having gone into teaching, advertising, and public relations instead of writing creatively. Sammy, whose Coney Island Jewish background resembles Heller's, is a more accepting version of Yossarian, reconciling himself to his work and milieu. Only the suicide of his maladjusted stepson and the death of his wife cause him much distress.

Lew Rabinowitz, Sammy's boyhood friend, is a less sophisticated version of Heller's other old men. Lew, however, considers himself more realistic, clever while Sammy is merely smart, a man of action rather than a thinker. When Sammy chooses the air corps during World War II, Lew picks the ground forces so that he can confront the Germans directly. Unfortunately, he ends up as a prisoner of war and survives the Allied bombing of Dresden. After the war, Lew prospers as a businessman, progressing from junkyard to lumberyard to plumbing-supply company. After fighting Hodgkin's disease for twenty-eight years, he decides to die.

Lew is most notable for his anger at the Germans for persecuting his fellow Jews. He flaunts his Jewishness in the prison camp, and after the war, he ridicules a German prisoner of war severely until his embarrassed fiancée forces him to quit. Lew's passion contrasts with the relative passivity of Sammy and Yossarian.

A fourth, less central old man is Albert Tappman, Yossarian's wartime chaplain. The most peaceful of men, Tappman is found to urinate heavy water and is "disappeared" by Milo and the government until they can determine how best to use his gift to create weapons.

The inclusion of Tappman and Milo and other references—in one case an entire scene—from *Catch-22* does little to advance Heller's observations about age, death, and the decline of civilization. For Yossarian to exist beyond the end of World War II, Heller must explain how he has gotten out of the predicament with which *Catch-22* ends. Heller does so by having him promoted to major and sent home because of his complaints, but this dissipates the existential pathos of the ending of the earlier work. Heller could have developed his themes through Sammy, Lew, and any other old men without dragging Yossarian back to this mundane world. The flatly satirical episodes involving Tappman and Milo are unnecessary.

Heller uses New York as a symbol of the moral morass into which civilization has allowed itself to fall: "Nowhere in his lifetime, Yossarian was bound often to remember, not in wartime Rome or Pianosa or even in blasted Naples or Sicily, had he been spectator to such atrocious squalor as he saw mounting up all around him now into an eminent domain of decay." Sammy, full of nostalgia for the Coney Island of his youth, remembers when WQXR, the radio station owned by *The New York Times*, proudly announced that it served a city "where seven million people live in peace and harmony and enjoy the benefits of democracy." Now the lack of peace and harmony threatens this democracy.

Heller's symbol-within-a-symbol is the Port Authority Bus Terminal (PABT), where homeless people, runaway teenagers, drug addicts, and prostitutes converge to mingle with commuters and other travelers. Yossarian is outraged that upon entering he is assaulted by people of all ages, sizes, and shapes offering to perform debased acts for coins. He is still sympathetic to their plight, however, for he sees the inhabitants of the PABT as "traveling automatically like spirits who would have chosen a different course than the ones they were following had they found themselves free to decide." Throughout Heller's fiction is a conflict between the individual's responsibilities for his fate and the forces willingly or accidentally out to destroy his individuality. Compared to the inferno imagined by Dante Alighieri, the PABT also recalls the decadence of the nighttime Rome through which Yossarian travels in *Catch-22*.

In addition to Milo's war toys, the main satirical device in *Closing Time* is the society wedding of M2, Milo's son. Such functions are often carried out in museums or other dignified locales. As a joke, Yossarian suggests using the PABT and is surprised to be taken seriously. The event, called "the Wedding of the Close of the Century," summarizes the American propensity for conspicuous consumption. There are 3,500 guests and 7,203 press passes. *The Temple of Dendar* is loaned by the Metropolitan Museum of Art in exchange for a ten-million-dollar donation. The fifteen-hundred-pound wedding cake costs another million. The PABT's usual derelicts are "replaced by trained performers . . . whose impersonations were judged more authentic and tolerable than the originals they were supplanting." The president of the United States is scheduled to give away the bride and act as best man, but he stays in the White House playing with his beloved video games until he accidentally launches a nuclear attack using Milo's supposedly nonworking, nonexistent bombers.

In the underground communities the government has built as shelters for the politically powerful, the president, whom everyone, including him, calls "Little Prick," has erected a nine-hole golf course and a Ben and Jerry Federal Ice Cream Depository so that he will, in the event of war, have ice cream and golf to go with his video games. Heller is outraged by the selfish recklessness of part of America and its disregard for those parts unlike itself: "Even in a recession, the country was awash in money. Even amid poverty, there was room for much waste."

As in *Catch-22*, the proximity to death makes life more valuable. In the midst of the accidental war, Yossarian leaves the safety of the underground world to look for Melissa. He is impelled by his naïve but admirable conviction "that nothing bad could happen to a just man. This was nonsense, he knew; but he also knew, in his gut, he'd be as safe as she was, and had no doubt then that all three of them, he, Melissa, and the new baby, would survive, flourish, and live happily—forever after."

Yossarian's charming optimism about making the best out of the worst of situations is one of several virtues of *Closing Time*, which include some humorous scenes involving Little Prick and his advisor/tutor G. Noodles Cook, an old advertising friend of Yossarian. Nevertheless, the novel is effective only in segments. Overall, the realistic Sammy and Lew chapters fail to coalesce with the absurdist humor of the Milo, Tappman, and Little Prick sections, with the Yossarian parts falling into both categories. It is as if Heller were trying to force a merger between the comedy of *Catch-22* and *Good as Gold* (1979), his Watergate satire, with the more conventional style of *Something Happened* (1974), a portrait of middle-class anguish. The conflicting tones work against rather than with each other, and Heller's criticisms of modern life do not seem particularly fresh. Too often, like its old men, *Closing Time* seems enervated.

Michael Adams

Sources for Further Study

The Christian Science Monitor. October 4, 1994, p. 14.
London Review of Books. XVI, October 20, 1994, p. 22.
Los Angeles Times Book Review. October 16, 1994, p. 3.
The New York Review of Books. XLI, October 20, 1994, p. 20.

The New York Times Book Review. XCIX, September 25, 1994, p. 1.
The New Yorker. LXX, October 10, 1994, p. 104.
Newsweek. CXXIV, October 3, 1994, p. 66.
Publishers Weekly. CCXLI, August 1, 1994, p. 69.
Time. CXLIV, October 3, 1994, p. 80.
The Times Literary Supplement. October 21, 1994, p. 21.

THE COLLECTED STORIES

Author: Grace Paley (1922-)
Publisher: Farrar Straus Giroux (New York). 386 pp. $27.50
Type of work: Short stories

This volume contains all the stories that originally appeared in Grace Paley's first three collections of short fiction

The first thing one notices about the short stories of Grace Paley is the voice that narrates them. It seems unmistakably the voice of a woman talking to other women. Paley once said in an interview that it was "the dark lives of women" that made her begin to write in the first place, adding that at the time she thought no one would be interested, "but I had to illuminate it anyway." In a preface written especially for *The Collected Stories*, she says that in 1954 or 1955, when she first felt the storyteller's need, she was not sure that she could write the important serious material that men were writing. Consequently, she says she had no choice but to write about what had been handed to her: "everyday life, kitchen life, children life."

Usually, the women in Paley's stories are unwed, widowed, or divorced; although they often have lovers and children, they are not defined either by marriage or by the desire for marriage. This focus on the female without men has resulted, say some critics, in stories that are feminist in point of view, language, and theme. In her new preface, Paley says that she agrees, at least to the extent that every woman writing during the decades of the 1950's, 1960's, and 1970's had to "swim in the feminist wave." Paley's stories are often unified by her focus on the voices of women engaged in conversation, gossip, jokes, intimacies, and above all storytelling. It is the power of this talk and storytelling, Paley insists, that bonds women together into a unified, collaborative force to make their voices heard. In an interview, Paley once said, "Our voices are, if not getting a lot louder, getting so numerous. We're talking to each other more and more." Paley believes that women, especially mothers, banding together and talking to one another constitute a powerful political force for social change. When one has children, one gets involved in community affairs, Paley says, for one becomes concerned for protection of the children. Indeed, in many Paley stories the community of mothers on the playground constitutes a central source of social consciousness.

Although Paley's stories show a concern for community and social responsibility, they are far from solemn social tracts or feminist polemics. Instead, they are characterized by an earthy awareness of urban folk culture combined with an often bawdy sense of humor. The women in Paley's stories rebel against the traditional role of woman as passive partner in sexual encounters, and at the same time they reject the egoistic image of men as the answer to all women's needs. As Mrs. Luddy tells the character Faith Darwin in the story "The Long-Distance Runner," men thought that they were bringing women a "rare gift," but it was just sex, "which is common like bread, though essential." As Faith and Mrs. Luddy talk, like many other women in

Paley's stories, one begins to realize that such collaborative talk among women fosters community and freedom.

Faith Darwin, Paley's alter ego, was first introduced in a pair of early stories in *The Little Disturbances of Man: Stories of Men and Women in Love* (1959) categorized as "two short sad stories from a long and happy life." The first one, entitled "The Used-Boy Raisers," begins with the typical Paley ironic voice—"There were two husbands disappointed by eggs"—and then continues with Faith's voice characterizing her husband and former husband, who are dissatisfied with the way she has fixed their eggs, as "Pallid" and "Livid" as they quarrel about the future of the Jewish race. At this point in Faith's life, she rarely expresses her opinion on any serious matter and says that she considers it her destiny to be, "until [my] expiration date, laughingly the servant of man." As the two husbands go off to face the "grand affairs of the day ahead of them," however, Faith's voice has managed to gently ridicule the pretensions of these "clean and neat, rather attractive, shiny men in their thirties."

In many ways, the various situations of Faith Darwin reflect the central thematic concerns of Paley's fiction. As Faith moves from egoistic self-pity to a broader identification and sympathy with women in general and women as an oppressed group in particular, she embodies Paley's own growing conviction that fiction can serve a powerful purpose in affirming community, hope, and love. Faith reappears in *Enormous Changes at the Last Minute* (1974) in the story "Faith in the Afternoon," where, recently abandoned by her husband, she visits her parents in a retirement home. Although she is very much aware of her family history, she holds herself aloof from family in this story, rejecting union and connection. Another story, "Faith in a Tree," finds Faith still holding herself aloof, this time symbolically sitting on the limb of a sycamore tree above an urban playground. By the end of the story, however, she is brought out of her lofty perch by her eight-year-old son's sympathetic identification with the purposes of a peaceful antiwar march and decides to change her distanced perspective to one of social and artistic involvement. In the final Faith Darwin story in *Enormous Changes at the Last Minute*, "The Long-Distance Runner," Faith jogs to her childhood neighborhood on Coney Island. Finding the area now populated by African Americans, she retreats to her old home place and stays for three weeks, uniting both with her past and with the black woman, Mrs. Luddy, who now lives there.

In "Friends," in Paley's third collection, *Later the Same Day* (1985), Faith goes with her friends Ann and Susan to visit another friend, Selena, who is dying. The story is a Paley experiment in creating a collective narrator; she has said in an interview that it is based on her own female friends, with whom she had a kind of collective existence. "Ruthy and Edie," also in *Later the Same Day*, begins with the relationship between two young girls who talk about the "real world of boys" and fight their fear of a strange neighborhood dog, then shifts to a period many years later at Ruthy's fiftieth birthday, when she invites three friends, including Faith and Edie, to her apartment for a celebration. The story ends with Ruthy's anxiety about her success as a mother as she struggles with the hopelessness of protecting her granddaughter from the hard world of "man-made time." Faith appears again in "The Expensive Moment," in which the network of women, a frequent theme in Paley's stories, broadens to include a Chinese woman whom Faith and Ruthy have met at a meeting of a women's governmental organization sponsored by the United Nations. Over tea in Faith's kitchen, the three women wonder whether they were right to rear their children as they did.

A number of Paley's stories are so short that they seem carefully crafted situations symbolic of the circumstances of women. For example, "Love" is an inconclusive episode in which a man tells his wife about his past loves, one of whom is a fictional character in her own book. "Lavinia: An Old Story" is a brief monologue in which a black woman tries to talk her daughter's suitor out of marrying her. "At That Time, or The History of a Joke" is, in itself, little more than a joke in which the Virgin Birth becomes the source of several satiric jabs at the Christian religion. The story "Anxiety" consists primarily of a woman's warnings to a young father taking his daughter home from school; "In This Country, But in Another Language, My Aunt Refuses to Marry the Men Everyone Wants Her To" is a two-page prose-poem in which a female child tries to understand whether her maiden aunt has a life of her own; "Mother" is a two-page reminiscence brought on by a woman's hearing the song "Oh, I Long to See My Mother in the Doorway." The two short pieces "A Man Told Me the Story of His Life" and "This is a Story About My Friend George, the Toy Inventor" are more like brief parables than fully developed narratives. In one, Paley tells of a man who, unable to fulfill his dream to be a doctor, saves his wife's life because of his diagnostic ability; in the other, a man invents a pinball machine that is a poem of the machine, its essence made concrete.

"Wants"—a three-page piece in which a woman meets her former husband at the library when she returns books that she has had checked out for eight years—effectively expresses a woman's basic desire to be the kind of person who returns books in two weeks, stays married to the same person forever, and addresses the Board of Estimate on the troubles of urban centers. In "Living," a woman friend calls Faith to tell her that she is dying, but Faith says that she is dying too, for her menstrual bleeding will not stop; the story is a poignant but restrained exemplum of female sympathy and identification. "Northeast Playground," another three-page story deals with a typical Paley social concern as she describes going to a playground where she meets eleven unwed mothers on relief who band together in a kind of play of their own.

When asked about these very short stories, which seem to challenge the limits of narrative structure, Paley has said that a story is more often likely to be too long than too short. She argues that stories should deal with more than the simple dialectic of conflict. "I think it's two events or two characters . . . bumping against each other, and what you hear, that's the story." That, she says, can happen in two pages.

Grace Paley is very much concerned with the nature of storytelling in her stories, for her narrator is often self-consciously aware of the fact that the characters in the stories are fictional creations. One of her most frequently anthologized stories, "A Conversation with My Father," is Paley's most explicit treatment of her view of story and its relationship to hope for the future of women. The protagonist of the story, a writer, is visited by her eighty-year-old dying father, who wants her to write a Chekhov-type story for him, one with a plot—a concept she despises because, she says, it takes away all hope. In order to please father, she tells two versions of a story of a woman who becomes a junkie so she can remain close to her son, who has become a junkie. Although the father sees the situation of the woman in the story-within-the-story as tragic, the narrator sees it as comic. As a result, the story is, like many of Paley's stories, tragic and comic at once.

What Paley rebels against in "A Conversation with My Father" is the inevitability of plot, which, because it moves toward a predestined end, is a straight line between two points. A basic difference between fiction and "real life," Paley suggests, is that whereas real life is open and full of possibility, fiction moves relentlessly toward its predetermined end. A basic difference between the father's reaction to the woman in the story-within-the-story and the author's reaction is that whereas the father takes her situation seriously, as if she had a separate existence in the world, the author knows that the woman is her own creation; thus, although she feels sorry for her, she never loses sight of the fact that as the author she has the power to alter her destiny.

For Grace Paley, writing is a collaborative, social act, not merely in the obvious sense of centering stories on social issues but also in the more complex and profound sense of writing as the creation of a community of speakers and listeners who share the same values. Not content to remain the prisoner of a language system based on the dominant male culture, Paley has devoted her art to the creation of a language-based community made up of talk by women to women.

Charles E. May

Sources for Further Study

Chicago Tribune. May 1, 1994, XIV, p. 3.
Commonweal. CXXI, May 20, 1994, p. 33.
Library Journal. CXIX, March 1, 1994, p. 122.
Los Angeles Times Book Review. April 3, 1994, p. 3.
The New York Review of Books. XLI, August 11, 1994, p. 23.
The New York Times Book Review. XCIX, April 24, 1994, p. 7.
Newsweek. CXXIII, April 25, 1994, p. 64.
The Wall Street Journal. April 25, 1994, p. A12.
The Washington Post Book World. XXIV, April 17, 1994, p. 3.
The Women's Review of Books. XI, July, 1994, p. 29.

THE COLLECTED STORIES OF LOUIS AUCHINCLOSS

Author: Louis Auchincloss (1917-   )
Publisher: Houghton Mifflin (Boston). 465 pp. $24.95
Type of work: Short stories

Spanning more than forty years of sustained activity, the author's selection of his "favorite" short fiction provides a useful point of entry into his subtly changing narrative universe

Although perhaps better known for his novels, especially *The Rector of Justin* (1964) and *The Embezzler* (1966), Louis Auchincloss has also worked long and hard at the art and craft of shorter fiction, often questioning and testing the boundaries separating the short story from the novel. Several of his many novels, including *The Great World and Timothy Colt* (1956) and *A World of Profit* (1968), were in fact expanded from shorter pieces already in print; conversely, some earlier collections of his short fiction, most notably *The Partners* (1974), have been published and marketed as novels. In preparing the current, somewhat misnamed volume ("selected" might well have been a better choice of adjective), Auchincloss has included one tale from *The Partners*, as well as "seed stories" for *A World of Profit* and also for *Watchfires* (1982). Explaining his choices in a brief, generally straightforward introduction, Auchincloss claims that the tales "simply jumped out at me from the ranks of their paler brethren." Unlike certain earlier anthologies, such as *The Stories of John Cheever* (1978), Auchincloss' volume makes no claim to completeness; on the other hand, it clearly sets forth a coherent "defense and illustration" of the shorter fictional form, directed toward the potential pleasure of reading. As essayist and critic, particularly in the volumes *Reflections of a Jacobite* (1961) and *Life, Law, and Letters* (1979), Auchincloss has long steered clear of the academic critical establishment, insisting that literature exists in order to be read and enjoyed rather than to be studied. His own work, as presented in the current volume, may thus also be seen as a companion to his resolutely extramural criticism, an illustrated lecture on the art and craft of short fiction.

To those who have followed his literary career over time, Auchincloss' selection of tales to be retold, or republished, appears generally sound, generally (but not always) observing chronological order of composition or publication. From the start, with *The Injustice Collectors* (1950), the tales included in each of Auchincloss' collections have tended to share a common theme or thread, or perhaps recurring characters or a single, unifying narrator; not surprisingly, they have tended also to reflect the concerns expressed in Auchincloss novels written around the same time. The earliest story, "Maud," dating from 1949 and included in *The Injustice Collectors*, clearly adumbrates the author's growing concern with the developing feminine consciousness, a concern further developed in his novels *Sybil* (1951) and *A Law for the Lion* (1953). The title character, Maud Spreddon, is in many ways a prototype for Sybil Hilliard and Eloise Dilworth, a thoughtful, restless young woman born around the time of World War I. Her expectations of life are quite at odds with those of her parents. Unlike her novelistic successors, however, Maud never quite musters the courage of her convictions, for she chooses self-sacrifice over the healthy self-assertion that is easily within her grasp. Other featured characters in the earlier tales belong to vanishing, now long-gone subspecies of the self-proclaimed New York aristocracy, into which the author himself was born in 1917.

As a practicing attorney on New York's Wall Street for more than forty years, balancing dual careers as lawyer and as writer, Auchincloss managed also, from the 1950's well into the 1970's, to afford his readers many enviable glimpses behind the scenes of power, where history is made or broken by the privileged few, often for the most trivial of reasons. Apprenticed by inclination and choice to the novel of manners tradition perfected by Henry James and Edith Wharton, Auchincloss in his middle years took double advantage of his professional activity and insider status to chronicle the initially gradual, eventually precipitate decline of the self-styled American aristocracy, itself a contradiction in terms. In *The Rector of Justin*, perhaps the most read and best remembered of his novels, Auchincloss addressed himself both ironically and empathically to the institution of the American prep school, an anomaly in that, modeled upon the misnamed British "public" school, it professes to promote democratic values despite high tuition and selective admissions policies. Still, it was just such institutions that provided the United States with most of its top and midlevel leadership well past the midpoint of the twentieth century.

In the present volume, "The Prince and the Pauper" best represents Auchincloss' sustained fascination with and analysis of the inevitable self-destruction of aristocracy in the "land of the free." Brooks Clarkson, a well-derived and well-placed attorney on the cusp of middle age, excuses his slide into alcoholism in part through his recognition of the vitality that he perceives in Benny Galenti, an office boy who dropped out of law school in order to support his growing family. Promoting Benny to office manager, lending him money to invest in hot prospects on the stock market, Brooks slides almost happily downhill. One of his cousins feels compelled to deny Benny's claimed debt to Brooks, who might well have taken for himself the stock tips that he passed to Benny. As it happens, Benny and his family will soon replace the Clarksons in an exclusive Long Island country club; these Italian Americans will be as easily assimilated as the Protestant ministers' sons who "infiltrated" the supposed aristocracy a generation earlier.

Included in *Second Chance* (1970), "The Prince and the Pauper" is described, in the author's introduction to the current volume, as "an effort on my part to write a story in the manner of John O'Hara" (a frequent competitor for reviewers' attention during Auchincloss' early years). Those familiar with the work of both writers in fiction both long and short, however, might have difficulty tracing O'Hara's possible influence; the piece could have been written only by Auchincloss. So too could "The Fabbri Tape," prepared a full decade after "The Prince and the Pauper" yet set back in time to the 1930's, at least in relation to the action described on tape years later by the narrator-protagonist, another American of Italian origin. Married early in his legal career to the daughter of a partner in his firm, Mario Fabbri (born around 1890) has spent the last years of his life disbarred but somewhat less than disgraced, having obligingly taken the fall for the misdeeds of his WASP "elders and betters." In many ways, Mario Fabbri's testimony recalls and even replicates the memoir of Guy Prime that opens and names *The Embezzler*, showing once again a master chronicler in well-modulated narrative voice, fully alert to all that he has witnessed both as lawyer and as writer.

Inexplicably omitted from *The Collected Stories* is "The Deductible Yacht," included in *Powers of Attorney*, in which an aristocratic lawyer will end up owing his partnership to a shady Middle Eastern client. It is no exaggeration to note that on Auchincloss' narrative watch (to borrow the terminology of his wartime naval service), the tenuous society into which he was born foundered onto shifting sands, ranging from Saudi Arabia to California, sands bearing with them the balance of power, occasionally whispering the news that New York was no longer the center of the Western world, or even of the New World. To his credit, Auchincloss has observed and recorded the gradual disappearance of his world with enviable detachment, keeping only the prose style, at once spare and somehow ornate, that he seems to have inherited quite willfully from James and Wharton, adding a few twists and touches uniquely his own that, in the more recent pieces, beg the question between parody and self-parody. Among the stuffier sentences to be found in the collection is "I should admit here that election to this club was the social triumph of my life. I could never see why Pussy and the children found it stuffy." The speaker/narrator, perhaps not surprisingly, is Mario Fabbri, the naturalized Italian American whose sense of duty, combined with his loyalty and ethics, led inevitably to his downfall.

When Auchincloss was first read and published, in the years immediately following World War II, he appeared, not implausibly, to be the next competitor to O'Hara and also to John P. Marquand, the latter a poor relation to self-styled aristocrats who claimed descent from Transcendentalists and shipowners alike. Unlike the two older writers, however, Auchincloss was not only a true insider but had also done his homework in the convention already known as the novel of manners. Although perhaps less consistently skillful as a writer of short fiction than O'Hara, he is somewhat more reliable as observer and chronicler, proceeding beyond mere observation toward analysis and explanation.

Ironically titled, "The Novelist of Manners" remains one of Auchincloss' most memorable and entertaining pieces, well worthy of its place in the current collection. Originally included in *The Partners*, where it could be seen as part of an episodic novel, "The Novelist of Manners" features Leslie Carter, a rising young lawyer with literary tastes and ambitions. Assigned to the Paris office of the firm featured in *The Partners*, Carter finds himself defending one Dana Clyde, the novelist of the title, against well-founded charges of libel. To be sure, Clyde is less a novelist of manners than a sensationalist and scandalmonger, the type of writer whose works are most often found in paperback at airport newsstands. As Carter gets to know his client while preparing his defense, he gradually persuades Clyde to take a furlough from the good life in France in order to write a work of true literary art.

When the book is at last ready to appear, with galley proofs mailed to Carter in his capacity as Clyde's attorney, Carter notes with surprise that the novel is little different from, or better than, the usual Clyde standard. Although well aware of his client's tendency to use real-life models, Carter is deeply stung to find himself cruelly caricatured as "Gregory Blake," a young lawyer driven to suicide by impotence on his wedding night. As Clyde's wife Xenia explains to Carter, "He can no longer kid himself that he could have written *Madame Bovary*. So he took his revenge." Notable for its ruminations on literature and the law, as well as for its ironic overview of the author's own characteristic subject matter, "The Novelist of Manners," removed from the original context of *The Partners*, manages to stand quite well on its own merits, more than justifying its republication in the current volume.

Taken together, the twenty stories in this volume provide not only an impressive literary testament but also a valuable chronicle of American society and politics from the Civil War to the end of the twentieth century. It is to be hoped, incidentally, that readers of the volume will be inspired to rediscover the strongest of Louis Auchincloss' novels, in particular *The Rector of Justin* and *The Embezzler*.

David B. Parsell

Sources for Further Study

Booklist. XCI, September 15, 1994, p. 110.
The Christian Science Monitor. December 30, 1994, p. 14.
Kirkus Reviews. LXII, September 15, 1994, p. 1218.
Library Journal. CXIX, October 15, 1994, p. 89.
The New York Times Book Review. XCIX, December 4, 1994, p. 62.
Publishers Weekly. CCXLI, October 10, 1994, p. 60.
Time. CXLIV, December 5, 1994, p. 96.

COLORED PEOPLE
A Memoir

Author: Henry Louis Gates, Jr. (1950-)
Publisher: Alfred A. Knopf (New York). 216 pp. $22.00
Type of work: Memoir
Time: 1950-1970
Locale: Piedmont, West Virginia

This memoir describes the experience of growing up "colored" in a small West Virginia town during the 1950's and 1960's

Principal personages:
HENRY LOUIS GATES, JR., the author
HENRY LOUIS GATES, SR., his father
PAULINE AUGUSTA COLEMAN GATES, his mother
ROCKY GATES, his older brother
JIM "NEMO" COLEMAN, his maternal uncle

In the preface to this memoir, Henry Louis Gates, Jr., states his objective explicitly: "As artlessly and honestly as I can, I have tried to evoke a colored world of the fifties, a Negro world of the early sixties, and the advent of a black world of the later sixties, from the point of view of the boy I was." The artlessness of the book lies in its easy colloquial language (nothing within the text itself reveals the author as an English professor at Harvard University) and its relaxed, digressive movement. Its honesty appears in the portraits not only of individuals (even the author's heroes, notably his mother, are presented as human and thus flawed) but also of a black culture in which the chief recreations are gossip and extramarital sex. Gates evokes the world of his childhood and adolescence—brings it to life in the imagination through image and narrative—as opposed to using it to make a point about race relations. It is a particular world he writes of: "This is not a story of a race but a story of a village, a family, and its friends." The point of view, however, is not consistently that of a boy; the adult author looks over his shoulder, offering perspectives of which his younger self was incapable and information of which he was unaware.

One such paradoxical perspective lies near the heart of the book. In the 1950's and earlier, Gates writes, life for black people in the Potomac Valley town of Piedmont, West Virginia had "a sort of segregated peace." He goes on to say that "what hurt me most about the glorious black awakening of the late sixties and early seventies is that we lost our sense of humor": a telling conjunction of positive and negative terms. Segregation is a basic affront to human dignity; yet ending it deals a crippling and in some ways fatal blow to a life-giving black community. Integration should, in theory, allow Gates and his family and neighbors the freedom to view and live racial issues individually, on their own terms. Yet nothing, as this memoir poignantly makes clear, is ever that simple. Race remains a tortuous issue. The deepest paradox, implicit in practically every sentence of *Colored People: A Memoir*, is embedded in the two words of the title. The blacks of Piedmont are colored, and race means everything; they are people, and it means nothing.

The division of *Colored People* into six sections, each containing three or four short chapters, seems to signal a tight structure. In fact, the book rambles along easily and amiably; the impression is that of a spontaneous monologue, with topics and anecdotes bubbling up one after the other by free association. Under the easygoing manner, however, lies a sharp intellect, surfacing from time to time in barbed irony, and a deep emotional awareness of loss and waste in the lives of the author's people.

In the fifty pages of the first section, "Will the Circle Be Unbroken?" Gates begins with an overview of the geography, natural and human, of his hometown of Piedmont: population 2,565, only three hundred or so of those colored, in 1950 when the author was born. Since then it has shrunk to less than half that; "completely bound up with the Westvaco paper mill," it appears now to be "a typical dying mill town." He goes on to describe the colored and white worlds of the town and how they impinged on one another; segregation as a formal institution; the importance of television, and how it brought the Civil Rights movement to Piedmont as a kind of spectator sport; his mother, with her great dignity and her implacable hatred of white people; and the extraordinary—and humorous, viewed from a distance—efforts of colored people to straighten their naturally kinky hair.

By means of brief, casual revelations, Gates snaps the reader to attention: "We called white people by their trade, like allegorical characters in a mystery play." Until the 1970's, "colored weren't allowed to own property." "*Everybody* loved *Amos and Andy*," because "their world was *all* colored, just like ours." Through anecdote, he brings his world to life. The first black valedictorian at the high school, during her freshman year at the University of West Virginia, gets on a motorcycle with a stranger and is never seen again. A racist businessman, a man weighing four or five hundred pounds, has "a heart attack one day while sitting in the tiny toilet at his place of business" and must be sawed out: By the time they "dragged out his lifeless body . . . it made little difference" to him that one of his rescuers is black. Whites are not the only victims of irony. A black man with diabetes drinks alcohol and eats fatty foods against his doctor's orders: "That high blood pressure stuff, he'd say, that only applies to white people. . . . They removed his second leg just after he went blind."

In the stories in the second section, "Family Pictures," members of the author's extended and nuclear families come to life. Once again, racial and human issues intertwine. For example, the salient fact about the Colemans, Gates's nine maternal uncles, is that they "were colored people"; the arresting physical descriptions of them specify precisely what color. They were "the last generation of our family conceived, born, and bred under segregation. . . . The soul of that world was colored," to the point where they "even fought to keep alive the tradition of the segregated all-colored schools." The result was a generation gap with racial features unique to that time: They "hated some of us, the first generation of integrated wannabes, recognizing us as the real threat to the ordered universe they had constructed with such painstaking care for such a long time." The paradox is that the real evil of institutional racism could not be rooted out without an equally real human cost.

Within Gates's nuclear family, racial issues receded, though only to a degree. His older brother was a fine athlete, whereas Gates himself was fat and flat footed; in that community, as in inner cities later, success in sports was a dream, a ticket out. The avid interest of father and sibling in baseball left the author feeling excluded—a story repeated in any number of families of every race. Gates, however, "early on developed an avidity for information about The Negro"; his father, on the other hand, was fond of saying that "niggers are crabs in a barrel." This section of *Colored People* poignantly evokes universal familial conflicts, with intraracial difficulties inextricably entangled.

The digressiveness of Gates's approach reappears strongly in "Over in the Orchard." Schools integrated in 1955, against black resistance; even so, color lines governed all social events, and racial barriers broke up the author's friendship with a white girl. His older brother was cheated out of a prestigious award because "the hotel where we would have had to stay in the state capital was segregated." The author discovered books, music, girls, and religion. Anecdote, once again, arrests the reader's attention. Human stories: The author, aged four, completely forgot the thirteen-word piece he was to recite in church. Racial ones: A black musician is described "up at The Barn, a redneck hangout, flirting with all the white women, gyrating and spinning those sinuous tones, making that saxophone into a snake"—and nearly getting lynched.

One of the most moving passages in *Colored People* occurs in the fourth section, "Saved," in which the author describes the breakdown suffered by his mother in middle life: "A veil passed over her life, dimming her radiance, and then never quite lifted away." She grew fearful, gained a great deal of weight, obsessively hoarded canned goods and bolts of cloth. "A sense of need, born of a childhood of scarcity, now came upon her, spurring a pack rat's notion of providence." The fear and confusion of the author, twelve years old as the crisis began, comes across vividly in his withdrawal from other children and his development of rituals, forlorn attempts to bring order into a life suddenly lacking it at the core. One day he challenged fate by crossing his legs the wrong way around—and that afternoon his mother suffered an attack of acute depression and went into the hospital, with no one knowing if she would ever return. When she did partially recover, his sense of guilt led him into the Methodist church: "For the next two years, I didn't play cards, I didn't go to dances, I didn't listen to rock and roll; . . . I didn't even lust in my heart—except once or twice for Brenda." The dry irony of the last phrase, mildly undercutting a serious moment, encapsulates the tone of this memoir.

In "Negro Digest," Gates turns abruptly to tales of his Uncle Jim, also known as Nemo, his favorite among his mother's brothers. A mighty fisherman and hunter, "not only was he the first colored man in Piedmont to own guns, but he got guns for everyone in the family." Despite being "*deathly* afraid of white people," he found the courage to ask permission to hunt on their land. "His fear and Mama's hatred," the author observes: "flip sides of the same coin." Yet Nemo was a World War II Navy veteran and in general a man of great prowess and standing among his own people. Gates evokes the tragedy of racism in a few trenchant words.

He goes on in the final section, "One Day Last Tuesday," to describe the energetic, courageous, and sometimes desperate ways in which he and his contemporaries challenged racism. During the summer of 1969, when he was nineteen, he often drove "to Rehoboth Beach, in Delaware, to see Maura." The pleasures they shared sound like those of any young man and woman; only in the next paragraph does the author mention, offhandedly, that "Maura was white," that they "were hassled at the beach," and that he "personally integrated many places at Rehoboth Beach that summer." Back home in Piedmont, they were "apparently the first interracial couple in Mineral County, and there was hell to pay," with people "making oblique threats, in the sort of whispers peculiar to small towns." To add to the tension, despite their well-founded fear and at risk of serious bodily harm, Gates and several of his friends "decided to integrate the Swordfish, a weekend hangout where all the college kids went." Rather than integrate, the owner closed it down.

Nevertheless, "for many of the colored people in Piedmont . . . integration was experienced as a loss." Nowhere is that clearer than in the final chapter, in which Gates describes the last colored mill picnic. When "the last wave of the civil rights era finally came . . . crashing down upon the colored world of Piedmont . . . its most beloved, and cementing, ritual was doomed to give way." In the image of the Civil Rights movement—in which the author himself so vigorously participated—as a destructive wave lies the abiding paradox of this time and place, and, implicitly, of Gates's relationship with and attitudes toward his family and neighbors.

A striking feature of this memoir is that it is very brief. Given the twenty-year time span and the number and richness of the lives that crossed the author's (or of which he heard stories), given moreover the racial crosscurrents and undercurrents that increased exponentially the complexity of this story, it could easily have been spun out to two or three times the length. Certainly the artistic choice Gates made, for all of his purported artlessness, has costs built into it: The emotional potential of many events, lightly touched on, remains largely untapped. Still, *Colored People* remains a major accomplishment. Gracefully told, it is an amiable tale with a darker subtext: a pleasure to read, a boon to understanding.

Edwin Moses

Sources for Further Study

Los Angeles Times Book Review. May 8, 1994, p. 3.
The Nation. CCLVIII, June 6, 1994, p. 794.
National Review. XLVI, August 29, 1994, p. 57.
The New Republic. CCXI, July 4, 1994, p. 33.
The New York Times Book Review. XCIX, June 19, 1994, p. 10.
Newsweek. CXXIII, May 23, 1994, p. 60.
Time. CXLIII, May 23, 1994, p. 73.
The Washington Post Book World. XXIV, May 15, 1994, p. 3.

THE COMPLETE PREFACES
Volume I, 1889-1913

Author: George Bernard Shaw (1856-1950)
Edited, with an introduction, by Dan H. Laurence and Daniel J. Leary
First published: 1993, in Great Britain
Publisher: Allen Lane/The Penguin Press (New York). 630 pp. $40.00
Type of work: Essays

This first volume of a comprehensive scholarly edition of Bernard Shaw's prefaces to his plays, collections of essays, and fiction contains, in chronological order, forty-two of Shaw's works, some previously uncollected

One of the most relentlessly prolific writers of the late nineteenth and early twentieth centuries, George Bernard Shaw habitually wrote prefaces, introductions, and forewords to his and others' works, sometimes to explain them, sometimes to argue points not fully covered in them, and sometimes to demolish criticism leveled at them. He also revised these prefaces over time, adding newer topical references to older works, deleting material he thought outdated, and at times exaggerating or misrepresenting events and opinions to suit his argument. The editors of *The Complete Prefaces: Volume I, 1889-1913* have followed Shaw's testamentary wishes by using the last printed versions of texts he authorized in his lifetime, although they have also restored some deleted passages, clearly indicating them as such. In addition, the editors have included judiciously chosen annotations to Shaw's more obscure allusions and references without cluttering the text with them.

Of the many kinds of prefaces in the volume, the editors identify three principal types in their introduction. They illustrate their categorization with detailed analyses of selected examples of Shaw's rhetorical, epistolary, and argumentatively journalistic modes of writing. In whatever mode, Shaw's prefaces appear to be living words, records of conversations that evolve in the course of his conversing on paper. Thus, he occasionally contradicts or undercuts himself, as if looking for another opening in the fray, taking another tack. He also appears to change his mind, at times savoring the witty phrase that does not quite convey his meaning but approximates it well enough in a nearly poetic vein.

The rhetorical Shaw is a lecturer in print, relying on an audience, engaging that audience, asking questions that may at first appear merely rhetorical but turn out to be precisely the sort of question an intelligent person might ask about the issues at hand. Moreover, his commands and exhortations to the audience, in which he asks them to direct their attention to something, to consider a point, to do their homework and read this or that commission report, are truly requests for cooperative, active listening and reading. He appears to work his audience adeptly, positing their anti-intellectual counterparts throughout London and the realm and allowing his hearers and readers to feel immensely superior to those unenlightened by him. Shaw is a propagandist, seeking to change minds, win approval, and prompt his readers to assert their own power to effect social change. This fits nicely with his own socialist agenda in his plays and essays, the gradualist strategy expressed in the motto of the Fabian Society: "Educate, Agitate, Organize." Shaw writes and seems to speak to the reader, then, as an educator who is interested in stirring up his audience, in provoking their indignation, and in organizing them into an effective band bent upon political reform. As the editors note, the prefaces to *Mrs. Warren's Profession* (1902) and *Major Barbara* (1907) are two among many examples of Shaw's highly rhetorical work.

The epistolary Shaw, in such prefaces as *Major Barbara*'s "First Aid to Critics," *John Bull's Other Island*'s "Preface for Politicians" (1907), and *Man and Superman*'s "Epistle Dedicatory" (1903), is a familiar, avuncular correspondent who addresses his readers personally, informally, cajolingly. Here Shaw takes his reader by the arm or elbow and converses with him or her as they walk together toward or from the theater. He creates an instant intimacy, at times confessionally, intimating that he has his own doubts about his work, his projects, his agendas in the plays. In some respects, Shaw distances himself from his work in the prefaces, almost looking for encouragement from the reader, occasionally encouraging the reader to disagree with him, all the while looking for a response, any response, to what he says. This is the same Shaw who, as the audience applauded wildly after one of his plays, noticed one man railing against it and agreed with him in his dissent, reportedly adding a sly rhetorical query about what they two could do against so many who approved of the play.

Additionally, Shaw used his vast experience as a journalist, book reviewer, and art, music, and drama critic to inform his prefaces. He is a master of the pungent phrase and a self-appointed tutor to the universe whose works teem with topical allusions to contemporary news and newspaper reports. The journalistic Shaw reports on events of the day as they relate to the play or essays he introduces, using headlines for subtitles, interrupting the flow of his preface with reports of late-breaking news, situating his work along the very pulse of national and international events. His familiar, journalistic style ranges from that of the reserved editorialist for *The Guardian* or *The Times* or *The Star* (for which he wrote) to the flamboyant headline writer for the tabloid press, teasing the reader into turning to the metaphorical back pages to continue reading about the scandal he introduces on page 1.

In all three of these modes, the prefatory Shaw remains the consummate dramatist, creating characters, giving them actual lines of dialogue, providing them with complications and reversals of fortune or expectation, and often enough, as in his plays, leaving the solution to the posed problem or the resolution of the snarled situation up to the reader. A controversial interpretation of many of his plays applies to many of his prefaces: Shaw is often accused of preachily solving the world's problems in both. A careful consideration of what he actually writes, however, often yields exactly the opposite finding, that he has no ultimate solutions and relies on the audience he educates and provokes to carry on the argument or thesis of the play and to find solutions for themselves. Shaw, as his prefaces attest, is not a systematic philosopher but a speculative one, often appearing more interested in the questions he raises than in the answers he might prefer they receive. A playwright who consciously strove to write uncomfortable plays, Shaw is also an essayist who frequently strives to make his readership uncomfortable with what he has to say.

Shaw the dramatist, for example, introduces both named and nameless reviewers into the prefaces to his plays and sets them in motion. He also alludes to characters from other plays and from novels, occasionally reproducing dialogue from those sources. He shapes and molds these characters—either his own inventions or his appropriations from others—as protagonists or antagonists in the drama of his own battles with reviewers of his plays. Not content to stop there, he uses what has been called his "compensating imagination" to create analogies among his prefatory characters, linking them in some obvious and some subtle ways. So in his preface to *Mrs. Warren's Profession* he links the jeweled vamp with the neighborhood bookmaker with those who donate to charities with the poorer girls in the gallery who watch his play and, by extension, with the critics and, just as surely, with the playwright himself. Money and the means of acquiring it are the common ground for all of these characters and for the essayist himself.

As the editors justly note, the creation of dramatic characters and situations is not the only element of the playwright's craft in the prefaces. The language of the stage, the cadencing of dialogue and monologue, and the crafting of cue lines are major if often unnoticed elements of the prefaces. The editors' treatment of Shaw's stylistics in their introduction underscores Shaw's own concern that his prose both on and off the stage be highly wrought art inspired by his vast knowledge of musical composition and his love of Wolfgang Amadeus Mozart's and Richard Wagner's music. Their careful analysis of a segment from the preface to *Man and Superman* is a paradigm for exploring the linguistic richness of Shaw's style, the circling of the operatic tenor and countertenor in the arias of his prefaces as well as of the plays. Like operatic arias, Shaw's prefaces build dramatically, sounding a theme and repeating it in variations until he achieves a dramatic close.

The abiding interest of Shaw's prefaces presented in this volume is not their considerable, quaint antiquarian value, nor their valuable clues to performing or viewing his plays, nor yet the window they afford for looking nostalgically into a past that has vanished. Rather, their interest and their strength lie in the painful relevance they have for the generations that have come after Shaw. The issues and problems in Shaw's plays and in his prefaces are universal issues and problems. Shaw himself recognized, in writing "To Introduce the Prefaces" (1934), with even more prefaces still to be written, that they were ahead of their time when he wrote them and remained ahead of their time in the 1930's. His prefaces to *Mrs. Warren's Profession* on economic realities, to *Man and Superman* on evolution, and to *Major Barbara* on revolution, for example, deal with concerns that are fundamental to the human condition. These prefaces typify the others in the volume in that their thrust and depth allow readers an entry into a consciousness that wrestled with the basic questions of human life and its meaning and influenced readers to do the same.

John J. Conlon

Sources for Further Study

Chicago Tribune. February 27, 1994, XIV, p. 1.
Choice. XXXI, July, 1994, p. 1724.
Library Journal. CXIX, February 15, 1994, p. 160.
New Statesman and Society. VI, July 16, 1993, p. 42.
The Times Literary Supplement. February 18, 1994, p. 5.
The Washington Post Book World. XXIV, February 13, 1994, p. 13.

THE CORRESPONDENCE OF WALTER BENJAMIN, 1910-1940

Author: Walter Benjamin (1892-1940)
Translated from the German by Manfred R. Jacobson and Evelyn M. Jacobson
Edited by Gershom Scholem and Theodor W. Adorno
Publisher: University of Chicago Press (Chicago). 651 pp. $45.00
Type of work: Letters
Time: 1910-1940

The first collected letters in English translation of the German-Jewish intellectual many consider the greatest literary critic of the twentieth century

Out of the 332 letters in this collection, only six are by Walter Benjamin's correspondents, all by Gershom Scholem and Theodore Adorno, who are also the editors of this volume. In all, Benjamin corresponded with more than thirty individuals, many of them world-renowned: In addition to Scholem and Adorno, they include Hannah Arendt, Bertolt Brecht, Martin Buber, Hugo von Hofmannsthal, Max Horkheimer, and other important central European intellectuals of the first four decades of the twentieth century. Because this collection consists of letters by Benjamin, the volume reads more like a monologue than the dialogue one would expect in the give-and take of a correspondence.

To read through these letters is to encounter thought in its richest texture. Benjamin not only shares his insights into writers and poets from Johann Wolfgang von Goethe and Charles Baudelaire to Marcel Proust and Franz Kafka, but also gives historical, political, ethical, and even metaphysical contexts for these insights that take readers further than literary interpretation. Literary texts for Benjamin were like archaeological fragments that could yield clues to meanings that the dark glasses of the present time have tended to obscure. The secrets Benjamin hoped to reveal were not limited to forgotten history. He was fascinated by semiotics and symbology, the structures and signs of language that encapsulated meanings beyond history. Indeed, he read phenomena like texts and saw in the artifacts of modern life—streets, shop windows, photographs—clues to mystical and political truths.

As Benjamin moved back and forth in his thought between theologically and humanistically centered ideas and social or political theories, he tended to center his thinking in people who embodied the ideas at hand. For example, Gershom Scholem came to stand for Jewish identification in Benjamin—not simply in personal or religious terms. Scholem's researches in the Kabbalah, the central text in Jewish mysticism, spoke to Benjamin's fascination with Jewish antiquity, its closeness to the semiotic origins of naming. In February, 1930, Scholem, who had used his influence to get Benjamin a stipend from the Hebrew University to study Hebrew in Berlin so that he could come to Palestine and pursue his Jewish studies there, was moved to remind his friend that he was not bound to his promise because of their personal friendship. Benjamin had repeatedly delayed his departure for Palestine, because he felt the tug of European culture and could not relinquish his dream of becoming Europe's major literary critic. Nevertheless, he could not bring himself to say no to

Scholem's expectations, even though Scholem insisted that it was in Benjamin's best interests to decide one way or the other. Benjamin, despite Scholem's emotional generosity, could not entirely depersonalize the situation: "I have come to know living Judaism in absolutely no form other than you. The question of my relationship to Judaism is always the question of how I stand . . . in relation to the forces you have touched in me."

This tendency of Benjamin to identify his thinking with a fellow thinker contradicts his oft-quoted remark to the effect that he did not relate to people, but only to things. The truth is that he related best to people who helped him in his search, through things, for the truths that define human experience. Just as Scholem was his "rabbi," Brecht was his instructor in Marxism and social observation. Benjamin was one of the first to recognize Brecht's genius; what attracted Benjamin was the poet's ability to use language in the service of social revolution in a manner that was as semiologically exciting as soviet realism was dull and propagandistic. Indeed, Benjamin found Brecht's Marxism so seductive that one could argue it cost him his life.

Instead of answering Scholem's call to Jerusalem, Benjamin lingered in Paris in the early 1930's—not only to work on his great "Passagen-Werk" (arcades project), a study of nineteenth century Parisian street life through which he hoped to unlock the social and historical secrets of Baudelaire's poetry and milieu, but also to be close to Brecht, who held court after Hitler's coming to power in a retreat in rural Denmark called Svendborg. It was there, on repeated visits, that Benjamin absorbed Brecht's satirical vision as well as his version of Marxist aesthetics. Both proved pertinent to his own Baudelaire project. By remaining in Europe into the mid-1930's, Benjamin finally was mired in the swamp of Nazi persecution. Max Horkheimer, who had found asylum in the United States, obtained a visa for Benjamin to teach at the Institute for Social Research, which had moved from Frankfurt to New York City. In late 1940, France's Vichy government made it extremely difficult for Jews, with or without visas, to escape. Benjamin fled across the Pyrenees and, under the mistaken assumption that the Spanish border guards would force him to turn back, committed suicide.

Can one generalize about these extraordinary letters? Do they have a quality that distinguishes them sharply from the correspondence of other modern literary figures? This is difficult to answer. Benjamin was unique in every sense of the word. His wide-ranging intellect, the mind of a polymath, enabled him to range over a wide variety of facts and allusions no matter what subject he was actually addressing. The remarkable thing is that his letters never seem pedantic or artificial, or, for that matter, unfocused. After a few personal remarks, Benjamin usually launches into a discussion of a text or project. He loves to discuss the distribution of his own writings: who has what essay; what is on the front burner and the back. In an introductory essay by Theodor Adorno, which was written originally in 1966 for the first German collection of the correspondence (published in 1978), Benjamin is described as follows: "[H]e seems empirically, despite extreme individuation, hardly to have been a person at all, but rather an arena of movement in which a certain content forced its way, through him, into language." This is a bit extreme, particularly when the tact and gently ironic qualities of Benjamin's personality—as revealed in his letters—are taken into account. Nevertheless, Adorno is pressing on the nerve of a quality in Benjamin that does seem prominent in his letters. They often appear as "an arena of movement" on which the entire range of his constantly working intellect is brought to bear. Benjamin is often spoken of as one of the last German Romantics. In the early letters to members of the Youth Movement, Benjamin reveals his youthful moorings in the salient concepts of German Romanticism: nature, symbol, and, above all, the power of the imagination. He reminds one of Samuel Taylor Coleridge, who was heavily influenced by the German Romantics and whose letters and notebooks bear a strong resemblance to Benjamin's own writings. There is the same fascination with disparate phenomena and a confidence in the shaping imagination that will eventually triumph.

This raises the most controversial and perennially interesting question revolving around Benjamin. Was he a humanist who yearned for an ultimate synthesis that would reveal the hidden truths of creation, or was he an inspired semiotician who delighted in displaying the indeterminacy of language and social experience? Postmodernism has made heavy use of the latter Benjamin. As postmodernism recedes from the center of the intellectual stage, it is possible that the other Benjamin may well rise as a corrective angel. If something like this happens, Walter Benjamin's correspondence will be reread, with all of his other works, with exactly the kind of deep reading he himself concentrated on the writings of others.

Peter Brier

Sources for Further Study

ArtForum. XXXIII, November, 1994, p. 35.
Chicago Tribune. July 17, 1994, XIV, p. 6.
Kirkus Reviews. LXII, April 1, 1994, p. 445.
Library Journal. CXIX, April 15, 1994, p. 84.
The Nation. CCLIX, October 31, 1994, p. 497.
The New York Times Book Review. XCIX, July 31, 1994, p. 13.
Publishers Weekly. CCXLI, June 13, 1994, p. 59.
The Washington Post Book World. XXIV, July 17, 1994, p. 5.

COSMOPOLITAN GREETINGS
Poems, 1986-1992

Author: Allen Ginsberg (1926-   )
Publisher: HarperCollins (New York). 128 pp. $20.00
Type of work: Poetry

Poems written by Allen Ginsberg since his sixtieth birthday, further illustrating his importance as a major figure in American cultural and literary history

Since Allen Ginsberg is in his seventh decade, a professor at the City University of New York Graduate Center and a member of the American Institute of Arts and Letters, it would not be surprising if his important work as a poet were behind him, if he had essentially retired from the field to enjoy the radical shift in literary sensibility that has moved the work of his fellow artists from the outer banks to the strongest currents of American literature. Yet in a volume that collects the poems he has placed in a very wide variety of periodicals and pamphlets since the publication of *White Shroud* in 1986, Ginsberg's immediately recognizable, distinctive voice retains the high energy and linguistic invention that has marked his writing since the groundbreaking "Howl" of 1956. This new poetry covers many familiar themes from the perspective of a "poet professor in autumn years," as he describes himself in "Personals Ad." The dazzling virtuosity with language, the heart-cheering spiritual generosity, the seriousness of political purpose, and the wry, self-reflective humor that characterize Ginsberg's extensive output are as striking in *Cosmopolitan Greetings: Poems, 1986-1992* as in any previous collection. Nevertheless, Ginsberg, who has always been extremely conscious of his physical presence ("the body/ where I was born"), has brought his concerns with the inescapable consequences of time's passage into poems illuminating the anxieties of an aging man trying to assess his own role in the cultural and historical patterns of his era. The exuberance and the antic humor that have always been a feature of Ginsberg's poetry of sexual candor remain, but there is a modulation in tone and mood toward the rueful and contemplative. Similarly, while the poems presenting strong positions about governmental policy are immediately contemporary, Ginsberg often refers to earlier works on related subjects as if he were adding links to a chain of historic commentaries.

In "Author's Preface, Reader's Manual," which he wrote as an introduction to his *Collected Poems: 1947-1980* (1984), Ginsberg referred to "strong-breath'd poems," which he saw as "peaks of inspiration" that occurred every few years. Using what he called his "Hebraic-Melvillian bardic breath," Ginsberg developed long, momentum-building line structures in poems like "Howl," "Kaddish," "Kral Majales," "Mind Breaths," and "White Shroud"—poems that are designed to pull the reader/listener into an emotional force field so that the intense conviction of the poet is, ideally, re-created in the mind and heart of the audience. *Cosmopolitan Greetings* does not contain any single poem with the historical sweep of the epiclike "Witchita Vortex Sutra," but Ginsberg still manipulates a strong, rhythmic base figure that accumulates power through repetition while a series of images gradually assemble a picture of a place or ecstatic moment. This strategy accounts for the success of poems such as "On Cremation of Chögyam Trungpa, Vidyadhara," "Improvisation in Beijing," "Get It?" and "Graphic Winces." The fundamental technique of these poems is either to sustain and expand an essential position through incremental addition or to place disparate images within a large framework so that the subject becomes a multidimensional construct with unlimited boundaries.

"Improvisation in Beijing," which Ginsberg has placed as a preface at the beginning of the book, is a poetic credo in the form of an expression of artistic ambition. Using the phrase "I write poetry because . . ." to launch each line, Ginsberg juxtaposes ideas, images, data, and assertion in a flux of energetic intent, his life's experiences revealing the desire and urgency of his calling. From the explicitly personal:

> I write poetry because my mind wanders subject to sex politics Bud-
> dhadharma meditation.
> I write poetry to make accurate picture my own mind.

to the overtly political:

> I write poetry because overgrazing sheep and cattle Mongolia to U.S.
> Wild West destroys new grass & erosion creates deserts.

to the culturally connected:

> I write poetry because I listened to black Blues on 1939 radio, Leadbelly
> and Ma Rainey.
> I write poetry inspired by youthful cheerful Beatles' songs grown old.

to the aesthetically ambitious in the concluding line:

> I write poetry because it's the best way to say everything in mind within
> 6 minutes or a lifetime.

Ginsberg has gathered, from a lifetime of reflection on the subject, his responses to a request for his "sources of inspiration." The rambling, discursive nature of the poem, with its abrupt shifts in focus, is designed to enable Ginsberg to emphasize one of his primary principles from Walt Whitman: "I am large, I contain multitudes." In this sense, he is continuing to function as a spokesman for an epoch, a time-honored tradition for the poet.

"On Cremation of Chögyam Trungpa, Vidyadhara," a tribute to a spiritual guide Ginsberg admired, reverses the structural thrust of "Improvisation in Beijing" so that its long lines beginning "I noticed the . . ." spiral inward toward a composite portrait built by "minute particulars"—Ginsberg's term for William Carlos Williams' injunction "No ideas but in things." He concentrates on specifics in tightly wound lines that present the observations of an extremely aware, actively thoughtful participant:

> I noticed the grass, I noticed the hills, I noticed the highways,
> I noticed the dirt road, I noticed car rows in the parking lot

Eventually he includes interjections that suggest the importance of the event for the poet:

> I noticed the palanquin, an umbrella, the stupa painted with jewels the
> colors of the four directions—
> amber for generosity, green for karmic works, noticed the white for
> Buddha, red for the heart—

The poem concludes with a summation of the impact of the event, a fusion of awe, delight, and wonder joining the mundane with the cosmic:

> I noticed the houses, balconies overlooking a misted horizon, shore &
> old worn rocks in the sand
> I noticed the sea, I noticed the music, I wanted to dance.

Again, Ginsberg is acting in a classic poetic position, speaking as the recorder who sees, understands, and appreciates the significance of important events, and who can find language adequate for their expression.

"Get It?" and "Graphic Winces" utilize similar forms, but without the immediately personal location of the poem in the consciousness of an "I" whose individual history is inherent in the subject. The staccato jabs of "Get It?" and the precise evocations of unsettling sensations in "Graphic Winces" indicate that this pattern, which Ginsberg described in "Notes for *Howl* and Other Poems" as "a base to keep measure, return to and take off from again," is sufficiently versatile for many different poetic occasions. Nevertheless, in spite of Ginsberg's pleasure with and expertise in this structural arrangement, his work has never been limited to or confined by any single signature style. In accordance with Robert Creeley's comment that "there's an appropriate way of saying something inherent in the thing to be said," Ginsberg fuses form and subject with the craftsmanship available to an artist who has not only worked steadily for four decades but also acquired a true scholar's knowledge of poetry in the English language.

The crucial issue for Ginsberg is that nothing is automatically unacceptable, that the open field of American poetry has been enriched by infusions of elements from many regions of cultural exploration. Thus, there are three poems set to a written musical accompaniment—"C.I.A. Dope Calypso," "N.S.A. Dope Calypso" and "Just Say Yes Calypso"— each with four-line stanzas and a recapitulating two-line chorus. They are followed by Ginsberg's "Hum Bom!" of 1971, with a second section written twenty years later that performs linguistic gymnastics on a core phrase, "Whydja bomb," to the point of hilarious, mindless syllabic absurdity. There is a comic-strip "Deadline Dragon Comix," in which primitive panels accompany what might be poetic lines cast in speech bubbles, notes, and comments. Is this a poem? There is another song, "Violent Collaborations," with four lines of music from a 1944 melody and (in collaboration with Peter Hale) erotic/scatologic improvisations. There are three pages of "American sentences," which are, in effect, a version of haiku, as in "Crescent moon, girls chatter at twilight on the busride to Ankara." There is a new set of verses to the "Internationale," in which Ginsberg pays homage to the dreams of a social republic of justice while parodying current manifestations of self-important salvationists. None of these may be examples of great poetry, yet they reflect the mental process that shaped the great poems, interesting in that sense and important to the poet as a part of his method of composition.

The poetry in *Cosmopolitan Greetings* that shows Ginsberg at his most effective beyond the "strong breath'd poems" occurs in two modes. Ever since his tribute to Walt Whitman, "A Supermarket in California," which was written at the same time as "Howl" in 1955, Ginsberg has used the lyric form as a means of conveying his deeply romantic vision of an idealized existence set in opposition to the social disasters he has resisted. These are poems of appreciation and gratitude, celebrating the things of the world that bring delight. "To Jacob Rabinowitz" is a letter of thanks for a translation of Catullus and recalls with satisfaction their initial love and continuing friendship. "Fun House Antique Store" conveys the poet's astonishment at finding a "country antique store, an/ old fashioned house" on the road to "see our lawyer in D.C." The lovingly evoked intricate furnishings of the store suggest something human that is absent in "the postmodern Capital." Both of these poems sustain a mood of exultation crucial to a lyric. In other shorter, sometimes fragmentary poems Ginsberg also achieves a feeling of heightened emotional response through the musical pulses of word clusters carefully placed for their pitch and duration, a demonstration of the poet's own application of the advice he includes in the title poem: "Syntax condensed, sound is solid./ Intense fragments of spoken idiom, best./ Consonants around vowels make sense./ Savor vowels, appreciate consonants."

The other mode that Ginsberg employs here is a familiar one. The opening lines of "Mescaline" were written in 1959:

> Rotting Ginsberg, I stared in the mirror naked today
> I noticed the old skull, I'm getting balder

They were harbingers of a continuing preoccupation in Ginsberg's poetry. Aside from the emphasis he has always placed on physical sensation and the exploration of how extremes of sensory response affect artistic consciousness, the poems that closely examine the self reflect the romantic concept that the poet is a register and recorder of common human existence, a witness to the world whose reactions give tongue to universal perceptions. The humor that Ginsberg has always brought to these meditations has darkened somewhat. In "Not Dead Yet," he counsels himself, "Drink your decaf Ginsberg old communist New/ York Times addict, be glad you're not Trotsky."

There is a note of desperation in the translation of the Bengali poet Lalon Shah, "After Lalon," where Ginsberg's characteristic hopefulness is overcome with soured self-recollection, implying that he has wasted his earthly gifts:

Then what's this heavy flesh this
    weak heart leaky kidney?
Who's been doing time
    for 65 years
in this corpse?

The poem concludes with one of the most disheartened cries in Ginsberg's writing: "Allen Ginsberg warns you/ don't follow my path/ to extinction."

This note of despair, however, is neither permanent nor pervasive. "Autumn Leaves," which cheerfully proclaims, "At 66 just learning how to take care of my body," and "In the Benjo," which expresses Ginsberg's appreciation for Gary Snyder's lessons in transcendent wisdom, have purposefully been located at the end of the volume, not merely because of their place in a chronological progression but also because they provide a note of affirmation. Ginsberg, after cataloging physical decline ("Return to Kral Majales"), loss of friends ("Visiting Father & Friends"), the sorry state of the world ("You Don't Know It"), the fraudulent nature of so-called leaders ("Elephant in the Meditation Hall"), and other afflictions, can still be powerfully moved by the possibilities of love and the promises of art—the twin poles of the cosmic compass guiding him through his poetic life.

The "poet professor" who describes himself in "Personals Ad" as "alone with the Alone" is still comforted and inspired by a visionary enthusiasm for human capability. As he says in "Now and Forever," the faith he holds, finally, is in language. Immortality may be reached

thru words, thru the breath
    of long sentences
loves I have, heart beating
    still,
inspiration continuous, exhalation of
    cadenced affection

Leon Lewis

Sources for Further Study

Booklist. XC, April 15, 1994, p. 1503.
Library Journal. CXIX, May 1, 1994, p. 107.
The Progressive. LVIII, May, 1994, p. 50.
Publishers Weekly. CCXLI, March 28, 1994, p. 87.
The Virginia Quarterly Review. LXX, Autumn, 1994, p. 134.

THE CROSSING
Volume Two: The Border Trilogy

Author: Cormac McCarthy (1933-)
Publisher: Alfred A. Knopf (New York). 426 pp. $23.00
Type of work: Novel
Time: The 1940's
Locale: New Mexico and Mexico

In elemental Mexico, sixteen-year-old cowboy Billy Parham pursues manhood, knowledge, justice, and adventure

Principal characters:
BILLY PARHAM, a teenage cowboy who roves Mexico for three years in search of revenge and life experience
BOYD PARHAM, his younger brother, who accompanies him in Mexico
THE MAN, a former Mormon philosopher and storyteller
THE BLIND MAN, a former revolutionary with scars and stories
THE DOCTOR, a scrupulous Mexican physician
THE GIRL, Boyd's Mexican girlfriend

Fame arrived late for the brilliant novelist Cormac McCarthy. His fiction had been in print for twenty-five years (*The Orchard Keeper*, 1965, was his first novel), but only his work published in the 1990's, *All the Pretty Horses* (1992) and *The Crossing*, has reached a wide audience. The tiny herd of readers devoted to his pre-1990's writing are divided over this ex post facto popularity. Some sense that McCarthy took the coldheartedness too much out of his work and became a Western-romance writer, while others are happy that their appraisal of McCarthy is now generally acknowledged. Suffice it to say, there is enough stern and genuine McCarthy genius in the later books to make it likely that the teenage cowboys he sets adrift on their pages will be engaging readers well into the twenty-first century.

When sixteen-year-old Billy Parham, the main character in *The Crossing*, feeds dry breakfast cereal to his horse, readers will recognize a detail (the cereal, not the horse) from their own lives. It will be one of few. The novel tells the story of Billy, a real cowboy and son of a real cowboy in southern New Mexico during the early 1940's, who travels horseback in Mexico for three years, long enough to become a twenty year-old man. Like the hero of the first book in McCarthy's Border Trilogy, *All the Pretty Horses*, Billy faces the archaic world—no McDonald's, few cars, no washing machines—but this time he has a sidekick, younger brother Boyd. Initiation is a theme, but adventurous escape seems even more the issue for McCarthy, his boy-men, and the reader. Billy and Boyd's presence in these wild, preconsumerist lands is the story, as much as what they do or whom they meet or how they develop as characters. Billy survives. That is sufficient.

Billy Parham's voyage into Mexico is the book version of a virtual-reality video game called Primal Contact. Here is a teenager who gets it into his head to return a wolf he has trapped to its Mexican mountains. The word "school" does not appear in the story, and Billy will learn real things, McCarthy implies, without books, pencils, or institutional organization of any kind. He faces the basic inhospitality of the world, not as an idea but as a fact. Primal contact means shooting a homemade arrow not for fun but out of desperate need of something to eat. It means living without consolation. Still, there is sweetness, tenderness, and longing in Billy's story, much as there is in *All the Pretty Horses*. This sweetness contrasts with the meaner tone of the earlier McCarthy novels, particularly *Blood Meridian* (1985), which features a minimally dimensioned teenage cowboy who learns how to scalp Apaches for bounty in the Mexican and Indian lands. McCarthy implies that Billy's life, harsh as it is, is enviable. Near the end of the book Billy says, "I been more fortunate than most. There aint but one life worth livin and I was born to it. That's worth all the rest."

In McCarthy novels, characters typically rove and forage in precarious surroundings. This is a condition of that good but dangerous life Billy must live. No telling when a tire iron will hit someone or a whiskey bottle gouge out an eye. Men are dangerous, the books say, some outright evil-from-Hell. Billy's sense of connection to the wolf detailed in the first hundred pages proclaims that men are loyal to the wild, the untamed. Men, like wolves, are also distinctive in their speech, sociable in tightly patterned ways, and competent at doing certain things well, When McCarthy shows competence in men it is archaic competence—working with horses, telling stories by a fire, dressing a bad wound. Men are good at the old things, readers are to understand, and McCarthy himself knows a hawk from a handsaw.

No generic descriptions exist in McCarthy fiction. He is as tangibly aware as his competent cowboys, and his remarkable knowledge of the Mexico they wander—its food, clothing, and speech—gives *The Crossing* and his other books powerful authenticity. McCarthy readers know to pack a good dictionary when reading his novels. The depth of immediate experience is forever being offered the reader in McCarthy's language, brought crafted to the feast with communal intention.

> They sat at a pine table painted green and the woman brought him milk in a cup. He'd about forgotten that people even drank milk. She struck a match to the circular wick of the burner in the kerosene stove and adjusted the flame and put on a kettle and when it had boiled she spooned eggs one by one down into the kettle and put the lid back again. The blind man sat stiff and erect. As if he himself were the guest in his own house. When the eggs had boiled the woman brought them steaming in a bowl and sat down to watch the boy eat.

The institutional will not protect Billy Parham. He will, from the first page of the novel to the end, be crossing most willingly again and again from the tame to the wild, from dependence to self-reliance. McCarthy says that it is in his blood, his innate manliness, to do so. Billy watches wolves in the middle of the night: "Their breath smoked palely in the cold as if they burned with some inner fire and the wolves twisted and turned and leapt in a silence such that they seemed of another world entire." He comes upon an Indian and finds in the stealthy hunter's eyes "that antique gaze from whence there could be no way back forever."

Billy traps a wolf that has been preying on his father's cattle and takes it to Mexico, where it is stolen from him and put to fighting all the big dogs of a Mexican rancher and his peasants. Billy shoots the wolf after hours of such fighting; he then wanders on horseback, touring empty landscapes and ancient mud villages, and returns to his now-vacant home. His parents have been murdered, the horses stolen. He locates his brother Boyd, and they set out for Mexico again.

There is "no way back forever." They ask directions at a town south of the border. They are hunting the horses, they half believe, and they will find them by chance or destiny but not by plan. This world is not mapped. God still runs the show. Asking directions assumes civic order.

> Such road as it was soon ceased to be road at all. Where it first left the river it was the width of a wagon or more and had in recent times been scraped or graded by a fresno and the brush cut back yet once clear of the town the heart seemed to have gone out of this enterprise and they found themselves on a common footpath following the course of a dry arroyo up into the hills.

Billy and Boyd's hunt for the horses is the novel's plot. Things happen in the course of this wandering—horses are found, Boyd gets a Mexican girlfriend, Boyd is shot, Billy meets a blind man whose eyes were sucked out of his head by another man during a war, Billy locates Boyd's bones and returns them to New Mexico. The story gripping the reader, however, is the page-by-page revelation of day and night, landscape, fires lit and slept by, visits to eroded villages where bad tacos are to be had. The story is how rudimentary Mexico is and Mexicans are, and it is told in endless convincing detail: "They wore homemade dresses and huaraches cobbled up out of leather scraps and rawhide. . . . Their skin was dark like an indian's and their eyes coal black and they smoked the way poor people eat which is a form of prayer." For Billy, "home had come to seem remote and dreamlike. There were times he could not call to mind his father's face."

The trip McCarthy takes in this novel is, the reader may sense, the same trip earlier American novelists have taken, from Herman Melville's *Moby Dick* (1851) to Mark Twain's *Adventures of Huckleberry Finn* (1884) to Jack Kerouac's *On the Road* (1957). Destination is irrelevant. Loss of the familiar, the conventional, the comfortable, the civilized, is the goal. A whaling voyage of three years is comparable to three years aboard a horse in Mexico without a shower, bathroom, suitcase, or lawn mower.

McCarthy, like his novelist forebears, knows that the road is better than the inn, but also that the solitary soul afoot will run into an interesting lot of Queequegs and Dukes, or the whole lot of fellow solitaries. A fine novelist can grip their words and serve them up for the equally solitary reader. McCarthy finds savorable voices all over Mexico, and they are not all Mexican.

> I am a Mormon. Or I was. I was a Mormon born.
>
> He [Billy] wasnt sure what a Mormon was. He looked at the room. He looked at the cats.
>
> They came here many years ago. Eighteen and ninety-six. From Utah. They came because of the statehood. In Utah. I was a Mormon. Then I converted to the church. Then I became I dont know what. Then I became me.

The humor of the interchange may mislead. This man is part of the novel's deep Beethovian bass theme of knowing things for oneself. His heresy is a sign of real learning. One knows because one lives, McCarthy hammers out, and not because one is taught. The former Mormon, like Captain Ahab, has begun to pursue God obsessively, with a summons for God to appear in court and explain Himself and the world He created.

The Crossing is a vastation upon ruins and time with a main character who never studied history much. He is getting it served up in a field trip he will never forget, which is making him into a permanent wanderer. "What kind of place is this," Boyd asks Billy of a town, and Billy responds, "I don't know." The reader does know, however, thanks to McCarthy's powerful imagination and power over language.

The Crossing, as well as other McCarthy novels, restores the legitimacy of the novel as a literary genre. It is not the form that is suspect but the one who fills the form. The novel demands of its writers a parallel between the world's depth and richness and the writer's imagination and inventiveness. As the world is full, so must the novelist be full. The first page of McCarthy's first novel, *The Orchard Keeper*, contains a sentence that illustrates this paralleling: "Far down the blazing strip of concrete a small shapeless mass had emerged and was struggling toward him. It loomed steadily, weaving and grotesque, like something seen through bad glass, gained briefly the form and solidity of a pickup truck, whipped past and receded into the same liquid shape by which it came."

The realness of the world is the witness of such sentences, and charting or inventing this realness has ever been McCarthy's assignment as a writer—an assignment evidently given by McCarthy's Creator, since he clearly has not done it, until recently, for the money. His insistence upon the archaic facts of characters' lives sheds a biblical light. Deserts, small portions, traveling and never arriving, close contact with animals, perpetual wariness—these elements testify to the destiny of humankind. Billy's story ends:

> It had ceased raining in the night and he walked out on the road and called for the dog. He called and called. Standing in that inexplicable darkness. Where there was no sound anywhere save only the wind. After a while he sat in the road. He took off his hat and placed it on the tarmac before him and he bowed his head and held his face in his hands and wept. He sat there for a long time and after a while the east did gray and after a while the right and godmade sun did rise, once again, for all and without distinction.

Bruce Wiebe

Sources for Further Study

Chicago Tribune. June 26, 1994, XIV, p. 5.
Library Journal. CXIX, June 15, 1994, p. 95.
Los Angeles Times Book Review. June 12, 1994, p. 3.

The New Republic. CCXI, July 11, 1994, p. 38.
The New York Times Book Review. XCIX, June 12, 1994, p. 1.
Newsweek. CXXIII, June 13, 1994, p. 54.
Publishers Weekly. CCXLI, April 25, 1994, p. 55.
Time. CXLIII, June 6, 1994, p. 62.
The Wall Street Journal. June 10, 1994, p. A8.
The Washington Post Book World. XXIV, June 5, 1994, p. 1.

DELUSIONS OF GRANDMA

Author: Carrie Fisher (1956-   )
Publisher: Simon & Schuster (New York). 260 pp. $22.00
Type of work: Novel
Time: The 1990's
Locale: Los Angeles, Paris, New York, Texas, and Las Vegas

In a sweetly amusing roman à clef *that combines diary entries to an unborn daughter with remembrances of the romance that caused her conception, best-selling author Carrie Fisher wryly comments on the state of contemporary relationships between women and men as well as mothers and daughters during the course of an unexpected pregnancy*

Principal characters:

CORA SHARPE, the protagonist, a successful Hollywood screenwriter and "script doctor" who finds motherhood easier to deal with than adult male-female relationships
RAY BEAUDRILLEAUX, an entertainment attorney who falls in love with Cora but refuses to take a backseat to her career and friends
BUD, her writing partner and best friend
VIV, her mother, a retired costume designer
BILL, her grandfather, who suffers from Alzheimer's disease
WILLIAM, her dear friend who is dying from acquired immune deficiency syndrome (AIDS)
ESME BING BEAUDRILLEAUX, her unborn baby (later named Lily)
CLIFF, her good friend, a successful entrepreneur
JOAN, her most famous friend

Delusions of Grandma, the third of Carrie Fisher's generally entertaining novels, examines life and love through a web of witty mega-metaphors and dramatizes the populist conviction that men and women have vastly different emotional needs and patterns of communication. In this case, the man and the woman are Cora Sharpe, witty and angst-ridden Hollywood "script doctor," and Ray Beaudrilleaux, steadfast southern gentleman turned Hollywood attorney. Their relationship feels doomed from the start, as they indeed seem to be from different emotional planets. For Cora and Ray, love cannot conquer all.

Inexperienced in being romantically involved with "normal" men, Cora constantly doubts her true feelings for Ray, who is neither neurotic nor narcissistic like her former husband and former lovers. Oblivious to Cora's insecurities, Ray's quiet nature surrounds her elusive heart as his presence insinuates some stability into her chaotic life. In turn, Cora's dazzling wit both fascinates Ray and keeps him at a distance, as she substitutes conversation for seduction. Yet physical contact—a first kiss in a parking lot leading eventually to sex on her sofa—silences her nagging mind at last, to Ray's delight and Cora's amazement.

After their first meeting at a friend's party in Los Angeles and a subsequent dinner at a trendy restaurant, Ray and Cora's unlikely pairing evolves through nightly trans-

Atlantic phone calls in which she does most of the talking and he does all the listening. In Paris to do a quick cable-film rewrite, Cora is surprised to discover how much she genuinely misses Ray. Absence making her heart grow fonder, she becomes aware of the inner depth lurking beneath Ray's "qualities of a good Scout." His reliability, earnestness, patience, and genuine interest in Cora prove unfamiliar to her, but her reluctance to let him love her begins to ebb nevertheless. Back in Los Angeles, Cora falls once again into the familiar verbal tap dance she choreographs to remain in control of her life—especially when love is at stake. Like water over stones, however, Ray continues to wear down her resistance to become involved. He does not take her reticence as seriously as she would like.

After Ray moves in with Cora, however, he discovers that their proximity does not entitle him to any more of her attention than he received when they were merely dating. He continues to ride in the backseat of Cora's life, the window seats being permanently occupied by her work and friends. Her vast network of friends includes her "committee," whose opinions and approvals Cora solicits whenever something threatens to undermine her control—such as falling in love with, God forbid, a lawyer.

As Ray's innate patience with Cora begins to wear thin, their already tenuous relationship starts to erode. He refrains from expressing his discontent, though, until Cora pushes him to admit that he wants a commitment from her. She glibly replies that she's a "weird enough girlfriend" but was a "disappointing wife" when she was married years before and has no desire to be one again. Ray valiantly argues in his own defense, battering down her emotional armor until he finally gets Cora to agree to an engagement "like in a Henry James novel" rather than an actual marriage. They'll work up to that, she hopes. When he makes the mistake of giving Cora an engagement ring, however, Ray fails to notice that she wears it like a ball and chain rather than a constant—and expensive—reminder of his love.

As Cora grapples with the unfamiliarity of this "normal" romance, her friendship with cowriter Bud suffers. Bud has known Cora for years, calls her "Caesar," and relies on her for advice and solace when his own doomed romances fail and he spirals into the pit of depression. Ray considers Bud a rival for Cora's attention, if not her physical affection, and it is clear that they will never be friends. Ray also becomes increasingly annoyed at Cora's inability to leave her friends' lives alone; he cannot understand her need to "fix" their problems when she cannot fix her own.

As tensions surface between them, Cora decides that their engagement is a big mistake. Her declaration of this news sends Ray storming off, leaving Cora to muse about the ideal relationship: "If only we didn't yearn for beginning things so damn close to the middle. Could be satisfied with a little more than a little. The warm toils in the hushed advancement of the clock. The mutual decisions. The carnival of compromise."

The carnival of compromise invades Cora's private space when William, her dearest friend who has only two T-cells left, comes to spend his last mortal days with her. Deeply affected by her decision to be William's caretaker, she suddenly wonders who will take care of *her*. Ray is the obvious choice, so she swallows her pride and calls him. He rises to the occasion, all southern gentlemanly forgiveness, and their proximity to William rejuvenates their romance. Clinging to each other as William gradually slips from this world in a matter of weeks, Ray and Cora try to pack as much of life's richness into his final days as they can. Ray remains pragmatic, however, sensing that witnessing William's illness has opened Cora's heart to him, but silently wondering what will bind them together once William is gone.

What happens next is inevitable—after William's funeral, which is attended by some of his relatives and lots of weeping, Cora unknowingly revives her old habit of keeping a proper emotional distance from Ray, and he refuses to accept it once more. This comes to a climax weeks later, when they drive in separate cars to a party given by Ray's friends, in case Cora wants to leave before he does. Ray proves to be the one who leaves first—not only the party but also her life. He has finally had enough of being second best.

What Ray does not know is that Cora has also had plenty of him—metaphorically speaking at least. She is pregnant with his child, conceived during the intense weeks leading up to William's demise, when life and death continually commingled. By the time Cora discovers her pregnancy, she has come to accept her inability to sustain a relationship with Ray and truly hopes that she can manage a relationship with his child instead. Certain that it will be a daughter, Cora names the baby Esme Bing Beaudrilleaux and writes her copious letters to explain how much she wants to be a good mother even though she is incapable of being a good wife.

When Cora informs her "committee" that she is having a baby sans wedlock, they are genuinely supportive and declare that she is doing a brave and wonderful thing. This makes Cora feel brave and wonderful, even when dealing with Viv, her somewhat eccentric mother, who is not exactly the maternal role model Cora would have designed for this occasion.

Ironically, at that very moment Viv is embarking on an odd quest of her own: to remove her aging father Bill (Cora's grandfather) from a nursing home in Santa Monica and take him to his boyhood home in Texas. Bill, who has Alzheimer's disease, has been expressing the desire to "go home," so Viv takes him literally and engineers his escape as if it were a major spy mission.

Viv enlists Cora to help her with Bill, and Cora enlists Bud, who is depressed because his latest romance has just dissolved. As Cora's pregnancy evolves and Viv mothers her own father, this odd quartet contemplates motherhood, friendship, and family as they travel by train to Texas. Cora discovers that Viv is far wiser than she has ever noticed before, although no less eccentric. In fact, Viv's next wild scheme is to buy a defunct Las Vegas hotel and renovate it as the site of an "amusement ride" based on costumes made famous in motion pictures, including those she designed in Hollywood's heyday.

Through their sudden proximity aboard a moving cross-country train, Cora comes to appreciate Viv's unique style of mothering without smothering. She even listens to Viv's assurance that Cora will instinctively know what to do when Esme arrives. Despite her natural tendency to fret, Cora begins to relax as they near Bill's hometown.

Months later, Cora's proudest creation is born in Viv's newly opened hotel. Playing the role of expectant father in Ray's absence, Bud forgets all of his birth preparation and comes unglued when Cora's water breaks. All goes well, however, and a darling baby girl, as predicted, emerges. Renamed Lillian (Lily for short) after Cora decides that Esme sounds like "nose noises," the baby instantly absorbs Cora's attention as no man—not even Ray—ever could.

Through this journey of the heart, Fisher draws Cora as a witty Everywoman who learns that love is an unexpected yet gradual happening over which no one truly has control. Fisher's amusing literary style keeps the reader engaged, watching Cora finally give up her need to control everything—and everyone—as her body is taken over by baby Esme.

As in her earlier works, *Postcards from the Edge* (1987) and *Surrender the Pink* (1990), Fisher gives her heroine an inner style of dialogue that hides the rather slim plot. Verbal interactions generally serve to define Fisher's characters while her story meanders through various incidents and episodes. In this case, these incidents and episodes remain disconnected to the very end. Readers must create their own connections between Cora's pregnancy and her cross-country train trip with Viv, Bud, and Bill; the links between these events are not as clear in Fisher's rendition of the events or Cora's interpretation of same as one might like.

Fisher's fluency with witty metaphors, however, propels the story along when the plot slows down. Her skill with verbal comparisons and turns of phrase is near-legendary and was prominent in her premier novel, *Postcards from the Edge*. In *Delusions of Grandma*, however, her similes seem self-conscious more often than not, as in the book's pun of a title. Overall, the writing feels full of effort, as if Fisher struggled to top her own witticisms at least once a paragraph, if not once a sentence. Sometimes the results are verbal gems; more often they feel like fool's gold. Fisher's description of how Cora feels about being pregnant is a case in point:

> She pulled mournfully at the clothes around her stomach and breasts. This was the onset of what she came to call her Pregnancy Humiliation. Something in her, quite apart from the baby, felt caught and foolish. She was a train track, and unless it was derailed, the little choo-choo on the distant horizon would grow larger and larger until it blasted right through her, leaving the place between her legs in ruins, her mind a blank. Someone who had oh-so-recently waddled could never be taken seriously again, she was sure.

While it is unlikely that readers will come away from *Delusions of Grandma* with the desire to begin an affair with a lawyer or become pregnant instead of married, the introduction of Cora Sharpe into Fisher's repertoire of heroines is greatly appreciated. Many readers surely hope that Cora will make a return visit in a future work so they can see how her life, her work, her committee of friends, and her penchant for metaphors are influenced by sharing her life and heart with Lily Bing Beaudrilleaux.

Barbara Elman Schiffman

Sources for Further Study

Boston Globe. April 3, 1994, p. 30.
Chicago Tribune. April 10, 1994, XIV, p. 5.
The Christian Science Monitor. May 9, 1994, p. 13.
Library Journal. CXIX, March 1, 1994, p. 117.
Los Angeles. XXXIX, April, 1994, p. 68.
New Woman. XXIV, May, 1994, p. 28.
The New York Times Book Review. XCIX, March 27, 1994, p. 15.
Publishers Weekly. CCXLI, February 21, 1994, p. 232.
The Times Literary Supplement. July 1, 1994, p. 22.
The Washington Post Book World. XXIV, May 1, 1994, p. 2.

D. H. LAWRENCE
The Story of a Marriage

Author: Brenda Maddox (1932-   )
Publisher: Simon & Schuster (New York). Illustrated. 620 pp. $30.00
Type of work: Biography
Time: 1908-1930
Locale: London, Cornwall, and other English locations; the Continent, chiefly Italy and Germany; Australia; Mexico; and Taos, New Mexico

Brenda Maddox traces the biography of the celebrated—and infamous—English writer from the period just before he met his future wife, Frieda, and experienced the defining moment of his life

Principal personages:
D. H. LAWRENCE, an English novelist, poet, short-story writer, and essayist
FRIEDA LAWRENCE, his wife, a German aristocrat and libertine
MABEL DODGE LUHAN, a wealthy American art patron in Taos, New Mexico
THE HONORABLE DOROTHY BRETT, a deaf, spinsterish English painter and a member of the Taos artists' colony
JOHN MIDDLETON MURRY, an English publisher and critic
ANGELO RAVAGLI, Frieda's lover, an Italian infantry officer

Brenda Maddox's *D. H. Lawrence: The Story of a Marriage* was published simultaneously in England as *The Married Man: A Life of D. H. Lawrence*. The latter is a more appropriate title for the work Maddox has produced. Although Maddox (the author of a biography of James Joyce's wife, Nora) has chosen to play down the "prophet of sex" approach taken by other Lawrence biographers, opting instead to concentrate on the writer's primary relationship, her book is by no means a dual biography. Frieda Lawrence is a vivid and compelling presence in *D. H. Lawrence*, which takes care to note her influence on her husband's life and works, but Lawrence himself takes up the bulk of Maddox's attention. Frieda, who lived on for twenty-six years after Lawrence's death, is the subject of only two of the biography's twenty-one chapters.

Nevertheless, Lawrence defined himself primarily as "a married man," and Maddox's focus on his years with Frieda is not misguided. The biography opens in 1908, just as Lawrence leaves his boyhood home in the English Midlands to take up a teaching post in a London suburb. Lawrence was apparently a dedicated and successful schoolmaster, but by this time he had already embarked on a literary career, producing in quick succession *The White Peacock* (1911) and *The Trespasser* (1912), as well as a succession of poems and stories. By the time he met Frieda, he had also had a brush with another defining aspect of his life, serious lung disease. Yet it was the meeting with Frieda in March, 1912, that would unalterably change his life's course.

At twenty-six, Lawrence had a reputation as a promising author of sexually oriented material drawing on modern German metaphysics. He was also desperately searching for a wife. When he met Frieda, she seemed a perfect partner for him—a notion she fostered by seducing him within twenty minutes of their first encounter. Frieda, a member of the aristocratic German von Richthofen family, was married to Nottingham University College professor Ernest Weekley and the mother of three young children. She was also a discreet libertine dedicated to the philosophy of Friedrich Nietzsche, which she had absorbed largely through a previous lover. Lawrence apparently made as great an impression on her as she did on him: Less than two months later, the two ran off together to the Continent.

It seems that initially there were no definite plans for a permanent union, at least in Frieda's mind. Lawrence, however, was determined to marry, pushing through a punitive divorce that robbed Frieda of the right even to see her children. Having secured his heart's desire, however, Lawrence proceeded to attack it. Not only did he repeatedly—even publicly—abuse Frieda verbally and physically, but he longed for a homosexual union as well. Although Maddox speculates that Lawrence may have had sex with a man only once in his life, he repeatedly addressed the subject of homosexual love in his fiction. The nude wrestling scene between the male protagonists in *Women in Love* (1920) is only one example. His writing also exhibited an increasingly strident misogyny, culminating with the story "The Woman Who Rode Away" (1925), in which the main character is ritually sacrificed to save the world's virility.

Nevertheless, Frieda, although not Lawrence's equal, was certainly a good match for him. At least as demonstrative as her husband, she usually held her own in their disputes, on one occasion even breaking a plate over his head. Blithely unfaithful, she continued to pursue sexual adventures of her own, unmindful of Lawrence's jealousy and the constancy he exhibited, if not espoused.

What Lawrence did espouse was a liberty of sexual expression in service of the eternal union between man and woman, an ideology he articulated most fully in his novel *Lady Chatterley's Lover*, which first appeared in 1928 but was not published in unabridged form until 1960, thirty years after the author's death. Although other women in Lawrence's life clearly served as partial models for the novel's heroine, Connie Chatterley, her unfettered embrace of physical love surely embodied much of what Lawrence had learned from his wife. At the same time, the two main male figures in the novel, the virile gatekeeper Mellors and the wheelchair-bound, impotent Sir Clifford Chatterley, are both Lawrence surrogates. While earlier in their marriage Frieda had helped Lawrence discover the kind of heightened sexual awareness displayed by Mellors, in the later years of their union his worsening tuberculosis kept them in separate beds because of his chronic cough and dwindling sexual appetite. Lawrence, like Clifford Chatterley, never was able to give his wife the child she wanted to have with him.

In 1926, Dorothy Brett, a Lawrence acolyte of long standing, finally achieved her wish of getting the high priest of love into bed. The encounter was an abortive one, and years later Brett would claim that Lawrence could be potent only with his wife. Her supposition is not accurate, according to Maddox's account, but it does reflect a fundamental truth about the Lawrence marriage: Despite his abuse and her infidelities, theirs proved to be an indissoluble union. After the first difficult years of their marriage, Lawrence published a series of confessional poems about that period under the title *Look! We Have Come Through* (1917); it is a credo that could be used to sum up their entire twenty-seven years together.

Throughout those years, Frieda was to follow Lawrence from country to country, even continent to continent, as he restlessly searched for relief from oppressive English attitudes and the even more oppressive English climate. Lawrence began to consider leaving his homeland for good after the suppression of *The Rainbow* (1915). He formulated plans for a utopian community of like-minded souls to be called Rananim, which he dreamed of establishing in some remote location. After Lawrence and Frieda were expelled from Cornwall in 1917 as spies (he because of his outspoken antiwar attitudes, she because of her German ancestry), he turned toward the New World.

Lawrence journeyed to America via a circuitous route, traveling first to Italy, where he and Frieda lived for two years while he tried to clear his lungs by moving ever southward, then to Australia, where, with customary dispatch, he turned his experience of a new land into literature, writing his novel *Kangaroo* (1923) in forty-two days. Finally, in 1922, the Lawrences arrived in New Mexico to take up the generous invitation of the wealthy patron Mabel Dodge Luhan (then Sterne) to join her Taos artists' colony. It would become the place with which Lawrence is most closely associated, but he remained there only three years (with lengthy side trips to Mexico to research *The Plumed Serpent* [1926]), failing to find Rananim or a return to good health. In February of 1925, his tuberculosis was irrefutably diagnosed, and seven months later he returned to England. He never left Europe again.

He did not, however, stop working. Of all the revelations about Lawrence contained in Maddox's book, perhaps none is as astounding as the evidence of his prolific literary output. In 1925, after a pulmonary hemorrhage felled him in Mexico City, he returned to the United States by Pullman train. During the grueling four-day journey, Lawrence was too weak to hold a pen, but he began a new novel anyway, dictating it to Frieda. Lawrence never finished this work, but, buttressed by Frieda, he continued to defy death by churning out work, in the summer following his collapse alone finishing his play *David* (1926), revising *The Plumed Serpent*, and writing a series of essays that appeared as *Reflections on the Death of a Porcupine and Other Essays* (1925).

The doctor in Mexico City had told Frieda that her husband had only two years to live, but the depth of her denial about Lawrence's illness was apparently as great as his own—and apparently as salutary. Both refused to alter their course in any significant way, with Lawrence spurning the conventional treatment for consumption, absolute rest, and Frieda—as much caught up in his drive and charisma as any of his disciples—enabling his behavior. Lawrence would live on for five more years, not two, producing scores of literary works and embarking on a new career as a painter. Among his last works was Frieda's annuity, *Lady Chatterley's Lover*.

After Lawrence's death on March 2, 1930, Frieda fought a hard but ultimately successful battle for control of his estate. She then returned to Kiowa Ranch, the property that Mabel Dodge had given the Lawrences in 1924 but that Lawrence had insisted be put in Frieda's name alone. Frieda organized a kind of shrine to Lawrence near the ranch and continued to serve his memory by drafting a memorable account of their life together, *Not I, but the Wind* (1934). It was a solid partnership to the end.

Brenda Maddox has done an admirable job of sorting through the complex web of relationships, travel, and literary output that constituted Lawrence's career after 1912, at the same time maintaining a sense of her subject's own drive not merely to live but also to transform his life into art. It is a fascinating life.

Lisa Paddock

Sources for Further Study

Booklist. XCI, November 15, 1994, p. 572.
Kirkus Reviews. LXII, August 15, 1994, p. 1104.
Library Journal. CXIX, November 1, 1994, p. 77.
London Review of Books. XVI, November 10, 1994, p. 24.
New Statesman and Society. VII, September 23, 1994, p. 24.
The New York Times Book Review. XCIX, November 27, 1994, p. 3.
Publishers Weekly. CCXLI, October 10, 1994, p. 53.
San Francisco Chronicle. November 13, 1994, p. DAT13.
The Times Literary Supplement. November 4, 1994, p. 4.
The Washington Post Book World. XXIV, November 27, 1994, p. 5.

DIPLOMACY

Author: Henry Kissinger (1923-)
Publisher: Simon & Schuster (New York). Illustrated. 912 pp. $35.00
Type of work: Political history
Time: The sixteenth through twentieth centuries
Locale: Europe, the United States, and abroad

Henry Kissinger addresses the contradictions between America's political idealism and the actualities of the situations with which it has had to deal as a twentieth century world leader

Principal personages:
THEODORE ROOSEVELT, twenty-sixth president of the United States (1901-1909)
WOODROW WILSON, twenty-eighth president of the United States (1913-1921)
FRANKLIN DELANO ROOSEVELT, thirty-second president of the United States (1933-1945)
JOHN FITZGERALD KENNEDY, thirty-fifth president of the United States (1961-1963)
LYNDON BAINES JOHNSON, thirty-sixth president of the United States (1963-1969)
RICHARD MILHOUS NIXON, thirty-seventh president of the United States (1969-1974)
RONALD REAGAN, fortieth president of the United States (1981-1989)
CARDINAL ARMAND JEAN DU PLESSIS RICHELIEU, a seventeenth century French statesman
PRINCE KLEMENS VON METTERNICH, a nineteenth century Austrian statesman
PRINCE OTTO VON BISMARCK, a nineteenth century Prussian statesman and first chancellor of the German Empire

Running in excess of nine hundred pages, Henry Kissinger's *Diplomacy* exemplifies a Teutonic tendency to provide extensive, sometimes ponderous, background material as the setting for the jewels that are a treatise's essence. On the one hand, *Diplomacy* is a speculative book that looks toward the twenty-first century with an eye toward assessing the international stature of the United States in the new world order that Kissinger identifies lucidly in his first and final chapters, each of which is a model of close reasoning and penetrating, usually brilliant, analysis. On the other hand, *Diplomacy* is a capsulized, if somewhat lengthy, history of international diplomacy as it has been practiced since the days of Cardinal Armand Jean du Plessis Richelieu and William of Orange; Kissinger devotes his third chapter to this pair.

In the book's second chapter, "The Hinge: Theodore Roosevelt or Woodrow Wilson," Kissinger sets up the diplomatic dichotomy that is to control much of the remainder of his argument. He presents Theodore Roosevelt accurately as a pragmatic practitioner of the *Realpolitik*, whereas he presents Woodrow Wilson, also with complete accuracy, as the idealist whose vision of a League of Nations, the precursor of the United Nations, won him a Nobel Peace Prize although he did not achieve sufficient domestic support for his own country to become a member of the league that he had spawned.

Herein, according to Kissinger, lies the major dilemma with which United States diplomats and statesmen have been forced to deal during the period of their country's ascendancy to the position of world power that it has enjoyed through most of the twentieth century. The great diplomatic tug-of-war for the United States has been between its ideals and the frequently daunting realities of the world situation. American ideals led the nation into involvement in Vietnam (to which Kissinger devotes three chapters, tracing the evolution of that conflict from the Harry S Truman administration to Richard Nixon's face-saving extrication of United States forces from the situation), in Somalia, and in Haiti. The specter of Vietnam, however, has kept the United States from further entangling involvements in Cuba, Serbo-Croatia, Rwanda, and other hot spots throughout the world.

Given the idealistic context of United States diplomacy during the mid-twentieth century, Kissinger does not fault the military and diplomatic advisers to Presidents John F. Kennedy and Lyndon Johnson who advised escalation of the Vietnam conflict, although such an escalation in retrospect proved disastrous. The bitter memory of Vietnam has had a profound effect upon United States involvement in regional conflicts for the last quarter of the twentieth century.

Early in his first chapter, Kissinger points to the inherent contradictions in the United States' practice of diplomacy. Born out of revolution against a monarchy, universally touted as a bastion of liberty and a land of incredible opportunity, the United States believes unerringly in political self-determination. So convinced are its citizens and its statesmen of the rectitude of its form of government, however, that they have spread its influence into every corner of the earth with a missionary zeal, sometimes imposing freedom upon populaces that had never been accustomed to living in a free society. The downside of this is evident, for example, in Haiti, where President Jean-Bertrand Aristide, elected by the people through a democratic process strongly encouraged and monitored by the United States, was for a long time unable to assume power, which was quickly grasped by a disgruntled military junta after the elections had made clear the will of the people.

Having set up his Roosevelt-Wilson dichotomy, Kissinger progresses to three historical chapters that deal with the international diplomacy of Cardinal Richelieu, William of Orange, and William Pitt the Younger (chapter 3); Prince Klemens von Metternich and the Congress of Vienna (chapter 4), the subject of Kissinger's earlier *A World Restored: Metternich, Castlereagh, and the Problems of Peace, 1812-22* (1957); and Napoleon III and Count Otto von Bismarck (chapter 5). In the first two of these three chapters, Kissinger presents approaches to international (read European) diplomacy devoted to preserving the balance of power in western Europe, a geographical area the size of Zaire, where cultural and language identities have always been clearly defined and where boundaries separate countries of essentially equivalent power and influence.

In the Napoleon-Bismarck chapter, Kissinger deals with the overambitious, often impetuous fool that Napoleon could be, juxtaposing him in sharp contrast to the intelligently analytical Bismarck, certainly the quintessential international diplomat of his era. Kissinger goes so far as to suggest that had it been possible for Bismarck to remain in power, the "doomsday machine" that led to World Wars I and II might have been derailed. In this chapter, Kissinger reveals his disdain for impetuosity and his respect for thoughtful analysis in governmental affairs, particularly those with broad international implications. Later in the book, he faults Adolf Hitler for his impetuosity and lack of analytical discernment.

Napoleon, like Hitler and many other notable politicians who have fallen in defeat, played to his public, devising strategies that would make him popular among the people. He played to the majority, paying little heed to minority voices—a tactic that pays immediate political dividends at the local level but sows seeds destined to germinate into poisonous plants. By implication, Kissinger suggests that the most recent presidential administrations in the United States suffer from the same virus that has infected failed regimes through history.

Kissinger's three historical chapters, coming as early as they do in the book, show clearly the difference between the tasks facing the controlling powers of the past two or three centuries and those that face the United States as the major world power of the twentieth century. France and Germany, undisputed world powers in the seventeenth and eighteenth centuries, dealt with an international world that was essentially confined to the European continent. The main challenge was to preserve the equilibrium between the nations of that continent. Great Britain, twenty miles across the English Channel from the mainland of Europe, was as staunchly isolationist during this period as the United States was in the last half of the nineteenth century and the first third of the twentieth.

During the nineteenth century, Great Britain became the dominant international force. Its colonial expansion (the sun never sets on the British Empire) and the riches it brought put it in the ascendant, but communication and transportation were still sufficiently slow to insulate England from many of the regional problems that now are transmitted instantly around the world. Television viewers today watch the starvation in Somalia and the wanton killing in Rwanda on a daily basis almost as it is happening. In slower times, such events would have been reported with little fanfare months after their occurrence.

As the United States moved into a position of world leadership in the first third of the twentieth century, it remained isolated and insulated from much that went on in Europe and Asia. Modern media brought news of world events to U.S. citizens, but two vast oceans separated them and removed from them the immediate threat of incursions on their territory. Isolationism kept the United States out of Woodrow Wilson's League of Nations. This isolationism persisted into the administration of Franklin Delano Roosevelt, which began in 1933.

As the clouds of conflict darkened over Europe, Americans looked on, but they issued no strident calls to enter a conflict that clearly had little immediate effect upon their lives. As American intervention became more and more an international necessity, Roosevelt's major task was to move his nation from one that believed in noninvolvement to one that realized the need to take a stand and become involved. The Japanese bombing of Pearl Harbor was Roosevelt's linchpin for gaining public support of his country's entry into World War II.

Diplomacy is not a record of Kissinger's service as Richard Nixon's assistant for national security or of his three and a half years as Nixon's secretary of state, although two detailed chapters, "Vietnam: The Extrication, Nixon" and "Foreign Policy as Geopolitics: Nixon's Triangular Diplomacy," do focus on the author's service during the Nixon Administration. Rather, *Diplomacy* provides an overview, though a selective one, of international diplomacy over the past three hundred years and assesses the role of the United States on the international diplomatic scene.

Using past United States diplomatic policy and action as his anchor, Kissinger also ventures forth with predictions of where United States foreign policy is (and should be) heading. It is in his last chapter, "The New World Order Reconsidered"—possibly the most important chapter in a highly significant book—that Kissinger proffers the advice he is uniquely qualified to give.

He warns of the danger of allowing any one nation to assume political or military dominance in either Europe or Asia. The People's Republic of China and the former Soviet Union were the two leviathans of their respective continents. Now that the Soviet Union has been dissolved, Kissinger urges the United States to encourage the territories of which it was composed to concentrate on internal development. A set of nations that stretch across eleven time zones have the space and resources for productive expansion. The United States can provide the technological expertise to encourage it.

In Western Europe, Kissinger sees the Atlantic Alliance and the European Union as modalities for promoting stability and prosperity. He recommends bringing more of Eastern Europe into the North Atlantic Treaty Organization (NATO) as a means of getting the former Eastern Bloc countries to look to such a consortium for the security that the Soviet Union previously afforded them.

Kissinger thinks that the United States should overlook Chinese violations of human rights (as popular as scrutiny of such violations is among many Americans) and should seek to help China develop the global strategies that will redound to its future benefit. As a part of this, Kissinger suggests that because of Chinese fears of a militarily strong Japan, the United States should keep Japan from arming itself significantly and should continue to be a strong military presence in Northeast Asia.

Kissinger applauds the North American Free Trade Agreement (NAFTA), the passage of which is probably the greatest triumph of the Clinton Administration to date. He urges the United States to strengthen NAFTA through active participation in and strenuous support of the General Agreement on Trades and Tariffs (GATT).

Kissinger warns that the economic dominance of the United States is unlikely to persist in its present form. He points out that the Third World is richer in resources and has a more abundant population than the United States and Europe. While its abundant population might hobble its development, spreading technologies must inevitably unlock its wealth of resources.

Looking ahead to the twenty-first century, Kissinger foresees that international diplomacy will be dominated not by one or two nations, as it was during the past three centuries, but by a group of entities that will likely include the United States, Europe, China, Japan, Russia, and possibly India.

R. Baird Shuman

Sources for Further Study

The Christian Science Monitor. April 27, 1994, p. 17.
Foreign Affairs. LXXIII, May, 1994, p. 132.
London Review of Books. XVI, July 21, 1994, p. 7.
Los Angeles Times Book Review. April 24, 1994, p. 2.
The New York Review of Books. XLI, May 12, 1994, p. 8.
The New York Times Book Review. XCIX, April 3, 1994, p. 3.
Newsweek. CXXIII, April 11, 1994, p. 42.
Publishers Weekly. CCXLI, March 14, 1994, p. 57.
Time. CXLIII, April 11, 1994, p. 80.
The Washington Post Book World. XXIV, April 3, 1994, p. 1.

DR. JOHNSON AND MR. SAVAGE

Author: Richard Holmes (1945-)
First published: 1993, in England
Publisher: Pantheon Books (New York). 260 pp. $23.00
Type of work: Biography
Time: The eighteenth century
Locale: London, England

A riveting study of the biographical process, probing the relationship between Samuel Johnson and the poet Richard Savage, Johnson's friend and first biographical subject

Principal personages:
SAMUEL JOHNSON, an English poet, critic, and pioneer in the field of biography
RICHARD SAVAGE, a minor but notorious poet who claimed that he was the bastard of a noble lady who denied him his birthright
LADY MACCLESFIELD, Savage's putative mother, who never acknowledged him as her son
ALEXANDER POPE, the greatest poet of his age and a supporter of Savage
LORD TYRCONNEL, a relative of Lady Macclesfield who became Savage's patron but eventually disowned him
JAMES BOSWELL, Johnson's famous biographer

Richard Holmes, author of distinguished biographies of Percy Bysshe Shelley and Samuel Coleridge and of a study of the biographer's method (*Footsteps*), here continues his discussion of biography as a Romantic form. He believes that the rise of biography as both a popular and a serious genre in the eighteenth century heralded the advent of Romanticism, a literary movement that prized the truth to be plumbed in the self. The poet turned inward, abandoning the standards of the neoclassical age (which elevated reason as the measure of things), and sought truth through individual experience, priding himself on the use of his imagination and often challenging the norms and strictures of the status quo.

Holmes concedes that the august Samuel Johnson is a strange figure to put forward as a harbinger of Romanticism. Johnson, an opponent of the American Revolution, sympathetic to the Jacobite cause (aimed at restoring the Stuart family to the throne and disestablishing the new Hanoverian line), and a devoutly religious man, hardly seems the prototype of a Romantic writer. Yet Holmes shrewdly demolishes this historical effigy of Johnson, proving in the process the extraordinary value of biographical thinking.

Holmes shows that the conservative Dr. Johnson was largely the invention of his biographer, James Boswell. Thirty years younger than his subject, Boswell craved the guidance of an all-wise mentor. The erratic biographer, lacking in discipline, saw in Johnson a steadying father-figure and exaggerated those elements of Johnson's character that suited his own needs. Holmes shows that Boswell consistently muted Johnson's insecure feelings, disputing or ignoring sources that revealed Johnson's immaturity and sexual needs.

Holmes portrays Johnson as an ungainly, hulking figure, subject to fits of depression and violent outbreaks of emotion. He failed several times as a schoolmaster, often frightening his pupils with his temper and with a grotesque physical appearance caused by the scrofula he had suffered as a child. Sexually frustrated, he pursued a number of well-born ladies—his princesses, as Holmes calls them. Johnson did not come into his own as a man or achieve success as a literary figure until his middle age, after struggling for several years in London. This is the Johnson who emerges from Holmes's narrative—a passionate but uncertain man who only gradually learned to subdue his demons.

Holmes's insistence on this more vulnerable and unpredictable Dr. Johnson helps him to explain Johnson's fascination with the minor poet Richard Savage, who by all accounts acted the part of a scoundrel. Scholars have wondered for ages why Johnson's biography treats Savage so sympathetically. Savage violated virtually every edict of the Augustan society Johnson revered. He spent much of his time drinking and whoring, shamelessly bilking friends of money and then libeling them, breaking numerous oaths to reform his profligate life, and accepting monies for books he never wrote. He crowned his dissolute career with a conviction for murdering a man in a tavern brawl. Holmes contends that Johnson's affinity with Savage has been obscured by Boswell's paternal image of him. In Savage, Holmes alleges, Johnson saw his other unreliable half. As Holmes admits, the title of his book alludes to the title of another key text in Romanticism, *Dr. Jekyll and Mr. Hyde* (1886). Savage, in short, was Johnson's dark, uncontrollable double.

Holmes is persuasive because he is able to demonstrate not only how aspects of Savage appealed to Johnson but also how Johnson projected parts of himself into his subject. All biographers do this, Holmes claims, even if they never let on that they are doing so. His position is, in fact, a Romantic conceit; that is, he is following William Wordsworth's notion (presented in his Tintern Abbey ode) that the poet half-perceives and half-creates his world, that human perception is a transformative process in which the self remakes the world (nature) through its insights—the word "insight" suggesting how truth has become an inward experience.

Holmes carefully explores Johnson's first years in London and shows how he came to know Savage at precisely the moment Johnson was seeking to establish his literary voice. In their long walks through London streets, Savage indoctrinated Johnson into the lore of literary London and impressed upon him the powerful myth of the forlorn and isolated poet, doomed to walk alone because he had offended the higher powers of society by speaking his unbridled mind. Such talk appealed to the young, struggling Sam Johnson, who could well believe that the mesmerizing Savage was a kind of fallen literary angel.

Holmes is on strong ground in presenting this bond between Johnson and Savage, even though (as he readily admits) there is not a single scrap of evidence that describes the two men together. Johnson and Savage had mutual friends, yet no description of the two writers together has come to light. What Holmes relies on, instead, is Johnson's own championing of Savage and numerous accounts of Savage's charming influence on others. Even though Savage disappointed his friends time after time, many of them, including Alexander Pope, continued to support him financially and spoke up in his favor.

After establishing Johnson's need to believe in Savage as the fallen poet, taken up and then spurned by society, Holmes shifts attention to Savage, attempting to build up a picture of him independent of Johnson's words. Savage told a powerful story. He had been born in humble circumstances and reared by a nurse. Only in his teens did he discover papers that proved he was in fact the son of Lady Macclesfield. His numerous attempts to interest her in his fate proved futile, Savage alleged. Indeed, she positively persecuted him and contributed to his penurious plight.

Savage broadcast his misfortune in a long poem, *The Bastard* (1728), and benefited from a sympathetic press. Although he libeled Lady Macclesfield several times, she never brought suit against him; this led some, including Johnson, to conclude that Savage told the truth. Yet no evidence apart from Savage's charges has ever been produced to support his case. Although Savage said that he had documents establishing him as the son of Lady Macclesfield, and one of his editors said that he had seen them, no papers have survived to corroborate Savage's story.

Indeed, Holmes points out (following the lead of other scholars) that the evidence that does exist exonerates Lady Macclesfield. She did have two illegitimate children, but they died in childhood. She had a reputable character and was never shown to have acted unjustly in any instance—except for what Savage maintained. Her refusal to take legal action against Savage may have resulted from a reluctance to increase the publicity that Savage clearly sought; she may have rejected the idea of placating him with financial support. Indeed, Holmes concludes that Savage's constant campaign against her amounted to an effort to blackmail Lady Macclesfield into providing him with hush money—not to suppress the truth but simply to ensure that he no longer troubled her.

As Holmes points out, the case against Savage is strong. Lady Macclesfield's nephew Lord Tyrconnel did aid the poet, but Tyrconnel never admitted the justness of Savage's claims against his aunt. The record plainly shows that Tyrconnel liked Savage, wanted to help him, and may have wanted to ease the embarrassment of his aunt, to whom Tyrconnel was devoted. After repeated insults and betrayals, Tyrconnel abandoned Savage, who had a talent for alienating his supporters.

Johnson had to ignore much evidence in order to produce his sympathetic portrait of Savage. For example, he had to blind himself to any explanation for Lady Macclesfield's silence except the explanation that she was the guilty party. Holmes is critical of Johnson's eagerness to credit Savage's stories, but in fairness to Johnson, Holmes also notes that Savage never wavered in his story and may have come to believe it himself. His lifelong adherence to his role impressed many others, especially Pope, who believed in Savage's talent and realized that Savage was often his own worst enemy.

The other argument Holmes makes for Savage arises from the biographer's reading of his poetry. Although Savage does not qualify as a major poet, his work is surprisingly modern in its personal intensity, its yoking of nature and the self. Part of Savage's sincerity, so to speak, arose out of his work, which impressed his contemporaries as injecting a new immediacy and intimacy in poetry. Johnson himself quoted Savage's poetry extensively in his biography of Savage. Holmes notes that this integration of life and work constituted a new biographical device.

Holmes reaffirms what earlier scholars have realized, that Johnson's biography of Savage portrays a poetic truth that transcends his errors of fact and sloppy research. Johnson's noble Romantic vision of the self-destructive poet has a beauty and coherence that far outshines his putative subject. Savage, however, is entitled to his defense, Holmes concedes, because of the obvious, if minor, merit of his verse, and because he seems genuinely to have identified with his story, no matter how much of it may have been false.

Holmes himself does a bit to make his book more dramatic and original than it actually is. For one thing, he rather exaggerates the sway Boswell has exerted over Johnson scholars. It is true that for many years Boswell held the field in thrall. Yet for the last two generations of criticism, at least, Boswell's idealizing of Johnson has been subject to rigorous scrutiny. Although Holmes does include a bibliography acknowledging previous scholarship, his failure to deal with the best of that scholarship—even in his notes—seems ungenerous. Certainly his narrative would have been spoiled by discussion of the body of criticism on Johnson, but a separate appendix would surely not have detracted from his story.

Holmes, then, is perhaps infected by the Romanticism he studies. He inclines to delving in inferences and to a creation of atmosphere that is downright novelistic. Like Johnson, even like Savage, Holmes is persuasive because his tone is personal and eloquent, passionate and authoritative, sweeping the rest of the field out of sight, claiming an originality that obscures the data on which his case actually rests. Romantics are great questers; they like to work up a great air of anticipation and revelation. By this measure, Holmes does not disappoint. He has written a provocative and even thrilling book.

Carl Rollyson

Sources for Further Study

Commonweal. CXXI, November 4, 1994, p. 32.
London Review of Books. November 4, 1993, p. 7.
Los Angeles Times Book Review. August 28, 1994, p. 3.
New Statesman and Society. VI, October 22, 1993, p. 37.
The New York Times Book Review. XCIX, September 4, 1994, p. 14.
The Times Literary Supplement. October 29, 1993, p. 11.
The Wall Street Journal. August 25, 1994, p. A10.
The Washington Post Book World. XXIV, September 4, 1994, p. 3.

DOLLY

Author: Anita Brookner (1938-)
Publisher: Random House (New York). 260 pp. $22.00
Type of work: Novel
Time: The 1930's to the 1990's
Locale: Primarily London

Ostensibly the story of the title character, this novel is also an intimate portrait of a family and the responsibilities that kin entails

Principal characters:

JANE MANNING, the narrator and legatee of the family burden
PAUL MANNING, her father, whose devotion to his wife is absolute
HENRIETTA MANNING, her mother, a true innocent who is capable of dying from pining for her lost companion
DOLLY, an opportunistic chameleon and a survivor
VIOLET LAWLOR, the Mannings' friend and housekeeper

Were one not cognizant of the fact already, one could divine from clues on the first page that Anita Brookner is a historian of art. She talks of "appropriation" and presence versus absence, two of the pet concepts of academic theorists in that discipline. She even has her narrator wander through the National Gallery and the Wallace Collection to find solace from the restlessness and insecurity that plague her as her world begins to fall apart. In the lovely but stagnant world of pictures she finds a sharp contrast to the inescapable realities of change and ugliness outside the galleries' walls.

Jane Manning narrates this quietly elegant reminiscence of her family. Aside from the fact that her mother, Henrietta, has inherited money, her parents are not extraordinary people. Paul, her father, works hard and devotes himself to his wife and daughter. In fact, what is perhaps most unusual about the Mannings is the absolute devotion of husband to wife and vice versa. Theirs is a staid existence: mother, father, daughter, housekeeper in a large but relatively modest apartment in one of London's unchic neighborhoods, "the middle of nowhere," as the title character uncharitably remarks on one of her rare visits. Jane's mother is content with her social isolation, happy to have found the love that she missed in her childhood. Paul enjoys his life of quiet, homey pleasures: reading with his wife, long walks, and slow meals.

Jane, who gains wisdom—probably from her reading—out of all proportion to her age, recognizes even as a child that her mild-mannered, thoroughly conventional parents are true innocents, unprepared for realities that are certain to intrude on their blissful communion. Jane knows that they will be hurt, and she wants more than anything else to protect them in their perfect union, one from which she knows that even she is excluded. "They were a placid reticent couple, and as time went by they spoke less and less, conferring with each other almost by osmosis, a process which was successful, since they rarely disagreed," Jane explains in order to illustrate the completeness of her parents' lives. Paul and Henrietta are

> like pale creatures newly liberated from engulfing darkness, slender pillars of English virtue advancing, hand in hand, towards the light of common day. Having effectively divorced themselves from home and family, they felt free to invent their lives, as if they were characters in Dickens. This meant doing the opposite of what they had been brought up to do, living lives of the utmost orderliness and decorum.

Jane calls her love for her parents "painful," precisely because she is a little impatient with their self-imposed otherworldliness, and she knows that their conscientious adherence to a regulated ordinariness ill-equips their daughter for the obtrusive realities of a society that is arbitrary, chaotic, and harsh in its demands.

She deduces, however, that in their oblivious avoidance of anything disruptive to their measured lives they, at least, are perfectly happy. They never seem to desire anything that they do not already have. In such mutual, exclusive dependence, the adolescent Jane foresees disaster. When Paul's mother dies, he is subdued until Henrietta points out, "Death is arbitrary, after all. No one is safe." Indeed, Jane's parents do resemble "Adam and Eve before the Fall." Consequently, Henrietta cannot adjust to a life without Paul after he succumbs to cancer. Not too long after her husband's death, Henrietta wastes away and dies, leaving her daughter with a substantial estate and one unexpectedly heavy obligation, her aunt Dolly, who makes it abundantly clear that she expects little from her niece in the way of family devotion but a considerable amount from her in the way of financial support.

Brookner devotes large sections of the novel to characterizations, and her portrait of her title character is masterful. Dolly is at once charming and irritating, self-absorbed and bullying. In sharp contrast to Jane's mother, she is a vibrant, forceful personality, one who expects and demands much from life, and she is relentless and single-minded in her ambition to get all she can from the situations into which circumstance throws her. As a child, Jane found her repugnant, objectifying her as "the" aunt, "for anything more intimate would have implied appropriation, or attachment." Jane remarks often on Dolly's ardor, finding evidence of her passionate nature in the details of her physical person. Dolly's hands are beautiful and predatory, and at one point, Jane imagines on her face "a plea for every kind of fulfillment." Yet on one of Dolly's visits to Jane's home, Jane notices Dolly's "carnivorous" teeth, anxious to bite into a more exciting life than the Mannings' staid tea party offers.

Although she is repulsed by Dolly's avaricious demands and ungenerous nature, Jane is also fascinated by this alarming and alluring creature who drifts in and out of her life. She "knows" Dolly before she really learns her history, and Brookner's frequent rehashings of Dolly's character are validations of impressions that the child Jane had already made. As Jane matures, she begins to understand—through further association with Dolly and greater knowledge of the personal history that has made her a somewhat desperate, lonely old woman—how experiences that her insulated existence did not allow could shape another woman's personality and manner of dealing with life. Brookner's narrator becomes more adept at psychological interpretations that, in the end, prove what the child had already read in the face, the hands, and the body of her aunt.

Dolly grew up in France, where her mother worked as a seamstress for the streetwalkers of the Rue St. Denis. Just as France was liberated after World War II, so too Dolly was freed from her virginal questioning of the world's ways by the American soldiers who occupied Paris. She was but sixteen and was set on a course from which she would not deviate through her long life. Men would be the means by which Dolly would get what she wanted, whether love, money, or position. American soldiers, however, usually had wives or girlfriends at home, and because Dolly and her mother had consorted with whores and collaborators during the war, they soon found it necessary to leave France for England. There, Dolly "landed" Hugo Manning; soon she moved with him to Belgium. Soon after Jane's childhood visit to Belgium, Hugo died and Dolly made her way back to London, where she exacted a monthly allowance from her mother-in-law, and after her death, from Henrietta.

When her mother dies, Jane assumes the responsibility of Dolly's allowance, a stipend that keeps her in a style that she wants to improve through marriage to a somewhat coarse suitor. Dolly's life is a round of bridge parties and weekend vacations, but she is far from idle. She is always grasping for something new, some way to better her condition, to keep from being bored. The one solution for a woman of her background is marriage, so she embarks on a pathetic courtship of the owner of a limousine service, whom she perceives as her last chance for happiness. Thoroughly self-centered, she manipulates Jane into the intrigue to wed this man; yet in her single-mindedness she estranges Jane, who is again revolted by her aunt's ruthless behavior.

Dolly is the one constant in Jane's life. Not always present even when Jane is in most need of family counsel or affection, Dolly is never really absent. The monthly remittance is the best reminder of her continued intrusion into Jane's attempts to fashion a life of her own. It is just as well that Jane has no expectations of her aunt's help in dealing with adult decisions:

> I never, during the years of my adolescence and young womanhood, managed to impose my presence on Dolly. I was the equivalent of those donor figures in religious paintings who look clumsy and out of place and whose presence seems barely justified, beside the saints and the madonna, except for the consideration of spot cash.

Jane's lonely wanderings in the great galleries of London once again provide her with an analogy, though an ironic one, for her all-too-human condition as the worldly support for a decidedly unsaintlike character who nevertheless lives on the assumption—the faith even—that she is worthy of adulation in the form of "spot cash."

Slowly, after the death of her parents, Jane begins to make her own way. Even though she is financially secure, well-off even, she works in a clipping service, goes on to university, and eventually becomes a best-selling author of children's books and a lecturer on the feminist circuit. Throughout her own rather timid odyssey, she has before her the example of her aunt. Where Jane sees the world as indifferent, Dolly finds it either challenging or hostile and reacts accordingly. Jane slowly becomes self-sufficient while Dolly, who has always been independent, pines for dependence, for marriage to Harry Dean and the glamour of his limousine-for-hire business.

Thwarted in that hope, and deluded as well, Dolly for once needs Jane, who observes almost sadly that her aunt finally becomes one of those faded English widows who have resigned themselves to cloth coats though once they had wanted mink. With her indecorous pursuit of Harry Dean, Dolly

> had perhaps overlooked or even buried that longing, that desire for fulfilment, for obedience, for a man's protection, archaic female longings which will not be banished, but which survive long after compromises have been reached and reality acknowledged.

Jane knows that she, too, has such longings, even though she has been successful in carving a niche for herself in a society that has yet to find a satisfactory place for the independent female. Ruefully, she remarks,

> Many a woman knows that on the level of her most basic imaginings she has not been satisfied; hence the look of cheerful forbearance which is the most recognisable expression on the face of the average woman, whereas if questioned she would confess to a certain mystification. Why must it be like this? A more romantic way would have been so much better.

Finally, then, Jane understands her aunt's courageous if vulgar admonitions to "dance," to seek glamour and excitement and to use whatever wiles she has to find security in a world unfriendly to lonely women. Dolly's one constant demand, even more than her thirst for money, has been for love. When she is finally denied it by Harry Dean and realizes the unlikelihood of having it at her age from any man, she acquires dignity. Jane sees Dolly's acquiescence to a quieter life among similarly aged women as the final chapter in her aunt's self-fulfillment. Formerly a stranger in the midst of her family, Dolly now becomes Jane's touchstone, a means by which she manages self-realization in her own fumbling attempts to make a room of her own.

Dolly is Brookner's thirteenth novel, and it is, like the others, a sophisticated study of twentieth century manners. Brookner has been compared to Jane Austen and Henry James, but it is probably in the works of Elizabeth Bowen that one finds a better comparison to Brookner's quiet, rather rarefied novels. Just as Bowen eschewed elaborate, action-laden plot for character dissection, Brookner finds real drama in the tensions of human relationships. As in her previous work *Fraud* (1993), family in *Dolly* is the structure in which she explores how the connections between people define identity. Brookner's truths are in no way small ones, even though her characters are rarely heroes in the traditional sense of the word. In the interplay between Jane Manning and Dolly, Brookner develops real suspense and passion, even though she is often accused of a dry detachment that renders her characters bloodless. As usual, her prose is elegant and spare, subtle yet piercing in her observations of the human condition. Dialogue is confined to a few well-chosen situations where it is necessary to advance the limited action. Brookner much prefers to describe and to explain through her narrator, and in so doing, she makes of Jane Manning less an omniscient observer than a real participant in the narration. It is in Jane's constant explications of

Dolly's motives and ambitions that readers learn most about Jane herself.

Jane is essentially a character whose own shy venturings are not likely to be understood. She has money, she is far from plain, and she is articulate and intelligent. Why is she so hesitant to make her way? Why is she so quick to absolve her aunt, who has willfully trespassed on her emotions? Dolly is so greedy and overbearing that Jane's reticence to cut her off is mystifying until it becomes clear that in the plight of these two individual women, whose lives are so intertwined, Brookner herself grapples with the *fin-de-siècle* roles of women in general.

William U. Eiland

Sources for Further Study

The Antioch Review. LII, Summer, 1994, p. 538.
Booklist. XC, October 15, 1993, p. 395.
Chicago Tribune. February 13, 1994, XIV, p. 6.
The Christian Science Monitor. February 22, 1994, p. 11.
Los Angeles Times Book Review. February 13, 1994, p. 10.
The New York Times Book Review. XCIX, February 20, 1994, p. 12.
The New Yorker. LXX, April 11, 1994, p. 99.
Publishers Weekly. CCXL, November 22, 1993, p. 50.
The Washington Post Book World. XXIV, January 9, 1994, p. 3.
The Women's Review of Books. XI, June, 1994, p. 23.

DOUBLE LIVES
Spies and Writers in the Secret Soviet War of Ideas Against the West

Author: Stephen Koch
Publisher: Free Press (New York). 419 pp. $24.95
Type of work: History
Time: 1933-1940
Locale: Germany, the Soviet Union, the United States, and Great Britain

An important, controversial investigation of the role that Soviet agents and their collaborators played in shaping public opinion in the West and in undermining Western political institutions

Principal personages:
WILLI MÜNZENBERG, a German Communist living in Paris who directed the subversive activities of Soviet agents and collaborators in the West
BABETTE GROSS, his widow, and one of Koch's primary sources
OTTO KATZ, his most important agent in the West
NOEL FIELD, an American Stalinist with links to the Soviet apparatus (system of spies and agents)
ANTHONY BLUNT, a member of the group of the "Cambridge spies" who conveyed the British government's secrets to the Soviet Union
ANDRÉ GIDE, the great French writer, at first a supporter of Stalinism and then its opponent

Double Lives: Spies and Writers in the Secret Soviet War of Ideas Against the West is one of a slew of books reviewing the significance of the Cold War in the wake of the Soviet Union's disintegration. What did the competition between the Soviet Union and the United States really mean? What were Soviet intentions? These questions have been asked since the Cold War's beginnings in the late 1940's. Indeed, similar questions have been asked ever since the 1917 Russian Revolution, when the Bolsheviks seized power and V. I. Lenin proclaimed the goal of world revolution. Yet historians have been hindered in studying Soviet strategy for several reasons. The Soviet Union was a closed society. No Western historian was permitted to examine Soviet archives or to interview Soviet officials (though some information leaked out through espionage). Soviet agents and their Western collaborators kept silent or denied their activities. Although some of them repudiated Stalinism and gave Western governments valuable information, it was difficult to verify their claims or to be certain that they were not double agents still working for the Soviet Union. Only after Soviet archives began to be opened and old Stalinists started talking more freely could students of the Cold War such as Stephen Koch begin to unravel the extent of what he calls the "Soviet war of ideas against the West."

Koch focuses on the period between 1933 and 1940, the years encompassing the advent of the Nazi regime in Germany, the Spanish Civil War, and the beginning of World War II. He makes frequent reference to the decades before and after this seven-year epoch, but he believes that Adolf Hitler's hegemony and Joseph Stalin's consolidation of authority through the purge trials of the mid-1930's are the proper frame for understanding Soviet treatment of the West.

The relationship between Hitler and Stalin has been fundamentally misunderstood, Koch argues. Until 1939, when Stalin and Hitler formed a nonaggression pact, many Western liberals believed that the Soviet Union was the major anti-Fascist force. Stalin had supported the government of the Spanish Republic against the attack of the Fascists, headed by Francisco Franco and supported by Hitler and Benito Mussolini. In what was known as the Popular Front, Stalinists made common cause with Western liberals in opposing Fascism. From his earliest days, Hitler had expressed his enmity toward Communists, suppressing the German Communist Party and putting on trial in Leipzig Communists whom he accused of setting fire to the Reichstag (the German Parliament). It is true that many liberals repudiated the Stalinists when they supported the nonaggression pact, but even then liberals were somewhat mollified by the argument that Stalin had been constrained to deal with Hitler because the pusillanimous West had failed to defeat Fascism in Spain. The Fascist victory there was regarded by virtually all parties as a prelude to a world war, which might have been prevented if the West had moved quickly against Hitler and Mussolini.

Koch argues that this Western liberal view of Stalinism (widespread but certainly not universal) is itself evidence of Stalinism's triumph in the war of ideas. He makes the following revisionist argument: Hitler and Stalin actually needed each other and abetted each other's tyrannical schemes under the cover of fierce propaganda battles against each other. This collusion of dictators began with the Leipzig trial. Although Hitler blamed the fire on the Communists, they were exonerated at the trial. Why? Koch asks. He does not really know, but he hypothesizes that at this early stage (1933) Hitler used the trial to discredit not the ostensible culprits—the Communists—but his own private army, the Sturm Abteilung (SA). Communist propaganda had blamed the SA for the fire, arguing that the SA constituted a menace not only to Germany but indeed to Europe itself, because the SA functioned as a gangster organization that threatened to supplant the traditional German army. Hitler himself had come to view the SA and its leader, Ernst Rohm, as a threat to his power, but in order to disguise his preparations for an attack on Rohm and the SA, Hitler allowed the Communists to set up the SA for the kill, so to speak. Stalin, who admired Hitler's ruthlessness, connived with him because Stalin did not want a strong German Communist party. He wanted weak parties, or weak governments (as in Spain), that he could exploit and easily bend to his will.

Koch goes on to argue that Stalin never really meant to oppose Hitler, that from 1933 until the nonaggression pact in 1939 he was angling for an agreement with Hitler. Stalin wanted Hitler to weaken, if not defeat, the Western governments that had been hostile to Communism, and thus to deflect Hitler from attacking the Soviet Union. The Popular Front, then, was an elaborate ruse, fomented by Stalin's agents—chiefly Willi Münzenberg and his colleague Otto Katz, who suavely preyed upon Western liberal opinion, establishing "fronts," various organizations that promulgated anti-

Fascism but also the Stalinist line, portraying the Soviet Union and Stalin himself as the bulwark of social democratic revolutions. At the same time, Stalin used these fronts to shield himself during the purge-trial period, when he liquidated all the old Bolsheviks and the officer corps of the Red Army so that there was virtually no one who could oppose him when he publicly committed himself to the pact with Hitler.

Koch does not deny that many Communists in the Popular Front were genuinely anti-Fascist; rather, he points out that as soon as the Popular Front was no longer needed, Stalin jettisoned it, making even his closest collaborators such as Münzenberg adopt a new political line or exterminating them. Münzenberg himself died in 1940—either a suicide or a victim of Soviet agents. Koch inclines to the belief that Münzenberg was murdered.

Koch presents a powerful but significantly flawed argument. Much of it is based on inference. His text is strewn with phrases such as "almost certainly" and "probable to a very high degree." This imprecise and often self-defeating verbiage means no more than he does not know, that he is speculating—a fact he acknowledges more often in his notes at the back of the book than in his text. He writes of history as a scenario; he presents persuasive scripts but not authenticated history. He may be right, but he has not presented a conclusive case.

Take his discussion of the Leipzig trial. He amply shows that in the eyes of Europe the SA was already discredited. Did Hitler really need a show trial before he committed himself to what has been called "the Night of the Long Knives," when he slaughtered Rohm and all the SA leaders? *Double Lives* reads too often like a film plot. Thus Münzenberg becomes the ace plotter, an incredible mastermind of an international apparatus that never seems to make a mistake. He is thwarted only when the likes of André Gide, the great French novelist, tours the Soviet Union and repudiates his former Stalinism. Otherwise, Münzenberg never missteps until Stalin decides that he must be liquidated; his life must end with the demise of the Popular Front. He has served his master's purpose.

Koch makes much of his interviews with Münzenberg's widow, the late Babette Gross. He does not take her word at face value, but he seems to regard her as a credible witness without saying why. She is quoted in the text, but she herself never comes alive as a character in the narrative. How reliable was her memory? How did Koch verify her information? Perhaps he quotes her only when he has other corroborating testimony, but this is not clear from his text or notes. In other words, she is heard from only when Koch finds her a convenient authority. Why he finds her so persuasive is not established.

Too often the style of the book does a disservice to its important argument. Koch, chairman of the Writing Division of the School of the Arts at Columbia University, resorts to clichés ("cooling his heels"), awkward phrases ("he had and wore a conspiratorial air"), and portentous, vulgarly melodramatic expressions: "Nemesis the goddess is fierce. Fierce—and ingenious." The crudeness of the style is not merely an unfortunate secondary feature; on the contrary, it undermines Koch's credibility. For example:

> One quite reliable report to the American State Department of 1940 asserts that Otto Katz had acted as a "go-between" for Bredow [a German intelligence agent] and the Soviets. This may or may not have been true: It *is*, however, a perfect fit for our available information.

This is a baffling passage. What has Koch demonstrated? What seems "quite reliable"—notice the use of "quite," a part of Koch's tendency to overplay his case—is smothered in speculation. What does it mean to have a "perfect fit for our available information"? Only that Koch has made a surmise or scenario that conforms to his thesis but does not prove it. Koch seems vaguely aware that his language runs him into problems, for his notes are usually far more scrupulous, but in the text he cannot resist reaching for emphatic language to bolster a tenuous point.

Nevertheless, Koch raises, page by page, provocative questions. He is right, for example, to probe the strange career of Noel Field and to suggest that he may have been far more connected to the Soviet apparatus than his seemingly meek demeanor has suggested to other researchers. Similarly, the duplicity of Anthony Blunt, a part of the Kim Philby-Guy Burgess-Donald Maclean group of Cambridge spies, receives a searching, astute analysis.

Most important, Koch demonstrates how widespread the Soviet apparatus became in the 1930's, simultaneously infiltrating the Spanish Republican government and the government bureaucracy in Washington, D.C. He shows how many literary figures, such as the novelist Josephine Herbst, were witting members of a Soviet conspiracy to use liberals and fellow travelers to condone Stalin's policies and to portray Western governments as decadent and weak. Koch's chapter on Spain at the end of the book makes the point most effectively. On the one hand, Stalin sent some military supplies to Spain—enough to make it seem as though he were supporting the Republican government when the West would not. On the other hand, he never supplied enough equipment to ensure a Republican victory. Indeed, he refused to extend the Republican government any credit, and his agents successfully smuggled the country's gold reserve to the Soviet Union, ostensibly for safekeeping, though it was not returned. Stalin's agents also systematically murdered anarchists and other leftists in Spain in order to ensure Stalinist dominance. Many Communists genuinely fought for the freedom of Republican Spain, but as Koch shows, their valiant effort had nothing whatsoever to do with Stalin's ultimate goals.

Although Koch does not prove active collusion between Hitler and Stalin, there is no question that he has opened up a fruitful line of inquiry. Other historians such as Alan Bullock in *Hitler and Stalin: Parallel Lives* (1992) have demonstrated that for all their differences in style and ideology, Fascism and Stalinism do share a fundamental resemblance as forms of twentieth century tyranny. Koch rightly suggests that his book is only the beginning. As Soviet archives are opened, much more will be learned about the origins of the Cold War, which consisted on the Soviet side as an attempt to soften up Western opinion for the Soviet interpretation of world affairs.

Carl Rollyson

Sources for Further Study

Commentary. XCVII, January, 1994, p. 65.
Journal of Military History. LVIII, July, 1994, p. 566.
The Nation. CCLVIII, May 30, 1994, p. 752.
National Review. XLVI, February 21, 1994, p. 56.
The New Leader. LXXVI, December 27, 1993, p. 14.
The New Republic. CCX, May 30, 1994, p. 37.
The New York Times Book Review. XCIX, January 23, 1994, p. 3.
Publishers Weekly. CCXL, December 13, 1993, p. 56.
The Wall Street Journal. January 17, 1994, p. A7.
The Washington Post Book World. XXIV, February 6, 1994, p. 8.

EACH IN A PLACE APART

Author: James McMichael (1939-)
Publisher: University of Chicago Press (Chicago). 63 pp. $20.00; paperback $9.95
Type of work: Poetry

The seamlessly gorgeous design of Each in a Place Apart *fills readers with the same kind of wonder as the balance and complex symmetry of higher math when we are shown its possibilities, making the long wait for new poetry from James McMichael well worth it*

Those who have been fortunate enough to have had James McMichael as a teacher have been told that in the free verse of contemporary poetry, the poet must invent the musical cadence with which his or her meaning is played. This, McMichael might say, makes it harder than writing in predetermined forms. This, he might also say, puts the responsibility on individual poets to create those cadences with their syntax and lines so their readers hear the music they intend when they write. Within such a framework, so much depends on tone, on the ear with which people hear the poetry they read. McMichael would say that is the poet's responsibility, that his line should create that tone, down to the slightest nuance of emphasis. Even the title of this book, *Each in a Place Apart*, is a terse syntactical and tonal puzzle, an encapsulation that is both intricate and precise, indicating that other people's experience of what we share with them is almost always outside of our own, and although we think it is otherwise, we are always surprised to realize our misinterpretation and subsequent emotional isolation.

As Frank Bidart writes in a blurb on the back cover, the book is a long poem, "a narrative about the genesis and dissolution of [McMichael's] second marriage." While there is all the tension of plot and situation that create a good narrative in a psychological style that, if it were a novel, could be equated with the scope and brilliant focus of someone like Henry James or James Joyce or John Fowles, the pieces of this narrative are not chapters, but single poems in the best vein of what free verse can offer. At the same time, they spring one from the other as a single story line, instead of being juxtaposed against one another, as in a collection of separate, more strictly lyric poems. They are lyric in the best and most fundamental sense of that term: they focus on feeling and encapsulate particular moment, using memory as a vehicle for a personal voice that is, contrary to Bidart's observation, confessional: It confesses "we read each other wrong"; "we made mistakes we did not know we were making." Such confessions are ones most readers live with as well, and so they do not impose intimacy with the poet's voice, but rather invite it.

The first of five sections in this narrative forms a personal family history that powerfully sets up the emotional landscape of the poems that follow. Since each poem in the collection arises out of the one that precedes it, reading the first poem closely and artfully is the key to unpacking meaning in the rest of the poems. By doing so, readers will have a guide to proceed through the longer and more complex poems that build on such a foundation. McMichael gives his readers cues, stitched seamlessly into the poem itself, that direct their reading of the emotional disposition so important to the narrative unfolding in each of the following poems. As readers follow the enjambment from the end of the second into the third line, they get an unmistakable cue about how important syntax is to interpretation. The sentence reads, "It meant/ I'd wear as a bandolier over my white T-shirt a red cotton sash." Informationally, this is a detail that fleshes out the importance of getting enough votes to be squad leader, facts that are given in the first two lines in simple declarative structures, made almost offhand by the contraction in "I'd gotten enough votes." Readers settle into this clarity almost instantly. It gives the air of trust needed to believe the speaker. By the third line, however, the syntax has turned a sharp curve. If the third sentence were written in the same declarative voice in which the first two sentences are written, it would read, "It meant I'd wear a red cotton sash as a bandolier over my white T-shirt." Why not keep the simple declarative statements of the speaker's boyhood memory? What "boy" would twist his syntax to read in such a way? This is McMichael's way of reminding readers that this is no boy speaking these lines, but a man looking back and resting on the detail of the red cotton sash by having it come last to emphasize that these statements arise out of a reverie remembered subjectively.

In terms of structure, twisting the syntax in that way is characteristic of how McMichael transforms sentences into lines. Without that twist, readers would not experience the enjambment that "snaps" the red cotton sash back against the seamlessly elastic "I'd wear as a bandolier over my white T-shirt." Moreover, readers need it so much as a piece of grammatical and factual information by the time they get to it, that they almost do not notice it is also quite powerful as an image of emotional confidence that gets transformed into shocked vulnerability at the "bottom" of the poem. This is what McMichael does most often with such images. Instead of showcasing them, he nearly hides them, so that like shadows and sunlight, structure of syntax becomes structure of line, and point of information becomes resonating image.

This oblique approach is comprehensive and essential to grasping the book's emotional center. Very clearly, this first poem is about the shattering news of his mother's death, made more shattering by the way in which it is revealed. Yet the title "mother" is never used. She is referred to simply as "she." Her absence is made more powerful and acute by this grammatical intimacy. The father and son share this "she"—in fact their closeness to each other seems almost entirely predicated on the presence of this "she" in their lives. Yet their understanding of what constitutes "better" for her is diametrically opposed. The shocked dislocation for the speaker that becomes a fundamental tenet of loving occurs when a single phrase, "she's better," is interpreted as differently as is possible in such a situation. The son hears it to mean: She must be recovering—maybe she will be coming home soon. The father means by saying it: She is dead, and that means she does not have to suffer anymore. The father understands something as "better" that is the worst possible scenario for the boy, even as he discovers his understanding of "she's better" is "wrong." The only possible comfort here is physical—at least he can sit on his father's lap while realizing he has misunderstood in the most blaring way imaginable. Such a jarring disjunction between the physical need for comfort and love and the emotional interpretation of words and the motivation behind them is the "square root" of the book.

Yet the poetry's algebra of emotion is not as simplistic as merely multiplying despair or disconnectedness in exponential ripples. There is a trigonometric relation between poems, a y-axis and an x-axis creating a single graph or function. One of the best examples of such inverse motion is the poem that begins "Three years not so much of squabbles as of routine." Although it comes close to the end of the narrative, it begins in the same declarative way as the very first poem and is, as such, even more transparent. The first six lines of this poem are entirely uncomplicated syntax, a tactic sustained for twice as long as the opening poem. The syntax does not actually turn its characteristic twist until the ninth line, when the news about the death of the speaker's father is delivered. In this dialectical opposite to the first poem, the "her" (rather than the "she") is Linda, the speaker's second wife, who does give comfort in words, does, for that instant, provide connection in what he beautifully articulates as "the fathomless spare nurturing/ 'O Jimmie'/ which I still hear in anything she says." While there simply is not a more stark contrast to "She *is* better. This is better," in the whole book, it is also, in a subtle way, its inverse companion. The "still" in the last line of the later poem lets us know this deliberate comforting on Linda's part is a thing of the past, something he still hears in whatever she is saying, in contrast to the immediacy of the memory described in the first poem. So while this poem differs in that it tells us comforting words are possible, it also reinforces disjunction by subtly reminding us, again through grammar and syntax, that the speaker is making his separate (and perhaps idiosyncratic) connection to these comforting words by merely hearing the sound of Linda's voice, even if she has not actually spoken such words for years.

This poem falls in the fifth and last section of the book, which is characterized by even more parched, jagged, syntactic structures, as in the poems that begin "I want her sense of me to be wrong" and "She likes to be out." Yet these poems, and the one that precedes them that begins, "As he often does when Linda holds him," share a water-rich language ("languidly," "fathomless") that balances and deepens the outcome of the book, and roots the disjunction so fundamental to understanding the poems in the swamps of familial history rather than in strictly marital dynamics, which are themselves formed by such history. The baby's finger game is described "languidly" and then more overtly when readers are told, "If he could make my fingers fit him as her water,/ if my fingers were her water, it would always have been/ his doing to have left it there, to have taken it away." Here, the emotional will with which humans substitute one reality for another is seen through a sleepy, mesmerizing, almost whimsical film, with the father granting the son the right to create such a world for himself. There is perhaps no more generous move made in any of the poems.

The other water word used to describe the phrase "O Jimmie" is "fathomless," obliquely recalling the image of the illusive trout in the high lake near the Inconsolable Mountains, and contrasting with the speaker's youthful but hypothetical assurance he knew exactly where they were:

> It was easy for me to translate into any equal
> volume of water the air inside the tall green
> handball court walls. Each was somewhere in a given cube.
> The water touched their noses, it touched their sides. Hungry,
> beautiful, and secret, they held to the beryl half-light,
> the sunken boulders opaline and faint.

This beautifully mysterious description of tracking the trout hidden somewhere inside the lake by imagining them inside using reference points from another setting relays poignantly how humans try to measure with what they know in their bodies, the truths of the heart they cannot ever completely "fathom."

As in the trout poem just quoted, the whole narrative provides readers with a rich terrain of settings and atmospheres, both hypothetical and actual, which form a rich backdrop to the narrative of the love affair and marriage. With the couple, readers travel to and feel the mood evoked by beachside apartments of Southern California, remote mountains in Idaho, a village in Switzerland, the English countryside, the bedroom in a small apartment in the middle of the night, or the medicine chest and its mirror in a suburban bathroom. In every case, these places are described in achingly beautiful and often intimate terms, as in the following excerpt, which takes place in Laguna Beach, California:

> I meet her at the Tic-Toc Market. My apartment's
> little more than the bed, and we can't wait.
> Safe-harbored, whispering, with always more to tell,
> we stay put, the dark catching up with us each week
> until it's there in our first hour. From upstairs,
> the muffled after-dinner clatter. Somebody's phone.

Later on, nearly dead-center in the narrative, is the only poem in which readers are taken completely into another situation, that of a hypothetical English couple living in another time-frame, whose story is meant to comment on the circumstances of the speaker and his second wife. Readers learn, by way of an explanation as oblique as the syntactical puzzle it is wrapped in, that "For as many/ hours as all its parts are by themselves,/ setting is the chance that something good might happen./ It's entire for that time, no person's there to see as/ different and overt the single gateposts, single/ free and leasehold fields."

The most detailed descriptions of setting are also the most abstract. They are hypothetical, like the souls "unconsulted" and "wet" outside of birth, or, as the speaker confesses, the environment of "the man [he] saw this week [he] fear[s] she'd like." Yet from the emotions evoked or at least implied by the spinning of such hypothetical scenes, the speaker decides to leave his wife.

An intricate image of water in the hypothetical landscapes just mentioned as "tight channeled in the iris rills, then underground" provides a bridge of metaphor connecting the couple's reunion and lovemaking with what might have been but was not in the lives of the hypothetical coupe. Thus, by a rare juxtaposition, readers are shown that sexual desire left unconsummated, wrongly discovered, and consequently denied is not their fate, is poignantly and acutely not the reason they could not stay together. This dense but brilliant axis in the middle of the narrative puts readers on the painful road to the end of the book, at which the speaker is, for all practical purposes, divorced, standing at the door to what was once his house, waiting to pick up his son. As he is remembering "the most forgettable of their outings [as a married couple]," he comes to this realization, which burns a trail back to the sparks flared in the first poem: "I wasn't thinking, at the time, how I/ fit into what she cared about: she fit for me. It comes/ back to me now because I have to change it, I'd/ gotten it wrong." Such a confession marks the clarity of tone that makes every line in this book worth savoring.

Perhaps more than any other poet writing, McMichael teaches readers what free verse has to offer, and what it must do to be essentially "free." It cannot apologize for itself, hanging limply line by line, relying on the ghost music of predetermined meter. Instead it must notate the individual music of the poet's voice with an excellence that compels the singularity of that voice to be heard and understood as itself by those who read it. The clear and fathomless quality of *Each in a Place Apart* allows each reader to find an undiscovered depth—both in terms of how it fits together as a single narrative as well as in the lyric immediacy of each poem.

Maria Theresa Maggi

Source for Further Study

Publishers Weekly. CCXLI, March 28, 1994, p. 91.

E. M. FORSTER
A Biography

Author: Nicola Beauman (1944-)
First published: Morgan: A Biography of E. M. Forster, 1993, in Great Britain
Publisher: Alfred A. Knopf (New York). 404 pp. $30.00
Type of work: Literary biography
Time: 1879-1970
Locale: England, Italy, Greece, and India

An impeccable, sensitive biography, concentrating on E. M. Forster's early years of great productivity as a novelist and making a credible case for his greatness

Principal personages:
E. M. FORSTER, a British novelist
LILY FORSTER, his mother
EDDIE FORSTER, his father
MARIANNE THORNTON, his formidable grandaunt
G. M. TREVELYAN, one of his Cambridge friends
CONSTANTINE CAVAFY, the great Greek poet, who became his friend in Alexandria
SYED ROSS MASOOD, an Indian friend who first suggested that he write a novel about India
MOHAMMED EL ADL, his lover in Alexandria
BOB BUCKINGHAM, Forster's most enduring love

E. M. Forster has enjoyed both a high reputation and popularity as a novelist. Several of his novels have been filmed—most notably *A Room with a View* (1908; film, 1986) and *Howards End* (1910; film, 1992). His first novel, *Where Angels Fear to Tread*, was published in 1905, and his last, *A Passage to India*, in 1924. Thereafter he published no fiction, although he lived another forty-six years. Why he should have experienced a twenty-year burst of creativity and then lapsed into silence cannot be entirely explained, but Nicola Beauman makes a superb effort, as well as demonstrating how complete Forster's career as a novelist actually was and why, even though he stopped producing fiction in middle age, he continues to be read and revered as a great writer.

Beauman begins her biography by showing how the themes and characteristic attitudes of Forster's life and work were grounded in his family background. His father, Edward Morgan, familiarly known as Eddie, was descended from Henry Thornton, a prominent member of the Clapham Sect, an influential group of evangelical and antislavery philanthropists. Forster, or Morgan—as Beauman calls him throughout her biography—felt his great-grandfather's influence largely through his grandaunt Marianne Thornton, known in the family as "Aunt Monie." Through her, Morgan inherited not only a fortune but also a powerful sense of society's conventions, of what was proper and what was not. He found her attitudes stultifying. She tried to interfere with his mother's upbringing of him and became even more of a menacing presence when Eddie Forster died, leaving his wife Lily to care for their four-year-old son. Yet

Morgan also respected his grandaunt and the strictures that bound society together. He even wrote his grandaunt's biography. He believed in change, but he preferred it to be gentle and gradual—liberal, not radical.

Morgan's ambivalent attitude toward his Thornton inheritance was greatly influenced by his mother, Lily. She had been a governess, and the Thorntons believed that their Eddie had married beneath himself. Lily never forgave or forgot this Thornton attitude, though in time the Thorntons accepted her—or perhaps decided that she would do. That she was initially made to feel unworthy, however, was communicated to her son, who became especially sensitive to class issues. Beauman explains that Morgan never felt comfortable with his wealth, never lived as a wealthy person, and in later life, when he finally was able to express his homosexuality, inclined toward working-class lovers.

Beauman does a considerable amount of educated guessing about Morgan's attitude toward his father. She has to make inferences because Morgan said remarkably little about Eddie. Eddie died when Morgan was four, but surely Morgan and Lily discussed him, and Eddie must have been a topic of discussion among the Thorntons. Morgan, a novelist, must have been curious about his father's character. That Morgan was so silent prompts Beauman to conclude that Morgan was hiding his true feelings—a justifiable deduction, since many people commented on his oblique manner and reluctance to give himself away.

Exactly what was Forster being silent about? Beauman speculates that at some point in his youth Morgan realized that his father was a homosexual. On Eddie's wedding trip to Paris, he had taken along his best male friend, and something had happened—exactly what no one knew, and Lily would not say. Beauman does not say it in so many words, but it is likely that Morgan blamed his father for his own predilection. There is ample evidence that like all adolescents, he wanted to conform to the norm; he also wished to be deemed worthy of his illustrious Thornton ancestors, even if he opposed many of their political and religious convictions. At a young age, then, Morgan learned to hide his feelings, to work by stealth. No rebel, he expanded his life by turning inward, writing novels about the conflicts he could not overcome in his daily life—the conflicts between wanting to be accepted by society and living by his own code of behavior. Morgan wanted friends and family. He wanted to belong. Yet his homosexuality and creativity made him the odd man out.

Morgan's extraordinary need for security, his timidity, and his inordinate attachment to the bases of his earliest years are revealed in his attachment to his mother. He lived with her (except for trips abroad) until she died at ninety (he was sixty-six). She often exasperated him by nitpicking and trying to run his life. He partially escaped by obtaining a room in London to which he could retreat from their suburban home. He also maintained some control by telling his mother little about his private life or his writing. His novels, as Beauman points out, are extraordinarily subtle in the way they criticize suburbia and conventionality. Morgan never launched a frontal attack; he sidled up to bourgeois society and subverted it through his characterization and scene setting. One of his female characters exhibits her independence, strength of mind, and talent by expertly playing perhaps the most difficult Beethoven piano composition. As Beauman notes, Morgan does not mention the work's unusual complexity; only a sophisticated reader would note that the very spirited execution of this piece is an affront to the middlebrow conventionality of the drawing room in which it is played.

Beauman argues that Morgan's novelistic touches are so light and deft in puncturing the pretensions of the status quo that he has been sometimes dismissed as a minor writer. Yet, she asks, is it not much easier to attack head-on, to bludgeon a subject, than to undermine it slowly and thoroughly? This is Morgan's great achievement, to be completely of the world he criticizes, to meld with it, and yet constantly to expose its weaknesses, providing a continuity of criticism that in the long run effects much greater changes than the overt revolutionary approach.

Morgan used guile, not brute force. Indeed, Beauman makes much of the fact that he disliked power and almost never used it to manipulate people. When he admits that in one of his sexual relationships he enjoyed abusing his partner, Beauman is shocked, because it is so unlike the pacific, low-key Morgan. Yet she has such a fine opinion of her subject that she cannot help praising him for his candor, for admitting that he too was susceptible to using someone as an object for his sadistic pleasure.

Morgan's great years as a novelist were also his unhappiest as a person. He does not seem to have awakened to the power of sex until his thirties and had no significant sexual experience until his forties. He seemed the epitome of the repressed male, an "invert" or "minorite" (two terms he used for his homosexuality) who was afraid of expressing himself sexually but became increasingly frustrated by his inhibitions. He gradually overcame his sexual impediment in the period between 1914 and 1924, when he spent three years working for the Red Cross in Alexandria and traveled to India. The exposure to other cultures began to liberate his feelings. In Alexandria, he met the great Greek poet Constantine Cavafy, who had been openly homosexual for thirty years. Cavafy wrote poems about homosexuality and published them, whereas Morgan wrote but suppressed *Maurice* (1971), a posthumously published novel based on a homosexual acquaintance who committed suicide. Morgan would never publicly admit his homosexuality, but he began to find pleasure in working-class young men—usually half his age—who had none of the constraints of his heritage.

Morgan's exposure to Alexandria, and then to India, resulted in his most famous novel, *A Passage to India,* which Beauman rightly treats as his culminating masterpiece. Here, on an international canvas, he was able to explore the restricted Englishness that was deeply embedded in his character in contrast to the open sensuality of Indians he had met both in England and in India. A close Indian friend, Syed Ross Masood, had been the first to suggest India as the topic for a novel. Masood seems to have realized that Morgan was the ideal writer to probe not merely the English role in India but also the Indian attraction to and influence on the English. Beauman supposes that Masood also realized that Morgan wanted a sexual relationship with him; this Masood would not countenance, but perhaps he realized that a novel on India would help Morgan to satisfy certain longings.

Morgan struggled ten years to complete his masterpiece. In part, World War I interrupted his work, but Beauman's narrative strongly implies that Morgan was coming to the end of his novelist's career. He had expressed his major themes in six extraordinary novels and had exhausted his insights. Shortly after completing *A Passage to India,* Morgan announced that it would be his last novel. He never seems to have been seriously tempted to write another. He developed a whole new career as reviewer, essayist, and sage, continuing to write beautiful, understated prose that spoke for the English in ways most other writers could not match. Again, as in his novels, Morgan's indirection made his views seem natural, right, unaffected, and unforced—quintessentially English.

Sometimes Morgan spoke so subtly and quietly, however, that he was misunderstood or dismissed as too tentative. He suggested, for example, that Adolf Hitler ought to be opposed because he could not tolerate any opinion other than his own. The statement seems naïve in the light of Hitler's monstrous crimes, but Morgan was speaking out for the essence of his liberal values. To him, a world with Hitler in control was unthinkable; civilization as Morgan knew it would vanish. His statement might seem mild, but Beauman suggests that its very decency and decorum worked to the values that Hitler would destroy.

Nearly all Beauman's biography is devoted to Morgan's first forty-five years, the years of his development and achievement as a novelist. Only three chapters and an epilogue are devoted to the remaining forty-five years. Yet the narrative does not seem rushed or truncated, for she has so firmly established who Morgan was, and how he continued the themes of his fiction in his nonfiction and his private life, that these last chapters are a very satisfying coda.

Especially interesting are the few pages she spends on Morgan's life with his last lover, Bob Buckingham. Bob was a twenty-eight-year-old policeman when he met Morgan. Their relationship lasted through the last forty years of Morgan's life. When Bob married a nurse, Morgan was upset, but he became reconciled to it when he found that Bob's affections for him did not flag. Then Bob's wife, May, became pregnant, and a distraught Morgan threatened to sever relations with him. Yet the baby, a boy, was given the middle name Morgan, and the author grew fond of his namesake. Indeed, Beauman suggests, anyone watching Morgan, May, Bob, and their child on an outing would have thought that Morgan was the child's grandfather.

Morgan and May became best friends. He sent her a note of commiseration when Bob had a brief affair with another woman. As Morgan lay dying, it was May who held his hand. Did May know the full story of Bob and Morgan's love affair? Beauman does not know. Nor does she say (although she must realize) that Morgan's life ended symmetrically. It is a little surprising that Beauman does not speculate about Morgan's last hours. Did he recall his father's wedding trip to Paris with his male lover and his new bride in tow? Beauman, like her subject, is a subtle writer, and she may prefer that her readers make such speculations and search for such symmetries for themselves.

Carl Rollyson

Sources for Further Study

Booklist. XC, February 15, 1994, p. 1034.
Choice. XXXII, September, 1994, p. 100.
The Christian Science Monitor. May 10, 1994, p. 15.
Kirkus Reviews. LXII, February 15, 1994, p. 184.
Library Journal. CXIX, March 15, 1994, p. 72.
The New Republic. CCXI, August 22, 1994, p. 40.
The New York Times Book Review. XCIX, April 3, 1994, p. 7.
Publishers Weekly. CCXLI, February 14, 1994, p. 73.
The Wall Street Journal. June 2, 1994, p. A12.
The Washington Post Book World. XXIV, April 3, 1994, p. 8.

THE END OF THE HUNT

Author: Thomas Flanagan (1923-   )
Publisher: Dutton (New York). 627 pp. $24.95
Type of work: Historical novel
Time: 1914-1934
Locale: Ireland and London

Relating the story of the Irish Troubles and the civil war that followed the Easter Rising of 1916, this is the author's third novel about pivotal events of Irish history

Principal characters:
PATRICK PRENTISS, an Irish Catholic barrister, onetime historian, and former British military officer
CHRISTOPHER BLAKE, a middle-class Irish Catholic, adviser to Michael Collins
JANICE NUGENT, a member of an old Irish Catholic gentry family, Blake's lover
FRANK LACY, the middle-class son of a newspaper editor, an Irish Republican Army (IRA) officer
ELIZABETH KEATING, Blake's assistant, a supporter of the Irish Republic
WINSTON CHURCHILL, a British politician, Secretary of State for War and the Colonies
MICHAEL COLLINS, the chief Sinn Fein/IRA military strategist during the Troubles
EAMON DE VALERA, the head of Sinn Fein and the president of the Irish Republic

In 1979, Thomas Flanagan was the winner of the National Book Critics Circle Award for fiction for his *The Year of the French.* That novel told the story of how the Irish failed, despite French assistance, to expel the British and create a republic in 1789, and how this event passed into myth. In 1988, Flanagan, again in fictional form, related the events of the 1860's Fenian rising against the British in *The Tenants of Time*. That rebellion, too, failed but also left a legacy of myth and symbol to affect another generation. In *The End of the Hunt*, Flanagan returns to an Irish rebellion against British rule, this time to the era of World War I and the Easter Rising of 1916 and its aftermath. As in the past, the Easter Rising was a failure in that it did not succeed in ousting the British, but the defeated rebels, who were executed by the victors, became martyrs who inspired further conflict by their shed blood. That conflict—the Troubles and the civil war—allows Flanagan again to explore the Irish past, which in Ireland is never past but always still alive in the present and seemingly never to be forgotten by future generations.

History and particularly its effects are the primary subjects of Flanagan's novels—not history for its own sake but its influence on later generations. It has been remarked that a happy nation is a nation with no history, but many in Ireland have nothing but their history (or histories). In *The Tenants of Time* Patrick Prentiss, a young Catholic Irishman trained in history at the University of Oxford, goes back to Ireland in 1904 to discover the true history—beyond poems and ballads—of the Fenian Rising of 1867. *The End of the Hunt* begins in 1919, with Prentiss returning to Dublin after losing an arm fighting in the British Army in the Great War, but he has abandoned academic history to practice law.

Christopher Blake is another young Irish historian, having written a respectable work on Irish Catholic gentry families of the eighteenth century. In 1916, however, Blake leaves academic history behind and joins Patrick Pearse and James Connolly at the General Post Office in Dublin. There Pearse proclaims the Irish Republic in what turns out to be a blood sacrifice—Pearse's and Connolly's blood.

Still another character in *The End of the Hunt* is wrapped up in history. Frank Lacy, whose father edits a newspaper in a small town in Ireland, is fond of the writers of ancient Rome, particularly Vergil, the epic poet of imperial Rome's heyday. On one occasion, Blake remarks that Lacy might be better off reading Plutarch rather than Vergil, for Plutarch concentrated upon the lives of the noble Greeks and Romans and, Flanagan intimates, history is the story of individuals and how they are caught up in the historical web of the past, present, and future.

Flanagan uses a number of literary techniques in *The End of the Hunt*. Each chapter usually focuses on a single individual, sometimes relating the present, sometimes events in the past, while occasionally the future is mentioned. At times Flanagan narrates events in the third person, as with Lacy's and Blake's experiences. Historical personages such as British Prime Minister David Lloyd George, War and Colonial Secretary Winston Churchill, and their Irish opponents Eamon de Valera and Michael Collins are also portrayed in the third person. Some of the fictional characters, however, tell their story through a first-person narrative, as when Prentiss returns to Dublin in 1919 after World War I, on the eve of the emerging civil war between the British government and the Irish revolutionaries, Sinn Fein and its military wing, the Irish Republican Army (IRA).

Interestingly, the key figure in *The End of the Hunt* is not one of the Irish politicians of Sinn Fein or one of the hard men of the IRA—Lacy, Blake, or Michael Collins—or even one of their British opponents, but Janice Nugent, from an old Irish Catholic gentry family. Widowed when the novel begins, she has been living primarily in London in recent years; her husband was killed in the Dardanelles in 1915. She and Blake begin an affair and fall in love. Much of the "history" of the novel is related by her, often through Blake's telling her of his experiences. Blake, a key adviser to Collins, is the man at the center of events, the onetime historian of Ireland's Catholic gentry families. Nugent, whose family is one of those chronicled by Blake, is little interested in history, particularly as exemplified by events such as the Troubles. Her husband died in that kind of history, and she fears that Blake may also be lost to the imperatives of history, not as a writer but as a maker. Her personal interest in history ended when she was a young girl playing historical roles with her sister on the family's estate in the west of Ireland. She no longer wants to listen to the siren song of history—Ireland and she have both had too much—but although she refuses to hear it, as her sister points out at the end of the novel, she cannot escape it. Blake dies violently, her father dies of old age, and she and her sister retreat from the public sphere into the declining world of her diminishing estate in the west.

What makes *The End of the Hunt* more than simply a historical novel is the continuing impact of that past on the events of the late twentieth century. It is a highly topical work. There is a direct connection between the events of Easter 1916, the Troubles, the Irish civil war, and the tragedies that still stalk Ireland and Britain. The Troubles, which begin in 1919, soon see much of the west and south of Ireland, along with Dublin, embroiled in war. The political movement or party called Sinn Fein is committed to Irish independence and a republican form of government. In response, the British government, no longer able to rely on the local constabulary, sends over numerous World War I veterans, soon to be known as the Black and Tans, to crush the IRA. The latter, under the inspired leadership of Collins, rely on guerrilla tactics. Both sides resort to assassination and other acts of terrorism. While in retrospect the actual number killed and wounded was relatively small—a few thousand—the conflict is pregnant with the assumptions, attitudes, techniques, and practices that will dominate numerous other twentieth century conflicts, in Ireland and elsewhere.

Along with the weight of the past on the present and the future, there is another major theme that Flanagan explores in *The End of the Hunt*: the conflict between reality and idealism, between the pragmatic compromise and the utopian vision, between politics and philosophy, between the historical present and the historical future, between fact and myth. This conflict has haunted and continues to haunt Ireland. In the summer of 1921, the Irish rebels and the British government agree to a truce ending the Troubles, and in December, representatives from both sides accept a treaty draft. It does not, however, create an Irish republic, but instead the Irish Free State, an independent state comparable to Canada, Australia, and New Zealand and within the British Empire, whose symbolic head is the British monarch. Never in recent centuries has most of Ireland been so free of British rule—it goes far beyond the concept of Home Rule in domestic affairs advocated by such Irish heroes as Charles Stuart Parnell—but the treaty does not establish a republic. The treaty is narrowly ratified by the Irish parliament, the Dail, but both Sinn Fein and the IRA are split in two. Collins gives his support to the treaty and the Free State, as does Blake, but de Valera, Lacy, and Keating remain committed to an idealized republic. The Troubles have apparently ended with the ratification of the treaty, but civil war is the result, a war fought between the Irish rebels, onetime allies and compatriots in the struggle against the British. Civil wars are often particularly bloody and bitter. Before this one ends in 1923 with the Free State victorious, many of the leading participants on both sides have been killed, including Collins and Blake.

Collins had supported the treaty and the Free State not because he believed that it was ideal or perfect, but because it was the best solution then attainable. British resources are still formidable, and the IRA is suffering from a lack of weapons and ammunition. Much practical independence has been achieved, more than most earlier Irish nationalists had ever dreamed about. As Collins envisioned, other steps can be taken in the future.

De Valera, a treaty opponent, rejoined the political arena in the late 1920's, becoming prime minister in the 1930's, and after World War II still other Irish politicians created the Republic of Ireland, or Eire. Yet the shadows of the 1921 treaty continued to bedevil Irish and British lives for generations. For decades the politics of Eire still revolved largely around stands that individuals had taken on the treaty, engendering bitterness, narrow-mindedness, and occasionally violence.

Paradoxically, those who rejected the treaty of 1921 focused their ire against the lack of a republic and the Free State's relationship to the British monarch as head of the British Empire. The symbolic republic and the failure to achieve it blinded many to what should have been a more crucial issue, the partition of Ireland. Six counties of Ulster became Northern Ireland and continued ties with the United Kingdom. As Collins foresaw, the Irish Free State was simply a way station on the road to an eventual republic, but a unified Ireland—undoubtedly desired by a majority of those in the Republic if not in Northern Ireland—is yet to be achieved. In the 1960's and 1970's, a new round of the Troubles, involving the IRA and the British, began in the north. If the symbolic quest for a republic had not divided the Irish nationalists in the early 1920's, perhaps a united effort directed toward the issue of partition would have led to a single Ireland. Or perhaps not, given the Irish penchant for remembering things past in particular ways.

Flanagan has written a brilliant novel. With the possible exception of Winston Churchill, who is something of a caricature, historical figures in the novel have been successfully incorporated with fictional characters. Michael Collins is especially realized. After three important novels about Ireland's history, Flanagan has indicated that he has completed his fictional ruminations about the Irish past. There is no happy ending to *The End of the Hunt*—it is about Irish history, after all—but its conclusion is not any sort of end: The events of those years continue to influence the Irish present as has nothing since, not even the new Troubles in the north.

Eugene Larson

Sources for Further Study

Booklist. XC, January 15, 1994, p. 875.
Chicago Tribune. April 3, 1994, XIV, p. 3.
Commonweal. CXXI, September 23, 1994, p. 22.
Kirkus Reviews. LXII, February 1, 1994, p. 84.
Library Journal. CXIX, February 15, 1994, p. 183.
The New York Times Book Review. XCIX, April 3, 1994, p. 1.
The New Yorker. LXX, June 6, 1994, p. 99.
Publishers Weekly. CCXLI, February 7, 1994, p. 69.
Time. CXLIII, May 23, 1994, p. 71.
The Washington Post Book World. XXIV, April 3, 1994, p. 1.

THE END OF VANDALISM

Author: Tom Drury
Publisher: Houghton Mifflin (Boston). 336 pp. $21.95
Type of work: Novel
Time: 1991-1992
Locale: Iowa

A sensitively written novel about a mythical Midwest county where a traditional way of life based on home, family, religion, soil, and the work ethic is decaying

Principal characters:
DAN NORMAN, a diplomatic, easygoing county sheriff
LOUISE DARLING, a photographer's assistant who divorces Tiny and marries Dan
TINY DARLING, a thief, drunkard, and ne'er-do-well
MARY MONTROSE, Louise's mother, a widow who lives vicariously by sharing her daughter's joys and sorrows

A famous cover of *The New Yorker* magazine, which has been enlarged, reproduced, and sold by the tens of thousands in poster shops, purports to show the typical New Yorker's mental picture of the United States: Beyond the Hudson River there is little but wasteland. The magazine itself was originally intended to be by New Yorkers, for New Yorkers, and about New Yorkers. Readers living in the hinterlands could expect to have trouble understanding many of the cartoons and would always feel a little like Dorothy dreaming of the Emerald City of Oz.

Over the years, however, the publishers found themselves subjected to economic and demographic pressures that were impossible to ignore. For one thing, many of the better-educated, better-paid New Yorkers were no longer living in the big, noisy, crime-ridden, expensive city but had fled to greener pastures. In order to accommodate their readers—and especially the advertisers of luxury goods and services who made the slick, sophisticated magazine possible—the editors were forced to take an increasingly broader view.

So *The New Yorker* discovered America about five hundred years after Christopher Columbus did. It began publishing stories and articles about strange places like Ohio and Texas with the attitude of a classical music connoisseur discussing the earthiness and sincerity of Dixieland jazz or country and western.

Eleven chapters of Tom Drury's *The End of Vandalism* were published as separate stories in *The New Yorker* between 1990 and 1994. This is a remarkable achievement for the young author, considering that under the radical regime of Tina Brown, who took over as editor in 1992, the magazine has drastically reduced the number of stories it prints. At one time it was publishing more than 150 stories a year (on one historic occasion it devoted almost its entire May 4, 1957, issue to J. D. Salinger's "Zooey.")

The chapters of *The End of Vandalism* that originally appeared as separate stories belong to the school of minimalism, which *The New Yorker* has cultivated to such an extent that the school and the magazine are inseparably identified. Ann Beattie is the magazine's most celebrated minimalist contributor. Her success is understandable because she writes about the kind of young, upwardly mobile Eastern urbanites who make up an important part of the readership. Before Raymond Carver's tragic death from lung cancer in 1988, *The New Yorker* had begun publishing his stories, even though they were about people and places a continent away. Minimalism seems to have provided a sort of golden key of admission: It is as if the staff is willing to recognize the existence of intelligent life west of the Hudson as long as that life is as feckless and melancholy as life on the side with all the skyscrapers.

The New Yorker has another reason for favoring minimalism: Such stories are, almost by definition, exceptionally short. Many sound as if the beginning and ending had been lopped off by some junior editor whose job was to conserve space. For example, one of the chapters of Drury's novel published in the November 19, 1990, issue under the title "The End of Vandalism" takes up only six pages of an issue that runs to 156 pages; it is the only story in the issue and shares those six pages with five large cartoons and a poem.

Grouse County is what New Yorkers would call "a good place to be *from*." Drury provides a map of the 296-square-mile county which seems intended to emphasize its deadly dullness. Most of it is planted in corn that is used to fatten hogs. The names of the mythical towns seem to have been chosen to indicate the county's insignificance: Names such as Pringmar, Pinville, Mixerton, Romyla, and Boris suggest a history that was never dramatic and has since become meaningless. Other features of this prairie county include the Rust River, the Lapoint Slough, and a number of gravel roads that cut through the landscape in uncompromising straight lines.

In an appendix the author lists the names and occupations of sixty-eight characters who appear in his book. *The End of Vandalism* has more characters than Count Leo Tolstoy's *Voyna i mir* (1865-1869; *War and Peace*, 1886), although it is less than a sixth as long. Drury's novel has the feeling of a panorama staged at a state fair, where an actor representing Buffalo Bill might gallop through waving his buckskin hat. Characters seem to appear and disappear into the opposite wing without contributing anything more than a fleeting impression of what their lives must be like in this inglorious environment.

The End of Vandalism is the kind of modular novel a minimalist story writer often assembles when he feels compelled to produce a novel. One might ask whether it is really a novel at all or merely a number of minimalistic short stories stuck together. This raises a bigger question, however, to which nobody knows the answer: What is a novel? The book is deliberately episodic. Like all minimalist fiction, it avoids dramatic confrontations and anything that would suggest that these episodes—or life itself—had "meaning."

In fairness to Drury, let it be said that although the book starts off as if it were going to prove unspeakably tedious, pointless, and dull, the reader eventually becomes absorbed in the very smallness and pettiness of modern-day prairie life. Minimalism is a kind of hyperrealism that makes some readers want to scream. Others relish the pointlessness and triviality because it reflects modern life. They consider that there is enough drama on television and that serious literature should divorce itself from the spectacular, because the spectacular is not truthful to the canned existence of contemporary life.

What saves *The End of Vandalism* from being as dreary as the environment it depicts is the author's talent. His dialogue is so natural-sounding, so appropriate to his unsophisticated characters, that one might suspect he had transcribed it from a concealed tape recorder. Certain striking observations betray a poetic sensibility that remains hidden most of the time behind his deadpan humor and monotone prose. Here is an example of Drury's quirky vision: "The windshield wipers worked, and sometimes they worked on their own, as if detecting a fine mist beyond Tiny's perception." Or again, "Marie was one of those eccentrics who travel the lonely highways of monotonous states and almost seem to have been hired by the tourism department to enliven the traveler's experience." Regrettably, however, Drury has a minimalist's addiction to throwaway lines like the following, which might be termed "consumerisms" or "Ann Beattie-isms": "Lenore told Dan about two cranes that had flown over her house early that morning, and Dan thought she was going to weep, but instead she shook her head and reached down to get some string cheese."

The reader comes to realize that *The End of Vandalism* deals not so much with individuals as with Grouse County itself and the whole region it represents. Drury's work shows the strong influence of William Faulkner, whose mythical Yoknapatawpha County was undergoing a parallel process of relentless evolution as a result of forces that could only be felt and not seen. Drury's little people are losing their religious faith, their work ethic, their sense of purpose, their sense of community, their family loyalty, their integrity—everything is being undermined by invisible modern forces that are producing an ugly homogeneity everywhere. It is especially disconcerting to see this decay in what used to be considered the heartland of America. Beattie's New York is decadent and Faulkner's Deep South is moribund, but Iowa always symbolized health, home, happiness, apple pie, Norman Rockwell, and the 4-H Club.

The "plot" of Drury's novel is almost rudimentary: Louise Darling breaks up with her no-good husband Tiny, a bully, drunkard, and petty thief. Sheriff Dan Norman must intervene in their domestic quarrels and ends up living with Louise and then marrying her. In the true spirit of minimalism, everything in the novel seems to happen by default. Tiny hovers around the perimeter smoldering with jealousy but never does anything except make a few telephone calls and show up at awkward moments, not unlike the inarticulate Burt in Raymond Carver's story "A Serious Talk."

Louise, who is in her late thirties, is shocked and then delighted to find that she is pregnant. Sadly, however, the eagerly awaited child is born dead. Louise goes off to mourn by herself—an indication of the alienation that exists even between people who are nominally in love—but eventually recovers and returns to Dan. They are virtually the only people in the book who have a reasonably conventional loving relationship. Drury reveals his banked-down powers as a writer in these moving scenes and makes the reader suspect that he is writing from personal experience.

The little episodes and anecdotes are tied together mainly through the official activities of Sheriff Dan, who has been compared by critics to the corn-fed television sheriff played by Andy Griffith. As an elected official, Dan is concerned about maintaining good relations with everybody in the county. The fact that the population is shrinking makes each constituent a more potent political unit. Dan is like half the people in modern America in fearing that his livelihood could be yanked out from under him, forcing him to look for a new career in the big, mirthless game of vocational musical chairs being played out in postindustrial American society. There is a real possibility that he could lose his job to an upstart who is running an aggressive campaign focusing on what is wrong with the county.

There is plenty wrong with the county, but there is not much Dan or any other elected official can do about it. Grouse County symbolizes the Middle West in general, and maybe the whole United States. Drury is an important American writer because he chronicles the changing Middle West. He understands how unseen forces are affecting the lives of its inhabitants.

Agribusiness with its relentless mechanization and absentee ownership is probably the main culprit. The federal government pays people not to work and pays farmers not to plant crops. The media are changing people's thinking, undermining traditional morality, and creating a pervasive consumer consciousness (one of the favorite subjects of minimalist writers). Education is stimulating younger people to despise manual labor, to forsake the land and move to the cities, where they can exchange rural idiocy for urban alienation. Automobiles are expanding people's worlds and making yesterday's quaint horse-and-buggy towns redundant.

Farmers no longer have to live on their land, and they certainly would not consider raising the food they eat. Shoppers can drive to malls and are no longer dependent on friendly little stores on Main Street and State Street. People in places like Grouse County all used to know one another; now they only know *of* one another. The churches no longer have the power to mold people's lives, because religious faith is dissipating. Businesses are closing. The fire department cannot even afford to buy new axes.

Significantly, there are hardly any children in Drury's long list of characters, except for an illegitimate infant abandoned in a shopping cart. This is no world in which to bring up children. It is obvious that in time towns like Grafton, Boris, and Pringmar will be derelicts with screen doors banging in the wind. There will be an end to vandalism because there will be nothing to vandalize and everyone, including the vandals, will have died or moved away.

Bill Delaney

Sources for Further Study

Booklist. XC, March 1, 1994, p. 1180.
Kirkus Reviews. LXII, February 1, 1994, p. 83.
Library Journal. CXIX, March 15, 1994, p. 100.

The New York Times Book Review. XCIX, March 20, 1994, p. 19.
Publishers Weekly. CCXLI, February 14, 1994, p. 78.
The Times Literary Supplement. August 26, 1994, p. 21.
The Virginia Quarterly Review. LXX, Autumn, 1994, p. 127.
The Wall Street Journal. April 5, 1994, p. A16.
The Washington Post Book World. XXIV, April 17, 1994, p. 7.

ENTRIES

Author: Wendell Berry (1934-)
Publisher: Pantheon Books (New York). 80 pp. $20.00
Type of work: Poetry

Entries, *Wendell Berry's tenth volume of poetry, presents a rich and varied selection of verse celebrating the poet's connections to his family, farm, and community*

Farmer, poet, novelist, and social critic Wendell Berry has offered a unique voice in contemporary American letters as a populist social critic, a defender of traditional family values, a spokesman for renewable agriculture, and a regional Kentucky writer. Though he began as a novelist and short-story writer, he first gained notice in 1963 for his Kennedy elegy, "November Twenty-six, Nineteen Sixty-three," and followed that with seven volumes of poetry and then *Collected Poems: 1957-1982* (1985). Since then, he has published *Sabbaths* (1987).

Though Berry began his career for the most part as a free-verse poet, his later work has shown more structure, particularly in *Sabbaths*, with its series of formal, rhymed meditations. There are forty-three new lyrics collected in *Entries*, arranged in four sections. Many of the poems are about his family—his wife, daughter, father, mother, and grandmother—and others are about friends. *Entries* has a distinctly regional, traditional tone, with a mixture of conservative and populist sentiments. Family, religion, and place are the cornerstones of Berry's work, here as elsewhere. There are a number of subtle but pervasive religious allusions, including epigraphs from Genesis and the Gospel of John and capitalizations of Heaven, Paradise, Kingdom, God, and Father, lending a meditative quality to what are otherwise personal lyrics.

Aside from "In Extremis," a series of poems in part 4 dedicated to Berry's father, there is otherwise little apparent formal structure to the arrangement of the poems. Part 1, "Some Differences," contains fifteen mostly personal lyrics; part 2 contains eleven mostly didactic occasional pieces; part 3 contains fourteen more short lyrics, including some delicate love poems addressed to the poet's wife.

Stylistically, Berry seems to be working toward a subtle and informal poetic structure with regular stanzaic form but little formal rhyme scheme, the occasional use of refrain, a regular rhythmic pattern, and a preference for slant or near-rhymes. Some of his didactic prose-poems use a verse-paragraph structure and resemble verse essays. Berry also returns to the elegy and experiments with a contemporary adaptation of the epithalamion, a classical and Renaissance verse form that he uses, without mythological allusions, in "A Marriage Song," a poem dedicated to his daughter Mary. Other pieces are as short as haiku and demonstrate an Asian cast. There are also sonnet variants, a verse epistle to a fellow poet, a dramatic dialogue, and a Whitmanesque/ Ginsbergesque free-verse poetic manifesto by Berry's "Mad Farmer" persona.

Part 1 is given the title "Some Differences" because its fifteen poems were originally published separately as a chapbook by Confluence Press in Lewiston, Idaho. The opening poem, "For the Explainers," rebukes the factual logic of cause and effect, which cannot answer the teleological question "What curled the plume in the drake's tail/ And put the white ring around his neck?" Instead, the poet urges a Zen-like acceptance of what is without explanation. "Voices Late at Night" dramatizes the poet's interior prayer, which may be likened to listening to the still, quiet voice within. In a series of five meditations, the poem contrasts worldly aspirations with the likelihood of poverty, strife, and ruin. Another Zen-like meditative lyric, "A Difference," contrasts the noise of heavy machinery that shakes the leaves on a young beech tree with the quiet tranquillity of ripples on the Kentucky River, below the road, which reflects the rustling leaves.

Three other poets are mentioned by name in the book: William Carlos Williams, Hayden Carruth, and Geoffrey Chaucer. The relationship suggested in two of the poems, "In a Motel Parking Lot, Thinking of Dr. Williams" and "To Hayden Carruth," is that of mentor and disciple. In an essay in *A Continuous Harmony* (1972) entitled "A Homage to Dr. Williams," Berry praised Williams' evocation of place, humble exactness of description, and sense both of the usefulness of poetry and of twentieth century culture's particular need for the voices of American poets. A person is most a poet, most a citizen, when he or she is most humanely exact in use of language.

"In a Motel Parking Lot, Thinking of Dr. Williams" extends this tribute in a two-part poem of seventeen three-line stanzas, written in Williams' characteristic accentual-syllabic verse. The poem seems to echo Williams' "Elsie" in its insistence that poetry dignifies cultural life by uplifting people's minds and reminding them of what is worth preserving: the human capacity to distinguish the permanent from the ephemeral, to cherish ordinary moments of transfiguring truth and beauty such as "the weighted/ grainfield, the shady street,/ the well-laid stone and the changing tree/ whose branches spread above." Berry, like Williams, complains of the impoverishment of culture and environment because of the inability of poetry to reach into and enrich the lives of ordinary Americans: "For want of songs and stories/ they have dug away the soil,/ paved over what is left."

Poetry is an important expression of cultural memory, the legacy of the common experience of ancestors that could enrich and ennoble people's lives and teach them to cherish their environment. Berry is a holistic thinker: Language, culture, and environment are part of a cultural legacy that must be cherished and preserved. Without poetry, human beings languish:

> The poem is important,
> as the want of it
> proves. It is the stewardship
>
> of its own possibility,
> the past remembering itself
> in the presence of
>
> the present.

In "To Hayden Carruth," Berry playfully greets the younger contemporary poet as a disciple, in language humorously reminiscent of Ralph Waldo Emerson's letter to

Walt Whitman after he had reviewed *Leaves of Grass* (first edition 1855). The verse epistle/poetry review praises Carruth's poems for the virtue of their necessity, for their wit, mastery, and verve. Reading Carruth's verse refreshes him, Berry affirms, as he sends his greetings from Port Royal, Kentucky, to Munnsville, New York. He urges Carruth to put aside thoughts of "career" for the hard work of poetic mastery, which must be achieved again and again. "On a Theme of Chaucer" is a more oblique, two-quatrain poem alluding perhaps to Chaucer's reaffirmation, at the end of *The Canterbury Tales* (1387-1400), of orthodox religious belief. Berry affirms that he, too, has never denied scriptural teachings about Heaven or Hell, but he will not speculate about the hereafter.

Many of the lyrics in *Entries* are autobiographical poems in the confessional mode, with personal, abstract, or elusive meaning. Age and mortality seem to be on the poet's mind in poems such as "A Parting," his elegiac tribute to his old friend, neighbor, and fellow farmer Arthur Rowanberry, who is lying in a hospital bed far from home, his body ravaged by cancer but his mind mercifully detached from his suffering as he prepares for his final journey. In "One of Us," Berry complains about the indignity of empty, moralizing, hypocritical funeral sermons that would steal the memory of the beloved dead from the mourners. Better to cherish one memory of the dead as she was when alive—standing by a fence holding turkey chicks in her apron, then tossing the hen over the fence so that the chicks would follow—than to submit to another dull eulogy.

The poet's own mortality troubles him as well, as in "Thirty More Years," where he contrasts the treelike aspirations of his youth with the humble, grasslike wisdom of middle age. He craves the forgiveness of his mother in "To My Mother," realizing that it was given so completely, in love, that it preceded any wrong that he might have done. His mother's forgiveness seems almost divine in its completeness.

Part 3 contains some subtle and beautiful love poems that show a deepening religious concern in their comparisons between eros and agape, human love and divine love. "Duality," perhaps the most interesting, is a nine-stanza confessional poem using an unrhymed nine-line stanza throughout. The poem opens with an epigraph from Genesis on the creation of man and woman in God's own image. The poem is cast in terms of "I" and "you": speaker and listener, lover and beloved, husband and wife. The speaker seems to be apologizing for the pain he has caused and asking for understanding. The poem explores the paradoxical nature of love, in that two people commit themselves to a relationship before they can possibly understand the nature of the commitment they have made. To love is to suffer, to give and receive suffering, as they express through their eyes the pain, anger, separateness, and frailty of their love. Their love is a light that passes between them, a burning of their bodies as their mortality is consumed in time. Human love is a reflection of divine love, an anticipation of the joy of Heaven. There are echoes in Berry's poems of the erotic love poetry of the Song of Songs, the passionate mysticism of Saint John of the Cross and Saint Teresa of Ávila, and the religious and love poetry of the English metaphysical poets—Robert Herrick, George Herbert, and Andrew Marvell.

Another religious poem, "Two Questions," recasts the parable of the wedding feast in Matthew 22, in which the Kingdom of God is compared to a wedding feast whose invited guests fail to attend, so the king invites those on the streets, both good and bad. In Berry's two-stanza retelling of the parable, he asks which would be more offensive: to have a marriage feast at which the thankless guests gobbled their food without tasting it, or to have finicky guests who picked over the food, refusing to enjoy the bountiful feast? Berry's version of the parable is clever, but the allegorical implications are unclear.

"Touch-Me-Not," a flower poem in this section, precisely describes the jewel weed (*Impatiens capensis*), which grows in wet, shady places and blooms from July through September. Its spotted orange blossom hangs like a pendant jewel, and its ripe seed pod pops at a touch. "Wild Rose," another apparent flower poem, is actually a beautiful and subtle love poem and tribute to the poet's wife, couched in terms of a conceit, an elaborate metaphorical comparison between the implicitness of their love and a wild rose "blooming at the edge of thicket, grace and light/ where yesterday was only shade."

The major work in part 4 is a series of twelve poems entitled "In Extremis: Poems About My Father," which presents an account of Berry's gradual reconciliation with his father, John M. Berry, a respected attorney and one of the founders of the Kentucky Burley Tobacco Growers Cooperative Association. At first resenting his strong-willed, demanding father with his high standards, Berry gradually came to understand that behind the difficulty of his father's demands was fear of losing the most precious things in life: children, home, and land. The first poem, a dramatic dialogue, describes how Berry and his father quarreled about the Vietnam War and were reconciled by Berry's admission that his father was the major influence in his life. Berry writes compassionately of his father's final years, characterized by gradual loss of health, mind, and dignity as he comes to live more in his past memories. Evoking the continuity of generations, Berry imagines his father, now an old man, as he might appear to his own parents if they returned from the world of the dead. Sometimes the old man forgets his age and infirmity, tries to go outdoors to work but cannot, and rages at the body that has betrayed him. He fears the end, which is always hard, and he calls out to the dead in his sleep. Finally, Berry reflects on what he has learned from his father: the difference between good work and sham; clear language and expression; honest service; a love of good livestock and good land. In this remarkable cycle of twelve poems, Berry expresses his father's fierce independence and integrity, his love of farming, his helplessness in old age, and his imagined apotheosis in fields, astride one of the horses that he loved.

Entries is a major poetry volume by a distinguished contemporary American poet. Wendell Berry's tenth poetry collection, a remarkably eclectic gathering of more than a decade's work, demonstrates once again that he is one of our necessary voices.

Andrew J. Angyal

Sources for Further Study

Booklist. XC, April 1, 1994, p. 1419.
Library Journal. CXIX, April 15, 1994, p. 81.
Publishers Weekly. XXIV, February 28, 1994, p. 77.

EXCURSIONS IN THE REAL WORLD
Memoirs

Author: William Trevor (William Trevor Cox, 1928-)
First published: 1993, in Great Britain
Publisher: Alfred A. Knopf (New York). Illustrated. 201 pp. $23.00
Type of work: Memoir
Time: The 1930's to 1991
Locale: Ireland, England, Switzerland, and Iran

Vivid essays on people and places as recalled by one of Ireland's most accomplished fiction writers

Principal personages:
WILLIAM TREVOR, an Irish writer
JAMES WILLIAM COX, his father
GERTRUDE DAVISON COX, his mother

William Trevor has been called England's greatest living short-story writer, an honor he shares, if such an honor can be, with V. S. Pritchett. Trevor (whose full name is William Trevor Cox) is, like many British writers, Irish by birth, but as he lived much of his adult life in England and has often written of English subjects, he has been adopted or at least hyphenated into Anglo-Irish. The question of national roots is not irrelevant, any more than is the fact that Trevor's family, like Pritchett's, moved frequently during his youth, upsetting his schooling, throwing him on his own resources, and making him (as a Protestant in a Catholic country) something of an outsider. The Irish writer as outcast or exile is a familiar figure.

The essays that constitute this memoir are appropriate to a writer whose accomplishments lie more in the short story than in the novel. The novelist creates the illusion of unity over time, of integration between characters and setting, characters and society. The short-story writer is usually concerned less with these illusions than in others: the momentary feeling of knowing a character or place from the inside, the sense of revelation or change experienced in a moment. These are the qualities of most of these essays, reinforced by the objectivity or detachment that seems intensified in, if not peculiar to, short-story writers, and in this case a writer who seems detached as a narrator and observer.

A case in point is Trevor's candid, moving reflection on the failure of his parents' marriage. Like most children, he can only speculate on what attracted this man to this woman; parental passion is as mysterious as the sources of parents' differences. Whatever their source, the differences were real, and they intensified over time. Periods of harmony became fewer, with the father taking refuge in clubs and drink, the mother in books and films. They remained together for the sake of their children, heroically bearing the strain of togetherness until it was no longer necessary. They died and were buried, as they had lived, separately and alone, tragic figures as Trevor presents them.

Surely here is the beginning, if not the only source, of Trevor's skepticism toward marriage in his fiction, his sense of the tragic and mysterious in human affairs. Perhaps, too, this is one source of the writer's precarious balance between involvement and objectivity, sympathy and cool analysis. What is striking about this account of a marriage gone bad is the absence of information about how it affected Trevor himself. Readers see the situation clearly and grieve at its tragedy, but can only speculate on what it meant for the children growing up in such a family and observing such a marriage.

For British writers, school is a particularly rich source of colorful, though usually disagreeable, memories. Unlike many of his peers, Trevor was sent most often to local schools, though he did spend several years at boarding school in Dublin. Life there was hell, for all the usual reasons—loneliness, bad food, a stale and outdated curriculum, a bully who liked to pretend to brand his victims with a hot poker. Yet school also had its share of memorable characters. One of the more endearing and fantastic of these was a headmaster nicknamed "the Bull" for his imposing size. He was a gentle and naïve giant who could think ill of no one, so his students blatantly hoodwinked him and secretly protected him from realities he could not understand.

The most moving and memorable of the school-life portraits is "The Warden's Wife." The headmaster at St. Columba's in Dublin (Ireland's only public school) held the title Warden. During Trevor's time, the office was filled by a round, red, bumptious clergyman whose unattractive, timid, scholarly wife was his opposite in every respect. Trevor touchingly sketches this mousy, marginal figure with her stooped posture, awkward manners, and bullied demeanor. He reveals much of the pettiness and nastiness of school life in his account of the gossip and speculation that surrounded her. Most important, however, are the surprising facts discovered years later—that the warden's wife was a graduate of the University of Cambridge, with a first-class degree in theology, and that all of her life she harbored a secret passion for horse racing. Trevor acknowledges that it was at St. Columba's that he first learned that human beings are composed not of black and white but of shades of gray. The warden's wife, so sympathetically portrayed here, must have been part of that lesson. As presented in this memoir, she is a striking and even tragic figure, re-created in memory with the dignity she often lacked in life. How exactly was it, though, that Trevor learned about shades of gray in people, and what part, if any, did the warden's wife play in this aspect of his education? Again, readers are left to speculate on the connection between cause and effect.

Other school portraits are briefer and less memorable, but no less engaging. There is the art master who insists that Trevor persevere with wood sculpture, even though its techniques elude him; the chaplain who quotes poetry and encourages precise language; the eccentric housemaster with a passion for the poetry of W. B. Yeats. Only one student claims an essay of his own, a handsome, socially precocious, well-dressed youth who enters the family business after school and over the years loses his youthful humor and declines into a kind of emotional oxymoron—a melancholy but happy man. University life at Trinity College in Dublin is described in much less detail; Trevor admits that he returns there now with a sense of regret over opportunities lost.

From this point onward, the autobiographical detail becomes more sketchy. "Summer, 1952" recalls a brief stint of teaching at a school that subsequently closed its doors. "A Public-House Man" pays tribute to Marchant Smith, copy chief at Notley's advertising agency and the man who gave young Trevor a job when he badly needed one in 1960. "In Search of Siri" is based on Trevor's attempts to understand the marriage between August Strindberg and Siri von Essen, about whom he was writing a play in 1970 or so. The author ceases to be the focus of interest and becomes instead the filtering consciousness. *Excursions in the Real World: Memoirs* slips away from being a memoir and becomes more a collection of personal essays.

Several of these essays focus on places. The most closely related to memoir, both in subject and in tone, are those relating to Ireland. "In County Cork" is the geography of Trevor's youth, "The Strand" a brief sketch about a beach near Ardmore in that county. "Visitors in Dublin" describes the city as it was until recently, a place where Trevor lived for several years but one that never felt like home. Though the city has changed architecturally since Trevor's time, its heart remains in its people. The Nire Valley, by contrast, is a timeless piece of County Tipperary. From these chapters the reader feels Trevor's Irishness, his sense of place and ethnic inheritance.

A number of other chapters are best described as travel pieces. "Blockley, Gloucestershire" creates a pastoral picture of the area where Trevor's wife (mentioned only in passing) grew up. Other chapters focus on Iran in the 1970's, New York City, the Valle Verzasca in Switzerland, San Francisco, and Venice. The most effective of these, "Out of Season," describes the English resort town of Hastings during the winter, when the town belongs to its inhabitants, not to tourists, and conventioning businessmen seem out of place. This is a lovely, wistful essay, in which the seedy resort town takes on the character of a living human being.

The pieces on the cities now seem dated, for they no longer exist as Trevor saw them. The rural subjects demonstrate a genuine feeling for the countryside, sometimes moralized with references to the comparative swiftness of human life. The tone is often pensive, verging on the nostalgic, but sentimentality is avoided by the clarity and grace of the writing, the incisive use of local detail, and hard-edged particulars of the losses and gains of "progress."

Apart from the autobiographical essays, the most consistently rewarding are those focusing on individuals. The most engaging of these are recalled from Trevor's childhood—the long-suffering housemaid Kitty and the gifted tutor Miss Quirke, whose breadth of knowledge and pedagogical originality left a deep impression. There are others equally memorable, though darker in tone. "Sarzy" is a tragicomic depiction of an Italian copywriter at Notley's, addicted to wine, astrology, and the saving of men who drank to escape their wives. She was devoted to others' happiness and to a belief in happy endings; once she carried a dead cat around the office, certain that it would recover. Finally, her unreliability and eccentricity were too much, even for Mr. Notley's humane agency, and she was pensioned off. She lived another ten years in spite of the wine and was missed by those who had known her. "Assia" evokes the unreality of London in the 1960's where fantasy ruled. Assia became—or fancied that she did—the other woman in a triangle including Ted Hughes and Sylvia Plath. Years later, having borne a child and been reduced to difficult circumstances, Assia rekindled her acquaintance with Trevor and then, shortly afterward, took her own life and the child's.

These and the other portraits already mentioned show the short-story writer's gift for rapid, vivid characterization, and in particular Trevor's preference for the tragic and mysterious in human nature. Another kind of portrait, the literary, makes up the balance of the book, but these chapters on Edith Somerville and Martin Ross, W. B. Yeats, Sean O'Casey, Samuel Beckett, James Joyce, and the failed novelist William Gerhardie seem a bit like filler. They have their merits as literary criticism and biography but seem out of place in what is billed as a memoir.

In the end, this is a book to be valued for its evocative writing and personal insights rather than as a source of autobiographical information. As individual and often as melancholic as Trevor's stories, *Excursions in the Real World* points to tantalizing clues about the relationship between the author and his fiction, the life and the art. Trevor is candid in the introduction that such a relationship exists, but he is cagey about particulars. Overall one can see the sources of his political ideas, his skepticism about marriage, and his belief in the resourcefulness and unknowability of other people, but a full understanding of the man behind the art will have to await the unlikely appearance of a full autobiography or the work of an energetic and resourceful biographer. Meanwhile, there is this book—rich, satisfying, tantalizing, and beautifully written. The pleasure of its prose is enhanced by Lucy Willis' complementary illustrations.

Dean Baldwin

Sources for Further Study

The Christian Science Monitor. March 10, 1994, p. 14.
London Review of Books. XV, December 16, 1993, p. 22.
Los Angeles Times Book Review. February 13, 1994, p. 6.
The New Republic. CCX, March 14, 1994, p. 38.
New Statesman and Society. VI, August 27, 1993, p. 40.
The New York Times Book Review. XCIX, February 13, 1994, p. 7.
Publishers Weekly. CCXLI, January 24, 1994, p. 48.
The Times Literary Supplement. September 17, 1993, p. 24.
The Wall Street Journal. March 2, 1994, p. A9.
The Washington Post Book World. XXIV, March 20, 1994, p. 13.

THE EYE IN THE DOOR

Author: Pat Barker (1943-   )
First published: 1993, in Great Britain
Publisher: Dutton (New York). 280 pp. $20.95
Type of work: Novel
Time: 1918
Locale: London and Manchester, England

An adept and sensitive neurologist in a London clinic helps three veterans of the Western Front in World War I heal their psychological scars

Principal characters:
BILLY PRIOR, a lieutenant in the Royal Army
CHARLES MANNING, a captain in the Royal Army
SIEGFRIED SASSOON, a lieutenant in the Royal Army
DR. WILLIAM RIVERS, a neurologist and social anthropologist and captain in the Royal Army Medical Corps
DR. HENRY HEAD, a colleague of Rivers
BEATTIE ROPER, a pacifist and former suffragette
HETTIE ROPER, Beattie's daughter, a pacifist and former suffragette
LIONEL SPRAGGE, a spy hired by the War Ministry to investigate Beattie Roper
HAROLD SPENCER, a captain in the Royal Army

In many respects *The Eye in the Door* is a sequel to Pat Barker's 1992 novel *Regeneration*. Barker found the sources for both novels in accounts of the lives of two historical figures—the famous antiwar poet Siegfried Sassoon and William Rivers, a neurologist who treated soldiers who had returned from the front in World War I. The real Rivers actually worked at Craiglockhart, a hospital in Scotland, and he did treat Sassoon there in 1917 and in London in 1918. Barker's imagination transforms these historical sources and creates complex literary characters who interact with one another and with a variety of wholly imagined characters. One of the imagined characters in *Regeneration* was Billy Prior, who suffered from shell shock, now known as post-traumatic stress disorder. He was discharged from the hospital and assigned to permanent home service. Sassoon was discharged to active duty in November, 1917. *The Eye in the Door* continues Barker's exploration of their lives and adds Charles Manning, an officer wounded in France and now suffering panic attacks. Prior is Rivers' patient in his London clinic, and Sassoon appears late in the novel when he is sent to an American Red Cross hospital in London after suffering a minor head wound at the front. Rivers is called in by Sassoon's attending physician because of recurring symptoms of emotional distress.

In *Regeneration* her focus was on the psychological impact of war on the combatants. The horrors of post-traumatic stress disorder are made vivid by the soldiers' nightmares and flashbacks. In *The Eye in the Door* Barker broadens her approach to include an indictment of repression and paranoia on the home front. The issues she raises reflect the contradictions and incongruities that are the basis of people's lives in a country at war.

Billy Prior's psychological crisis dominates *The Eye in the Door.* After successful treatment at Craiglockhart, Prior is discharged and sent to London to work in an intelligence unit in the Ministry of Munitions. There he investigates the activities of notorious pacifists. The woman he is sent to interview in a prison outside London is Beattie Roper, an elderly woman with whom he lived for a year when he was a small child. Her daughter, Hettie, was one of his closest friends. Prior's return to his roots forces him to address the question of his allegiance—to the people he grew up with and to his country.

When Prior interviews Beattie, he begins to suspect that she was framed. He knows that she is a pacifist who hides deserters and helps provide them safe passage to Ireland. She is in prison, however, because she has been implicated in a plot to assassinate the prime minister. Actually, she had no part in such a plot: An informant, Lionel Spragge, hired by the Ministry of Munitions, altered the facts to implicate her. Why this need to imprison an old woman for life? Prior suspects that the Ministry of War has made Beattie a scapegoat. She will be a lesson to others. Clearly, Beattie is not under the control of German spies or other agents of a secret British organization. Her allegiance is to her children and to the young men she believes should not be sent to die in the trenches of France. In a time of war, however, governments will not tolerate any actions that may be construed as attacks upon the established order. Everyone must be on the same side; thus Beattie is sacrificed to "the cause."

Another instance of the government's repression is its treatment of homosexuals during the war. Certain people within the War Ministry believed that gays and lesbians were part of an intricate German plot to undermine the foundations of British culture and the British government. One of the people most afraid of exposure is Charles Manning. He returned from the front with a severely damaged knee and knows that he will never be sent back to the trenches. Still, he has repeated flashbacks of horrific scenes, and he suffers from panic attacks. Manning is happily married, and he loves his children, but he also has a secret life as a gay man. He has come to accept that part of his identity, but he is vulnerable because his homosexuality defines him as a pervert and as a criminal. He is terrified that someone will turn him in.

The fears that are provoked when paranoia and repression hold sway are evoked by the guiding metaphor of the novel, the eye in the door. In the prison cells that hold war deserters and pacifists there is a literal eye on the door; that is, around the circular opening of the keyhole is a painting of a realistic eye. The eye suggests that someone is always watching the imprisoned person. Who is watching? The guards? The State? God? One's conscience? A spy? Billy Prior first encounters the eye in the door when he visits Beattie Roper in her prison cell. At first he is disconcerted by this crude metaphor; then he is deeply troubled by it. He even has a nightmare about the eye in the door. What does the metaphor mean? Certainly it represents the power of the government to spy on its citizens, to oppress those whose viewpoints do not conform to the "party line." The eye in the door also may refer to the fear felt by people like

Manning, who are oppressed in a society that condemns homosexuality as a crime and a perversion.

The metaphor of the eye in the door is given another meaning in Prior's psychological crisis. After visiting Roper in prison, Prior meets her daughter Hettie and an old childhood friend, Paddy MacDowell, who is a deserter. Days later, Prior discovers that there are gaps in his experience that he cannot recall. Some gaps are thirty minutes long; some are as long as three or four hours. Eventually he realizes that he has multiple personalities. He fears that a shadow self is controlling him. Perhaps his shadow self is a monster, a Mr. Hyde. Perhaps Prior has murdered someone and does not even know it.

In the headnote to the novel, Barker quotes *The Strange Case of Dr. Jekyll and Mr. Hyde* (1886), by Robert Louis Stevenson. In that novel Dr. Jekyll learns that his character is intimately related to the character of his shadow self. For Prior the "eye in the door" represents his fear that his shadow self is a cruel, sadistic force watching his every move and dominating his life. In one of his nightmares he strikes at the eye in the door with a knife, as if to destroy a part of himself that is monstrous.

Fortunately for Prior, Rivers is able to assist him in resolving these fears. Late in the novel Prior's alter ego confronts Rivers and claims to know everything about Billy Prior. He maintains that he is superior to Prior because he feels no fear and feels no pain. Eventually Rivers discerns that this personality is called forth by Prior in the face of overwhelming traumatic events. The logic of Prior's unconscious is absolute: If he cannot stand the pain or fear, his other personality will bear it for him. Prior began resorting to this safety valve in order to cope with horrifying experiences in the war. Actually, he has called forth this personality before, when he was a child and felt helplessness and anxiety when his father brutalized his mother. Through therapy he learns that his shadow self is neither evil nor sadistic.

Throughout the novel Rivers struggles to help the men in his care overcome the demons that control their lives. When Manning's panic attacks persist, Rivers hospitalizes him and provides aggressive therapy to help him face the horrors of life in the trenches. In reliving his story and admitting a terrible deed, a "mercy killing" of a young recruit, Manning begins to free himself from another "eye in the door"—his self-imposed guilt and anxiety.

The third character who faces a psychological crisis is Siegfried Sassoon. Sassoon and Rivers are the most complex characters in the novel. Their interactions are subtle, challenging, and deeply felt. It is evident that they are fond of each other. Sassoon sees Rivers as his father confessor, someone who can rescue him from his guilt and anxiety. Rather like Prior, Sassoon found that the only way he could survive at the front was to split his consciousness into two parts—one a gung-ho commander, the other a loving father-figure. Now he tells Rivers he fears that he will not be able to save all of the men in his care.

Rivers understands Sassoon's dilemma. In some respects he faces a similar crisis himself. His role is analogous to a company commander on the Western Front. He heals patients so that—in many cases—they can be sent back to fight again. His fate is the same as Manning's, Prior's, and Sassoon's: These officers have witnessed unspeakable slaughter, but their job is to send men over the tops of the trenches again and again. Neither Rivers nor the officers can do anything to save the young men running into the line of fire. These contradictory and irreconcilable truths are at the core of the madness of war and the psychological disabilities felt by men in war.

How to resolve this dilemma? Rivers notes that in time of war the love between men is glorified in order to form community among the troops, but this arouses anxiety because of society's fears of homosexuality and deviance. Finally, he concludes, his allegiance is to the men in his care, just as the allegiance of the company commanders is to the men in their care. In both cases, the feelings of love for those in one's care is a vital and positive force against the brutality of war.

Regeneration and *The Eye in the Door* are companion novels, best read in order. The latter completes the stories that were introduced in the former. In both novels Barker conveys the sense that war is an all-encompassing experience that is impossible to communicate to anyone who has not experienced it, and perhaps too overwhelming to be understood by those who have experienced it. In some respects they are classic antiwar novels, because they admit to the ambiguities and complexities of the individual's and the society's responses to war.

Robert Yahnke

Sources for Further Study

Chicago Tribune. May 22, 1994, XIV, p. 1.
Kirkus Reviews. LXII, March 15, 1994, p. 317.
Library Journal. April 15, 1994, p. 108.
London Review of Books. XV, October 21, 1993, p. 22.
New Statesman and Society. VI, September 10, 1993, p. 40.
The New York Times Book Review. XCIX, May 15, 1994, p. 9.
The New Yorker. LXX, September 5, 1994, p. 111.
Publishers Weekly. CCXLI, March 14, 1994, p. 63.
The Times Literary Supplement. September 10, 1993, p. 21.
The Washington Post. May 20, 1994, p. C2.

FAMILY

Author: Ian Frazier (1951-)
Publisher: Farrar Straus Giroux (New York). Illustrated. 386 pp. $23.00
Type of work: Biography
Time: 1638-1990
Locale: Ohio and Indiana

An unusual blend of social, community, and family history, focusing on the Midwest from the Civil War era to 1990

Principal personages:
IAN FRAZIER, the author
DAVID FRAZIER, his father
MARGARET (PEGGY) KATHRYN (KATE) HURSH FRAZIER, his mother
EDWIN RAY FRAZIER, his paternal grandfather
CORA WICKHAM FRAZIER, his paternal grandmother
HARRY EDWIN FRAZIER,
LOUIS W. WICKHAM, and
OSINANDER AMARIAH SYLVESTER (O. A. S.) HURSH, his great-grandfathers
OSINANDER (OSIE) CHAPMAN HURSH, his maternal grandfather
FLORA ("BARBAR") EMILY SOPHIA BACHMAN HURSH, his maternal grandmother

Ian Frazier's book, which bears the naïve title *Family*, is considerably more complex than its title suggests. It is neither a purely biographical study of family history, nor an overview of town life in the Midwest, nor an examination of technological growth in the United States, although it is partly all of these. Some readers may find its eclecticism disconcerting; its organization is prismatic rather than chronological, and the immediate effect upon a reader can be bewildering, akin to that of a guest who arrives late at a party of strangers. Names come in quick succession, as well as something of personalities, associations, and accomplishments, but it takes half the evening before the strangers acquire significance more meaningful than they had upon introduction.

Such diachronology has the advantage of highlighting patterns, however, and this is clearly what Frazier intends. None of his antecedents achieved exceptional fame, although several approached greatness. None attained vast wealth, although one named Fanny Benedict (Frazier's great-great-great aunt) married Ohio oil magnate Louis Severance. Even so, the generational characteristics that apply in variation to every individual mentioned in this family album are those of earnest hard work, a predisposition to do what appeared to be the right thing, and a trust (sometimes pathetic) in institutions. Events in the larger world touch their lives, and prevailing social standards influence the decisions they make. Collectively, they are the essence of America's heartland, individuals with whom many readers can identity.

Both sides of Frazier's family spring from the Ohio and Indiana towns of the Western Reserve, that band of territory stretching westward from the original thirteen colonies theoretically as far as the Pacific Coast. Connecticut was among the last of the Colonies to surrender its claims on western land to national jurisdiction, with the result that many of the earliest settlements in the territory bear names identifiable with the eastern origins of their settlers.

Charles P. Wickham, the author's great-great-grandfather on his father's side of the family, was, for example, a leading citizen of Norwalk, Ohio, a town that has perennial associations for the Frazier family. Wickham was a brevetted lieutenant colonel in the Union army during the Civil War, a two-term congressman, and a judge of the Huron County Court of Common Pleas. His son, Louis W. Wickham, born the year after the Civil War, married Ellen Eliza Benedict, the great-granddaughter of Platt Benedict, who originated from Connecticut and founded Norwalk, Ohio, in 1817.

Both Wickham men were attorneys, the son working in his father's firm, and the family became prosperous in the years following the Civil War, primarily as a result of defending railroad interests in the enormous number of damage claims filed by people who had lost relatives, limbs, or property as the railroads pushed westward. Since the railroads never paid a claim until they had taken a plaintiff through every court possible, the Wickham firm, as regional representative of the railroads for Huron County, prospered steadily. Apparently, the fact that the firm's senior partner was also a judge never created a conflict-of-interest question in these many cases.

Frazier uses the Benedict line as a springboard for two excursuses, one on the continuous movement of westward settlement that begins following the Revolutionary War and slows only during the Civil War, to resume with even greater energy after 1865. The Benedict who founded Norwalk, Ohio, was among a number of individuals whose families had received financial settlements as a result of claims made against the states for damages incurred during the Revolutionary War. When Connecticut sold three million acres of the Western Reserve to the Connecticut Land Company in 1795, Benedict bought what land he could, and as he prospered, he bought more. Frazier devotes considerable space to evoking the everyday life of people during this period, using particularly the moving personal history of Comfort Hoyt (the great-grandfather of Frazier's great-great-grandmother), whose Danbury, Connecticut, home and property were destroyed during the Revolution. Hoyt journeyed into the Ohio wilderness entirely on his own, built a one-room log cabin for his family, then returned to Danbury to accompany them back to Ohio the following year. They discovered, upon arriving, that the cabin had been burned to the ground during their absence. Undismayed, Hoyt rebuilt his cabin and prospered.

Frazier's second excursus deals with the fate of the Norwalk, Ohio, volunteers recruited by Charles P. Wickham to serve the Union cause during the Civil War. In this even more detailed account, the author concentrates on the hardships endured during several nearly forgotten engagements, as well as the celebrated one at Chancellorsville, Virginia, which virtually decimated the Ohio men. His hour-by-hour narration of this bloody encounter is already hauntingly familiar to readers of Civil War historiography, and much of it is adapted from Shelby Foote's *The Civil War: A Narrative* (1963), but Frazier intersperses the familiar story with letters written by Wickham as well as with anecdotes from his own 1990 visit to the battlefield. His experiences and interviews there reveal much about what Americans choose to remember and forget. One can hardly ignore that fact that there were enormous numbers of dead on both sides—the physical evidence of military cemeteries is simply too great—but it is more difficult to find specific locations meaningful to the Ohio volunteers. Weeds, interstate highways, suburban developments, and even a threatened theme park often obscure or attempt to sanitize the personal aspects of history.

As the paternal side of Frazier's family had produced farmers whose children became lawyers, the maternal provided nineteenth century America with ministers and academics. These, too, had Ohio associations, though with German and German-Swiss origins. Johannes (John) Bachman, the author's great-great-grandfather, was pastor of the First German Reformed Church, in New Knoxville, Ohio. The church building remains much as it was when Bachman preached there in the late 1890's, despite several renovations and additions; however, New Knoxville itself, a town approximately one hundred miles southwest of Norwalk, is no longer the community of German-speaking immigrants who constituted its original population. It remains a small town, considerably smaller than Norwalk, yet has lost its ethnic German identification. The tiny congregation of its church has become fundamentalist, like many others in the Midwest and South. Its original congregation had been staunchly Lutheran.

Osinander Amariah Sylvester (O. A. S.) Hursh, the author's great-grandfather on his mother's side of the family, reflects this Lutheran tradition. He grew up on a farm near Ithaca, Ohio, taught in a country school to earn money for college, and eventually became a professor of Greek and Latin at Heidelberg College in Tiffin, Ohio, and later a minister in the German Reformed Church. He remained engaged in both teaching and the ministry throughout his life and, although he never had a congregation of his own, rode the length and breadth of Ohio to serve as substitute minister to the numerous small Lutheran parishes scattered about the state. This arduous schedule of preaching and teaching probably taxed his health, for he succumbed suddenly to typhoid fever after a tour of speaking engagements, and died in 1881 at the age of thirty-five.

The pattern that emerges in the author's genealogy is a superb blending of practical and visionary elements, what becomes identifiable as American character. None of Frazier's antecedents was afraid to take chances, and although none succeeded conspicuously, each clearly contributed a thread to the nation's human tapestry. The author's more immediate family, his parents and grandparents, continue in the same vein. Sohio, the regional company that arose after the dissolution of the Standard Oil trust, becomes both employer and investment vehicle for these later generations. The family continues to prosper, quietly and moderately. Here again, Frazier provides an excursus, focusing on the rise of John D. Rockefeller compared to the less spectacular but noteworthy success of his distant cousin by marriage, Louis Severance.

David Frazier, the author's father, struck out boldly in his youth, earning a doctorate in chemistry at Stanford University. He completed his studies just in time to volunteer for the Navy during the final year of World War II, although he saw no action and did not use his training in chemistry until after the war, when he returned to his home state and found a position in research in the company that would become Sohio. His work in fuel recovery processes and synthetics was distinguished, yet it was accomplished as part of a research team.

Margaret (Peggy) Kathryn (Kate) Hursh, the author's mother, provided a perfect counterpoint to the chemist's practical nature. She had a lifelong passion for the theater, but as a woman of the 1950's put aside these ambitions to rear five children and live in an Ohio suburb. Their home was comfortable, yet in most respects indistinguishable from those that surrounded it. Both of the author's parents recognized a certain aridity in their environment, but they take satisfaction from the promise their children's future seems to offer. As the author re-creates their story, their lives seem filled with small happinesses and occasional tragedies, the most poignant of the latter being the death of Fritz, the author's younger brother.

When Fritz succumbs to cancer, Ian Frazier is an undergraduate at Harvard, and the latent searching that had always been present in the generations of Fraziers, Wickhams, and Hurshes finally surfaces. One sees it first in the author's academic career, as he shifts from the sciences to the arts and ultimately to the almost sinister comprehensiveness of what comes to be called American Studies. Perhaps middle-class affluence of the 1960's allowed less definite goals than previous generations had had. Possibly, too, the war in Vietnam disillusioned the author's generation in ways more permanent than even his great-grandfather had experienced during the Civil War. Social inequities among the races also play a part in the author's discontent, as he becomes increasingly sensitive to the aspirations of people who had never had his advantages.

Family concludes in this disquieting minor key. As if recognizing that a meaningful life is not consequent upon possessions, the author's mother and father leave their Hudson, Ohio, home and move to a small apartment. His maternal grandparents retire to New Mexico. Frazier himself moves first to Manhattan, then to Montana, and finally to Brooklyn, New York, marries in his early thirties, and ultimately decides to become a full-time writer.

While at Harvard, he had achieved notoriety as one of the founding editors of the *National Lampoon*, the nationally published derivative of the *Harvard Lampoon*, the celebrated humor magazine. Frazier masterminded the concocted photograph that the magazine published of a naked Henry Kissinger, and this brought him to the attention of the national media. As an adult, Frazier has become considerably less brash, and his work focuses on forgotten elements of the mundane and personal past as seen through larger, dominating world events. Undoubtedly, his gift for perceiving importance in what many would discard as insignificant has supplied his authentic, distinctive voice as a writer. With this understood, *Family* is the logical, perhaps the only possible sequel to his previous book, *Great Plains* (1989).

One genuinely comes to know and like the Frazier clan through this book, all of them in all their generations. One weeps at the sad, intimately described deaths of two children (the author's brother and a boy who would have become Frazier's uncle). The death by suicide of Frazier's elderly grandmother, the Alzheimer's disease that afflicts his father in the 1980's, and his mother's death from cancer in 1988 are no less affecting. Still, if a reader's first reaction is regret for all the unrealized possibilities almost within the grasp of each of these people, one also senses the indomitable hope that each new generation carries. Although Frazier's mother never realized her dream of attending the Yale Drama School, she did raise a son who attended Harvard, a successful author who describes in the final pages of *Family* his unrestrained joy when he feels his unborn child moving in its mother's womb.

Robert J. Forman

Sources for Further Study

Chicago Tribune. November 13, 1994, XIV, p. 5.
Commonweal. CXXI, December 2, 1994, p. 24.
Library Journal. CXIX, October 15, 1994, p. 69.
Los Angeles Times Book Review. November 27, 1994, p. 3.
National Review. XLVI, December 19, 1994, p. 57.
The New York Times Book Review. XCIX, November 6, 1994, p. 9.
Newsweek. CXXIV, November 7, 1994, p. 73.
Publishers Weekly. CCXLI, November 14, 1994, p. 49.
The Wall Street Journal. November 30, 1994, p. A16.
The Washington Post Book World. XXIV, October 16, 1994, p. 3.

FATHERALONG
A Meditation on Fathers and Sons, Race and Society

Author: John Edgar Wideman (1941-)
Publisher: Pantheon Books (New York). 197 pp. $21.00
Type of work: Memoir; essays
Time: The 1940's to the 1990's
Locale: Pittsburgh, Pennsylvania; Greenwood, South Carolina; and Amherst, Massachusetts

In essays describing the search for his father and their common Southern roots, John Edgar Wideman lays out a number of important ideas about race relations in the United States

Principal personages:
JOHN EDGAR WIDEMAN, a fifty-year-old African American novelist and short-story writer, living and teaching in Amherst, Massachusetts
EDGAR WIDEMAN, his father, who has been separated from the family for some years
BETTE, his mother, still living in the Pittsburgh neighborhood where Wideman grew up
HARRY WIDEMAN, his paternal grandfather, who moved north from South Carolina, and who died in 1978

With *Fatheralong: A Meditation on Fathers and Sons, Race and Society* John Edgar Wideman takes his place—with James Baldwin and, before him, Richard Wright—as an African American novelist and short-story writer who is raising a persistent and eloquent voice in the debate on race in America. The six essays collected here not only tell several poignant personal stories but also raise questions in a voice that will be hard for any sensitive reader, white or black, not to hear.

The five essays that make up the short memoir proper are prefaced by "Common Ground," an essay that defines the terms and assumptions of the whole collection. Here Wideman makes his most important statements about race and society in America. The "common ground" that African Americans share as "survivors," Wideman notes, includes "a continent, a gene pool, a history" but also "the higher ground, spiritual and material, we strive to gain." What stands in the way of black progress is the "paradigm of race—a vision of humankind and society based on the premise that not all people are created equal and some are born with the right to exploit others." Race not only reduces the complexity of black cultural history and "preempts our right to situate our story where we choose" but also confuses and cripples people of any color.

> So race ain't it. Huh-uh. The common ground is elsewhere: the bonds we struggle to sever, discover, invent, sustain, celebrate. If we pay attention, we hear many stories of black people trying to work out ways of living on the earth. Taken together the voices sing out a chorus of achievement.

One antidote to the distorting "paradigm of race" is thus this book itself. The stories Wideman tells here can help African Americans in their struggle to "reinvent" themselves by giving them "a glimpse of common ground where fathers and sons, mothers and daughters can sit down and talk, learn to talk and listen together again."

Wideman is attempting to "replace the paradigm of race," to understand what human beings might be without it. Thus he proposes to write about "fathers, color, roots, time, language."

The memoir itself is less theoretical and more personal, but bears out the ideas about race and racism that Wideman has outlined in this preface. In essence, the five essays of *Fatheralong*—"Promised Land," "Fatheralong," "Littleman," "Picking Up My Father at the Springfield Station," and "Father Stories"—describe trips that Wideman takes with his father: short ones, as when his father drives him to the Pittsburgh airport after a family visit; longer ones, as when the two fly to South Carolina to find their Wideman roots; and celebratory journeys, as when the whole family converges on Amherst for the wedding of one of Wideman's sons.

Put in socioeconomic terms, the book is thus about places and about the history of African Americans' getting to them: to America as slaves in the distant past, to the crossroads town of Promised Land, South Carolina, as survivors during Reconstruction, to Pittsburgh as black migrants in the beginning of the twentieth century looking for better work, and back to South Carolina as adults trying to understand something of "the miracle and disgrace" of this complex history. The book is thus a personal course on reading history and geography. As Wideman writes about the crucial trip south with his father, "Perhaps Promised Land is one of the maps I've returned to South Carolina with my father to learn to read. Or draw, even as we search."

The trips described in *Fatheralong* are not only geographical and historical; they are emotional and psychological as well. They describe Wideman's attempt to understand his father, their common roots, and thus himself, and finally his relationship to his own sons. (*Fatheralong*, appropriately, is dedicated both to Wideman's father and to his sons.) The book is a personal memoir of fathers and sons, a geography of growing up black in the United States, and thus a story about living in the richest country in the world but not sharing that wealth.

Edgar Lawson Wideman left his family when his children were still in various stages of growing up. The author does not give all the reasons for this breakup, but readers witness instead the consequences: the difficulties of family visits and gatherings, when John Edgar and his own family return to Homewood, the black section of Pittsburgh where he grew up; the complex maneuvering to see everyone, and then the guilt that he has not spent enough time with his father during these visits. Part of this emotion, perhaps, prompts his suggestion to his father that they take a trip together to Greenwood, South Carolina, and trace the family roots back to where Wideman's grandfather started. Much of *Fatheralong* concerns that trip and its successful conclusions: the friends they make, the history they uncover, and the relationship they establish.

Yet simultaneously all these trips are also connected to racial history, Wideman argues.

> Let me say it again, in the simplest terms. This country, as it presently functions, stands between black fathers and sons, impeding communication, frustrating development, killing or destroying the bodies and minds of young men, short-circuiting the natural process of growth, maturity, the cycle

> of generations. This country, as it's constituted today, its basic institutions and values, or rather the corrupted versions of these institutions and values produced by the paradigm of race, has abandoned its children.

Among its many scars, the paradigm of race denies black diversity and "transforms color into a sign of class, culture, and inferiority." In the course of *Fatheralong*, Wideman reveals not only his own personal history, the unique cultural background he shares with his family, and the rich ethnic history he shares with so many others but also—as he writes at the end of a letter to his own son in the last chapter—these effects of racism,

> a wall between my grandfathers and myself, my father and
> me, between the two of us, father and son, son and father.
> So we must speak these stories to one another.
> Love.

Readers will share Wideman's continuing attempts to penetrate his father's pride and to describe his dignity. In the United States, Wideman demonstrates, neither is an easy task.

Fatheralong is filled with wonderful family detail: of the great-grandfather, the Reverend T. W. Wideman, who died with his mouth wide open; the memorable residents of Promised Land whom Wideman and his father meet, such as James "Littleman" Harris and Bowie Lomax; the cemetery they visit where other Widemans rest. Like his best fiction, Wideman's essays balance ideas and images easily. Readers share the memories of Wideman's Pittsburgh childhood, see him visiting his father at work, sitting on his shoulders at a snowy Thanksgiving parade. They also feel the conflict between his parents, the pull of loyalty and betrayal, the tension between competing parental philosophies of life. ("The first rule of my father's world is that you stand alone. Alone, alone, alone . . . My mother's first rule was love. She refused to believe she was alone.") Wideman vividly describes his younger self standing outside his father's bedroom listening to him sleep during the day, and later studying the bodies of the women in his family as he tries to discover who and what he is.

Several incidents here have found their way into Wideman's fiction: the autobiographical story of visiting his father in the restaurant of Kaufmann's department store, where Edgar works as a waiter, for example, was originally told in the short story "Across the Wide Missouri," published in the collection *Damballah* (1981). Much of the history of Wideman's jailed brother Robby was earlier related in the powerful nonfictional *Brothers and Keepers* (1984). Many of Wideman's novels and short stories are set in the Homewood section of Pittsburgh he visits in *Fatheralong*.

Throughout the memoir, Wideman analyzes or comments on a great number of current social and political problems: prejudice and violence; the economic geography of Pittsburgh, where Wideman grew up and which, like so many cities, still stultifies human lives; gangs and their clothing—which cries out, as Wideman writes, "*we're still kids.*"

As in his fiction, Wideman's writing style is perfect for conveying his personal story. His prose is full of long, rich sentences that wind around the complex, convoluted family history related here. His use of repetition brings readers closer to the family history—lists of people and places encountered—that he relates. His voice is lyrical throughout, even when it is angry.

In many ways, Wideman may remind readers of other contemporary African American writers—Alice Walker, perhaps, and the South she renders in *The Color Purple* (1982), or Toni Morrison, especially her novel *Song of Solomon* (1977), in which a son searches for his father's roots in the Deep South. Yet *Fatheralong* also rings with the reverberations of works by male writers, such as Philip Roth's *Patrimony* (1991) and Richard Rodriguez' *Days of Obligation: An Argument with My Mexican Father* (1993), both part of an emergent literary consciousness of male roles and gender history.

Like Richard Wright and James Baldwin before him, then, John Edgar Wideman is making a wake-up call to America about race and racism. Like Roth, Rodriguez, Robert Bly, and others, he is also giving a call about the sons who have been abandoned along the road of American progress, a renewed call about the responsibilities of fathers for their children—and the responsibility of the culture for that deteriorating relationship. At a time when politicians talk easily about taking children from parents on welfare, Wideman's book contains an important message.

> Father stories are about establishing origins and through them legitimizing claims of ownership, of occupancy and identity. They connect what's momentary and passing to what surpasses, materiality to ideal. . . . Men's stories, women's stories. How they are about blood and roots and earth, how they must be repeated each generation or they are lost forever.

Wideman has told his own stories in one of the most powerful books of 1994, a book that, one hopes, will have a lasting effect on American culture.

David Peck

Sources for Further Study

American Visions. IX, October, 1994, p. 38.
Atlanta Journal Constitution. December 4, 1994, p. N8.
Chicago Tribune. October 23, 1994, XIV, p. 8.
Ebony. L, January, 1995, p. 22.
Los Angeles Times Book Review. December 25, 1994, p. 2.
The New York Times Book Review. XCIX, November 13, 1994, p. 11.
Publishers Weekly. CCXLI, August 8, 1994, p. 406.
USA Today. November 2, 1994, p. D7.
The Wall Street Journal. December 23, 1994, p. A8.
The Washington Post. December 12, 1994, p. B1.

FIGURES IN A WESTERN LANDSCAPE
Men and Women of the Northern Rockies

Author: Elizabeth Stevenson (1919-)
Publisher: The Johns Hopkins University Press (Baltimore). 222 pp. $25.95
Type of work: Historical biography
Time: 1830-1903
Locale: The northern Rocky Mountains

This series of biographical sketches focuses on the way its subjects responded to the landscape of the northern Rockies and created the human history of the region

Principal personages:

MERIWETHER LEWIS, a Western explorer who was murdered on the Natchez Trace in 1809
OSBORNE RUSSELL, a Maine native who kept a journal of his fur-trapping in the Rockies
JOHN KIRK TOWNSEND, one of the first naturalists to go west (in 1834) and describe his findings
JOHN OWEN, a trader who helped settle the Bitterroot Valley in what is today Montana
FATHER PIERRE JEAN DE SMET, the first Catholic missionary in the northern Plains and Rockies
JAMES and GRANVILLE STUART, brothers who were early settlers in Montana
THOMAS DIMSDALE, a visionary Englishman who edited a newspaper and started a school in Montana
HENRY PLUMMER, a Montana sheriff who was hanged by vigilantes
GEORGE CROOK and JOHN GREGORY BOURKE, U.S. Army officers who were prominent in the High Plains Indian wars
PRETTY-SHIELD, an Indian medicine woman
NANNIE ALDERSON, a Montana settler wife
PARIS GIBSON, the founder of Great Falls, Montana
CHARLES M. RUSSELL, a famous painter of the American West
CALAMITY JANE, one of the West's legendary figures, born Martha Jane Cannary Burke in Missouri

Elizabeth Stevenson is Candler Professor of American Studies, Emeritus, at Emory University. She was born in Montana in 1919 to one of "a colony of six related families transplanted from the yeoman farming country of hilly north Georgia" and left Great Falls in 1932, when her family returned to Georgia. Her Montana childhood shaped her imagination for life, and in 1979 she returned to the region "to look at a remembered landscape and see it again with a kind of critical questioning." She approached history as biography and explains of *Figures in a Western Landscape: Men and Women of the Northern Rockies*, "I saw a basic fact as underlying all theories [of the American western movement]: that the dry regions west of the ninety-eighth or one hundredth meridian are different from the wetter and more humid regions of the East and that this difference would largely determine the kind of life that could be lived in this vast space."

The first figure in Stevenson's landscape is Meriwether Lewis. In 1809, a few years after his return from his famous Western expedition with William Clark, Lewis was robbed and murdered at age thirty-five on the Natchez Trace between Memphis and Nashville. Stevenson finds in Lewis' journals a compound of Enlightenment rationalism and the romanticism of his day. Whereas Clark was straightforward and objective in both his life and his journal accounts, Lewis was introspective and sometimes self-consciously literary. Stevenson calls Lewis "a man of the advent of a new age, that of the romantic view impinging on the useful, rational view of landscape and life."

Osborne Russell was a Maine Yankee who went west in 1834 with a party of fur trappers led by Nathaniel Wyeth, and he took off into the mountains on his own the next year. The life he lived among Indians and occasional whites was cruel and harsh. What interests Stevenson about Russell is the awareness of his surroundings that he reveals in such journal remarks as "the scenery now spread out before me put me somewhat in a Poetical humour."

John Kirk Townsend shared Russell's ardor for mountain landscapes and surpassed him as an observer and a naturalist. Townsend left Independence, Missouri, in 1834 with a companion naturalist, Thomas Nuttall, and overcame a natural fastidiousness to plunge into the brutal life of the region. Stevenson describes him as a rationalist who sought to fit the West into "the grand rational scheme," and who as "the new scientist was thus as much an enemy of the way of life of the Indians as the thoughtless and speculative trapper."

Two important figures in the Bitterroot Valley between the 1840's and the 1870's were the first Catholic missionary to the northern Plains and Rockies, Father Pierre Jean De Smet, and "Major" John Owen, a trader who bought an abandoned mission and turned it into a social center as well as an economic influence. Stevenson sees De Smet and Owen as part of "an early phase in Anglo western life," intermediaries between the first explorers and early settlers like the Stuart brothers, James and Granville, who had left their native Iowa for the California gold fields and made their way to Montana in 1857. The Stuarts were the kind of solid citizens who would travel 150 miles to buy five books for five dollars each: Shakespeare, Byron, a life of Napoleon, a French Bible, and Adam Smith's *The Wealth of Nations* (1776).

Two lives unusually intertwined were those of Thomas Dimsdale and Henry Plummer. Plummer came to Bannack in 1862 and immediately distinguished himself as a fast man with a six-shooter when he killed a man in a shootout. He was tried, acquitted, and then elected sheriff. Another new arrival in Montana, Thomas Dimsdale in nearby Virginia City, edited the first newspaper in the territory, the *Montana Post*. Dimsdale's life intersected Plummer's when he wrote up the story of Plummer's hanging by vigilantes. Whether justice was done in the execution of Plummer, who was accused of conniving with outlaws, is still debated. What interests Stevenson is the sympathy with the vigilantes revealed by Dimsdale, "a man who loved civility and culture, yet was fascinated by evil and excused violence."

Lieutenant John Bourke went to the northern Plains in 1875 as aide-de-camp to General George Crook. Their mission was to subdue the Cheyennes and the Sioux, but the military tradition that they inherited was hardly a heroic one: "What people behind the frontier never realized was that most of the battles in the 1860s and early 1870s had not been and would not be formal military engagements, but a series of U.S. Army attacks upon unarmed, usually sleeping, Indian settlements in which women and children, as well as whatever men happened to be in the village, were killed."

When Crook's units began harassing the Cheyennes and the Sioux, these tribes joined forces to fight back beyond what had been expected of them. Although Crook was an accomplished officer, he loathed the whites whose behavior toward the Indians he regarded as contemptible, and he earned the respect of his enemies. Bourke's feelings were similar. He liked his Shoshone foes better than the riffraff of the mining towns.

The result of these two officers' experience with Indians was unexpected. When Crook retired, he became a spokesman for Indian rights and defended them as "the intellectual peer[s] of most, if not all, the various nationalities we have assimilated." Back in Omaha in the 1880's, Bourke married and settled down but yearned for the old days on the Powder River. His affinities for Indians led him back to the Rockies and to the Southwest and serious study of Indian cultures. So it was that in 1891 Bourke published *Scatalogic Rites of All Nations*, a new edition of which Sigmund Freud published in Vienna in 1913 with his own introduction.

Two women whom Stevenson admires as survivors were Pretty-Shield and Nannie Alderson. Pretty-Sheild was a Crow medicine woman whose husband, Goes-Ahead, had been one of General George Custer's scouts. When Pretty-Shield told her story in the 1930's, she repeated the account of Custer's defeat as it had been told to her by Goes-Ahead. Pretty-Shield's backward look at her life "had seemed to signal a closing down of any way toward freedom, spontaneity, opportunity, purpose." For Nannie Alderson, who came to Indian country as the young wife of a rancher, what she saw looking back was a life of hardship that opened up into promise for the future. Stevenson catches the pathos in the two women's stories, one defeated and skeptical, the other sober but hopeful.

Stevenson effectively juxtaposes the lives of Paris Gibson and Charles M. Russell to tell how the modern city of Great Falls grew up in a lonely region of Montana. Gibson, born in Brownfield, Maine, in 1830, left the Maine legislature for life in the West. After founding two mills and becoming a civil mainstay in Saint Anthony Falls (later Minneapolis), Gibson in 1879 moved west again, this time to a life of sheep ranching on the Missouri River in Montana. Impressed by Lewis and Clark's account of some waterfalls upriver from his domain, Gibson traveled to the falls in 1880 and determined to build a city there. He did just that, helped along by clever politicking in the Benjamin Harrison Administration.

In 1920, the ninety-year-old Gibson was honored by a celebration in Great Falls, and the prairie cemetery where he is buried bears a stone marker reading "Paris Gibson, Founder of Great Falls." Among the participants at the ceremonies for Gibson was Charles M. Russell, born in St. Louis in 1864 and a dropout from a New Jersey military academy and a St. Louis art school. His father sent the sixteen-year-old Russell to

Montana to settle him down, but Russell took up with an old hunter, became a skilled horse wrangler, and from then on was "lost to civilization."

In 1888 Russell went north to Canada, where he lived with Blood Indians and became fluent in both their spoken language and their sign language. Enamored of the frontier life, Russell poured his vision into his paintings, many of which were sold by two bars in Great Falls, the Silver Dollar and the Mint. The valuable Mint collection was bought by a Texas millionaire and is now in the Amon Carter Museum of Western Art in Fort Worth. Russell's funeral in 1926 was "a poignant celebration of a myth"; his body was pulled to the cemetery by horses in an ancient glass-bodied hearse, and his own horse, Redwing, was led behind with reversed stirrups. He was buried across the cemetery from Paris Gibson, with a large boulder giving his name and dates and a foot marker reading simply "C. M. R." Stevenson acknowledges that the prosperous city of Great Falls fulfills Gibson's "dream of the good life," but "it is Russell's feckless dream of irresponsible freedom in the great space surrounding this urban center which still has mythical power."

Stevenson's longest and most scholarly endeavor comes in the chapter "Who Was Calamity Jane? A Speculation." Martha Jane Cannary Burke was born in Missouri in 1852, moved west with her parents in 1865, and two years later was an orphan about to become a frontier myth. She died in South Dakota in 1903 and was buried in Deadwood next to Wild Bill Hickok, with whose life she is problematically linked.

Of the many mysteries surrounding Jane's life, the most tantalizing emerged in 1941, when a woman calling herself Jean Hickok McCormick appeared with a collection of unsent letters that she claimed had been written to her by Jane. McCormick claimed that she was the legitimate daughter of Jane and Hickok and had been given away in infancy to an Anglo-Irishman named James O'Neil. The letters, written between 1877 and 1903, had been sent to O'Neil in 1903, and he had given the collection to his foster daughter in 1912, so McCormick claimed. The letters present an interesting case: If genuine, they reveal a much more complicated person than the myth had before sustained; if faked, they are a superb literary creation. Stevenson says that judgment must be suspended, but she sees in the letters an image of the myth of Calamity Jane itself: a story of the frontier in which the real and the imagined are inseparable. This is the story that Stevenson has told well here, of larger-than-life individuals posed against a sublime backdrop.

Frank Day

Sources for Further Study

Choice. XXXII, September, 1994, p. 199.
The Christian Science Monitor. April 8, 1994, p. 13.
History Today. XLIV, April, 1994, p. 57.
Wilderness. LVII, Spring, 1994, p. 32.

THE FINAL MARTYRS

Author: Shūsaku Endō (1923-)
Translated from the Japanese by Van C. Gessel
Publisher: New Directions (New York). 199 pp. $21.95
Type of work: Short stories

The second collection of stories by the well-known Japanese Catholic novelist to be translated into English

The fact that Shūsaku Endō is a Christian in Japan, a country in which Christians have always been a small minority, is the most important single influence on his writing. Best known as the author of *Chimmoku* (1966; *Silence*, 1969), a novel about the persecution of Japanese Christians in the early seventeenth century, Endō has been called one of the most accomplished writers in Japan. *Stained-Glass Elegies*, Endō's first collection of short stories, originally published in 1965 and translated in 1984, primarily focuses on spiritual issues of guilt, commitment, and ego-denying love. This second collection continues those preoccupations, featuring stories mostly written between 1968 and 1985.

Although basically realistic, the pacing and style of Endō's stories may be somewhat unfamiliar to readers accustomed to the minimalist realism of the Chekhov tradition or the magical realism of the Kafka tradition. Endō's stories seem more old-fashioned; they are somewhat leisurely and ruminative, most often characterized by the steady voice of an older man narrating a simple story or recalling a past event. There are no cryptic ellipses here to make the reader wonder what is being left out, nor are there any uneasy departures into alternate realities that make the reader wonder just exactly where he or she is. Because these stories move casually along with no strong, motivated direction nor an emphatic sense of closure, they may seem less structured than most Western short stories. As much as they seem to be merely realistic vignettes, however, they are in fact heavily weighted with theme, usually the theme of spiritual struggles, particularly from within a Catholic perspective.

The title story is perhaps the most conventionally moral in terms of its exemplary generic type and its straightforward structure and theme. Told in simple narrative fashion, it is set in the nineteenth century during one of the times of persecution of Japanese Christians. The central character is Kisuke, a giant of a man who is clumsy, ineffectual, and easily frightened. On July 15, 1867, at the start of what is known as the fourth persecution at Uragami (a district near Nakasaki), Kisuke's village is raided by government agents to seek out and punish anyone who has violated the prohibition against Christianity. Those who are captured are tortured to make them recant their religion. Although most hold firm, Kisuke's cowardice makes him quickly give, and he trudges away from the village, transformed into a Judas figure who has betrayed his savior. Unable to bear the guilt of his actions, two years later, Kisuke, now a beggar, returns to the prison where his friends are kept, for he has heard a voice telling him that all he has to do is go with the others; even if he is afraid of the torture and runs away again, it is all right. Kisuke's return, in spite of his terror, reaffirms to the others that they have been right to uphold their faith, for it indicates the power of Christian forgiveness; Kisuke's friend tells him that it is all right if he apostatizes again, that Jesus is pleased just because he came. Thus, Kisuke becomes one of the most loved of the final martyrs, because he came back even though he was the most frightened.

Several of these stories are somewhat autobiographical, in that the narrator is a novelist like Endō himself who explores the motives and mysteries of those around him. For example, "Shadows" is in the form of a long unsent letter written by a novelist to a Catholic priest that he knew in his youth and has only recently seen again. The narrator tells the priest that he is one of the important narrative figures in his fiction and that although he has written about him three times previously, the works have been failures because he did not have a firm grasp on who the priest really is. The epistolary story is an exploration of the writer's memories of the priest to try to discover what fascination he holds for him. The narrator's central concern is the fact that the priest became involved with a Japanese woman and thus betrayed not only his faith but those, such as the narrator, who looked up to him as an idealized image. The story ends as it begins, with the narrator's having seen the priest recently in a restaurant, and having watched him quickly and inconspicuously cross himself before eating his meal. After all his efforts to recall his relationship with the priest and to discover his essential nature, the narrator ends by saying that the one gesture is all that he really understands about the priest now. Given the mystery of faith, perhaps this is all that he can know.

In his first collection, *Stained-Glass Elegies*, Endō included one story entitled "A Forty-Year-Old Man," which recounts the experience of a seriously ill man (Endō was once hospitalized for a period with lung disease) who discovers a symbol of Christ's pity and love in a mynah bird. In this new collection, he includes a story entitled "A Fifty-year-old Man" and another entitled "A Sixty-year-old Man." The first also focuses on a man's relationship to an animal, in this case an old dog who serves as a reminder of the protagonist's own advancing age, but whose death at the end of the story stands for a kind of Christian sacrifice that symbolically allows the protagonist's ill brother to live. The sixty-year-old man of the second story is a writer who is rewriting a book entitled *The Life of Jesus*, and who is dissatisfied with the way he has previously explained how Jesus' followers could have abandoned him so readily. He finds his answer after meeting a young girl about whom he has sadistic dreams; he knows that his wish to defile the girl in his dreams is because of the jealousy of a sixty-year-old man toward a young woman whose life still stretches ahead of her, and he knows that those who spat on Jesus did so because of the same envy. The central line in the story is his realization that "the ugliness of old age is the inability to be free of such wretched attachments to life."

Other stories also deal with increasing age and impending death. The narrator of "Heading Home" is a writer whose brother has recently died and who must make arrangements to have his ashes buried in the same grave as that of his mother. Having felt that as long as his brother was alive he stood between him and death, now he feels death looming like a "black barricade" on the path ahead of him. After his brother's burial, he stands before the tombstone and notes that a large empty space has been left between the names of his mother and brother, and he accepts with equanimity the fact that one day his name will be etched there.

The story "Life" focuses on a young boy whose parents' marriage is disintegrating, a recurring theme in Endō's stories. To show his anger toward them and his mother's harsh treatment of him, the boy steals a ring that his mother treasures and allows the theft to be blamed on a Manchurian houseboy who has been devoted to him; the boy must then deal with the guilt that results from his betrayal.

Although Endō usually does not make use of metaphoric devices to communicate his theme, nor does he often focus on the more complex theological implications of Catholic symbolism, the story "The Last Supper" does focus on the paradox of the communion—eating the body of Christ. In the story, a psychiatrist listens to the confession of a soldier who, during the war, ate the flesh of a dead comrade in order to survive. This story is then connected to another one about a plane crash in the Andes mountains in which a priest, knowing that he is going to die, tells the survivors that they must eat his flesh so that they can be saved. The Christian symbolic implications are obvious here—the sacrifice of the one so that the others can live, and the willingness to participate in the communion in which to eat the body is to eat the love that the sacrifice implies.

The final story in the collection, "The Box," moves even more closely toward a mystical treatment of Christian eschatology, and is perhaps the story most similar to those in the Western tradition. It centers on a central symbolic object and takes place in a world that is simultaneously both real and the realm of desire. The central theme of the story is stated emphatically when, after relating an anecdote about talking to his plants, the narrator says that humans and animals are not the only ones that have hearts and language and faculties; even things humans think of as simple objects—sticks and stones—have some kind of power living inside them. The story begins when the narrator, once again a writer, finds an old wooden box in an antique shop, which contains, among other things, a Bible with some postcards inside and a photograph album. He is especially interested in the postcards addressed to a woman with the French-sounding name of Mademoiselle Louge, and some photographs in the album that show an old deserted highway from before the war.

Being a writer and curious about such things, he inquires about who the woman was. He learns that Mademoiselle Louge had been tortured during the war by the Japanese military police for not agreeing to spy for them. After the war, when American soldiers question her about this and confront her with her torturers, she denies that they did anything to her. When the narrator goes back and looks at the postcards, he notes that their return addresses are actually references to passages in the Bible, which in turn are allusions to the war and peace efforts sent to Mademoiselle Louge and then passed on to others. He believes that the postcards had taken on a will of their own and had been waiting patiently for someone like him who could reveal their truth. He ends the story by explaining that this is why he speaks to his plants, for he thinks that plants must converse with each other and that trees and rocks and even postcards "saturated with the thoughts of men must speak to one another in hushed voices."

Although the work of Shūsaku Endō is not so well known in the west as the fiction of his countrymen Yukio Mishima or Ryunosuke Akutagawa, this fact may change with the release of the film version of his novel *Silence*, which has been in production under the direction of Martin Scorsese. In a world that is rapidly becoming more and more multicultural, Western readers need to read a writer such as Endō, who has long struggled with the difficult connection between two cultures, and has successfully integrated them into a unified world of human experience.

Charles E. May

Sources for Further Study

America. CLXXI, November 19, 1994, p. 28.
Christianity Today. XXXVIII, October 3, 1994, p. 44.
Far Eastern Economic Review. CLVII, January 27, 1994, p. 37.
Kirkus Reviews. LXII, July 1, 1994, p. 865.
Library Journal. CXIX, September 1, 1994, p. 217.
Los Angeles Times Book Review. September 18, 1994, p. 13.
National Catholic Reporter. XXXI, November 18, 1994, p. 23.
New Statesman and Society. VI, April 30, 1993, p. 44.
The Observer. August 29, 1994, p. 53.
Publishers Weekly. CCXLI, August 15, 1994, p. 88.

A FISH IN THE WATER
A Memoir

Author: Mario Vargas Llosa (1936-)
First published: El pez en el agua, 1993
Translated from the Spanish by Helen R. Lane
Publisher: Farrar Straus Giroux (New York). 532 pp. $25.00
Type of work: Memoir
Time: 1936-1990
Locale: Peru

In this dramatic and intricately structured memoir, Vargas Llosa juxtaposes the rise and fall of his Peruvian presidential candidacy with youthful memories of his artistic growth

Principal personages:
MARIO VARGAS LLOSA, an internationally known Peruvian writer
ERNESTO J. VARGAS, his father
AUNT JULIA, his aunt and first wife
PATRICIA, his present wife
ALAN GARCÍA, a former president of Peru
ALBERTO FUJIMORI, Vargas Llosa's political opponent in the Peruvian presidential race

In August, 1987, Mario Vargas Llosa suddenly found himself popular enough to consider running for president of Peru. He had published an essay, "Towards a Totalitarian Peru," in the *El Comercio* newspaper objecting to the government's recently declared intention to nationalize businesses, and an unexpected outpouring of public support for his position led him to consider entering politics. He believed that free-market economic reform could save Peru from its declining fortunes, so he energetically set about creating a plan for governing from his principle. He campaigned for three years, forming his Freedom Movement Party, giving speeches at rallies, and traveling to visit foreign dignitaries, until he lost the election to Alberto Fujimori on June 10, 1990. The rise and fall of his candidacy and his ambivalent reactions to his immersion in politics form the backbone of this memoir, but he complicates matters by interspersing his story with an account of his youth in Peru. Vargas Llosa humanizes and particularizes what might have been a dry and somewhat bitter campaign record with memories of his childhood and apprentice years as a writer.

A Fish in the Water: A Memoir has twenty chapters, with odd chapters chronicling Vargas Llosa's early autobiography and even chapters describing the presidential campaign. He used basically the same structure in his novel *La tía Julia y el escribidor* (1977; *Aunt Julia and the Scriptwriter*, 1982), half of which is devoted to an autobiographical story and half to soap-opera plots. In both books, the alternating plots speak to one another and tease the reader into unraveling their unstated correspondences. Showing a true storyteller's craft, Vargas Llosa often ends chapters on cliff-edge dramatic moments. The first chapter ends with the young Mario first learning to fear his father, while the second chapter concludes with the older Vargas Llosa standing in triumph before his first successful rally. The tones of the two juxtaposed narratives sometimes contrast with each other. A happy period from his youth plays against a bleak period from his campaign, and vice versa. The book's structure keeps the reader off balance, shifting between the particulars of memory and the generalizations of political commentary.

This dual structure of the memoir reflects a thematic split in Vargas Llosa's life between his strong interests in politics and literature. As the title of his memoir suggests, Vargas Llosa has a deep ambivalence about immersing himself in a protracted campaign, though he admits that he could become wholly impassioned about and committed to politics. He devotes most of one chapter to describing his undergraduate participation in a clandestine Marxist organization at the University of San Marcos until he realized the "inanity" of the group's discussions. He titles another chapter with his nickname, "The Fierce Little Sartrean," in acknowledgment of his youthful devotion to Jean-Paul Sartre and Sartre's credo in favor of political commitment. He worked as a speechwriter and political journalist for years. His first short story drew inspiration from a school protest, setting the pattern for the large political strain in his novels such as *Conversación en la catedral* (1969; *Conversation in the Cathedral*, 1975), *La guerra del fin del mundo* (1981; *The War of the End of the World*, 1984), and *Historia de Mayta* (1984; *The Real Life of Alejandro Mayta*, 1986). When the opportunity for running for president arose, Vargas Llosa was naturally inclined to try. His wife Patricia warned him against trying to "live out" a great novel instead of writing one, and the memoir validates her warning by depicting the many problems a writer encounters in a political arena.

Difficulties arose when Vargas Llosa turned from writing his platform to trying to lead. Old world Peruvian politics and its corruptions, forms, and rituals kept interfering with Vargas Llosa's attempts to carry his ideas to the people. He learned early that all that most politicians desire and think about is power—how to get it and keep it for as long as possible—and not about innovative reform. He mistakenly enlisted the help of two established parties, the Popular Action and the Christian Popular Party, even though political advisers had told him that a large part of his initial appeal stemmed from his lack of affiliations with politics as usual. Vargas Llosa found himself unable to get along with the party bosses who dominated the smaller districts of Peru. He characterizes them as a "type" with "tight-fitting suits" and "ridiculous little hairline mustaches" and found it very difficult to cultivate them as political allies. He realized with some bitterness that the Peruvian people do not vote according to ideas but according to obscure whims in part created by the images and personalities of candidates conveyed by the press. By the time the Fujimori campaign turned to slandering Vargas Llosa's tax records and questioning his agnosticism, he despaired over the way such "dirty war" tactics caricatured and parodied the electoral processes of other countries.

In terms of political ability, Alberto Fujimori provided an interesting contrast to Vargas Llosa. To all of Vargas Llosa's plans for governing, Fujimori brought almost nothing except his lack of any obvious ties to established politics (although Vargas Llosa suspected that Fujimori had the hidden support of Alan García and the Apristas, the party then in power). Fujimori was so much the dark-horse candidate—a former rector seen riding around on a tractor proclaiming Honesty, Technology, and Work—that the poor of Peru almost perversely began to vote for him en masse. Fujimori's evangelical background and Japanese heritage brought issues of race and religion to the forefront of the campaign, and Vargas Llosa's pale skin became a liability, associating him with the "white" upper class. After Fujimori's strong showing in the first election, Vargas Llosa realized that the Apristas would throw all of their state-controlled media support behind Fujimori. By keeping the populace's attention focused on the peripheral issues of race and religion, they turned the election toward Fujimori's favor.

In the process, Vargas Llosa learned of the complete incompatibility between writing and politics. During the campaign, he had no time to write or even think; he was cut off from his accustomed walks around the city of Lima. Every visit to a restaurant or motion-picture theater became a media event. Surrounded by security guards, he had no privacy at home. This sense of constant intrusions on his psyche may best explain the title of the memoir; politics is a matter of submersion within a milieu that gives one little time or ability for reflection or taking a longer view. One is at the mercy of opinion polls, freakish accusations, day-to-day campaign crises, and anxieties of the populace. For example, Vargas Llosa found himself forced to respond to questions of religion in the campaign's latter phases because Fujimori's evangelical background placed the support of the Catholic church squarely on Vargas Llosa's agnostic shoulders. Vargas Llosa found it difficult to say or do anything on this matter without seeming to manipulate the highly volatile religious issue in his favor. Thus, when the pope offered him an audience, he refused to see him, even though he would have enjoyed the audience out of literary curiosity. Vargas Llosa learned that as a politician he was no longer free, that his every word and gesture carried the weight of thousands of witnesses and their contradictory interpretations.

How objective is Vargas Llosa in portraying his capabilities as a politician? He argued persuasively for the benefits of a free-market economy by citing recent successes of Japan, Taiwan, South Korea, and Singapore. He conscientiously drew up extensive plans for governing and reform, taking on Peru's public school systems, its terrorist groups, and its national debt. While his programs for reform appealed to the middle class, he had difficulty earning support from the poor, who perceived him as an aloof, proud candidate for the rich. Clearly, something was lacking in his campaign style. His political advisers said that he was one of the worst politicians they had ever encountered. He published an erotic novelette, *Elogio de la madrastra* (1988; *In Praise of the Stepmother*, 1990), around the time of the campaign, giving fuel to his opponents. He showed a certain inflexibility sometimes when it would have been politically expedient to adjust his policy. When not conveying aloofness, he betrayed a kind of innocence in his refusal to engage in any of the arm-twisting dirty work of politics. As much as he describes himself as a "fish in the water" submerged in politics, he was also making a bid for power, but he seems reluctant to consider his campaign in those terms. While he can convey many ideas, he had a hard time conveying a sense of himself to the voters—a problem exacerbated by the necessary duplicity of an author. These memoirs are, in part, a belated attempt to fulfill this mission.

This inability to connect with his voters may have been the impetus for the dual text juxtaposing early memories alongside the campaign. Peruvians perceiving him as rich can learn of the many periods of poverty in his life, the many jobs he had to hold down during college: a reporter for several newspapers, a writer for television and radio, a compiler of gravestones, a teller in a bank. They can see how he was exposed to the different strata of Peruvian society at the Leoncio Prado Military Academy and in his journalistic labors, before his success as a writer allowed him to lead a more international lifestyle in Europe and North America as well as Peru. He leaves out his later years as a successful international writer, perhaps to keep his story focused on Peru, perhaps because writing in exile would be less interesting than his struggle to become that writer.

Vargas Llosa counterbalances his initial campaign successes with early memories of being terrorized by his father. After his father left his mother during her pregnancy, Mario was reared by her side of the family, the Llosas, in indulgent, carefree surroundings, with many surrogate fathers to make up for the loss of the real one. Then, however, Ernesto J. Vargas returned to take back his wife and son, and young Mario was plunged into a new home filled with his father's jealous rages. Ernesto Vargas instilled in his son a deep rebellion against authoritative regimes and a corresponding love of literature, which can serve as a "form of resistance to power" in its ability to question and subvert. In the new isolation of his father's household, Mario turned to books for escape and wrote poetry in surreptitious revolt against his father's wishes. His father's hatred of the socially superior Llosa family first introduced Mario to Peru's complex levels of racism among whites, mestizos, Indians, and blacks. Mario turned his resentment and fear of his father to his literary advantage, mining narratives out of family conflicts.

The youthful memories include numerous gems about how a young writer forms his aesthetics. He wrote his first erotica in the Leoncio Prado Military Academy, selling this sensual prose as a way to win friends. Later this sensual side formed a major theme of his art, as he explains in his book on Flaubert, *La orgía perpetua: Flaubert y "Madame Bovary"* (1975; *The Perpetual Orgy: Flaubert and "Madame Bovary,"* 1986). He recounts how the memory of the Academy formed the basis of his novel *La ciudad y los perros* (1963; *The Time of the Hero*, 1966) (in what he calls a "very free distorted version" of the original). His experiences as a crime reporter for *La Crónica*, a newspaper in Lima, formed part of the basis for *Conversation in the Cathedral*. The chapter entitled "Aunt Julia" recounts Vargas Llosa's dramatic first marriage to a woman fourteen years his senior that would later find novelization in *Aunt Julia and the Scriptwriter*. His discovery of William Faulkner's works led him to pay close attention to complex narrative forms that would help his fiction reflect the labyrinthine realities of Peru. The European literary tradition helped him distance himself from his country's provincialism. The novelist, in Vargas Llosa's view, "subtly arranges" the world "in accordance with his most secret appetites."

Beyond these aesthetic concerns, *A Fish in the Water* chiefly conveys Vargas Llosa's disillusioned reassessment of his home country. He describes this book as being "difficult to write," and no wonder: He worked for years to put into effect a free-market economy with multiple other programs to improve Peru, and then the poverty-stricken people of the country elected a little-known Japanese agricultural engineer instead. Vargas Llosa is very conscious of Peru's tendency to live up to its own caricature as a "beggar sitting on a bench made of gold," a country without the sense enough to free itself from its heritage of dictators, nationalization, terrorism, and mass poverty and use its plentiful natural resources to join the advanced countries. His political experiences confirm Peru's intractability, its repetition of the mistakes of the past. Soon after Fujimori took power, he dissolved the senate and declared himself dictator, ruling by decree. In Princeton, New Jersey, Vargas Llosa found himself forced to conclude that "there is nothing new under the sun."

A Fish in the Water addresses two audiences: the Peruvian voters, who witnessed every distortion of his character in the media, and Vargas Llosa's international literary readership. To the voters, the memoir allows him to defend himself by pointing out aspects of his life in Peru that he could not express during the campaign. In this way he reaffirms his ability as a writer, since he can better explain himself in books than in speeches (indeed, he may not be suited for politics in Peru). On another level, the memoir educates his foreign literary audience about Peruvian politics. He shows how politics saturates all aspects of Peruvian life and inevitably forms a large part of his own aesthetics. Literature, on the other hand, provides an escape from Peru's labyrinthine power struggles. Toward the end of the memoir, Vargas Llosa juxtaposes his campaign loss to his first joyful trip to Paris in 1958 on the winnings of a literary award. On the day after his defeat in 1990, he flew to Paris again to resume his literary career and convert his political loss into this successful and intriguing memoir.

Roy C. Flannagan III

Sources for Further Study

Booklist. XC, March 15, 1994, p. 1299.
Commentary. XCVIII, August, 1994, p. 54.
Kirkus Reviews. LXII, March 15, 1994, p. 385.
Library Journal. CXIX, May 1, 1994, p. 114.
The New York Review of Books. XLI, May 26, 1994, p. 19.
The New York Times Book Review. XCIX, May 15, 1994, p. 10.
Publishers Weekly. CCXLI, April 11, 1994, p. 49.
Time. CXLIII, June 13, 1994, p. 75.
The Times Literary Supplement. June 17, 1994, p. 11.
The Washington Post Book World. XXIV, May 22, 1994, p. 5.

THE FOLDING STAR

Author: Alan Hollinghurst (1954-)
Publisher: Pantheon Books (New York). 424 pp. $24.00
Type of work: Novel
Time: Chiefly 1976 and 1992
Locale: Belgium and England

This second novel by one of England's finest young writers takes gay fiction into an altogether new, less polemical, and more far-reaching phase

Principal characters:
EDWARD MANNERS, a writer and teacher
LUC ALTIDORE, his student
MARCEL ECHEVIN, another student
PAUL ECHEVIN, a curator at the Orst Museum
MATT, "VIM VERMEULEN," a pornographer
EDGAARD ORST, an artist
RALPH, "DAWN," one of Edward's former lovers

"My life was in a strange way that summer, the last summer of its kind there was ever to be," says William Beckwith, the spoiled and rakish narrator of Alan Hollinghurst's highly acclaimed first novel, *The Swimming-Pool Library* (1988). "I was riding high on sex and self-esteem—it was my time, my *belle epoque*—but all the while with a faint flicker of calamity, like flames around a photograph, something seen out of the corner of the eye." It is not only the coming of AIDS that makes the summer of 1983 a turning point for the twenty-five-year-old Beckwith, guilty of nothing worse than his own "mindless randiness and helpless sentimentality." This is the summer that Beckwith, out cruising Kensington Park, saves the life of eighty-three-year-old Lord Nantwich, who later invites him first to lunch and then to write his biography. The difference in their ages, a variation on a theme from Oscar Wilde's *The Picture of Dorian Grey* (1891), proves less significant than their considerable similarities, in education, in clubs, in sexual orientation. The temptation to write the biography of a man who had been friends with gay eminences such as Evelyn Waugh and Ronald Firbank is great but not great enough—not because Beckwith has anything better to do with his time but because of what he discovers in reading Nantwich's journals: that Beckwith's grandfather was "really the driving force" of the 1950's "crusade to eradicate male vice." The crusade failed (a failure paid off with a peerage) but not before Nantwich had been arrested and imprisoned. "The one unspeakable thing that no one had been able to tell me threw light on everything else, and only left obscure the degrees of calculation and coincidence in Charles's offering me his biography to write—a task he must have known I could never, in the end, accept."

The Swimming-Pool Library is a startling, amazingly accomplished, and ambitious first novel, but *The Folding Star*, shortlisted for the Booker Prize, is an even better book, clearly indebted to the earlier yet in every way its superior in its artful exploration of homosexual desire. Neither polemical nor prurient, Hollinghurst's treatment of gay life has at least as much in common with the postmodern novels of Peter Ackroyd, John Banville, and Julian Barnes as it does with the gay fiction of Edmund White. At once intricate, explicit, and elegiac, *The Folding Star* succeeds as both an engaging literary tour de force and a sad comedy of unrequited love and unfulfilled promise. Chief among its many strengths—its formal symmetry, verbal precision, attentiveness to the male body, and sheer intelligence—is the manner in which Hollinghurst creates and sustains, occasional humorous touches notwithstanding, a strangely, perhaps perversely inviting atmosphere, at once lucid and "tenebreaux." As Hollinghurst has explained in *Granta*, "The writers whom I revere are grand and shadowy—Navokov, Proust, James. . . . I like things to reverberate, be suggestive."

The novel is set in two shadow-filled locales, the small English town of Rough Common (as in "rough trade") located southeast of London and, more important, the small and unnamed Belgian city with its bars (the Cassette for gays, the Golden Calf for old men), its Catholic gloom (St. Narcissus, St. Vaast, St. Caspianus), its small museums, its factories and baths, its working-class districts and the faded splendor of its once-grand houses and park, the Hermitage, now a cruising ground. In a world at once specific and spectral, the hero is right to claim, even late in the novel, that he knows "nothing of this country." "To me," he says, "it was a dream-Belgium, it was Allemonde, a kingdom of ruins and vanished pleasures, miracles and martyrdoms, corners where the light never shone. Not many would recognise it, but some would"—more, one suspects, by way of Edgar Allan Poe's gothic stories than by perusing Fodor's and Michelin's travel guides.

As the story opens, Edward Manners, the novel's thirty-three-year-old narrator, has arrived in Belgium, his motives "too tenuous to explain" though ostensibly to tutor two boys: seventeen-year-old Luc Altidore, recently expelled from St. Narcissus, and sixteen-year-old Marcel Echevin, too sickly to attend. Overweight and shortsighted, a writer of limited abilities and financial resources, Edward is (his homosexuality aside) everything that William Beckwith is not. Longing for a future but locked in the past, he is only as self-deceived as he is self-aware, his life "one of understandings based on sex and misunderstandings based on love." Even as he becomes infatuated with Luc, he takes on, or alternately is taken on by, a succession of sexual partners, including Cherif Bakhtar, a Moroccan from Paris, and Matt, also known as Vim Vermeulen, a confidence man and pornographer specializing in videos, stolen underwear, and most recently a telephone service at which Edward proves rather adept—disconcertingly so for Hollinghurst's readers, if not for Matt's clients.

Edward plays various roles—voyeur, vampire, victim, and more specifically in relation to Luc, mentor, father, lover. Clearly, Cherif, Matt, and the others only serve as substitutes for the adored and mistakenly idealized Luc, who as it turns out is himself a substitute, most obviously for Edward's lost youth and more important for the doubly lost love of his life.

The latter becomes apparent only in the novel's middle section, when Edward returns home to Rough Common for the funeral of his friend Dawn, né Ralph. Once back, he begins to recall his past. He thinks about his father, a singer of some ability but not quite enough; he recalls his own early promise as a poet, encouraged by his Aunt Tina and her friend Perry (Peregrine) Dawson, the one a minor novelist, the other an equally minor poet. Finally, he remembers his earliest homoerotic and homosexual experiences culminating in 1976, when he was seventeen and his father was dying of cancer, with Dawn, dead now in an automobile accident a few months before he would have died of AIDS. The driver, Dawn's lover, "should have known the problem with [the car] in the wet." The same may be said of Edward, who buys condoms once, more out of boredom than out of any commitment to safe sex, and seems to use them not at all.

Dawn looms large in *The Folding Star*, even though he figures in it directly very little. In this he is like virtually all the novel's characters (and there are plenty of them), who do not so much enter and exit as in a stage play as float in and out, materializing and then dematerializing as in a dream (a more or less bad dream, though a decidedly good novel). Only briefly sketched, they are remarkably real if never quite realistic. They are figures in a world that manages to be both physical and psychological, a world not unlike Alice's Wonderland, a virtual reality of comic terror. Luc's mother, for example, "the most prolific needlewoman in Belgium," has transformed her house into "the shrine and workshop of an obsession." No less grotesquely, Marcel has been struck not dumb but asthmatic by the unusual circumstances of his mother's death:

> I didn't quite make the story out at first, I was chivvying him and making him repeat words without knowing I was taking him back, like some kinder and wiser analyst, to the scene of a childhood tragedy. It turned out he had been shopping in the town with his mother: he was only six, it was ten years ago, in the summer. They had gone into a florist's and were waiting to be served, when he saw a bee hovering around his mother's shopping-basket. He knew she mustn't be stung by a bee, but she was talking to a friend and she told him not to interrupt. He tried to flap it away, but only frightened it, and as his mother turned to him it flew up and stung her in the face. She groped for the antidote in her handbag, but she'd brought the wrong bag. She fell to the floor in front of Marcel, and within a minute she was dead.

Then there is "Rodney Young, Researcher," whom Edward frequently encounters and especially loathes—as well he might, for this bête noire is Edward himself, slightly older, slightly less occupied, slightly more lecherous.

More intriguing and more important to the narrative is Marcel's widowed father, nearly fifty years older than his son. Paul Echevin gave up a promising career as an art historian to become the curator of an obscure museum devoted to the work of a once-famous but now largely and perhaps justly forgotten local artist, Edgaard Orst. Devoted to and overprotective of his subject, yet well aware of the relative insignificance of this labor of perverse love (the brainchild of Orst's spinster sister), Paul finds in Edward "the right person" to confess both his misgivings and his darkest secret, which transforms his devotion into an act of penance. During the Occupation, when he was seventeen and his parents were active in the Resistance, Paul fell in love with a man who turned out to be a member of the fascist militia. As the Allies advanced,

Paul tried to save the lover he now despised. Instead, however, he inadvertently betrayed an elderly couple and the half-Jewish invalid for whom they had been caring, the artist Orst.

Edgaard Orst is the novel's most fascinating character, even more than Dawn, its absent center. Though he had once been famous and wealthy enough to build his fantastic Villa Hermes, a House of Usher (now fallen) in this City by the Sea, he lived out his last days "a premature ghost," syphilitic, blind, forgotten. He lives on in the museum that attracts few visitors, in the catalog Paul seems unable or perhaps unwilling to finish, and finally in Paul's efforts to complete the museum's collection, particularly the enigmatic triptych entitled *Autrefois*. One of the panels depicts the love of Orst's life, the actress Jane Byron, whom he met in 1899 and who died within the year, drowned at sea. Her body was never recovered except figuratively by the painter, who found a prostitute to play the divine Jane's part, the model filling in for the absent actress. If, as Paul contends, "Orst's tenacious remembrance of Jane was an ideal form of the collector's passion," then it was a passion that had "taken the fatal turn into fixation"—a fixation that all too closely resembles Edward's pursuit of Luc, the simulacrum of his long-lost Dawn. Looking "at the familiar panel of Jane," Edward sees

> a dream of beauty, glimmering silk, folded angels, troughs of velvety dusk. Then I pictured her splayed successor, the plunge from reverence to cruelty. I assumed that, after once being robbed of what he loved, Orst had needed to chain his girl down (Marthe she was called), to insist on his power while he could, with a kind of futile force—it was like watching the angel of bereavement hugely delayed. I met the face in the dark oval of the mirror, and caught my breath as much at my own stupidity as at the halting gaze of chrysanthemum eyes.

The Folding Star is itself a triptych, a tenebrous imitation of life, a series of mirror images that both reflect and distort. The novel is all done with mirrors, an art of self-conscious conjuring that alternately reveals and disguises itself in its cunning relay of duplicate characters, parallel scenes, and intertextual echoes. Here history occurs not twice but thrice: first as tragedy, then as farce, and finally as something other. Thus when Luc runs away, his mother outfits Edward in her son's too-tight clothes and sends him off in doubly hot pursuit in her car, which he nearly crashes when a jealous Cherif tries to jump out just before Marcel (at Paul's insistence) gets in. The chase, worthy in its way of the Keystone Kops, comes to naught. Edward learns soon after that although Luc was indeed running away, he was not running away from Edward after they spent a night together; he was running from his friend Patrick, whom he loves but who does not love him, for Patrick loves Sibylle, who loves Luc. Worse still, Edward learns by chance that Matt has been using Luc, presumably for his nefarious commercial purposes. Yet not even this knowledge quite prepares the reader for the novel's final revelation.

The Folding Star may derive its title from John Milton's 1634 masque *Comus* ("The Star that bids the Shepherd fold") and its plot from Thomas Mann's *Der Tod in Venedig* (1912; *Death in Venice*, 1925), but its power to intrigue, seduce, and astonish the reader derives from Alan Hollinghurst's extraordinary narrative skills and compelling psychological insights.

Robert A. Morace

Sources for Further Study

Australian Book Review. July, 1994, p. 52.
Library Journal. CXIX, October 1, 1994, p. 114.
London Review of Books. XVI, June 9, 1994, p. 6.
New Statesman and Society. VII, June 10, 1994, p. 37.
The New York Review of Books. XLI, November 3, 1994, p. 23.
The New Yorker. LXX, October 24, 1994, p. 95.
The Observer. June 25, 1994, p. 15.
Publishers Weekly. CCXLI, July 25, 1994, p. 31.
The Spectator. CCLXXII, May 28, 1994, p. 38.
The Times Literary Supplement. May 27, 1994, p. 19.

THE FOLLOWING STORY

Author: Cees Nooteboom (1933-)
First published: Het Volgende Verhaal, 1991, in The Netherlands
Translated from the Dutch by Ina Rilke
Publisher: Harcourt Brace (New York). 115 pp. $14.95
Type of work: Novella
Time: The latter half of the twentieth century
Locale: Lisbon, Amsterdam, and Brazil

Combining mystery and metaphysics, the magical and the matter-of-fact, The Following Story *is one of those rare fictions—whether long or short or in-between—that manage to be both narratively enticing and intellectually stimulating*

Principal characters:
HERMAN MUSSERT, a classics teacher and travel writer
LISA D'INDIA, a student
MARIA ZEINSTRA, a biology teacher who is briefly Mussert's lover
AREND HERFST, her husband, a poet, teacher of Dutch, and basketball coach
PROFESSOR DENG, one of Mussert's fellow passengers, a devotee of Qu Yuan, a poet of the feudal age

At one end of the fiction continuum is the short story, accorded new respect thanks to the influence of Donald Barthelme, the critical and commercial success of *The Stories of John Cheever* (1978), and the understated artistry of Raymond Carver. At the other end is the novel, for many reviewers and critics still *the* measure of a fiction writer's stature. Then, at that more or less theoretical point where the short novel and the long story meet, there is the novella, also (pejoratively) known as the novelette. Given its relatively brief if venerable history—one that includes Herman Melville's "Bartleby the Scrivener," Fyodor Dostoevski's "Underground Man," Leo Tolstoy's "The Death of Ivan Ilich," Stephen Crane's "The Monster," Henry James's "The Beast in the Jungle," Joseph Conrad's *Heart of Darkness*, Thomas Mann's *Death in Venice*, Franz Kafka's "The Metamorphosis," Bohumil Hrabel's *Closely Watched Trains*, John Gardner's *Grendel*, and Samuel Beckett's *Company*—it seems both ironic and unfortunate that the novella should be going the way of the dinosaurs.

Novellas are still written. Some are still published separately—Robert Coover's *A Political Fable* (1980) and *Spanking the Maid* (1981), John Cheever's *Oh What a Paradise It Seems* (1982; a novella by default, a fatal bout with cancer having cut down the "bulky novel" Cheever claimed to be writing in size, if not in impact), and Malcolm Bradbury's aptly titled *Cuts* (1987). Others appear in collections of short fiction—E. L. Doctorow's *Lives of the Poets* (1984), several of Guy Davenport's books—or more rarely in collections of novellas—Stanley Elkin's triptych *Van Gogh's Room at Arles* (1993). Yet as the entrepreneurial spirit continues its rapid advance in Hrabel's Eastern Europe, as the number of outlets for novella-length fiction continues to decline in the United States and the United Kingdom (*TriQuarterly* and *Granta* being the most notable of the handful of holdouts), and as readers, particularly American readers, continue to demand more pages of bang per buck, the novella becomes less and less viable, first commercially, then aesthetically.

Thus there is something akin to poetic justice in the fact that a book that measures only 4½ by 7½ inches and that contains 115 less-than-densely-printed pages should have had a notable success in this postindustrial age of corporate downsizing, of minimalist stories and maximalist novels. The title of Cees Nooteboom's *The Following Story* plays a variation on the "who's on first" routine made famous by the comedy team of Abbott and Costello. As popular in his native Holland as he is prolific, Nooteboom has since 1956 written more than thirty books—novels, poetry, essays, travel writing—in addition to a film and two plays. Seven of the books have been translated into English, the majority published by Louisiana State University Press. The eighth, *The Following Story*, published by a major commercial house (Harcourt Brace) and thus assured of reasonably wide circulation, arrived on American shores by an even more curious route. Commissioned by the organizers of the Dutch Book Fair to produce a work that would be given free to anyone who spent a specified amount at participating booksellers, Nooteboom had to keep his story short in order to keep the sponsors' production costs down. Unlike music, books written to order on commission, like those written by committee, seem destined for failure: they may be curiosities but are not expected to become classics. Thus it is passing strange that Nooteboom's small gift book soon metamorphosed into an international hit winning the European Literary Prize for Best Novel and shortlisted for the English newspaper *The Independent*'s Foreign Fiction Award.

All this leaves readers who have been looking for a good contemporary novella rather nicely situated—far better, certainly, than *The Following Story*'s understandably confused though generally genial narrator, Herman Mussert. In brief, his dilemma, or story, is as follows. Having gone to bed as usual in Amsterdam, he wakes up the next morning in a hotel in Lisbon, with his wallet full of Portuguese money. In fact (which is to say in this fiction), the room is the very one in which he had stayed twenty years earlier with his lover Maria Zeinstra, a colleague as well as a colleague's wife. "Lovers," however, does not quite describe their relationship. After all, Herman believes himself—or wants to believe himself—incapable of love, and Maria is mainly interested in getting back at her husband, Arend Herfst. When not otherwise occupied teaching Dutch, coaching the school's basketball team, and writing poetry, Arend is busy having an affair with one of his students, Lisa d'India, biologically the daughter of an Italian steelworker but literarily a descendant of Dante Alighieri's Beatrice, Vladimir Nabokov's Lolita, and Edgar Allan Poe's Annabel Lee. That the lovely, intelligent, but prematurely graying Lisa is also enrolled in Maria's biology and the narrator's classics classes only makes matters a bit more complicated—and comical.

The narrator's name is Herman Mussert, "same as our national traitor," the Nazi puppet Anton Mussert. "Obedient by nature," he is modest, even self-deprecating, but also at times rather haughty, as in his assessment of Maria's "putty-faced husband, a giant built up from slabs of veal." Then again, Mussert is often just as critical of himself. He lives alone with his cat Bat in a world of books, nourished by food he spoons from cans, disdaining, perhaps fearing, actual life, which he finds too contingent, too formless. This former teacher of classics at a provincial grammar school prefers the grace and economy of a dead language, Latin. Not unlike T. S. Eliot's J. Alfred Prufrock or Ezra Pound's Hugh Selwyn Mauberley, he understands his predicament almost too well. "We are descendants," he laments, "we do not have mythical lives, but psychological ones." Before his students he play-acts the parts of his doomed heroes, Socrates and Phaeton, and unintentionally that of Odysseus as he resists the siren song of the beautiful Lisa d'India. He is a sadly comic figure, worshiping beauty from afar, later dragged from his classroom and roughed up by Maria's husband, the adulterer turned cuckold.

Arend's bit of machismo ends (to the extent that anything in *The Following Story* ends) with Mussert, Maria, and Arend fired and Arend carrying, or rather driving, Lisa off into the sunset. In the space of a sentence there is an accident; Lisa dies; Maria and Arend go off to South America; and Mussert loses the three loves of his life (Maria, Lisa, and teaching). Out of necessity he embarks on a new career as a writer of popular travel guides under the nom de plume Dr. Strabo, after the author of the *Geōgraphica* (c. 7 B.C.; *Geography*, 1917-1933) who had as it were a foot not only in two cultures (Greek and Roman) and two centuries but in two eras as well.

Together the novel's two parts follow the course of the last two seconds of Mussert's life. In part 1, events of the previous twenty years or so "flash" before his eyes in a fifty-seven-page slow-motion sequence. In part 2, Mussert sets off on the last leg of a dream journey that is at once linear and circular, and that takes him from one Belem, in Portugal, to another in Brazil, its former colony. Trip here is also trope, as the epigraph to part 2, from Nabokov's *Transparent Things*, neatly and playfully points out: "This is, I believe, *it*: not the crude anguish of physical death but the incomparable pangs of the mysterious mental maneuver needed to pass from one state of being to another. Easy, you know, does it, son." Mussert does pass, easily and slowly. As the shadowy ship crosses an Atlantic-wide River Styx and nears a Brazil that is less a geographical place than a myth like Tartarus, a fantasy like Terry Gilliam's *Brazil* (1985), each of Mussert's five fellow passengers tells his story, including the story of his death, and then disappears, leaving Mussert to tell his tale to no one but "you," his ideal narratee, Lisa d'India.

Having found it quite difficult to speak his mind earlier in his life, he now proves understandably garrulous, at once an impatient Walt Whitman upbraiding himself for loitering so long and a reluctant and wily Scheherezade not quite willing to end his story and with it his life (one of them anyway). He explains in the final sentences of the understandably long paragraph that serves, paradoxically enough, both as coda to all that has just been told and as prologue to all that will follow,

> It was not my soul that would set out on a journey, as the real Socrates had imagined; it was my body that would embark on endless wanderings, never to be ousted from the universe, and so it would take part in the most fantastic metamorphoses, about which it would tell me nothing because it would long since have forgotten all about me. At one time the matter it had consisted of had housed a soul that resembled me, but now my matter would have other duties. And I? I had to turn around,

> I had to let go of the ship's rail, to let go of everything, to look at you. You beckoned; it was not difficult to follow. You had taught me something about infinity, about how an immeasurable space of memories can be stored in the most minute time span, and while I was permitted to remain as small and coincidental as I was, you had shown me my true stature. You needn't beckon me any longer, I'm coming. None of the others will hear my story, none of them will see that the woman sitting there waiting for me has the features of my dearest Crito, the girl who was my pupil, so young that one could speak about immortality with her. And then I told her, then I told you
>
> the following story

What exactly is *The Following Story*? It is Nooteboom's means for meditating on time even as he plays with it. Pitting memory against metamorphosis (Kafka's no less than Ovid's), this chastely yet joyously written novella simultaneously collapses twenty years into 115 pages while stretching two seconds over the same now impossibly expansive space. Moving seamlessly back and forth between grand vision and Grand Guignol, *The Following Story* manages to be both lyrical and ludic, enthralling and erudite, fabulous and philosophical. This is speculative fiction at its very best, every bit as intellectually and metaphysically stimulating as it is intertextually and metafictionally intriguing.

Robert A. Morace

Sources for Further Study

Australian Book Review. February, 1994, p. 45.
Boston Globe. October 26, 1994, p. 83.
Los Angeles Times Book Review. October 9, 1994, p. 6.
New Statesman and Society. VII, January 21, 1994, p. 40.
The New York Review of Books. XLI, December 1, 1994, p. 19.
The New York Times Book Review. XCIX, October 16, 1994, p. 13.
The Observer. January 9, 1994, p. 18.
Publishers Weekly. CCXLI, August 22, 1994, p. 40.
The Times Literary Supplement. January 21, 1994, p. 20.
The Washington Post Book World. XXIV, October 30, 1994, p. 7.

FOREGONE CONCLUSIONS
Against Apocalyptic History

Author: Michael André Bernstein (1947-)
Publisher: University of California Press (Berkeley). 181 pp. $22.00
Type of work: Literary criticism

Writers of history and historical fiction should not allow their knowledge of an event that occurred after the time period about which they are writing to influence their description and interpretation of life before that event

Michael Bernstein's *Foregone Conclusions: Against Apocalyptic History* delivers many insights about several extremely sensitive topics. He focuses on fictional works about what he prefers to call the *Shoah*, the murder of European Jews in German concentration camps during World War II, and related topics. Unfortunately for the reader, several of Bernstein's stylistic idiosyncracies often obfuscate the subtle and elusive points he tries to make. Many of Bernstein's sentences are eight or more lines in length. One paragraph on pages 115-116 begins with a sentence in excess of seven lines and concludes with sentences more than eight lines long. The tortured clausal contortions within those excessively long sentences require multiple rereadings. The author also overworks a number of favorite words and phrases (such as "prosaics of the quotidian") to the point that some readers may become irritated and driven to distraction. Nevertheless, the importance of what Bernstein has to say makes the book worth the significant effort required to read it.

Bernstein's primary thesis is that many historians and writers of historical fiction employ what he calls "backshadowing" which completely distorts the nature and meaning of the historical era about which they are writing. By backshadowing, Bernstein means that the authors use their own and their audience's knowledge of an apocalyptic event which occurs after the epoch about which they are writing to interpret the actions of their real or imaginary characters. (How backshadowing differs from the more familiar term "foreshadowing" is not entirely clear.) As examples of backshadowing, Bernstein critiques two recent biographies of Franz Kafka by Ernst Pawel and Frederick Karl, and a historical account of Viennese Jewry before the *Anschluss* in 1938 by George Berkeley.

According to Bernstein, both Pawel and Karl interpret Kafka's life and work primarily in terms of the fate of European Jews during World War II. Both biographers, he says, frequently resort to backshadowing to remind their readers that the society in which Kafka lived would soon perpetrate a monstrous act against the entire Jewish population of Europe. As an example of this backshadowing, Bernstein points out that Pawel, while describing the birth of one of Kafka's sisters, mentions that Adolf Hitler had been born earlier in the same year. Karl's biography, Bernstein argues, makes an even more pernicious use of backshadowing by portraying Kafka's literary works as prophetic of the triumph of Nazism. In the case of Berkeley's account of the Viennese Jews, Bernstein notes that in recounting the sensational murder/suicide of Austria's crown prince and his lover in 1889, Berkeley made note that Vienna's Jewish community should have been more concerned with Hitler's birth in that year than with the royal scandal.

The sort of backshadowing Bernstein illuminates in the works of Pawel, Karl, and Berkeley represents the primary target of his criticism of apocalyptic themes in formal historical writing. Bernstein argues persuasively that to view the lives of Kafka and his contemporaries only in the light of the ultimate fate of Europe's Jews distorts the meaning and nature of Jewish life and culture before 1939. Similarly, to suggest that Viennese Jews should somehow have recognized the significance of Hitler's birth in 1889 and have consequently begun an exodus from Austria grotesquely distorts the richness of the fabric of Jewish culture.

Bernstein then turns his attention to fictional accounts of Jewish life in Europe before the Nazis. He maintains that society's understanding of the *Shoah* derives much more from fictional literature than from formal historical studies. He therefore argues that those who write fictional accounts of the *Shoah* must scrupulously avoid distorting its nature and meaning through intentional or unintentional foreshadowing or backshadowing. In this regard, Bernstein especially criticizes the work of the celebrated Israeli novelist Aharon Applefeld.

According to Bernstein, Applefeld deliberately uses his audience's knowledge of the *Shoah* to portray the lives of assimilated central European Jews before World War II as having been meaningless. Because they were destined to perish in one or the other of the concentration camps, Bernstein thinks Applefeld's characters appear as superfluous, their activities trivial and meaningless. Bernstein maintains that this portrayal of the lives of assimilated Jews in prewar Europe is misleading, untrue, and distorts the nature and meaning of the *Shoah*. Instead of using backshadowing to trivialize the lives of those Jews, Bernstein insists that writers should use what he calls "sideshadowing" to illuminate pre-*Shoah* central European Jewish culture.

Bernstein's concept of sideshadowing (he credits Gary Morsen with coining the term) constitutes one of the several important insights in this volume. Bernstein argues that the nature and qualities of a culture such as that of prewar European Jews cannot be judged or understood only in the light of an apocalyptic event such as the *Shoah*. To portray their lives as trivial because of the catastrophe they could not foresee is tantamount to blaming them for their fate, a tendency Bernstein sees as much too common among Jews and gentiles alike. Their culture must be understood through their mundane, everyday activities, all of which have dignity and worth regardless of events in the future which must remain unfathomable. As Bernstein points out, the future exists only as an infinite array of possibilities. No one can foretell with certainty what will transpire tomorrow or next week or next year. Therefore, Bernstein insists novelistic accounts of the *Shoah* should explore the multiple possible futures as they appeared to the Jews of Europe before World War II in order to expose the true richness of their culture. Such an exploration, Bernstein argues, will add a new dimension to human understanding of the breadth of the tragedy that was the *Shoah*.

Bernstein also makes a powerful statement about what he calls "victimization" in fictional accounts of the *Shoah* and its aftermath. He argues once again that history (especially Jewish history) should not be portrayed as a series of horrible, wrenching events interspersed with unimportant daily affairs, but rather as daily affairs punctuated occasionally by an event that interrupts the much more important routine of life. Many of the fictional accounts of the *Shoah* and related themes become nothing more than sadomasochistic attempts to appeal to the most base of the human instincts of the reader, according to Bernstein. Being adversely affected by one of the periodic calamitous events does not imbue a person or a culture with any special moral virtue nor impart a right to those so affected to expect special considerations from anyone not involved in the victim's problem, Bernstein argues. These contentions may become the most controversial in the book.

Bernstein spends several pages decrying what he perceives as the "competition" between groups that perceive themselves to be victims of some historical apocalypse. These groups (including but not restricted to Jews) compete in establishing their degree of victimhood and the special treatment they believe to be merited because of injustices done to them or their ancestors. Bernstein uses as an example a recent series of tragic events in New York City involving confrontations between African Americans and Jewish Americans. Bernstein in part blames apocalyptic backshadowing in both fiction and formal historical accounts for the ensuing and (to Bernstein) distasteful competition between the two groups as to which of them had endured the greater injustices. He is careful to warn that the actual victims of an event as profound as the *Shoah* will understandably be prone to interpret history in an apocalyptic way. The rest of us should, says Bernstein, try to understand the victims' viewpoints and show compassion for them, but not be seduced into writing or interpreting history or historical fiction in that way.

In an effort to show how fiction should be written using sideshadowing to illuminate what he considers the truly important aspects of life on the eve of an apocalyptic event, Bernstein devotes most of a chapter to an analysis of Robert Musil's unfinished novel, *The Man Without Qualities*. Published in three parts in 1930, 1933, and 1943, Musil's novel portrays a number of interesting characters in 1913 Austrian society. Rather than using backshadowing to make the actions of his characters seem ridiculous through his own and his reader's knowledge that their world was about to collapse in the firestorm of World War I, Musil uses sideshadowing, according to Bernstein. Sideshadowing allows Musil to show that even the most inane activities of everyday life have meaning and value. Bernstein thinks Musil's technique and the time he chose to write about illuminate the flavor and texture of Austrian society to a much greater degree than could a novel written about the society during the war or the postwar years.

All of Jewish history including the *Shoah*, Bernstein concludes, should be approached using Musil's techniques. To interpret the high degree of culture attained by Spanish Jews before Ferdinand and Isabella only in the light of the Inquisition would do a monstrous injustice to the generations of Jews who lived and prospered before the *auto-da-fé*. Similarly, to dismiss the many and notable attainments of pre-Nazi European Jews as meaningless destroys them more surely than did the Nazis. Bernstein's argument that any particular moment in time has an infinite array of possible futures is particularly pertinent to his conclusion: Each life, no matter how exalted or how debased, has worth and meaning beyond any apocalyptic historical event. The everyday lives of a society's members should be the prism through which that society is viewed and interpreted. Bernstein reviews the works of several writers, including Paul Celan and Yehuda Amichai. Published recently in Israel, the works of these writers show how sideshadowing should be used to explore the many dimensions of Jewish culture in Europe before and after the *Shoah*, according to Bernstein.

Many of Bernstein's pronouncements throughout the book will certainly offend some readers. He is critical, for example, of what he describes as the Zionist tendency to use the *Shoah* and other apocalyptic events in Jewish history to argue that Jewish life among the populations of nations other than Israel is doomed to a recurring cycle of judeophobia and pogroms, and ultimately destruction. Bernstein sees this interpretation of history as nothing more than scare tactics used by some Zionists to bring financial support and immigrants to Israel from the Jewish communities around the world. Several different groups in the United States and Israel are likely to level criticism at Bernstein for adopting this position. His suggestion that those who denounce pre-1939 European Jews for not foreseeing their fate and consequently leaving Europe represent a form of anti-Semitism is unlikely to be universally applauded. His criticism that those who denigrate the Jewish communities of Europe for not fighting with more vigor against their fate are themselves anti-Semitic may not be well accepted among yet other circles in Israel and elsewhere.

Whether or not Bernstein manages to please or convince everyone concerned with writing about the *Shoah*, he has made a powerful contribution to the debate about the nature and meaning of history. His contention that writers of fiction have considerable influence in shaping popular concepts concerning historical events and the ways in which history should be interpreted is also an important point. Bernstein obviously believes that the influence wielded by writers of historical fiction imports to them a responsibility to illuminate the past with a compassionate understanding of the human condition.

Paul Madden

Source for Further Study

The New York Times Book Review. XCIX, October 30, 1994, p. 40.

FRANCO
A Biography

Author: Paul Preston (1946-)
First published: 1993, in Great Britain
Publisher: BasicBooks (New York). Illustrated. 1002 pp. $37.50
Type of work: Biography
Time: 1892-1975
Locale: Spain

An exhaustively researched and authoritative account of the life of Francisco Franco, who ruled Spain as a dictator from 1936 until his death in 1975

Principal personages:

FRANCISCO FRANCO, the caudillo, or leader, of Spain from 1936 to 1975
CARMEN POLO Y MARTINEZ VALDES, his wife
RAMON SERRANO SUNER, his brother-in-law, a government minister
LUIS CARRERO BLANCO, a longtime associate of Franco
DON JUAN DE BORBON Y BATTENBERG, the pretender to the Spanish throne
JUAN CARLOS I, the son of Don Juan and Franco's designated successor

Few historical episodes stir as much passion as the Spanish Civil War of 1936-1939. The war represented the breakdown of an intensely polarized society. Rightists based in the army launched a rebellion against the left-wing government of the Spanish Republic. The ensuing struggle, brutally waged by both sides, devastated Spain and cost the lives of more than 600,000 people. The Spanish Civil War would be notable as yet another moral disaster of the Iberian Peninsula, but it did not remain an internecine brawl. It was quickly internationalized, and absorbed into the wider political currents of the 1930's. The fascist powers of Germany and Italy championed the authoritarian crusade of the Nationalist insurgents, while the Soviet Union came to the defense of the beleaguered Republic. The Spanish agony became a tragedy into which outsiders read foreign meanings. The war was used as a martial laboratory for the great powers, and German and Soviet "advisers" experimented on the dusty plains of Castile with the weapons and tactics that would be unleashed to greater effect during World War II. The Spanish conflict early on came to be regarded as the opening phase of the general war all too many people anticipated in the tumultuous 1930's. Hence thousands of idealists traveled to Spain to fight on the side of the Republic, and against the Nationalists aligned with Adolf Hitler and Benito Mussolini. Others, more frightened by Joseph Stalin's Russia than Hitler's Germany, or shocked by anticlerical atrocities in the Republic, thrilled to the steady advance of the Nationalist conquistadors. To a remarkable degree, the struggle became a Western as well as a Spanish civil war.

As a consequence, few accounts of the Spanish Civil War are unbiased. In Great Britain and the United States, most historians have favored the cause of the doomed Republic. The ghosts of George Orwell and Ernest Hemingway still dominate the Anglo-American memory of the Spanish conflict. Although both of these men wrote unsparingly of the moral and practical failures of the wartime Republic, they nevertheless enshrined its brief and embattled career as a theater of romantic heroism. Francisco Franco, the dour and portly general who commanded the Nationalist armies that overwhelmed the republican experiment in Spain, comfortably fit his traditional billing as the villain in this exemplary drama. The occasional British or U.S. hagiographer of the caudillo invariably founders on the icy rock of his implacable ruthlessness. Even a figure as unlovely as Francisco Franco, however, must ultimately command our attention, and with it some measure of guarded respect. Victor in a bitter war, contemporary and associate of Hitler and Mussolini, Franco managed to weather the storm of World War II and outlast by decades both his friends and enemies, ruling Spain until his death in 1975. Perhaps perversely, Franco ended his days as the most successful member of his generation of 1930's tyrants. After maintaining his exhausted nation's neutrality in World War II, for which he earned the undying gratitude of Western statesmen such as Winston Churchill, Franco gradually escaped international isolation. The onset of the Cold War highlighted Spain's strategic importance. Franco's determined anticommunism made him an acceptable ally for the United States, which in the 1950's began leasing military airfields in Spain. Finally, the man who gave the fascist salute to Adolf Hitler endured to preside over the economic rebirth of his homeland, and its reintegration with the Western community of nations. In the years since his death, a few conservative voices in England and the United States have gone so far as to assert that Franco, for all his cruelty, was ultimately a benefactor to his nation and the West.

Paul Preston's authoritative *Franco: A Biography* provides a welcome reappraisal of the Spanish dictator's life and accomplishments. Preston brings impressive credentials to the task. He has spent years studying modern Spanish history, and is the author of numerous books on the Spanish Civil War and its aftermath. The result of Preston's labors is a massive tome that refutes the arguments of recent apologists for the dictator. Preston presents a damning portrait of Franco as a man and as a leader. The Franco who emerges from his pages is a talented but fundamentally mediocre man, who, through luck and guile, aggrandized himself at the expense of a nation. In fundamental harmony with the traditional Anglo-American historiography of the Franco years, Preston's book brilliantly transcends it. Preston makes no secret of his own political sympathy with the battered Republican movement in Spain, but he refuses to allow this to obscure his scholarly accomplishment. His book is solid academic history, not a polemic. He exhaustively researched *Franco*, and painstakingly documents all his assertions. Preston's special grace is to ground conventional wisdom on Francisco Franco firmly in fact.

Preston also endeavors always to be fair to Franco, and he does not begrudge him credit for his virtues and his successes. Preston never allows his study to degenerate into the record of a monster. His Franco is always a fully rounded and comprehensible human being. Ultimately however, Preston is unable to fully capture the essence of Franco's character. As he trenchantly remarks, Franco remains an enigma. Francisco Franco was a reserved and intensely private man. He lived his life behind a series of masks, which he rarely chose to lift, and only then to his closest relations. Men who worked with him for decades admitted that the caudillo was ever a mystery to them. Further effacing the record of his private life was Franco's delight in reworking his personal history, a penchant he indulged in more freely during the years of his dictatorship. The elusiveness of Franco's personality reinforces the plausibility of those who assert that the dictator was a wise and farseeing ruler. Preston copes with this human conundrum by meticulously sifting through the sources, and at times tracing Franco's decision-making process on a day-to-day basis. While Preston fails to get inside his subject's head, he has compiled a monumental record of Franco's activities, which he mines to buttress his own judgments.

Francisco Franco was born December 4, 1892, into a family of naval administrators. Spain at that time was a nation torn by its inability to change. The political class in Spain was corrupt and hopelessly divided. Regional drives for autonomy threatened to split the country apart. The vast gap between the haves and have-nots in Spanish society kept alive the terrifying specter of revolution. Then, in 1898, came humiliating defeat in a war with the United States, and the loss of the remnants of Spain's Asian and American empires. Growing up in a military family, Franco keenly felt Spain's weakness. Like other young men of his class and generation, he was determined to assist a rebirth of Spanish glory and power. Franco entered the army hoping to become a latter-day conquistador.

Ironically, the only field of glory open to Franco was Morocco, where the Spanish authorities waged a desultory and largely unsuccessful war against recalcitrant Moorish chieftains. This third-rate colonial conflict became Franco's element, and his experiences in Africa forged the man who would one day rule Spain. Franco quickly proved himself an officer of unusual ability and courage. His exploits in Morocco read like a military romance, and made him a national hero. More important, Franco imbibed a colonialist mentality. His later callousness toward the suffering of ordinary Spaniards, his cruelty to prisoners and political opponents, and even his notable skill in dividing and ruling his allies, all can be traced back to lessons learned in Morocco. His service in Morocco also inspired Franco's sense of destiny. His many victories and brushes with death convinced him that Providence had singled him out, sparing him for some great task. Franco's self-importance was fed by popular adulation and rapid promotions. Early in his service, Franco won command of the Spanish Foreign Legion, a band of desperadoes so tough that their motto was "Long Live Death." In 1926, Franco was appointed the youngest general in Europe.

The collapse of the Spanish monarchy and the advent of the Republic in 1931 shook Franco's world. Although his career did not suffer under the new order, Franco became convinced that Spain was on the road to destruction. He shared the antipathy of his class to democratic politics. He believed the leaders of the Republic to be a collection of communists, Freemasons, and Jews, all equally dangerous in his blinkered vision. Hence, Franco was one of the authors of the military putsch that attempted to overthrow the government in July, 1936.

Preston rightly points out that Franco's rise to the leadership of the Nationalist movement was not foreordained. The designated leader of the rebellion was killed in a plane crash, leaving Franco, based in his old haunt of Morocco, in command of the largest body of rebel troops. He solidified his central position by embracing Germany and Italy as allies. Their technical assistance enabled him to ferry his army to the mainland, and their patronage gave him prestige his rivals lacked. Once acknowledged as the head of the Nationalist state, Franco created a totalitarian regime modeled on those of his fascist benefactors. While indebted to Hitler and Mussolini, Franco was not governed by them. He frustrated his patrons by his deliberately slow and systematic approach to conquering the Republic. Franco did not want a rapid victory because he saw the war as a crusade, the goal of which was to cleanse Spain of the evils he believed afflicted her. To accomplish this, he intended to kill as many of his Republican opponents as possible. So the old "Africanista" intentionally waged a colonial war of extermination against his own people.

Franco declared victory in April, 1939, only months before the outbreak of World War II. Spain's neutrality during that conflagration is often cited as one of Franco's greatest achievements. Preston casts a jaundiced eye on this claim. He argues that Franco was eager to join his German and Italian friends in their career of conquest, but because Spain was militarily and economically shattered by three years of civil war, Franco lacked the means of fulfilling his ambitions. The only way Franco could join the conflict was with extensive assistance. Hence his famous demand for a mountain of equipment and supplies when Hitler asked him to enter the war. What some have seen as a masterful bluff to put off the German request, Preston argues was simply the measure of Spain's genuine military needs, and of Franco's inflated sense of his own importance. Whatever the truth, Hitler did not value Spanish belligerency so highly, and so Franco sat out the war, officially neutral while covertly assisting the Axis.

Preston devotes only a third of his book to Franco's life and rule from 1945 to 1975. This was the period when history seemed ready to rehabilitate the caudillo. The Cold War made Spain a valued partner of the United States. With time, Franco allowed the more overtly fascist trappings of his regime to lapse, outlawing the straight-armed salute and letting his once revolutionary partisans age into governmental time-servers. The late 1950's saw a return of economic prosperity to Spain. Often credited to Franco's policies, the Spanish boom of the 1960's, like neutrality in the war, Preston attributes to a frustration rather than a fulfillment of Franco's desires. Since the end of the Civil War, he had pursued a policy of economic autarky modeled on that of Nazi Germany. Preston argues that the result of this quixotic program was to prolong the wartime impoverishment of Spain for two decades. Popular unrest with miserable living conditions finally forced Franco to turn the economy over to a new generation of technocrats, who then engineered the Spanish economic miracle.

So Franco held on, maintaining to the end, as Preston ruefully notes, his ability to juggle alliances and adapt to changed circumstances. Franco hoped in his last years that his regime would be continued after his death by Prince Juan Carlos, grandson of King Alfonso XIII, whom he had designated his successor as a sop to monarchist sentiment in the country. This, like so many of Franco's dreams, was not to be. As king, Juan Carlos superintended the return of democracy to Spain. So long did Franco rule, and so different was the world when he left, that his passing was not greeted in the United States with rejoicing, or even much interest, but instead with an absurdist joke on *Saturday Night Live*. Franco remains a historical figure of multifaceted ambiguity. It is a tribute to Paul Preston's scholarship that *Franco* illuminates so well the Machiavellian paradoxes of its subject's career.

Daniel P. Murphy

Sources for Further Study

The Christian Science Monitor. January 26, 1995, p. B2.
The Economist. CCCXXIX, November 27, 1993, p. 98.
History Today. XLIV, May, 1994, p. 56.
Library Journal. CXIX, October 1, 1994, p. 88.
London Review of Books. XVI, March 24, 1994, p. 11.
National Review. XLVI, November 7, 1994, p. 72.
The New York Review of Books. XLI, November 17, 1994, p. 14.
The New York Times Book Review. C, February 19, 1995, p. 37.
The New Yorker. LXX, October 17, 1994, p. 116.
Publishers Weekly. CCXLI, September 5, 1994, p. 97.
The Times Literary Supplement. October 22, 1993, p. 3.
The Washington Post Book World. XXIV, October 30, 1994, p. 4.

GEORGES PEREC
A Life in Words

Author: David Bellos
First published: 1993, in Great Britain
Publisher: David R. Godine (Boston). 802 pp. $45.00
Type of work: Literary biography
Time: 1936-1982
Locale: France, Israel, Tunisia, the United States, and Australia

This work chronicles the life and work of the novelist, poet, and dramatist Georges Perec, winner in 1965 of France's prestigious Prix Renaudot for Les Choses: Une Histoire des années soixante (Things: A History of the Sixties, *1967) and renowned for his experimental prose*

Principal personages:
GEORGES PEREC, the French novelist, poet, and dramatist
DAVID BIENENFELD, his uncle
PAULETTE PETRAS, his wife
CATHERINE BINET, his companion
RAYMOND QUENEAU, a French writer

The publication in 1965 of Georges Perec's novel *Les Choses: Une Histoire des années soixante* (*Things: A History of the Sixties,* 1967), which was eventually translated into twenty languages from Catalan to Estonian, marked the beginning of a prolific career that produced more than twenty works during a decade and a half of sustained effort. His first published work, in addition to being awarded the Prix Renaudot, enjoyed enormous commercial success and continues to sell, in the original French version, tens of thousands of copies annually. Despite the diversity and radically inventive nature of Perec's writing, it has received little critical attention.

Georges Perec: A Life in Words presents a captivating portrait of an enigmatic writer. David Bellos re-creates in minute detail the historical and social evolution of twentieth century France, and in particular of the literary world of the 1960's and 1970's, while being equally meticulous in recounting Perec's development from the orphaned young boy, unremarkable in many ways, to the writer, mischievous and deeply committed to the ideal of originality.

Georges Perec was born to Icek (Izie) and Cyrla (Cécile) Perec, Polish Jews, on March 7, 1936, in Paris. He spent his first years in Paris in a multilingual environment, with French, Yiddish, Polish, and German being the most commonly used languages within the extended family and snatches of Russian, Czech, Hungarian, and Romanian heard in the streets. There is evidence that Perec understood and spoke some Yiddish and that he knew some words of Polish as well. In *W ou le souvenir d'enfance* (1975; *W: Or, The Memory of Childhood,* 1988), Perec recounts the rapture of his family when, at the age of three, he pointed to a Hebrew letter and called it by its name. This evanescent memory of the first letter of his life is one of the initial signs of his fascination with language and the written letter.

When France and Great Britain declared war on Germany after Adolf Hitler's invasion of Poland in September, 1939, Izie Perec, thirty years old, was one of many thousands of Jews who quickly enlisted. In *W,* Georges Perec describes his father as a doughty fighter with foolish bravado. On June 15, 1940, Izie's regiment suffered many casualties, and Izie himself was killed. The effect of this death on the young Perec, also known as Jojo, is not known, but for Izie's wife Cécile, his mother Rose, and his sister Esther, it was a grievous blow.

Defeated and divided in 1940 and having no civil records identifying the Jewish community, France required Jews to declare themselves at police stations or, failing to do so, be liable for unspecified penalties. Perec's uncle David Bienenfeld, an influential pearl dealer, declared himself, his wife Esther, and their two daughters. It is likely that at the same time Cécile declared herself and Georges at the local commissariat. By the end of 1941, 139,979 people in the Paris region alone had declared themselves to be Jews. The French police were now able to retrieve four categories of information regarding the registrants: name, address, nationality, and profession. This Tular Index greatly facilitated the first arrests of Jews in Paris in May, 1941, when 3,700 out of a possible 6,494 individuals received summonses requiring them to undergo an *examen de situation.* Those who responded were immediately interned in French camps at Pithiviers and Beaune-la-Rolande. In this way, the prolonged persecution of Jews within French borders began.

During the occupation of France, Perec's mother, interned at Drancy in January, 1943, was deported by order of the German authorities. At the end of the war, it was learned that Cécile Perec had been transported by cattle truck to Auschwitz, where she was taken with other Jews directly to the gas chamber. Without mother or father, Georges became the ward of David Bienenfeld.

In 1945, after the end of World War II, Georges returned to Paris from Vercors, a mountainous region in southeastern France, and settled with David and Esther Bienenfeld and their children, Bianca and Lili, in the family's comfortable apartment on Rue de l'Assomption in the sixteenth arrondissement. In the early years, Georges profoundly missed the affection of his biological parents. Nevertheless, he developed strong ties with Bianca, for whom he felt great brotherly affection. His relationship with his uncle David was more problematic; arriving in Paris at the age of nine, and not having had a father figure for six years, Georges was hardly nurtured by Bienenfeld's rigidity and lack of warmth.

From 1948 to 1951, Perec attended boarding school at the Collège Geoffroy-Saint-Hilaire at Etampes, about fifty kilometers south of Paris. During these years, Perec visited Israel during summer vacations and was introduced to classical music, modern painting, the works of the German writer Thomas Mann, surrealism, and the formally innovative modern novel of France, called the new novel. By the age of sixteen, Perec had been to England, Israel, Austria, and Switzerland and had traveled across France from the Atlantic coast to the Alps. He was fond of cycling, detective fiction, jazz, and cinema. At this time, he also read the works of the French existen- tialist writer Albert Camus, winner of the Nobel Prize in Literature in 1957, and of Honoré de Balzac, whose enormous corpus of works, *La Comédie humaine* (1829-1848; *The Human*

Comedy, 1885-1893), paints a minutely detailed picture of nineteenth century France.

By the age of eighteen, Perec had decided to be a writer. This decision had probably been taken during his last two years of secondary education. In *Je suis né* (1990; I was born), he claims not to have understood this decision and, indeed, questions the very nature of a writer's activity.

Perec did extremely well in his examinations for the *baccalauréat* and won the school prize for philosophy in 1954. Since the young man had not carried on his Greek studies, he was unable to enter the finest of France's *grandes écoles*, the Ecole Normale Supérieure in Paris. As a consequence, he attempted to gain admission to the slightly less prestigious Ecole Normale Supérieure de Saint-Cloud by entering the preparatory class, *hypokhâgne*, at Lycée Henri-IV in the Latin Quarter of Paris. At the end of the 1955 school year, he was informed by school authorities that his time at Henri-IV was over. Immediately following this, he enrolled for a degree in history at the Sorbonne, where he spent several lackluster months before terminating his academic career. His failure to succeed at Henri-IV meant that he would not be admitted to a *grande école* or be a candidate for the *agrégation*, a rigorous set of national examinations that often served at that time to support the writing life of academics and to grant admission to the French establishment's intelligentsia.

In early 1955, Perec began publishing literary reviews through the encouragement and publishing connections of Jean Duvignaud, his philosophy teacher at Etampes, in the *Nouvelle NRF*, the new version of the monthly *La Nouvelle Revue Française*, founded long before by the French writer André Gide. During his student years in Paris, the foundations of Perec's literary culture, mainly French, were laid. His interests did not limit themselves exclusively to French literature, though, since he also read the Irish poet and novelist James Joyce and the American novelist John Dos Passos.

Begun in the summer of 1955, when the war against Communist insurgents in Guatemala was at its height, and finished before mid-February, 1956, "Les Errants" (the wanderers) was Perec's first unpublished novel. Set in Guatemala, it recounts the death of four itinerant jazz musicians. Never submitted to a publisher, the manuscript is nevertheless present in *La Vie mode d'emploi* (1978; *Life: A User's Manual*, 1987) and was the subject of a lecture Perec gave in Australia in 1981, as an example of how not to write.

In 1960, Perec married Paulette Petras, a student at the Sorbonne. In 1961, Perec secured a position as a scientific archivist, which he would keep for nearly two decades, in a laboratory for medical neurophysiology. Among his many tasks, Perec was expected to type documents of various kinds. Here the writer took over the archivist's domain. Perec would often systematically modify colleagues' scientific reports by inserting puns, spoonerisms, and misspellings. His games with English involved inserting French words apparently at random and applying spelling distortions to written English that represented the sound of atrocious French accents. Scientific pseudo-English was attacked with zeal, and he delighted in using incremental indentations to compose diamond-shaped, E-shaped, and triangular-shaped texts. Eventually, Perec received a tenured position as archivist and, despite his unorthodox typing results, retained his position in the laboratory.

When Perec published *Things*, it was admired for its realism of situation, for its story of poverty bound up with the image of wealth, for its combined sociological and aesthetic dimensions. Bellos believes it represents in one sense the last chapter of Perec's autobiography. With few exceptions, what he wrote after *Things* draws on material from earlier periods of his life.

In *Things* there is no psychological probing into the lives of the young couple Jérôme and Sylvie. A sharp focus on the things desired by the couple unveils the emptiness of their lives, from which passion of any kind is absent. Consequently, the novel creates a profound sense of melancholy that invades the reader's sensibility.

In 1967, Perec was co-opted as a member of OuLiPo (Ouvroir de Littérature Potentielle; workshop for potential literature), founded in 1960 by a group of writers and mathematicians who wished to fashion new tools for writing and to refurbish old and forgotten ones. Perec's adoption by OuLiPo was significant, since it demonstrated that the group recognized him as one who could endorse and develop the objective of literary innovation.

La Disparition (1969; the disappearance)—an eloquent example of such an attempt, for it is written without the use of *e*—is about a man who disappears and whose friends, trying to locate him, also vanish one by one. Perec wished to see if *e*-less French could invent its own story and vindicate the potential not only of that constraint but also of the very principle of constraint. Although *La Disparition* was not well received, news of it spread by word of mouth among the literary avant-garde rather than by critical notice.

By the end of 1969, Georges and Paulette had separated. Settling eventually into an apartment above her husband's in Rue Linné on the Left Bank, Paulette remained Madame Perec in law and was a central member of the writer's family of friends. In 1975, Perec began a relationship with Catherine Binet, a woman eight years his junior who was a film writer and director. Binet proved a faithful friend, to whom Perec would read the drafts of *Life: A User's Manual*, until his death seven years later.

Life was written in less than eighteen months following a meticulously prepared plan that had taken years to establish. The work is interwoven with a seemingly endless array of different types of fiction: fairy tales, an adventure narrative, a family drama, a detective story, and a dream sequence, among others. Many nonnarrative forms of writing are incorporated, including a dictionary entry, a newspaper résumé, and an equipment catalog. Perec's talent as a writer of pastiche is clearly evident, as are his skills in multiplying narrative and linguistic styles. For this work, his last unique contribution to modern French literature before his death in Paris from cancer in 1982, he was awarded the 1978 Prix Médicis.

David Bellos has re-created with acute precision and a wealth of documentation the literary career of Perec and, to a lesser degree, has produced a psychological portrait of the man. That Perec was able to sustain a prolific writing career despite a lack of financial stability is testimony to his commitment to his deeply felt desire to write and, while doing so, to create a type of all-encompassing literature that could transcend stultifying ideologies. *Georges Perec: A Life in Words* is a rich chronicle of the inimitable position Perec has come to occupy in modern French literature.

Kenneth W. Meadwell

Sources for Further Study

Australian Book Review. February, 1994, p. 46.
Choice. XXXI, May, 1994, p. 1440.
Los Angeles Times Book Review. December 12, 1993, p. 3.
New Statesman and Society. VI, December 3, 1993, p. 38.
The New York Review of Books. XLI, November 3, 1994, p. 47.
The New Yorker. LXX, March 7, 1994, p. 99.
Publishers Weekly. CCXL, October 11, 1993, p. 75.
The Review of Contemporary Fiction. XIV, Spring, 1994, p. 235.
The Times Literary Supplement. December 3, 1993, p. 3.
The Washington Post Book World. XXIV, January 9, 1994, p. 5.

GHOSTS OF MANILA

Author: James Hamilton-Paterson (1941-   )
Publisher: Farrar Straus Giroux (New York). 279 pp. $22.00
Type of work: Novel
Time: 1993
Locale: Manila, the Philippines

Lonely, anxious Filipino, British, and American men and women try to survive from day to day in the politically corrupt, crime-ridden, rapidly expanding city of Manila

Principal characters:
JOHN PRIDEAUX, a middle-aged anthropology student doing fieldwork in the Philippines
INSPECTOR GREGORIO DINGCA, a burnt-out policeman trying to remain reasonably honest in a corrupt system
EPIFANIA TUGOS, a shrewd Filipino woman who runs a sewing cooperative in one of Manila's biggest squatter colonies
EDSEL "EDDIE" TUGOS, Epifania's husband, a heavy-drinking, irresponsible, but charming man
VIC AGUSAN, an investigative newspaper reporter who specializes in exposing police and political corruption
YSABELLA BASTIAAN, a snobbish young British archaeologist doing fieldwork with a local museum
SHARON POLICK, a worldly young American archaeologist
FATHER NICOMEDES HERRERA, an eccentric, garrulous homosexual posing as a Catholic priest
LETTIE TAN, a powerful Chinese "dragon lady" involved in drug smuggling and other criminal activities

James Hamilton-Paterson is a former journalist who writes novels like a poet. He has published two books of poetry and won the Newdigate Prize for poetry from Oxford University, his alma mater, in 1964. He worked as a free-lance journalist and for *The Times Literary Supplement* and *New Statesman* from 1968 to 1974. He was born in England but has chosen to live in foreign lands—mostly in the Philippines and Tuscany—for much of his adult life.

Ghosts of Manila, his thirteenth published work, reads more like a poetic travelogue than a novel. The slow-paced plot, told from many different viewpoints, is sometimes hard to follow. The book becomes fascinating, however, because the author knows his subject thoroughly and writes with great visual intensity. The lethargic pacing seems appropriate to the subject: It mimics the spirit of an ancient land that has seen Spanish, American, and Japanese conquerors come and go while the resilient native people remain relatively unchanged.

The author's anonymous third-person narrator has a charming sense of humor reminiscent of Graham Greene, another English writer who forsook his bland little island and traveled the world in search of exotic settings and colorful characters. It is impossible to convey an accurate impression of Hamilton-Paterson's style without a few quotations. Here is his throwaway description of a fighting cock: "Its wattles glowed with rich blood; the sun burnished its metallic plumes until they bled gold and copper and bronze; the proud arch of its tail dribbled inky lights." Here is a casual glimpse of the background in a Chinese restaurant: "In tanks along one wall mournful eels gulped and furious crustacea attacked each other in slow motion." Hamilton-Paterson's humor is wry: "This was a Squires Bingham .38 [pistol] of local manufacture, generally rated as life-threatening to all except the person being fired at." "The economic position [of the Philippines] might be summarised as that of a banana republic which imports its bananas."

The author clearly knows Manila. The reader is left with the impression of having seen the Philippine capital more thoroughly than any tourist who jets in and jets out after staying at the Philippine Plaza Hotel and visiting the obligatory attractions. Many of the sights the author unveils are not pretty. His opening pages describe a small factory where the Chinese proprietors chop up human bodies and reassemble the boiled, dried, and lacquered bones into skeletons for export to medical schools. The skeleton-makers prudently do not ask where the corpses come from but are no doubt aware that some were murdered for the specific purpose of being sold to their "chop shop."

The most appalling business of all is child prostitution. Manila, according to Hamilton-Paterson, is a mecca for perverts who not only enjoy sexual intercourse with children but get an added thrill from murdering them afterward. Boys and girls are kidnapped off the streets; others are purchased from ignorant peasants who believe that their offspring will be given vocational opportunities in the big city. Life is cheap in the Philippines.

These victims are some of the "ghosts" of Manila. Others are workmen killed in badly designed, graft-ridden construction projects funded by the corrupt government. Still others are petty criminals who are brutally murdered by the police in order to save the time, trouble, and expense of trials and incarceration.

Hamilton-Paterson's story mainly deals with the life and death of San Clemente, an enormous squatter colony built out of salvaged wood, metal, cardboard, concrete blocks, and anything else the more affluent Manilenos have thrown away or neglected to lock up. The book opens with a description of Manila as a tourist might see it, coming in for a landing near what the author describes as "the pinchbeck Manhattan of a new commercial centre" and roaring over San Clemente without noticing the barefoot children playing amid pools of raw sewage crossed by duckboards. It ends with a description of another jetliner taking off with another group of tourists, who are equally oblivious of all the stories that were being played out in that city-within-a-city before it was gutted by the holocaust that forms the climax of the novel.

The most prosperous Clementeno is Epifania Tugos, who runs a cooperative workshop in her jerry-built home. There women turn out shirts and other garments on a piecework basis on ancient sewing machines. Epifania unwittingly sets the wheels of tragedy in motion by asking her husband and a few of his layabout drinking buddies to dig a cesspool. The excavators turn up some pottery and children's skeletons, which prove to be of archaeological interest because they date back to A.D. 1100.

Immediately San Clemente becomes the focus of outside interests seeking to capitalize on the findings. There is talk of bulldozing the entire colony and turning it into a gigantic mall featuring the archaeological dig in the center—a tourist attraction like the La Brea Tar Pits in Los Angeles. Before the snorting bulldozers can rip through the shanties, however, a fire breaks out and rages through the entire colony, killing a number of people in the process. The author's description of this climactic inferno displays his flair for vivid imagery.

> As Vic stood, panting, a swag of greenery above him burst into fire with a sound of Chinese crackers and drops of gum began falling around him sputtering tiny blue flames. . . . Now and then came a loud thump as though a bottle of kerosene had exploded and for an instant a tighter crimson bud opened its individual blossom above the general rags and tatters of incandescence.

Everyone knows the fire was set by agents of the Chinese crime boss Lettie Tan, who bears a grudge against the squatters for tapping the water line that runs into her family mausoleum in the adjacent cemetery. Lettie is rumored to own all the land on which San Clemente has been built. One of the Clementenos, however, gets revenge for the entire colony by hot-wiring a bulldozer and driving it straight into the ornate Tan family mausoleum, exposing incriminating contraband that should cause serious trouble for Lettie and her henchmen.

John Prideaux, the main character in *Ghosts of Manila*, seems to be the author himself, thinly disguised as an expatriate British anthropology student who feels himself getting old before he has managed to find himself either vocationally or in a romantic relationship. The only person he has ever loved is his daughter Ruth, who is attending school eight thousand miles away in England. Prideaux lives an unusual life as an expatriate but is otherwise not much different from many other men who believe that they are sexually maladjusted because they are vocationally maladjusted and vice versa.

For years Prideaux has been trying to gather data for a projected dissertation about the phenomenon he refers to as *amok*: the madness that suddenly overwhelms certain individuals and causes them to commit murder and mayhem against strangers, friends, foes, and family members. Like many another academician, Prideaux has the unpleasant suspicion that he has gotten entangled in a subject that is far too complex to handle in a single work. He has also begun to suspect that he is using this projected work as an excuse for leading a life of idleness and fruitless introspection; sooner or later, he fears, the truth will come out and he will be left without even this counterfeit purpose for living.

It may be that the city of Manila itself is sapping his energies in a way similar to that described by Joseph Conrad in *Heart of Darkness* (1902). The most important "character" in the novel is Manila itself, one of the numerous Third World cities that are expanding in all directions without any sort of planning because of the hordes of people who are abandoning fields and villages and swarming to urban areas.

Hamilton-Paterson writes like an American but thinks like a European. His tone reflects the cynicism, fatalism, and world-weariness of Englishmen who have seen an empire built through centuries washed away like sand castles in less than fifty years. His beautiful prose is full of Americanisms, but the complexity of his thinking and his ineluctable melancholy bespeak a mind like that of Greene, who knew that there are no easy answers to the world's problems and that empire-building Americans who assume that money can fix everything will find out how wrong they were. In fact, *Ghosts of Manila* closely resembles *The Comedians* (1966), Greene's tragicomic novel about Haiti. Hamilton-Paterson's hidden thesis, like Greene's, seems to be that the so-called developing nations will never really develop into "developed nations" because the people are so lovably incorrigible. Like Greene, he is not a neocolonialist but a sort of postcolonialist, a rueful onlooker who thinks that the world might have been a better place if the European empires had been left to run it.

James Hamilton-Paterson is an author worth knowing about—and he is not nearly as well known as he should be. A journalist who writes like a poet and tries to be a novelist, who drifts around the world like Conrad's Lord Jim, is just the sort of maladjusted individual who may actually find himself one day and become famous. Hamilton-Paterson, who wrote this book in his early fifties, may have his best work ahead of him. The patient reader cannot help wishing him well. This sensitive, solitary, gifted author may be out of step with the rest of the world, but he is as true to himself as it is possible for anyone to be in postmodern times.

Bill Delaney

Sources for Further Study

Booklist. XCI, October 15, 1994, p. 400.
Kirkus Reviews. LXII, August 1, 1994, p. 50.
Library Journal. CXIX, October 1, 1994, p. 114.
The New York Times Book Review. XCIX, November 27, 1994, p. 38.
The Observer. May 15, 1994, p. 17.
Publishers Weekly. CCXLI, October 3, 1994, p. 50.
San Francisco Chronicle. January 8, 1995, p. 95, p. REV9.
The Spectator. CCLXXII, May 21, 1994, p. 35.
The Times Literary Supplement. May 20, 1994, p. 13.
The Washington Post. December 30, 1994, p. C3.

GOING NATIVE

Author: Stephen Wright (1946-)
Publisher: Farrar Straus Giroux (New York). 305 pp. $22.00
Type of work: Novel
Time: The 1990's
Locale: The suburbs of Chicago; the highways of Nebraska; Cool Creek and Denver, Colorado; Las Vegas; Borneo; and Los Angeles

A tour of the western United States, beginning in the Chicago suburbs, detouring into the jungles of Borneo, and ending in Los Angeles, with a collection of disparate characters

Principal characters:
WYLIE JONES, a husband and father who disappears inexplicably after dinner one night
RHO JONES, his wife
TOM HANNA, their neighbor and friend
GERRI HANNA, Tom's wife
MR. CD, a small-scale drug and music dealer
BILLY CLAY, a homicidal hitchhiker
AERYL CHASE, a teenage runaway
PERRY FOYLE, a cinematographer
DRAKE COPELAND, a Hollywood producer
AMANDA COPELAND, an actress, his wife

One could say that American literature was founded on the road; Mary Rowlandson, James Fenimore Cooper, and many of the American novelists of the nineteenth and twentieth centuries have sent their heroes out on a journey. American society is congenitally mobile, and the road has been the home of its most memorable characters. It is therefore only fitting that Stephen Wright would situate his *Going Native* characters out on the highways of the western United States; however, their journey is into the eye of the nation's nightmares.

The novel opens with a woman preparing dinner in her well-appointed suburban home outside Chicago and awaiting her guests, Tom and Gerri Hanna. Wylie Jones, her husband, eventually arrives after surviving a day he describes as "murderous." There is an air of strained uneasiness that explodes when Wylie and Tom run out to a convenience store and find a dead body in the parking lot. After dinner Wylie wanders about the house, visits his two sleeping children, and then vanishes into the night.

This first chapter represents the first of eight separate though related stories that make up the narrative, each of which involves Wylie in a series of personas. The second chapter shifts three blocks away to another, decidedly seedier, suburban house where a pair of crack addicts, Mr. CD and Latisha Charlemagne, quarrel, make love, drive to the mall, and score more dope, each locked into a private fantasy. As they travel into chemical oblivion, Mr. CD grows increasingly paranoid, convinced that an intruder is hiding behind a tree on his front lawn. This section ends with mouthfuls of abuse, broken furniture, and mayhem, as someone steals Mr. CD's green 1969 Ford Galaxie and drifts off into the dark.

Chapter 3 is set somewhere west, most likely Nebraska, where a hitchhiker named Billy Clay is rousted by state troopers and then hitches a ride with Randy Sawyers, a truck driver who insists that his passengers entertain him with constant conversation or be subjected to enduring his Madonna tapes. When Clay remains taciturn, Sawyer turns on the music and is then stabbed in the chest. Clay hitches one or two more rides and eventually settles into a green Ford Galaxie heading nowhere. The driver appears to be the next of Clay's victims until he reveals that he has stolen the car. Clay panics, insists that he stop the car, and leaps out.

The scene shifts to the Yellowbird Motel in Cool Creek, Colorado, where the proprietor, Emory Chase, spends his days checking tenants in and out and mentally revising the screenplay to "The Syn Man," his ticket out of obscurity and Cool Creek. Eluding his observation is the fact that his family is quickly receding from his grasp: His wife has been drifting into aimless affairs, and one of his daughters, Aeryl, is running away with Lazlo, devotee of heavy metal bands and dime-store Satanism. The two hitch a ride with a man named Tom in a green Galaxie and proceed to insult him and make love in his backseat. When Lazlo demands that they make a rest stop, Tom and Aeryl drive off, stranding him.

The next chapter opens with Perry Foyle, cinematographer manqué, videotaping unsuspecting lovers through a hole in the wall of his hotel room. Foyle collects his tapes and heads over to a bacchanalia at the Rainbow Bridge, where Freya, porn star turned director, purchases the tapes and demands that Foyle stay and photograph a short that she is about to shoot. The vignette teems with Foyle's brief encounters with the decadent glitterati, each more hopelessly narcissistic than the last. Frustrated in his attempts to secure a companion for the night, he returns to his room and begins filming a new tryst that suddenly turns deadly when a man sets a hooker on fire. Foyle falls over in shock and is then visited by the man, who shoots him.

The scene shifts farther west, to Las Vegas, where Jessie Horn, survivor of a pair of abusive relationships, lives with Nikki, whom she met after witnessing a horrible car accident, and her two children. The two women work for Nikki's parents at the Happy Chapel, and all seems idyllic until a couple, Tom and Kara, arrive and ask to be married. After they leave, Nikki discovers that a number of rings have been stolen, and she and Jessie wrangle over whose fault it is.

Chapter 7, a rewriting of Joseph Conrad's *Heart of Darkness* (1902), is the longest of the book, and on the surface it is unlike the others. It is novella length and is set in the jungles of Borneo, where Hollywood producer Drake Copeland and his actress wife Amanda leave the tourist trail and hike into headhunter country. There they take up brief residence in a village of the Pekit tribe, who entertain them with a videotape of *Batman* (1989), a gift from their friend Jack Nicholson after one of his visits. While Amanda suffers from the heat and the local food and drink, Drake strives to become one of the villagers, submitting to a painful sexual mutilation and accompanying the tribe on a pig hunt.

Abruptly the scene jumps to Hollywood, where the Copelands are entertaining friends. Their dinner is interrupted by a pair of strangers, Tom and Kara, who demand money. Dissatisfied with the take, Tom, like Perry in Truman Capote's *In Cold Blood* (1966), suddenly snaps. Walking through the house, he methodically executes the Copelands and their guests.

The final chapter is set in an unidentified Southern California beach community where unemployed Will Johnson lives in bored splendor with his wife, Tia, and her son, Todd. John wanders from health club to exclusive gun club to trendy bars, assuming various disguises and personas and unsuccessfully attempting to seduce women. The novel ends as he argues with Tia over his old car and prowls the house late at night in one of her dresses. He moves out to the garage and sits in the dilapidated old Galaxie, feeling suddenly in control and realizing that "there was no self, there was no identity, there was no grand ship to conduct you harmlessly through the uncharted night."

This observation reveals the novel's central theme and its form. Wright has written a modern picaresque, a form that grew out of a sense of social dislocation and has proved for centuries to be an infinitely adaptable fictional mode. Picaresques have always concerned themselves with rogue heroes, isolated figures who live outside the bounds of traditional morality, exploiting, using, and manipulating circumstance and other people whenever necessary. Their lives are testaments to the conviction that the social arrangement is fundamentally unfair and human relations deceptive. The world has no solid, fixed points, and people are never who or what they appear to be. As Jessie grimly realizes after her unexpected argument with Nikki, people will never be immune to "the plentiful and venomous relationship diseases."

In such a threatening world, the picaro soon learns that survival is the only true means of triumph and that survival comes through unscrupulousness and a quick wit. The picaro is usually a protean figure, a shape shifter who can become anyone and thus moves easily among all levels of society. Wylie Jones, an otherwise undistinguished figure (a "guy who looked like any other guy"), becomes a malevolent personification of his friend Tom Hanna, then Will Johnson, Larry Talbot, Ridley Webb, Lyle Coyote, and eventually a drag queen impersonating his own new wife. For him "a name was a prison . . . binding you to a place even after you were dead." In these ways the novel is reminiscent of one of American literature's overlooked masterpieces, Herman Melville's *The Confidence-Man* (1857). Besides an episodic plot and shape-shifting protagonist, the two novels share an acidic view of moral corruptibility and exploitative relationships.

All of this may sound like a latter-day version of existentialism, but Wright is suggesting something quite different. Where Jean-Paul Sartre posited the notion of a changing self to meet mutable situations, Wright reveals an absence of self, a vacuum at the heart of being, and his character's shifting personalities and identities are attempts at existential evasion. To fill this void, character after character invokes actors, plots, and films from Hollywood. The novel teems with references to motion pictures—*The Big Sleep* (1946), *Murder, My Sweet* (1944), *The Terminator* (1984), and *The Raven* (1935), to name only a few—and characters are often defined by the number of televisions they own and the shows they watch, which they gladly quote or summarize upon receiving only the slightest encouragement. The novel insists that films have so invaded modern consciousness that people use them as the informing metaphors for existence. Even the Pekit in the jungle take delight in videotapes and visitors acting out parts played by characters in films they have never seen.

Some members of the tribe, however, offer an important counterpoint to the allure of cinema. One night the chief explains the myth of the tree. A tree, he says, is a paradigm of the cosmos, and forests are the true homes of people. When human beings wander too far away from their home, they cannot return. Then they destroy their home. "Once all the trees are gone, there will be no way to get back to God. Then there will be no God." The village healer, after ministering to an ailing Amanda, offers a more succinct explanation: "American lady sick from too much movie . . . Movies are visions sick people have before they die." Sick Wright's characters are, as they desperately define themselves by the ephemeral images that flicker through their daily lives.

Just as important as the novel's themes is its style, which is lush, vibrant, and hypnotic. Wright is a compelling stylist; his sentences shimmer with original images and observations. He does a masterful job of capturing the evanescent nuances of a moment, and the novel resonates with one quotable passage after another. For one character, a transitory moment of joy "came inexplicably out of nowhere and was gone by the time she got home, a psychic comet in elliptical orbit from that parallel universe her real emotional life, the good one, seemed to inhabit." The novel reveals the complex currents of thought and emotion that surround even the smallest events. Wright conveys a richness found not simply in dramatic outward events but also in the minute inner workings of experience.

In these ways the novel can be compared with those of writers such as Paul West, Thomas Pynchon, and Don DeLillo. Unfortunately, however, the relentless attention Wright pays to human degradation becomes overworn. *Going Native* needs more of the ironic humanism that DeLillo and Pynchon's best works convey. Nevertheless, this is a novel with few faults, proof of a prodigious talent. *Going Native* is like a thrill ride into darkness that shocks yet maintains the reader's rapt attention.

David W. Madden

Sources for Further Study

The Antioch Review. LII, Spring, 1994, p. 364.
Chicago Tribune. March 13, 1994, XIV, p. 5.
Los Angeles Times Book Review. January 30, 1994, p. 3.
The New York Times Book Review. XCIX, January 23, 1994, p. 8.
The New Yorker. LXIX, January 17, 1994, p. 89.
The Review of Contemporary Fiction. XIV, Summer, 1994, p. 202.
The Wall Street Journal. February 8, 1994, p. A16.
The Washington Post Book World. XXIV, February 27, 1994, p. 6.

THE GOOD HUSBAND

Author: Gail Godwin (1937-)
Publisher: Ballantine Books (New York). 468 pp. $22.95
Type of work: Novel
Time: 1990-1993
Locale: Aurelia, New York

Gail Godwin offers a close study of four individuals whose lives intersect as each faces an emotional and/or spiritual crisis

Principal characters:
MAGDA DANVERS, a noted scholar who studies her life as she faces death
FRANCIS LAKE, her husband, a former seminarian who takes care of her
HUGO HENRY, a novelist who must come to terms with writer's block and a disintegrating marriage
ALICE HENRY, his wife, who regains her equilibrium after the death of her son by becoming involved with Magda and Francis

Gail Godwin's novels tend to explore the fabric of relationships—particularly the peculiar give-and-take between two people that sustains love, remakes personalities, and lifts individuals out of isolation. In her early novels, particularly *The Odd Woman* (1974) and *Violet Clay* (1978), Godwin probes the consciousness of a single female protagonist who struggles to maintain some autonomy within a potentially damaging relationship. Similar themes appear in *A Mother and Two Daughters* (1982) and *A Southern Family* (1987), Godwin's more expansive novels of the 1980's. Their characters, mostly women, search for personal freedom within the larger context of a family. By utilizing multiple points of view, Godwin can demonstrate the effects of her characters' choices on others and explore tangential themes of how environment, family, and social milieu influence one's choices. Godwin returns to exploring a single consciousness in *Father Melancholy's Daughter* (1991), but with a new psychological probing of the protagonist's struggle for autonomy as she searches for her mother.

In *The Good Husband*, Godwin continues to write in this intense psychological vein. In many stylistic ways, the novel is typical of Godwin's earlier work: The main characters are, for the most part, carefully constructed with exacting and evocative detail, and part of the plot concerns relationships and the making of a good marriage. Yet this novel reaches beyond Godwin's usual concerns. With potent illustrations of death and other forms of loss, Godwin forces the reader to consider large issues in a much more direct and, unfortunately, obvious manner than in her earlier novels. Her heavy-handed attempt to project multiple meanings on the slightest of actions further flaws the text, creating in the process some less than realized characters and unbelievable plot developments.

Structurally, *The Good Husband* is divided between the consciousnesses of its four main characters—Magda Danvers, Francis Lake, Hugo Henry, and Alice Henry. There are minor players in this novel—a college president and his political wife, a wealthy benefactress, the stoned daughter of a famous critic—but they offer only slight commentary on the major events. One consciousness generally rules a given chapter, but the four main characters' lives become so intricately intertwined that eventually their voices are separated only by breaks within chapters. Each of the four faces a major crisis and must come to terms with his or her individual Gargoyle, the name Magda gives to her cancer.

For Magda Danvers, a professor of English at Aurelia College and noted scholar of visionary poets, the crisis is immediate and impassable—she is dying of ovarian cancer. Electing to forgo chemotherapy, she opts to study her life rather than her disease. Her sections of the novel are a crosshatch of reminiscences, ramblings, and graphic descriptions of how cancer ravages a body. As the cancer destroys her body, Magda occupies herself with her favorite pastime: determining the motivations and multiple meanings of everyone's actions—past, present, and future—using symbols from the works of the great poets. She reads all actions like a Talmudic scholar, believing that every action, planned or unplanned, displays several meanings at once. As long as she believes that all things have significance, she can exist happily, even though she is dying. Out of this quixotic spiritual quest comes one of the central points of the novel: The mind, even the brilliant mind, cannot survive death. All actions, understood or misunderstood, lack relevance in the end. Perhaps these truths are passé, but Godwin forces the reader to look hard at what death really does to the body, a truth well beyond the abstract notions of dying that Magda's mind offers at the onset of her disease.

Unfortunately, Godwin works too hard at the symbology that Magda proposes is prevalent in life, and the multiple layering is often too obvious. For example, Magda wears all black when she goes to speak at the seminary where Francis meets her. He thinks that she looks like a nun, and she *is* a type of nun of the academy, putting all of her power into the creation of her academic work. By marrying her, Francis releases her from this type of life, but as a consequence, her work is never the same. Another equally obvious moment occurs when Alice dreams of her brother and hears Francis' voice saying, "They were meant to be together, but they got separated . . ." The conspicuous association here of Francis with Alice's beloved dead brother, Andy, forces the reader to notice Alice's developing attachment to Francis. Godwin has not trusted her readers to make such discoveries for themselves.

Another problem with this novel lies in Godwin's rather noticeable delineation between givers and takers, those who are ego-centered and those who are egoless. Francis Lake, Magda's "good husband," is as passive as Magda is active. He explains to Magda early in their relationship that he likes to take care of things, and that is exactly what he does—takes care of Magda, keeping her grounded in day-to-day concerns. Francis' crisis is coming to terms with the loss of his beloved Magda. Indeed, taking care of her is all he has ever done. Godwin, however, does not allow the reader to care much for Francis. Because his depiction is relatively brief and his interior monologues offer little insight into what really motivates him, one begins to wonder whether he really exists at all.

This could be Godwin's point. Yet Francis' passivity makes it nearly impossible to imagine him with Alice Henry in the romance that culminates at the end of the novel. Furthermore, the success of this relationship seems necessary in order to justify another of the novel's increasingly blatant main points: Individuals can switch roles in different relationships; they need not be only givers or only takers. Here Godwin never quite convinces the reader, primarily because Francis lacks the textual reality that she gives to her other characters. One never forgets that Francis is a character in a novel.

Alice Henry, also a giver in her marriage to Hugo Henry, does not lose her vitality because of her passivity. Her interior monologues create a more believable emotional landscape than Francis'. Her crisis occurs with the stillborn death of her first baby, made more poignant by the fact that her mother, father, and brother died when she was younger. After the death of her child, she begins to suffer some of the numbing depression that overcame her with those earlier deaths. Alice does work through this new grief believably, though, and her story demonstrates Godwin's skill at showing the reader the most horrible thing and then forcing him or her to relive it. The scenes of the birth/death of her baby and Alice's remembrances are the most powerful in the novel.

The decision that Alice reaches through her crisis seems designed to free and help her—to disengage from her marriage to Hugo and find another mate who can be a comfort to her and allow her to be a comfort to him. In theory, her choice of Francis seems viable, but her falling in love with him seems too pat. Given Magda's judgmental personality, it seems unlikely that Magda would actually like Alice enough to invite her to her home while she is dying. Yet these meetings must occur to allow Alice access to Francis. Godwin's writerly manipulations at times seem all too forced.

Hugo Henry, a novelist, is the second "taker" or egotist in the novel. Unlike Magda's ego, which unravels things, Hugo's ego thrives on creating things. His crisis, then, rather necessarily involves his inability to write, to find anything worth retelling. One first expects to hate Hugo because while his wife grieves unconsolably over the loss of their son, he focuses mostly on his own grief at being unable to write. As the novel progresses and one becomes privy to Hugo's thoughts, one learns that he is not emotionally capable of giving anything except to his fictional creations. He is redeemed, however, because he tries. During the course of the novel, he tries to reach out to his son by his first wife. This young man, he unexpectedly discovers, is gay. By watching his son with his lover, Hugo learns another of the lessons of the novel: A person can be transformed and renewed when paired with a suitable mate. This realization prompts him to precipitate a separation from Alice. In a metafictional scene at the end of the novel, Hugo muses on how the beginning, middle, and end of a novel are like the beginning, middle, and end of a marriage. Godwin uses his words about writing to discuss her own work, since most of his dictums for good writing are followed in *The Good Husband*.

When Hugo recognizes that writing is the most precious thing in his life, he also realizes that he cannot stay married to Alice, because he believes that she deserves to be the most precious person in someone's life. At the end of the novel, Hugo is, rather implausibly, serving as writer-in-residence at the library in his hometown, enjoying the patronage of a local woman who is dying of lupus, and happily at work on his next novel.

The strengths of *The Good Husband*, like the strengths of Godwin's other works, lie in her creation of plausible characters who endure plausible situations. When Alice asks the midwife to help her open her dead baby's eyes so that she can see their color, her emotional anguish becomes vivid. When Godwin juxtaposes Hugo's and Alice's interior monologues doing silent emotional battle, she lays bare the emotional substance of a relationship. Certainly her expertise at sketching characters in internal emotional combat is evident throughout this novel, particularly in Magda's struggle to face the inevitability of death.

Yet this novel seems overloaded with emotional crises. At one point Hugo considers the potential problems of using his wife's calamitous life in a fictional creation, particularly after the death of their son: "Jesus Christ, he'd think twice about visiting such a nightmare on characters in a novel. Particularly if one of them had already been given Alice's history of loss: it would seem like overdone punishment on the novelist's part." This insight seems true for much of the excessive catastrophe and crisis, the search for "big answers," that permeates this novel. Eventually the reader begins to feel the orchestration of the author. Sometimes the answers seem too easy or too obvious. For example, Hugo discovers how important writing is to his happiness only near the end of the novel, yet even the self-absorbed Hugo should have been able to grasp this fact much earlier. In the case of the Alice-Francis relationship, the coupling seems too implausible and too forced. At one point near the end of the novel, Francis suddenly remembers a time when he felt intense hatred for Magda. Nothing has prepared the reader for this revelation, which conveniently frees Francis from emotional ties to his dead wife and clears the way for Alice. Ultimately one simply grows tired of so much anguish without credible relief. Godwin fails at what she has done so well in other novels—allowing her readers to uncover answers without feeling the novelist's pressure to find them.

Rebecca Hendrick Flannagan

Sources for Further Study

Chicago Tribune. August 28, 1994, XIV, p. 3.
The Christian Century. CXI, November 16, 1994, p. 1088.
Los Angeles Times. September 8, 1994, p. E7.
The New York Times Book Review. XCIX, September 4, 1994, p. 5.
Time. CXLIV, September 26, 1994, p. 82.
The Times Literary Supplement. November 4, 1994, p. 22.
The Washington Post. September 16, 1994, p. F2.

THE GREEN KNIGHT

Author: Iris Murdoch (1919-   )
First published: 1993, in Great Britain
Publisher: Viking (New York). 472 pp. $23.95
Type of work: Novel
Time: The early 1990's
Locale: London and its suburbs

The lives of a tightly knit group of middle-class Londoners are disrupted and changed when a man accidentally wounded by one of them forces his way into their lives and makes them all confront the emptiness of their collective existence

Principal characters:

LOUISE ANDERSON, a widow rearing her three daughters in a fashionable section of Greater London
ALETHEA (ALEPH) ANDERSON, her oldest daughter
SOPHIA (SEFTON) ANDERSON, her middle daughter
MOIRA (MOY) ANDERSON, her youngest daughter
HARVEY BLACKET, a family friend of the Andersons, Sefton's suitor
JOAN BLACKET, Harvey's mother and Louise's close friend
CLEMENT GRAFFE, a family friend of the Andersons who loves Louise
LUCAS GRAFFE, Clement's adopted brother, a university professor
BELLAMY JAMES, a friend of Clement and of the Andersons
PETER MIR, a businessman wounded accidentally by Lucas

In an essay on *Message to the Planet* (1991), Karen A. Kildahl remarks that "part of the interest" in reviewing a novel by Iris Murdoch lies in charting "the intense reactions it invariably provokes among reviewers." An Oxford professor, Murdoch has used her vast store of knowledge about literature and philosophy to give her novels a sense of intellectual depth not always present in popular fiction; on occasion, however, critics have found this smattering of erudition simply window dressing aimed at making the commonplace seem more significant than it really is. It is hardly surprising, then, to see that comments about Murdoch's 1993 novel *The Green Knight* are widely divergent: One reviewer praises Murdoch for her novelistic skills, while another warns readers of the superficial schlock to which they will be subjected if they pick up this book.

Such remarks could be predicted, given the task Murdoch sets for herself in this novel. In *The Green Knight* the author attempts to blend two distinct literary genres: the Arthurian romance and the realistic novel. She is not the first to try the merger—among contemporary works, Mary Stewart's novels of the Arthurian cycle immediately come to mind—but her choice of subject is particularly noteworthy. The curious medieval tale "Sir Gawain and the Green Knight" has long been recognized as one of the premier literary productions of the late Middle Ages. Penned by an unknown author whose only other writings are bound in manuscript with this story of one of Arthur's chief lieutenants in a single extant copy now in the British Library, this northern English romance tells how Sir Gawain defended the honor of Arthur's court against an intruder who had, in essence, called everyone at Camelot a coward. Some of the best medieval scholars of the nineteenth and twentieth centuries have devoted considerable attention to exploring the philological and psychological aspects of this tale. A number of fine modern translations have graced the shelves of academic bookstores and private libraries for more than a hundred years. Though the outline of the story may not be known to that loosely defined group known as the general reading public, the story of Sir Gawain's encounter with the mysterious green giant Sir Bertilak is household fare in the halls of academe.

Readers not versed in medieval literature may miss the significance of Murdoch's narrative if they read quickly and only for "the plot." Murdoch's story involves the aftermath of a curious incident in which a university professor, Lucas Graffe, kills a man in self-defense when—according to Lucas—the man tries to rob him. This is his story at a trial held while the would-be thief turned victim lies dying in the hospital. After the trial, Lucas disappears. His friends and family, especially his stepbrother Clement, worry greatly for Lucas' safety, especially when they find themselves being watched by a stranger. What the circle of friends discovers when Lucas finally returns to London is that the stranger is actually the man who had supposedly died at Lucas' hand. Peter Mir, the returned-to-life victim, tells a different version of the assault: He claims that he was struck when he tried to stop Lucas from killing Clement. Forcing Clement to admit that he is correct, Peter then blackmails Lucas into introducing him into the professor's circle of friends—the Andersons and the men who have attached themselves to the Anderson clan.

No one is quite sure what Peter wants; it turns out that he desires a curious form of revenge, in which Lucas is made to acknowledge his crime to those who are closest to him. He demands further that the principals involved in the original altercation replay the scene a year later. In the same field where he had been bludgeoned, Peter pulls a knife on Lucas but merely nicks him. Then, at what ought to be the denouement, a lavish dinner party at Peter's home, the group learns that Peter is actually an escapee from an asylum, where he has been undergoing treatment for mental illness brought on by the attack. Peter is summarily whisked off to his sickbed—and dies within weeks. The Andersons, the Graffes, and others in their group must now come to terms with the significance of Lucas' attempted murder of Clement and Peter's death. All's well that ends well, though; two of the Anderson daughters and their widowed mother find appropriate husbands (Lucas takes the oldest sister off to America), and the entire group can now presumably go on with their angst-filled existences.

If this plot summary sounds more like domestic realism than medieval romance, that is precisely what Murdoch intends. Her novel is consciously written to operate on two levels. First, it is a study of modern middle-class Londoners, that group often called "shabby genteel," who maintain the façade of sophistication but whose problems mirror those of the population at large: a widowed mother bringing up three precocious daughters, several men (most approaching middle age) who struggle with their identity and their sexuality, all close friends in what seems to be an extended family relationship where intergenerational romance is the norm rather than the exception. The petty jealousies, anxieties, aspirations, and concerns that knit the group together make them appear to be the cast of some highbrow soap opera. Murdoch spices up the story by creating a pair of siblings (one adopted, the second the natural child of loving parents) whose rivalry leads the older one to attempt fratricide. That act, foiled by the intervention of a mysterious stranger, generates the primary plot complication and introduces into this social circle the title character of the work.

The similarities to the Arthurian romance are introduced in the details. Murdoch does all that she can to provide subtle parallels between her story and its medieval source. Her mysterious stranger dresses in green (sometimes a dark green suit, sometimes merely a waistcoat) and carries a green umbrella—which serves as a sheath for an unusual knife, the weapon used late in the novel to inflict the retributory wound on the would-be murderer Lucas. Other characters (who, like most middle-class denizens of London, are exceptionally well read) observe the similarities between Peter Mir and the shadowy figure of medieval romance. To be sure that her less well educated readers get the point, near the end of the novel Murdoch provides a brief synopsis of the Green Knight's story, allowing Clement to point out both the similarities and the differences between the romance and the much more realistic modern reenactment.

Yet this is no slavish retelling of the legend. Unlike many modern Arthurian tales, Murdoch stays away from simply dressing up medieval characters in three-piece suits. Rather, she uses some of the incidents present in the fourteenth century tale of Sir Gawain's adventures with the Green Knight to explore modern problems. The differences are noteworthy. In *Sir Gawain and the Green Knight,* the green giant arrives at King Arthur's court at Christmastime, wielding a mighty ax, and challenges any knight to exchange blows with him. Gawain takes up the challenge, cutting off his head. The knight picks up his head and demands an equal opportunity; the next year Gawain sets off to give his opponent his due. Arriving at the home of the Green Knight (though he does not yet know that he has come to the right place), Gawain is fêted by the host and his wife, the latter a temptress who woos Gawain unsuccessfully but convinces him to wear a magic girdle (a sash) to shield himself from the blow he will receive from the Green Knight. When the knight finally delivers the blow, he merely nicks Gawain, then tells him that the blow is retribution for the Arthurian champion's failure to resist all the temptations of the wife, who has been working in collusion with her husband.

Only a few of the plot details from this medieval story find their way into Murdoch's novel. Gone is the wife, and with her any notion of sexual temptation. Predictably, the beheading scene is transformed into something more palatable in a realistic novel—a case of simple battery performed with a cricket bat. Gone too is the Arthurian setting. Instead, the group oriented around Louise Anderson and her daughters serves as the "court" into which the modern-day Sir Bertilak interjects himself. Sir Gawain has been replaced by a self-centered academic whose crime against the Green Knight is accidental, a by-product of his failed attempt to kill his stepbrother. As is expected in realistic novels, every character has a motive for his or her actions, and every seemingly mysterious occurrence has a logical explanation. The suggestiveness of setting and the symbolic qualities of natural settings evoked by the romance become extended descriptions of the everyday—elaborate explanations of room furnishings, table settings, and dinner courses, minute detailing of apparel and hairstyles. Such is the stuff of realistic novels, and Murdoch must provide these trappings to remain faithful to the genre that ultimately dominates this work.

In the transformation of the story from the fourteenth to the twentieth century and from the realm of romance to hard-core realism, there are inevitable losses as well as gains. If Murdoch must provide rational explanations for every character's actions to satisfy modern readers' expectations of the novel, she is forced to demystify one of the most enigmatic characters in the history of her nation's literature. As a result, *The Green Knight* is destined to meet with mixed reviews: Fans of Murdoch the novelist will applaud her deftness in reshaping old materials to fit her modern purposes, while devotees of medieval literature may well bemoan the fate of the Green Knight in the hands of a twentieth century novelist. Unfortunately, that is the risk one runs whenever one attempts to tamper with a legend.

Laurence W. Mazzeno

Sources for Further Study

Chicago Tribune. January 23, 1994, XIV, p. 1.
Commonweal. CXXI, April 8, 1994, p. 21.
The Economist. CCCXXVIII, September 25, 1993, p. 99.
London Review of Books. XV, November 4, 1993, p. 25.
Los Angeles Times Book Review. February 20, 1994, p. 2.
New Statesman and Society. VI, September 17, 1993, p. 39.
The New York Times Book Review. XCIX, January 9, 1994, p. 7.
Publishers Weekly. CCXL, November 1, 1993, p. 64.
The Times Literary Supplement. September 10, 1993, p. 20.
The Washington Post Book World. XXIV, January 9, 1994, p. 3.

GREEN RIVER RISING

Author: Tim Willocks (1957-   )
Publisher: William Morrow (New York). 352 pp. $23.00
Type of work: Novel
Time: The late twentieth century
Locale: East Texas

An intelligent, compassionate doctor wrongfully convicted of rape becomes involved in a bloody race riot deliberately orchestrated by a psychotic prison warden

Principal characters:
RAY KLEIN, an orthopedic surgeon deprived of his license and wrongfully imprisoned for rape
JULIETTE DEVLIN, a visiting prison psychiatrist who falls in love with him
JOHN CAMPBELL HOBBES, the mentally unstable warden of Green River State Penitentiary
CLAUDE (CLAUDINE) TOUSSAINT, a black bisexual prisoner
NEVILLE "NEV" AGRY, the sadistic leader of the white prisoners
HENRY ABBOTT, a psychotic giant serving multiple life sentences for murders
EARL "FROGMAN" COLEY, the tough but conscientious black trustee in charge of the prison infirmary where Klein works as a nurse/paramedic
HECTOR GRAUERHOLZ, a psychopathic killer who leads a mob trying to break into the infirmary

Tim Willocks prefaces his novel with a quotation from William Shakespeare's *Richard II* (c. 1595-1596): "I have been studying how I may compare this prison where I live unto the world." His fictitious Green River State Penitentiary in East Texas—overcrowded, seething with racial hatred, ready to explode—is intended as a microcosm of the United States, if not the entire shrinking, overpopulated globe.

The reader does not have to turn many pages to realize that Willocks is an exceptionally intelligent, well-educated, and talented author. His descriptions and psychological insights are frequently impressive. He has an unusual background for a thriller writer. He was born in England, studied to become a physician and surgeon, and finally decided to specialize in psychiatry, focusing on the treatment of addiction. He lives and works in London.

It would appear that Willocks' knowledge of Americans is largely based on a fondness for popular American films and hard-boiled American novels. The cadences of his prose are definitely American, reflecting the powerful influence that American literature has had on British writers in recent decades. There is, however, still something very British about the fine quality—the "high gloss," as Henry James might put it—of Willocks' prose. He is such a good writer that the reader may wonder what this British psychiatrist is doing tossing together such a premeditatedly commercial product. The doctor-author seems quite capable of writing high-quality mainstream fiction and may go on to more ambitious projects after getting this fantasy out of his subconscious.

The writer Willocks most closely resembles is Stephen King. The Briton and the American share the same apocalyptic vision and enjoy adding conflict after conflict to a smoldering concoction until it must inevitably explode. *Green River Rising* will remind the reader of King's *Needful Things* (1991) in the way it builds and builds to catastrophe and of King's "Rita Hayworth and the Shawshank Redemption," published in *Different Seasons* (1982) in the way it pits an idealistic white middle-class intellectual convict against an unscrupulous warden.

Warden John Campbell Hobbes has become psychotic under the strain of trying to run a modern American penitentiary on principles suggested by Jeremy Bentham, the British philosopher and theoretical jurist who recommended that in a model prison the inmates should be made to sense that they are under around-the-clock surveillance. Hobbes, a white racist, attributes most of his administrative problems to the animalistic nature of his African American and Latino prisoners. In his madness, Hobbes has decided that the only solution is a race riot to release the tensions that have been building up in this overcrowded, superannuated institution since the advent of the soaring crime rate in the 1970's. Hobbes resembles the infamous Charles Manson, still incarcerated in a maximum-security California prison for masterminding the murders that he hoped would trigger a massive race riot he called "Helter-Skelter." Hobbes hates African Americans and lets them know it in no uncertain terms before "locking down" their section of the prison and turning off the air-conditioning to increase their rage.

Ray Klein, a doctor who lost his license when jailed on a bogus rape charge, is well aware that the warden has stopped taking the medication prescribed to keep his psychosis under control. Klein is the only person among the twenty-eight hundred prisoners who is accepted by all three racial factions: whites, blacks, and Latinos. His status is based on the fact that he provides medical treatment impartially and has the skill to provide better care than the visiting prison doctor, whose feelings about the prisoners are not much different from those of Warden Hobbes. Klein knows that an explosion is coming but intends to go on being a model prisoner and minding his own business until the parole board decides to let him go.

Klein is falling in love with Juliette Devlin, an idealistic visiting psychiatrist who tries to provide counseling and therapy but is hopelessly overburdened by the size of her workload. When the riot finally breaks out, she is trapped in the prison infirmary and becomes the target of a horde of sexually frustrated redneck convicts because she not only is a beautiful woman but happens to be the only woman in the institution.

Willocks, unlike Stephen King, pulls no punches when it comes to describing sex, and rather than avoiding four-letter obscenities he goes out of his way to use them. In many scenes he describes both homosexual and heterosexual encounters in painstaking detail without departing from the vernacular. He is more hard-boiled than any hard-boiled American writer, with the possible exception of Jim Thompson.

In the course of the last chapters, a large contingent of the most macho of the white convicts is intent on breaking through several heavy doors that separate them from Juliette and the AIDS patients, whom they intend to murder because they identify

AIDS with homosexuality. They tell Juliette in their own colorful language that they are going to gang-rape her until she dies from the physical abuse. Only she and convict-paramedic Earl "Frogman" Coley stand between the murderous mob and the bed-ridden patients.

When the riot explodes, Klein judiciously holes up in his cell. Until he learns about Juliette's predicament, his main problem is trying to stay alive while the riot burns itself out. He has been granted parole and will soon be released if he can make it apparent that he had no involvement in the disturbance. His instincts as a doctor, however, force him out of his isolation. He manages to save a number of guards from being murdered and gives first aid to some of the wounded. He is also able to serve as a negotiator between the various groups of prisoners, as well as between prisoners and the armed guards who are waiting to retake the prison by whatever means necessary.

The riot intensifies. Murders lead to thirst for more blood. Many of the convicts realize that they have thrown away their chances of parole and will have years added to their sentences; this creates a general fatalistic frenzy. The prisoners are doing exactly what Hobbes wanted: They are venting their hatred of society on one another, proving by their wild behavior that they are wild men who deserve the inhumane treatment they have been receiving.

When Klein learns that Juliette is in danger, he focuses his attention on the problem of getting to her. This seems impossible, because the normal route to the infirmary is blocked by the dozens of drunken, drug-crazed convicts who are intent on breaking into it. Klein is aided by Henry Abbott, a psychotic white convict whose devotion he has earned by befriending him when both convicts and guards were treating the giant like a rabid dog.

Abbott's work assignment involves maintenance of all the underground plumbing. No one else wants to go down into these Stygian regions, known as the Green River. He leads Klein through this labyrinth of rat-infested tunnels and shows him how to get up inside the infirmary by a secret route. Then, willing to sacrifice his life for his friend, he turns to confront the gang of black convicts who have been pursuing them.

Willocks' descriptions of violence, like his descriptions of sex, are lengthy and elaborate. Klein—a basically gentle soul who happens to have studied karate for many years in case it should come in handy—does more than his share of bone-smashing and eye-gouging when he finally gives up his efforts at diplomacy and neutrality. One problem with the novel is that the violence, when it finally breaks out, is so unremitting that the reader tends to become inured. The love story does not provide enough contrast. Juliette herself is no passive sex object: She thinks up ways of inflicting death and mayhem that surprise even the toughest convicts.

Embittered by his false imprisonment, Klein had decided to do his work, mind his own business, and pray for an early parole, ignoring the gang rapes, murders, beatings, mutilations, and other atrocities that occurred almost daily at Green River. Now, however, having found true love for the first time in his life, the defrocked doctor is willing to risk his freedom and even his life to defend Juliette and to accept her commitment to life by helping her protect the helpless AIDS patients.

Willocks is a better writer than King but lacks King's naïve, almost juvenile zest for the macabre. If a category novel is too well written, it runs the risk of being too highbrow for the lowbrows and too lowbrow for the highbrows. Willocks seems to be trying too hard. His characterization, for example, is exhaustive—he is, after all, a psychiatrist—yet most of his characters, including the warden himself, remain one-dimensional. They are stock figures who are incapable of change and seem pinned to the pages like exotic lepidoptera.

Nevertheless, *Green River Rising* has found a distinguished publisher in William Morrow, and the film rights have been sold to Alan J. Pakula/Warner Bros. The novel has obvious cinematic potential along the lines laid down in the film *Brute Force,* which starred a youthful Burt Lancaster in 1947, and it goes a step further by adding the volatile element of racial animosity.

The subject of race relations is of urgent contemporary interest. King avoided this issue in his "Rita Hayworth and the Shawshank Redemption," made into the film *The Shawshank Redemption* in 1994, by setting his story in an earlier time and in his home state of Maine, which had and still has only a small nonwhite population. The film version of Willocks' *Green River Rising*, like the book, will offer plenty of thrills and suspense, yet in the end it will avoid making any significant points about the critical problems of crime, prisons, or race relations.

Bill Delaney

Sources for Further Study

Booklist. XC, August, 1994, p. 1993.
Kirkus Reviews. LXII, July 1, 1994, p. 885.
Library Journal. CXIX, September 1, 1994, p. 217.
New Statesman and Society. VII, July 1, 1994, p. 39.
The New York Times Book Review. XCIX, October 23, 1994, p. 12.
The New Yorker. LXX, December 5, 1994, p. 149.
Publishers Weekly. CCXLI, July 18, 1994, p. 234.
San Francisco Chronicle. October 10, 1994, p. E5.
The Washington Post Book World. XXIV, October 16, 1994, p. 15.

HALF ASLEEP IN FROG PAJAMAS

Author: Tom Robbins (1938-   )
Publisher: Bantam Books (New York). 386 pp. $23.95
Type of work: Novel
Time: Easter weekend in the early 1990's
Locale: Seattle, Washington

By the end of one frantic weekend, Gwen Mati may have lost her job as a result of the stock-market crash, but she may also have found the key to future happiness

Principal characters:
GWENDOLYN MATI, a twenty-eight-year-old Filipina stockbroker
Q-JO, her friend, a three-hundred-pound tarot reader
BELFORD DUNN, her boyfriend, a lumberjack turned fundamentalist realtor
LARRY DIAMOND, a former stock trader and now a guru with cancer
DR. MOTOFUSA YAMAGUCHI, a Japanese scientist who has apparently found a cure for cancer
ANDRÉ, Belford's pet macaque (rhesus monkey)

This Tom Robbins novel has all the ingredients readers have come to expect from his earlier fiction. *Half Asleep in Frog Pajamas* comments on life in the United States through characters who are slightly unmoored from it and who seem to be traveling on some other astral plane. The author, in lively lyrical style, comments on both the characters and their worlds with almost nonstop slapstick and verbal humor. What is most unusual about *Half Asleep in Frog Pajamas*, perhaps, is that Robbins directly addresses the central character, so that the novel can be described as written in second person (with third person used when the central character is "out of earshot"), as here, in an early description of Gwen Mati:

> "Here!" you yell, and wave your arms. The phone is attached to the wall at the far end of the bar, and you set out for it, gingerly threading your way through the mob. As soon as you are out of earshot, which is a matter of inches, Ann Louise turns to Phil and says, "That girl is finished in this business."

Gwen Mati may be finished in the stock brokerage business, but then again, so may everyone else in the Bull & Bear restaurant and lounge, a crowded watering hole in the heart of Seattle's financial district, where all the brokers have retreated after a nine-hundred-point crash in the stock market. It is the evening of Easter Thursday when the novel begins, and no one knows what will happen when the market reopens on Monday. All the brokers face a painful weekend of waiting.

The weekend will be more painful, and much more complicated, for Gwen. Apparently she has been "unethically churning . . . accounts" and may lose her job as well as her savings. To complicate matters, her boyfriend, Belford—whom she has promised herself to dump by July 4—has lost his pet macaque; he has enlisted Gwen to try to find the animal while he is out of town for the weekend. Q-Jo, a psychic whom Gwen has been counting on to help her move into the very uncertain future, also chooses this particular moment to disappear. Much of the novel's action thus takes place on the wet weekend streets of Seattle, as Gwen searches for friend or animal.

In her distress, Gwen turns to Larry Diamond, a burned-out stock trader turned spiritual guru who has just returned from Timbuktu, the legendary city in Mali, in western Africa. Diamond lives under a bowling alley and suffers from cancer of the rectum. The novel is, on one level, a frantic chase sequence, as Gwen searches for other characters and for help and rapidly becomes involved with the charismatic Diamond, who may have the answer to her financial questions though he has as yet no solution to his own more serious medical problems. "Every single thing in my life has gone totally haywire," Gwen confesses to the former trader. Yet by the end of the novel, and with the help of the mysterious Larry Diamond, she is aware that "for some reason, the world around [her] seems alive in a way it never was before."

A large chunk of the novel, unfortunately, consists of lectures that Diamond (a.k.a. Tom Robbins) gives to Gwen on the limitations of yuppie notions of life and work. "We're job junkies, and not one of our institutions is prepared or qualified to help us kick the habit." "All Uncle Larry is saying is that individuals have to accept responsibility for their own bad choices." The main problem, he explains to Gwen is

> the Lie of Progress. The Lie of unlimited expansion. The Lie of "grow-or-perish." Listen. We built ourselves a fine commercial bonfire, but then instead of basking in its warmth, toasting marshmallows over it, and reading the classics by its light, we became obsessed with making it bigger and hotter. . . . Did we really believe capitalism was exempt from the laws of nature? Did we really confuse endless consumption with endless progress?

Larry Diamond is also in love with her. "Gwendolyn," he says, "you're like a handsome, expensive television set that can only bring in two or three channels. I want to hook you up to cable, sweetheart. I want to be your satellite dish." Much of the novel consists of their heated encounters, in whatever room or vehicle they find empty. In between clutches they search for André and Q-Jo, and Larry also tries to locate Dr. Motofusa Yamaguchi in order to obtain his miraculous cancer cure. All the mysteries are not solved by the end of the novel, but the recovered André (formerly owned by a Belgian jewel thief) may help Gwen—to steal a Van Gogh drawing and save her life.

In addition to its talkiness, *Half Asleep in Frog Pajamas* suffers from a serious problem of character development. Half her waking day, Gwen is a docile, submissive Asian American woman, worried about her future; yet she can become an aggressive broker or lover in a wink. Robbins never reconciles this split personality in his yuppie stock trader. Born in Oakland, reared in Seattle, Gwen has her M.B.A. from the University of Washington and can recite the Dow Jones industrial index like a mantra. Her mother, a poet, committed suicide some years ago; her father now recites his dead wife's poetry in Seattle nightclubs. This strange mix is apparently waiting for the New Age message from the reformed, if now infirm, Larry Diamond.

Other characters suffer from the same cartoon cut-out quality. Larry Diamond, as a legendary 1980's stock manipulator turned guru, sounds rather like Michael Milken reincarnated as Peter Fonda in *Easy Rider* (1969). While neither Q-Jo nor Belford

Dunn stays around the novel long enough to become boring, neither shows much promise of becoming a full-fleshed, well-rounded character either. Robbins, in short, is working with a stacked tarot deck, in which his players are almost all allegorical bit-player cards—the Fool, the Bozo, and so on.

Yet readers have never followed Robbins for his consistency or his verisimilitude. What one gets from a Robbins novel is a psychedelic linguistic rush. Like Belford's monkey, the language in *Half Asleep in Frog Pajamas* can sometimes get loose and run wild, in wordplay, poetic imagery, and colorful motifs. No description is ever straight; all involve elaborate figuration. Urination, for example, becomes "the meeting of the waters"; an afternoon can last "approximately as long as fourth grade"; thoughts "play bumper cars in your brain"; a kiss is "like a Mexican wedding dress"; a look becomes "a smile that could paint a doghouse," or, in an earlier passage, "a smile a girl could bring home to mother, if she had a mother; a smile a girl could pet like a pony, sip like a lemonade, hum like a popular tune; a smile a girl would feel safe with in a dark alley."

If Robbins' language is often out of rational control, so too is the content beneath. The message that Larry Diamond conveys to Gwen Mati is a rather simple one: *Carpe diem,* seize the day, by ditching the frenzied financial rat race. That message is couched, however, in a convoluted cosmology involving not only stars (particularly Sirius B) but also African mythology, frogs, lily pads, and mushrooms, as well as some traditional Christian symbolism (such as Easter Sunday). The novel is delightful to read, in short stretches, but it clearly involves a fundamental leap of New Age faith.

Interestingly, what *Half Asleep in Frog Pajamas* most closely resembles is the kind of fictional romance (like Robert James Waller's enormously popular *The Bridges of Madison County*, 1992) that has drawn a huge readership in the United States. Robbins would undoubtedly resist being lumped in such saccharine company, but when readers scratch the surface of slapstick and wordplay in this novel, they find the same simplistic characterization and worldview.

Tom Robbins novels have always had the same essential ingredients. Like his most famous *Even Cowgirls Get the Blues* (1976), Robbins in *Half Asleep in Frog Pajamas* creates an alternative universe, a kind of shadow world to the one readers know, where life is happier, sex and drugs are worry-free, language flows like music. In both novels, there are gurus (in *Even Cowgirls Get the Blues* it was the Chink; here it is a transformed stock dealer who has returned from Africa with a mystical message for the world). The earlier novel's motifs were thumbs, whooping cranes, and feminine sprays; here they are dogs, the tarot deck, and thunder. The two novels offer the same message and medium: A man lectures women on how to achieve nirvana, and it predictably involves a male fantasy of unfettered sex. While some writers who started roughly in the 1960's—one thinks of E. L. Doctorow, Joyce Carol Oates, and Larry McMurtry—have moved on to larger playing fields, others—such as Ken Kesey, Joseph Heller, and Kurt Vonnegut, Jr.—seem mired in their past. Robbins is clearly in the latter group.

Yet in *Half Asleep in Frog Pajamas* Robbins acknowledges how much the world has changed in the interim. His descriptions of Seattle's financial district, for example, take note of the street people who populate any American urban center, and some of them actually become key characters. Robbins seems grounded in stock manipulations and urban problems at the same time as his characters talk about astral travel and tarot readings. It is a schizophrenic fictional world. In one typical passage, Robbins informs readers that

> the city can no longer adequately fund its service agencies. Everywhere, everywhere, the infrastructure is deteriorating. Fiscal funeral directors circle America's largest municipalities like buzzards, archaeologists are pointing shovels at towns that aren't even buried yet.

At the end of the novel, his characters, perhaps partially in response to these urban conditions, take off for the legendary city of Timbuktu. Since *carpe diem* hardly can help panhandlers, perhaps escape is the only answer. As Larry Diamond warns readers, "At our present level of development, largely oblivious to our origins and our destination, we are half-asleep in frog pajamas."

David Peck

Sources for Further Study

Booklist. XC, August, 1994, p. 1992.
Chicago Tribune. November 17, 1994, V, p. 2.
Kirkus Reviews. LXII, August 15, 1994, p. 1081.
Library Journal. CXIX, September 15, 1994, p. 92.
Los Angeles Times Book Review. September 25, 1994, p. 3.
The New York Times Book Review. XCIX, October 30, 1994, p. 27.
Publishers Weekly. CCXLI, August 15, 1994, p. 86.
San Francisco Chronicle. September 6, 1994, p. G6.
USA Today. August 26, 1994, p. D1.
The Washington Post Book World. XXIV, December 18, 1994, p. 5.

HARDY

Author: Martin Seymour-Smith (1928-)
Publisher: St. Martin's Press (New York). Illustrated. 867 pp. $35.00
Type of work: Literary biography
Time: 1840-1928
Locale: England

Seymour-Smith narrates the life of an important Victorian novelist and provides a critical assessment of his works

Principal personages:
THOMAS HARDY, a British author
EMMA GIFFORD HARDY, his first wife
FLORENCE DUGDALE HARDY, his second wife

Among British authors of the late Victorian period, Thomas Hardy enjoys a critical reputation as a serious writer of primary importance. Born into a middle-class home in Bockhampton, he was educated in the village school and in nearby Dorchester; afterward, rather than attend a university, he became an apprentice architect. Yet because he had acquired a passion for reading and cherished the ambition of becoming a poet, he abandoned a promising career as an architect to try writing fiction. He achieved initial success with novels and short stories set in the south-central region of England.

Throughout his career, his fictional settings remained primarily agrarian Dorsetshire, which he called Wessex, an area removed from the rapid industrial and commercial development of the late Victorian era. Beginning with *Far from the Madding Crowd* (1874), Hardy produced a series of highly successful novels, the most important including *The Return of the Native* (1878), *The Mayor of Casterbridge* (1886), *Tess of the D'Urbervilles* (1891), and *Jude the Obscure* (1895). Although he often offended public taste by writing frankly of sexuality, he became financially independent through the sale of his work. After 1896, he could afford to devote his efforts largely to a less remunerative literary form, poetry. Although his poems do not rank among the greatest in English literature, or even among the best in British Victorian poetry, they were well received, and volumes like his *Wessex Poems* (1898) enhanced his literary reputation. When he died in 1928, Hardy was recognized as one of the world's leading authors.

Martin Seymour-Smith, who has previously written extensively on Victorian and modern literature, has produced a massive critical biography of Thomas Hardy. In doing so, Seymour-Smith has furnished a thorough account of the life, a critical assessment of the works, and a partial evaluation of the most important Hardy scholarship. As a critic, he shuns the theoretical for a more commonsensical approach and an insistence on logic. Early in the work, he cites Ockham's Razor as an important guide, a principle named for the fourteenth century English monk William of Ockham. It holds that when several conflicting or contradictory explanations are possible, the simplest that accounts for all elements is likely to be the correct one. It is the bane of scholars and sophists, who are attracted to abstruse, improbable, and arcane theories and speculations. Yet, contrary to reasonable expectation, its application by no means creates brevity in Seymour-Smith's text; instead it increases the length because he employs the principle to refute numerous improbable conjectures by earlier biographers.

When the truth is not known, he attempts to weigh the probabilities involved and to offer conclusions reached through inference. Since his knowledge of the Victorian era, the modern period, and Hardy's English setting is vast, he is able to establish priorities among the probabilities convincingly, although he advances his views with caution. When he has to make inferences supported only by educated guesses, he uses the biographer's normal qualifiers—expressions such as "he must have" and "we may fairly guess." When he makes conjectures that are highly speculative, he usually labels them accordingly.

As a personality, Hardy, although not a recluse, was somewhat withdrawn and shy. In narrating his life, Seymour-Smith is enough of a Freudian to find significance in early traumatic events, as one can discover in his biographies of Robert Graves and Rudyard Kipling. Thus he discerns the seeds of Hardy's pessimism in early life. At his birth, the attending physician mistakenly assumed Hardy to be dead and laid him aside, where he remained without moving or crying until an attentive nurse detected signs of life. Inclined to despondency in his youth, Hardy once expressed the hope that he would not live to maturity. He was below average in height, and from early youth his keen interest in reading became an avenue to self-education. He was quiet if not serene by temperament, and not at all given to outbursts. Following his father's taste, he enjoyed music and dancing from an early age. While he acquired many friends during his long life, he was not gregarious, and his adventures, such as they were, fell far short of those of his admired romantic hero, George Gordon, Lord Byron. When W. Somerset Maugham attempted to portray him as Edward Driffield in his popular novel *Cakes and Ale* (1930), he created a respected but private, colorless man of letters.

In his religious outlook, Hardy became a pessimist and an agnostic, yet, as Seymour-Smith points out, he retained a lifelong emotional attachment to the Church of England and regularly attended services. Despite his frequent denials and efforts to downplay its importance, Hardy was influenced by the pessimistic philosophy of Arthur Schopenhauer, whose *Die Welt als Wille und Vorstellung* (1818; *The World as Will and Representation*, 1883-1886) cast a long shadow over late nineteenth century European thought and aesthetics. Following Schopenhauer, Hardy found it necessary to reject the providential view of history, which assumed that the creation and continuation of the universe were designed for man's benefit. Having rejected an optimistic view of the world, he found comfort in absorbing work, human relationships, natural and artistic beauty, and, significantly, pets.

The depiction of an impersonal, uncaring deity in his fiction and poetry induced alarm among contemporary readers, but the popular reaction had little effect on either his success or his good fortune. As was true of another skeptical intellectual whom he admired, Charles Darwin, popular opposition to Hardy's views did not prevent his burial in Westminster Abbey.

The tone of pessimism permeates most of Hardy's novels, so much so that his biographer believes it the reason he was never awarded a Nobel Prize in Literature. His most noteworthy recognition was the Order of Merit, conferred by the British monarch. Hardy's pessimism is not limited to a cosmic view involving a malignant or an indifferent fate. The English class system, a fruitful source of comedy to many fiction writers and dramatists, became, for Hardy, a theme for tragedy. In *The Mayor of Casterbridge*, Michael Henchard claws his way into the middle class, only to fall from power when an incident from his past life is cruelly exposed. *Tess of the D'Urbervilles* depicts the despair associated with nobility that has declined financially and morally. Even Gabriel Oak in *Far from the Madding Crowd* struggles against adversity for so long that his marriage into the upper-middle class seems hardly worth it, however deserved.

Perhaps deliberately, perhaps because years of research have made the subject familiar to him, Seymour-Smith normally refers to Hardy as "Tom" in the biography, and the stylistic difference is significant. While "Hardy" is sometimes used to refer to the eminent man of letters, the usual "Tom" suggests a somewhat reserved yet vulnerable individual, one who is approachable and uncomplicated. Although showing Hardy as retaining few of his early coarse country manners, Seymour-Smith indicates that he preferred the quiet life of rural England to the more stimulating London, and spent most of his time at Max Gate, a country house he designed and built near Dorchester. After achieving success and fame, he routinely rented a London flat where he spent a few weeks or months annually. He was hypersensitive to the strictures of reviewers, yet accepted the requirements of serials editors that he bowdlerize his novels in order not to offend the sensibilities of middle-class readers, the Mrs. Grundys of the reading public. Except for his extraordinary success as a writer and the remarkable quality of his work, there is little to notice about Hardy.

In the account of his personal life, Seymour-Smith offers a reassessment of Hardy's first marriage to Emma Gifford, who was his wife for thirty-eight years, until her untimely death. Her importance in Hardy's life and supportive role to the author has, he believes, been generally neglected by other biographers and scholars. Seymour-Smith traces the flawed views about Hardy's first marriage to his first official biography. The book appeared shortly after his death and was attributed to Florence Dugdale Hardy, his second wife, who before their marriage had been Hardy's secretary. Biographers have long recognized that although she was thirty-eight years younger than her husband, she was inadequate to the task of producing the biography. It had been ghost-written almost entirely by Hardy himself, who had remained active as a writer until within a few weeks of his death. He wanted to do everything possible to set the record straight and to discourage ill-founded speculation. Florence Hardy had, however, edited the work extensively. In her role as editor, she suppressed or omitted numerous favorable references to Emma, and the result was to lessen Emma's contributions to Hardy's success.

A further complication is found in the work of subsequent biographers. Knowing that the first marriage became troubled after Hardy published *Jude the Obscure*, later biographers have attempted to discover evidence of troubles much earlier. One factor cited was Hardy's inclination, after the age of fifty, to carry on flirtations with younger women. As Seymour-Smith points out, this activity was not very unusual. He demonstrates that Emma was supportive of her husband throughout many years, and cites records and correspondence to illustrate that their marriage functioned effectively in a spirit of mutual support. Drawing upon his profound knowledge of Victorian manners and customs, Seymour-Smith dismisses the circumstantial evidence cited by earlier biographers that suggests otherwise. Even after 1896, Hardy continued to be solicitous of a spouse increasingly troubled by illnesses and instability; her erratic behavior late in life prompts Seymour-Smith to suggest, with little supporting evidence, that she suffered from Alzheimer's disease. The marriage survived until her unexpected death in 1912.

In his examination of Hardy's writings, Seymour-Smith explores both issues of relevance to biography and those that are purely literary, and one discerns a clear distinction between the discussions of prose and those of poetry. The book offers quotations from numerous poems, some a few lines or several stanzas, others an entire lyric. The text usually includes little analysis, and Seymour-Smith does not really attempt to assess Hardy's contributions to poetry. The one important exception is the chapter devoted to Hardy's long epic drama on the Napoleonic era, *The Dynasts* (1903-1908). It should be noted, however, that Hardy's romantic lyrics seem to require little by way of explication. Often relying heavily upon images and subject matter from nature, they are neither complex in theme nor rich in poetic figures. Seymour-Smith quotes them largely as analogues to events in Hardy's life, such as his attraction to a young woman, his growing love of his wife, grief over the death of a favorite cat, or forebodings about the future. Other lyrics are cited because they reflect his opinions and attitudes on subjects such as war, philosophy, and cruelty to animals. The poems afford little specific information about the life, but Seymour-Smith suggests that they do serve to convey emotions that the author probably experienced at the time.

While his approach to the novels is varied, Seymour-Smith normally gives a more comprehensive account than he does for the poems, and for the major novels he usually provides a full chapter of discussion. Even a few of the lesser-known novels, such as *The Trumpet-Major* (1880), *Two on a Tower* (1882), and *A Pair of Blue Eyes* (1872-1873), receive significant attention. He gives factual information concerning publication of each and assesses the reception by reviewers and the public. The biography usually also includes a discussion of the plots, major characters, and themes. Where critical controversies have been significant, Seymour-Smith outlines the important issues and offers his own view as to the correct interpretation. In comparison to earlier Hardy scholarship, the discussion of setting is minimal, although locale is by no means ignored.

Seymour-Smith attempts to blend a scholarly approach with one congenial to the general reader. The limited documentation occurs within the text, and while this proves no difficulty for a reader, it is less than satisfactory for the scholar. The book, however, is largely successful in its effort to enhance Hardy's stature as an author and show his decency as a human being.

Stanley Archer

Sources for Further Study

Booklist. XCI, December 15, 1994, p. 730.
Chicago Tribune. January 15, 1995, XIV, p. 5.
London Review of Books. XVI, September 8, 1994, P. 18.
Los Angeles Times Book Review. January 15, 1995, p. 1.
The New York Times Book Review. XCIX, December 18, 1994, p. 3.
Publishers Weekly. CCXLI, October 24, 1994, p. 47.
Time. CXLV, January 16, 1995, p. 74.
The Times Educational Supplement. February 4, 1994, p. A12.
The Times Literary Supplement. March 18, 1994, p. 3.
The Wall Street Journal. December 27, 1994, p. A14.
The Washington Post Book World. XXV, January 15, 1995, p. 3.

HARRIET BEECHER STOWE
A Life

Author: Joan D. Hedrick (1944-)
Publisher: Oxford University Press (New York). 507 pp. $35.00
Type of work: Biography
Time: 1811-1896
Locale: The United States and Europe

A compelling feminist interpretation of Harriet Beecher Stowe's works, her politics, and her role in nineteenth century American popular culture

Principal personages:
HARRIET BEECHER STOWE, an American author
LYMAN BEECHER, her father, a prominent Congregationalist minister
CATHARINE BEECHER, her sister, a pioneer in the education of women
CALVIN ELLIS STOWE, her husband, a nationally recognized biblical scholar

When most people hear the name Harriet Beecher Stowe, they think not of the woman herself but of her most famous creation, *Uncle Tom's Cabin: Or, Life Among the Lowly* (1851-1852). Nearly every American is familiar with this novel's staunch abolitionist stance and the role it had in shaping the antebellum popular imagination. The blatant sentimentality of the book—its flagrantly emotional appeal to popular tastes—and its deft manipulation of stereotypes in its portrayal of African Americans have served to obscure Stowe's achievements. Even Abraham Lincoln's praise for her as "the little woman" who was responsible for the Civil War has a condescending ring to it. Joan D. Hedrick, in an impressive act of scholarship, reexamines the life of Harriet Beecher Stowe, revealing a detailed portrait of one of the first female professional writers in America.

As Hedrick observes, Stowe's long life (1811-1896) spanned nearly all the nineteenth century. As the seventh of the thirteen children that were eventually born to Lyman Beecher, Stowe is to be credited for finding her own voice amid this large and talented brood. Hedrick is quite adept at reconstructing her childhood, a crucial phase in the future writer's life. Though large families were the norm at this time, the Beecher family was anything but typical. A contentious Congregationalist minister and a spellbinding orator, Lyman Beecher pursued a lifelong mission to affect American popular culture through his Calvinist beliefs. His first wife, the intelligent, educated, and worldly Roxana Foote, tried to bring order to the domestic turmoil caused by his public activities. Hedrick makes much of this patriarchal atmosphere, and with justification. Lyman Beecher was a patriarch in a double sense—not only in the legal aspect as head of the household but also in the biblical fashion. Roxana, on the other hand, fully embodied the feminine ideal of the period. Sacrificing her intellectual pursuits in favor of her growing family, she became a paragon of self-denial and died when Harriet was but a small child. As Hedrick's text makes clear, Roxana's complaisance was reflected in Harriet's behavior: The latter never balked at her father's ministerial demands or her sister Catharine's educational schemes.

Harriet's education, too, was of a very high order. This came in part through self-study and overhearing her father instruct her brothers. Education of a different sort—learning of the misery of the underprivileged—came through her association with the bonded servants who were always a part of the family. This was an important factor in her later involvement in abolition and in her creation of the most explosive text of the antebellum period, *Uncle Tom's Cabin.*

Yet Hedrick underscores the fact that even in formal education the young Miss Beecher was far ahead of most women of her time. Harriet was most fortunate in being sent to Sarah Pierce's school, a girls' school with a national reputation. Hedrick, noting the patriarchal tone of this era, demonstrates that women were not educated for their own good but to enable them to serve their future husbands well. It was fortuitous that Harriet was born into the Beecher clan, because this family's dedication to education was second only to spreading the gospel. Her sister Catharine was a pioneer in the education of women. Thus, when Catharine founded the Hartford Female Seminary, it was only natural that Harriet should attend. Hedrick devotes a considerable amount of space to Harriet's time at this institution. The Hartford Female Seminary was one of the nation's foremost schools for women at this time. During a period when the yoke of patriarchy forced "free" women to live lives little better than slaves, Catharine created and operated an all-female institution that was "a school of equals."

According to Hedrick, Harriet's attendance at the school provided a relief from the oppressive patriarchal atmosphere that locked women into predetermined roles in the outside world. One of this biography's chief merits, among many, is Hedrick's emphasis on the limited and even bleak outlook for women during this period. Aside from marriage, with the life-threatening prospect of childbirth and domestic slavery, an educated woman could look forward only to the celibate spinsterhood of a life of teaching. Thus Hedrick correctly centers on Harriet's life at the Hartford Female Seminary as being crucial to her development as a woman and as a writer. Here Harriet began her role as a teacher, became editor of the school newspaper, and had charge of her students' spiritual growth. Hedrick clearly shows that Harriet's role as a teacher and preacher to the public in her fiction (particularly in *Uncle Tom's Cabin*) had its roots in her education.

Catharine Beecher's nervous breakdown from overwork in 1829 provides one of the most fascinating episodes in the book. Rather than turn her duties over to a man during her absence, Catharine decentralized authority in the school, effectively creating "a self-conscious Republic of Women." Each teacher led a small group of students in one department of study, with "the personal influence" of the instructor taking precedence over competition. Harriet, as Catharine's sister, became the de facto head of the institution. At a time when women had few legal rights, these students proved that they could effectively govern themselves. Hedrick brilliantly examines this episode as a precursor of Harriet's future as a leading voice in the moral conscience of the nation.

How Stowe gained the training and experience to be a professional writer constitutes the most enlightening part of the book. In the antebellum period, the parlor was the social center of the home, a gathering place that included much domestic literature. Hedrick terms this forum for fiction, poetry, and letters "parlor literature." Letters in particular were a sine qua non of this body of work. Harriet's dwelled on the finer details of daily life and employed a narrative voice that would be realized in her published fiction. Indeed, these well-crafted works were intended to be read aloud in the performance area of the parlor. Hedrick is correct when she states that, "the trifles that were the delight of their letters were also the stuff of realistic fiction." Yet this is only partly true. Stowe, like Louisa May Alcott, could create vivid domestic scenes through the selective use of familiar details. In addition, Stowe had an unerring ear for dialects, something she shared with her friend Samuel Clemens. It would be a mistake, however, to confuse Stowe's sentimental fiction with, say, the crisp realism of Stephen Crane's work. Moreover, Hedrick's criticism of Ralph Waldo Emerson's call for an American poet who would celebrate the mundane is rather unfair; her claim that American women were already doing this in the parlor seems somewhat disingenuous. Parlor literature was directed at a strictly limited audience. It is true that Harriet's involvement with the Semi-Colon club, a literary group, was a more formal and public version of parlor literature, but Emerson was clearly speaking of published works. Undoubtedly, some of the parlor literature was of high quality, but it would remain unknown to the reading public.

One of the strengths of this biography is the manner in which Stowe's life is seen as paralleling the sweeping changes that were affecting her country as a whole. In her life, Stowe witnessed the transition from precious homespun to cheap, factory-made clothing and the shift from New England culture to such disease-ridden boomtowns as Cincinnati. In her fiction, Stowe often served as the literary counterpart of Nathaniel Currier and James Merritt Ives, creating finely drawn pictures of regional scenes in an emerging national culture. Hedrick is at her best when exploring the social context for Stowe's work and in her analyses of the novelist's fiction. Her observations are often brilliant, such as when she states that in *Uncle Tom's Cabin* Stowe "created a highly effective medium that combined literary realism, political satire, and sermonic power." Hedrick sometimes stumbles, though, as when she claims that "the great nineteenth-century novels were in fact letters to the nation." Such a sweeping statement requires more proof than she provides.

Moreover, Hedrick would have benefited from a broader knowledge of the popular literature of Stowe's time. When she refers to *The Scarlet Letter* (1850), she observes that "models for ministerial impiety were close at hand in the 1840's." This is an understatement of the first order. As David S. Reynolds demonstrates in *Beneath the American Renaissance* (1988), the "reverend rake" was a stock character in antebellum literature. Hawthorne's masterpiece succeeds in part because the Reverend Arthur Dimmesdale transcends this stereotype. It is unfortunate that Hedrick's otherwise superb bibliography is marred by the omission of Reynolds' work.

Despite the deaths of four of her seven children, frequent periods of ill health, and a supportive but inept husband, Stowe persevered and even thrived in the competitive world of magazine writing. Indeed, her first book of fiction, *The Mayflower* (1843), was a collection of her magazine stories, and they highlighted her gift for regional dialects. Hedrick's book also makes clear Stowe's shrewd ability to perceive what her audience wanted at precisely the right time. Like Charles Dickens, Stowe wrote much of her fiction in serial form under the constant need for more money, and this is how *Uncle Tom's Cabin* came into being. Yet in the novel she also transformed her grief over the death of her son Charley with biblical imagery, creating a potent combination of "realism, high purpose, and mythic power." Hedrick's analysis of the novel is superb, particularly when she highlights the empathy between Stowe's domestic slavery as a woman and the chattel slavery of African Americans.

The decade preceding the Civil War and the years immediately following constituted the high point of women's writing in the United States. In fact, Harriet Stowe was the sole source of her family's income from 1863 on. Hedrick's text is particularly useful for its charting of the decline of women's writing in general and Stowe's reputation in particular. Stowe's *Lady Byron Vindicated* (1870) did nothing to help her last political cause, women's rights, in that it served to reinforce a stereotype, "the Victorian angel in the house." There was also the simultaneous rise of the male canon—those works that are regarded as "classics." The decline of Stowe's reputation, according to Hedrick, was largely the result of the rise of such male-oriented periodicals as *The Nation*. Staffed by men who often congregated at men-only clubs, they drew a clear distinction between high (male) art and low (female) art. Hedrick correctly notes the outrageous behavior of such reviewers as Henry James, who rejected the works of women writers without having read them. With increasing emphasis placed upon originality rather than the oral tradition—Stowe's trademark—her later works, Hedrick claims, were not regarded as "serious" by her male judges. Hedrick cites convincing evidence for her stance: *Oldtown Folks* (1869) sold well with the general public, even as it was rejected by male critics.

Hedrick believes that this was wholly a male response to "the decades-long dominance of women in the parlor and the press." David Reynolds holds, however, that women did not dominate the field of fiction between 1830 and 1860 and that sensational literature—not sentimental domestic fiction—was the norm from 1774 to 1860. Also, Reynolds claims, there were many men who wrote domestic fiction and a number of women who wrote in the sensational mode.

This is not meant in any way to detract from the significance of Hedrick's achievement. Hers will undoubtedly stand as the definitive biography of Stowe, and she has done much to restore Stowe's reputation in American letters. It merely demonstrates the fact that the role of gender in nineteenth century American literature is still a much-debated issue.

Cliff Prewencki

Sources for Further Study

America. CLXX, March 19, 1994, p. 25.
Choice. XXXI, June, 1994, p. 1578.
The Economist. CCCXXX, February 5, 1994, p. 92.
The Nation. CCLVIII, May 16, 1994, p. 676.
The New York Times Book Review. XCIX, February 13, 1994, p. 3.
Publishers Weekly. CCXL, November 29, 1993, p. 50.
The Times Literary Supplement. June 3, 1994, p. 13.
The Wall Street Journal. March 22, 1994, p. A12.
The Washington Post Book World. XXIV, February 27, 1994, p. 3.
The Women's Review of Books. XI, April, 1994, p. 13.

HIGHER SUPERSTITION
The Academic Left and Its Quarrels with Science

Authors: Paul R. Gross (1928-) and Norman Levitt (1943-)
Publisher: The Johns Hopkins University Press (Baltimore). 314 pp. $25.95
Type of work: Current affairs; science

Two scientists defend science against attacks by American academic humanists and social scientists

Paul R. Gross and Norman Levitt, a biologist and a mathematician respectively, are disgusted with doctrinaire attacks upon science generated by humanists and social scientists who are ignorant of both the workings and the content of the physical and biological sciences. They also believe that some political activists have been unfairly assailing science. In *Higher Superstition: The Academic Left and Its Quarrels with Science*, a blatantly polemical counterattack, Gross and Levitt take on a diverse group of critics of science. Their targets include sociologists and historians of science who advocate cultural constructivism, postmodernist literary critics and philosophers, feminist theorists, radical environmentalists, some gay activists, supporters of animal rights, and partisans of Afrocentric curricula.

The subtitle of the book is misleading. Not all the designated members of the "academic left" are literally academics (many of the political activists have no connections with academia), nor do Gross and Levitt mean to criticize all academics who are politically left of center. They target only those leftists "whose doctrinal idiosyncracies [sic] sustain the misreadings of science, its methods, and its conceptual foundations that have generated what nowadays passes for a politically progressive critique of it."

The authors are witty and persuasive when they focus on logical inconsistencies, outrageous claims, descent into jargon, and scientific ignorance of any particular target. Some of their sharpest reproaches are aimed at the pretentiousness, scientific confusion, ahistoricism, and emptiness of literary criticism based on postmodernism and deconstructionist philosophy. Some of the critics of science whom Gross and Levitt refute, such as N. Katherine Hayles and Stephen Best, lack knowledge of both science and the history of science. Other worthy targets of the authors include some writings on the relationship between science and feminism, including the efforts by critics to justify a "feminist algebra," the hysteria generated by radical environmentalists such as Jeremy Rifkin, and the distortions of science and history presented in some Afrocentric history of science, including the work of Hunter Adams. They highlight numerous examples of bad science, bad history, bad logic, or—quite often—simply unreadable arguments. Many of these critics of science share a disdain for clear writing. Obscure and jargon-laden prose is the norm.

Gross and Levitt are less successful when they attempt to take on the proponents of cultural constructivism and a multicultural approach to knowledge. Gross and Levitt anchor their attacks on cultural constructivism—which argues that all knowledge systems, including science, are culturally determined or constructed—on the thesis that science (by which they always mean what social constructionists and multiculturalists would designate "Western," "European," or "Euro-American" science) is a privileged knowledge system. Unlike other knowledge systems, which they acknowledge might be local in nature and culturally bound, science is universal and true. The authors define a principle of science as "*an objective truth about the world*." Science is "a uniquely accurate way of finding out about the world." In other words, "science *works*." In defending the truth of the uncertainty principle, they contend that if it were not true, "there would never have been so much fuss about it!" They admit that arguments of past intrusions of ideology or other cultural elements into scientific discourse are "reasonable in principle" and may even have influenced science in the very short term, but they dismiss the significance of such intrusions in the long-term development of science. They also contend that the possibility that such intrusions might occur in the future is very slight because scientists have developed an "always-increasing awareness of the danger."

Unfortunately, this is not convincing. Most cultures have "science," if one means by that a knowledge system defined in terms of observation of physical phenomena with the intent of explaining and controlling those phenomena. Within its cultural context, each of these sciences works just as well as Western science does in its cultural context. Each is as logically consistent. So why are the results of Western science objective truths and those of other knowledge systems not? Gross and Levitt never say. In addition, Gross and Levitt's attempt to equate "making a fuss" with truth simply does not hold. Historians can point to a number of theories in science, religion, or philosophy about which a great fuss was made. Indeed, in religion, millions have died in conflict over doctrinal theories. But to nonbelievers, all the fuss proved is that within a particular cultural context or among a certain group of people, these theories were (or are) true. Finally, historical evidence for the social construction of science in the form of case studies is much stronger than the authors concede.

In their counterattacks, the authors discard a certain type of scholarly rigor. They are rigorous in the sense of providing citations for quotations and a bibliography for further reference. What they have disposed of is the intellectual rigor exhibited when one takes on the best argument one's opponent can offer and demolishes it. They hold most of their targets in intellectual disdain; as a result, they look for absurdities to ridicule and dismiss, not strong arguments to counter. Central among the sources mined for quotations to demonstrate the inanity of the academic left are unpublished lectures (presumably the authors are relying on the notes they took at the time) and polemical works that have already been subjected to criticism in the scholarly literature. Sometimes the authors simply ignore the larger body of scholarly writings created by a scholar to focus on a more vulnerable publication. For example, in considering the thought of Donna Haraway, whom Gross and Levitt call "one of the greats of the business" of feminist science criticism, the authors disregard her extensive bibliography of historical articles in peer-review journals which lay out the basis for her theories. They even ignore her more polemical essays, a collection of which has been published and reviewed in scholarly journals. Instead, they rely solely upon a published interview, not the best medium for expressing one's ideas. In a polemic, this is fair play, but it is simply not as persuasive as a more reasoned approach.

This book would also have been much stronger if Gross and Levitt had narrowed their focus. The range of critics of science taken on by the authors is far too diverse and broad for any single label and perhaps any single book. The only unities among them are their generally left-of-center political positions and their apparent hostility toward science (or perhaps more accurately, hostility toward the current social construction of science; what is being attacked by these critics is the perceived sexism, racism, and exploitiveness of Western science). In their effort to find solidarity among the critics, Gross and Levitt conveniently overlook fundamental differences. For example, the social constructionists challenge the fundamental notion that science should be a privileged form of knowledge system in Western culture, while the advocates of Afrocentrism highlighted in *Higher Superstition* accept that special status for science. Afrocentrics complain, however, that current understanding of the history of science is inaccurate because of racial bias; the discoveries of Africans and African Americans or their contributions to the development of Western science have been systemically ignored or suppressed by the white, male, Euro-American scientific establishment.

When the evidence is overwhelming that there is nothing approaching consensus among the critics on a particular issue, the authors search hard for any link between the members of the academic left, no matter how tenuous or unrepresentative. For example, the existence of one issue of a feminist journal which linked ecofeminism with animal rights is sufficient for them to argue that animal-rights advocates should be included among the critics of science on the academic left. Yet Gross and Levitt readily admit that many if not most members of the academic left are completely indifferent to the set of issues they designate "animal rights." As a result, their concept of an "academic left" seems very artificial.

Gross and Levitt repeatedly assure their readers that the critics they are responding to are influential, representative, and effectual, and thus dangerous to the well-being of science. Nevertheless, the very breadth of their counterassault leaves open the question whether all the critics are important either intellectually or in terms of campus politics. Those who are familiar with the literature in the respective fields will find most of the important figures at least enumerated, if not selected for detailed refutation. Yet Gross and Levitt present neither literary (quotations) nor quantitative (citation analysis) evidence that any, let alone all, of these critics are in fact influential beyond relatively small portions of their respective disciplinary spheres. Nor is there any hint in *Higher Superstition* that many historians, philosophers, and sociologists of science— the scholars best equipped to judge the writings of the critics—view at least some of the particular critics as extremely controversial.

The influence and significance of the critics becomes relevant because the authors have a political agenda—political in the sense of campus politics. Like many polemics, *Higher Superstition* whines about the unfairness of life and lays out some suggestions for changing things for the better. The authors complain repeatedly about how the members of the academic left, despite their obvious ignorance of science, illogical arguments, unclear writing, and pretentiousness, get contracts from major university presses, jobs, tenure, promotions, and grants. The corollary, one assumes, is that the scientists, the real intellectual leaders of academia, who have been subjected to the criticism of the academic left, have not been getting their fair share of contracts, jobs, tenure, promotions, and grants. No evidence is given for the claim of the relative success of the academic left except for the anecdotal.

The whining would not be important, except that Gross and Levitt end the book with a concrete call for action in the realm of academic politics. As a result, the cynical reader may conclude, perhaps with some justification, that the whole point of the book was to justify the authors' charge to physical and biological scientists to exert more influence in the hiring and promoting of humanists and social scientists. Such a suspicious view of their motivations is probably unfair to Gross and Levitt. They are truly offended by the arrogance of some of the academic left. To this they have responded, however, with an arrogance of their own.

Marc Rothenberg

Sources for Further Study

The Chronicle of Higher Education. April 27, 1994, p. A15.
Commentary. XCVII, June, 1994, p. 53.
National Review. XLVI, October 10, 1994, p. 70.
Nature. CCCLXVIII, March 31, 1994, p. 409.
New Scientist. CXLII, June 11, 1994, p. 45.
New Statesman and Society. VII, May 20, 1994, p. 38.
ORBIS. XXXVIII, Fall, 1994, p. 673.
Science. CCLXIV, May 13, 1994, p. 985.
The Wall Street Journal. April 19, 1994, p. A18.
The Washington Post Book World. XXIV, May 22, 1994, p. 13.

A HISTORY OF RUSSIAN SYMBOLISM

Author: Avril Pyman
Publisher: Cambridge University Press (New York). 481 pp. $79.00
Type of work: Literary history; literary criticism

The first full-scale history, in English, of the Symbolist movement in Russian literature

In *Century's End: A Cultural History of the Fin de Siècle from the 990s to the 1990s* (1990), Hillel Schwartz tells us that the phrase *fin de siècle* made its "popular debut" in France late in 1885. From France it spread rapidly throughout Europe and even to the United States, so that by 1891 an *Atlantic Monthly* contributor was complaining that "Everywhere we are treated to dissertations on fin-de-siècle literature, fin-de-siècle statesmanship, fin-de-siècle morality."

The fin de siècle was protean in its aspects. Seen from one perspective, the 1890's were "years of nervousness, decadence, boredom, and thrill-seeking, suicide and Ferris wheels, faithlessness and occult philosophies, anarchy and artificiality." Some saw the waning of the century as emblematic of the end of an epoch in Europe's history. Meditations on the close of the nineteenth century mixed with prophecies about the century to come. The prospect of radical change, heralded by stunning technological developments, was celebrated by some, while others regarded it with foreboding.

Throughout Europe the arts were strongly marked by the fin de siècle. In Russia, this mood was most strongly expressed in the Symbolist movement. In *A History of Russian Symbolism*, Avril Pyman traces the history of this movement from its beginnings in 1892 to 1910, when the "Symbolist rebellion against utilitarianism and simplistic belief in progress" began to open out "into a delta of many streams." Pyman, author of a two-volume biography of the poet Aleksandr Blok (*The Life of Aleksandr Blok*, 1979-1980), the greatest figure in the Symbolist movement, defines her approach here as "that of the chronicler rather than the critic." She quotes extensively from the works of the Symbolists, both poetry and prose (poems are given in Russian with English translation). The main text is supplemented by a thirty-page year-by-year chronology, which is very helpful; this is followed by notes, a primary bibliography, and an unusually full index. A tour de force of meticulous scholarship, Pyman's book will be indispensable to students of Russian literature and of the fin de siècle.

Russian Symbolism took its name from the French movement associated with Stéphane Mallarmé, Paul Verlaine, and others (and strongly influenced by Charles Baudelaire). As Pyman shows, however, many previous treatments of Russian Symbolism have exaggerated the influence of the French movement. (Consider for example the beginning of the entry on Symbolism in the *Handbook of Russian Literature*, edited by Victor Terras, 1985: "a literary movement which originated in France and which had ramifications in several national literatures and a florescence in Russia between 1900 and 1910.") "Russian Symbolism was not an imitation of the French," Pyman writes, "but part of a wider European movement" of the fin de siècle. It needs to be seen in that larger context and, at the same time, in the context of specifically Russian matters—in particular, the demand for a socially concerned "literature of the people."

The founding manifesto of Russian Symbolism was Dimitrii Merezhkovsky's "On the Reasons for the Decline and on New Trends in Russian Literature," a set of two lectures delivered at the end of 1892 in Saint Petersburg and published at his own expense in 1893. Earlier in 1892, a collection of poems by Merezhkovsky, entitled *Simvoly* (symbols), had been published. In his lectures, Merezhkovsky suggested that art offers access to realities that cannot be comprehended by science or any other form of strictly rational discourse—truths otherwise incommunicable. "Symbolism," in Pyman's summary of his lectures, "was not a matter of describing one known thing in terms of another. It was a breakthrough."

Rejection of the ordinary, the utilitarian, the purely rational; art as the revelation of incommunicable truths ("The thought, once spoken, is a lie," a line from a precursor of the Symbolists, Fedor Tiutchev, "became a Symbolist slogan," Pyman notes): These were at the essence of Symbolism in all its manifestations. Pyman acknowledges the great diversity among the writers she treats—Blok, Merezhkovsky and his wife, Zinaida Hippius, Vladimir Solovev (not a Symbolist, but one of the predecessors who most deeply influenced the movement), Andrei Bely, Konstantin Balmont, Valerii Briusov, Fedor Sologub, Vasilii Rozanov, Viacheslev Ivanov, Lev Shestov, and other lesser-known figures—but also shows how they were shaped by similar preoccupations. Indeed, at the height of the movement, through correspondence, regular meetings (such as the Wednesday evening gathering at Ivanov's apartment, "the Tower"), and intense interrelationships, many of them were engaged in what Pyman calls "collective creation."

In his account of "The Symbolist Ambiance" in *Modernism and Revolution: Russian Literature in Transition* (1994), Victor Erlich, drawing on the French Slavist Georges Nivat, identifies three primary strands within Symbolism: decadent, theurgic, and apocalyptic. Not always easily distinguishable, these three strands nevertheless highlight different emphases. In the decadent vein, exemplified in the poetry of Briusov, Symbolism was characterized by "forbidden" themes (semipornographic treatment of sex, with a heavy dose of sadomasochism; demonism and "going beyond good and evil"), exoticism (foreign or otherwise exotic settings, foreign or rare words), and provocative aestheticism.

The theurgic strain of Symbolism, represented above all by Bely, celebrated art—and poetry in particular—as a means to attain mystical knowledge; art became the fulfillment of or a substitute for religion, and the poet became a magus, a high priest, an enchanter, all in one. In its apocalyptic voice, prominent in Bely, Blok, and many others, Symbolism articulated what Pyman describes as "a new kind of nostalgia: for the distant, the far future which would come into being after some great catastrophe." (When the Revolution came in 1917, virtually all the Symbolists welcomed it, though many were soon to become disillusioned.)

Two other characteristics of the Symbolist movement (cutting across distinctions among the decadent, theurgic, and apocalyptic strains) deserve special mention. The first is the emphasis on music, which the Symbolists regarded as the highest form of art. "In the beginning there was music," Blok declared. Especially through Blok, but through others as well, the Symbolists revived the music of Russian poetry, preparing the way for Anna Akhmatova, Osip Mandelstam, Boris Pasternak, and Marina Tsvetaeva.

The second is the Symbolist tendency to blur the line between life and art. This was expressed in many ways, all of them destructive and all in some way reflecting a mixture of spiritual pride and foolishness. It is at once excruciating and irritating to read about the Symbolists' entanglements, their betrayals and perversities, all carried out amid lofty philosophizing. One longs for the pungent voice of Nadezhda Mandelstam, who makes some sharp observations on Ivanov and the Symbolists generally in *Hope Abandoned* (1974). Scorning the Symbolists' inflated view of the artist as "the vehicle of divine revelation," Mandelstam does not mince words in describing the disastrous effects of their teachings ("You are free, Godhead—everything is permitted, only dare"). Near the end of her narrative, Pyman summarizes a lecture that Blok gave in 1910, in which he concluded that "the artist must stop mixing art and life," a belated recognition that many of his fellow Symbolists never achieved.

Pyman's study is historical; she leaves it to her readers to ponder resonances between the 1890's and the 1990's, between the fin de siècle and the end of the millennium. Certainly there is much in the Russian Symbolist mood and ethos that finds echoes in the 1990's. The parallels are not exact, of course, and perhaps readers can learn as much from the differences as from the similarities.

Consider for example a *New York Times* review (December 12, 1994) of a concert by Trent Reznor and his band, Nine Inch Nails, at Madison Square Garden. The oxymoronic title of the review—"Nihilistic Sing-Along with Nine Inch Nails"—nicely expresses a tension that Lionel Trilling identified in his essay "On the Teaching of Modern Literature." Trilling, writing in the 1960's, was struck by the way in which his students casually accepted the alienation and the contempt for "ordinary life" that characterize the canonical texts of modern literature. "I asked them to look into the Abyss," Trilling wrote, "and, both dutifully and gladly, they have looked into the Abyss, and the Abyss has greeted them with the grave courtesy of all objects of serious study, saying, 'Interesting, am I not? and *exciting*, if you consider how deep I am at my bottom.' " Nihilism had become domesticated.

Three decades after Trilling made that observation, bands such as Nine Inch Nails are playing to sold-out concert halls and selling millions of albums. Their audience may include the equivalent of Trilling's college students, but it also includes many younger listeners, in junior high and high school. The themes of the Symbolists, in poetry stripped of nuance and cultural memory and accompanied by "a flurry of adrenaline-fueled riffs and jackhammer drumbeats," are commonplace in the 1990's; twelve-year-olds tap their feet to the apocalyptic crescendos of Nine Inch Nails'

"Burn." And Reznor himself, dressed all in black, "[tearing] apart the stage in choreographed fits of rage," is surely a Symbolist spellbinder on speed.

John Wilson

Source for Further Study

Russian Literature. XXXVI, November 15, 1994, p. 371.

A HISTORY OF WALES

Author: John Davies (1939-   )
First published: Hanes Cymru, 1990, in Great Britain
Translated from the Welsh by John Davies
Publisher: Allen Lane/Penguin (New York). Maps. 718 pp. $34.95; paperback $14.95
Type of work: History
Time: 1170 B.C. to A.D. 1989
Locale: Great Britain and continental Europe

A chronologically presented history encompassing the earliest archaeological and written testimony as well as contemporary evidence on the state of Wales and its people

Written histories of Wales, until the appearance of John Davies' masterful volume, have had a severely restricted focus, a distorted and subjective point of view, or a markedly Anglophilic agenda. Davies' *A History of Wales*, despite its simple title, is a work of massive and complex scholarship which presents a comprehensive examination of Wales, its people, and its distinctive identity, and it achieves this without any of the shortcomings of its predecessors. Indeed, the volume knows virtually no limits in its consideration of Wales and things Welsh, and it remains remarkably unbiased in its patient examination.

The 1970's and 1980's produced ten historical studies on Welsh history. Davies cites this modern historiography in the appropriate places, though he begins by considering the land area that would be called Wales as it existed during the Paleolithic, Mesolithic, and Neolithic periods. Geological evidence points to 6000 B.C. as an approximate date for the appearance of a coastal configuration comparable with that recognizable on modern maps. Tacitus, the second century Roman historian, records a Roman attack in A.D. 48 upon the Deceangli, a pre-Welsh tribe. The territorial name for Wales, Cymry, appears in runic form in 580, approximately 180 years after the legendary royal houses of the territory, while the precise date of 790 marks the construction of Offa's Dyke, which separates the Cymric from the Brythonic kingdom.

Davies merely arranges and presents this information, but one may draw certain reasonable inferences. First, it is clear that though long nomadically inhabited, Wales evolved from a nomadic to a monarchic society in less than half a millennium. Second, the legendary Welsh kingdoms, by their relatively quick diminution, quickly perceived a common ethnic identity, underscored both by adoption of a collective name and by topographical segregation from their Brythonic neighbors. The astonishing vitality of the Cymric tongue amid the overpowering linguistic influences of the Brythonic, Celtic, and Norman languages testifies to the historical perception of Welsh separateness.

The historical fact of Welsh separateness is not nearly so absolute as its perception. The legends of King Arthur had their origin among the Welsh, but the king and his knights became the common property of England and France by the Middle Ages.

These legends so proliferated in France that Sir Thomas Malory culled the French rather than British sources for the writing of *Le Morte d'Arthur* (1485). Offa's Dyke notwithstanding, Davies' examination proves that Welsh history is tied to that of England and that it was so from the earliest period of its national identity.

By 1105, during the reign of Henry I, the so-called Marcher Lords held firm possession of parts of the kingdom of Wales. The March, a central element of Welsh history, was essentially a massive colonizing move that situated families loyal to the English king at various points within Wales. Radnorshire, Breconshire, Pembrokeshire, Monmouthshire, Flintshire, and Montgomeryshire are several of the English seats established on Welsh soil by the twelfth century as a counterweight to Welsh nationalism. Collectively they bore the designation Marchia Wallie to distinguish them from those parts of Wales specifically under Welsh rule, the Purae Walliae.

In the short term, the March served the purpose the Crown intended: dispersal of power. Even so, less than a century had elapsed before the Marcher families, estranged from native Welsh culture though they were, began to perceive their own identity as hybrid, neither wholly Welsh nor wholly English. One recognizes in this ambivalence a pattern that appears repeatedly in British imperial history; it emerges in the Anglo-Indian of the Raj and the Anglo-African of Rhodesia, now called Zambia. Since the Marcher Lords began very early in their tenure to think of themselves as princes, English monarchs soon saw the governing value of a royal presence among their number, and it was for this reason that Edward I began a vast castle-building program in Marchia Wallie in the latter part of the thirteenth century. The most remarkable of these projects is Caernarfon, a magnificent castle of light-colored stone with octagonal towers that recall the massive fortifications of Constantinople. Edward also created the title Prince of Wales, traditionally awarded to the heir apparent of the British throne. Caernarfon remains the official seat of the Prince of Wales and the site of his installation. The title and Caernarfon, taken with Edward's other castles in Wales, represented a bold and on the whole successful attempt to join the destiny of Wales with that of England.

Much as it tended to restrain the Marchers, even Caernarfon could not still the voice of native Welsh patriotism. Twelfth and thirteenth century Welsh patriots abound; Llywelyn, Dafydd, Rhys Fychan, Maelgwn, Owain Brogyntyn, and Owain Madog all spring fiercely from Davies' pages, and most met violent and bloody ends. If Davies' study had had no other value (though it has many others indeed), it would have been in putting to rest the implication of most modern historiography that nothing worth recording happened in Wales during the late Middle Ages. Davies proves that these were centuries filled with distinctive, bold personalities wholly committed to the separate identity of their country.

That the Welsh ultimately adopted an attitude of resigned acceptance in regard to their connection to England, a posture roughly equivalent to that of the Scots, apparently resulted from several factors relating to geography, religion, language, industry, and system of education. Ireland shared none of these particulars, and centuries of history have borne witness to the sad consequences. First, geography itself tied the fate of Wales and England. Henry VIII, founder of the House of Tudor, recognized this by conciliating the Welsh princes whenever he could, proclaiming his Welsh ancestry when it suited the political tides, and benignly standardizing Welsh law with that of England, particularly in the area of inheritance. The Welsh tended to share Henry's view of Roman Catholicism too, though they had eliminated monasticism in the late Middle Ages primarily because they perceived that it had fallen away from the scholarship and asceticism that had constituted its original mission. While the Irish came to view allegiance in religion to Rome as a mark of defiance of England, the Welsh preferred to assert their theological independence by adherence to the various Nonconformist churches. These, particularly Methodism with its reliance upon popular participation, made great inroads into the religious life of the country by the early eighteenth century.

None of this implies that the Welsh ever became masters of their own governance. Though the representation of Wales in Parliament grew steadily between the fifteenth and nineteenth centuries, those with mixed English and Welsh blood were its representatives. Whether through formal oaths of allegiance to the Crown or, in later centuries, by informal understandings and educational qualifications, Wales found itself governed, even on the local level, by a political establishment that was British rather than Welsh in its general outlook. Since the Oxford and Cambridge colleges accepted only young men willing to profess Anglicanism, a university education remained unobtainable for even the most promising.

Indirectly, however, such restrictions had a positive effect on the culture of Wales, for they forced its internal development from inward resources. Though higher education remained a dream unobtainable until establishment of the University of Wales and its university colleges at Abcrystwth, Bangor, Cardiff, and Swansea in the nineteenth century, primary schooling thrived at least a century and a half earlier, thanks to the church-affiliated schools established by various Nonconformist congregations. Because these remained independent, their effectiveness varied; yet all committed themselves to teaching the Welsh language in tandem with English. The Welsh were always few in number relative to the English, but their cultural life, diluted though it was at various periods by English incursions, never faced the concerted onslaught Ireland had to endure. Hence the Welsh language remained viable, even as Irish Gaelic, despite Ireland's larger numbers, has struggled for retention among its people.

One could say, too, that the topography of Wales has both blessed and cursed it. On the one hand, its bountiful supply of iron, coal, building stone, and running water made it the spawning ground of the Industrial Revolution in eighteenth century Britain. On the other, its proximity to numerically superior England made it a supplier of raw materials rather than an exporter of finished goods. Generations made their way to its mines, quarries, and docks, and this maintained a caste system of labor underwritten by the nature of English classism. The psychological restrictions this has historically imposed upon the Welsh people are as regrettable as the scarification three centuries of violent industrial development has done to the land.

Modern Wales has continued to experience these mixed blessings at every juncture of its history. Just as the wool and cattle industries promised a degree of autonomy Wales had never enjoyed, the railway boom started in England. By the middle of the nineteenth century, rails made in England, ironically from Welsh ore, extended to even the most inaccessible regions of Wales. While this provided a ready market of sweater-wearers and beef-eaters, the railroads literally tied Wales to England. With more markets assured for Welsh wool and beef, acreage reserved for locally consumed grain declined dramatically after 1850. The immediate result was a drastic decline in farmworkers, from more than seventy-three thousand in 1851 to fewer than forty-five thousand in 1871. Here again Davies' perceptiveness emerges. Anglophilic historiographers hasten to argue that Victorian Wales experienced unparalleled prosperity, and so it did if one considers only the capital infusion that the railways initiated. Davies proves that most of the country's new wealth found tangible expression in buildings. New chapels, public buildings, and manor houses became almost commonplace. In essence, the railroad money found its way to the landowners who endowed these projects, and the prosperity remained one-sided.

The gap between the wealthy and the economically marginal classes of Wales, always pronounced, continues noticeably even into the contemporary era. When Oliver Cromwell signed the Act of Union in 1536, his professed reason was uniformity of administration among the countries of the British Isles. The lasting consequence for Wales was a system of administrative gentrification that has endured in various guises for nearly half a millennium. Periods of prosperity, when they occur, originate from without rather than within the country; moreover, they develop from the top rather than the base of the economic structure. This never augurs well for the sustained well-being of the general populace. When historiographers note that Wales never suffered the devastating effects of massive emigration by its youngest, most talented people (as Ireland has), they overlook the fact that for Wales to lose even a minuscule amount of its young talent predisposes it to the economic stasis that has marked its history.

Despite all these negative factors, modern Wales has remained steadfastly loyal to Great Britain in times of external crisis. Irish nationalists were unable to persuade Wales to adopt a neutral stance during the two world wars. From a purely practical point of view, it would have caused economic suicide. Since 1945, faced with a moribund coal industry, Wales has promoted tourism with some success, but even this has led to externally originated gentrification by the English middle class. Whole regions seem more English than Welsh, and again one hears the lament that Welsh culture will not survive; yet, this is a cry as old as the time of the Marcher Lords. Remarkably, despite all the onslaughts history has brought, Wales has remained the enviable, distinctive country Davies describes in this impressive history.

Robert J. Forman

Sources for Further Study

Booklist. XC, December 15, 1993, p. 735.
The Economist. CCCXXVII, April 3, 1993, p. 86.
History. LXXIX, February, 1994, p. 106.
History Today. XLIII, April, 1993, p. 53.
Kirkus Reviews. LXI, November 15, 1993, p. 1433.
The New York Review of Books. XLI, December 22, 1994, p. 61.
Publishers Weekly. CCXL, December 20, 1993, p. 62.
The Spectator. CCLXXI, November 27, 1993, p. 35.
The Times Literary Supplement. March 12, 1993, p. 10.

HOLE IN OUR SOUL
The Loss of Beauty and Meaning in American Popular Music

Author: Martha Bayles (1948-   )
Publisher: Free Press (New York). 453 pp. $24.95
Type of work: Cultural criticism; history
Time: The 1950's through the 1990's
Locale: The United States

This provocative and well-argued critical history argues that popular music has been corrupted by "perverse modernism," a long-established tendency to denigrate aesthetic and moral values in art, and that performers and listeners need to rediscover the rich wellspring of the Afro-American tradition

Principal personages:
LOUIS ARMSTRONG,
MUDDY WATERS,
BIG BILL BROONZY, and other purveyors of relatively authentic styles of the Afro-American musical idiom
ELVIS PRESLEY,
JERRY LEE LEWIS,
THE BEATLES,
THE ROLLING STONES, and other white American and British imitators of the Afro-American idiom
FRANK ZAPPA,
ANDY WARHOL,
IGGY POP,
THE VELVET UNDERGROUND,
THE SEX PISTOLS, and other artists who infected popular culture and music with the sensibility of "perverse modernism"

The cultural and musical legacy of the 1960's, like that decade's political legacy, is a smorgasbord of balkanized sociocultural enclaves, each doing its own thing, apparently with little or no heed for or communication with its several adversaries. By the mid-1990's, popular music was well into a distinctly postmodern period, characterized by the insufferable preening and mugging of indistinguishable maudlin young "alternative" bands; an endless string of all-star tributes resembling high-school reunions, in which once genuinely great artists such as Eric Clapton and Tina Turner rub shoulders with latter-day mediocrities such as Bryan Adams and Paul Young; yet more albums from the Rolling Stones, amid jokes about Boy Scouts helping Mick Jagger and Keith Richards across the street; all too much "dance music" accompanying semipornographic videos; vulgar and violent rap; and an assembly line of cookie-cutter Nashville stars sporting seemingly made-up names like Clint Black and Garth Brooks. By 1994, many an aging lover of good, original, lively popular music—and many not-so-aging—could be heard to mutter beneath the din, "What's going on? What went wrong?"

Martha Bayles, a former teacher of writing at Harvard University and arts critic for *The Wall Street Journal*, articulates the exasperation others may not have known quite how to put into words and suggesting that a hopeful way forward just might exist. Indeed, probably the most substantial achievement of *Hole in Our Soul*—the title is from the old saying "If you don't like the blues, you've got a hole in your soul"—is simply that to the extent that it is read and discussed seriously, it will have shifted the boundaries of discussion and (so the author obviously hopes) fostered in readers a renewed respect for the Afro-American musical tradition that is the very lifeblood of almost all music that can legitimately be called American.

A reviewer who shares Bayles's distaste for cant can be grateful that she insists on using the relatively old-fashioned term "Afro-American" rather than the fashionable "African American." Bayles has something particular in mind: she uses "Afro-American" to refer to the American musical tradition as a whole, as opposed to the European classical or "serious" tradition. Her point is well taken: American music, like American history and culture in general, simply cannot be understood in any meaningful way without rigorous and respectful study of the history of black people and black music in the American context. Thus Bayles uses "Afro-American" quite pointedly as a near-synonym for "American." The interaction of this (Afro-)American tradition with certain European or quasi-European habits of mind and assumptions about high and low culture constitutes the history of American popular music. This interaction and its motley legacy is the subject of Bayles's trenchant critique.

She structures her polemic both chronologically and thematically, in four sections, starting with a discussion of "The Three Strains of Modernism," moving through "The Obstacle of Race," "The Taint of Commerce," an appreciative discussion of the history of jazz, the transition from 1950's rock 'n' roll to 1960's rock and the counterculture of the late 1960's (of which she is not fond), to critiques of the major strains of post-1960's music, including headbanging, disco, punk, the eclectic post-punk "new wave" of the early 1980's, and hip-hop or rap. She lambastes rappers such as Ice-T and 2 Live Crew for using sexual vulgarity, violence, and outlaw personae as cheap publicity tools. "Anyone, black or white, who worries that the outlaw culture is encouraging American society to disinvest in black youth, can only feel dismay at this particular marketing gambit," she writes. She ends by observing that there is hope, as evidenced by many young black performers—among them rappers dissatisfied by the limitations of their genre—consciously reaching back into the wellspring of their musical heritage, and performers in their forties or older who "share a deep traditionalism that has helped their music endure," whom she calls "root doctors."

Two central confrontations have shaped the development of American popular music, according to Bayles. One is "the blood knot," the inescapable historical fact that whites and blacks in America share an ineradicable cultural and indeed genealogical heritage from which none can escape, try as one might. Attempts to escape the blood knot result in the intellectual dishonesties of black cultural separatism on one hand, white "racism" on the other. (The word "racism" is rendered in quotes here because it is a term few writers ever bother to define. The unfortunate evasion, of which Bayles partakes, will be discussed below.) Bayles is by no means the first critic to take note of the blood knot, as she readily acknowledges. Her very welcome contribution is to have taken the trouble to untie it carefully and cogently. Noting the very real physical and sexual power white men exercised over black women under slavery, and the humiliation this entailed for white women, she writes that "Proper white Southerners condemned R & B as "nigger music" because they associated it not just with black sexuality, but also with the habit of white men to go 'slipping around' with black women." This, she argues, helps explain the extraordinary popularity of the young Elvis Presley:

> Now let me ask: How would these [white] women be likely to react if a white man suddenly appeared who could not only sing as seductively as a black R & B star, but who also made it clear (as no black R & B star could, or would) that his singing was directed not at black women but at *them*? What if, being white himself, this singer made it possible for white women to turn the tables on their men, to reduce those arrogant creatures to passive onlookers while they, the women, abandoned themselves to the sighs, whispers, and screams of "alien ecstacy"? To find the answer, we need only recall that one of the biggest problems on Presley's early Southern tours was security. Along with the frantic adulation of his female fans, he was also endangered by the frantic resentment of the males, who understood all too well that the Hillbilly Cat was not playing by the rules.

The blood knot probably has been mostly a salutary influence on American music. Not so "perverse modernism," a posturing stance which Bayles traces to the nineteenth century French poet Arthur Rimbaud. She narrates the history of this self-conscious tendency among artists in various fields who have flattered themselves that they were on the artistic as well as political cutting edge. Although she does not mention the graphic artist Robert Mapplethorpe, he comes to mind when Bayles writes that

> Today's perverse modernists identify shame with repression because they are committed to obscenity as the only reliable way to get a shocked reaction from the public. They flatter themselves that this reaction is akin to the great scandals of the modernist past. . . . Most people feel a trace of shame and a strong need for either ritual or privacy when eating, eliminating, making love, suffering, and dying. If that makes them unable to appreciate "art," then the word has lost its meaning.

Bayles claims that perverse modernism was introduced into rock music by Lou Reed, Frank Zappa, and John Lennon (via Yoko Ono), and that it pervades the self-righteous nihilism of punk as well as the self-conscious vulgarity of rap. "Performers such as Ice-T and Madonna are not working in the medium of music, hoping to attract a critical mass of listeners who like what they're doing," she argues. "They're working in the medium of publicity, testing the resistance of a public that generally dislikes what they're doing, but that can be forced to pay attention through the skillful application of sexual, sometimes violent, obscenity." The term "postmodern" is superfluous, she says, because "the tendencies it describes have been present since the dawn of modernism. Specifically, the postmodernist injunctions to break with the past, to attack aesthetic standards, to shock the audience, and to erase the line between art and life, are the essence of perverse modernism."

Like the thoughtful and literate polemicist she is, Bayles almost never fails to define her terms carefully. The single exception is a word almost never defined adequately: racism. With all due caveats made, it is reasonable to ask: Just what is racism? Bayles does discuss the phenomenon intelligently over several paragraphs, but what, precisely, does the word mean?

This question is indeed pertinent if Bayles is going to claim, as she does, that country music's "fear of polyrhythm" is "rooted in white racism." Not so fast, a lover of country might respond. Are you calling me a racist? Bayles does observe that "the best country musicians use their eminence to reaffirm their Afro-American roots. And these reaffirmations, whether [Willie] Nelson doing a TV special with Ray Charles or Randy Travis singing a duet with B. B. King, contain none of the leering primitivism found in the standard postpunk rock 'tribute.' " It might well be asked: Were country music to be more eclectic than it is, at what point would it cease to be country music? Purism is almost always stifling and exclusive. Yet if, as Bayles argues persuasively, all or most American music is pervaded by the Afro-American sensibilities fostered by the blood knot, and if these sensibilities, expressed in jazz, the blues, soul, Motown, and other genres, can be described as expressions of "blackness"—in a very positive sense of that term—then does not American music have some room for what might be called "whiteness"? What, a hypothetical country fan might justifiably ask with some resentment, is inherently wrong with whiteness, after all? This is a very difficult topic to discuss without opening oneself to charges of (usually undefined) racism. It is also the only place in her argument where Bayles's lively and confident style of disputation yields to timidity.

Bayles writes with a blend of erudition and common sense that is the hallmark of the best criticism, leavened heavily with a palpable enthusiasm for her topic. Like the best and timeliest books in any form or genre, *Hole in Our Soul* helps readers to see a way forward, precisely because it takes a sustained, unblinking look back to determine how popular music reached such a seeming impasse. She ends on a hopeful note, without straining unduly. "The most timely ideas are routinely resisted by the commercial powers that be, with their tidy categories and rigid marketing systems," she writes. "But if commerce is the logjam, it is also the river. Break things up, I say, and let the fresh current flow." Hope can be found in young black performers such as Boyz II Men, and in root doctors who, growing up in the 1950's and 1960's, "fell in love with Afro-American music and remained stubbornly loyal to it without being purist." Among these, Bayles includes Van Morrison, the Neville Brothers, Dr. John, Bonnie Raitt, and Ry Cooder.

This list must be understood also to include two white artists of the 1990's who receive far too little critical appreciation: John (formerly "Cougar") Mellencamp and Tom Petty. Both began hitting their stride artistically in the mid-1980's—Mellencamp with his superb album *Scarecrow* (1985), Petty with *Southern Accents* (1985)—and both went from strength to strength in the decade that followed, Petty becoming a close associate and eager protégé of Bob Dylan. It also should be noted that all artists operate under formal and generic constraints, often of their own making or choice. Bayles has no kind words for Nirvana, a "grunge" band that might have developed in admirable ways had not lead singer Kurt Cobain committed suicide in April, 1994. Van Halen rises above the mostly undistinguished pack of hard rock bands, especially since the talented songwriter Sammy Hagar replaced David Lee Roth in 1986.

On popular music in general, Bayles surely would endorse lyrics from Petty's 1994 album *Wildflowers*: "It's time to move on, it's time to get goin'/ What lies ahead I have no way of knowin'/ But under my feet, baby, grass is growin'/ It's time to move on, time to get goin'."

Ethan Casey

Sources for Further Study

Boston Globe. May 21, 1994, p. 27.
Chicago Tribune. July 20, 1994, V, p. 2.
Choice. XXXII, September, 1994, p. 122.
Commentary. XCVIII, August, 1994, p. 59.
Library Journal. CXIX, March 15, 1994, p. 73.
National Review. XLVI, May 16, 1994, p. 68.
The New Republic. CCX, May 2, 1994, p. 39.
The New York Times Book Review. XCIX, August 14, 1994, p. 10.
Publishers Weekly. CCXLI, March 14, 1994, p. 61.
The Washington Post. April 14, 1994, p. C2.

THE HOT ZONE

Author: Richard Preston (1954-)
Publisher: Random House (New York). 302 pp. $23.00
Type of work: Science
Time: 1960-1993
Locale: Kenya; Zaire; Sudan; Washington, D.C.; and Reston, Virginia

Richard Preston records the electrifying story of how the Marburg and Ebola viruses afflicted Europeans and Africans and, in 1989, threatened the Reston, Virginia, area with a plague worse than AIDS

Principal personages:

CHARLES MONET, a French expatriate in Western Kenya
LIEUTENANT COLONEL NANCY JAAX, a veterinarian
COLONEL JERRY JAAX, her husband, also a veterinarian
EUGENE JOHNSON, the chief of logistics and safety for a biohazard operation in Reston
DAN DALGARD, a veterinarian at a Reston primate facility
PETER JAHRLING and
TOM GEISBERT, codiscoverers of the Ebola Reston virus
COLONEL CLARENCE JAMES PETERS, the overall military leader of the Reston biohazard operation
MAJOR GENERAL PHILIP K. RUSSELL, the physician who authorized the Reston biohazard operation

Those who read the opening chapter of *The Hot Zone* may find it difficult to realize that what they are reading is not science fiction but documented scientific fact. Charles Monet, a fifty-six-year-old expatriate Frenchman living in western Kenya near the Nzoia River, is spending his Christmas vacation on Mount Elgon with a woman from nearby Eldoret.

On New Year's morning of 1980, the pair wander into Kitum Cave, host at night to herds of elephants that come for the salt they can ferret out of its rocks, which they pulverize with their tusks. Monet and his friend spend the entire day exploring this huge, mysterious opening in the earth, home to bats, rats, and various other animals and insects.

Seven days later, Monet is racked with pain. His eyeballs and head ache so monumentally that he stays home from work. Aspirin does not relieve the headache. Soon Monet develops a throbbing backache as well. By the third day of his illness, he is running a fever and vomiting, finally bringing up no solids or fluids but continuing to have dry heaves. He sinks into an uncharacteristic passivity. His face becomes masklike; his eyelids droop. His eyeballs, looking ready to pop, redden; his skin yellows and develops red blotches.

When some of his fellow workers look in on him, it is apparent to them that he needs to be rushed to the hospital at Kisumu, on the shore of Lake Victoria. His illness baffles the physicians there, who give him antibiotics to no avail. They recommend that he go to Nairobi Hospital, the best medical facility in that part of Africa.

Although he is becoming increasingly ill, Monet boards a jammed Kenya Airways flight to Nairobi. During the flight, he becomes violently ill, vomiting into a sickness bag and coughing up a slimy red substance flecked with black spots similar to coffee grounds. Before long, his vomit is black. His body has been invaded by a filovirus more virulent and much faster-acting than the acquired immunodeficiency syndrome (AIDS) virus, whose incubation period can be as long as ten years.

Richard Preston's descriptions and detail have a clarity reminiscent of the best writing of Lewis Thomas, Loren Eisley, or Barry Lopez. He explains simply but never condescendingly what a filovirus is and how it acts. He notes that one hundred million such viruses can fit into a space the size of the period at the end of a sentence. They are almost as old as Earth. Their primary purpose is to replicate themselves in the cells of their hosts. They can jump species, perhaps using insects, bats, or rats as hosts, but quickly moving to primates, including humans, when the need arises.

Viruses like those that consumed Monet had emerged in other places. In Marburg, Germany, thirteen years earlier, a man who cleaned monkey cages at the Behring Works, a vaccine factory, evidenced symptoms similar to Monet's. Two weeks later he died. Thirty-one other people in or near Marburg contracted the virus. Seven of them died.

Before the plane lands, Monet's blood is clotting in all of his organs and in his intestines. He is bleeding from every orifice, and with the blood come huge amounts of tissue from his tongue and his intestines. Because his brain is being compromised by the clotting, he feels little pain.

Still ambulatory, although barely so, Monet stumbles to a taxicab outside Jomo Kenyatta International Airport and mumbles, "Nairobi . . . Hospital." Once at the hospital, Monet, now bleeding profusely through the mouth, nose, eyes, gums, nipples, and anus, is attended by Dr. Shem Musoke, who is soon soaked with Monet's virus-laden blood. A blood transfusion does Monet no good. He slips into a coma and dies. It is January 15.

Nine days later, Musoke begins to have the symptoms that presaged Monet's illness. He goes through most of the stages of Monet's illness, but somehow survives. An autopsy has revealed that Monet's major organs were affected, that his liver had ceased working days before his death, and that his kidneys had failed. Some of his organs, including his liver, had begun to liquefy, as had much of his body tissue.

Such is the beginning of *The Hot Zone*. Preston presents this gripping case study in vivid detail that recalls some of the most nightmarish paintings of Hieronymus Bosch or Gustave Doré's depictions of the lower circles of the Inferno about which Dante Alighieri wrote. The immediacy of Preston's prose evokes a gruesome horror reminiscent of the more extreme physical descriptions in John Foxe's *Actes and Monuments: The Book of Martyrs* (1563).

Against the backdrop of this case study are others set in Zaire, Sudan, and Kenya that Preston presents intermittently throughout the book. In Kenya, a fourteen-year-old Danish boy who visited the same Kitum cave in which Charles Monet had spent New Year's Day seven years earlier died in 1987 after displaying symptoms almost identical to Monet's. Preston, however, focuses his fullest attention on the drama that is the major thrust of his book: the threat of an Ebola contamination in the Washington, D.C., area in 1989.

After monkeys brought from the Philippines and held in the quarantine facilities of Hazleton Research Products in Reston, Virginia, began dying at an accelerated rate, Dan Dalgard, chief veterinarian of the Reston primate facility, sent samples of their blood and tissue to the nearby Army research facility in Washington, where they were examined by Peter Jahrling, a civilian virologist who worked for the United States Army. Tom Geisbert examined them at 125,000 times magnification on his electron microscope.

Lieutenant Colonel Nancy Jaax was, like her husband Colonel Jerry Jaax, a veterinarian. She became chief of pathology at the Army research facility in 1989. She had experienced a dangerous brush with the Ebola virus six years earlier, when, dissecting an infected monkey in the level 4 isolation room, she found a hole in the glove of her space suit, which all personnel at level 4—labeled a "hot zone" by the Army—are required to wear. Although she was saved from infection by extra gloves she wore beneath those of her space suit, she came face-to-face with the possibility of being infected by the dreaded filovirus, an event whose outcome could be a horrible death.

Jaax was called into the Reston situation after samples that Dalgard sent to the Army research facility appeared to be Ebola Zaïre, a string of the filovirus that kills nine out of ten primates—including humans—who are infected with it. The less virulent Ebola Sudan has a 50 percent death rate, and Marburg, the least virulent, kills still fewer.

As it turned out, Ebola Reston, named by its codiscoverers for the Virginia town where it was first detected, appeared to be nonlethal to humans. Four monkey handlers at the Reston facility, clearly a hot zone, tested positive for the virus but did not exhibit the dire symptoms associated with other strains, although two did come down with suspicious ailments during the height of the primate facility's Ebola outbreak.

All the major personages in his account are accorded physical descriptions that help readers establish a relationship with them. One sees Nancy Jaax not only as a military pathologist but also as the mother of two young children and as the daughter of a Kansas man who was dying of cancer. When his death became imminent, at the height of the Reston crisis, his daughter was forced to decide whether to return to his bedside or to stay and fulfill her obligations as chief pathologist. She opted for the latter, but not without undergoing considerable inner conflict.

Two of the military researchers, Peter Jahrling and Tom Geisbert, sniffed a vial that contained a culture from the infected monkeys before they realized that the animals were carrying the deadly virus that the two of them would finally discover and name. They were faced with an ethical problem. Should they report their exposure to the virus, thereby taking themselves out of the action, or should they keep mum about it and hope that they remain asymptomatic?

Their blood tests gave a negative reading. They knew that if they reported their exposure, they would be confined to the "Slammer," a quarantine facility so isolated that some of its inmates turned suicidal after being there for only a few days. The typical length of stay was thirty days.

The two decided not to report their possible exposure, because they needed to be involved in the intricate decontamination operation about to occur in Reston. In the end, the strain of Ebola filovirus that killed many monkeys at the primate facility and forced the military decontamination was found to bear a striking resemblance to Ebola Zaïre but proved to have a slightly different genetic code from the strain fatal to humans.

No one died as a result of what happened in Reston. For several days, however, it appeared that a huge population in Fairfax County and the surrounding Washington, D.C., area was at substantial risk. The primate facility was decontaminated, which involved euthanizing some 450 monkeys and safely disposing of their cadavers. The building was returned to the company that occupied it.

Every page of *The Hot Zone* is filled with dramatic events that Preston presents with skill sufficient to make his exploration of a technical subject read like a highly charged adventure story. He structures his book by dividing it into discrete sections, most dated, that interweave the Reston story with related information about the filovirus in Africa and Europe.

After Preston's first essay about Ebola and filoviruses appeared in *The New Yorker* in 1992, Twentieth Century-Fox earmarked fifty million dollars for a film version of the story, based only upon the twenty-two-page essay out of which the present book grew. This project, however, has been sidetracked.

Preston illustrates the incredible dangers that may lurk in unknown places, waiting to attack humans. Given the accessibility of air travel, no place in the world is currently remote. As contagious a virus as Ebola Zaïre can be loosed upon the world population by any world traveler exposed to it; the AIDS virus, for example, entered the United States through a promiscuous flight attendant working international routes. The results can devastate—and, in the case of Ebola, devastate with meteoric swiftness.

Why have viruses of this sort come out of dormancy lately? Preston blames human incursions into rain forests and other isolated habitats throughout the world. Nature's defense, he postulates, is to annihilate the infection caused by humans upon Earth's surface. He suggests that the human race might be facing a period during which nature engages in a protective process aimed at clearing away human threats to its well-balanced ecosystem.

R. Baird Shuman

Sources for Further Study

British Medical Journal. CCCIX, October 29, 1994, p. 1168.
Library Journal. CXIX, August, 1994, p. 121.
Los Angeles Times Book Review. September 25, 1994, p. 4.

Nature. CCCLXXII, November 17, 1994, p. 294.
New Scientist. CXLIV, November 19, 1994, p. 45.
The New York Times Book Review. XCIX, October 30, 1994, p. 13.
Newsweek. CXXIV, September 19, 1994, p. 64.
Publishers Weekly. CCXLI, June 27, 1994, p. 61.
Scientific American. XXVII, November, 1994, p. 114.
Time. CXLIV, September 5, 1994, p. 66.

HOW WE DIE
Reflections on Life's Final Chapter

Author: Sherwin B. Nuland
Publisher: Alfred A. Knopf (New York). 278 pp. $24.00
Type of work: Current affairs

As Sherwin B. Nuland describes how people die from heart attack, cancer, AIDS, and other diseases, he also offers a realistic yet compassionate philosophy to help people cope with death and dying

One by one, vast numbers of people die every day and night. They do so in thousands of ways. As long as human life exists on earth so it has been and always will be. Death is nothing new, and neither are books about it. Because death takes so much from human beings—often in pain-filled if not untimely ways—it leaves not only a corpse behind but also senses of loss and grief so deep that nothing quite can fill them. Still, if words are never sufficient to meet the needs that death and dying create, they can help us to cope. So there is no lack of writing about death, most of it seeking to provide consolation.

How We Die: Reflections on Life's Final Chapter breaks the mold. In more ways than one, this book about death and dying is new and different. What accounts for the book's distinctiveness is the fact that its author, Sherwin B. Nuland, brings five different but related perspectives to this study. First, Nuland has had a long and distinguished career as a successful surgeon. He also teaches the skill of surgery at Yale University's medical school. Thus, the most up-to-date medical knowledge informs his book.

Second, this surgeon is an accomplished scholar. In particular, Nuland's teaching encompasses the history of medicine. His book draws on that history to restore death to its ancient place in human existence.

Third, this surgeon-scholar is also a caring and compassionate doctor who is dedicated to more than the life-saving techniques of surgery. His practice of medicine aims at keeping the whole person well. Therefore his book counsels healthy people as well as dying patients and their friends and families. Specifically, Nuland wants to equip all people to make informed choices that enhance life's quality.

Fourth, Nuland is a gifted, eloquent, and even poetic writer. His book combines unsparing descriptive detail with unsentimental insight about how we die, much of it drawn poignantly from his own rich experience and the sensible skepticism it has produced about unlimited medical progress against death and dying. To cite just one example that keeps Nuland on guard against overoptimism, he reports that in the mid-1970's some members of the public health establishment thought that the threat of bacterial and viral disease might become a thing of the past. Little more than a decade later, the AIDS epidemic arrived, and, says Nuland convincingly, "There has never been a disease as devastating as AIDS." Nuland's purpose in citing such examples is not to crush hope. Far from that, he turns realism and skepticism into common sense that helps humans understand what to expect as their bodies inevitably fail them.

Finally, Nuland's book shows its author to be a wise and compassionate man who has suffered with family and friends whose lives could not be saved even by the latest medical techniques. His "reflections on life's final chapter," as the book's subtitle calls them, reveal a philosophy about living and dying that contains wisdom we all should have.

The wisdom begins with an epigraph Nuland chose to govern the book's themes. It comes from John Webster, a seventeenth century writer, who observed that "death hath ten thousand several doors/ For men to take their exits." Nuland cannot operate on all the ways people die, neither in his medical practice nor in the pages of his book. Instead, he stresses that no sooner has a life begun than its dying is also under way. Good health, strength, vitality— all may grow and flourish for a time, even for a long time, but humans are physical creatures, and their bodies are not immune to the weakening that results in death.

Embodied selves that humans are, their bodies are besieged, not least of all by their own carelessness. Their frailty becomes apparent in Webster's "ten thousand" ways. Nuland concentrates on the ones that most commonly kill humans. Among them are disease categories such as heart attack, stroke, cancer, Alzheimer's disease, and AIDS. He also discusses clinically what happens when people die a violent death—criminally or accidentally—and how death can overtake people through an aging process in which vital body parts eventually lose their vitality.

Whatever the general category into which one's death falls, whatever the details of one's dying, Nuland shows that "the weapons of every horseman of death" involve "certain universal processes that we will all experience as we are dying." Those processes include circulation stoppage, organ failure, and diminishing brain functions. What drives them all is the fact that human lives depend on oxygen. Lack of oxygen is at the bottom of how we die. One way or another, disease, trauma, or aging will find a way to rob us of the breath of life.

In his guise as a historian, Nuland notes that nothing fundamental has changed since the time of Hippocrates, the ancient and legendary Greek father of medicine, when it was known that man is an "obligate aerobe," a creature, like all known terrestrial animals, whose life depends on air. Yet everything has changed as one medical advance after another has promoted better health and extended the time during which death is kept at bay. Nuland's historical scholarship provides an important perspective by keeping before readers both the progress of medical expertise and the recognition that the history of medicine shows that nothing human can stop death indefinitely. In fact, not even the ugliness and anguish of dying can be prevented completely by any medical advance. The dying that awaits us all involves deterioration, destruction, and decay. Just as we start dying from the moment we are born, the inexorable processes of the body's demise may be checked, arrested, even in some ways reversed for a time, but only for a time because they are the ways that nature takes with us.

Repeatedly Nuland reminds readers that they are not destined to live forever. To the contrary, whatever brought each one to life, the truth remains that humans are perishable creatures whose living is also a process of dying. Nuland reminds his readers of this fact because the amazing medical advances that have occurred as generation after generation of physicians and researchers have battled disease so often dispose people to keep life going at any price in the hope that death does not have to arrive—at least not yet.

As a doctor who cares for patients living and dying, Nuland counsels that such refusal to accept what is inevitably coming, understandable though that is, ultimately proves as unwise as it is futile. The emphasis, he believes, should be on the quality, not the sheer duration, of one's life. Where it can cure disease, Nuland insists that treatment should definitely be used. Where medical intervention can truly enable one to live better, it ought to be employed. But as far as life's quality is concerned, unavoidably times come when the "cure" will be worse than the disease and the dying it brings. As much as possible, Nuland believes, physicians, patients, and their families should work together to discern the differences in these situations, to understand the available options, and to take the realistic decisions that have the best chances to make people's dying days as meaningful, good, and full of joy as they can be.

In his professional capacity as a doctor, Nuland cares passionately about life. He truly wants it to be as good as possible for all. Like doctors everywhere, however, he has seen much more death than most people have, and he has seen it up close. Understating what his experience has taught him, Nuland writes that he has "not often seen much dignity in the process by which we die." That observation becomes a key point of departure for the work of Nuland the writer.

Nuland has not produced what might have been, in his words, "a horror-filled sequence of painful and disgusting degradations," but neither does *How We Die* mince words. Readers learn more than they might like to know about the physical details of dying, especially now that hospitals and the intensive care that modern medicine provides have done so much—wrongly, Nuland insists—to isolate the dying person and to insulate family and friends from the processes that result in death. There is nothing beautiful, not even much that is tranquil, about the dying that Nuland describes. Human bodies do not give up life easily. Even when the battle is a lost cause, the lingering is not completely passive. As far as our bodies are concerned, the poet Dylan Thomas need not have worried. As long as it can, the body keeps raging "against the dying of the light" with the result that few of us go gently into the night. The idea of death with dignity, much in vogue at the time of Nuland's writing, is much more an imagined possibility than anything that happens as death approaches.

Nuland says that he wrote to "demythologize the process of dying." To do so, he takes his readers to meet the persons and to visit the places where he has seen people die—sometimes virtually alone—from diseases that have ravaged them and their loved ones. Nuland's detailed accounts of the physical, mental, and spiritual deterioration that various diseases bring creates a reading experience that is often disconcerting and even frightening.

Death, as Nuland says, conveys the idea of "a permanent unconsciousness . . . in which there is simply nothing. It seems so different from the nothing that preceded life." Thus, impulses to put this book down, to wonder why one is reading it, are likely to be felt. Yet readers do not have to fight these impulses in order to keep on with the reading. Once the reading starts, this book is not one that many readers are likely to set aside. There is even a reluctance to have it end. Nuland's narratives are gripping as little else could be; in addition, one soon senses that their goal must not be missed. Nuland does not miss his mark, and the reader's apprehension is changed into awareness that the author's demythologizing realism, including its skepticism about unending medical progress, contains reassurance.

As surgeon, scholar, doctor, and writer, Nuland becomes a wise friend who guides readers through what Psalm 23 calls "the valley of the shadow of death." His is a counseling guidance based on a philosophy of living and dying that makes sense. The key to the sense that Nuland makes about how we die is found in a line of poetry that he cites at the beginning and again at the ending of his book. It serves as a counterpoint to the book's seventeenth century epigraph. John Webster spoke of the "ten thousand several doors" through which death may take us. Yet Nuland also loves the thought of the great poet Rainer Maria Rilke, who once wrote simple words that ask, "Oh Lord, give each of us his own death."

Nuland loves this line not because he expects Rilke's prayer will be answered in any way that we can—or even God will—control. What Nuland knows, however, is that each of us will have our own death, and because that is true, he wants each of us to know how we die. To the extent that we have this knowledge and share it with one another in care and compassion, not only our dying but also our living will be less anxious, less driven by unjustified expectations, and thus more honestly and intensely human.

"We die," says Nuland, "so that the world may continue to live." Each of us has a gift of life. Nuland wants us to make the most of it. To do so we cannot live forever, at least not on this earth. We have to do what we can in the time we have and then take leave so that others can have their turn. Before the breath of life is taken from us, Nuland wisely stresses, we ought to live so that no one is left to die alone, so that no one is left to die in needless pain, and so that others, especially those we love and care about the most, will have good and worthy reasons to appreciate what we have been. If those things are true of us, then the right words in response to our death can rightly include the profound benediction that comes from Nuland's Jewish tradition: "May his memory be for a blessing."

John K. Roth

Sources for Further Study

JAMA: The Journal of the American Medical Association. CCLXXI, June 22, 1994, p. 1966.

Los Angeles Times Book Review. March 6, 1994, p. 6.

Nature. CCCLXX, August 4, 1994, p. 340.
The New York Review of Books. XLI, March 24, 1994, p. 14.
The New York Times Book Review. XCIX, January 30, 1994, p. 11.
The New Yorker. LXX, February 28, 1994, p. 92.
Publishers Weekly. CCXLI, January 3, 1994, p. 64.
Time. CXLIII, February 21, 1994, p. 66.
The Times Literary Supplement. May 27, 1994, p. 7.
The Washington Post Book World. XXIV, February 27, 1994, p. 1.

HOWARD MUMFORD JONES AND THE DYNAMICS OF LIBERAL HUMANISM

Author: Peter Brier (1935-)
Publisher: University of Missouri Press (Columbia). 178 pp. $32.50
Type of work: Literary criticism

An examination of the intellectual legacy of a leading literary and cultural historian

Howard Mumford Jones had a distinguished career as a historian and critic of American arts and society. At home in several literatures, he stressed transnational literary relations not only between the United States and the Atlantic community but also between the United States, Latin America, and Asia. He made himself an immensely erudite comparativist, on a level with such great European-born scholars as Erich Auerbach, Werner Jaeger, Leo Spitzer, and René Wellek. Like his colleague at the Johns Hopkins University, Arthur Lovejoy, Jones wrote seminal essays showing the impact of European thought on American writers and thinkers. Throughout his long life, he vigorously defended the tradition of humanistic rationalism and the necessity for the broadest, most cosmopolitan scholarship in American studies. He served ably as president, at various times, of the Modern Language Association, the American Academy of Arts and Sciences, and the American Council of Learned Societies.

Peter Brier, professor of English at California State University, Los Angeles, has written an ambitious study that seeks to serve several purposes. It is an affectionate biography of Jones the scholar and teacher, it expounds and explicates his most important ideas, and it raises the ghost of Jones as "a strong scholar of the recent past to challenge the present discourse in cultural and literary criticism."

Howard Mumford Jones was the son of an insurance agent who died when the boy was fourteen and left his Wisconsin family in near-poverty. Jones received his B.A. from the University of Wisconsin, then an M.A. in 1915 from the University of Chicago. His master's thesis was an essay on and translation of the great German poet Heinrich Heine's lyric cycle "The North Sea." For the next decade he taught at the Universities of Texas, Montana, North Carolina, and Michigan. He worked on a doctoral dissertation for Chicago's graduate school, researching the relationship between French and American culture. When his dean insisted that Jones take courses that he had already taught in the university's summer program, he refused and abandoned his Ph.D. candidacy. The fifteen honorary degrees he was to receive in later years surely compensated Jones for his lack of a doctorate. He had the satisfaction of having the University of North Carolina Press publish his non-Ph.D. "dissertation" in 1927; *America and French Culture, 1750-1848* becoming a standard work in the field. In 1974, the University of Chicago awarded him its prized Alumni Medal.

In 1936, Harvard University's president, James B. Conant, did Jones two significant honors: He invited him to receive an honorary degree at the grand celebration of the university's tercentenary, and he requested Harvard's English faculty to consider him for an appointment as full professor. In what turned out to be the middle year of his life, forty-four, the Midwestern Jones joined a brilliant cadre of specialists in American literature at Harvard: New Englanders Perry Miller, F. O. Matthiessen, and Kenneth Murdock. Brier states that Jones's teaching left few students with mild responses. Some resented what they considered his overbearing pedagogy, as he hurled armies of facts at them and insisted that they take lecture notes in a prescribed manner and notebook. Behind his back they derided him as "Howard Mumford Duck." Others, however, admired his energy, verve, enormous learning, and devotion to the highest standards of scholarship; they found his kindness of heart equally present with his intellectual rigor.

Jones regarded literature as a Dionysian art that defies binding definition, and was not particularly interested in literary theory. For him, literary criticism teaches society much about its culture, which is largely delineated by its art. History mattered far more than aesthetics, cultural typology far more than the organicism of the New Critics, who regarded literature as a self-enclosed, special kind of language often opposed to the language of science. Jones thought that literature and science should be allies, just as literature and history are. Formalist critics accused him of tending to desert the text in order to illustrate shifts in sensibility and cultural taste. Jones insisted that he served the text best by locating its meaning in the broadest possible historical perspective and sophistication. Brier states that "Howard Mumford Jones not only trusted in the past as a source for the information and ideas that would enable him to interpret great literary art, but he also believed that holding on to the legacy of humanism was the best insurance against cultural and social decline."

Like the literary historian Van Wyck Brooks, Jones believed in a "usable past," and that past was, centrally, European culture. His aim was to show how the United States could achieve the highest hopes of European civilization. The founders of the United States thought in terms of the Enlightenment and, in Jones's words, "believed this republic could live only on a principle of rationality." In his later years he became increasingly worried that America's rational-humanistic society would succumb to the temptations of the irrationalism and moral relativism espoused by European modernism. By the 1960's, Jones, as an honest historian, knew that he could no longer uphold a Jeffersonian model for his country's literary sensibility, which he acknowledged to be now possessed by "melancholy," "loneliness of the soul," and "imaginative rushes of violence, brutality, horror, and despair." He agonized that a nation that produced writing such as Henry Miller's *Tropic of Cancer* (1934) no longer had the right to proclaim "a special moral or aesthetic or intellectual virtue of its own."

Jones preferred to return to the era between 1865 and World War I, and he did so in a major study written in retirement, *The Age of Energy: Varieties of American Experience, 1865-1915* (1971). Instead of Mark Twain's pejorative title for American society in the late nineteenth century, "the Gilded Age," Jones preferred the phrase "the Silver Age" for an era that he saw as a significant incubator for the flourishing of American culture, particularly a vital, popular one.

Brier organizes a spectral "debate" between Jones and Hayden White, a prominent postmodern historian influenced by Jacques Derrida's deconstructionist philosophy of language. In *Tropics of Discourse: Essays in Cultural Criticism* (1978), White declares that "the language and styles used by historians, rather than their command of facts and philosophical inclinations, will determine what their texts convey *as history*; the discourse itself is the true subject." Jones, who died in 1980, never read White's book; his view of history was totally opposed. For him the subject shone through the prose, not the prose through the subject. He strove to write colorfully, lucidly, and wittily so that his vast subject matter would not sink into a morass or turgid rhetoric. Whereas White's historiography invites the rumination of the unconscious mind, Jones's insisted on rationally organized writing whose vivid details sparkled. White's notions of historical thought are tragically shaped by his reading of G. W. F. Hegel, Sigmund Freud, and Martin Heidegger; Jones went back to the epic mode in pursuit of reason, virtue, justice, and love, committed to the ethical qualities of literature which could educate Americans to their heroic potential.

Brier stresses Jones's focus on what Jones termed "the Anacreontic world," named for the sixth-century B.C. Greek author of love poems and drinking songs. In his last major text, *Revolution and Romanticism* (1974), he saw the Anacreontic strain of youth, health, joy, love, and wine as a bridge between Enlightenment and Romantic sensibility, stretching from, say, John Keats to Edna St. Vincent Millay. He regarded it as a "human cry" that overshadowed the comic, tragic, and satiric modes, sounding instead the heroic note. No wonder that Jones opposed Freudian determinism and such contemporary expressions of alienation as the theater of the absurd, averring, "I think men are often irrational, but I think man is rational." He remained committed to a Hellenic passion for *paidea*, the belief that a culture can achieve perfection through education. He rejected Henry Adams' vision of a tragic tension between unity and multiplicity. Instead he opted for both variety and richness in American life, for both national order and regional autonomy, for both the Virgin and the Dynamo.

In the last and longest chapter of his book, Brier uses the example of Howard Mumford Jones to do battle against what he considers—and is certain that Jones, were he alive, would deem—literary and cultural influences that seek to subsume the humanities to the social sciences, refuse to grant literature any meaning divorced from its localized or anthropological expression, and therefore estrange it from any general value system that would connect its nature to universal human needs. Brier deplores a "relativizing of value judgments [that] has its roots . . . in combinations of linguistics, anthropology, new varieties of psychoanalytical theory, feminism, Marxism, multiculturalism, and . . . postmodern historiography." What Brier attacks, through the agency of Jones's views, is an assemblage of antihumanist critiques of knowledge that derive largely from the concepts of the Heideggerian Jacques Derrida, the Nietzschean Michel Foucault, the Freudian Jacques Lacan, and the Marxist Roland Barthes. These theories assert that the existence of the individual subject is illusory and that the repressive forces of language and culture are so pervasive that they are unknowable and uncontrollable. They suspect that Western rationality, universalism, and humanism are mere covers for the domination of white men over women and nonwhites.

Brier points out that at least a generation before feminism and multiculturalism had become fashionable academic causes, Jones had lauded the novelists Willa Cather and Ellen Glasgow and had urged the study of Asian and Latin American civilization in undergraduate courses. As one of the founders of American Studies programs, Jones would have been delighted with multicultural research that was truly scholarly. He would, by the same token, have scorned the notion that tribalism can be an end in itself, disdaining it as superficial, recriminatory, and aimed at fragmenting American society instead of unifying it. In 1942, Jones delivered an address titled "Tribalism" at Wellesley College. In it he warned against the Nazis' tribalistic use of "the monstrous Nordic myth" but also attacked the more genteel but still pernicious myth of Anglo-Saxonism. As Brier eloquently cautions: "When the group and conformity to the group are given metaphysical sanction, tyranny is in the wings."

At a symposium sponsored by *The Partisan Review* in 1991, Catherine Stimpson, one of the most prominent academic advocates of multiculturalism, defended it as "the recognition that we live, nationally and internationally, with many cultures, defined both anthropologically and aesthetically." Brier indicates that Jones would have agreed with Stimpson's plea for tolerance and openness but would have disagreed with her bracketing of cultures between historical and aesthetic boundaries. He preferred a creed of universal humanity to the explicit tribalism of an anthropological ideology or a postmodern aesthetics of conflicting indeterminacies. Jones championed the determinacy of the epic Enlightenment philosophy held by the founders of the American republic.

Brier mounts his own attack on multiculturalism by lamenting its rancorous tone and its penchant for stigmatizing its opponents as racists or sexists or, at best, reactionaries. What the partisans of multiculturalism achieve, all too often, is a multiplication of the nation's differences into separatism, denying the idea of a common culture and a single society. Jones, on the other hand, insisted that America's differences are subsumed by a common European cultural heritage, but this heritage is one of inclusion, not exclusion, with the country's Anglo-Saxon base modified, enriched, and reconstituted by transfusions from other nations, continents, and civilizations.

Brier points out that Jones's cultural world is cosmopolitan and transcends ethnocentrism. Jones's achievement was to use his historical research and writing to convey a sense of the variety, continuity, and adaptability of cultures, yet fundamentally to enable his students and readers to understand an American identity that will always be in the making but does share common institutions and ideals.

Brier's study is learned, incisive, and—excepting occasional excursions into tangled mazes of critical theory—gracefully written. He has joined such literary scholars as Henry Louis Gates, Jr., David Bromwich, and Bernard Knox in defending American scholarship against the drive to reduce the humanities to ideological power politics. Many readers will find his argument convincing.

Gerhard Brand

Sources for Further Study

Choice. XXXII, January, 1995, p. 776.
Reference and Research Book News. IX, September, 1994, p. 44.

HULA

Author: Lisa Shea (1953-   )
Publisher: W. W. Norton (New York). 155 pp. $15.00
Type of work: Novel
Time: The summer of 1964 to the summer of 1965
Locale: An undesignated Virginia suburb

Narrated by a young girl describing the summers of her ninth and tenth years, this novel blends a child's unreflective lyricism about the natural world with her bewilderment at the adult behaviors to which she is subjected and the bodily changes disrupting her sense of self

Principal characters:

THE NARRATOR, an unnamed girl, about ten years old, who describes her troubled home life in the mid-1960's

HER UNNAMED SISTER, approximately two years older, for whom the stresses of early puberty intensify the family conflicts

THEIR FATHER, a World War II veteran subject to bizarre and violent behavior

THEIR MOTHER, a shadowy, languid presence unable for most of the novel to provide a reliable buffer to her husband's instability

Among the many strengths of *Hula,* winner of the Whiting Writers' Award in 1993, is the way it depicts how children in harrowing circumstances encode the sinister atmosphere in which they live within the ordinary surfaces of their imaginative play. Lisa Shea tells this story through the first-person narrative of the younger of a pair of sisters in a severely troubled family. Relying primarily upon their sibling bond for emotional reinforcement, the two must negotiate the constant threat to their well-being posed by a father whose World War II head wound has left him deranged, the metal plate in his skull suggesting "a bomb in his head that keeps going off." Hospitalized repeatedly, he supports his family through unspecified work at the local American Legion post. Their economic and social marginality is made visible in the wasteland landscape of junked cars and open drainage ditches that becomes the children's playground.

The father routinely satisfies his lust for violence by staging conflagrations of the refuse that makes its way to their ditch. With the gun he keeps on hand, he engages in drunken shooting sprees whose scattered bullets become the objects of a perverse treasure hunt—one of many examples of how the children transmute the fear he inspires into the taming rituals of their games. They are not deluded, though, about their reality: The older girl bluntly describes their circumstances as war, and as in every war, battles often assume the form of surreal, sadistic games. In an episode reminiscent of Flannery O'Connor's *Wise Blood* (1952), the father dons a gorilla costume at dinner and grabs food from the girls' plates, his sole effort at "play" within the text really an exercise in intimidation. Later the girls surreptitiously watch as he beats a newly purchased sheep to death, his inexplicable assault on the dumb animal a graphic reminder of their own helplessness. While his habit of pounding his head against a wall in arguments with his wife injects pathos into the mix of emotions he arouses, his unrelenting tyranny toward the women in his household suggests that although a victim of apocalyptically yielded male power himself, he champions an unfettered patriarchy whereby irrational masculinity unconstrainedly imposes its authority on everyone around.

Not surprisingly, he proves most aggressive in attempting to control female sexuality. Although his future wife was a dance instructor when he met her, he now forbids her even to teach her daughters graceful dances like the hula. When he discovers the girls with grass skirts, he angrily consigns the toys to his fires. His older daughter's tap dancing earns no such condemnation, presumably because of its less sexualized nature, but her adolescent forays into the woods with boys so enrage him that he first tries to imprison her in their yard and then whips her when she defies his edicts. That he is in a losing battle to curtail her hormonal urges is made obvious by the way he recedes from the narrative as the scenes involving her sexual adventurism multiply.

The children's mother fails to offer an effective female counterforce to their situation. Most of the time she is markedly absent from the text, the narrator commenting in a typical moment of crisis that "my mother could be anywhere." A housewife and part-time staffer at the local dance studio, she lets inertia shape her responses to her husband's terrorism. Ironically, she remains a greater enigma in her aloofness than the father, for while his metal plate provides a tangible if incomplete explanation for his worst excesses, there is no comparable route into her subjectivity except for the tears and hand-wringing impotence to which she occasionally resorts. Pretty, gentle, dreamy, she is doted upon by her similarly dreamy younger child, whose fantasy of escaping into a world inhabited by just the two of them hints at the deprivation of affection she suffers. The older daughter far more resistant to the cult of female passivity, vacillates between a childish hope that her mother will repudiate her chronic lassitude and a rebellious adolescent conviction that she herself will break her father's hold on them.

To both girls' surprise, their mother finally yields to the urgings of a friend and moves herself and her daughters to a cheap motel decorated in a Hawaiian motif recalling the forbidden hula. The book ends, however, with ominous hints that she will not sustain this independence. Telling the girls obliquely that "we might stay at the Waikiki another week," the mother triggers the narrator's fears of the powerful male force irresistibly drawing them back to the status quo: "I don't see our father in the picture, but I know he's there, waiting to find us. . . . He'll come after us with tears in his eyes, just like we never left."

While it is predictable that the girls turn to each other for security, their complex relationship eschews any sentimental idealization of sisterhood. The narrator's bond with her sibling serves as the emotional center of her life, making the older child's inexorable march toward sexuality and its betrayals all the more bewildering and painful for the younger. Shea vividly captures the dance of intimacies, dependencies, and antagonisms that characterize the girls' daily interactions and exposes the serious struggle for dominance beneath their childish quarrels. In many ways the girls reenact the sadomasochistic dynamic at work between their parents, for the narrator generally submits to the often brutal bullying of the older girl and becomes adept at placating her sister's easily aroused temper. Whereas the older girl cannot resist announcing her rebellious presence, the narrator typically resorts to running away or hiding in an effort "to act invisible" as an antidote to her vulnerability. When she periodically refuses the docile role, she quickly pays the price for disturbing the power alignment with her sister. Having snatched her sister's jumprope and refused to return it, she is subjected first to near-suffocation and then to a display of indifference that erodes her victory and makes clear that power flows to she who has the least to lose, the least invested. In another grisly game the child practices her ability to endure self-inflicted pain as a test of her character: "I light a match and watch it burn down to where it almost touches my fingers. It's a game my sister taught me. . . . Even when the pain comes, I hold on." Such thinking makes her habit of clutching her fleeing sister's talismanic ponytail doubly poignant as it ceases being a gesture of girlish dependence and becomes a futile protest against the loss of childhood.

If the girls' father creates the external conflict propelling the episodically minimalist narrative, it is the urgency of the girls' own sexual maturation that produces the interior rhythms of the novel. The narrator, after all, has already devised strategies of coping with her parents but is at a loss about how to manage her contradictory feelings about the impulses she sees acted out by her sister and vaguely experiences in herself. Shea superbly documents the way children become aware of sexuality, first in the world outside themselves and then within their own bodies. From their beloved dog Mitelin, the girls learn how the unselfconscious physical affinity linking them to the animal is disrupted by sex and its irrevocable consequences: In heat, the devoted Mitelin becomes "prey" for the dog next door, and their mating "dance" transforms her into a vicious beast who turns on the girls when they approach her too soon after coitus. The pregnancies that result dramatize sexuality's pricetag and magnify the disjunction between Mitelin as asexual childlike buddy and mature female. When the girls' mother suffers a miscarriage, she offers more proof that sex is dangerous, as does their father's explosive suppression of femininity. Most significantly, the boys who begin to hover around them project an atmosphere of threat that unnerves the younger child even as it lures the older one. In the very bushes where they had once found a safe haven there now lurk masturbating youths eager to initiate them into the phallic hijinks of "Mr. Romeo." To the narrator's chagrin, her sister collaborates in mysterious exchanges with them that she haughtily refuses to describe even as she warns her "babyish" sibling that such sinful pollution awaits her too, regardless of her Catholic holy water rituals.

Because the narrator is undergoing her own preliminary physical changes, she regards her sister's budding hips, breasts, and pubic hair with an envy steadily eclipsing her original fascinated revulsion. She also knows the bittersweet pleasures of sublimation: As she moons over record-album portraits of Frédéric Chopin, she inadvertently croons the name of a local boy whose look of near-religious ecstasy while masturbating upends her neat dichotomies of right and wrong. Trying to maintain some vestige of sisterly solidarity in the face of this hormonal onslaught, she joins the secret rendezvous with the boys in the woods but then rejects any contact with them, regressing into the game of horses she and her sister have played for years, only to discover that her sister has abandoned the game (itself ironically suggestive of the sexuality, though unselfconscious, of preadolescent girls).

The narrator's puzzling over sex derives from her larger concern with the precariousness of life itself, a tendency revealed in the poetically succinct imagery of her thoughts. Shea admits that numerous sections of the book began as prose poems, and her spare sentences strip away distracting detail to allow the basic facts of a scene to resonate with heightened significance, much as a child's sharply focused perception of the seemingly mundane can explode its familiarity and demand new readings. The narrator's reliance on certain images reveals them as central to her imaginative effort to interpret the world and creates a subtle lyrical unity beneath the fragmentary narrative action. This is not an unreflective child, for all that she lacks the linguistic sophistication to explain her concerns. Death is an ever-present reality made tangible to her by the ubiquitous ashes to which her father's fires reduce everything from lawn debris to the corpses of beloved puppies to the mutilated sheep carcass. Similarly, the badly working and malodorous sump pump buried in their yard continually reminds her of the corruption into which life steadily slides, an observation that her rudimentary Catholicism reinforces. Other images become more nuanced and symbolically complex; the ditch that serves as refuse dump, incineration site, treasure trove, and hiding place, for example, ultimately comes to hint at the terrain of female sexuality itself, complete with drainpipe where the girls toss dismembered doll bodies and the narrator hides from her father and Frankie Blackmore. The prominence of fire in the sections devoted to her father yields to the water motifs that dominate the latter third of the book, when the girls' irrepressible sexuality asserts itself. Dances and games also assume richer associations as their contexts shift, provocatively sketching the distance between childhood and adolescence. Even the narrator's propensity for hiding comes to express her flight from the twin dangers of being a small child in a violent household and a maturing female in a sexually predatory world.

Finally, the relentlessness of time itself haunts this girl, undermining her reliance on the familiar elements that have sustained her fragile sense of security. The bodily alternations affecting every female she knows, from Mitelin to her sister to herself, merely offer an aggressive form of the temporal flux ultimately moving all life toward death, and *Hula*'s narrator, unable to sleep because "anything could happen if I close [my eyes], anything at all," is left with only the power of her imagination to hold reality at bay.

Barbara Kitt Seidman

Sources for Further Study

The Antioch Review. LII, Spring, 1994, p. 375.
Booklist. XC, November 15, 1993, p. 603.

Kirkus Reviews. LXI, October 15, 1993, p. 1291.
Library Journal. CXVIII, November 15, 1993, p. 101.
Ms. IV, January, 1994, p. 73.
The New York Times Book Review. XCIX, January 16, 1994, p. 11.
The New Yorker. LXX, February 21, 1994, p. 119.
Publishers Weekly. CCXL, November 1, 1993, p. 64.
The Washington Post. February 3, 1994, p. C2.
The Women's Review of Books. XI, July, 1994, p. 47.

IMPERFECT THIRST

Author: Galway Kinnell (1927-)
Publisher: Houghton Mifflin (Boston). 81 pp. $19.95
Type of work: Poetry

The intensity of these poems lies in the delicate balance between the shimmering transparency of the present and the inescapable presence of memory

Galway Kinnell's latest collection of poetry is generally elegiac in tone, in keeping with the direction his poetry has taken with *The Past* (1985)—less visceral and hard-edged, more introspective and subtle, yet still a vigorous play of sound and sensuousness. Esoterica are less in evidence. Whitmanesque expansiveness has given way to an interior universe of memory and relationship. Kinnell's poetry, after crashing upon the world with powerful, salty force, is drawing back into the rich sea from which it came. The intensity of these poems lies in the delicate balance between the shimmering transparency of the present and the inescapable presence of memory. Their long, quiet lines draw out a moment over time, or draw time into a moment, and achieve an overall sense of place and continuance.

Imperfect Thirst is divided into five parts of five poems each. The whole is preceded by a proem called "The Pen," which introduces the themes to be explored: memory, relationship, youth, age, love, regret, death, regeneration. In Kinnell's hand, the pen becomes an organism. Its heartbeat is an "alternation of lifts and strokes." At the end of a line its direction of movement is that of memory—"backward and downward." Its blood is ink, the blood of fallen gods—Adam, Icarus—who sacrificed immortality for the "clarity of knowing." The ink sometimes proves inadequate to the task of revealing what it knows, speaking nonsense sometimes, or imposing comprehension on things, like death, that are incomprehensible. The curse is that the ink runs dry.

The blessing, although bound by death, is that the ink is replenished by common humanity. Another poet speaks of her grief, and Kinnell is again able to write about his own. Ink, agent of thought, transcends loss, enabling the poet to continue "to speak the unspeakable."

Part 1 invokes the ghosts of Kinnell's parents. Two poems about his mother frame three about his father; all reveal estrangement, repression, and loss. Two are particularly poignant. "Showing My Father Through Freedom" illuminates the moment in which a child's innocence begins to dissolve in the sudden light of knowing—a knowing that, in its infancy, is more a glimmer than a glare. Something open and free becomes a secret; that which has been spoken of becomes unspeakable. The irony of freedom is clear.

"The Man in the Chair" carries further the tragedy of that which is unspoken. An allusion to an earlier poem identifies the man in the chair as Kinnell's father. "Memories of My Father" (*When One Has Lived a Long Time Alone*, 1990) opens with the image of driving "a spike too weak into wood too hard." This image is carried over in the form of a hammer trying to extract a spike from *lignum vitae*—the tropical "wood of life" characterized by extraordinary hardness. The man's rigidity, slackness of the neck, shaking, and jerking also identify him with the man of "Parkinson's Disease," found in part 4. The latter poem is a soft portrait of an aged father who totters on the edge of bliss in the gentle care of a daughter. Yet the detached acceptance in "Parkinson's Disease" is not evident in "The Man in the Chair." The point of view here is that of a boy who struggles to suppress the complexities of his need for his father, who is absent both physically and emotionally. This neediness is counterbalanced by a recognition of the father's struggle, although the boy, like the father, is powerless to speak. The pen that bears down through the paper to dark realms below recalls the pen of the proem, which presses down, "thickening the words that attempt to speak the unspeakable," words that have "a mineral glint, given by clarity of knowing, even in hell."

Part 2 continues the theme of relationship on a more earthy plane. The connections are those of love, although differing in kind and in degree, and in each there is an element of danger, violence, or betrayal. Violence and ecstasy are juxtaposed in "Running on Silk," where a voice behind the escaping couple calls "*bop! bop!* like a stun gun, or a pet name," and again in "The Cellist," where "The music seems to rise from the crater left/ when heaven was torn up and taken off the earth," and where the particulars of the manufacture of catgut cello strings are deftly and remorselessly conveyed. "The Night" ascribes to lovemaking the utter and dangerous vulnerability of children and hatchlings. In "Trees," an oak's maternal care of the boy overrides what the man knows and the boy does not—that the boy will grow into a man, and men will rape the forest.

The middle poem of this group, "The Deconstruction of Emily Dickinson," at first seems out of place. The setting is a classroom in Amherst; at issue between professor and protagonist is the reason why Dickinson's poems were not published in her lifetime. The protagonist has a personal relationship with Dickinson that recalls breakfast with John Keats in "Oatmeal" (*When One Has Lived a Long Time Alone*); however, "Dickinson" takes a much darker turn. The professor is imperious, his language incomprehensible. The protagonist, despite coaching from his muse, cannot articulate the truth. The violence is intellectual. The professor violates the language and denigrates Dickinson's intent—deconstruction as rape. The protagonist betrays Dickinson with silence, and is punished with desertion.

In the poems of part 2, the lines that separate human from animal, or animal from plant, are blurred, recalling "The Bear" and "The Porcupine" (*Body Rags*, 1968). Also blurred are the lines between past, present, and future. The lovers of "The Night" "have been lying on this bed since before the earth began." In "Trees," the oak is an hourglass, and time "falls, and does not fly." "Running on Silk" jumps a span of forty years in memory. In "The Deconstruction of Emily Dickinson," Emily speaks to the protagonist across a century, and the tragedy hangs on forcing a word to assume a meaning that is out of time.

The blurring of time carries over to part 3, a group of poems that take the form of Persian *ghazals*. This group, the book's centerpiece, is probably the most difficult, and ultimately the most compelling, of the collection. The prevailing theme is death. The poems are paradoxical and deeply personal, as Kinnell's invocation of his own name in each signifies. The lines are of varying lengths; each line is self-contained, a complete sentence. The images presented in each line are seemingly out of joint, yet taken as a whole they create a fabric of images that transcend time, place, and linear thought, approaching a state of "pure poetry," that washes over, rather than speaks to, the reader. This is "to speak the unspeakable" in the highest sense, requiring the poet's utmost skill, authenticity and courage.

Part 4 is a collection of love poems that balances those of part 2. The element of danger does not appear; rather, it is replaced by a sense of connection with things larger than the things at hand. In "Parkinson's Disease," past, present, and future arrive at a stillpoint in the image of the daughter walking backward, supporting her father as he walks forward, tottering on the edge of heaven: "At this moment, he glints and shines,/ as if it will be only a small dislocation/ for him to pass from this paradise into the next." "Telephoning in Mexican Sunlight," a delightful reprieve, binds birds, words, and technology in a shimmering moment of correlation. "The Music of Poetry" is a tour-de-force of connections, both ontological and grammatical; the entire poem is one sentence. "Rapture" links lovemaking with the movement of the earth—a tired metaphor—so sweetly that we don't mind; besides, Kinnell makes it obvious that he knows what he is doing: "The two mounds of muscles for walking, leaping, lovemaking,/ lift toward the east—what can I say?/ Simile is useless; there is nothing like them on earth." The final poem of the section, "The Road Across Skye," like the *ghazals*, is a temporal spillway where disparate images join and merge to elicit a pure, nonverbal response. Taken altogether, the soft and steady luminosity of these poems relieves the shadowed contours of the others.

The longer poems of part 5 are a curious mixture of silliness and sublimity. They revisit the subjects of the proem and part 1, finishing what was begun there. "Flies" and "Holy Shit" forsake elegy for highbrow humor, but stop short of nonsense. "Flies" touches with delicate fingers the source of familial pain—a mother's "craving for love in her own life" and a father who "righted himself out of the muck" of a war knowing that "no one who rights himself out of it/ and walks and feels OK/ is OK." "Holy Shit" puts a wry finger on the cure for human arrogance: "Let us sit bent forward slightly, and be opened a moment,/ as earth's holy matter passes through us." "Lackawanna" is a tortuous, courageous exploration of sexual abuse, where salvation is achieved in the singing of the poem. "The Striped Snake and the Goldfinch" is another time-traveling poem in which the child of the Seekonk Woods, for whom "the lights in the valley/ seem farther away than the stars," reconciles himself to the adult in the Garden, who knows that a wine-filled glass is "the upper bell of the glass/ that will hold the last hour we have to live."

The final poem, "Neverland," is a stunning memorial for his sister Wendy, the "little mother" of the proem. Where an early and moving elegy for his brother ("Freedom, New Hampshire" in *What a Kingdom It Was*, 1960) searches memory for an afterlife, and finds none, "Neverland" looks closely and tenderly at the moments just before death, and then moves ahead to "the region she passes through." He goes as far as he can go, in lines that intermingle sight and sound:

> I hear her voice,
> calling back across the region she passes through,
> in prolonged, even notes, which swell and diminish,
> a far landscape I seem to see as if from above,
> much light, much darkness, tumbling clouds,
> sounding back to us from its farthest edge.
> Now her voice comes from under the horizon,
> and now it grows faint, and now I cannot hear it.

Imperfect Thirst is an extraordinary book. Graceful, grieving, relational, solitary, earthbound, visionary—these poems are figures for what is profoundly and deeply human. Kinnell stands again in the fragile space between here and there, singing of what is with great skill, integrity, and compassion.

Louise Grieco

Sources for Further Study

Booklist. XCI, October 15, 1994, p. 395.
Library Journal. CXIX, November 1, 1994, p. 80.
Publishers Weekly. CCXLI, December 5, 1994, p. 56.

IN A TIME OF VIOLENCE

Author: Eavan Boland (1944-)
Publisher: W. W. Norton (New York). 70 pp. $17.95
Type of work: Poetry

Eavan Boland continues to explore the themes that have guided her mature poetry—the relationships between her gender, her identity as an Irishwoman, and her calling as a poet

Eavan Boland has frequently identified the central concerns of her work as the process of discovering the interrelationships of her gender, her national identity, and her art. Boland has noted that the woman poet in Ireland faces particular challenges in these respects. First, Ireland has been slow to embrace feminism, a fact that sometimes has led readers and reviewers to dismiss as insignificant any subjects (such as home and family relationships) that they consider characteristically "female." Moreover, the Irish woman who writes poetry has few models from her own country. Only since about 1970 have women been much represented in the rich list of Irish poets.

Understanding one's origins is an essential element of claiming one's identity. For the Irish, that process has required reexamining and reclaiming their history, in many cases rejecting the interpretation of Irish affairs promoted by England, whose colonial rule of Ireland spanned more than three centuries until it ended in 1949.

Concern for that history has formed a recurrent theme in much contemporary Irish poetry. As a diplomat's daughter, Boland was more than usually cut off from Irish culture. She was schooled in London from 1950 to 1956; for the next three years she was educated in New York City. The effect was a distance between her and her country and its past. Boland's poems have frequently been her means of overcoming that distance. "The Achill Woman," a poem from her collection *Outside History: Selected Poems 1980-1990* (1990), relates an event from Boland's university days which illustrates this process. The poem describes her conversation with an elderly country woman who brings her water. When their conversation ends, the speaker goes indoors to study the court poets of the Silver Age—poets such as Sir Thomas Wyatt and Sir Walter Raleigh—oblivious, Boland says, to the ironies the situation suggests.

In an essay for *American Poetry Review* (March/April 1990), Boland talks further about this conversation. The woman had told her about how local people struggled to survive in the terrible years of the 1840's famine, sometimes moving closer to the coast in order to eat seaweed. It was Boland's first intense encounter with her country's past, and in the essay she proposes the old woman and her own youthful self as emblems of what the poet, particularly the Irish woman poet, must integrate if her work is to be meaningful.

The poems of *In a Time of Violence* continue to examine the problems of that integration as well as Boland's desire to move beyond poetry that merely records experience to poetry that is experience itself. Boland describes that goal in the collection's first poem, "The Singers," which seems to stand as an epigraph to the book's three parts. In the poem she talks of "women who were singers in the West," who endured the dangers of the coast, the ocean, and its storms. Boland wonders whether there must not have come some moment of revelation for them, a realization that "rain and ocean and their own/ sense of home were . . . one and the same." Such a revelation, she thinks, would have let the singers know that their voice and their vision were identical, the goal Boland has claimed for her own songs.

The first section of the book is titled "Writing in a Time of Violence," and its seven poems are described as "a sequence." The epigraph to this section is Plato's famous condemnation of poets as those who indulge people's "irrational" natures, but the poems here suggest that times of violence themselves lead people to the inability to discriminate that Plato ascribed to poetry. The first poem, "That the Science of Cartography is Limited," describes a "famine road," a road that was make-work assigned to the starving Irish by relief committees in 1847. "Where they died, there the road ended," Boland says. Although the map can represent the road that ends meaninglessly in a forest, it can never communicate either the sweetness of the trees or the agony of those who died among them.

Painting is often a powerful metaphor for Boland, whose mother was an artist. "The Death of Reason" imagines the burning of an eighteenth century portrait of a woman ("anonymous beauty-bait for the painter"). As the picture burns—the woman's silk dress, her face and mouth—so Ireland is burning "from Antrim to the Boyne," ignited by the death of reason, which motivates violence from both the Peep-O-Day Boys (a secret agrarian society of Ulster Protestants) and the English colonial rulers in Augustan London. Boland's poem joins two ironies. First, reason dies in the midst of the age that is named for it, and second, its death is represented by the "death" of the picture of a woman who for the painter and his public was anonymous but who comes in the poem to represent Ireland itself, ablaze with violence.

"March 1 1847. By the First Post" explores much the same theme, this time in the form of a letter written by a young woman in Dublin to her sister in London, bemoaning the trivial discomforts and boredoms she faces while the Irish starve. The reference to the dress of copper silk that the writer is sending her sister is one among many such descriptions in these poems. Boland is always conscious of fabrics. "In a Bad Light," for example, describes a setting in a St. Louis museum. The speaker thinks of Dublin as she looks at a display representing an elegant steamboat passenger of 1860, headed for New Orleans in crepe, satin, suede, and silk. While the passenger enjoys her luxuries and ignores rumors of war, Boland imagines the Irish seamstresses who worked in bad light to create those clothes. They seem to be sewing their own obliteration—sewing "the salt of exile," sewing the coffin ships into which starving emigrants were crowded to their deaths, sewing "history's abandonment" of themselves and their country.

All the poems of the section emerge from the violence of Ireland's history. "The Dolls Museum in Dublin" merges the image of the cracked and "wounded" dolls with the wounds of those who were broken in the Easter Uprising of 1916. Boland summons up the pictures of dolls in the arms of little girls, walking with their families on the

Green after Easter Sunday worship. All the details suggest lives of refinement and ease. Nevertheless, "rumor and alarm at the barracks" recall the bloodshed of that Sunday. Now the dolls lie in their museum, having outlasted the terrible events, "the hostages ignorance takes from time."

The final poem of the section, "Writing in a Time of Violence," joins all these themes in a meditation on language. It stands as a conclusion to the ideas of "The Singers," where voice and vision merge. In this latter poem, however, language becomes deceptive, perilous. The language of persuasion, even the "satin phrases" that have decorated Ireland's past, now conceal a language of violence waiting to strike, incapable of being discriminated.

Boland has always been interested in myth. The poems of "Legends," the second section of this collection, suggest the many sources of legend beyond the Greeks. Legends can emerge even from the scene of the quiet suburban evening described in "This Moment" when it is described with Boland's meticulous detail. In "Love," Boland's speaker tells her husband the tale of their marriage and their early life together in the American Midwest (Boland was associated with the International Writing Program at the University of Iowa), where one of their children experienced life-threatening danger and was later healed. The town's river is described as the river that forms the boundary of the underworld. The hero who crosses the boundary, perhaps to be questioned by the dead, is her husband. The question she would ask him is the question of epic, now asked by the middle-aged wife: "Will we ever live so intensely again?" Even the hero cannot answer such a question, cannot even hear it.

Three other poems from this section demonstrate how legend can encompass territory as wide as ancient history and as specific as the poet's mother or her grandparents. "In Which the Ancient History I Learn Is Not My Own" pictures the speaker as a child in London, learning about the Roman Empire and the Delphic Oracle. In the midst of that English classroom she suddenly realizes that what she really longs to learn is "the weave of my own country," its place names, even the location of her old house. In contrast to that wide scope, "The Parcel" reconstructs minutely the details of her mother's craft in wrapping a package, a dying art. "Lava Cameo" uses the emblem of the carved brooch to communicate the catastrophe of her grandparents' lives, another family legend. "Legends," the last poem in the section, is dedicated to Boland's daughter, to whom she says, "Our children are our legends./ You are mine. You have my name."

"Anna Liffey" is the first and longest poem in the last section. The name Anna Liffey uses the name of Dublin's river, the Liffey, and the story that it was named for the mythical woman Life; it also recalls one of the versions of the name Anna Livia Plurabelle, the figure of universal woman in James Joyce's *Finnegans Wake* (1939). Boland uses this evocative image to suggest her complex relationship to her city, her country: "A woman in the doorway of her house./ A river in the city of her birth." Together they make an emblem for the speaker herself, a woman in her middle age, an Irishwoman, a poet. She has come to a time when she knows the limitations of language at the same time she knows that the river, the place, and its history will be communicated to others only through language, only through the voice of the poet.

That theme of the dual nature of language, at once limited and yet the only means by which the poet can turn myth into experience, also informs "Story" and "What Language Did." The need for language to become experience itself seems most powerfully represented, however, in the volume's last poem, "A Woman Painted on a Leaf." The odd little painting—not exactly a picture, no longer a leaf—suggests what a poet must overcome. Boland does not want to record experience; she wishes the poem to be the experience: "I want a poem/ I can grow old in. I want a poem I can die in." She wishes to return the leaf to the autumn air, where it will become leaf mold, where the painted mouth of the picture can call out for death.

The music of Boland's poems rises from her subtle use of stanzas, slant rhyme, and sound effects such as the echoes in the phrase "faces, stars, irises, Narcissus" ("The Water Clock"). The remarkable range of her poetic voice can be understood if one compares the lyricism of "Anna Liffey" with the petulant voice of the cosseted young woman in "March 1 1847. By the First Post."

Eavan Boland's American reputation soared with the publication of *Outside History* in 1990; that volume showed American readers the depth and range of her poetic concerns. *In a Time of Violence* continues to validate Boland's insistence that poetry can incorporate gender, nation, history, and the poet's own sense of mortality. In doing so, poetry becomes myth and works the way myth has always done, to communicate a truth that somehow transcends the details of its history. In "Story," Boland uses the Tristan and Isolde legend, which, as she writes it, mysteriously enters the Dublin suburbs, enters her own garden, to become new all over again through the power of poetry. That is what can come from writing in times of violence.

Ann D. Garbett

Sources for Further Study

Booklist. XC, March 15, 1994, p. 1322.
Irish Literary Supplement. XIII, Fall, 1994, p. 23.
Library Journal. CXIX, March 1, 1994, p. 90.
The Nation. CCLVIII, June 6, 1994, p. 798.
The New York Review of Books. XLI, May 26, 1994, p. 25.
Poetry. CLXV, October, 1994, p. 41.
Publishers Weekly. CCXLI, February 28, 1994, p. 77.
The Times Literary Supplement. August 5, 1994, p. 19.
The Women's Review of Books. XII, November, 1994, p. 19.

IN PHARAOH'S ARMY
Memories of the Lost War

Author: Tobias Wolff (1945-)
Publisher: Alfred A. Knopf (New York). 221 pp. $23.00
Type of work: Memoir
Time: 1967-1968
Locale: My Tho, a Vietnamese town in the Mekong Delta; Washington, D.C.; San Francisco; Oxford, England; and various military bases stateside

Memoirs of the author's coming of age and his tour of duty in Vietnam

Principal personages:
TOBY, a young American lieutenant in the Green Berets
SERGEANT BENET, his African American aide, roommate, and protector in My Tho
CANH CHO, his pet dog in My Tho
HUGH PIERCE, his best friend in flight school, who dies in Vietnam
STU HOFFMAN, another friend from flight school, who deserts rather than go to Vietnam
KEITH YOUNG, a buddy who dies in action
DOC MACLEOD, a bitter medical volunteer in Vietnam
PETE LANDON, a Foreign Service officer who befriends Toby in Vietnam
CAPTAIN KALE, Toby's pompous replacement at My Tho
VERA, Toby's moody and erratic girlfriend
GEOFFREY, his older brother, who works for *The Washington Post*
ARTHUR (DUKE), his disreputable father

Pharaoh's army is the United States Army in Vietnam. The soldier is Toby, a late adolescent who joins the army on a whim. Despite the title's negative association of the United States with the oppressive pharaoh of the biblical exodus, this memoir contains no vitriolic antiwar tirade. The purposelessness of the American presence in Vietnam and the young soldier's own lack of solid dedication to the war effort are, indeed, a backdrop to events in *In Pharaoh's Army: Memories of the Lost War*, but the real focus is the young soldier and his search for himself.

In this memoir, Tobias Wolff continues the autobiographical reflections that he began so successfully in *This Boy's Life* (1989). In these earlier memoirs Wolff described his turbulent childhood, centering on his parents' divorce, his abusive stepfather, and his disappointing career at various boarding schools. While strong maternal figures such as Toby's real mother Rosemary and her friend Marion played a major role in *This Boy's Life*, *In Pharaoh's Army* deals much more with male relationships and male bonding. Indeed, except for his doomed friendship with Vera, Toby concentrates *In Pharaoh's Army* on his ties with other men, with his army buddies, with his older brother Geoffrey, and especially with his geographically and emotionally distant father.

Toby's narrative voice dominates the book and spares no one its stark criticism. Toby sees the flaws in army procedure, in American policy, and in human nature. He coldly describes a grudge-bearing fellow shipmate, who tries to kill him before his army days, and the misdeeds of his wayward former-convict father. He spares little sympathy for the likes of Pete Landon, a Foreign Service officer who demonstrates his culture and sophistication at the expense of his fellow officers, or Captain Kale, Toby's insensitive and know-it-all replacement at My Tho. Both Landon and Kale suffer for their sins in appropriate ways but ways that implicate Toby. Landon loses a valuable antique Chinese vase, and Kale makes a gross error of misjudgment by which some Vietnamese homes are unnecessarily destroyed. In each case Toby probably could prevent disaster if he wishes to do so, but he does not.

Indeed, Toby is harshest on himself. In the opening scene, he describes himself bearing down on a group of Vietnamese peasants in his speeding armor-plated truck. His closing references are still self-critical as he mentions his aimless, postwar student days at the University of Oxford. Toby is acutely conscious of his own deficiencies, his lack of courage in war, his weakness as an officer and troop leader, and his many social shortcomings.

The first-person voice of the narrative strengthens the self-critical tone of the narrator. Recollecting events from the perspective of adulthood, Wolff is able to add the wisdom of maturity to his commentary on the deeds and misdeeds of the young Toby in Vietnam.

The only joys in this book are bittersweet. There are memories of long conversations and nights on the town with Toby's buddy Hugh Pierce, who never makes it back from Vietnam, and of Toby's last visit with his father before he dies. The humor is macabre and battle-scarred, as when Doc Macleod, a veteran medical volunteer in Vietnam, recognizes and mocks Toby's naïveté. Personal relationships are frustrating: Toby's association with Sergeant Benet cannot become true friendship because of their inequality of rank. All these events are narrated in *In Pharaoh's Army* with both a sense of pleasure past and of opportunity lost.

In Pharaoh's Army begins *in medias res*, with Toby's wild adventures on Thanksgiving Day in 1967 in My Tho. The narrative takes the reader through a series of personal war stories, of Toby's near-misses with death, of life in a provincial Vietnamese city, and of the crude behavior of fellow Americans toward Vietnamese civilians and military. The infamous Tet Offensive of January, 1968, is the only significant historical event that intrudes into Toby's story. As My Tho is destroyed, mostly under American fire, Toby realizes that in the eyes of his fellow Americans, there is little difference between the Viet Cong enemy and the South Vietnamese civilian. Both are Asian. Both are foreign. The lives of both are dispensable.

Only a few months following Tet, Toby's tour of duty in Vietnam comes to an end, but his narrative does not. Wolff brings himself back home, to an encounter with his father in San Francisco, a final confrontation with Vera, and his own aimlessness. In the end, Wolff leaves Toby studying in Oxford, England, with no clearer purpose in life than a vague ambition to become a writer.

Toby's real story, however, is not strictly the one told in chronological order. Rather, the true focus of *In Pharaoh's Army* is a journey of self-reflection in which

Wolff forces the reader to leap back and forth between Vietnam and earlier events in the United States. Narrative time fluctuates between the year of Toby's Vietnam service and the circumstances that led him there.

A series of individual vignettes dominate the narrative and provide it with structure. The first is the hare-brained plan Toby shares with Sergeant Benet on Thanksgiving Day in 1967 to acquire a large color television set. The absurdity of their desire to watch a *Bonanza* special that evening, in the middle of war-torn Vietnam, is equaled only by the illegality of their action. They trade contraband rifles for the television set and deceive a brutish captain at the guard shack. As Wolff recalls this foolhardy enterprise, his thoughts return to the circumstances leading to his receipt of the "safe" post in My Tho, to his early days in the town, and to Sergeant Benet's background and character. He acknowledges his own weakness and lack of integrity as he spontaneously promises the newly acquired television set to a Vietnamese woman and her son and then takes the set back home to watch *Bonanza* instead.

In the sad tale of Canh Cho, Toby's Vietnamese dog, the narrator recognizes his unequal relationship with his South Vietnamese allies, who see humorously through Toby's uniform to his human weaknesses. All too conscious of the Americans' affection for dogs and aversion to eating them, the Vietnamese tease Toby by naming the beast Canh Cho, which means "dog stew." In order to save the pup from the flames of the cooking fire, Toby has to pull rank. Afterward, he suffers from gestures and jokes of culinary innuendo whenever the Vietnamese see him with Canh Cho. The pathos and irony of the situation reaches maturity only when Toby's tour of duty at My Tho is up and he shares his final meal with his Vietnamese colleagues. Like Atreus in Greek mythology, Toby learns too late that the menu includes his old friend Canh Cho. Unlike Atreus, and to Toby's credit, he manages to continue the meal and even to enjoy it.

Just before the Tet Offensive, Toby's father sends his son a belated Christmas card in which he mentions how proud he is of Toby. This card rouses another tale, one that takes Toby back to his final days in the United States and the unsatisfying farewell between father and son. Toby had not seen his father for years, partly because the older man had spent several years in prison for fraud and partly because Toby and his brother had been avoiding him. Nevertheless, while waiting in San Francisco for his flight to Vietnam, Toby looks up his father. The encounter is filled with pained silences and an inability to communicate.

As he recalls his father's card and farewell, Toby also remembers another father-son relationship, one in stark contrast to his own. On the same trip to San Francisco, Toby and an army buddy named Stu Hoffman wander aimlessly in San Francisco and find their way to Haight-Ashbury, where they encounter troops of hugging flower children. They dine with Stu's father, who, like the hippies, clearly opposes the war and resents sacrificing his son to the cause. It comes as no surprise to Toby that Stu fails to report for his bus to the airport the next morning and is listed as a probable deserter. For Toby, Stu's disappearance is less a commentary on the war than it is on fathers. On the bus trip to the airport, he hallucinates a hijacking by fathers of the

Vietnam recruits, having come to rescue their sons and take them home. It is only after the war, when Toby visits his father in San Francisco again, that father and son reach an understanding and an equilibrium.

Toby's relationship with his father is not the only relationship that frames *In Pharaoh's Army*. Another one is his friendship with Hugh Pierce, the flight-school buddy who becomes Toby's best friend and soul mate. Hugh is shipped to Vietnam first. Several months before his own tour of duty begins, Toby finds Hugh's name listed in the newspaper among the dead. The pain of Hugh's death continues to haunt Toby, not only during his stay in Vietnam but also afterward.

In fact, it is recollection of Hugh that draws Toby, the character in *In Pharaoh's Army*, back into identity with his creator, the middle-aged Tobias Wolff. As he brings these memoirs to a close, Wolff describes how he still remembers Hugh. At the same time, he imagines his dead friend not as he was in 1967, but as he might have lived decades later, as the father of a young son and the child of aging parents. Memory replaces might-have-been as Wolff abandons his thoughts of a middle age that Hugh never lived to see and ends his memoir with recollections of a youthful Hugh jumping out of a training airplane while shouting, "Are we having fun?" So, in a masterful stroke, Wolff the writer merges past and present. Hugh's joyful leap from the airplane is identified with his leap from life into Wolff's memory. The dead Hugh is revived in the imagination of his old friend.

Toby himself represents a similar reincarnation. In writing these memoirs, Wolff leaps back into his past and connects with his own youthful dreams, aspirations, and anxieties. The young Toby had always yearned to be a writer. *In Pharaoh's Army* confirms that the mature Wolff has satisfied these hopes.

Thomas J. Sienkewicz

Sources for Further Study

American Heritage. XV, November, 1994, p. 120.
Boston Globe. October 23, 1994, p. 14.
Library Journal. CXIX, October 15, 1994, p. 66.
Los Angeles Times Book Review. October 16, 1994, p. 3.
The Nation. CCLIX, November 21, 1994, p. 618.
New Statesman and Society. VII, December 9, 1994, p. 39.
The New York Times Book Review. XCIX, November 27, 1994, p. 10.
Newsday. October 16, 1994, p. F33.
Newsweek. CXXIV, October 24, 1994, p. 77.
Publishers Weekly. CCXLI, October 24, 1994, p. 45.
Time. CXLIV, October 31, 1994, p. 81.
Virginian-Pilot. December 4, 1994, p. J2.

IN SEARCH OF EQUALITY
The Chinese Struggle Against Discrimination in Nineteenth-Century America

Author: Charles J. McClain
Publisher: University of California Press (Berkeley). 385 pp. $35.00
Type of work: History
Time: 1850-1900
Locale: California

Refuting the stereotypical image of the Chinese as passive victims of discrimination, this well-documented study shows that from the outset they were persistent and resourceful in seeking redress in the courts

In the textbook version of American history a generation ago, Chinese Americans were virtually invisible. Indeed, as Charles McClain observes in the introduction to this invaluable study, even the scholarly works that focused on the first Chinese immigrants to the United States tended to view them as curiously passive, stoical victims of discrimination—if not invisible, still far from being seen as actors on the stage of history. Increasingly, however, as McClain notes, scholars have sought "to see the Chinese more as subjects and shapers than as objects of history." In that vein, he argues that "the conventional wisdom concerning the Chinese and their supposed political backwardness needs to be stood on its head. . . . Far from being passive or docile in the face of official mistreatment, they reacted with indignation to it and more often than not sought redress in the courts."

By chronicling the tenacious resistance against discrimination carried out by the Chinese and their lawyers in nineteenth century America, McClain greatly enriches our understanding of the early Chinese American community. At the same time, he situates the Chinese experience in a larger historical context. "To ignore Chinese legal initiatives," McClain writes, "is . . . to ignore an important facet of U.S. constitutional history in general. The cases brought by the Chinese raised immensely interesting questions of constitutional and statutory interpretation. Many of them contributed significantly to the molding of American constitutional jurisprudence."

Although a handful of Chinese had settled on the East Coast earlier in the nineteenth century, the first substantial Chinese immigration to the United States was spurred by the Gold Rush of 1849 and was heavily concentrated in California. Almost from the beginning, the Chinese had to contend with strong opposition to their presence, manifested both by intimidation and violence and by discriminatory legislation.

McClain traces the Chinese struggle against discrimination from roughly 1850 to 1900, by which time Japanese immigration had become the focus of nativist sentiment. His study is divided into four parts. Part 1 surveys the first anti-Chinese laws in California, enacted in the 1850's and 1860's, and the vigorous Chinese response; this is followed by a detailed account of a number of test cases from the 1870's.

Parts 2 and 3 are devoted to the 1880's: Part 2 deals with cases in which the Chinese sought equal protection of the law as guaranteed by the Fourteenth Amendment, while part 3 chiefly centers on attempts by the Chinese to challenge federal exclusion laws. (The Chinese Exclusion Act of 1882 marked the first time that entry to the United States was restricted on the basis of race or ethnicity; it was followed by a series of federal acts that further limited Chinese immigration.) Under the heading "Century's End: Last Episodes of Sinophobia," part 4 analyzes the case of *In re Lee Sing* (1890), in which the Chinese successfully challenged a San Francisco ordinance enforcing residential segregation, and an outbreak of bubonic plague in San Francisco in 1900, as a result of which the Chinese were once again forced to fight for equal protection.

A handful of the cases McClain discusses will already be well known to students of constitutional history—most notably *Yick Wo v. Hopkins* (1886). This case grew out of several San Francisco laundry ordinances adopted in the early 1880's. Beginning in the 1870's, the many Chinese-operated laundries in San Francisco had drawn the attention of nativists. Several ordinances clearly directed against Chinese laundrymen were tested in court and found unconstitutional, only to be followed by new ordinances with the same aim.

A serious fire which broke out in a Chinese laundry in 1880 provided the pretext for regulations intended to put the Chinese out of the laundry business altogether. The law required that all new buildings erected for use as laundries must be constructed of brick or stone. Already existing laundries—except those made of brick or stone—could not continue to operate without having obtained a permit from the board of supervisors. Virtually all of the Chinese laundries were in wooden buildings. Some two hundred Chinese laundrymen applied for a permit to continue in business; all were denied. Meanwhile, more than eighty Caucasian-owned laundries in wooden structures were allowed to carry on business as usual.

Yick Wo, who had operated a laundry at the same location for twenty-two years, applied for a permit and was denied. Like a number of other Chinese laundrymen, he continued to operate his business in defiance of the law; he was arrested and convicted in August, 1885. His case went all the way to the U.S. Supreme Court, which handed down its decision in May, 1886. Finding in favor of Yick Wo, the Court ruled that the disparity in treatment of Chinese-owned and Caucasian-owned laundries rendered the San Francisco ordinances unconstitutional. The decision established an important principle in interpretation of the Fourteenth Amendment: "that racially discriminatory enforcement of the law offended the constitutional mandate of equal protection just as much as did a law that discriminated in its terms."

While *Yick Wo* has long held a significant place in constitutional history, most of the cases McClain discusses will be known only to specialists in Asian American Studies. He marvels at the extent to which this history remains unknown: "The Chinese readiness to resort to the courts to remedy perceived wrongs is an aspect of their experience in the United States barely touched on in the published literature. Yet it is surely one of the most salient and defining features of that experience."

In filling that lacuna, McClain's book implicitly makes a powerful case for the kind of revisionary history that has drawn the fire of conservatives in recent years—most emphatically following the release of the first national standards for American history, in October, 1994. Lynne Cheney, former director of the National Endowment for the Humanities, denounced the standards as a "travesty," charging that they omitted important figures and topics from the traditional American history curriculum in favor of a politically correct agenda. Cheney wrote that, "from this document, you'd think we were a nation that only experienced oppression and failure." Others—not all of them conservatives—echoed Cheney's criticisms; in turn, scholars and educators who had participated in the creation of the standards issued rebuttals.

The controversy over the standards is important, for they are likely to exert a powerful influence on the teaching of American history in the next generation. Much of the debate, however, is mere rhetorical posturing. A book such as McClain's helps to clarify the issues involved in deciding how the nation's story should be told. What is essential? What can be omitted? What overarching framework will govern the telling? Cheney and other vocal critics of the standards have made much of the omission of figures such as Paul Revere, Daniel Webster, Robert E. Lee, and Thomas Edison—all white males and thus dispensable in the revisionists' judgment. But what about the gaps in "traditional" histories of America?

At a time when the United States has experienced an enormous increase in immigration (the influx of immigrants—legal and illegal—and refugees since the landmark Immigration and Nationality Act of 1965 exceeds even the totals for the comparable peak period early in the twentieth century), especially from Asia, it is essential to include in the curriculum the experience of groups such as the Chinese Americans. As McClain shows, the "new history" can deepen our understanding of some of the classic themes of American history—here in particular the remarkable role of constitutional interpretation in shaping American society as it exists in the late twentieth century.

Yet if the criticisms of the national standards for American history—and, more broadly, the approach to history they represent—are in some respects misguided, in other respects they are fully justified. The problem with much revisionist history is not that it brings the experience of women and minorities, for example, into greater prominence. The problem is that its telling of the American story is badly skewed by the contemporary ideology of victimhood.

The historical experience presented in McClain's book defies reduction to a simplistic morality tale. The old rosily idealistic vision of America greeting immigrants with open arms does not fit the evidence of *In Search of Equality*, but neither do the currently fashionable one-sided jeremiads about America's legacy of racism and violence. By their immediate recourse to the American legal system (for which there was no counterpart in their homeland), the early Chinese immigrants decisively disproved one of the prime contentions of the anti-Chinese movement: that the Chinese were so utterly foreign to "our" culture that they could never be assimilated. At the same time, the responses of the courts, which were often—though not always—

responsive to Chinese claims of injustice, refutes the myth of a monolithic discriminatory society. In short, *In Search of Equality* does what good history often does: upsets preconceptions all around.

John Wilson

Sources for Further Study

Choice. XXXII, October, 1994, p. 354.
San Francisco Chronicle. October 23, 1994, p. REV9.

IN THE LAKE OF THE WOODS

Author: Tim O'Brien (1946-)
Publisher: Houghton Mifflin/Seymour Lawrence (Boston). 306 pp. $21.95
Type of work: Novel
Time: 1986 and late 1960's
Locale: Minnesota and Vietnam

Centering on the sudden disappearance of the wife of a Minnesota politician and Vietnam veteran, this novel explores the haunted past of the veteran and his country, and the dark side of human nature

Principal characters:
JOHN WADE, a prominent Minnesota politician, amateur magician, and veteran of the My Lai massacre during the Vietnam War
KATHY WADE, his wife, who vanishes without a trace during their vacation in the northern Minnesota wilderness
LIEUTENANT WILLIAM CALLEY, the real-life officer responsible for the My Lai massacre; Wade's commanding officer in this novel

Tim O'Brien's novel *Going After Cacciato* (1978), which won the National Book Award, and his collection of stories *The Things They Carried* (1990), chosen by *The New York Times* editors as one of the best books of 1990, have established him as one of the finest fiction writers to explore the Vietnam War and the psychological scars that left their marks on many combatants, including O'Brien himself.

The central action of *Going After Cacciato* is escape: The title character simply decides one day to walk away from the war, and his squad pursues him through the dense Vietnam jungles and across Europe, all the way to Paris. The narrative is drenched in realistic detail, but it becomes increasingly dreamlike as the action moves away from the jungles.

The Things They Carried is also about escape, or, more precisely, what cannot be escaped. In the autobiographical episode "On the Rainy River," O'Brien explains, with painful honesty, why he reported for duty after being drafted instead of fleeing to Canada, as he wanted to do. He went to Vietnam, he says, because he was a coward; because he was too weak to withstand the loss of love and respect that would have resulted from dodging the draft. Unlike a Cacciato, O'Brien himself could not walk away from military duty with a smile on his face; he could only imagine doing so. As he relates so vividly in the *The Things They Carried*, those who fought in Vietnam carried a heavy burden during and after the war. While in combat they bore with them, in addition to the physical implements of war, powerful emotions: fear, grief, anger, and guilt. After their tour of duty, the survivors left Vietnam, but Vietnam remained in them; "They all carried ghosts."

In the Lake of the Woods is also about ghosts, personal and national, and about the impossibility of escaping them. The central character, John Wade, has much in common with O'Brien himself: like O'Brien, Wade grew up in Minnesota; like O'Brien, he went to Vietnam because he feared losing the love of his family and friends if he did not serve; like O'Brien, he did "bad things" in the war in order to be loved and respected by his comrades in arms; like O'Brien, he cannot escape the past. Yet Wade is not O'Brien. Whereas O'Brien confronts his ghosts through the act of writing—exposing his guilt and shame for public view—Wade is an expert at suppressing the past and at making all disagreeable memories disappear.

Disappearance is a major motif in the novel. Wade, who is nicknamed Sorcerer, is an amateur magician. In his youth, his magic tricks helped him escape the pain caused by his alcoholic father's verbal abuse and eventual suicide (he hanged himself when Sorcerer was fourteen). Sorcerer learns at an early age that magic is power: the power to deceive, trick, and manipulate others. In Vietnam, Sorcerer made entire villages disappear with a few magic words and heavy explosives; after the My Lai slaughter—which O'Brien renders in vivid, gory detail—Wade makes his name disappear from the company roster. Back in the United States, he puts his magic and trickery to use as a politician; he is on the verge of winning a seat in the United States Senate when the Vietnam past that he has buried deep inside his mind comes back to haunt him. The discovery and news reports of his participation in the My Lai incident cost him the election.

O'Brien reveals Wade's haunted past in bits and pieces. The novel opens in its present time frame (1986) with Wade and his wife, Kathy, trying to cope with the election defeat by secluding themselves at a cottage at the Lake of the Woods in the northern Minnesota wilderness. In love since college, when John compulsively spied on her, they now try to deceive themselves into believing that they can forget the past and build a new future out of the ashes of the defeat; but strong tension and anxiety run just beneath the placid surface of their daily routines. There have been too many secrets and betrayals. The Lake of the Woods, with its "secret channels and portages and bays and tangled forests," thus functions as a metaphor for the Wades's psychological state.

One morning Kathy vanishes from the cottage, without leaving a trace. Much of the subsequent narrative focuses on her disappearance: Did she get lost in the wilderness or accidentally drown? Did she commit suicide? Did she run out on Sorcerer? Perhaps Sorcerer made her disappear, and is now concealing that terrible fact from himself. The stage is set for a gripping mystery drama. This is not, however, a mystery novel, at least not in the conventional sense, because O'Brien refuses to solve the mystery; there is no climactic discovery or denouement to satisfy the reader's curiosity. Like life itself, *In the Lake of the Woods* is a fascinating and frustrating mystery without any absolute truth. O'Brien emphasizes that what humans call "facts" and "truth" are mental constructions that can never be isolated from the perceiver's point of view; just as the angle of light from the sun determines the color of the Lake of the Woods, the author's angle of vision shapes the reality projected in a novel. As in his earlier works, O'Brien intentionally blurs the boundary between fact and fiction, suggesting that the latter can be more truthful than the former.

Toward the end of the novel, readers are told that everything that has been related is hypothesis. Several of the chapters in fact bear the title "Hypothesis." In them,

O'Brien dramatizes possible scenes of Kathy's disappearance—she gets lost in the Lake in the Woods, she is murdered by John, and so forth. Other chapters are titled "Evidence." The evidence in each includes testimony about John and Kathy by their family, friends, and acquaintances—testimony that is inconclusive and often contradictory. Similarly, the material facts of the case cannot prove or disprove any of the hypotheses. The "Evidence" chapters, moreover, do not restrict themselves to the novel's fictional world, for they contain quotations from Miguel de Cervantes, Fyodor Dostoevski, Nathaniel Hawthorne, Sigmund Freud, Harry Houdini, Richard Nixon, Woodrow Wilson, and a host of other novelists, historians, psychologists, and famous personages. All the quotations are cited in footnotes, as if they were part of a scholarly book rather than a novel. Thus the "evidence" reaches out into the "real" world of history. Yet history, as the quotations and source notes signify, is itself textual, a verbal reconstruction of past experience that is no longer immediately accessible. By embedding his novel in the intertextual web of other narratives that comment on war and war crimes, evil, love, and other ideas that are at the core of *In the Lake of the Woods*, O'Brien paradoxically makes his fiction a part of history and of the "real" world.

The "Evidence" chapters also contain footnote comments by O'Brien himself, or rather by his persona, which discuss the writing of the novel and express opinions on the issues it raises. In his final self-reflexive footnote, O'Brien explains why he refuses to solve the mystery he has created: "Nothing is fixed, nothing is solved. The facts, such as they are, finally spin off into the void of things missing, the inconclusiveness of conclusion. Mystery finally claims us. Who are we? Where do we go?"

O'Brien's refusal to provide a tidy ending to his tale; his insistence that all truth is a mental construction and therefore never "universal"; his mixing of genres and intentional blurring of the lines between fact and fiction; his self-reflexive footnotes—all these are common traits of the postmodernist novel, for example, E. L. Doctorow's *Ragtime* (1975) or John Fowles's *The French Lieutenant's Woman* (1969). Readers unacquainted with or hostile toward postmodernism might therefore lose their bearings in *In the Lake of the Woods*.

Even those whose taste leans toward traditional realism will be gripped by O'Brien's brutally realistic descriptions of Vietnam, which are supplemented by the appalling testimony taken from transcripts of Lieutenant William Calley's court-martial proceedings, and from historical documents detailing inhumane acts in other wars. Any lover of fiction will appreciate the novel's splendid dialogue, especially the dialogue that suggests more than it explicitly states (in this regard, O'Brien rivals another teller of love-and-war stories, Ernest Hemingway). O'Brien also has a gift for startling images, such as that of two snakes swallowing each other (the image is a metaphor of John and Kathy's self-devouring love for one another). Most readers will be captivated by the novel's unflinching glimpses into the dark side of human nature, a dark side that is often brought into action by feelings of love rather than hate. Ironically, this postmodernist novel, which questions the existence of objective truth, seems almost unbearably true at times.

In the Lake of the Woods closes with the question of whether John Wade was a monster or merely a man. That question points to a problematic issue in the novel. On the one hand, O'Brien emphasizes that Sorcerer got lost in the moral jungle long before he went to Vietnam; his obsessive need for love and his bent toward secrecy and deceit stem from his relationship with his alcoholic father and from the father's suicide. On the other hand, if Sorcerer's psychological problems are rooted in his particular childhood experiences, then why does O'Brien suggest at other points in the narrative that Sorcerer is the embodiment of a dark self that lurks within all human beings? The novel seems to be at odds with itself as to whether Wade is to be viewed as a figure of abnormal psychology or as universal human nature.

In 1994, O'Brien, who had patrolled the My Lai area the year after Calley's company committed the atrocities there, returned to Vietnam and to My Lai itself. Writing about the trip in *The New York Times Magazine* (October 2, 1994), O'Brien states that the Vietnam War was like a long horror film that would not end for him, and that he hoped his return to the site of his painful memories would "make the bad pictures go away." *In the Lake of the Woods*, which took O'Brien six years to write, is an imaginative return to the tragedy of Vietnam, with the same purpose as the physical trip: to make the bad pictures go away, to finally put to rest the ghosts that have haunted him, and his country, since his return from that war. Whether the novel can perform that magic feat must remain a mystery.

Lawrence J. Oliver

Sources for Further Study

The Atlantic. CCLXXIV, November, 1994, p. 46.
Booklist. XC, August, 1994, p. 1992.
Library Journal. CXIX, August, 1994, p. 132.
Los Angeles Times Book Review. October 2, 1994, p. 3.
The New York Times Book Review. XCIX, October 9, 1994, p. 1.
The New Yorker. LXX, October 24, 1994, p. 111.
Newsweek. CXXIV, October 24, 1994, p. 77.
Publishers Weekly. CCXLI, July 11, 1994, p. 61.
Time. CXLIV, October 24, 1994, p. 74.
The Washington Post Book World. XXIV, September 25, 1994, p. 5.

IN THE PALACE OF THE MOVIE KING

Author: Hortense Calisher (1911-)
Publisher: Random House (New York). 448 pp. $25.00
Type of work: Novel
Time: The last decades of the twentieth century
Locale: Eastern Europe and the United States

The adventures of a European director provide the author with a means to meditate on the meanings of art, politics, geography, and life from the perspectives of outsiders

Principal characters:
PAUL GONCHEV, the protagonist, a film director and expatriate
VUKISCA GONCHEV, his wife, a former actress
ROKO, his Japanese translator and mistress
DANILO, Vukisca's twin brother
JOHN PERKINS PFIZE, an agent of "the Department," who monitors Paul's American experiences
LAURA GONCHEV, Paul and Vukisca's daughter, who emigrates to America
KLEMENT GONCHEV, Paul and Vukisca's son, who betrays his mother during her escape attempt
MALKOFF, a Russian émigré scientist who acts as Paul's host in California and his guide to American culture

Hortense Calisher is the author of more than twenty books, a well-respected teacher and recipient of two Guggenheims, a past president of PEN, and a member of the American Academy and Institute of Arts and Letters. Despite her achievements, she has not really received the critical attention that her work deserves and is not as well-known as one might expect. In addition, Calisher has consistently written books about the life of ideas and uses a complex and ambiguous style; these characteristics, while no doubt having a negative effect on the numbers of her readers, make her novels, in particular, treasures worth excavating. *In the Palace of the Movie King* is no exception.

Calisher novels generally explore the yearning for a sense of place in the complex multiverse of the twentieth century. *In the Palace of the Movie King* adds a postmodern twist to this theme by focusing on a hero whose identity is consistently marginal and whose experiences are always shaped by his understandings of the realities of borders—geographical, emotional, and interpersonal. Central to this work—and to a number of others in Calisher's oeuvre, in particular the novels *Textures of Life* (1963) and *Queenie* (1971) and the biographical *Herself* (1972)—is the process of the journey made by a protagonist. Calisher's main characters find themselves moving from an existence in which order is created and enforced by imaginative philosophies or emotional aloofness to life in a world of perpetual upheaval where bewildering and challenging realities must be engaged.

In the Palace of the Movie King is a novel of quintessential social drama, clearly inspired by the work of Slavic writers such as Milan Kundera, Václav Havel, Danilo Kiš, Mikhail Bulgakov, and Witold Gombrowicz. The term "Kafkaesque," referring to a particular perspective on the modern condition, is also certainly applicable to this novel. Like many of the works of the Czech writer Franz Kafka, this narrative is peopled by characters who find themselves at the mercies of bureaucracies and systems that emphasize the frailty and tenuousness of their expectations and experiences.

In the Palace of the Movie King also calls to mind Henrik Ibsen's play *Peer Gynt* (first presented in 1867), which inspired Edvard Grieg's incidental music of the same name (the two were first played together in 1876). Both the play and the musical work are represented in the novel. Like Ibsen's play, Calisher's book is episodic, following a picaresque, egocentric hero on a physical and emotional odyssey that involves a variety of adventures all over the world. While the hero wanders, his love waits and suffers. The play, the music, and the novel end with the hero reunited with his true love, basking in her tender affection.

Paul Gonchev is born in Vladivostok, grows up in Japan, and makes films about European cities he has never visited at a mountain studio he names Elsinore, built for him in Albania. Within this environment, he is king of all he surveys, manipulating all of his interactions with others and directing the careers of his students as well as his own films. In the face of changing political and social realities, his wife arranges to have him "hijacked" by Americans. He is so traumatized by this experience that he is unable to speak any of the seven languages he knows except the Japanese of his boyhood. John Perkins Pfize, his "Department" contact and the engineer of his "escape," arranges for the services of an interpreter, the lovely Roko, who becomes Paul's mistress. Paul becomes a professional dissident, spending time in California with the cynical Malkoff and his wife, Daria, and experiencing his first earthquake. At last, he ends up in New York, where his daughter Laura has found sanctuary and a boyfriend.

His wife, Vukisca, is imprisoned in Albania after a botched escape attempt during which she is forced to shoot her son, Klement, who does not want her to defect. Vukisca is rescued by her twin brother Danilo, who switches places with her. Disguised as Danilo, she is spirited out of the country and finally reunited with Paul in New York City during the marriage ceremony of Roko and her Korean groom. Paul's return to his beloved and his attachment to her over any political or artistic allegiance reveal the limitations of adventuring and the meaninglessness of the boundaries and borders he has both constructed and crossed.

Music is an important element of the novel. Paul's father was a concert pianist, and there are a number of references to specific pieces and musical experiences. As a matter of fact, the title of the book is a reference to a movement in Grieg's *Peer Gynt* entitled "In the Hall of the Mountain King," and refers to scenes in which Peer Gynt encounters an elf-king and his daughter, whom he marries and deserts, and the Great Boyg, who symbolizes the complex paradoxes of life.

There is a symphonic, even operatic, quality to the novel, and its organization has much in common with the structure of a fugue. *In the Palace of the Movie King* is divided into two main sections, each with a slightly different focus. The first is concerned with Paul as a film director of uncertain citizenship who is content with his life even while he realizes its ritualistic and artificial qualities; the second part, after his kidnapping, shows the unraveling of his sense of purpose and connectedness, the negative effect of his "defection" on his family, and finally the resolution of his quest for accommodation and order in his reunion with Vukisca. The chapters act as organizational and thematic subdivisions, and the threads of various ideas and images reappear and entwine as variations on the novel's central motifs.

Plot, as such, is not particularly important to this novel. Paul Gonchev undertakes both psychic and physical journeys, though not always simultaneously, nor especially willingly. He is always at the center of the action even when he is not present, and the significance of any of the other characters is measured in relation to Paul's experiences and interpretations. The narrative develops out of the behaviors of each character and focuses on the inconsistencies, paradoxes, and unexpected meanings that accompany and result from each action and reaction.

The author's voice and commentary are central elements of the novel. The book opens with a five-page prologue that describes Gonchev from an unidentified third-person perspective. Narrative commentary emphasizes the ideas, decisions, and accidents that have impact on the lives of the characters. Calisher develops the characters in a thematic way, rather than analyzing their emotions in any great depth. There is an almost cinematic quality to the narrative, as though the author and readers were the audience at a screening of Paul Gonchev's life. The effect is an elegant detachment that is a matter of style as much as narrative.

While Paul is, at least, nominally a European film director who has adventures and experiences in several nations, finally ending up in the United States, the novel is really an extended meditation on the meanings of place, politics, art, language, and relationships. This is basically an existential novel, and Calisher's examination of a variety of human complexities is contextualized within the larger forces of modern life such as psychology, history, and philosophy. Themes of distance and difference run through the entire novel. Paul is painfully aware of his own marginality. As a matter of fact, in the opening chapters, it is clear that he has cultivated and refined "outsiderness" to a fine art and uses it as a shield in his dealings with others. Gradually, he comes to understand this separateness as a basic human quality, not reserved for only exiles and émigrés. Paul spends considerable time and effort trying to understand the reasons for this isolation and its effects, but he is ultimately unable to "arrange" a satisfactory system of explanations or meanings.

"Arrangement" is a significant word and an important theme in *In the Palace of the Movie King*. Paul's identity as "the Director" in the novel's first section is not merely a matter of film vocabulary. His responsibilities and privileges are clearly related to his desire and ability to orchestrate and command assemblies of crews, props, committees, even entire film-lot city facades. Once he has been "kidnapped" and finds his way to the United States, he realizes the futility and falseness of an arranged/arrangeable environment. Paul and his wife decide to live in America, and to embrace the uncertainties and dislocations of life that are illustrated in American speech, political affairs, ideology, and even in landscape, wonderfully delineated in a description of a California earthquake.

There is a deceptive naturalism to the novel, as in the passage devoted to the earthquake, which reflects the complexities of the concepts and experiences with which Calisher is concerned. Although the novel is almost photographic in its realism, there are subtle and beguiling metaphoric developments in *In the Palace of the Movie King*, which can overwhelm the unwary reader. In this book, as in much of Calisher's work, words often carry multiple meanings, and simple sentences must be read twice. The manipulation of language and words and the inadequacies of speech as a form of communication are recurrent themes. Seemingly simple conversations are always cryptic. For example, early in part 1, Paul has a ritualistic exchange with his assistant, whom he knows to be a spy who records his every word and deed. The conversation follows predictable lines as Paul carries on a very different exchange with the man in his imagination. Words cannot be trusted. Gonchev speaks Japanese, English, Serbian, and Russian, yet chooses film and images, rather than literature and language, as his medium of expression.

In the Palace of the Movie King is an expertly constructed work. In the character of Paul Gonchev, Calisher takes full advantage of her remarkable powers of observation and expression to create delicate nuances of scene and characterization. In some ways, *In the Palace of the Movie King* reads like a novel by Henry James or Marcel Proust, with elegant and often rarefied sentences devoted to organizing and justifying the worldviews and psyches of the characters. At the same time, however, this is a novel that is clearly rooted in the modern consciousness, perhaps even in postmodernism. The narrative's conflicts center in an awareness of the impossibility of truly communicating individual experience, and the frustration and exhilaration that accompany any effort to make sense of the human condition. This is the paradox of Paul Gonchev's story and also the center of its power. How might people unite and make sense of the worlds of art and politics, the private and the public, the old and the new? What will personal experiences ultimately mean to humans, as individuals and as a species?

J. R. Donath

Sources for Further Study

Booklist. XC, September 15, 1993, p. 126.
Kirkus Reviews. LXI, October 1, 1993, p. 1217.
Library Journal. CXVIII, August, 1993, p. 148.
Los Angeles Times. April 4, 1994, p. E6.
The New York Times Book Review. XCIX, February 20, 1994, p. 12.
Publishers Weekly. CCXL, October 11, 1993, p. 69.
The Review of Contemporary Fiction. XIV, Spring, 1994, p. 216.
The Washington Post. February 11, 1994, p. B2.

IN THE TENNESSEE COUNTRY

Author: Peter Taylor (1917-1994)
Publisher: Alfred A. Knopf (New York). 226 pp. $21.00
Type of work: Novel
Time: 1916 to the 1990's
Locale: Tennessee and various college campuses

A sheltered boy is frightened by an older, less conventional cousin and remains obsessed with the other man throughout his life

Principal characters:
NATHAN TUCKER LONGFORT, the narrator, a scion of a prominent Tennessee family, an art critic, and a failed artist
MELISSA LONGFORT, his wife, a writer
AUBREY TUCKER BRADSHAW, the illegitimate son of his granduncle, a scapegrace and gigolo
GERTRUDE "TRUDIE" TUCKER LONGFORT, his solicitous mother, the daughter of a United States Senator
AUNT BERTIE and AUNT FELICIA, Trudie Longfort's sisters and Nathan's protective aunts
BRAXTON "BRAX" BRAGG LONGFORT, the youngest of Nathan's four children, an artist

Peter Taylor was for years regarded by critics as the premier writer of short stories during the latter third of the twentieth century. Shortly before his death late in 1994, he published his second novel, *In the Tennessee Country*. Like much of his earlier fiction, this novel is set in his native Tennessee; also like most of his earlier fiction, it is retrospective, presenting as a central figure a person who looks back over significant events in his life, regretting some, comforted by others. Like all of Taylor's fiction, *In the Tennessee Country* is low-keyed, beautifully crafted, and deeply perceptive.

On the funeral train bearing the body of Senator Nathan Tucker, former governor of Tennessee, from Washington back to his native state for burial, the senator's four-year-old grandson and namesake, Nathan Tucker Longfort, is struck by the animosity in the look given him by a mourner in his early twenties. The man, Aubrey Bradshaw, remains in Nathan's memory as stories about the older man accumulate in his mind. Aubrey, bastard son of the senator's brother and a hill girl, had served as a kind of secretary to the elder Nathan Tucker when the politician was governor and had accompanied his uncle to Washington for his term in the United States Senate. Aubrey had paid court to each of the governor's three daughters; he had especially been a suitor of Nathan's mother while she was a teenager and had planned to elope with her. In the end, the elopement did not take place, and Aubrey left Tennessee—one of many men who simply disappeared and did not return. He reappeared secretly in Tennessee only for family funerals, at which he did not make himself known to his relatives.

Nathan Tucker Longfort grew up in households dominated by women. His father sickened and died when Nathan was still a boy, and the husbands of both of his aunts also met early deaths. The men in the family left him only the memory of lives dominated by regrets at their having missed the heroics of the Civil War.

Trudie Longfort made sure that her only child was looked after. She and her older sisters sheltered him from harsh realities and encouraged his artistic talent, hoping that he would become a famous painter. In grade school, a strong and athletic older boy took Nathan under his wing and taught him how to play baseball and football, so that the younger boy was accepted by his youthful peers. When he was old enough, Nathan was sent to a private boarding school; during these years he spent his weekends with his aunts and his mother, still under their care and guidance.

When the time came after his graduation from the University of Virginia, Nathan found an appropriate wife in Melissa, who would eventually reserve a corner of her life for the writing of short fiction, but who for the most part subordinated her own ambitions to take care of Nathan and supervise the rearing of their three sons and daughter. For most of his adult life, Nathan would continue to paint, reserving a time every morning to go to his studio for an uninterrupted hour or two, but he early gave up the notion of devoting his life to his own art, choosing instead a career as an art critic and writer about art.

This career, at which he was eminently successful, provided Nathan with increasingly important positions at various colleges and universities, from Indiana University and Kenyon College to the University of Virginia; he was in sufficient demand to be able to reject offers from Harvard and Yale universities. His early success, Nathan came to believe, was the source of envy and antagonism from faculty colleagues, and he welcomed the friendly overtures of the president of one of his universities. Realizing that he had come to the president's attention because of his growing reputation in the academic world, Nathan nevertheless became a supporter of the president during some difficult times. His position during a particularly bitter controversy (based closely on an episode observed by Taylor at Ohio State University) caused great resentment among his colleagues and led to his accepting a position elsewhere.

Nathan's special relationship with his youngest son, Brax, developed early. Brax alone in the family felt free to go to Nathan's studio in the mornings when his father was painting, and Nathan allowed him to stay. Nathan, in his recollections, hardly seems to know the names of his other sons, but Brax is frequently present in his thoughts. Brax's own interest in painting came in part from his early experiences, but his abilities and goals were far beyond Nathan's limited aspirations. The father never tried to teach his son anything about painting, nor did the son ask for any instruction, as if he knew that he would learn only the value of work habits from the older man.

Nathan's growing obsession with his cousin Aubrey led to an intense disagreement with Melissa and with Brax. The young son, as he moved away from his family and forged his own successful career, became less and less tolerant of Nathan's continuing references to Aubrey and his attempts to follow his older cousin's career. It is clear that Brax has some of the same need for independence from the family that led to Aubrey's self-exile. He seems to believe that Nathan's obsession in some way reflects a need to prevent his son from following in Aubrey's footsteps. Ironically, Brax, living in Washington, D.C., strikes up an acquaintance with a stranger who turns out to be

Aubrey Bradshaw. Eventually, Brax brings his father to see the older man, hospitalized and poor.

The fact that Aubrey is indigent is something of a surprise to Nathan. When the older man had appeared at family funerals, he had seemed well dressed and prosperous. In the newspaper pictures Aubrey appeared in, always in the company of a wealthy woman, he had also seemed confident and well-to-do. Once Nathan sees him, however, it becomes clear that the rumors he had heard that Aubrey was a gigolo, dancing attendance on rich older women, were all true. Nathan makes several trips to Washington to see his cousin and learns about his family history from the viewpoint of a man who chose to live apart from what he saw as the suffocating family. Nathan makes plans to pay the hospital bills and to take Aubrey back to Charlottesville to live with him and Melissa.

In the climactic scene, Aubrey rejects Nathan's offers of help. He has made arrangements to marry one of his still fascinated older women, who will pay his bills and give him a place to live for whatever remains of his life. In a bitter outburst, Aubrey makes it clear that he has always resented the comfortable, carefully arranged world in which Nathan has spent his life. His attempt to induce Trudie to elope with him and leave that life behind was a manifestation of that resentment; his glaring look at Nathan on the senator's funeral train reflected his hatred of the life to which Trudie had remained bound. Nathan, in a belated understanding of his own life, recognizes that the security his mother and aunts had provided and that he had relied on has deprived him of the independence and daring that could have led him to success as a painter. That success, in turn, would have provided him with the fulfillment that his criticism and academic success have failed to give.

In the Tennessee Country is nicely balanced between the opposing poles of Senator Nathan Tucker's world and that of Aubrey Bradshaw, the senator's illegitimate nephew. The senator never appears in the novel except in the memories of his daughters, but the public nature of his success and the sense of family pride that he engendered remain of great significance to his grandson. More than anything else, the respectability demanded of a Southern politician and his family during the period between the two world wars makes it nearly inevitable that Nathan would accept the coddling and careful attentions of his mother and aunts, that he would choose an "appropriate" woman for a wife, and that his career would be based on writing about other people's art rather than on breaking artistic ground on his own.

It is clear, however, that the Nathan Longfort who narrates the novel recognizes that such acceptance was not entirely inevitable. His obsession with Aubrey Bradshaw shows that he has been intrigued not only by his cousin's hatred for him but also by the alternative kind of life that Aubrey has chosen. To a considerable extent, Nathan's focus on Brax to the exclusion of his other children results from his early recognition that Brax has the character to follow in Aubrey's footsteps and the talent to forge an original style in painting. Nathan wishes to keep Brax close to the family and at the same time hopes that Brax will break away and become the artist Nathan lacked the courage to become.

Yet the ironies of *In the Tennessee Country* do not end here. Brax does not disappear from view, as had Aubrey and such early Tennessee "bolters" as a banker and Texas pioneer Sam Houston, who completely lost touch with their former lives. Brax goes to Washington but remains in constant contact with his family. Once he has achieved success as a painter, his two brothers, both art dealers, are his representatives; Brax has not entirely broken away. A further irony lies in the fact that Melissa, who had enjoyed a mild success as a writer of short stories, encounters a writer's block when Nathan and Brax are at odds, a block that dissolves when the father and son are reunited. Melissa decides, however, that she will write no more once Nathan has recognized what his own life has become. His egotism has drained her strength and obliterated her own art.

To a considerable extent, *In the Tennessee Country* is an extended short story. It contains no chapter divisions and no distinct breaks in the narrative flow, which unfolds as the seamless recollections of the narrator. Fittingly, it is a low-keyed novel, reflecting the quiet and easy passage of Nathan's life. He goes from the protective care of his mother and aunts to a sheltered academic career. As an adult, he accepts without question the shelter provided by his wife and his academic sponsors. He remains blissfully self-centered: He has no friends, he virtually ignores three of his four children, and he is an academic without genuine colleagues. He seems not to notice the extent of his isolation, even when he subconsciously envies Aubrey's ability to break away from the family. The novel is a carefully constructed and smoothly written study of a barren life.

John M. Muste

Sources for Further Study

Booklist. XC, June 1, 1994, p. 1726.
Chicago Tribune. September 11, 1994, p. 3.
The Christian Science Monitor. August 26, 1994, p. 13.
Library Journal. CXIX, July, 1994, p. 130.
Los Angeles Times. October 3, 1994, p. E4.
The New York Times Book Review. XCIX, August 28, 1994, p. 6.
Publishers Weekly. CCXLI, June 13, 1994, p. 49.
Time. CXLIV, August 22, 1994, p. 86.
The Times Literary Supplement. September 9, 1994, p. 21.
The Washington Post Book World. XXIV, August 21, 1994, p. 3.

IN THE TIME OF THE BUTTERFLIES

Author: Julia Alvarez (1950-)
Publisher: Algonquin Books of Chapel Hill (Chapel Hill, North Carolina). 325 pp. $21.95
Type of work: Novel
Time: 1938 to 1994
Locale: The Dominican Republic

This fictionalization of the murder of three of the four Mirabal sisters in the Dominican Republic during the waning of Rafael Trujillo's regime is chillingly factual

Principal characters:
DON ENRIQUE MIRABAL, the father of the Mirabal sisters
DOÑA MERCEDES REYES VIUDA MIRABAL, his wife
PATRIA MERCEDES MIRABAL GONZÁLEZ, the eldest Mirabal sister, born in 1924
PEDRITO GONZÁLEZ, her husband
DEDÉ MIRABAL, the second Mirabal sister, born in 1925
JAIMITO, her cousin and husband
MINERVA MIRABAL, the third Mirabal sister, born in 1926
MANOLO, her husband
MARÍA TERESA "MATE" MIRABAL RODRÍGUEZ, the youngest Mirabal sister, born in 1935
LEANDRO, her husband
RAFAEL LEONIDAS TRUJILLO, dictator-president of the Dominican Republic, 1938-1961

Julia Alvarez's butterflies are the four Mirabal sisters, whose code name in the revolutionary underground was Mariposa, Spanish for butterfly. These women, daughters of Don Enrique Mirabal, a landed merchant-farmer who became prosperous and socially prominent, and his wife, Doña Mercedes, referred to as "Mamá" throughout the novel, were born into a rising middle class.

In the early 1930's, an ambitious military man, Rafael Leonidas Trujillo, barely literate and from humble origins, rose to be Dominican Chief of Military Operations. He seized the reins of government precipitously, declaring himself president after instigating the downfall of his predecessor.

Trujillo's meteoric rise to power had begun in the army. He advanced quickly as those in line before him mysteriously disappeared. As second in command, he assured his ascendancy to Chief of Military Operations by devious means. He knew that his superior was having an affair with another man's wife. One night he learned where the illicit couple planned to rendezvous. He informed the husband, who, lying in wait, killed the lovers in a jealous frenzy.

Trujillo thus became the second most powerful person in the country. He arranged his final ascent by engineering an uprising against the sitting president, then failing to respond to calls for help from the palace. As president, Trujillo, from whose regime Julia Alvarez's family fled to the United States in 1960 when she was ten years old, retained power in two major ways: He annihilated his opposition without conscience, and he spent public money in visible ways to create an illusion of civic progress.

Alvarez tells the story of the Mirabal sisters in the first person. Each division of the book is headed by the name of one sister and by one or more dates. This structural device permits rounded development of each character because each sister speaks for herself in the first person but is also revealed as others see and comment about her.

Alvarez's use of time is essentially sequential, although in some cases, as in Dedé's opening section, it involves two or more nonsequential dates, in the latter instance 1994 and 1943. This is necessary because Dedé, the sister who survives the atrocity that killed the other three, is being interviewed by Alvarez, who remains much in the shadows more than three decades after the murders around which the novel revolves.

The technique Alvarez has developed results in readers' coming to know the Mirabal sisters intimately, almost as people know members of their immediate families. As this feeling of intimacy grows, knowledge of the story's outcome becomes agonizingly wrenching.

The novel poses a number of universal social questions. Most obviously, it is a strident statement about human rights and human dignity. It also becomes a forceful feminist statement. Minerva, the most independent of the daughters, is a feminist in every respect. Dedé, a submissive wife until she joins the revolutionary movement, divorces her husband and, after the political troubles have died down, becomes an extremely successful insurance agent, something she could never have done in the Dominican Republic as Jaimito's wife.

Whereas Patria wants only to be married—she gains her desire at an early age—and have children, Minerva, who does not marry until she is twenty-nine, insists on attending the university and taking a law degree. Dedé and María Teresa, generally called Mate, begin as passive, conventional Hispanic women beholden to their husbands, as Mamá has been to her husband, although, as Alvarez reveals, Papá is the weakest member of the immediate family. Only once in Enrique's lifetime does Mamá, who has never learned to read, publicly assume the control of which she is fully capable, and that is when Papá's (and the family's) future is severely threatened.

Alvarez deftly develops the theme that demonstrates how a bit-by-bit erosion of freedoms eventually eradicates them totally. She shows how a nation in the grips of a dictator becomes a fawning, paranoid society in which no one is secure. The walls have ears. People must put their minds in neutral and devote themselves to glorifying the megalomania of a dictator who makes their lives alternately—and at his own whim—sweet and bitter.

Early in the lives of his daughters, Don Enrique becomes a wealthy man. He owns a car and a truck and is prominent in his community, Ojo de Agua, whose lachrymose name suggests the inner torment of his family. The eldest Mirabal sisters are sent to a convent school to be groomed as submissive matrons. Even the fiercely independent Minerva, Papá's favorite, submits partially: Upon graduation at age eighteen she returns home rather than going to the university as she wishes.

The turning point for Minerva comes when Trujillo invites Don Enrique to a

Discovery Day Ball at his palace, requesting that Minerva accompany him. This addendum ignites suspicion: Trujillo is legendary for his appreciation—and exploitation—of virginal beauty. The Mirabal sisters remember how he whisked the beguiling seventeen-year-old Lina Lovatón from their convent school. He established Lina in a remote mansion and commanded the nuns to give her a diploma in absentia, placating them by contributing substantially to their school and building its gymnasium, named for Lina.

Minerva, uniquely successful at getting her way through her skilled use of logic, rebuffs the president's advances at the ball and, when they become flagrant on the palace dance floor, she slaps his face with all her might. By doing this she gains his respect but engenders his smoldering animosity.

Minerva tells Trujillo that she wants to attend law school. He discourages her but eventually arranges for her admission. Four years later, she receives her diploma, but, revealing his strong upper hand, Trujillo withholds from her the necessary Dominican license to practice law.

Minerva marries Manolo, two years ahead of her in law school but five years younger. He becomes a leading figure in the Dominican underground, in which she also serves as an enthusiastic worker. She learns the code language of the movement, stores large quantities of arms and propaganda in her house, and becomes increasingly engrossed in seeking Trujillo's downfall.

When the youngest sister, Mate, enters the university, Minerva has little difficulty involving her in the revolutionary movement. Patria, who during adolescence considered becoming a nun, is drawn less easily into revolutionary activities. Eventually, however, she all but loses her religious faith and joins in resisting the repressive Trujillo regime. Her house is destroyed by secret police. Her husband and seventeen-year-old son are arrested and detained.

Dedé leans toward joining the movement, but her husband, Jaimito, who turns out to be the mainstay of the extended family during its most trying times, strongly resists involvement. Wanting to save her marriage, Dedé holds out for as long as she can, but she finally decides that she must leave her husband and join the underground.

Pervasive in the novel is the closeness of the Mirabal family, reminiscent of Judith Ortiz Cofer's representation of the cohesiveness of Hispanic families in her novels *The Line of the Sun* (1989) and *The Latin Deli* (1993). Alvarez demonstrates remarkable skill in leading her readers through the various stages of the sisters' conversion from conventional Hispanic wives and mothers to women fighting for a cause.

Eventually, Minerva and Mate are arrested, as their husbands and Patria's have been. After they are held at La Victoria Prison without access to attorneys, a kangaroo court sentences the two to five years' imprisonment, which is finally reduced to a humiliating house arrest in Ojo de Agua. This house arrest permits them two excursions a week, provided that the sleazy representative of the secret police in Ojo de Agua, Tío Peña, issues them passes. They may go to church on Sundays, and they may visit their husbands at La Victoria on Thursdays.

During all this time, Trujillo, whose regime is crumbling, is obsessed by the Mirabal sisters, who are rapidly gaining celebrity as symbols of the resistance. He transfers Manolo and Leandro from La Victoria Prison to a prison in Puerto Plata, closer to home but accessible only over dangerous roads. Every Friday, the two women and their driver, Rufino, visit Puerto Plata without Mate, because she goes every Thursday to La Victoria and does not return home before they leave.

On November 25, 1960, however, Mate, returning on Thursday night, joins Patria and Minerva for the drive to Puerto Plata. The journey assumes ominous aspects from the start. A store clerk who sells them purses slips them a warning. At a deserted mountain pass, they spy Peña's Mercedes parked outside one of Trujillo's palaces. Nevertheless, they arrive in Puerto Plata safely.

After visiting Leandro and Manolo, they decide, despite bad weather, not to stay overnight with relatives, whose business has declined as a result of harboring them. By 4:30, they leave for home. At the pass near where they had seen Peña's automobile, the road is blocked by secret police thugs. They grab the three sisters and their driver, beat them, and strangle them. The attackers then cram their corpses into their Jeep and push it over a cliff.

Dedé, who was unable to join her sisters on this trip, is now the only surviving Mirabal daughter. She and Mamá share responsibility for rearing the children of the dead sisters, who quickly are enshrined as symbols of the liberation movement.

Trujillo is assassinated in 1961 and replaced by a president who is little better. Manolo, released from prison, goes into the hills to organize opposition against the new president. In 1963, he dies there in a hail of bullets.

In the Time of the Butterflies is unerringly factual, based upon the transformation of one prosperous, God-fearing family from law-abiding citizens to revolutionaries who risk, and eventually give, their lives to overthrow a totalitarian regime. The story, fast-moving and spine-tingling, captures the drama of the evolution to revolution.

Alvarez understands the folklore of the Dominican people, as reflected in Fela, a black servant of the family, who, after the sisters die, begins communicating with their spirits and engaging in magical acts that border on voodoo. The book is replete with folk sayings, such as "Until the nail is hit, it doesn't believe in the hammer," and folk ways such as bringing a broom to the door when one wants guests to leave. When three of his daughters are about to go to boarding school, Papá complains that daughters are needles in the heart because they leave their fathers.

One heartening subplot in the story involves Papá's infidelity. He keeps his mistress and three illegitimate daughters in a house on his land. Mamá learns of this and is devastated, although as a wife, Catholic, lacking marketable skills, she cannot realistically consider leaving her husband. Eventually Minerva discovers her father's secret and is outraged. She confronts Enrique but soon grows sympathetic to the mistress and to her stepsisters. Finally she insists that they be educated, and she and Patria help pay for their schooling from their inheritance. Eventually Patria, now a pharmacist, helps smuggle luxuries to her stepsisters and their husbands in prison.

R. Baird Shuman

Sources for Further Study

Booklist. XC, July, 1994, p. 1892.
Chicago Tribune. October 24, 1994, V, p. 3.
The Christian Science Monitor. October 17, 1994, p. 13.
Kirkus Reviews. LXII, July 1, 1994, p. 858.
Library Journal. CXIX, August, 1994, p. 123.
Ms. V, September, 1994, p. 79.
The Nation. CCLIX, November 7, 1994, p. 552.
The New York Times Book Review. XCIX, December 18, 1994, p. 28.
Newsweek. CXXIV, October 17, 1994, p. 77.
Publishers Weekly. CCXLI, July 11, 1994, p. 62.
The Washington Post Book World. XXIV, November 27, 1994, p. 7.

IN TOUCH
The Letters of Paul Bowles

Author: Paul Bowles (1910-)
Edited, with a foreword, by Jeffrey Miller
Publisher: Farrar Straus Giroux (New York). Illustrated. 604 pp. $30.00
Type of work: Letters
Time: 1928-1991
Locale: The United States, Europe, Africa, Asia, and South America

This superbly edited collection of lively and provocative letters shows an extraordinary writing career in the making, as well as a writer at the peak of creativity and descriptive power

Principal personages:
PAUL BOWLES, a controversial American writer
RENA BOWLES, his mother
CLAUDE BOWLES, his father
JANE AUER BOWLES, his wife, a successful writer
WILLIAM BURROUGHS, a fellow experimental writer
AARON COPLAND, a distinguished composer
ALLEN GINSBERG, a controversial poet
GERTRUDE STEIN, an influential expatriate writer

Paul Bowles has lived a fascinating life, one that has stretched across continents and cultures. In novels such as *The Sheltering Sky* (1949) and in the rich array of shorter works assembled in his *Collected Stories, 1939-1976* (1979) and *Too Far from Home: The Selected Writings of Paul Bowles* (1993), Bowles has entertained, startled, and enlightened six decades of readers. While his life story has been recounted in the unauthorized biography *An Invisible Spectator* (1989) and Bowles's cautious autobiography *Without Stopping* (1972), readers and critics have always sensed that there was another story to be told, one of greater emotional honesty and immediacy. That story is now disclosed in the letters that make up *In Touch: The Letters of Paul Bowles*. Jeffrey Miller has done a superb job of selecting pieces that capture a life of great risk-taking, heartache, and fulfillment. Drawing from more than seven thousand pages of correspondence and working with the full cooperation of Bowles himself, Miller has assembled more than six hundred pages of letters, ones that contain revealing passages of personal, cultural, and social commentary and that make for consistently riveting reading.

Beginning with correspondence from Bowles's adolescence, Miller has chosen letters that illuminate the influences on, insights of, and trials endured by a reclusive writer, whose guarded nature stands in remarkable contrast to the shocking frankness of many of his fictional works. Bowles's juvenilia offers clues to this peculiar combination. Letters from the 1920's and 1930's to his parents and friends reveal Bowles's painful sense of isolation and tendency toward introspection but also his need to perform in ways that compel others' attention. From a childhood in New York to the beginnings of a writing career nurtured during college in Virginia and trips to

France, Mexico, and North Africa, Bowles demonstrates a remarkable descriptive talent and keen ability to mock hypocrisy and vacuous forms of social conformity. At the same time, he is haunted by restlessness and a feeling of hollowness. He is caught up in a search for emotional and aesthetic fulfillment that takes him on voyages across the globe, even as he is left perpetually unsatisfied, agitated, and insecure.

Bowles's writing matures and his mood improves dramatically with his discovery of Morocco as a personal paradise. In the relative sexual freedom allowed to men there, he finds a space that accommodates his bisexuality. In the exotic sights, smells, and sounds, he finds balm for an overwhelming sense of ennui. Yet in the apartness that an expatriate lifestyle allows, he manages to retain the outsider's perspective that feeds his creative talent. Furthermore, in his marriage to fellow writer and bisexual Jane Auer in 1938, he finds a soothing combination of emotional support and personal autonomy. Bowles's trials and successes are both memorable and inspirational, for they demonstrate that the individual when refusing to bow to social norms, can succeed at creating a happy and productive life, one that may not be easy or materially comfortable but that meets deep needs for emotional, spiritual, and aesthetic fulfillment.

For Bowles, many of these needs have been met through remarkable friendships with some of the most inventive and insightful artists of the twentieth century. Bowles first corresponded with Gertrude Stein in late 1930, asking her to contribute to a literary magazine that he was guest-editing at the University of Virginia. He paid a visit to Stein in Paris in 1931 and began a fulfilling relationship with the brilliant writer and her companion, Alice B. Toklas. Like Stein, Bowles has retained a lifelong fascination with the conventions of language. His letters from this period demonstrate an eager playfulness, as he experiments with rhythm, punctuation, capitalization, and word order. Similarly productive was his long, close friendship with the composer Aaron Copland, who encouraged Bowles's interest in new sounds and forms, influencing not only his literary works but also his musical compositions, which have been highly acclaimed.

As Bowles's writing skills were honed and his publication record became distinguished, he found an even wider circle of friends, who have continued to fertilize his talent but whom he has influenced as well. His correspondence with similarly avant-garde writers such as William Burroughs and Allen Ginsberg shows an eagerness to exchange ideas about literary genres, an active engagement with social issues and world politics, and a continuing experimentation with the exotic and dangerous. He writes often of his drug use, his travels across Asia and Africa, and his sometimes stormy relationships with Moroccan citizens and their government; all of these have fed fictional works that center on violent acts and tortured relationships. His marriage to Jane, whose painful battles against depression and ill health are the subjects of numerous letters, is revealed to be part of the fabric of a life and body of work internally consistent, at least in its fascination with extremes.

Indeed, Bowles often seems to be the eye of a hurricane, remaining in most of his adult letters remarkably calm and reasonable during even the most tumultuous circumstances. His letters informing others of Jane's death are surprisingly matter-of-fact, though never insensitive. His writing appears to be a mechanism through which he exercises control over difficult events, describing them brilliantly and analyzing them thoroughly without an immediate admission of personal attachment or impact.

His emotional engagement does emerge, however, in subtle ways, in nuances and single lines that stand in stark contrast to the general dispassion. In one of the many letters telling of Jane's demise, he suddenly reveals that his "degree of interest in everything has been diminished almost to the point of non-existence," a startlingly honest statement after pages of absolute calm. His resilience is also apparent, however, for in the next letter he tells of his recent misadventures with what he thought was a letter bomb, the raucous parties he has attended with Tennessee Williams, and the delight he is finding in reading. Even so, he also gives hints of a continuing process of emotional recovery, for in explaining why he has not traveled recently, he states quite revealingly, "You have to run as fast as you can to stay in one place, let alone try to get to another."

Bowles's letters are engaging and highly literary, abounding in well-turned phrases and insightful comments. Beyond the interest these letters hold for those looking for biographical detail or scandalous and amusing anecdotes, they are also beautifully written, with intricate descriptions of beaches, gardens, deserts, and cities. Read as a narrative, *In Touch* is partly a travelogue, partly a recounting of historical incidents and personal adventures. The hardships of wartime, the dangers of success, the excitement of discovering an exotic new landscape, the exhilaration of a trip through Asia—all these components make Bowles's letters a literary feast and sure delight for the armchair traveler. Miller is to be commended for his success in constructing a volume that is wide-ranging and comprehensive, but never dull or repetitious.

For Bowles scholars, however, the volume offers particular rewards. Sprinkled among the travel narratives and lovely descriptions are items of clear scholarly importance. Not infrequently, Bowles incorporates creative material into his letters: a short story here, a poem or sketch there. He offers insightful interpretations of and reactions to the works of contemporaries, novels and plays from the past, and, perhaps most important, his own fiction. While he seems reluctant to discuss any piece that he is in the process of creating, he does respond quite liberally to reviews and comments concerning published work. For example, he embraces the word "decadent," which has been used often to describe his fiction, with the express demand, however, that readers understand that his decadence reflects that of a time period, not his own degenerative state. He energetically denies having been influenced by the writings of the Marquis de Sade, a connection made by many; he claims, as of 1978, never to have read anything written by the seventeenth century libertine. In other letters, he reveals his dislike of William Faulkner and his respect for the novels of John Dos Passos. Such points of clarification and revelations of influence and intent make *In Touch* a valuable addition to the library of any scholar of twentieth century American literature.

As the volume draws to its end, the letters become briefer and more irregular. Bowles refers time and again to his ill health and tardiness in returning correspondence. His reflections remain fascinating, as when he discusses his favorites among popular rock musicians in 1983 and his joy at seeing *The Sheltering Sky* made into a film in 1989. Yet one is left with the feeling of a career approaching, though certainly not quite reaching, its close. The last letter included in the collection contains some amusing reflections on the Gulf War of 1991, but ends with the question "When will we see each other?" in Spanish—a fittingly open-ended but evocatively tentative finish to a book that can have no conclusion, for at publication its "subject" was still very much alive, even if slowing down perceptibly.

In Touch is a well-shaped, delightful, and useful edition. It is reader-friendly, not only in its presentation of consistently interesting correspondence but also in its abundant peripheral material. Miller includes a useful "biographical glossary" to explain references and correspondents who are not generally known. His impressive index makes individual references and letter recipients easy to locate. The generous and insightful introduction sets up the broad outlines of Bowles's career in a way that aids the reader's assimilation of the primary material that follows. Both Bowles and Miller deserve praise for *In Touch*, a work that truly touches the reader and lingers in the mind.

Donald E. Hall

Sources for Further Study

Booklist. XC, December 15, 1993, p. 734.
Chicago Tribune. February 13, 1994, XIV, p. 3.
Kirkus Reviews. LXI, November 1, 1993, p. 1360.
Library Journal. CXIX, January, 1994, p. 116.
Los Angeles Times Book Review. February 20, 1994, p. 2.
New Statesman and Society. VII, November 4, 1994, p. 40.
The New York Times Book Review. XCIX, June 26, 1994, p. 1.
Publishers Weekly. CCXL, December 6, 1993, p. 62.
The Review of Contemporary Fiction. XIV, Fall, 1994, p. 235.
The Washington Post Book World. XXIV, August 14, 1994, p. 11.

IRRAWADDY TANGO

Author: Wendy Law-Yone (1948-)
Publisher: Alfred A. Knopf (New York). 290 pp. $23.00
Type of work: Novel
Time: The 1940's to the 1990's
Locale: Myanmar (formerly Burma), Thailand, and the United States

A picaresque chronicle of an Asian American woman from girlhood in Southeast Asia through her development to champion tango dancer, then wife of her country's military dictator, hostage and convert of a guerilla movement, wife to an American, and finally assassin of the dictator

Principal characters:
IRRAWADDY MEW TANGO, a Burmese woman
SUPREMO, her first husband, the dictator of Burma
BOYAN, a guerrilla leader, her lover
THURANI, her cousin
LAWRENCE, her American husband
REX, her shiftless American companion

Irrawaddy Tango, the second novel of Asian American writer Wendy Law-Yone, follows her well-received *The Coffin Tree* (1983). Both are told through first-person female narrators and set in Law-Yone's native Burma (Myanmar) and in her adopted homeland, the United States. *Irrawaddy Tango* tells a gripping tale of a Southeast Asian woman's experience of physical, mental, and political abuse with brilliant physical detail, psychological penetration, and erotic candor. *Irrawaddy Tango* is not flawless, however, having longueurs of plot and a sometimes unsympathetic protagonist.

The novel's title derives from its protagonist's nickname. As "Irrawaddy" suggests, the novel's fictional country is modeled on Myanmar/Burma. The novel's historical events are also readily recognizable as Burmese: colonization by the British, invasion and occupation by Japanese in World War II, national independence followed by a military coup, and ongoing guerrilla warfare. One supposes that Law-Yone chose to fictionalize the novel's country because the protagonist, Tango, marries her country's dictator, who would, in actual life, be General Ne Win.

Although current Burmese events are not sufficiently calamitous to merit world media attention, they have an intrinsic interest. In 1994, the Nobel Peace laureate Aung San Suu Kyi was still under house arrest there. Democracy-minded youths are forced to seek asylum in neighboring Thailand and often end up being unspeakably exploited by their so-called hosts. Moreover, Myanmar remains (unofficially) the chief source of heroin bound for the United States. Law-Yone's family was close to the center of political turmoil in Burma in the 1960's; her father, Edward Law-Yone, then publisher of Burma's foremost English-language newspaper, was imprisoned and exiled. Yet the atmosphere of Burmese politics, although integral to Wendy Law-Yone's novel, is only peripherally so. The novel primarily focuses on the evolving career and character of its protagonist, Irrawaddy Mew Tango.

Tango's picaresque career seems to pass through four phases, analogous to recognizable popular archetypes of female identity: first, an Evita (Peron) phase during which a small-town girl becomes a dictator's wife; second, a Patty Hearst phase during which a wealthy woman socialite is kidnapped by guerrillas and then converts to her abductors' cause; third, a joyless-luckless Asian American woman phase (à la Amy Tan) where an émigré woman discovers the anomie of existence in America; and fourth, a spiderwoman phase in which a woman empowers herself sexually, mates, and demolishes her mate. Through these phases, Tango's character moves and develops, like the dance itself, full of exhilarating dips and lifts of fortune, dizzying turns and reversals of plot, in movements charged with a sinister power and unassuaged sensuality, all performed by a character cool to the point of superciliousness.

In the sophisticated and suspenseful beginning of the book, the novel opens near the end of its action, with Tango returning as a political prisoner to Daya after twenty-five years' domicile in the United States. The details are vividly and strategically evoked: the garish airport frescoes mythologizing the nation's history, in which Tango reads a cruel and bloody national character, Tango's journey blindfolded through the sounds of a tropical night, the dreary particulars of her cell, the mind-boggling bureaucracy that requires her to sign a receipt for her body's being in captivity. Once the reader's interest is aroused by initial situation and character, the first-person narrative flashes back to the antecedent stages of Tango's career.

Tango's Evita-like maturation in the small town of Irrawaddy is delineated with captivating vividness. The river boats laden with rice and elephants, the tethered gibbon at the Indian dry-goods store, the playmate with the soft spot in her head, the boy with a "pet worm" that emerges from his pants for Tango to fondle all become palpable presences in Law-Yone's descriptive pages. Against this backdrop Tango's moral and psychological character is formed. She emerges as a self-asserting, even egocentric individualist embedded in a Buddhist setting of self-denial and transcendence. Her father has nicknamed her Mew because, as he explains, "You *acted* like a cat. No love for anyone but yourself." This almost callous egocentricity is confirmed by Tango: "From time to time I felt a hardening inside, around the very spot warmed supposedly by love and goodwill." It allows Tango to mock her father's imperfect English and her mother's poor musical taste. After a particularly stormy confrontation with the teenage Tango, her mother decides to transcend the material world and retreat to a Buddhist nunnery. By contrast, Tango embraces the material world and uses her physical talents to ascend from her humble origins.

Tango's developing interests and talents have bifurcated into opposed career pathways: piano playing and tango dancing. Unfortunately, piano playing deadends in a fiasco of a national musical exhibition. (Law-Yone herself had been an accomplished music student but was prevented by politics from accepting a scholarship to the Soviet Union and one to Mills College in California.) Tango develops a passion for the Argentine dance, which, unlike Asian dance forms, allows her to be and to assert herself:

> "a dance that allowed me to stand . . . tall. It didn't oblige me to crouch as if . . . my back had just been broken. I wasn't pulled by invisible strings; I was guided and wooed by a partner who strode and leapt as one with me. A partner from whom I could swivel or twist away in seeming pique but could still trust to sweep me off my feet."

Tango and her instructor, Carlos, enter a national talent competition. Though they perform brilliantly, the prize goes to a politically correct native dance. Still, Tango attracts the attention of a bemedaled colonel. She marries him, and he soon becomes General Supremo, then military dictator of Daya.

Tango quickly discovers, however, that existence at the top of her material world leaves much to be desired. Her public life of languid poolside preening and glittering diplomatic balls soon palls. Her private life with Supremo is a hell of mental and physical abuse: She must obey Supremo's every wish, even petting a crocodile at his command and fanning the fading embers of his virility by urinating on their bedroom floor.

There is a sudden tangolike reversal of plot direction when, at the apogee of Tango's social and material ascendancy, she becomes the hostage of a dissident Christian guerrilla tribe improbably named the Jesu Liberation Army (JLA). Supremo ignores the JLA's conditions for his wife's release and makes no effort to rescue her. In time, Tango becomes, with some ambivalence, one of the sexual partners of the JLA president, Boyan—he at least is physically capable if not emotionally fulfilling for Tango. She becomes a helper and, after Boyan's death, a leader of the JLA.

Tango's fortunes then undergo a dizzying dip as Supremo's henchmen kidnap her from her former abductors. Law-Yone describes their torture of her in chillingly intimate detail, the low point of their inhumanity being a game of Russian roulette played with a pistol in her vagina.

A heady lift and reversal of fortunes occurs when Tango is rescued from her harrowing, hellish experience by an American named Lawrence, who works for a pacifist organization with the acronym INRI. Tango and Lawrence are married with a modicum of mutual attraction, though she appears largely motivated by dreams of freedom in America and he by a wish to possess an entrée to Asia by marrying an Asian. Their attempt to make a blockbuster Hollywood film peters out, and Tango discovers that her American Lawrence (not unlike the Arabian one) has eccentric sexual tastes (masturbation is his preferred form of excitation). So they drift apart—he to relief work in Asia, she to her dream of freedom in Washington, D.C.

Tango gradually realizes, however, that freedom and fulfillment in America is an empty dream for her. Thus Law-Yone's protagonist joins the unhappy band of émigrés who haunt so many pages by Asian American women writers, ranging from Maxine Hong Kingston's lunatic aunt Moon Orchid in *The Woman Warrior: Memoirs of a Girlhood Among Ghosts* (1976), to Amy Tan's unhappy mothers and daughters in *The Joy Luck Club* (1989), to Bharati Mukherjee's deranged and murderous protagonist in *Wife* (1975). Indeed, Tango's existence in America reeks with alienation, ennui, and anomie, almost to the point of dementia. Tango is unable to relate to the Dayan émigré community, drifts through relationships with one American after another (even conceiving a stillborn child with a nameless one-night stand), and sleeps in other people's houses in the company of a homeless caretaker, Rex. To be sure, Tango is free from the Southeast Asian horrors of Daya, but she has not become free to find fulfillment in America. The stark psychological truthfulness of these pages is searingly painful as Tango's egocentricity and sense of superiority keep her from bonding with anyone around her and prevent her readers from sympathizing with her.

On this latter point, one especially unattractive trait of Tango is her snobbishness about her superior command of English. Her narrative asides constantly make cruel fun of stereotyped ways in which Asians allegedly mispronounce and misuse English—for example, a Thai calling a priest a "wery holy man. He fart [fast] all day." Yet Tango's own narrative is not devoid of solecism. She uses the ethnic slur "Chinaman" unapologetically. Awkward archaisms occur, such as "Just trodding the ground . . . felt familiar." Further, Tango seems unable to resist puns or wordplays, however inappropriate: for example, the horror of beating an obnoxious man to death with a fan is trivialized into "*the fan hit the sh*——."

Eventually, Tango returns to Asia to realize the climactic phase of her identity. She becomes a sexually empowered, avenging spiderwoman. This opportunity comes when the Dayan astrologers foresee the approaching end of Supremo's power and decide that the event may be forestalled by a reconciliation between him and "the first woman sanctioned to receive his sacred life milk"—Tango. Approached by the Dayan embassy, Tango agrees to return to Daya, where she is kept as a prisoner until the propitious hour of attempted reconciliation. The ensuing episode, which concludes the novel, is a graphic piece of erotic writing detailing Tango's heroic measures of sexual resuscitation as she brings the desiccated Supremo to tumescence and even ejaculation. The novel then climaxes with Tango's supreme act of self-empowerment: As her mate lapses into a postcoital slumber, Tango uses duct tape to wrap him in an insectlike cocoon and terminates him.

In sum, *Irrawaddy Tango* is a worthwhile successor to Wendy Law-Yone's earlier *The Coffin Tree*. Despite its less than sympathetic protagonist and some doldrums in its later action, *Irrawaddy Tango* is assuredly the product of a considerable talent. Law-Yone is a gifted evocator of places and their spirit, a candid searcher of the psyche who develops her protagonist's character with piquant allusions to a variety of archetypal female identities. Notable, too, is the finesse with which Law-Yone uses eroticism in her narrative, an attribute rare among serious Asian American women writers (Law-Yone's success in this vein has been recognized by her inclusion in the 1992 collection *Slow Hand: Women Writing Erotica*, edited by Michele Slung). Finally, *Irrawaddy Tango* performs a signal service by shedding light and focusing attention on the political plight of a too often ignored area of darkness in the heart of Southeast Asia.

C. L. Chua

Sources for Further Study

Belles Lettres. IX, Spring, 1994, p. 17.
Booklist. XC, February 1, 1994, p. 995.
Far Eastern Economic Review. CLVII, May 5, 1994, p. 46.
Kirkus Reviews. LXI, November 15, 1993, p. 1413.
Library Journal. CXIX, January, 1994, p. 162.
The New York Times Book Review. XCIX, February 20, 1994, p. 22.
The New Yorker. LXX, February 28, 1994, p. 101.
Publishers Weekly. CCXL, November 22, 1993, p. 48.
USA Today. February 18, 1994, p. D5.
The Washington Post Book World. XXIV, January 16, 1994, p. 1.

IT ALL ADDS UP
From the Dim Past to the Uncertain Future
A Nonfiction Collection

Author: Saul Bellow (1915-)
Publisher: Viking (New York). 327 pp. $23.95
Type of work: Essays
Time: The late 1940's to the 1990's
Locale: Paris, Illinois, Vermont, Spain, Israel, and Italy

A Nobel Prize winner in literature collects his travel pieces, biographical sketches, speeches, and essays in cultural and literary criticism

Nearing his eightieth year, Saul Bellow can look back at his fifteen or so novels with a deep sense of a job well done. No other American writer of the later twentieth century will leave behind a more distinguished and inspiring oeuvre. To make such claims for Bellow in the mid-1990's may strike contemporary readers as somewhat exaggerated. Later novellas such as *A Theft* (1989) and *The Bellarosa Connection* (1989) struck many readers as representative of a decline in inventiveness that was already apparent in *More Die of Heartbreak*, Bellow's last true novel, published in 1987. In addition, his harshly comic treatment of women in his fiction—from Madeleine and Ramona in *Herzog* (1964) to Renata in *Humboldt's Gift* (1975) and beyond—was bound to strike feminist readers, whose perspective has dominated literary criticism in the late twentieth century, as objectionable. In a similar vein, Bellow's lack of interest in multicultural literary values that denigrate the classics of the past has not endeared him to ethnically and racially centered critics.

Those who believe, however, that Saul Bellow will reemerge as one of the true giants of twentieth century literature when trendy ideologies pass from the scene will find support for their convictions in ideas and feelings that Bellow underscores in his nonfiction. The main subtitle of *It All Adds Up* is *From the Dim Past to the Uncertain Future*. Bellow means to contextualize different experiences, people, and places in his own mnemonic life. The range of his memory serves as a guide to what a truly engaged human being may call his or her life—in the end no richer than what is remembered, no matter how dimly. The "future" is "uncertain" because the "past" is "dim." This is unavoidable, but the challenge it represents is precisely what moves Bellow to make the effort to remember, both at the time he wrote the various pieces collected here and now at the time of their final stringing on a common thread. That thread is Bellow's fascination and love for "the mysteries of our common human nature." On the spine of this book, there is a space between "Adds" and "Up"—a pause that has the effect of stressing the second word and bringing out its two meanings: summation and hope.

Chicago is Bellow's Jerusalem, and this is so despite the moving tribute to the true Jerusalem in his acclaimed travel book *To Jerusalem and Back* (1976). In that book, he reflected in a disinterested way on the passion and tragedy of the holy city, past and present. Bellow cannot be disinterested or objective, however, when it comes to

Chicago. He found his voice as a novelist in *The Adventures of Augie March* (1953), and that novel not only embodies the Chicago of Bellow's youth but also captures the strange way in which the ugliness, smells, dirt, crowded tenements, and, all in all, the quintessential urbanness (not urbanity) of this great American city inspired Bellow to define himself as an artist. The religion of Bellow's art has its shrine in Chicago.

In a short piece on Chicago originally written for *Life* magazine in October, 1983, Bellow stands at the site of his childhood home on Le Moyne Street. There is only a vacant lot and not a single physical reminder of the past. Chicago's "transformations" are central to its being and therefore do not really frighten Bellow: "It forces you inward, to look for what endures. Give Chicago half a chance, and it will turn you into a philosopher."

Six years earlier, in 1977, Chicago did for Bellow exactly what he remembered in 1983; the city provided him with a philosophical perspective for his memorable Jefferson Lectures in Washington under the auspices of the National Endowment for the Humanities. The lecture is largely a narrative of Bellow's historical experience of the city and how its elemental cosmopolitanism, the great ethnic neighborhoods, turned him into a writer. As he describes the streets and monotonous architecture, the reader begins to understand the full force of what drove Bellow deep into inwardness. He muses on the way Chicago's racial and ethnic character has changed from central and eastern European to Latin and African; this "transformation" strikes Bellow as foreshadowed in the way Henry James turned away in dismay from the "antics" and "gabble" of Bellow's own ethnic ancestors on the Lower East Side of New York. The changes that Chicago absorbs strike Bellow as a secret pact between American history and the individual artist's ever-deepening search for his or her own inwardness.

Throughout his life in art, Bellow has always maintained that the literary artist has a sacred responsibility in the modern world to keep alive the human center of things, to provide an alternative to the dehumanizing forces of technology and the politics of conformity. In his acceptance speech for the Nobel Prize, delivered in Stockholm on December 12, 1976, he inveighed against Alain Robbe-Grillet's aesthetics of "choseisme" ("thingism") and the notion that "character" is an obsolete concept. Bellow has also, however, drawn a careful distinction between character and individualism. In an early essay on Fyodor Dostoevski, Bellow agrees with the great Russian novelist that Western civilization has rationalized selfishness as an expression of individualism and violated that other great revolutionary war cry, fraternity. Here is a clue to the heart of Bellow's art. The height of humanity and the secret of true self-mastery is to use the power of individuality to serve others. This insight fuels all Bellow's fiction. The test of a great novel is its "aesthetic bliss," but for Bellow this is not a detached art-for-art's-sake emotion; on the contrary, the bliss he is talking about can take hold only when the novelist persuades his readers that he has passionately imagined the other.

Bellow's sensitivity to the "transformations" of places like Chicago makes him value the same power in other people, particularly writers. In a eulogy for John Cheever, Bellow notes Cheever's striking ability to transform himself; his later fiction is truly different from his early work. "Rereading him . . . it becomes apparent to me . . . how much of his energy went into self-enlargement and transformation and how passionate the investment was."

Without the example of such investment of genius in human exploration, the world threatens to succumb to the chaotic "distractions" of the information revolution. Drowning in the "noise" of what passes for communication, today's people are lost without writers such as Cheever, John Berryman, Allan Bloom, and William Arrowsmith. These writers and friends of Bellow all remained true to the intimations of growth and transformation. In his moving tributes to their memory, it is clear that Bellow acknowledges them as models for his own life as a writer. Indeed, the need for Bellow to master the self-expanding power of the transforming artist becomes a moral imperative that answers the world's need. "The writer cannot make the seas of distraction stand still, but he can at times come between the madly distracted and their distractions. He does this by opening another world."

To expect this much of art after the "moronic inferno" of the twentieth century may be too reminiscent of high modernism and the confidence of the great poets and writers after World War I. If there is anything reactionary about Saul Bellow, it is his refusal to give up the great claims for art made by Gustave Flaubert, Joseph Conrad, and their followers, and his firm conviction that postmodernist skepticism, particularly in its deconstruction of classic texts, has inaugurated the "Kingdom of Frivolity." Surely this is defiance rather than reaction.

In an interview dialogue in 1990, Bellow made the following remark:

> The classics themselves are shooting, not drifting, Letheward. We may lose everything at this rate. . . . Do I look or sound despairing? My spirits are high as ever. Not despair—anger. Contempt and rage. For this latest and longest betrayal by putty-headed academics and intellectuals.

Peter Brier

Sources for Further Study

The Christian Science Monitor. April 28, 1994, p. 14.

Commentary. XCVII, June, 1994, p. 38.

Library Journal. CXIX, February 15, 1994, p. 158.

The Nation. CCLIX, August 8, 1994, p. 168.

The New Republic. CCX, May 2, 1994, p. 37.

The New York Times Book Review. XCIX, April 10, 1994, p. 9.

The New Yorker. LXX, May 16, 1994, p. 108.

Publishers Weekly. CCXLI, January 24, 1994, p. 42.

Time. CXLIII, May 9, 1994, p. 80.

The Washington Post Book World. XXIV, March 27, 1994, p. 3.

I'VE KNOWN RIVERS
Lives of Loss and Liberation

Author: Sara Lawrence-Lightfoot (1944-)
Publisher: Addison-Wesley/Merloyd Lawrence (Reading, Massachusetts). 654 pp. $25.00
Type of work: Biography; social history
Time: From mid-century to the 1990's
Locale: The United States

In telling their stories to a responsive interviewer, six middle-aged, middle-class African Americans challenge stereotypes regarding the black bourgeoisie

Principal personages:
ORLANDO BAGWELL, a documentary filmmaker
KATIE CANNON, an ordained Presbyterian minister and tenured professor of theology at Episcopal Divinity School in Cambridge, Massachusetts
FELTON (TONY) EARLS, an epidemiologist and psychiatrist at Harvard University's School of Public Health
CHARLES OGLETREE, a criminal defense lawyer, political activist, and professor at Harvard Law School
M. ANTOINETTE (TONI) SCHIESLER, a research chemist and former Roman Catholic nun, who has married and has become a candidate for the Episcopal priesthood
CHERYLE WILLS, an entrepreneur and community activist
SARA LAWRENCE-LIGHTFOOT, a professor at the Harvard University Graduate School of Education

Sara Lawrence-Lightfoot's *Balm in Gilead: Journey of a Healer*, published in 1988, won a Christopher Award and was recognized in *The New York Times Book Review* as one of the Notable Books of the Year. The subject was obviously meaningful for the author: the life of her mother, Margaret Morgan Lawrence, one of the first African American child psychiatrists in the United States. Yet the book also remains notable for its method. It was based on a regularly scheduled series of long tape-recorded interviews, which were then selected, edited, and commented on by Lawrence-Lightfoot. The emphasis was on the personal rather than on the public, and the story that emerged, as the author herself affirms, was that of the daughter and author as well as of her mother. Storytelling, the name Lawrence-Lightfoot gives to her method, represents an alternative to more conventional academic methods of social science. Some critics have even suggested that the author has invented a new literary genre.

The triumph of *Balm in Gilead* rests to a considerable degree on the striking match of method and matter. Throughout the book, a tension between detachment and intimacy, reflecting the author's dual identity as social historian and daughter, generates drama and insight. By the end of the book, readers come to know two remarkable women with a kind of clarity that could hardly have been achieved in any other way.

What remained uncertain after the achievement of *Balm in Gilead* was whether the methods so triumphantly employed there would work as well for subjects with which the author was less personally involved. Insofar as *I've Known Rivers: Lives of Loss and Liberation* can be regarded as providing an answer to that question, the issue is still in doubt.

I've Known Rivers is based on long tape-recorded interviews conducted over extended periods with six subjects, all of them middle- to upper-middle-class African Americans in their middle years. There is no family connection between the author and her subjects, yet it remains true here as in *Balm in Gilead* that the story told by the book as a whole is the story of its author as well as of her subjects. As she reminds readers, the description of her subjects fits her as well. In fact, that is one of the problems of this book. The sense of the author-interviewer's personality that made *Balm in Gilead* a compelling portrait of a relationship of mother and daughter can, in *I've Known Rivers*, seem merely an intrusion. One review of *Balm in Gilead*, while generally laudatory, regretted that readers are not permitted to hear the voice of Margaret Morgan Lawrence unfiltered and undiluted. Since the relationship of interviewer and subject lacks the intrinsic dramatic interest of that of mother and daughter, the reader of *I've Known Rivers* may feel a similar, but more intense, regret with regard to the six human beings whose stories are filtered on this occasion through the consciousness and values of Lawrence-Lightfoot.

These subjects certainly constitute a sufficiently interesting group in themselves, and the author's method of interviewing over an extended period means that readers observe the six storytellers living their lives as well as narrating them. Katie Cannon, the daughter of North Carolina sharecroppers, for the first time writes a letter to her illiterate father. Cheryle Wills suffers the pain of divorce. Toni Schiesler carries on her struggle to achieve ordination in the Episcopal Church. These stories-in-process yield moments of genuine dramatic intensity.

These are also men and women of dedication and accomplishment. Charles Ogletree has enjoyed a remarkable record of success as criminal defense lawyer; in ten years as a public defender in Washington, D.C., he never lost a case. Now he seeks to integrate his position as a member of the faculty of Harvard University, that most elite of elite white academic institutions, with his commitment to equal justice for all. Tony Earls, also a member of the Harvard faculty, applies his scientific intelligence by attempting to document the major sources of crime and violence in society and prepares his major creative work, a study of how large urban environments constrict development. Orlando Bagwell, known for the two-part public television production *Eyes on the Prize* (1987-1989), works on a film that seeks to discover the real Malcolm X. Speaking as a father, he resolves that his kids will grow up to be the kind of African Americans society will love to embrace.

These are extraordinary people, so much so that it would be hard to claim that they represent much beyond themselves. While acknowledging that her six subjects hardly constitute a representative sample of anything, Lawrence-Lightfoot is nevertheless concerned to place them within several more general contexts. In everything that is individual, that is special, about them, these people challenge all attempts to stereotype the black bourgeoisie. Such stereotypes originate not only from white racists, but from within the black community as well. A common theme is that members of the black middle class forget their origins, dilute their racial identity, and abandon solidarity with their less fortunate brothers and sisters. Not only do such myths circulate within vernacular culture, but they also have gained academic respectability through the influential work of African American sociologist E. Franklin Frazier. His book *Black Bourgeoisie: The Rise of a Middle Class* (1957) portrays the members of the black middle class as materialistic assimilationists, whose inauthentic lives are motivated above all by the desire to rise in a world whose rules and standards have been set by the white majority. As Lawrence-Lightfoot makes clear, both in the book and in a number of interviews, whatever other significance it may have, *I've Known Rivers* can be read as an answer to Frazier.

But if the author is determined to explode the categories created by Frazier, she is not prepared to liberate her subjects from categorization as such. She has a project of her own. As she puts it: " 'we' must begin to construct a more authentic and complicated narrative about 'our' lives—one that challenges the distorted, narrow caricatures of 'successful' blacks." Her book is successful to the extent that her subjects are permitted their complexities. Yet that success is compromised by the author's determination to make her subjects fit her notion of the authentic. The story the seventh storyteller, the author, wants to tell is the story of the reconciliation, in the lives of people like herself, of roots and destinations. Each subject in turn becomes an illustration of the need to base forward movement through life's journey on a connection to culture, roots, and ideology. One need not quarrel with the values thus expressed (even if one entertains doubts about the fit between "ideology" and her other keywords) to question the inevitability of the pattern and to wonder whether the imposition of such a pattern was in any way required.

It is, in any event, the author's pattern, the pattern demanded perhaps by the story she wants to tell, the story in which she wants to be a character. For it is, to a sometimes disturbing extent, the voice of the author that dominates here. A process of homogenization occurs as these six remarkable individuals are, one by one, presented, explained, justified, at times even apologized for, by their anxious interviewer. They are not, under any circumstances, to escape her thematic net.

Are the blanks that remain in these narratives a direct result of Lawrence-Lightfoot's program, or do they simply arise from a combination of respect for her subjects' privacy and mere indifference, perhaps unconscious, to certain aspects of their lives?

The author acknowledges that there are topics she has elected not to pursue out of consideration for subjects who have given her their trust, but her choices seem erratic and often far from protective. When readers hear of a middle-aged professional woman's fixation on the man who took her virginity years before, they may be embarrassed at what can seem regressive and irresponsible behavior. When the woman arranged a meeting with this man, by now married and a father, he wanted to know if he should bring a condom. In fact, their relationship at the time the book was written is not sexual, but, at least on the evidence of this book, it is the most important emotional relationship in the woman's life. What do she and this man of limited education and accomplishments talk about? What effect does this relationship have on the man's marriage? It may be that there are very good answers to these and similar questions, but, having exposed the relationship, Lawrence-Lightfoot refrains from exploring it, thus blocking any possibility of discovering what may be authentic in it. Surely this is precisely the wrong decision, the one that is least protective of a woman who has trusted her.

There are some topics, of unquestionable importance to her subjects, about which the author simply does not seem very interested. Religion is one of them. If she acknowledges the existence of a religious dimension of human experience, which is not necessarily the same as affirming the existence of God, there is no evidence of it in this book. From one point of view, of course, this is her business. Yet Katie Cannon is an ordained Presbyterian minister and professor of theology; Toni Schiesler is a former nun who aspires to the Episcopal priesthood. When Cannon refers to herself as an agnostic, Lawrence-Lightfoot is not moved to ask for clarification or to inquire into the issues of spiritual and intellectual integrity that such a position might involve for a minister. When Toni Schiesler declares that she would regard ordination as a stamp of approval for herself, Lawrence-Lightfoot seems unaware that ordination to the priesthood might have any other sort of meaning. Can she be as naïve as she seems? She affects surprise that a woman who is interested in science can trust the canons of faith. What century has she been living in? Perhaps readers should be warned when she observes that Toni Schiesler does not conform to her fantasy of what a former nun should look like. People who have fantasies about what former nuns look like seldom have interesting things to say about the varieties of religious experience.

Finally, the book is simply too long. There is too much repetition, too much commentary in relation to what is being commented upon, too much putting into the author's own words what has already been more effectively uttered in the words of the subjects. It is as though Lawrence-Lightfoot is involved in an unacknowledged and perhaps unrecognized struggle with her subjects, from which she is determined that she will emerge as the master storyteller. Perhaps her next project should be an autobiography—direct, undisguised, without apologies.

W. P. Kenney

Sources for Further Study

Afro-American. October 29, 1994, p. B6.
Boston Globe. September 4, 1994, p. 14.
Kirkus Reviews. LXXII, July 1, 1994, p. 906.
Library Journal. CXIX, September 1, 1994, p. 202.
Ms. V, September, 1994, p. 77.
The New York Times Book Review. XCIX, November 13, 1994, p. 69.
Publishers Weekly. CCXLI, September 5, 1994, p. 80.
The Washington Post. November 8, 1994, p. E2.

JAMES BALDWIN
A Biography

Author: David Leeming (1937-)
Publisher: Alfred A. Knopf (New York). Illustrated. 442 pp. $25.00
Type of work: Literary biography
Time: 1924-1987
Locale: New York City; Paris and Saint-Paul-de-Vence, France; and Istanbul, Turkey

David Leeming's biography connects James Baldwin's literature to his life and times and shows the continuing moral witnessing that links them all

Principal personages:
JAMES BALDWIN, an African-American novelist, essayist, playwright, and civil rights activist
DAVID BALDWIN, his brother and closest friend, who helped to keep the writer's life in order
BEAUFORD DELANEY, a black painter, Baldwin's friend for more than forty years
LUCIAN HAPPERSBERGER, a Swiss friend and lover with whom Baldwin would have a stormy relationship for three decades
MARY PAINTER, an early Paris friend
ENGIN CEZZAR, a Turkish actor and friend

David Leeming knew and worked with James Baldwin for the last twenty-five years of the writer's life, and that intimacy has helped him to produce a biography that gets beneath the celebrity to the writer and the man below. Leeming accurately sees Baldwin as an Old Testament prophet, a biblical witness or "voice in the wilderness." Baldwin's "essays stand out as among the most articulate expressions we have of the human condition in his time," Leeming writes, and Baldwin's three plays, six novels, and many short stories create "parables to illustrate . . . the words of his essays."

Leeming also portrays the private Baldwin, a man who sought love unsuccessfully throughout his life and who suffered terrible bouts of depression and loneliness for most of it. Almost from birth, Baldwin faced multiple strikes against him. Illegitimate—he never knew who his biological father was—and reared by a stepfather who became increasingly mad in a Harlem with few escapes even for the sane, Baldwin in the end used these very conditions "as starting points for a lifelong witnessing of the moral failure of the American nation—and of Western civilization in general—and the power of love to revive it." In the telling titles of his works, Baldwin became the persona of *Nobody Knows My Name* (1961), *No Name in the Street* (1971), or "Stranger in the Village," the outsider who could see and depict so clearly the social conditions in his own country.

Baldwin was fortunate as a youth to have his talent recognized early by mentors, white and black—the poet Countée Cullen, for example, and Orilla ("Bill") Miller were both influential early teachers. He needed such support, for he carried a double burden, not only his blackness but his emerging homosexuality as well. At the age of fourteen he became an apprentice preacher, but his religion was really a temporary escape from his emerging sexuality. As Leeming demonstrates here, however, it was in the pulpit that Baldwin first learned to use rhetoric effectively, and "the Word" would become the foundation of a prose style that would be used as a powerful instrument, not only in his literature but in his country's moral development as well. "Baldwin was a writer who could combine the cadences of the King James Bible and Henry James with what he liked to call the 'beat' of African-American culture." No prose style has had a greater impact on modern American life.

After graduation from high school, Baldwin lived in and around New York, took on a series of dead-end jobs, and worked on his writing. (His first published piece, a review of Maxim Gorki's short stories, appeared in *The Nation* in April, 1947.) His earliest influences were Beauford Delaney, the African American painter, who would introduce Baldwin to jazz and the blues, and Richard Wright, the African American novelist, who would provide Baldwin with a writing model but whom he would in a few short years have to reject as a literary father figure.

After eight years in New York, Baldwin left for Paris and the exile that would be his state for much of the remainder of his life. Like Ernest Hemingway, F. Scott Fitzgerald, and other American expatriates twenty-five years earlier, Baldwin found Paris an exciting, creative place, even if he was too poor to experience all of it. As often happens, Baldwin really discovered his American identity there; while on one level his exile may have been an escape, it also brought him face-to-face with himself and with his Americanness. His early works reflect that truth. In 1953, his first (and possibly best) novel *Go Tell It on the Mountain*, appeared, based on his religious experiences in his Harlem adolescence, and two years later, *Notes of a Native Son*, the collection of essays that would make his name thereafter synonymous with civil rights, was published—only a year after United States schools had been desegregated in *Brown v. Board of Education*.

Baldwin's career was launched, and in the next twenty years he would be a lightning rod for his country's moral and social problems. For long stretches of time he lived in France and in Turkey, but again and again, the civil rights struggles of the 1960's and 1970's drew him back to the United States as witness. His portrait on the cover of *Time* magazine on May 17, 1963, said as much about his importance as a spokesman for African Americans as about his writing.

Leeming does a masterful job of linking the literature to the life. In particular, he does extended literary analyses of all Baldwin's fiction and nonfiction, connecting it not only to his troubled personal life but also to the life of the world around him. He shows that despite Baldwin's growing fame, his personal problems continued. In fact, as his international celebrity increased, so did his troubles, for it became harder and harder to find a quiet place to work, and the entourage of hangers-on grew accordingly. Meanwhile, Baldwin's search for love, his aloneness, did not end.

Leeming sees the importance of love for Baldwin, both as a man and as a writer:

> Love is at the heart of the Baldwin philosophy. Love for Baldwin cannot be safe; it involves the risk of commitment, the risk of removing the masks and taboos placed on us by society. The

> philosophy applies to individual relationships as well as to more general ones. It encompasses sexuality as well as politics, economics, and race relations. And it emphasizes the dire consequences, for individuals and racial groups, of the refusal of love.

Leeming is also good at demonstrating how much of Baldwin's energy went into an obsession with the theater that never really paid off for him. Toward the end of his life, Baldwin would tell Leeming that he wished he had concentrated on drama to the exclusion of all else. Never completely successful in the theater and film projects he energetically pursued, Baldwin had a love of the theater that remained unrequited.

Leeming shows that all of Baldwin's works—drama, fiction, essays—are connected by characters and themes, for he witnessed in fiction as well as in essays: in *Giovanni's Room* (1956) and *Another Country* (1962) as well as in *Nobody Knows My Name* and *The Fire Next Time* (1963). His critical and popular successes crossed traditional literary boundaries. Leeming notes that "*Another Country* became a best seller and, with *The Fire Next Time*, one of Baldwin's two most successful books in terms of sales." Leeming recognizes that Baldwin's novels "are best described as modern parables—or as segments of a long parable." His essays established him "not only as a reliable commentator on racial conditions in America but as a witness to the whole dilemma of what it meant to be American in the context of those conditions." His interest in fiction and nonfiction alike, Leeming demonstrates again and again, "was always in the inner workings of people." Baldwin's best novels and short stories are psychological studies of social problems; his best essays get inside the minds and hearts of all Americans, white and black.

In his last decades, Baldwin's roles as public figure and spokesperson for African Americans almost overtook his writing. He debated William Buckley at the Oxford Union and took meetings with Robert Kennedy, Martin Luther King, Jr., Marlon Brando, Black Panther leaders, and other figures in the Civil Rights movement. He taught, at Bowling Green and the University of Massachusetts, and lectured. "'I've been here 350 years,' he told his audiences, 'but you've never seen me.'" With Baldwin's help, the United States began to see him, and the voice of the African American began to be heard, loud and clear, in the land.

At the end, as he was dying of cancer in Saint-Paul-de-Vence, near Nice, France, Baldwin's life appeared tragic. He had never found the love he had longed for, only a series of troubled personal and sexual relationships. Yet he was surrounded by an alternative family that had grown over the years and that included his brother David and other loyal friends. When he died, he "did not belong any longer to his close friends, to his lovers, or even to his family, but to the many thousands gone and to the many millions still struggling to be free. These had always been his people. Now, in death, he was to be theirs."

Leeming's biography is not without its limitations. Because he did not have the authorization of the Baldwin family, he is not able to quote from letters and manuscripts; this leaves a hole at the center of the book. Baldwin's voice, in particular, is often missing from his life. On the other hand, Leeming's friendship with Baldwin renders the writer, especially at the end of his life, in living detail. Leeming's perceptive analyses as a literary critic—he is professor of English and comparative literature at the University of Connecticut at Storrs—provide a number of valuable insights into individual literary works, as well as an accurate overview of Baldwin's oeuvre. His generous selection of photographs from Baldwin's life adds detail to this life.

It is interesting that three solid biographies of Baldwin have been produced in the few years since his death. W. J. Weatherby, a writer at the British *The Guardian* newspaper, produced a good study of the writer in 1990, and a few years later the Scottish writer James Campbell published a second useful life. If the authorized biography has yet to be produced, these three early works fill an important void and speak to the importance of Baldwin to his times. No American writer looms larger in pointing to the center of the country's postwar problems. Leeming is as eloquent as any of the three biographers in his recognition of Baldwin's importance: "In his personal life and his work, he took the side of those who were made into exiles and outcasts by barriers of race, sex, and class or who turned away from safety and chose the honorable path of tearing down such barriers."

David Peck

Sources for Further Study

Booklist. XC, March 1, 1994, p. 1138.
The Christian Science Monitor. May 10, 1994, p. 15.
The Economist. CCCXXXI, June 18, 1994, p. 97.
Essence. XXV, July, 1994, p. 46.
Kirkus Reviews. LXII, February 15, 1994, p. 202.
Library Journal. CXIX, April 1, 1994, p. 98.
The Nation. CCLVIII, May 2, 1994, p. 596.
The New York Times Book Review. XCIX, May 15, 1994, p. 30.
Publishers Weekly. CCXLI, February 28, 1994, p. 67.
The Times Literary Supplement. June 17, 1994, p. 13.

JAPAN IN WAR AND PEACE
Selected Essays

Author: John W. Dower (1938-   )
Publisher: New Press (New York). 368 pp. $30.00
Type of work: Essays; history

A medley of essays on Japanese twentieth century history, some of them important both for the specialist in Japanese history and for the student of contemporary events

John Dower's collection of essays covers many topics; because they do not present a unified argument, the reader may want to read or consult some but not all of them. The subjects of the essays are the wartime origins of Japan's successful economy; Japanese cinema as a propaganda vehicle during World War II; Japan's attempt to develop an atomic bomb; dissident thought in Japan during the war; the postwar occupation of Japan by the United States (1945-1952); Shigeru Yoshida, twice prime minister during the postwar period; racism in World War II; and Japanese-American relations.

The most original and provocative essay is "The Useful War," first published in *Daedalus* magazine (summer, 1990). The essay locates World War II in the context of twentieth century Japanese and Asian history. Dower argues that many institutions responsible for Japan's dominant position in today's global economy had their origins in the rapid military industrialization of the 1930's, and not in the postoccupation period, as many have assumed.

Dower presents World War II in Asia not as a clash of cultures but as a clash of interests. "Culture was not the critical issue; power, wealth, and security were." The Japanese attack on Pearl Harbor in December, 1941 (which Dower calls "audacious" and "successful"), was a single event in a chain of earlier events, part of an extended period of struggle for national interests and economic development.

American and British historians tend to treat the 1930's as a decade of relative "peace," contrasting it to World War II and the violent attacks against England and the United States in 1940 and 1941. For many countries in Asia, however, the dividing line between war and peace has to be drawn much earlier, if at all. The Japanese historian Fusao Hayashi has written that World War II was the last stage of a hundred-year war against the Western presence in Asia.

Japan had been at war long before Pearl Harbor. It had had an expeditionary force in China ever since 1931. Both Korea and Formosa (present-day Taiwan) had been Japanese colonies since the end of the nineteenth century. In the 1930's, the Japanese government became increasingly militarized, and this coincided with a successful push for economic and industrial development. According to Dower, it is incorrect to refer to the Japanese economic "miracle" of the 1960's as an event without precedent. The notion "belongs to mythology rather than serious history"; there was an economic "miracle" that was just as important in the 1930's. In Asian terms, Japan was not a late bloomer.

The period between 1930 and 1945 was a time of growth for Japan, with profound changes in the structure of capital and labor. It was not a time of economic depression. In the late 1930's, Dower points out, the United States was still attempting to regain the production level of 1929, but Japan's average annual growth was 5 percent throughout the 1930's. Mobilization of the U.S. economy for World War II helped pull America out of the Depression, but Japan had had a comparable mobilization of its economy a decade earlier. The government made direct investments in industry.

> Growth was particularly rapid in metals, chemicals, and engineering. . . . By 1937, Japan was constructing most of its own plants, including many kinds of machine tools and scientific instruments, and was largely self-sufficient in basic chemical products. Dower's conclusion is that on the eve of Pearl Harbor, Japan had one of the most rapidly growing economies of the world.

Dower sketches in the pre-1945 history of some of the postwar Japanese corporate giants, demonstrating that most of them were prospering in the 1930's. In this part of his study he follows work done by the economists G. C. Allen, Hugh Patrick, Henry Rosovsky, and Takafusa Nakamura. Of the eleven major auto manufacturers in postwar Japan, ten came out of the war years. Only Honda was a pure product of the postsurrender period. Three of the other ten firms—Toyota, Nissan, and Isuzu—prospered as the primary producers of trucks for the military after legislation passed in 1936 drove Ford and General Motors out of the Japanese market. Nomura Securities, which grew to be the second wealthiest corporation in Japan after Toyota, was founded in 1925. Its breakthrough in investment trust operations came in 1941. Hitachi, Japan's largest manufacturer of electrical equipment, was established in 1910 but emerged as a vertically integrated producer of electrical machinery in the 1930's. Toshiba, second in rank after Hitachi in electrical products, dates back to 1904, but became a comprehensive manufacturer of electrical goods only after a 1939 merger under the military campaign to consolidate and rationalize production.

Mobilization for war stimulated a spectacular concentration of capital. As military orders came to play an increasing role in the economy, the four "old *zaibatsu*"—the huge conglomerates Mitsui, Mitsubishi, Sumitomo, and Yasuda—were challenged by the emergence of a group of "new *zaibatsu*" dependent on military contracting. In 1937, these ten largest *zaibatsu* controlled 15 percent of total paid-in capital in Japan. By the end of the war, this had risen to more than 35 percent.

An important feature of Dower's analysis is to show the continuity of wartime economic organization after 1945. As he notes, the "big capitalists did not evaporate after Japan surrendered." Although there was some diversification during the occupation period, many of the key enterprises remained close to one another through a variety of formal and semiformal relationships. War had strengthened the bureaucracy, and the nearly seven-year occupation that followed strengthened it further. MITI—the Ministry of International Trade and Industry, which had its greatest influence in the 1950's and 1960's—first orchestrated industrial policy in the 1930's. The mobilization of labor under umbrella organizations began under the notorious "Sampo" association during the war. The contemporary system is what Dower calls a "transwar phenomenon." Both war and peace, he writes, fostered an intense preoccupation with national security and a commitment to the necessity of guided change.

The economic bureaucrats pose a challenging question for political analysts. Dower asks,

> What sort of capitalism have the Japanese been practicing since the 1930s? Clearly, it is not laissez-faire in the manner associated with Adam Smith. On the other hand, state ownership is not the issue, for in fact this is minimal in Japan. The question is really one of laissez-faire in a box—that is, how (and how much) control is imposed on the market—and in recent years numerous phrases have emerged which all suggest that the box is very intricately constructed indeed. Japan is said to be a plan-rational as opposed to a market-rational nation, a mixed capitalist state, a capitalist development state, a technocratic state, a neomercantilist state, a "smart" state, a network state, a corporatist . . . state. . . . In Chalmers Johnson's phrase, since the 1930s Japanese development has been powerfully guided by an "economic general staff"—a most effective metaphor for conveying both the historical and the ideological mesh of war and peace that lies behind the so-called Japanese miracle.

Yet it would be a mistake to exaggerate the military or bureaucratic metaphor for the contemporary Japanese state. It remains a strong capitalist state, its version of capitalism "brokered by conservative interests" so as to retain the market "while controlling 'excessive' competition and promoting nationalistic goals." The conservative elites that work the system are no longer militaristic. Yet "a great many of their institutions, ideas, practices—and leaders—were formed in the crucible of war."

The half-dozen shorter essays that conclude Dower's collection are less provocative than the opening piece, and some might be described as "bridges." The essay on Yoshida is a spin-off from Dower's first scholarly book, *Empire and Aftermath: Yoshida Shigeru and the Japanese Experience, 1878-1954* (1979); the essay "Race, Language, and War in Two Cultures" is a summary of his prizewinning book *War Without Mercy: Race and Power in the Pacific War* (1986); and "Occupied Japan and the Cold War in Asia" is a sketch for a forthcoming book about the occupation period.

One warning should be issued regarding both the essay on race and *War Without Mercy*: Dower's concept of "race" is extremely broad. Attempting to prove that both the United States and Japan were "racist," Dower mixes very different categories. He compares newspaper cartoons to philosophical works, war reporting to religious mythology, mass media propaganda to serious literary works, expressions of offensive war to those of defensive war. Failure to distinguish among different contexts sometimes produces confusion and many false analogies.

The last essay in Dower's collection is excellent and timely. "Fear and Prejudice in U.S.-Japan Relations" is a contribution to the widespread debate in the American media about trade conflicts with Japan. Dower's main argument is that Japanese "capitalism" is genuinely different from that of the United States. The Japanese leaders believe in what Dower calls "the visible hand." This is a reference to Adam Smith's concept of a competitive market as an "invisible hand." Dower quotes a Japanese economist:

> Instead of standing back passively and letting Adam Smith's "invisible hand" take its course, they prefer to play a more active role in shaping the directions that the market takes. In doing so, they routinely draw on a broader array of policy instruments than their American counterparts. . . . The mixture of market and organization in Japan is strikingly different from that in the United States.

"Japan," Dower concludes, "is not a market economy in the American sense."

Are the interlocking *keiretsu*, then, "cartels" that restrain free trade? This is still in the process of negotiation and has yet to be decided. Will countries with open markets continue to trade with a Japan that has closed markets? Some will; others almost certainly will not, or will erect punitive barriers.

Dower admits that differences in basic philosophy and practice are conspicuous. These cannot be wished away or swept aside with emotional assertions. They are the subject of one of the most important contemporary debates, and Dower has made a significant contribution; it is well informed, firmly based in historical scholarship, and worth readers' attention.

John Carpenter

Sources for Further Study

The Christian Science Monitor. March 7, 1994, p. 15.
Foreign Affairs. LXXIII, September, 1994, p. 126.
The Journal of Asian Studies. LIII, May, 1994, p. 552.
Kirkus Reviews. LXI, November 15, 1993, p. 1433.
Library Journal. CXIX, January, 1994, p. 140.
Publishers Weekly. CCXL, December 20, 1993, p. 60.
Reference and Research Book News. IX, September, 1994, p. 8.
The Washington Post Book World. XXIV, August 7, 1994, p. 3.

JOE PAPP
An American Life

Author: Helen Epstein (1947-   )
Publisher: Little, Brown (Boston). Illustrated. 554 pp. $24.95
Type of work: Biography
Time: 1921-1991
Locale: New York City and Los Angeles

In this biography of one of America's most important producers, Helen Epstein produces an evenhanded portrait of a brash, idealistic champion of popular theater

Principal personages:
JOE PAPP (JOSEPH PAPIROFSKY), the founder of the New York Shakespeare Festival and the Public Theater
GAIL MERRIFIELD PAPP, his wife, an officer of the Public Theater
ROBERT MOSES, the commissioner of parks for New York City
BERNARD GERSTEN, Papp's longtime associate at the New York Shakespeare Theater

In the introduction to *Joe Papp: An American Life*, biographer Helen Epstein presents contrasting descriptions of her subject, the late American director and producer: "Joe leapt into action driven by passion and rage and adrenaline," says one close associate in a eulogy addressed to an audience packed with well-known actors and theater people. "Great numbers of us here spring from him, have learned from him, have loved and hated him, . . . have wept because of him and have triumphed with him. And we are his legacy." Upon reading the fulsome obituaries of Papp, however, a former associate of the director rages, "Who would say, today or tomorrow, that the emperor had no clothes—that Joe Papp was just one more fast-talking con man who latched onto the nonprofit structure? . . . Arrogant and anti-intellectual autodidact, have done with you!"

It is one of the great triumphs of Epstein's book that the author has succeeded in balancing these conflicting views of Papp's complex personality and remarkable accomplishments. Joe Papp was perhaps the most vivid and important figure in American theater in the nearly forty years that followed his establishment of the New York Shakespeare Theater in 1954. He was arrogant, brash, energetic, and idealistic, loved by the many actors, directors, and writers whom he supported over the years but disliked as well, often by those who nevertheless continued to admire him and his accomplishments. A champion of Shakespearean drama for the poor of the city and a defender of multicultural casting in a period when this was unusual enough to be considered radical, he lived to see many of his ideas succeed, but he also saw some of them begin to lose their power in a city increasingly dominated by economic and cultural forces that threatened the survival of traditional theater. His successes and failures epitomize both sides of the American dream: the idealism that drives accomplishment and the cost demanded by the achievement of a goal.

Joseph Papirofsky was born in Brooklyn in 1921, the child of immigrant parents who lived on the margins of the working class. Although his brother and sisters later cast some doubt on the accuracy of his portrayal of family life, his own memories were of a cold and depressed household, characterized by poverty and a certain grimness. Social ties and a sense of community were scarce, and young Joseph spent most of his adolescence avoiding home. Although he was not a good enough student to get into Brooklyn College when he was graduated, school offered him at least the appreciation of teachers and a strong feeling for William Shakespeare, whose plays were taught and read as early as junior high school. His sense of isolation and poverty drew him, Epstein points out, to sympathy with the Communist Party and lay behind his activities as a union organizer when he took his first job, but they also resulted in a lifelong habit of denial, particularly at first where his Jewish background was concerned.

Papirofsky married early. His many relationships with women are discussed only briefly in this book—he married four times and fathered at least one child outside of marriage—but it is clear that the restlessness and quickness to judge that characterized his professional life were part of a personal pattern as well. After only a few months with his wife, he enlisted in the navy in 1942. His success in directing military entertainments led to an interest in acting. After leaving the navy in 1946, he was able to use the benefits of the G.I. Bill to enroll in the new Actor's Laboratory School in Los Angeles, an integrated institution that was run by several former members of the Group Theater and had a reputation for radical politics. Papirofsky thrived on the atmosphere and made friends who would be close to him for years, but red-baiting and an investigation by the House Committee on Un-American Activities closed the school and put an end to Papirofsky's only formal education beyond high school.

Settling in New York with, at first, a second wife and then, soon after, a third, Papirofsky was hired as a stage manager at CBS. His real life, however, soon began to develop after hours, in a theater company he founded with several friends in the back of the Emmanuel Church on the Lower East Side of New York. Although his earliest New York productions had been of plays by Sean O'Casey and Federico García Lorca, he was now able to do the Shakespeare he had always dreamed of. Unable, unfortunately, to raise money for the *Romeo and Juliet* he had planned, he produced instead two evenings of Shakespearean scenes, one starring the then unknown actress Colleen Dewhurst. He signed the press release with a shortened form of his name: Joe Papp. Once he obtained a charter from the New York State Board of Regents, a new institution was under way.

The Shakespeare Workshop of 1954 was in some ways characteristic of all of Papp's later enterprises. It was ambitious in name and concept, and its plans exceeded its ability to fund its activities. Somehow, Papp seemed always able to come up with the money he needed, but it was almost always after the fact—a situation that eventually resulted in some serious personal and professional antagonisms. Throughout the early years of the theater, while Papp was still working at CBS, he roped his colleagues into helping with scenery and production. Soon, he was proposing to the municipal government that he present a summer season of Shakespeare in the abandoned amphitheater near the East River. He did, and his reviews fueled an expansion of the workshop, first to a mobile theater on a van and then to Central Park.

It was over the Central Park theater that Papp fought his most spectacular and probably most remembered battle. Robert Moses, the commissioner of parks in New York City who had for as long as anyone could remember been indirectly in charge of how ordinary New Yorkers spent their leisure time, insisted that Papp's theater pay its own way. Papp, both for idealistic reasons and for the practical reason that charging admission would make him subject to union rates for the actors, refused to institute an admission charge. The battle was joined by philanthropically minded New Yorkers, government officials, and the press. Moses exploited the fact that Papp's Communist sympathies had caused him to lose his job at CBS (although, at the insistence of the union, he was quickly rehired). When Papp was forcibly ejected from a Parks Department office, he sued Moses. The latter won, but Moses' cause was lost. The commissioner surrendered, and in a brilliant stroke of generosity, Papp invited him to go with him to the Board of Estimate to ask for funding. The Delacorte Theater, named for a sympathetic donor, began construction.

The fifteen years that followed Papp's victory over Moses were marked by a series of less visible but perhaps equally important successes for Papp. By tying his need for a permanent theater to a vision for the reuse of the condemned and decaying Astor Library on Lafayette Street, Papp was able both to secure a physical home for his increasingly varied activities and to gain the support of New York's uptown community of preservationists. He continued his summer Shakespeare productions, but he also provided a home for the counterculture theater activists who were beginning to voice the nervous anger of their generation. His productions of plays such as *Sticks and Bones*, *No Place to Be Somebody*, *Hair*, *for colored girls who have considered suicide/when the rainbow is enuf*, and *Short Eyes* brought middle-class subscription audiences to plays that they might not have sought or found on their own. New actors and actresses, such as Raul Julia and Meryl Streep, developed their skills on the stages of the Public Theater, and new playwrights, in particular, benefited from Papp's vigorous support.

In the 1960's and 1970's, the Public Theater was above all a playwright's theater. This might have been expected from Papp's obsession with a populist Shakespeare, presented to reach ordinary people, but it came as a surprise to many and was the source of friction between the producer and the many actors and directors who wanted a greater emphasis on the skills and details necessary for coherent theatrical productions. The lack of the latter often resulted in uneven realizations of works and terrible reviews. Papp, however, believed in writers. Despite the objections of his friends, he gave new playwrights the freedom to experiment and develop their ideas, a process that was perhaps most effectively realized in Michael Bennett's development of the successful musical *A Chorus Line* out of a Public Theater workshop, but it also played an important part in the early careers of writers such as Thomas Babe, David Rabe, David Mamet, and John Guare.

The financial success of *Chorus Line* and, later, of *Two Gentlemen of Verona* and *The Pirates of Penzance* led, in a perhaps predictable way, to greater and more costly ambitions. Papp took over the leadership of Lincoln Center's Beaumont Theater, but despite the critical success of some productions (*A Doll's House*, *Threepenny Opera*, *The Cherry Orchard*), the venture was not a successful one. Papp's luck seemed to have changed. His resignation from the Beaumont was, in Epstein's words, the first time many New Yorkers had seen the producer retreat. There were quarrels and breaks with longtime associates in the 1980's, and many of the new generation of actors and playwrights who had been too young to realize the excitement of the early festival years began to find the Public exclusionary or out of touch with change. Papp lost a long battle with cancer in 1991, but the real struggle of his last years was against the decline of the New York theater.

The Papp presented in *Joe Papp: An American Life* is a scrappy, abrasive character who could scarcely have succeeded anywhere but New York and who already seems like a creature from the distant past. Although his multicultural agenda has been adopted throughout the nation, his confidence in the survival of his institution may have been misplaced. There are few people in the nonprofit world today who can take the risks that Papp took in his enterprises, and fewer still who relish the public battle.

Epstein's biography is skillful and interesting. The author makes clear her personal connection with Papp and his widow, whom she met in the 1970's, yet she does not gloss over her subject's less-than-admirable traits. Papp's public life, not his private one, is her subject; although this may be frustrating for some readers, there is abundant material to explore without exploiting the personal. Conventional footnotes are missing, but discursive notes do give a useful context for the quotes, and the index of the book is reasonably complete. A checklist of New York Shakespeare Festival productions, 1954-1991, is a useful addition for researchers.

Jean W. Ashton

Sources for Further Study

American Theatre. XI, December, 1994, p. 70.
Booklist. XC, July, 1994, p. 1911.
Chicago Tribune. August 28, 1994, XIV, p. 1.
The Christian Science Monitor. September 26, 1994, p. 13.
Kirkus Reviews. LXII, June 1, 1994, p. 751.
Library Journal. CXIX, June 15, 1994, p. 71.
The New Republic. CCXI, September 5, 1994, p. 36.
The New York Times Book Review. XCIX, August 21, 1994, p. 1.
Publishers Weekly. CCXLI, June 13, 1994, p. 54.
The Wall Street Journal. December 29, 1994, p. A8.

JOHN MAYNARD KEYNES
Volume II: The Economist as Saviour, 1920-1937

Author: Robert Skidelsky (1939-   )
First published: 1992, in Great Britain
Publisher: Allen Lane/The Penguin Press (New York). Illustrated. 731 pp. $37.50
Type of work: Biography
Time: 1920-1937
Locale: England

The second in a three-volume biography of John Maynard Keynes, Great Britain's most influential twentieth century economist

Principal personages:
JOHN MAYNARD KEYNES, a British economist
WINSTON CHURCHILL, British Chancellor of the Exchequer, 1924-1929
LYDIA LOPOKOVA, a Russian ballerina who married Keynes in 1925
JAMES RAMSAY MACDONALD, Prime Minister of Great Britain, 1924 and 1929-1935
VIRGINIA WOOLF, a British novelist and a member of the Bloomsbury Group

John Maynard Keynes has been the subject of numerous biographies and economic studies. Why then another book on Keynes? Part of the answer is that most previous studies have been primarily about Keynes's economic theories and his contributions to the making of economic policy. Robert Skidelsky has had access to a considerable body of new and unpublished material that enables him to discuss in much greater detail the other aspects of Keynes's life and to integrate them with his activities as an economist.

Skidelsky suggests that the playing of multiple roles constituted one of the central themes of Keynes's life. During the interwar period, Keynes taught economics at King's College, Cambridge. Despite his other commitments, he missed teaching only one term between 1919 and 1937. He also became the bursar (chief financial officer) of his college and made investments that added considerably to its wealth. In the 1920's, he supplemented his teaching salary by writing frequently for the press. He also served on the board of directors of influential journals such as *The Nation* and took an active interest in making it the mouthpiece of a revived Liberalism. Finally, in addition to authoring several important books during the 1920's, he was already such an influential economist that he was repeatedly called to London to provide economic advice to the government.

Keynes first became widely known as a result of *The Economic Consequences of the Peace* (1919), in which he warned that insistence that Germany make huge reparations payments to the Allies would impede Britain's economic recovery from the war. As this work was an important factor in turning public opinion against the government's policy, it is understandable that previous historians have suggested that Keynes became *persona non grata* to the British government. While some did view Keynes's book as virtually an act of treason, Skidelsky stresses that Keynes continued to be consulted by policymakers during the 1920's.

Skidelsky claims that despite *The Economic Consequences of the Peace*, Keynes had greater influence on British governments during the 1920's than he did in the 1930's. David Lloyd George refused to have anything to do with Keynes for several years, but when he resigned as prime minister in 1922, he was replaced by Andrew Bonar Law, with whom Keynes had been friends since both served in the Treasury Department during World War I. During the renegotiation of German reparations payments in 1922, Keynes actually provided advice to both the British and the German governments. Even Lloyd George eventually reconciled with Keynes, and Keynes had a major role in drafting the Liberal Party program that Lloyd George put before the electorate in the 1929 general election.

Was Keynes a New Liberal? Peter Clarke claimed that Keynes continued the pre-World War I left-Liberal tradition of social reform. Skidelsky disagrees, pointing out that Keynes viewed the New Liberal social theory, based on Oxford idealism, as a confused muddle. Also, Keynes was concerned with ensuring the stability of capitalism rather than with the redistribution of wealth that New Liberals urged. A full-employment economic policy might result in a degree of redistribution of wealth, but for Keynes this was a relatively insignificant consequence of a policy that he urged on other grounds. Furthermore, while New Liberals valued democracy for its own sake, he believed that the formation of wise economic policies requires a level of knowledge beyond that of the average voter; thus he preferred the state to be run by an elite of experts.

Because Keynes was homosexual, his friends were astonished at his marriage to Lydia Lopokova, a Russian ballerina, in 1925. They were even more disturbed by the woman he chose than by his sudden display of heterosexuality. Keynes belonged to the Bloomsbury Group, a small circle of artists and writers who prized conversation of a highly intellectual nature. As Lydia was not a native English speaker, she was at a considerable disadvantage in the group and was ridiculed by Virginia Woolf and other members. Although Keynes remained a member of the Bloomsbury Group, its members' behavior toward Lydia was a continuing source of tension. He was deeply in love with her and sought to defend her against their criticism.

When Ramsay MacDonald became prime minister in 1929, he established an Economic Advisory Council of leading economists, including Keynes, to advise him. This gave Keynes the opportunity to influence the Labour Government's economic policy as the Great Depression took effect in Britain. When the economists could not agree among themselves, however, the opportunity slipped by, for MacDonald used their disagreement as a rationale for inaction.

Skidelsky maintains that the debates among the members of the Economic Advisory Council and the government's Committee on Finance and Industry did serve a valuable purpose. Keynes's inability to persuade other economists to accept his proposals made him realize that he must show them why the theory behind their arguments was mistaken. This awareness led directly to his decision to begin writing what became *The General Theory of Employment, Interest, and Money* (1936), his greatest work.

How did Keynes accomplish the intellectual revolution presented in *The General Theory of Employment, Interest, and Money*? Some, including Clarke, have suggested the ideas presented in that book came from Keynes's wrestling with classical economic theory without much reference to the economic crisis of the 1930's. Skidelsky disagrees. He views the book as a direct response to the problem posed by the Great Depression: Why was unemployment continuing at such a high level when, according to classical economic theory, capitalism contained self-regulating mechanisms that should have restored near full employment?

According to Skidelsky, Keynes's magnum opus primarily has to do with the theory of employment. From the very beginning, however, readers understood it in widely different ways. Though Keynes actually argued that low interest rates were key in increasing the level of employment, the earliest self-styled Keynesians claimed that his work justified higher levels of public spending as the most effective means of stimulating higher employment. Economists by no means accepted *The General Theory of Employment, Interest, and Money* uncritically, and Skidelsky devotes a full chapter to their responses. Few were more critical than William Beveridge, who with Keynes is sometimes considered the chief theoretician of the Liberal welfare state. Beveridge, then director of the London School of Economics (LSE), considered Keynes a "quack." When a professorship in economics became available at the LSE in 1931, he appointed Friedrich Hayek rather than Keynes.

Ironically, Keynes was considerably less prominent in public life in the 1930's, when his most important book was published, than he had been during the previous decade. In part this stemmed from the fact that Keynes was a Liberal, and the Liberal Party was no longer a significant political force after 1931. The politician most committed to Keynesian economics in the 1930's, Oswald Mosley, lost his seat in Parliament and launched the British Union of Fascists. Although MacDonald remained prime minister until 1935 and continued to seek advice from Keynes, MacDonald was dependent on the support of right-wing Conservatives and was thus not free to implement Keynes's policy advice.

Even though Keynes voted Labour in the 1935 general election and believed that it was more likely to follow his policies than the Conservatives were, he never joined the Labour Party. Although he urged increased state intervention in the economy, he did not think public ownership generally a good idea. Labour economists in the 1930's were preoccupied with economic planning as an alternative to market forces, whereas Keynesian economics was designed to restore capitalism to good health through full-employment policies. Skidelsky suggests that Keynes would not have received a warm welcome from the Labour Party even if he had wished to join, because of his upper-class manner and his close association with two men who were thought to have betrayed the Labour Party, Lloyd George and Mosley.

Discouraged by his lack of influence on British economic policy, Keynes turned his attention elsewhere. He was fascinated by Franklin Delano Roosevelt and hoped that Roosevelt would be more responsive to his views. Keynes wrote to Roosevelt, urging him to delay reform measures until after the economy revived and recommending higher public spending and low interest rates. Although other historians have concluded that Keynes had little influence on New Deal policies, Skidelsky claims that the United States government did lower interest rates as a result of Keynes's advice.

Although Keynes was a cultured urbanite whose powerful intellect intimidated many who met him, during the 1930's he became much more conservative in his personal life. Surprisingly, he developed a romantic view of rural life and took up breeding pigs on a three-thousand acre farm. He acquired hunting rights over the wooded area and, according to Skidelsky, began to see himself as a country squire.

During 1936 and 1937, Keynes suffered from repeated health problems. He had had an attack of pleurisy in 1931, and when he began having chest pains later in the 1930's, he assumed that he was suffering a recurrence of the pleurisy. Though he found it impossible to take even short walks without suffering extreme exhaustion and chest pain, he continued to work until he collapsed in May, 1937, with severe angina, apparently caused by a narrowing of the coronary arteries. Although Keynes recovered, he remained weak and relatively inactive during the following two years.

John Maynard Keynes, Volume II: The Economist as Saviour, 1920-1937 was awarded the 1992 Wolfson Prize for the best book on history published in Britain that year. This is not surprising, as Keynes played a significant role in public life during the interwar period, and Skidelsky provides a full and well-informed account of his contributions to policy making. It is in his discussion of Keynes's private life, however, that Skidelsky adds most to knowledge of Keynes. He makes extensive use of the correspondence between Keynes and Lydia Lopokova to reveal this personal dimension. This is the second of a projected three-volume biography and is likely to become the definitive biography of Keynes.

Harold L. Smith

Sources for Further Study

America. CLXXI, July 16, 1994, p. 29.
Canadian Journal of Economics. XXVI, November, 1993, p. 993.
Choice. XXXI, May, 1994, p. 1481
Economic Journal. CIV, January, 1994, p. 138.
The English Historical Review. CIX, April, 1994, p. 395.
Los Angeles Times Book Review. December 26, 1993, p. 4.
The New York Review of Books. XLI, March 3, 1994, p. 6.
The New York Times Book Review. XCIX, January 23, 1994, p. 1.
Publishers Weekly. CCXL, December 6, 1993, p. 63.
The Washington Post Book World. XXIV, January 2, 1994, p. 1.

JOSEPH BRODSKY AND THE CREATION OF EXILE

Author: David M. Bethea (1948-)
Publisher: Princeton University Press (Princeton, New Jersey). 317 pp. $35.00
Type of work: Literary criticism

A critical study of the exiled Russian poet and essayist who received the Nobel Prize in Literature in 1987 and served as poet laureate of the United States from 1991 to 1992

Set apart by his genius and his Russianness, Joseph Brodsky is a powerful and distinctive presence among contemporary American writers. To the extent that "set apart" implies lack of recognition, conjuring up images of a lonely figure working in isolation, the description does not fit Brodsky, who has been showered with literary awards and honors. A frequent panelist at national and international symposia, he counts many prominent writers among his friends. His poems and essays appear regularly in the leading English-language periodicals. Nevertheless, by what matters most to him—his conception of poetry and the poet's role, and especially the poet's relation to language—Brodsky *is* set apart.

Joseph Brodsky and the Creation of Exile is one of the first full-length studies in English of this major writer. (The first was Valentina Polukhina's *Joseph Brodsky: A Poet for Our Time*, published in 1989.) David Bethea is the author of two previous books: *Khodasevich: His Life and Art* (1983; see *Magill's Literary Annual*, 1984) and *The Shape of Apocalypse in Modern Russian Fiction* (1989; see *Magill's Literary Annual*, 1990).

Bethea describes Brodsky as "an American poet laureate whose primary audience is in another language and culture and, in some cases, not even of this world." An audience "not even of this world"? Bethea reminds readers that Brodsky "has never sought solidarity with any group or 'interpretive community' other than his own private 'dead poets' society.' Homer, Virgil, Ovid, Martial, Catullus, Horace, Dante, Donne, Mandelstam, Akhmatova, Tsvetaeva, Auden, Frost, Lowell—these are his jury of peers, his writing must meet their standards." This begins to suggest the way in which Brodsky is set apart both by circumstance and by vocation, and leads into Bethea's statement of his themes: "The present book is about Joseph Brodsky, the metaphysical implications of exile, and the poetry that is written when the first and second enter into dialogue."

In his first chapter, billed as "A Polemical Introduction," Bethea outlines his approach and lays the groundwork for what follows. Before offering a biographical sketch of his subject, he issues a caveat. Brodsky himself would strenuously resist "any outside attempt to place a causal conjunction ('because,' 'as a result of') between the facts of his life and, as he puts it in an English phrase that owes its birth to the Russian (*izgiby stilia*), his 'twists of language.'" Yet while rejecting a reductive causal connection between life and work, Bethea observes that it is impossible to grasp Brodsky's sense of himself as a Russian poet "in the vatic mode" without taking into account the "facts of his life" and the shaping of his "biographical legend."

Brodsky was born in Leningrad in 1940, the only child in a nonobservant Jewish family. His father, a photojournalist, became a naval officer in World War II; his mother worked as a clerk for a local council. Both suffered from the anti-Semitic campaigns that followed the war in the Soviet Union. Brodsky has memorably described the family's life in a communal apartment in his collection of essays *Less Than One* (1986).

At the age of fifteen, Brodsky left school. He traveled all over the Soviet Union, holding a variety of short-term jobs, including stints with geological expeditions. First arrested in 1959, he was tried for "social parasitism" in 1964 and sentenced to five years of hard labor. (Prior to the trial, he was sent to a psychiatric hospital, where, like many others who ran afoul of the Soviet state, he was tortured in the guise of "treatment.") After serving about a year and a half of his sentence in a remote village in the far north—during which, self-taught, he read a good deal of poetry in English—Brodsky was released early. In 1972, however, he was expelled from the Soviet Union.

In 1961 or 1962 Brodsky had first met the poet Anna Akhmatova and her lifelong friend Nadezhda Mandelstam, widow of the poet Osip Mandelstam (who died in a Soviet labor camp in 1938) and herself a writer of unforgettable memoirs. Both saw the young Brodsky as a successor to Osip Mandelstam (a "second Osya"). In exile, Brodsky found another mentor, W. H. Auden, who recognized his exceptional gifts and did much to smooth the way for him. Settling in the United States, Brodsky continued to improve his English, establishing himself as a major bilingual writer and international man of letters.

Told thus, Brodsky's story has an unreal quality, as if scripted. Presumably the day-to-day living was quite different. To begin with, this account does not do justice to the experience of estrangement from all that is familiar. After the fall of communism and the collapse of the Soviet Union, Brodsky could have returned to Russia (though as of 1994 he had not chosen to do so); technically he is no longer an exile. The bulk of his mature life has been spent outside his homeland, however, and that is irrevocable.

Bethea notes that Brodsky rejects the notion that, as a poet in exile, he suffered a particularly poignant fate. "Whether we like it or not," Brodsky wrote in a statement for a conference on writers in exile (a conference that he did not attend), "*Gastarbeiters* and refugees of any stripe effectively pluck the carnation out of an exiled writer's lapel. Displacement and misplacement are the century's commonplace. And what our exiled writer has in common with a *Gastarbeiter* or a political refugee is that in either case a man is running from the worse to the better."

This no-nonsense statement fits with Brodsky's definition of exile, not as a condition to be passively accepted but rather as an opportunity to exercise one's freedom. What is not suggested by his brusque tone is the way that the experience of exile has informed his poetry from the beginning. Even before he was expelled from the Soviet Union, Brodsky was metaphorically an exile, an outsider.

Bethea's procedure, then, is to consider Brodsky's career from a series of diverse yet complementary perspectives, each illuminating in some fashion the centrality of exile and "otherness" in his poetry. Along the way, Bethea demonstrates the inadequacy of several of the critical paradigms that govern current academic discourse about literature, including the psychoanalytic criticism of Julia Kristeva, the political criticism of Edward Said, and the feminist criticism of Hélène Cixous and Luce Irigaray.

As suggested above, what most distinguishes Brodsky as a poet-critic is his relation to language. In an essay on Osip Mandelstam in *Less Than One*, Brodsky asserts that "what dictates a poem is the language, and this is the voice of the language, which we know under the nicknames of Muse and Inspiration." In an essay on Auden in the same volume, Brodsky writes that the "mask" of Auden's idiom (Auden "disguised himself as an observer of public mores," dispensing "witty comments") "had less to do with matters of style and tradition than with the personal humility imposed on him not so much by a particular creed as by his sense of the nature of language." This notion of language as a repository of wisdom is utterly foreign to most contemporary poets and critics; those who affirm it (Brodsky is one, Geoffrey Hill another) seem to have alighted here from another era.

For Brodsky, one consequence of this relation to language is an emptying of the self, resulting in the "impersonality" that strikes every reader of his poetry. He often hears the "voice of the language" in the words of his great predecessors, and they in turn speak through him. This process is brilliantly analyzed in Bethea's chapter "Brodsky's Triangular Vision: Exile as Palimpsest."

To illustrate what he means by "triangular vision," Bethea provides an in-depth reading of Brodsky's poem "December in Florence" (published in 1980 in *A Part of Speech*, his first collection written in exile). The poem is addressed to an unnamed "you," clearly meant to be Dante Alighieri, and there are echoes of Dante throughout. At the same time, the poem alludes to Mandelstam (who identified himself with the Italian master in his great essay "Conversation About Dante"). Bethea explains that Brodsky's "vision can be called triangular in that a Russian source, say Mandelstam, is subtly implanted within a Western source, say Dante, so that each source comments on the other, but as they do so they implicate a third source—Brodsky himself."

Bethea shows that this pattern—so frequent in Brodsky as to constitute "a kind of signature"—is fundamental to understanding what Brodsky has made of exile. From Mandelstam, Brodsky inherited a "nostalgia for world culture." Rejecting the official Soviet culture, he claimed for himself the classical Western tradition, the "outsider" tradition of Russian poetry, and the Anglo-American tradition (from John Donne to Thomas Hardy, Robert Frost, T. S. Eliot, and Auden). Thus, "Dante's exile is mediated by Mandelstam's, which in turn is mediated by Brodsky's. All are different . . . yet all are also the same, each in its own way reflecting the central paradox of banishment: 'an exile is someone who inhabits one place and remembers or projects the reality of another.' "

Bethea concludes with an afterword, quoting from Brodsky's proposal to place an inexpensive anthology of American poetry in supermarkets and indeed wherever people congregate; he suggests a printing of 50 million copies. As he often does, Brodsky plants a trap for readers who are nudging one another, deriding his impracticality and his grandiose pretensions. The books will not sell all at once, he concedes, "but gradually, over a decade or so, they will sell. Books find their readers. And if they will not sell, well, let them lie around, absorb dust, rot, and disintegrate. There is always going to be a child who will fish a book out of the garbage heap. I was once such a child, for what it's worth." One trusts that Bethea's superb study will also find its readers, if not in a garbage heap then in the dim stacks of university libraries, or in the yet-to-be-imagined limbo to which such artifacts will be consigned when the technology of the book becomes obsolete.

John Wilson

Sources for Further Study

Choice. XXXII, November, 1994, p. 461.
Library Journal. CXIX, April 1, 1994, p. 96.
The Times Literary Supplement. July 8, 1994, p. 21.
Washington Times. April 24, 1994, p. B8.

JOSEPH CORNELL'S THEATER OF THE MIND
Selected Diaries, Letters, and Files

Author: Joseph Cornell (1903-1972)
Edited, with an introduction, by Mary Ann Caws
Foreword by John Ashbery
Publisher: Thames and Hudson (New York). Illustrated. 480 pp. $35.00
Type of work: Diary, letters, and notebooks
Time: 1940-1972
Locale: Flatbush, Queens, New York City

A generous selection from the voluminous diaries, letters, and files of Joseph Cornell, the eccentric and distinctive American artist best-known for his "boxes" constructed from the diverse materials he collected tirelessly during visits to Manhattan

In *Joseph Cornell's Theater of the Mind: Selected Diaries, Letters, and Files*, Mary Ann Caws, a distinguished American scholar of Dada and Surrealism, successfully performs the daunting task of shaping a representative and manageable selection out of the vast store of Cornell's papers and other materials deposited in the Smithsonian Institution's Archives of American Art. Cornell was an energetic diarist and correspondent. Much of what this celebrated packrat accumulated, typically on visits to used bookshops such as those on Manhattan's Fourth Avenue or the thrift shops and stalls along Canal Street, he turned into art. Many of his whimsical boxes and collages became gifts bestowed on friends and those he admired. Caws presents the fragments of Cornell's life in a handsome illustrated volume that includes appreciations of Cornell by Robert Motherwell and John Ashbery.

Joseph Cornell was born in 1903 in Nyack, New York, to a moderately prosperous family. Yet the last years of his father's life were marked by illness and financial ruin. Cornell was able to enter Phillips Academy in 1917, the year of his father's death, but left school without a diploma in 1919, at about the time the Cornell family moved to Queens. During the 1920's Cornell worked for a textile firm, and in 1925 he experienced a profound religious conversion to Christian Science. He was to remain a devoted member of this denomination until his death.

In 1929, his family moved to a white frame house in Flushing, Queens. Cornell remained here for the rest of his life, caring for his invalid brother Robert (who suffered from cerebral palsy) until the latter's death in 1965. His mother died in 1966. Cornell left the family home regularly to venture into Manhattan, where he frequented used and rare bookshops and secondhand stores. Although he nurtured throughout his life a love for the French language (with which he had considerable facility) and modern French literature, Cornell never traveled abroad, let alone to other parts of the United States.

By the early 1930's, Cornell had begun to create collages (he called them "montages") in response to the photomontages of Max Ernst. He also made his first film and began to fashion the boxes that remain his artistic signature. Viewing the dreamlike arrangements of objects in Cornell's boxes, one can easily understand how his work came to be associated with Surrealism. In 1942 Cornell met a number of Surrealist artists, many of them refugees newly arrived in the United States. He also worked briefly in a defense plant during the war.

After a sampling of undated entries, the material Caws presents begins in 1940, when Cornell was emerging into the ranks of American modernists, especially those associated with the Surrealist movement in exile. The memorable 1938 Museum of Modern Art exhibition "Fantastic Art, Dada, Surrealism" had included some of Cornell's work, bringing his art to the attention of a wider public. His new admirers included émigré artists such as Marcel Duchamp and Pavel Tchelitchew, as well as the poet Marianne Moore. Letters exchanged between her and Cornell provide some of the high points of this volume's war-era correspondence.

Cornell's correspondents were a varied and interesting lot. Besides those of Moore, early letters reproduced here include those between Cornell and poet Mina Loy, critics Parker Tyler and Charles Henri Ford (for whose magazine, *View*, Cornell occasionally designed covers), and Robert Motherwell. In later years, he engaged in lively exchanges with Dore Ashton and Susan Sontag, who, like all Cornell friends, received boxes as gifts.

In his letters, the artist is sweet and charming, usually decorating the pages with bits of collage. Cornell seems to have struck others as a kind of exceptionally gifted child, and indeed he retained to the end the spontaneity and lack of pretense one associates with childhood. In *Dime-Store Alchemy: The Art of Joseph Cornell* (1992), Charles Simic noted the effect Cornell had on critics, "disarming" them with his originality and genius. "When it comes to Cornell," he wrote, "there are no axes to grind." Though he never married, Cornell enjoyed children immensely.

Whether writing a letter or a diary entry, Cornell reports on such commonplace activities as eating sweets, going for walks, and riding the subway. He describes his moods—"feeling of *felicity*" is a typical phrase. He recounts the late-night bouts of concentrated work that often followed periods of quiescence. He comments on his musical passions, often mentioning Wolfgang Amadeus Mozart or Claude Debussy. He collected records, along with everything else, and would describe a new purchase from the Record Hunter excitedly to his friends.

Apparently Cornell strongly tested others' friendship through long, rambling telephone conversations. The artist would carry on a frenzied monologue, thinking out loud, while his exasperated friend waited him out (even napping, receiver to her ear, in one case). This irritating quirk points to one of the many complexities that made the man. He was far from the recluse his legend would have him to be, for he valued friends immensely and went to great lengths to stay in contact with them.

Among other complexities or paradoxes the reader confronts in this volume, Cornell combined religious devotion with a finely tuned erotic sensibility. In later years, he was increasingly open about his erotic obsessions, complaining at times about the degree to which they distracted him and even recording ruefully the fact of his occasional masturbation. Nudes appeared more frequently among his images, encouraged in part by his friendship with artist Carolee Schneemann, one of the first

American artists (in the 1950's) to combine nudity with "performance art."

Cornell was fiercely attracted to ballerinas, opera divas, and film starlets such as Lauren Bacall, to whom he dedicated a famous box. Attractive young women working in stores, restaurants, and cafeterias became objects of excessive fascination and aesthetic inspiration, like so many Beatrices to his Dante. He referred to them as "fées" (fairies) or "sylphs." He would endow someone he had glimpsed in the most commonplace setting with an exaggeratedly fanciful title. The girl behind a counter of stuffed rabbits at Grant's Five and Dime became the "fée aux lapins," for example. In one case, he even invited Joyce Hunter, a cashier at Ripley's Believe It Or Not in Manhattan, to come and live in his house. She did so, and later stole several of his boxes and other works. When she was apprehended, Cornell refused to press charges. After Hunter was tragically stabbed to death, Cornell paid her funeral expenses and visited her grave regularly.

Given current heightened awareness of child sexual molestation, Cornell's friendly attention to little girls may give readers serious pause. He extolled the delicate beauty of young girls and invited friends to bring their daughters to his home, where he would serve them pastries and show them his works in progress. Dore Ashton recounts telephone conversations with Cornell during which he would inquire after her daughters. Neither Caws nor any other biographer gives the slightest hint that there was anything untoward or unsavory in the delight Cornell took in little girls.

Cornell's desires and appetites were held in check by his observant religious life. Very late in his life, he testified publicly to the gratitude he felt for his Christian Scientist faith. He read daily from the Bible and from Mary Baker Eddy's *Science and Health, with Key to the Scriptures* (1875). He devoted himself unselfishly to his incapacitated younger brother Robert, and, according to his diaries, always felt more than rewarded by his sweet disposition and "radiant" countenance. After Robert's death, his older brother memorialized him in a box that incorporated René Magritte's *Time Transfixed* (1939), whose locomotive image pays homage to Robert's passion for model trains.

Christian Science is a uniquely American religion, and Joseph Cornell remains a uniquely American artist, a genuine native eccentric like Charles Ives or Emily Dickinson (one of his great literary passions). Yet Cornell was also a committed Francophile. His quotidian routines and experiences continually led him to invoke a pantheon of modern French authors whose refined aesthetic sensibilities matched his own. The diaries and files are replete with references to and quoted material from their writings. He was very much drawn to Gérard de Nerval, the tragic nineteenth century author and prototypical *poète maudit* whose *Aurélia* (1855; English translation, 1932) was one of his favorite books. He admired and emulated the great poet Stéphane Mallarmé's devotion to his art, a trait shared by Marcel Proust, with whose cloistered existence Cornell much identified. He also shared Proust's rapturous appreciation of music.

Proust's work, which Cornell read and reread faithfully, is filled with instances of persons transported to otherwise inaccessible psychic and emotional states through aesthetic experience, such as the keenly experienced hearing of a certain passage of music. The concept of synesthesia, the ability of certain sensations to induce such a state, was introduced by Charles Baudelaire, one of the poets Cornell most admired. In some ways, Cornell's regular urban forays recall Baudelaire's *flâneur*, the poet's term for an idler who takes in the city's stimuli in a random, unhurried fashion. Cornell's interventions, however, were at least marginally more purposive. He was gathering supplies for his boxes and collages. In any case, Cornell may be said to have been something of an American symbolist.

Mary Ann Caws possesses the requisite expertise in modern French letters to highlight the strong Francophilic tendencies Cornell exhibited in his work—to which he often gave French titles and in which bits of text from French newspapers and books routinely appeared—and in his daily life. Cornell lived amid a welter of debris and material saved for eventual use in his art or to be sent in collagelike letters to his cherished friends. Late in life, he employed several assistants to supervise this mountain of curious fragments. Cornell also filed away all sorts of scraps of writing, not only journals and notebooks. One can only begin to imagine the formidable labors that faced Caws as she set about to cull this unique archive to produce the appropriately named *Joseph Cornell's Theater of the Mind*.

Cornell's daily jottings show that he could experience ecstasy or "epiphany" over a bit of graffiti glimpsed above the tunnel near Penn Station. He describes in detail his appreciation of certain classical music recordings and mentions specific orchestras, conductors, and soloists. One has the sensation of browsing through a friend's record collection. In later years especially, he returns again and again to favorite books. Wallace Fowlie's *Rimbaud* (1966) is mentioned repeatedly, and always there is *Science and Health* and the Christian Science he embraced with a quiet but ever mounting fervor.

There are a few surprises in Cornell's diaries and letters. He rarely mentions world events, despite having lived through much of a remarkable and turbulent century. A rare exception occurs when he notes the national mourning for Robert Kennedy in June, 1968—there is nothing about John F. Kennedy's assassination five years earlier. Also absent for the most part are comments about his work's critical reception. When he does mention one of his pieces, it is usually to discuss its status as a gift, either actual or imagined (sometimes he designated a work as a gift to a long-dead historical figure, such as Emily Dickinson). It would seem that Cornell did not possess the oversized ego for which all too many celebrated artists are known.

This quietly determined man was one of the most unforgettable and enduring artists of the twentieth century. *Joseph Cornell's Theater of the Mind*, with its rich essays, illustrations, helpful chronology, and bibliography, is an outstanding addition to an already distinguished body of critical literature on Cornell.

James A. Winders

Sources for Further Study

Artforum. XXXII, Summer, 1994, p. S1.
Choice. XXXI, July, 1994, p. 1711.
Library Journal. CXIX, March 15, 1994, p. 70.
The Observer. April 3, 1994, p. 20.
The Review of Contemporary Fiction. XIV, Fall, 1994, p. 235.
The Times Literary Supplement. April 8, 1994, p. 11.
The Village Voice Literary Supplement. March, 1994, p. 6.

JULIP

Author: Jim Harrison (1937-   )
Publisher: Houghton Mifflin/Seymour Lawrence (Boston). 275 pp. $21.95
Type of work: Novellas
Time: The 1990's
Locale: Florida, Georgia, Wisconsin, Michigan, and Arizona

In Julip, *his third collection of novellas, Jim Harrison firmly establishes himself as a contemporary master of the form*

Many of the best contemporary writers have never written (or at least published) a single short story. Cormac McCarthy immediately comes to mind, and several other names quickly follow: Toni Morrison, Paul Auster, Robert Stone, William Gaddis. The list goes on. There are exceptions—writers who have concentrated solely, and with unwavering fidelity, on the short story, including Raymond Carver, Grace Paley, Andre Dubus, Alice Munro, and Stuart Dybek.

Although Jim Harrison is known best as a novelist, he occasionally narrows the scope of his storytelling powers in an effort to scale down plot and action—the sibling conventions of the typical Harrison novel (excluding his densest, most complex novel, *Dalva* [1988])—in favor of a more streamlined narrative that finds its expression best in the shape of the novella. The novella has intrigued the world's greatest writers (Leo Tolstoy, Anton Chekhov, Thomas Mann, William Faulkner, Gustave Flaubert, Herman Melville, Joseph Conrad, William Gass). Among the top ranks of contemporary writers, the novella remains that rarest of half-breeds, a bird that once flourished, then plummeted to near extinction, even though writers such as Harrison, Rick Bass, Andre Dubus, and Ellen Gilchrist are attempting to save it.

In *Julip*, Harrison's third and most recent collection of three long stories, he continues to breathe new life into the lost art of the novella. Although the canvas is small (two of these novellas run under one hundred pages), here Harrison appears willing to expand the boundaries of his imagination. Prior to the appearance of *Legends of the Fall* in 1979, Harrison's previous work romped over familiar stomping grounds: the backwoods country of Michigan's Upper Peninsula, all-night forays in mid-1970's Key West. These novels were built around whiskey, dope, and the bedding down of beautiful women—moments, it should be noted, that rise above the inherent pitfalls of country-western music, lifted by the lyricism and lucidity of Harrison's prose. In *Legends of the Fall*, though, he broadened the scope of his vision by allowing his imagination to take him into interior Mexico ("Revenge"), corporate New York ("The Man Who Gave Up His Name"), and pre-World War I Montana ("Legends of the Fall"). Each of these stories possesses a mythic quality, a larger than actual life dimension—the first sure sign that Harrison is a master, a writer who will last. The publication of *Legends of the Fall*, which is Harrison's most publicized book (two of the novellas have been adapted into Hollywood films), was a turning point in his career.

The books that followed—most notably *Sundog* (1984), *Dalva*, and *The Woman Lit by Fireflies* (1990)—as well as Harrison's seven books of poetry, earned for him further critical and commercial success. Critic Bernard Levin climbed out on a ledge when he claimed that Harrison is a "writer with immortality in him." Harrison's permanence still remains to be seen. One thing is certain: With each subsequent new book—as he proves once again in *Julip*—Harrison continues to break new ground, ground that always comes up fertile.

It is true that Harrison's early work is shadowed and perhaps even shackled by Ernest Hemingway's ghost. Harrison, who was born and reared and continues to live and sometimes to write about places and rivers immortalized by the postwar wanderings of Nick Adams, is fond of taking brazen jabs at Hemingway, proclaiming much of his work dated, worn to parody over time. Unlike Hemingway (whose later work, aside from *A Moveable Feast* [1964], is stiff and stilted), Harrison is determined not to repeat himself. Nowhere does this desire to find a new story to inhabit assume a more palpable presence than in *Dalva*, *The Woman Lit by Fireflies*, and *Julip*, books that explore the roles that strong, vivacious women play in the lives of men who desperately need to be saved.

The men in these three novellas, most of whom are over forty, find themselves in the crisis-stricken grips of middle age. In "Julip," the three main male players (to whom the narrator refers as the Boys)—a painter, writer, and photographer—ritually head down to Key West to play out their boyish fantasies as faux outdoorsmen. They spend their days fishing for tarpon and tooting cocaine under a sun that scalds bald spots; at night they hop from bar to bar in their pursuit of that not-so-elusive bed partner. The morning after, hung over, they manage to find time for telephone calls home to their wives. Twenty-one-year-old Julip, a dog trainer, eventually gets involved with all three of these men, and all of them court her with gifts and money and false promises of marriage. These are men that in the hands of another writer, say Hemingway or even a younger Harrison from the days of *Wolf* (1971), *A Good Day to Die* (1973), and *Warlock* (1981), would have been billed as heroic; the Harrison of *Julip*, however, sees them clearly for who they are, "petrified babies suspended in dreamless sleep." Julip, who is the product of a "schizophrenic upbringing," child of an "alcoholic marriage," is forced to pick up the broken pieces after her blood-lusting brother Bobby shoots and wounds the three men who had "defiled my sister." What Bobby fails to realize, though, is that Julip can take care of herself; he is the one in need of help. Julip is the only one resilient enough to live not only with the world but with herself as well. Although she is the youngest, Julip is the one character who understands how the world works—that sometimes one must work with the world in order to get out of it what one wants.

Unlike Julip, B. D., better known as Brown Dog, the backwoods malcontent from "The Seven-Ounce Man," was "born not to cooperate with the world." B. D. is a highly likable stray, a mutt who has been kicked around for most of his forty-two years, though he keeps coming back for more as if someday somebody were bound to throw him a bone. In this novella, Harrison returns to the north woods of his native state,

Michigan, to tell a picaresque tale. B. D. is "a true mongrel," a card-carrying member of the "plain pissed-off residue of society." Years ago, at nineteen, B. D. had studied to become a preacher at the Moody Bible Institute in Chicago, but had dropped out after he had "blown his tuition on a hooker."

The tale of Brown Dog was first heard in an earlier novella, "Brown Dog," from *The Woman Lit by Fireflies*—a frolicking roll-in-the-hay memoir that begins when B. D. finds the body of a drowned Indian, "a big one . . . sitting . . . on a ledge of rock in about seventy feet of water" in Lake Superior. B. D. admits, "I don't amount to much, and you can't get more ordinary, but no one ever called me stupid." Yet he is naïve in the ways of the world. A good-looking graduate student in anthropology at downstate's University of Michigan tricks him into revealing the exact whereabouts of a sacred Native American burial ground, following his lust rather than the foresight and wisdom born of a reasonable mind.

"The Seven-Ounce Man" picks up the tale during "the darkest and coldest summer of the century in the Upper Peninsula." It has been six months since Brown Dog first told his story, and now he is looking back over the chain of events that were "predestined by everything that had happened to him in the past two years." He is introduced to unfamiliar readers as "a desperado falsely accused." His mug shot graces the Outstate section of the *Detroit Free Press*, so that he is tracked and heckled by "the unpleasantness of fame." The media mislabel Brown Dog as the spokesperson for a radical "Red Power" group based in the political underground of Wisconsin or farther west. For fun, Brown Dog feeds the myth. He gets courted into action in defense of the ancient burial site by Marten, a smooth-talking Native American filmmaker and petty drug smuggler whose films carry titles such as *Will Whitey Ever See Red?* Comically, the novella comes to an explosive, firecracking conclusion when the Red Power advocates plan a dawn's early light attack against the team of Ann Arbor anthropologists, who are in the interest of "digging up my grandparents."

Harrison is one of the few serious writers of contemporary fiction who are successful at blending pathos with humor. Like Brown Dog, who is not above laughing at himself, Harrison pokes fun, as he did in "Julip," at a world where male heroics are governed by an adage that is true for all males, canine or human: "A hard dick has no conscience."

The world found in the third novella, "The Beige Dolorosa," is an academia strangled by the claustrophobic clamor of political correctness. Phillip Caulkins is a fifty-year-old English professor at a small liberal arts college located in southern Michigan ("liberal," in this case, is the operative word—a major misnomer), a school proudly labeled "'the Swarthmore of the Midwest.'" Caulkins is a hanger-on to worn-out mythologies, an Old School advocate, the last of his department who does not own or know how to use a word processor, a heavy smoker in a health-obsessed environment. This is a world, an ivory tower of stodgy learning, whose ruling ideology has been antiseptically cleansed by connotative meanings and dead-ended discursives regarding the veiled undercurrents of certain potentially offensive words: a world, in short, to which Caulkins no longer belongs.

> My reality had betrayed me, the reality to which I had devoted my life had disappeared. I no longer had control of the world I lived in. . . . A world that had welcomed me for three decades had shown me the door, and at fifty I owed that world nothing but my contempt.

Like Brown Dog, Caulkins heads west to live on an Arizona ranch owned by the wealthy father of his daughter's husband. There, in a world where actions speak louder than words, where the body is used more than the mind, Caulkins' spirit is slowly, from midwinter to spring, restored through his daily intercourse with the natural world—a relationship that is spawned, at least in the beginning, by his daughter's encouragement. Caulkins finds a sense of redemption by setting himself the grandiose task of renaming the birds of North America. Here is an echo of one of Harrison's favorite poets, Rainer Maria Rilke, who wrote in *Duineser Elegien* (1923; *Duino Elegies*, 1930), "Maybe we're here only to say: *house,/ bridge, well, gate, jug, olive tree, window—/* . . . but to say them, remember,/ oh, to say them in a way that the things themselves/ never dreamed of existing." It is clear that Caulkins himself never would have dreamed that he—a stuffed shirt by trade—would find solace in the desert wilderness, away from the comforts of books and classrooms.

What is not so surprising is the wide-ranging territory and the shifting of narrative voices and landscapes that Jim Harrison covers in *Julip*, his third collection of novellas. He has established himself as the contemporary master of the form. In *Julip*, Harrison is working at the height of his powers. With each new book, he rises without fail to the occasion, fulfilling the hopes of a legion of faithful readers who know immortality when it looks them square in the eye. *Julip* is further evidence that Harrison is a writer built to last.

Peter Markus

Sources for Further Study

Booklist. XC, March 1, 1994, p. 1139.
Chicago Tribune. May 8, 1994, XIV, p. 5.
Kirkus Reviews. LXII, February 15, 1994, p. 163.
Library Journal. CXIX, April 1, 1994, p. 136.
Los Angeles Times Book Review. August 14, 1994, p. 8.
The New York Times Book Review. XCIX, May 22, 1994, p. 41.
Publishers Weekly. CCXLI, February 28, 1994, p. 71.
The Washington Post Book World. XXIV, April 17, 1994, p. 7.

KAY BOYLE
Author of Herself

Author: Joan Mellen (1941-   )
Publisher: Farrar Straus Giroux (New York). Illustrated. 670 pp. $35.00
Type of work: Literary biography
Time: 1902-1992
Locale: The United States and Europe (England, France, Austria, and Germany)

This biography counterbalances the personal myth that Kay Boyle created in her lifetime, thus revealing a new aspect of this complex, original author

Principal personages:
KAY BOYLE, an author and political activist best known for her fiction and poetry
KATHERINE EVANS BOYLE, her mother, whose ambition inspired yet perhaps harmed her daughter
RICHARD BRAULT, a Frenchman, Boyle's first husband
ERNEST "MICHAEL" WALSH, Boyle's Irish American lover, who died of tuberculosis after a few months with her
LAURENCE VAIL, an avant-garde artist and author, Boyle's second husband
JOSEPH VON FRANCKENSTEIN, the Austrian baron who became an American soldier, a diplomat, and Boyle's third husband

Kay Boyle, author of some forty books of prose and poetry, was an American who lived for more than twenty years in Europe, was on the cutting edge of poetry in the 1920's, and in the 1930's was hailed as "Hemingway's successor" by critic Mary Colum. Joan Mellen's book is the first complete biography published since Boyle's death in 1992. Unlike Sandra Whipple Spanier's earlier *Kay Boyle: Artist and Activist* (1986), which offers a literary assessment of her work, Mellen's book focuses on Boyle's life and relationships. She examines Boyle's writing, which she finds strongly autobiographical, only as it reflects and illuminates her life. Mellen draws upon extensive personal and phone interviews with Boyle and her family and friends; letters and private papers; contemporary accounts; and Boyle's own poetry and prose.

Boyle's life was not a quiet one. Married at twenty, she sailed with husband Richard Brault to France, became involved in the literary life of Paris, and then met and fell in love with poet-editor Ernest Walsh, father of her first child. After Walsh's death, she married Laurence Vail, whose spontaneous nature first enchanted and later alienated her, and by whom she had three more daughters.

When the Nazis invaded France, the Vails fled to America, where Boyle soon married Joseph von Franckenstein, an Austrian who had tutored her children in France and who became an American espionage agent during World War II. They had two more children. After the war, they returned to occupied Germany, where Franckenstein held a civilian post and Boyle served as correspondent for *The New Yorker*. Both underwent loyalty hearings during the 1950's; when he lost his government position, she supported them with her writing. In subsequent years, she became known for her outspoken political activism.

Mellen shatters the image that Boyle carefully cultivated. Boyle presented herself as a fascinating woman, successful author, and devoted wife and mother. Upon her 1941 return to America at the peak of her literary reputation, she was perceived as a glamorous expatriate and was the subject of several interviews. Mellen exposes her, however, as stubborn, self-centered, attractive to men, yet indifferent to her children, whom she abandoned emotionally and often physically. She did not care for her family herself but hired domestic help, while she followed her own rigorous writing schedule.

In contrast, Mellen notes Boyle's surprisingly conventional ideas on bearing children, suggesting that sex to her meant babies. Mellen is extremely harsh toward her subject for not taking precautions to avoid pregnancy (though at times Boyle did) and for not taking a loving interest in the children she had. She also chastises Boyle for openly preferring her son (by Franckenstein) to her five daughters.

Mellen examines the irony that "a writer who had spent forty years chronicling the emotions of men and women with sensitivity should perceive so little about her own children." Boyle did not understand why her children felt abandoned, as their comments repeatedly testify. She believed that she was rearing them appropriately, even after three daughters and one stepdaughter attempted suicide. When one of her lovers seduced two daughters, she forgave him. Years afterward, her daughter Clover wrote, "What is the sense of saving the children of Biafra if you can't save your own children?"

If at times Boyle appears monstrous by her indifference to her children's needs, such a point might not even be raised in a discussion of a male writer. Nevertheless, looking at Boyle in the total context of her family, Mellen blames her (perhaps rightfully) for the children's problems. She finds Boyle withholding approval from her children even in her eighties.

Frequently Mellen reminds the reader that Boyle was not only author of herself but a fabricator too. She loved to embellish a good story, even to the point of contradiction. She rewrote her own history with Ezra Pound, from her initial meeting, where she "liked him more than I ever have," to her public statement, "I disliked him then," made fifty years later. She exaggerated her closeness to James Joyce and Samuel Beckett, among others, claiming Beckett as her oldest, dearest friend, though they met only once in 1931 and not again for many years. To her children, she even implied an affair with him, which he was generous enough not to deny.

Mellen points out numerous errors of fact and omission in the autobiographical chapters that Boyle added to poet Robert McAlmon's memoir of the Paris years, *Being Geniuses Together: 1920-1930* (1968, 1984). Boyle never studied to become an architect, as she stated, though she did take some classes in mechanical drawing. Discrepancies in names, ages, and dates appear, possibly through Boyle's carelessness, although Mellen suggests that her errors were deliberate. Boyle did modify truth to serve her own purposes, eliminating of some of McAlmon's passages that she thought reflected poorly on him, especially those referring to his homosexuality. Her changes were substantial enough that Mellen finds the book is "best read as a work of fiction."

As other writers have done, Boyle also mythologized herself in the heroines of her stories and novels. Although Boyle frequently said that her life could be known through her work, Mellen relies on that work as if it were fact. She writes that Boyle's long fiction "offers . . . mirrors into the author far more accurate than anything she might have said about herself then or later." That is, fiction is truer than fact.

Boyle took a slightly different position. For her, fiction *was* fact. Thus she denied any hint of incest in her story "Wedding Day" or homosexuality in "The Bridegroom's Body" and *My Next Bride* (1934), even though these themes are clearly present. Boyle knew the people and events on which her stories were modeled; there could be no more than what she saw. Mellen views her denial as a typical contradiction, for "no writer of her day wrote with such sensitivity about the love between two people of the same sex."

Perhaps the strongest example of Boyle's mythologizing occurs with respect to her mother, Katherine Evans Boyle. Boyle dedicated her first novel, *Plagued by the Nightingale* (1931), to "My Mother and Her Undying Flame"; she also praised her mother as a frail, heroic figure in *Being Geniuses Together* and in her 1984 memoir. Yet Mellen believes that Katherine was in many ways a negative influence on her daughter. A permissive mother, she allowed Boyle to stay home from school so that she never received a formal education; instead, she read and went to galleries. Because Katherine uncritically praised Boyle's childish scribbles as art and poetry, Mellen infers that any attempt Boyle "made to develop as an artist and a thinker was blunted by her mother's unqualified endorsement of everything she said." She concludes that Boyle resented her mother's artistic dreams for her and unconsciously tried to fail as a writer. Like Katherine, Boyle became a cold and distant grandmother.

Characteristically, Boyle reacted on the basis of emotion rather than logic. In the 1930's, she passionately championed the supremacy of the individual and stayed away from politics, strongly rejecting Marxism. She moved from an apolitical to an intensely political stance as the McCarthy-driven loyalty hearings nearly destroyed her life. In *The Long Walk at San Francisco State and Other Essays* (1970), Boyle chronicled the infamous strike called by the Black Student Union to demand a black studies program at San Francisco State College.

Mellen offers quite a different perspective on that event. In her own book, Boyle failed to mention that the faculty curriculum committee had already agreed to a black studies program before the strike was called. When a fellow faculty member tried to explain this to her, she refused to listen and joined the picket line with her students. "I don't mind dying for a worthy cause," she told a reporter. She then plunged wholeheartedly into demonstrations on behalf of César Chávez's farm workers and against the Vietnam War.

Boyle was notoriously unsympathetic to women as writers or students. In her classes she attacked the work of Anaïs Nin, Sylvia Plath, and Tillie Olsen. In a 1964 interview she observed, "I don't think women should try to write like men but I think they should try not to write like women . . . presenting the woman's instead of the human point of view." For her, the "human" view was unquestionably male. She spurned the women's movement as "reactionary" and showed little empathy for women who were seeking their own voice and fulfillment. "Well, I could do it, with my children," Boyle said, believing her own myth.

Mellen's work is excellent when she is dealing with facts. The research and scholarship of this biography are impressive, with sources cited for nearly every quotation. Unfortunately, the author indulges in some mythmaking of her own, such as the "sexually tinged" relationship she finds between Katherine Boyle and her father-in-law. She does not adequately document her explanations for Boyle's professional and personal antipathy toward other women, her lack of concern for her children, or her unconscious need to fabulate. An example of Mellen's tendency to go too far can be seen when she dramatically interprets the facial expressions of the Vail children as they arrive in the United States, comments not borne out by the accompanying Associated Press photograph.

At the same time Mellen attempts a balance, for she clearly admires her subject. She credits Boyle with the creation of the so-called *New Yorker* story, which disdains traditional rising and falling action, focusing instead on a single intense moment. She praises Boyle's courage in what was surely a difficult life and records the literary honors given her: two O. Henry Awards for fiction; two Guggenheim Fellowships; grants from the National Endowment for the Arts, the Before Columbus Foundation, the Fund for Poetry, and the Lannan Foundation; and membership in the National Institute of Arts and Letters and the prestigious American Academy of Arts and Letters.

Both Spanier and Mellen have sought to explain why Boyle's literary reputation dimmed. Spanier claims that Boyle was a victim of faulty timing, a political liberal in a conservative era, and that her work was trivialized because it was woman-centered. Mellen finds Boyle's European settings a barrier to her readers, her work less timely as American concerns shifted to Korea and the Far East. But more important, when Boyle decided in the 1940's to write commercial stories for magazines such as *The Saturday Evening Post*, she lost her ability to move easily between commercial fiction and art. *Avalanche* (1943), her only popular success, was the novel that impelled many critics to reject her as a serious writer.

This biography is critical, though not unsympathetic. Mellen counteracts the personal myth that Boyle created and that Spanier largely accepts, thus revealing new dimensions of this complex, original author. Spanier's biography stresses Boyle's very real literary achievement. Taken together, these works re-create Kay Boyle's remarkable life and talent.

Joanne McCarthy

Sources for Further Study

Booklist. XC, April 15, 1994, p. 1500.

Kirkus Reviews. LXII, February 1, 1994, p. 122.

Library Journal. CXIX, April 15, 1994, p. 76.
Los Angeles Times Book Review. August 7, 1994, p. 4.
The New York Times Book Review. XCIX, May 1, 1994, p. 11.
Publishers Weekly. CCXLI, February 7, 1994, p. 77.
The Washington Post Book World. XXIV, July 17, 1994, p. 13.
The Women's Review of Books. XI, July, 1994, p. 33.

KING OF RAGTIME
Scott Joplin and His Era

Author: Edward A. Berlin
Publisher: Oxford University Press (New York). Illustrated. 334 pp. $25.00
Type of work: Biography
Time: 1868-1917
Locale: Texas, Missouri, New York City

The story of composer Scott Joplin, "King of Ragtime," who as part of the first post-Civil War generation of African Americans used music as a means of transcending poverty and low social class

Principal personages:

SCOTT JOPLIN, an African American composer
FREDDIE JOPLIN, his first wife
LOTTIE STOKES, his common-law wife who helped arrange business affairs in the later years of his life
JOSEPH E. LAMB, a white composer and friend who, along with Joplin and James Scott, was one of the "Big Three of Classic Ragtime"
ARTHUR MARSHALL, a former Joplin student who became a noted Midwest pianist-entertainer and lifelong Joplin friend
SAM PATERSON, a Joplin protégé and friend who collaborated on "Swipesy Cake Walk" (1900)
JAMES S. SCOTT, a prominent African American pianist-composer
JOHN STARK, a music dealer from Sedalia, Missouri, who published Joplin's most famous work, "The Maple Leaf Rag"
JULIUS WEISS, Joplin's German-born piano teacher

Edward A. Berlin's meticulously researched *King of Ragtime: Scott Joplin and His Era* is a welcome addition to the growing literature on American popular music. Berlin, a noted musicologist whose *Ragtime: A Musical and Cultural History* (1980) established the writer as one of ragtime's preeminent scholars, sets an ambitious agenda in *King of Ragtime*. First and foremost, Berlin aims to set the record straight on Joplin, separating the man from the legend, assessing his accomplishments as well as his failures.

Berlin's foil is the pioneering work of Rudi Blesh and Harriet Janis, *They All Played Ragtime* (1949). While a still valuable resource, largely because Blesh and Janis based their book on interviews conducted with actual ragtime veterans, the authors never really question or cross-check their subjects' stories, a particularly egregious shortcoming given the frailties of human memory and the tendency to "rewrite" history so as to promote one's place to a more prominent position. Another problem is the authors' partisanship which ends up distorting its subject by privileging ragtime above other African American inflected musics such as swing and bebop. More serious is the fabrication of "facts" and "dialogue" that Blesh and Janis apparently added in order to construct more compelling or complete stories. Thus, while still shedding much light on the temper of the decades bracketing the turn of the century when ragtime reigned, *They All Played Ragtime* must ultimately be categorized as a kind of fictionalized history comparable to the facts-*cum*-fiction docudrama biographies produced routinely by the film and television industries.

In contrast to the avid fandom of Blesh and Janis, Berlin, who has an earned Ph.D. in musicology, brings the research skills of a trained historian to his task. Most important, Berlin has done the hard work of checking the record by carefully scrutinizing the public archives and newspapers of the period in order to document Joplin's actual comings and goings. As a result, readers are given a much clearer idea of the peripatetic lifestyle lived by Joplin during his early professional years as he moved from his home of Texarkana, Texas, to Sedalia, Missouri, "the cradle of ragtime," to such bustling Midwestern cities as St. Louis, Missouri, and, eventually, on to New York City. Readers also come to appreciate the subtle intricacies of ragtime as a specific and idiosyncratic musical form. Thanks to Berlin's copious musical examples and clear explanations, even a nonmusician comes away with an enhanced appreciation of ragtime's syncopated and pianistic nature, where deftly executed "off-beat" right-hand figures dance playfully over metronomic "oom-pah, oom-pah" bass lines.

Like other members of the new generation of popular culture historians who are squeezing the ballyhoo and press agentry out of their fresh and scrupulously researched chronicles of American music and movies, Berlin never claims more than his facts allow. For example, in his quest to precisely establish Joplin's date and place of birth, Berlin, in spite of having combed the public records in and around Texarkana, can only narrow Joplin's birth date to within a year of November 24, 1868, the standard but inaccurate birth date assigned the composer. Though perhaps a relatively minor point, the pains taken to ascertain the correct date are emblematic of Berlin's persistent detective work and his unwillingness to rush to judgment. "Gaps remain," he states in the preface, "for every answer that I might provide brings its own host of new questions."

As Berlin's saga unreels, it becomes clear that Joplin was the right man, at the right time and place. Indeed, improvements in the technology of printing suddenly made possible the inexpensive mechanical reproduction of sheet music which, in turn, made possible the phenomenon of Tin Pan Alley. Located in the heart of New York City's bustling show-business district, Tin Pan Alley engineered a promotion and marketing of popular music that reached unprecedented heights. Nevertheless, it was an enterprising white music dealer in Sedalia, Missouri, named John Starks who first brought Joplin to the public's attention. Having fallen in love with the lively syncopations of ragtime emanating from the town's brothels and show tents, Starks took a chance with an unknown African American and published Scott Joplin's "Maple Leaf Rag" in 1899. It proved a propitious moment, as Joplin's ebullient piano composition became the first piece of sheet music to sell more than one million copies. Imitation, that dubiously dubbed mode of "sincere flattery," manifested itself in the form of countless other rags of uneven quality.

For Joplin, there were many successful follow-ups. "Elite Syncopations" and "The Entertainer" (both 1902), "The Chrysanthemum" and "The Cascades" (both 1904), and "The Wall Street Rag" (1909) were among the Joplin rags that achieved popularity upon publication. Ragtime's success, as Berlin points out, was a mixed blessing. On the one hand, it was viewed as the first true American musical style. Indeed, it seemed to fulfill the advice of observers of the American music scene, including celebrated European composer Antonin Dvořak, to forge an indigenous style based upon the musics of African Americans and Native Americans. One critic cited by Berlin typifying the positive response to ragtime by "serious" commentators praised Joplin's work as "the beginning of American music," if American music was to be more than a mere reflection of European influences.

Other critics objected to the "wild" syncopations of ragtime in no small measure because of the music's African American origins. "Can it be said that America is falling prey to the collective soul of the negro through the influence of what is popularly known as 'rag time' music?" one white writer asked. Such attacks came from members of the country's white and black cultural elites. One of the cruelest ironies for Joplin was the assault on ragtime from educated blacks who worried about the music's harmful and distracting effects on their children. Having absorbed many of the cultural values of the white educated elite, many black leaders were concerned that ragtime would detract from their efforts to instill essentially European cultural standards in the black community.

For Joplin, who argued tirelessly for "high class" ragtime as an artistic expression of racial pride, there was yet another irony. Like other black leaders, Joplin was a staunch proponent of education. Indeed, as a child growing up in Texarkana, Texas, he drew inspiration from Julius Weiss, a German music teacher who gave the promising youngster free piano lessons. In the process, Weiss also shaped Joplin's ambitions toward lofty artistic goals by imparting an appreciation of music as an art as well as a mode of entertainment. As a result of those ambitions, and the constant attacks upon his short-form ragtime successes, in the cruelest irony of his career, Joplin fixed his sights on writing an opera. He would fight his Eurocentric critics by tackling Western music's most demanding long from. At the same time, he wanted his opera to reflect his racial pride and his commitment to ragtime.

In 1911, Joplin published the two-hundred-thirty-page opera *Treemonisha* at his own expense. There was a highly favorable review in the *American Musician and Art Journal* in which the author noted the abilities and progress of "the colored race," using Joplin's opera as an example of this evolution. As Berlin points out, Joplin wanted to demonstrate his ability to transcend ragtime and black music. Although Joplin uses ragtime and gospel sparingly to help establish the setting, an 1884 Arkansas community of former slaves, *Treemonisha*'s primary musical materials derive from European operatic models. Significantly, as a work revealing something of its creator, education is at the core of Joplin's libretto. Indeed, the heroine Treemonisha was educated by a white woman just as Joplin had been educated by the German-born Weiss and at the white-administered Smith College in Sedalia, Missouri.

Despite the praise of writers such as the critic of the *American Musician and Art Journal*, Joplin was never to see a full-blown production of his intended masterwork.

Expending his own funds to try to interest potential backers and suffering the ravages of syphilis, Joplin died in New York City in 1917, a broken and largely forgotten man. Nevertheless, Joplin's legacy lives on.

Historically, ragtime, though not invented by Joplin, was put on America's musical map through the unprecedented success of such "hits" as the aforementioned "Maple Leaf Rag" and "The Entertainer." Though there have been periodic revivals of ragtime, whose heyday spanned the late 1890's to the late 1910's, the most important boost in its postwar popularity came in 1973, with the blockbuster motion picture hit, *The Sting*. Along with its stars, Paul Newman and Robert Redford, the George Roy Hill film received an unanticipated assist from composer-arranger Marvin Hamlisch, whose arrangement of "The Entertainer" became, some seventy years after its first splash, a musical hit once again. In the wake of the success of Hamlisch's (and Joplin's) Oscar-winning score, Joplin's rags have become "standards" in the repertoires of contemporary keyboardists and, in lavishly expanded arrangements, orchestras and bands as well.

Berlin's careful accounting of Joplin's life, his achievements as well as his failures, is greatly enhanced by a generous array of photographs, reproductions of the covers of sheet music, programs and advertisements of events in which Joplin participated, census records, legal documents such as marriage certificates, and Joplin's music itself. Also significant is Berlin's use of informative "sidebars," textual asides providing valuable backgrounds on such subjects as "Minstrelsy," "Prostitution in Sedalia," "Joplin and Coon Songs," "On the Road with a Black Company," "Emancipation Day in Sedalia," "Ragtime in the White House," and "The New York Sheet Music War." Berlin's copious and annotated notes, his comprehensive bibliography, and a listing of music collections containing Joplin's works are further assets.

The story of Scott Joplin, while central to the story of ragtime itself, is also significant in the evolution of twentieth century American popular music as a vibrant, multicultural embodiment of America's democratic, melting pot ideal. While it is nothing less than America's "first uniquely national style of music," to cite Berlin, ragtime is also significant as a precursor of jazz. Berlin's accomplishment is perhaps best summed up by the author himself: "In the end, Scott Joplin, the King of Ragtime Writers, remains elusive. So many of the artifacts that might have provided answers have been destroyed or lost. But while we do not reach a goal of pristine clarity, we do come to a greater understanding and appreciation of the ragtime world and of Scott Joplin."

Charles Merrell Berg

Sources for Further Study

Booklist. XC, July, 1994, p. 1910.

Chicago Tribune. September 18, 1994, XIV, p. 4.

Houston Post. September 25, 1994, p. C5.
Kirkus Reviews. LXII, June 1, 1994, p. 746.
Library Journal. CXIX, July, 1994, p. 95.
The New York Times. July 20, 1994, p. C16.
Publishers Weekly. CCXLI, July 25, 1994, p. 42.
San Francisco Chronicle. September 18, 1994, p. REV5.
Time. CXLIV, September 19, 1994, p. 80.
The Wall Street Journal. August 12, 1994, p. A8.

KNOWING WHEN TO STOP
A Memoir

Author: Ned Rorem (1923-)
Publisher: Simon & Schuster (New York). Illustrated. 607 pp. $30.00
Type of work: Memoir
Time: 1923-1951, with a brief interlude in 1988
Locale: Chicago, Mexico, Philadelphia, New York, Paris, and Morocco

Ned Rorem recounts, often in more detail than one might desire, the course of his first twenty-eight years, beginning with his childhood in the Hyde Park section of Chicago and ending with his travels and extended residence in France and Morocco

Principal personages:
NED ROREM, an American composer and author
CLARENCE RUFUS ROREM, his father, an economist
GLADYS MILLER ROREM, his mother
ROSEMARY ROREM MARSHALL, his sister and only sibling
VIRGIL THOMSON,
AARON COPLAND,
LEONARD BERNSTEIN,
MARC BLITZSTEIN,
SAMUEL BARBER, and
GIAN CARLO MENOTTI, American composers
PAUL BOWLES, an American composer and author

Early in this sprawling autobiographical volume, Ned Rorem writes, "In autobiography, as in any crafted work, technique lies in omitting. Not omitting through tact, but through a sense of shape. Actual life repeats and repeats and repeats itself." Elsewhere in this memoir, Rorem contends that people are who they pretend to be. He claims that people decide early in life what roles they will play and that these roles, which they play forever, become second nature to them.

These contentions reveal much about Rorem and, perhaps more significantly, about how he relates to people. There is throughout this memoir a notable lack of profound penetration of human nature. Rorem's ego often blocks the path that might lead to the deep understandings of human nature that historically have distinguished some of the truly great biographies and autobiographies.

Rorem frequently writes about interesting surfaces. The intellectual milieu in which he was reared during his father's tenure as professor of economics at the University of Chicago and the artistic milieu to which he was subsequently exposed in Mexico, Philadelphia, New York, Paris, and Morocco provide sparkling backdrops to the story of Rorem's development as an artist. He writes enticingly about these surfaces but seems incapable of penetrating beneath them to glean analytically the still more enticing motivations for many of the behaviors that he and the characters in his memoir display.

His facile division of the world into German and French attitudes and habits, while an interesting notion, quite often leads Rorem to simplistic conclusions that entertain rather than enlighten readers. Rorem is astute in his observation that the technique of autobiography lies in omitting. In this case, however, one might wish that Rorem had omitted more or included less. This six-hundred-page book is awash in detail, much of it extraneous, some of it inherently uninteresting. Rorem has preserved oceans of paper during his lifetime, and in *Knowing When to Stop: A Memoir*, he seems bent on using as much as possible of the material he has squirreled away in his voluminous files.

Although the organization of his book is essentially chronological and easy to follow, the organization within chapters is often chaotic, suggesting a lack of disciplined planning, careful editing, and thoughtful revision. The chapter about Martha Graham, for example, begins and ends with this renowned choreographer, but the heart of it—some twenty-five pages—strays far from the topic in a way that exceeds the casual and borders on the out-and-out chaotic.

One must admire the candor with which Rorem discusses his homosexuality. On the surface, he appears comfortable with his sexual orientation. One must question, however, whether, if he is really as well adjusted to being gay as he would have his readers believe, he would feel the need to re-create in detail so many of his sexual encounters as he moved through his teens and twenties. One must also question whether it is fair to identify by name many of his former lovers and gay associates. More than a few of the people he names are quite circumspect homosexuals who would, in all likelihood, prefer to avoid the sort of "outing" in which this memoir seems to delight. The sort of exhibitionism that seems necessary for Rorem suggests a troubled—or at least a conflicted—psyche.

Despite these reservations, *Knowing When to Stop* depicts as well as any contemporary book the artistic and intellectual tone and temper of New York City and Paris in the period immediately after World War II. The artistic ferment that bubbled up on both sides of the Atlantic and of which Rorem was fundamentally a part during the postwar years comes to life vigorously in the pages of this memoir. Rorem captures with considerable authenticity the closeness and camaraderie that characterized the artistic world of that period. One gleans fully the sense of a world-within-a-world that characterized the musical community of the late 1940's and early 1950's.

Rorem gained his most important entrée into that world when he was studying counterpoint with Rosario Scalero at the Curtis Institute of Music in Philadelphia. Scalero, old enough to have once met Johannes Brahms, was a traditional teacher under whose tutelage Rorem chafed. Nevertheless, through other associates at Curtis Institute, the callow young transplant from the Midwest came to know Leonard Bernstein, and, through him, many of the most notable musicians of his day.

Rorem began to spend as much time as he could in New York City, sleeping on Bernstein's living-room floor. At the end of his first year at the Curtis Institute, he left Philadelphia to take a poorly remunerated job in New York as Virgil Thomson's copyist. Although he did not respect Thomson's artistry, Rorem liked Thomson and through him gained access to the scintillating musical world around whose fringes he had been hovering.

Rorem's upbringing prepared him well for the musical world in which he was to live his life. His parents were gifted intellectuals, unfailingly liberal in their outlook. They mingled socially and publicly with blacks, although, in the 1930's, this was not commonly done even in enlightened Hyde Park. Rorem's father specialized in the economics of health care. The original Blue Cross was organized based on his scholarly work. Clarence Rufus Rorem was, throughout much of his life, a well-respected economist who served in important consultative capacities well into old age.

Ned Rorem was born in Richmond, Indiana, early in his father's career as a beginning faculty member at Earlham College, a Quaker institution. The Rorems belonged to the Society of Friends, and although Ned became outspokenly atheistic, many of the moral tenets of Quakerism have remained with him through the years. He certainly has always held to the fundamental Quaker belief in pacifism. Although the Rorems discovered early that their son was homosexual, they made no commotion about this revelation. They accepted Rorem for what he was and allowed him the friends that he preferred, often becoming quite close themselves to their son's friends and associates.

As responsible parents concerned about their son's future, the Rorems encouraged Ned to attend college, although his grades at the renowned University High School were so marginal that he was denied acceptance by Oberlin College. His father finally arranged for him to be admitted to a baccalaureate program in music at Northwestern University, where he studied for two years in a program that was far too traditional for his tastes. Rorem wanted to study his own times and the music of these times rather than history and classical music.

Finally, on a business trip to Philadelphia, Rorem's father left one of the young man's musical compositions with administrators at the Curtis Institute. In 1943, Rorem was offered a scholarship, and Rosario Scalero agreed to work with him. Thus Rorem was given the opportunity to take the initial step out of the Midwest into the more highly charged musical atmosphere of the Northeast.

It is interesting and revealing that part 1 of *Knowing When to Stop* ends not with the chapter in which Rorem begins university studies or with his completing two years at Northwestern University, which marked the end of his life in the Midwest, but with the chapter he entitles "Philadelphia 1943." Clearly, the great turning point in his life came early in 1944, when he met Leonard Bernstein and through him gained access to the musical world of New York City.

At this point, Rorem had to reach a decision that was more difficult for his father than it was for him. He had to decide whether to leave school, which was impeding his career, and to sign on as Virgil Thomson's copyist. He was sure that although this course correction would not lead to the academic degree his father wanted him to earn, it would become a fundamental building block in the career he wished to establish for himself.

Had Rorem not made the difficult career decision he did, he might never have emerged as the celebrated musician he became. He opted for education by means of apprenticeship rather than by means of formal instruction, although, in time, he resumed his baccalaureate studies at the Juilliard School of Music and also studied in the summer programs at Tanglewood.

In the United States of the first half of the twentieth century, New York City was the sort of magnet for artists of all kinds that Paris long had been in Europe. Rorem did not begin to come into his own until he became attuned to the musical world of New York City. Having imbibed the most that he could from New York, he ventured abroad in 1949, and Paris became his artistic base. He remained there for the better part of the next eight years, living during several of these years in the mansion of Marie-Laure de Noailles, perhaps the most artistically acute woman in Europe. It is upon this part of his career that part 3 of *Knowing When to Stop* focuses.

In his mid-twenties when he went to Paris, Rorem was instantly transfixed by the electricity of the city's substantial international artistic community. In Paris, as in New York, Rorem found the world-within-worlds that artists, gathered in a hub, tend to inhabit. He soon was part of the select circle that revolved around Nadia Boulanger and Pierre Boulez. Francis Poulenc and Jean Cocteau became his friends.

Rorem began to make trips to Morocco, where he became the lover of a French physician living in Fez. Guy Ferrand loved Rorem more than Rorem loved him, but in his extended stays in Morocco, Rorem was able to work effectively. He also fell into the society of Paul Bowles and, through Bowles, met Truman Capote. Perhaps the Moroccan adventures, more than any other element in his life, helped Rorem to be the writer that he eventually became. Bowles had been a musician, but after the publication of *The Sheltering Sky* (1949), he gained more celebrity as an author than music had ever brought him. Today he is more remembered as a writer than as a musician.

Knowing When to Stop presents in its three parts contrasting vignettes of what it is to be an artist in the Midwest, in the Northeast, in Paris, and in Morocco. The geography is important. Artists tend to cluster in places in which they feel at home and in which they find kindred spirits. Rorem's memoir extends beyond its author's individual development as an artist and, with considerable deftness and verisimilitude, presents valuable generalizations about the artist's place in society.

R. Baird Shuman

Sources for Further Study

American Theatre. XI, December, 1994, p. 82.
Chicago Tribune. November 27, 1994, XIV, p. 8.
Los Angeles Times. September 18, 1994, p. CAL55.
The New York Times Book Review. XCIX, November 13, 1994, p. 58.
Opera News. LIX, December 24, 1994, p. 41.
Time. CXLIV, October 17, 1994, p. 81.
The Wall Street Journal. August 31, 1994, p. A10.
The Washington Post Book World. XXIV, September 25, 1994, p. 1.

THE LANGUAGE INSTINCT

Author: Steven Pinker (1954-)
Publisher: William Morrow (New York). 494 pp. $23.00
Type of work: Linguistic theory

An exploration into how children learn language, how language has evolved, how it changes, and how the mind creates and computes it

The publication of Noam Chomsky's *Syntactic Structures* (1957) changed forever the way people concerned with language would look upon it. Within a decade of its publication, the teaching of the new Chomskian transformational-generative grammar was being widely mandated in schools throughout the United States. A cottage industry developed to produce textbooks based on the transformational-generative approach to language, some in series that had one book for each grade from three through twelve, such as the series created by Paul Roberts and published by Harcourt Brace.

The appearance of these series, however well-intentioned and intelligent they were, backfired in many instances because teachers, unable to understand the highly technical approach to language promulgated by Chomsky, even as simplified for popular consumption by Roberts and others, in many cases simply gave up teaching grammar, even though all sorts of summer workshops on the new grammar attracted hordes of participants, as did the workshops offered by publishers trying to promote their new, highly lucrative product. The books sold briskly. For the most part, however, they collected dust on classroom shelves.

Chomsky contended in *Syntactic Structures*, as well as in his later *Aspects of the Theory of Syntax* (1965), *Language and Mind* (1968; rev. ed. 1972), and *Rules and Representations* (1980) that language as it is used universally is governed by "super rules." Individual language groups—Romance, Germanic, Oriental, Arabic, African—possess their own distinguishing characteristics and vocabularies, but underlying all language, according to Chomsky, are universal rules and sounds that constitute human language.

Children born into a given language environment quickly assimilate and use the characteristics peculiar to the language environments into which they are born, but all languages and families of languages have common elements, syntactic structures, of which every human in some mysterious way has an underlying awareness. More than any other factor, it is human beings' ability to use language that distinguishes them from other biological forms.

The Language Instinct explores many of the areas of language into which Chomsky and his followers had long been delving. Steven Pinker warns his readers that his book is about spoken rather than written language, and that it is not about the English language per se. *The Language Instinct* does not deal with the niceties of grammar, punctuation, usage, or other schoolmarmish considerations. Rather, it is a broad, well-informed study that considers language as it exists among, and is used by, human beings throughout the world. It poses pertinent questions about how human language came into being.

Pinker, a psychologist at the Massachusetts Institute of Technology, where he directs the Center for Cognitive Neuroscience, and where, incidentally, Chomsky has spent his professional career, has long been interested in language acquisition among young children. He contends that language is genetically programmed into human beings, who then develop the ability to speak the particular varieties of language present in their environments.

In support of his highly controversial thesis, Pinker points out that people begin to talk in much the same way that spiders begin to spin webs: no one specifically teaches them language, yet they seem genetically predisposed to developing an ability to use it. Fully understanding what a highly charged word "instinct" is to educated people, and especially to psychologists, Pinker nevertheless makes the conscious decision to use that word when he speaks about how children learn to talk.

Those with opposing views might contend that children learn to talk by imitating the people who surround them, and, up to a point, even Pinker would admit to the partial validity of such a statement. Imitation, however, does not explain why two-year-olds reared in an environment in which relatively standard English is spoken consistently will say things like "they drived" or "I drinked," when certainly that is not the form of the past tense of these irregular verbs used by the people around them.

Pinker also suggests that young children in their most egocentric stages do not imitate the behaviors of adults. Their parents may be sedate, considerate airline passengers, for example, whereas their two- or three-year-olds may be noisy hellions, annoying everyone within earshot of them.

No one has taught these same two- or three-year-olds in any formal way such grammatical structures as subordinate clauses, compound and complex sentences, or the subjunctive, yet, by the time children reach those ages, they are employing quite naturally every grammatical structure their language possesses. Something inherent apparently drives them linguistically.

On the other hand, if their language requires sounds strange to some ears, such as the glottal click of some African languages or the umlaut in German, they quite naturally use the glottal click or the umlaut, presumably because they are imitating the sounds they most commonly hear in their environments. Ten-year-old Albanians, having grown up in an environment in which the glottal click is not used would have great difficulty trying to acquire it at their linguistically advanced age.

Pinker deviates from many earlier linguists by pointing out that language is not a cultural artifact like telling time or understanding the workings of the internal combustion engine. These are abilities that can be, and frequently are, taught. Language, however, develops naturally in young children. In the language they develop, communicating is the only criterion of correctness. If they say, "He don't got none," they are communicating. The nonstandard forms they use—the double negative, "got" for "have," and "he don't"—do not mask the meaning of the sentence. It is only an artificial cultural overlay that makes that sentence seem incorrect to some people. It would be more valid to call it, in some cultural settings, inappropriate.

A grammatical error in English occurs if someone says something like, "To New

York going accountant the was." No native speaker of English would structure a sentence in this way because, by violating the inherent genetic code of which Pinker speaks, it obscures meaning.

Language study has flourished since the publication of *Syntactic Structures* largely because of the rise of a relatively new field of study, cognitive science, a burgeoning interdisciplinary field that uses the most sophisticated tools of psychology, computer science, linguistics, philosophy, and neurobiology to unlock the mysteries of how humans function mentally. The rise of computers and the need to program them in highly sophisticated ways have led armies of scholars to deep understandings of what constitutes human intelligence, as such scholars have groped their way along in their highly complex attempts to devise artificial intelligences.

Pinker explains how inductive processes help children, as well as more mature speakers, to make incredibly sophisticated language categorizations. He notes that the verb "fly," in English, is a strong (irregular) verb whose past tense is "flew": "I fly home once a week"; "I flew home yesterday." Within a given cultural context, the irregular past tense is usual.

On the other hand, in a different cultural context, that of the baseball stadium, "fly" has a regular past tense: "The batter flied out twice in one game." One might argue that "fly out" is a different verb from "fly," therefore it is not governed by the same conventions. For whatever reason, it does not take great linguistic sophistication for the average person over the age of five to make the distinction between these two possible past tenses.

Pinker cites Theodore M. Bernstein as mentioning in *The Careful Writer: A Modern Guide to English Usage* (1977) that "flied out" is used rather than "flew out" because in this instance, "fly" has a specialized meaning. This explanation, however, does not satisfy Pinker, who mentions that "see a bet," "cut a deal," and "take the count" all have specialized meanings, but that their past tenses use the irregular form of the verb as it is used in more conventional contexts.

Similarly, with a nominal like "life," the plural is made by adding *-s* but also requires an internal change: "lives," spelled the same as the third person singular of the verbal "live," yet pronounced differently. Native speakers quickly learn to make the pronunciation distinction between nominal and verbal forms of "live," although they do not consciously ask themselves whether they are using a noun or a verb. They intuit the appropriate form.

They also know that if they use "life" in a compound form such as "low-life," the plural is "low-lifes" in most dialects of English. They may, regardless of their social levels, however, have difficulty with "hoof/hooves" and "roof/roofs," because the conventions governing these two pairs are not clear-cut to most people, although in each instance above, the plural form given is the preferred one.

Such considerations have become increasingly important as industrial countries have moved into a society whose very existence depends upon the accuracy of computers. Despite their ability to store and process mountains of information, computers cannot intuit, as anyone realizes who has typed in a ":" where a ">" is required. Cognitive scientists since Chomsky have sought to dissect language and to analyze linguistic behaviors in such minute ways as to approach understanding how the finest linguistic distinctions are made.

The human intellect, which has the ability to intuit, understands from context the difference between the word "bank" as it is used in sentences such as, "They put their money in the *bank*," "They sat on the *bank* of the river," "Don't *bank* on having a car waiting when you arrive," "The pilot should *bank* his plane to the right before trying to land," and "Please *bank* the snow toward the end of the driveway." Computers programmed to translate documents from one language to another often produce bizarre translations when confronted with such variations in the meanings of specific words that appear in the texts they are programmed to translate. Pinker is most concerned with understanding the intricate thought systems and responses that make humans able to intuit meaning in such situations.

Chomsky focused initially on understanding the deep structures through which language and linguistic variations are generated. Pinker, however, has moved beyond such considerations (as did Chomsky in his later work) into a concern with the dynamics of language as they relate to understanding, particularly in some of the eerie reaches of linguistic sophistication whose unlocking modern technology makes possible on the one hand, and, on the other hand, persistently demands.

Chomsky is a linguist's linguist, whereas Pinker has made a conscious effort to be a populist linguist, writing, certainly, about exceptionally complex and intellectually demanding topics, yet writing always with a keen sense of what examples and explanations are required to allow reasonably intelligent general readers to understand what he is saying. He writes with wit, stylistic vibrancy, and an undisguised enthusiasm for language. General readers will not breeze through his book in a single sitting. They will, however, find themselves richly rewarded if they make the effort to read the book closely and studiously.

R. Baird Shuman

Sources for Further Study

Antioch Review. LII, Summer, 1994, p. 534.
The Atlantic. CCLXXIII, March, 1994, p. 130.
The Chronicle of Higher Education. June 15, 1994, p. 8.
The Economist. CCCXXXI, April 9, 1994, p. 95.
National Review. XLVI, April 18, 1994, p. 50.
Nature. CCCLXVIII, March 24, 1994, p. 360.
New Republic. CCX, January 31, 1994, p. 19.
New Scientist. CXLII, June 25, 1994, p. 28.
New Statesman and Society. VII, April 8, 1994, p. 36.
The New York Times Book Review. XCIX, February 27, 1994, p. 7.

LINCOLN IN AMERICAN MEMORY

Author: Merrill D. Peterson (1921-   )
Publisher: Oxford University Press (New York). Illustrated. 449 pp. $30.00
Type of work: History
Time: 1865-1993
Locale: The United States

Merrill D. Peterson chronicles Abraham Lincoln's fame and reputation from his assassination to the late twentieth century

Principal personages:
ABRAHAM LINCOLN, the sixteenth president of the United States, 1861-1865
MARY TODD LINCOLN, widow of Abraham Lincoln
ROBERT TODD LINCOLN, the Lincolns' son, custodian of Lincoln's official papers
JOHN MILTON HAY, Lincoln's secretary and official biographer
JOHN GEORGE NICOLAY, Lincoln's official biographer and personal secretary
IDA TARBELL, an American muckraker, author of numerous books on Lincoln
WILLIAM H. HERNDON, Lincoln's law partner, author of an early biography

Although he discouraged personal legends and mythmaking during his lifetime, Abraham Lincoln, the sixteenth president of the United States, became the most celebrated and revered of American political leaders following his death in 1865. The biographical facts of his life firmly laid the groundwork for posthumous fame. A frontiersman by birth, whose parentage was obscure and whose early hardships had to be surmounted, he became the essence of the American success story by rising to the most powerful position in the nation. Self-educated as a lawyer, he possessed a sharp natural wit, a sense of humor, a genius for storytelling, and a dignified, eloquently cadenced prose style for oratory and writing. These qualities became assets to him when he found it necessary to debate important issues or to address subjects of the utmost importance to the nation. His personal life, though not without its ambiguities, was devoid of any hint of scandal or blame. While not all biographers would agree, the majority have viewed Lincoln as an exception to the generalization that greatness is accompanied by great flaws.

On issues of nationalism and of freedom Lincoln held decidedly idealistic positions. A lifelong opponent of slavery, he presided over its demise in the United States. Although he was denied the opportunity of implementing his vision of economic development, it was his destiny to lead the nation successfully through the terrible crisis and war that jeopardized its survival. In his role as commander-in-chief, made the fateful wartime decisions that led to a Union victory in the Civil War. The Founding Fathers had drawn up the Constitution; Lincoln assured its continuance by preserving the nation. Crowned with success, he died at the hands of an assassin. Taken together, the facts of his life constitute a greater claim on fame than that of any other American leader.

Merrill D. Peterson, professor emeritus of history of the University of Virginia, traces Lincoln's fame and reputation from his assassination to the early 1990's. Before undertaking this formidable task, he produced a similar study of Thomas Jefferson in the book *The Jefferson Image in the American Mind* (1960). In tracing Lincoln's legacy in the mind of humankind, he has demonstrated that fame has cast Lincoln in the form of five great archetypal images: the savior of the Union, the Great Emancipator, the self-made man, the man of the people, and the first American.

Yet, as Peterson also demonstrates, not all the Lincolns reflected in the light of fame were accurate. Assorted movements attempted to claim him as one of their own, invoking his life or words in support of controversial and conflicting points of view. Crosscurrents in his fame and reputation arose when opposing movements seized upon him for opposite purposes.

As Peterson's account shows, the course of Lincoln's posthumous fame follows a path that one generally finds among people who have achieved renown during their lives. In the first stage, which Peterson labels apotheosis, there are elaborate obsequies, memorializing, and projected monuments. The fallen hero takes on the aura of sainthood as plans are laid for monuments to ensure that his fame endures. In Lincoln's first period, poets such as Walt Whitman produced a multitude of dirges and elegies. A second stage occurs when contemporaries who knew the person begin to write their memoirs and reminiscences. At about the same time there are those who initiate collections of memorabilia—all the personal items, papers, and mementos that they can find. Also during this period, one or more biographies sanctioned by the family may appear.

Only later do professional scholars and historians begin a meticulous examination of the reliable records. For Lincoln this stage was delayed longer than usual because of the great number of journalists and acquaintances who wrote about him in an earlier phase and also because his papers were not accessible to scholars for many decades after he died. This delay was the wish of his son and executor Robert Todd Lincoln, who severely limited access to the papers until 1947. Even after delivering them to the Library of Congress in 1919, he stipulated restrictions that kept the papers from historians until long after his own death. When they were made available to scholars, they proved to contain little information that was entirely new.

Scholarly examination of the extant documents changes the complexion of the developing myth. As studies become more specialized and detailed, the heroic figure gradually recedes into memory, still hallowed and honored but no longer a presence in the contemporary popular myth. Though granted a secure place in history, the hero seems less relevant to the present.

The Lincoln monuments, planned shortly after his death, are known to millions and remain popular attractions, though not all contemplated during the first phase were completed expeditiously. Peterson narrates the story of each of the four major monuments: the Lincoln National Monument in Springfield, Illinois, featuring bronze figures and a 117-foot obelisk, dedicated in 1874; the boyhood home in Hodgenville, Kentucky, sheltered by an impressive classical revival temple in granite, completed in 1911; the Lincoln Memorial in Washington, D.C. (1922); and the massive Mount Rushmore sculpture in South Dakota's Black Hills (1937). For each of these structures, there is an account of the organized effort to raise funds and to produce the finished monument. In addition, Peterson recounts the history associated with the monuments themselves. The memorial in Washington, for example, is recalled, appropriately, as the setting for important events in the history of civil rights, including the Marian Anderson concert in 1941 and the "I Have a Dream" speech of Martin Luther King, Jr., in 1963.

Among other monuments, numerous statues scattered about the eastern United States depict Lincoln as the frontiersman, as the Great Emancipator, as a father-figure to his people. While Lincoln sculptures are abundant, living portraits are scarce, since he did not like to sit for them. He attained, however, an advantage over national heroes such as George Washington and Thomas Jefferson, of whom numerous portraits exist, for widespread use of cameras in his time meant that numerous photographs were taken. The 120-odd photographs that survive provided artists with numerous likenesses for popular reproductions and depictions.

Among the written tributes to Lincoln, biographies occupy the most substantial place. Crosscurrents in the account of his life began to develop as biographers took different approaches. The popular Lincoln myth became a well-known Horatio Alger story, as Lincoln served as an inspiration and model for youth in a spate of popular biographies. This continued the trend of early biographies and memoirs that depicted Lincoln as a saint. William Herndon, his law partner, sought to set the record straight by writing a biography that revealed some of his frontier humor and earthy expression. Herndon's long-delayed biography also introduced new information about Lincoln's obscure life as a merchant in New Salem, Illinois, including the poignant story of his early romance with Ann Rutledge, an account that Herndon narrated in a version probably exaggerated. Herndon's work was perceived by the family as an attack on Lincoln's character, although he had no intention of diminishing Lincoln's stature.

The official biography by John George Nicolay and John Milton Hay appeared in 1890, in ten volumes. As they were the only biographers permitted unlimited access to Lincoln's papers, their work introduced much new material about the presidency and remained the standard for decades, until Carl Sandburg's lengthy and comprehensive work eclipsed it. Sandburg, however, like many subsequent writers on the subject, freely incorporated myths. As scholars began producing academic studies, books about Lincoln became increasingly specialized, so that most studies were eventually limited to a very small part of his life and career.

Lincoln in the popular imagination—an image supported by history, images on coins and bills, advertisements and company logos, and countless place-names—has waxed and waned over the decades since his death. He has been accorded acclaim worldwide, especially by champions of liberty. At home his popularity has also been susceptible to change, but his stature has grown. He has been more acclaimed in the

East than in the West, for reasons of history, since much of the West was still territory during his lifetime.

As Peterson shows, Lincoln's reputation in the South underwent perhaps its most important change. At first, he was viewed as the man responsible for the Civil War and the destruction it wrought. Then some Southerners came to believe that Lincoln's magnanimity would have made Reconstruction less oppressive than it was, that Lincoln would have dealt more gently with the South, and so the bitter attitudes waned. In the early twentieth century, the New South movement, stressing economic progress and industrialization, praised Lincoln for his role as preserver of the nation and a far-sighted nationalist. Over time the positive image of Lincoln prevailed over the negative memories of the region.

The temperance movement of the early twentieth century that led to Prohibition invoked Lincoln as a patron saint because of his moderation. In response, the saloon interests produced a document showing that Lincoln obtained a license for the sale of liquor in his store in New Salem, and they claimed him for their side. Religious groups claimed him as a born-again Christian, one who had intended to enter the Presbyterian church had he lived. Freethinkers, on the other hand, embraced Lincoln as the president who had no religious affiliation and whose occasional comments on religion, though ambiguous, revealed a skeptical mind at work. Such contradictions resulted from the desire to appropriate his fame without balancing all available evidence.

Among African Americans, Lincoln has always been accorded an honored status, primarily for his emancipation of the slaves and for his earlier outspoken opposition to slavery. Yet because his opinions on race were tinged with the views of his time, some of his writings have been disquieting. The emergence of recognized national leaders from the black community also, according to Peterson, means that African Americans now have less need to look to the past for heroes. Perhaps most important, to many Americans Lincoln no longer seems as relevant to current issues as he once did. For better or worse, modern youth are inclined to find their role models among sports or popular culture heroes rather than among historical figures. While Lincoln's place in history remains unshaken, his presence in the daily lives of Americans has diminished with time.

Peterson's book is a useful contribution to Lincoln studies, for it offers a chronologically ordered account of the Lincoln legacy. It describes the memorials that a grateful nation has showered on one of its heroes and attempts to assess his place in the American mind. Anyone seeking to know about poetry, biography, and monuments devoted to him might well begin with this book. Peterson weaves the diverse strands of his subject admirably, capturing not only the detailed and concrete memorials but also the changing spirit behind them. Thus he has made a contribution to the social history of the nation as well.

Stanley Archer

Sources for Further Study

American Historical Review. XCIX, October, 1994, p. 1281.
Choice. XXXII, October, 1994, p. 354.
The Christian Science Monitor. March 22, 1994, p. 12.
The Economist. CCCXXXII, July 30, 1994, p. 80.
Los Angeles Times. July 22, 1994, p. E6.
The New York Review of Books. XLI, April 21, 1994, p. 7.
The New York Times Book Review. XCIX, June 26, 1994, p. 24.
Publishers Weekly. CCXLI, March 7, 1994, p. 58.
The Wall Street Journal. March 31, 1994, p. A12.
The Washington Post Book World. XXIV, March 20, 1994, p. 3.

LOCAL PEOPLE
The Struggle for Civil Rights in Mississippi

Author: John Dittmer (1939-   )
Publisher: University of Illinois Press (Urbana). Illustrated. 560 pp. $29.95
Type of work: History
Time: 1945 to 1968
Locale: Mississippi; Washington, D.C.; Atlantic City, New Jersey

The author tells in great detail the inspiring story of the activists who struggled to win access to public accommodations and the right to vote for blacks in one Southern state

Principal personages:
ROBERT PARRIS MOSES, a New York-born member of the Student Non-Violent Coordinating Committee (SNCC)
FANNIE LOU HAMER, a Mississippi-born black woman activist and co-founder of the Mississippi Freedom Democratic Party
MEDGAR EVERS, a Mississippi civil rights leader who was assassinated
JAMES MEREDITH, the first black to attend University of Mississippi
JOHN FITZGERALD KENNEDY, president of the United States, 1961 to 1963
LYNDON BAINES JOHNSON, president of the United States, 1963 to 1969
AARON HENRY, a Clarksdale pharmacist and black civil rights leader
MARTIN LUTHER KING, JR., the well-known black civil rights leader
HODDING CARTER III, a white liberal politician in Mississippi

To understand race relations in the United States in the 1990's, one must be aware of the blatant injustices to which blacks were subjected in the South until the late 1960's; one must also know something about the Civil Rights movement, which arose to fight against such injustices. As the 1960's have become ever more distant in time, more and more academic historians have begun to write about the movement.

At first, historians wrote either biographies of the most famous civil rights leader (Martin Luther King, Jr.) or studies of the major national civil rights organizations. Later on, historical studies of the Civil Rights movement in individual states, counties, and cities began to appear in print. Examples include William Chafe's *Civilities and Civil Rights: Greensboro, North Carolina, and the Black Struggle for Freedom* (1980) and Robert J. Norrell's *Reaping the Whirlwind: The Civil Rights Movement in Tuskegee* (1985). Both activists from other parts of the United States and native-born black Mississippians, the author suggests, were necessary to make the successes of the movement possible. Dittmer, who taught in Mississippi for twelve years, ascribes these successes to the courage of ordinary people, as well as to the genius of Martin Luther King, Jr., or President Lyndon Johnson.

Dittmer portrays presidents John F. Kennedy and Lyndon Johnson not as sincere champions of civil rights, but as practical politicians who had to be prodded to do the right thing. Kennedy is faulted for trying to dissuade Freedom Riders from going to the South instead of protecting them when they did so; for failing, in the fall of 1962, to intervene to protect black college student James Meredith's right to enter the hitherto all-white University of Mississippi until the last possible moment; and for failing to protect the black activists who conducted voter registration drives in Mississippi against violent attacks by whites. Readers of this book may remember President Johnson as the man who spared no method, fair or foul (including wiretapping), to defeat the challenge by the black-run Mississippi Freedom Democratic Party (MFDP) at the Democratic Party Convention in Atlantic City in August, 1964, and as the man who used the military, in January, 1966, to disperse starving rural blacks who had occupied an abandoned Air Force base near Greenwood, Mississippi, to publicize their plight. Unfortunately, Dittmer pays much less attention to Johnson's role in pushing the Voting Rights Act of 1965 through Congress.

Martin Luther King, Jr., visited Mississippi only once in his career: in June, 1966, to complete a civil rights march from Memphis, Tennessee, to Jackson, Mississippi, that had been begun by James Meredith, and had been interrupted when Meredith was wounded by a sniper. Because of his assassination in April, 1968, in Memphis, Tennessee, many Americans in the 1990's remember Martin Luther King, Jr., as a martyr for the cause of civil rights. Yet there were also, Dittmer shows, several black Mississippian martyrs: Medgar Evers, field secretary for the National Association for the Advancement of Colored People (NAACP), who was ambushed on June 12, 1963; George W. Lee and Lamar Smith, who were killed in 1955; farmer Herbert Lee, who was murdered in 1961; James Chaney, who was killed in June, 1964; and Vernon Dahmer, asphyxiated when his house was fire-bombed in January, 1966. Activists who did not meet violent deaths, Dittmer shows, often endured jailings and beatings; until 1965, ordinary blacks who tried to register to vote often risked losing their jobs.

Dittmer's periodization of the history of the Mississippi movement is itself a contribution to scholarship. He dates its beginning from July, 1946, when a young Medgar Evers, accompanied by a few other black World War II veterans, tried unsuccessfully to register to vote in Decatur, Mississippi. The 1950's are seen as a time when white repression dashed the hopes raised by the Supreme Court school desegregation decision and deterred all but a tiny portion of the black middle class from joining the movement, then dominated by the NAACP. Dittmer perceives the beginning of the second phase in the spring and summer of 1961, when the freedom rides occurred and Robert Moses, of the Student Non-Violent Coordinating Committee (SNCC), began a voter registration drive among the state's blacks. The author sees the conclusion of the second phase in August, 1964, when the MFDP failed to unseat the regular Mississippi delegation at the Democratic Party Convention. Unlike many historians, Dittmer does not end the story of the Mississippi movement in 1964; instead, he concludes it in 1968, when a biracial delegation containing remnants of the MFDP replaced the segregationists at the Democratic Party convention in Chicago.

Such black SNCC activists as Robert Moses, a mathematics teacher from the New York City area, were young men when they began their activist careers. Dittmer shows, however, that young SNCC activists, far from waging generational war against their elders, deliberately sought their assistance. Thus Amzie Moore, a middle-aged postal worker and civil rights worker in Cleveland, Mississippi, helped Moses win the acceptance of local blacks.

Dittmer breaks new ground in his discussion of the role of women in the Mississippi movement. Throughout the 1950's, he asserts, its leadership was almost completely male. During the early 1960's, men continued to dominate the new SNCC leadership; nevertheless, women, especially rural women, began to assume prominent roles. These women included Annie Devine, Victoria Gray, and the indomitable and much-loved sharecropper's daughter, Fannie Lou Hamer.

White supporters of the movement, Dittmer points out, were at first rare in Mississippi; even most white Protestant ministers were staunch segregationists. Whites who joined the movement in its early stages included the Reverend Edwin King, a chaplain at Tougaloo College, a hotbed of civil rights activism with an all-black student body; John Salter, a young sociology teacher at Tougaloo, who took part in a May 28, 1963, lunch counter sit-in in Jackson; a maverick attorney, William Higgs, who fled Mississippi in 1963 to escape trumped-up criminal charges; and at least one crusading newspaper editor, Hazel Brannon Smith. Not until the passage of the Civil Rights Act in 1964 and the Voting Rights Act in 1965, Dittmer suggests, did white Mississippians with moderate-to-liberal racial views (such as Hodding Carter III, son of a prominent newspaper editor) begin to take an active part in mainstream Democratic Party politics.

White college students from the North played a crucial role in the movement during the Freedom Summer voter registration campaign of 1964. The decision by Robert Moses to invite them (ratified by the movement leadership on January 10, 1964) was, Dittmer shows, a controversial one: A minority of Mississippi's leading black activists argued in vain against it. Long after 1964, the controversy continued among those who remembered the civil rights struggle. The author, who tries to deal with this sensitive issue as evenhandedly as possible, is concerned primarily with the good or harm done to the movement itself by the presence of the volunteers; to learn about the effect of participation in the struggle on the future careers and political activities of the volunteers themselves, one should consult sociologist Doug McAdam's *Freedom Summer* (1988).

Dittmer expresses admiration for New York City volunteers Mickey Schwerner and Andrew Goodman, who, together with the young black activist James Earl Chaney, were murdered by members of the Ku Klux Klan, with the collusion of the local police, in Neshoba County in June, 1964. Dittmer finds that warm friendships, lasting long after 1964, developed between some white volunteers and their black host families; that bonds of camaraderie sometimes arose between volunteers and black movement workers as they fought shoulder to shoulder against white racist attacks; and that the Freedom Schools—hastily improvised institutions in which white volunteers and black activists taught—often had long-term beneficial effects on the children who attended them.

Weighing conflicting memoir testimony, the author concludes that relatively few white female volunteers had sexual affairs with black movement coworkers; yet the affairs that did develop were, he suggests, highly disruptive of morale. He finds evidence, from memoirs and other sources, that at least some of the volunteers were so arrogant that they alienated their black coworkers. By the autumn of 1964, he argues, relations between the remaining volunteers and their black movement coworkers had come close to the breaking point. The withdrawal of Robert Moses from movement activity in 1965, Dittmer asserts, was one symptom of the increasing disarray.

Two other signs of the black-white split within the movement, noted in previous histories, are SNCC activist Stokely Carmichael's utterance, during the June, 1966, civil rights march, of the slogan of Black Power; and the decision of the SNCC national leadership, in December, 1966, to expel all white members. Providing a much-needed grassroots perspective, Dittmer asserts that the antiwhite extremism that arose among the national SNCC leadership did not filter down to the MFDP, whose growth SNCC had encouraged. During all of its short life (it was moribund in the late 1960's), the author argues, the MFDP welcomed white volunteers.

Dittmer perceives friction within the movement, not only between blacks and white liberals, but also among blacks themselves. Making an original contribution to historical scholarship, Dittmer traces this friction among blacks to social class resentments. From the summer of 1964 onward, he argues, the relatively well-educated urban middle-class blacks who had been in the movement since the 1950's began to pull away from the poorer rural blacks who had been mobilized by the young agitators of SNCC. The clash between Aaron Henry, a pharmacist who became a civil rights leader, and Fannie Lou Hamer at the Democratic Convention in 1964 (Henry was willing to accept a compromise offered by northern liberal Democrats on the question of seating the MFDP delegation; Hamer indignantly rejected it) is seen as one symptom of this split.

After 1965, Dittmer shows, Aaron Henry and Charles Evers (Medgar's brother) joined forces with Hodding Carter III, a leading white moderate, in a two-front struggle for control of the local Democratic Party against the segregationists, on the one hand, and the MFDP (now led by onetime SNCC activist Lawrence Guyot) on the other. The MFDP was drained of resources by its unsuccessful struggle (from January through September, 1965) to get Congress to deny seats to the Mississippi congressional delegation. The Voting Rights Act of 1965, by making it easier for blacks to take part in politics, also made it easier for blacks to dispute the dominance of the MFDP. By 1968, Dittmer makes clear, the MFDP had lost; its remnants united with the Carter-Evers-Henry wing to choose a slate for the 1968 Democratic national convention, which easily gained the right to replace the segregationists.

The divisions among blacks, Dittmer concedes, did not prevent changes favorable to blacks from occurring in the late 1960's and beyond. The barriers of public accommodations discrimination finally began to fall, and, under court pressure, Mississippi finally began to integrate its public schools. Mississippi's whites tired of Ku Klux Klan violence: a turning point was the decision of an all-white jury, in 1967, to convict several men for violating the civil rights of Goodman, Schwerner, and Chaney in 1964. In 1967, a black schoolteacher, Robert Clark, was elected to the Mississippi legislature; by 1992, Dittmer points out, the state of Mississippi would have more than 825 black elected officials.

Such undeniable progress in politics, Dittmer notes, was accompanied by stagnation, and even deterioration, in the economic condition of Mississippi's poor blacks. In the chapter on "CDGM and the Politics of Poverty," Dittmer points to the rift within the black leadership as one explanation for this paradox. The author sees the Johnson Administration's decision, in the fall of 1966, to divert federal antipoverty funding from one organization devoted to compensatory education, the Child Development Group of Mississippi (CDGM), to another such organization, Mississippi Action for Progress (MAP), as a deliberate effort to promote the fortunes of the Carter-Evers-Henry alliance at the expense of the MFDP. The fight between CDGM and MAP, he contends, undermined the entire antipoverty effort in the state. Dittmer also recognizes a nonpolitical reason for worsening black poverty: the increasing use of the mechanical cotton picker and of chemical herbicides, reducing the need for unskilled labor.

In this exhaustive work, the author seems to mention every site of civil rights battles within the state; every sit-in, protest march, or confrontation between would-be black voters and recalcitrant white registrars; every killing by white racists; every act of police brutality; and the name of every movement activist. The general reader can easily become confused trying to keep track of the turf struggles not only between civil rights activists and white racists, but also between different civil rights organizations, and even between different individuals within the same organization.

Dittmer's book, like many other scholarly monographs, fails to provide a broad perspective. Although Dittmer mentions the Alabama and Georgia movements briefly in the final chapter, the reader who wants a more thoroughgoing comparison of the movement in Mississippi with the movement elsewhere in the South, or in the North, should consult Fred Powledge's *Free At Last?: The Civil Rights Movement and the People Who Made It* (1991) and Steven Lawson's *Running for Freedom: Civil Rights and Black Politics in America Since 1941* (1991). Dittmer fails to probe deeply into the psychology of Mississippi's white racists, to determine why so many were willing to use violence to stop the Civil Rights movement. Journalist Adam Nossiter's *Of Long Memory: Mississippi and the Murder of Medgar Evers* (1994), which examines the life of the civil rights leader's killer (Byron de la Beckwith), comes closer to providing this type of analysis.

Local People, which took eight years to write, rests on an impressive body of research. Besides consulting published memoirs and local newspapers and interviewing surviving civil rights activists, Dittmer has mined the John Fitzgerald Kennedy and Lyndon Baines Johnson libraries, the archives of various government agencies, and the collections of private papers of individuals involved in the movement.

The book includes maps, photographs, and an excellent index. The seventy-two pages of endnotes, which are almost as informative as the text itself, provide a mine of bibliographical information.

Paul D. Mageli

Sources for Further Study

Booklist. XC, June 1, 1994, p. 1767.
Detroit News and Free Press. August 7, 1994, p. B1.
Kirkus Reviews. LXII, April 15, 1994, p. 518.
Library Journal. CXIX, June 1, 1994, p. 130.
The New York Times Book Review. XCIX, July 24, 1994, p. 16.
Publishers Weekly. CCXLI, May 16, 1994, p. 56.
The Washington Post Book World. XXIV, June 26, 1994, p. 3.
Wilson Library Bulletin. LXIX, October, 1994, p. 101.

THE LONGINGS OF WOMEN

Author: Marge Piercy (1936-)
Publisher: Fawcett Columbine (New York). 445 pp. $22.00
Type of work: Novel
Time: The 1980's and 1990's
Locale: Cambridge and Boston, Massachusetts

The story of three women, all disappointed and betrayed by men, as they attempt to fulfill their need for happiness

Principal characters:

LEILA LANDSMAN, a middle-aged sociology professor
NICHOLAS (NICK) LANDSMAN, her philandering husband, a theatrical director
REBECCA (BECKY) SOUZA BURGESS, a young woman who murdered her husband
SAM SOLOMON, a high school senior, Becky's lover and accomplice
ZAK SOLOMON, a veterinarian, Sam's uncle and Leila's lover
MARY FERGUSON BURKE, a homeless woman employed by a cleaning service and assigned to Leila

In her much-admired novel of World War II, *Gone to Soldiers* (1987), Marge Piercy sought to recapture the spirit of a past era by describing the lives of ten individuals. *The Longings of Women* is not as long or as complex as the earlier book, nor is it historical in nature. Piercy's method, however, is much the same. In this work she follows three women through a critical period in their lives, as they try to find happiness that does not depend upon the love or approval of men.

Leila Landsman is a forty-five-year-old sociology professor at a college in Cambridge, Massachusetts. Although she is the primary breadwinner of the family, throughout the twenty-four years of their marriage she has been subservient to her husband, Nick, who directs plays at regional theaters and occasionally picks up additional money by teaching. From the beginning, Nick has insisted on having his sexual freedom, and Leila has settled for whatever attention he chooses to give her. Now, with her only child in college in California and her best friend dying of cancer, Leila needs the kind of support from her husband that she has always been only too happy to give him. Nick is too busy with a play opening in New York and, even more important, with his affair with one of the young actresses. When Leila sees how Nick has failed her, she is at first devastated. Then she begins to reassess her life.

Piercy's second protagonist, Mary Ferguson Burke, long ago gave up not only on her husband but on her children as well. Once Mary had been a suburban housewife, married to a prominent and prosperous geologist. When she was forty-five, her husband left her for another woman. Though she had a college degree, Mary was not really prepared to earn enough to support herself. When she was evicted from her apartment, she lost what little she had left. Although she finally found a job working for a cleaning service, she cannot afford to pay rent. At sixty, she spends her nights in airports, laundromats, church basements, or unlocked garages. She is too proud to admit the truth to her two married children, who answer her occasional pleas for money with descriptions of their own minor financial difficulties, and she is too canny to let her various "ladies" know that she is living in the streets, for their revulsion toward the homeless would result in her immediate dismissal. Mary looks forward to nights and weekends when her employers are out of town, for then she can move into their homes to bathe, eat, and sleep in comfort. Yet Mary never forgets that these pleasures, like everything else about her life, are merely temporary. When the worst happens and she becomes ill, she has to face the fact that unless she finds a home, she will die.

Unlike Leila and Mary, who devoted themselves to pleasing men only to be betrayed by them, it takes only one experience of being used to persuade Becky Souza Burgess that it was wiser to use men than to be used by them. Although she likes Terrence Burgess, Becky does not love him. Nevertheless, after maneuvering him into marriage, Becky makes her husband's happiness her first priority. Only when he loses his job and refuses to get another, so that she must supply his every need while he sleeps in front of the television or sneaks out to date other women, does Becky decide that he is worth more dead than alive. At the beginning of the novel, Becky has been arrested for killing Terrence with the help of Sam Solomon, a seventeen-year-old high school senior whom she has seduced for the purpose.

Even though one may understand why Becky is angry, it is difficult to think of her as a victim. In one way, however, she is not unlike Leila and Mary. Again, a woman is betrayed by a man—or, in her case, by two men: first Terrence, who was too self-centered to give her the affection she craved, then Sam, who, however unintentionally, led the police to her by being too frugal or too stupid to jettison the television and the videocassette recorder supposedly stolen by Terrence's unknown killer. Admittedly, Becky is a cold-blooded murderer; admittedly, by her actions she destroys the lives of two men. Yet like Leila and Mary, she is also the victim of social assumptions about gender. If her initial mistake is the result of trusting a man with her life, her second error is shocking society by behaving like a man. To her surprise, Becky finds the jury unsympathetic, not primarily because of her deviousness or her brutality but because, as a female, she demonstrated the predatory behavior that society expects and encourages only in males. By crossing the gender line, Becky has made her conviction inevitable.

In *The Longings of Women*, Marge Piercy again demonstrates her mastery of technique. For example, throughout the novel she uses third-person narration, but by focusing on only one protagonist in each chapter, she achieves an effect of immediacy that is ordinarily found in stories told in the first person. Moreover, although the events that take place during the course of the novel are related in chronological order, with the exception of thoughts and memories, in fact Piercy maintains not one, but two, time schemes. The chapters dealing with Leila and Mary are set in the present and move onward, while those in which Becky is the primary character take place in the past and move up to the present. Thus although at the time of the novel Becky is actually twenty-five, at her first appearance she is still in high school. Step by step, then, the author shows her moving toward murder, until, very late in the book, Becky's life has come to the point where the novel actually begins.

In another way, too, Becky's story is handled differently from those of Mary and Leila. Not only does the omniscient author reveal the truth about Becky's motivations and her actions, but she also follows a fictional author as she attempts to write a nonfiction book on the same subject. Because Leila has published a book about women in prison, she is asked to produce a work about the sensational Burgess case. This presentation of Becky from two perspectives, one authoritative and one tentative, the product of speculation, has some interesting results. Since Piercy has already entrusted her readers with the facts, there is a strong element of comic irony in Leila's fumbling interviews. In the difference between what is true and what Leila's subjects say they believe, the author also dramatizes one of her major themes, the tendency of human beings to delude themselves, especially when their emotions are involved.

Fortunately, an omniscient author is exempt from human illusions, at least on the pages of her book. Piercy's method of maintaining her authorial presence in *The Longings of Women* is particularly interesting. While it is evident that this is a novel with three protagonists, all of equal importance, it is significant that the novel begins and ends with Leila. She seems to have two major functions. First, her place in the plot is pivotal: Leila is the only one of the three protagonists who knows both of the others. Leila is connected with Becky because of the book she is writing, and she is involved with Mary first because she is one of the women whose house Mary cleans, and later because it happens to be Leila's house in which Mary collapses. Even more important, Leila is uniquely suited to speak for the author. Even though she may not always see her own situation clearly, she has an analytical mind, and as a sociologist, she has been trained to view people and situations objectively. Therefore it is not surprising that in the chapters about Leila one finds most of the comments that illuminate not only her own situation but also those of the other women in the novel.

Indeed, one of the points Piercy makes is that women who in many respects are very different have more in common than they realize. Her three protagonists have been trapped because they believed the common assumption that a woman's worth is derived from her relationship with a man. Mary spent her youth catering to the whims of her husband, only to be dropped for another woman; then she attached herself to another man, who repeated the pattern, firing her when he no longer needed her to set up his business or to warm his bed. Leila may not be financially dependent on her husband, but like Mary she made him much the center of her life. Leila is happiest when she is helping Nick analyze the characters in one of his plays; in other words, she feels most valuable when she is serving him. With her radio newsman, Becky is just as slavish as the other women in the novel, and even though she is not emotionally tied to her husband, for some time she finds her identity not in her job but in preparing meals he likes and doing laundry to his satisfaction. Abandoning her old dream of becoming a television personality, Becky hurries into marriage, hitching her wagon to Terrence's star. By living with him and becoming like him, she intends to achieve her goal of rising into upper-middle-class society.

By implicitly suggesting that it is foolish for a woman to define herself as a handmaiden to a man, Piercy is not urging her gender to become self-centered and selfish. Becky is not unhappy when she is helping to support her family, who, unlike Terrence, appreciate her efforts. Both Leila and her son take great pleasure in their relationship, which is based on mutual respect. Yet when the family becomes one's only reason for living, the situation is as unhealthy as dependence on a single individual. Therefore it is better for Leila that her friend's orphaned daughter chooses not to move in with her. Deprived of a chance to start another family, Leila learns to be happy with her cats, who give her more love than Nick ever could, and with her writing. For the first time in her life, Leila is doing what she wants to do, rather than what she feels she must do. Certainly she enjoys seeing Sam's appealing uncle, Zak Solomon, put Nick in his place, and she enjoys his company and his lovemaking. Yet even if Leila does eventually make a commitment to Zak, she will never become as emotionally dependent on him as she was on Nick.

Because of circumstances, the other two women in the novel do not attain the degree of independence that Leila does. Mary lost too much time depending on her husband, and now she is too old to become fully self-sufficient. Nevertheless, her life does improve immeasurably after Leila arranges for her to move to California, where she becomes a housekeeper for Leila's sister. Even though she must still depend for her survival on her power to please, in this case it seems unlikely that Mary will fail. Becky, too, has lost her chance for independence, at least for a number of years, and, like Mary, she must survive by catering to others. The reader's glimpse of Becky is as a prisoner, gamely setting about to make the right friends and coldly calculating the chances of an escape.

By using not a single protagonist, but three, Piercy has enriched her novel immeasurably. Regardless of whether the author intended it, *The Longings of Women* can be seen as an illustration of the golden mean, the concept described by the Greek philosopher Aristotle and adopted as truth by most great minds of the Middle Ages and the Renaissance. Mary represents one extreme, total subservience to one's mate, while Becky represents the other, self-assertion to the point of disregarding the rights of others. It is Leila who epitomizes the golden mean, the ideal, by learning how to nurture without losing her own identity, how to assert herself without destroying others.

Rosemary M. Canfield Reisman

Sources for Further Study

Booklist. XC, December 1, 1993, p. 660.
Boston Globe. March 13, 1994, p. 92.
Chicago Tribune. April 17, 1994, XIV, p. 3.
Kirkus Reviews. LXI, December 15, 1993, p. 1546.

Library Journal. CXIX, January, 1994, p. 164.
Los Angeles Times Book Review. April 3, 1994, p. 5.
The New York Times Book Review. XCIX, March 20, 1994, p. 23.
Publishers Weekly. CCXL, December 13, 1993, p. 61.
The Washington Post Book World. XXIV, March 27, 1994, p. 5.
The Women's Review of Books. XI, July, 1994, p. 46.

LOOKING AT THE SUN
The Rise of the New East Asian Economic and Political System

Author: James Fallows (1949-   )
Publisher: Pantheon Books (New York). 517 pp. $25.00
Type of work: Current affairs

A well-informed overall view of what the author calls "the Asian system": Japan and the Pacific Rim countries that are following its model of largely state-directed economic development

James Fallows' *Looking at the Sun: The Rise of the New East Asian Economic and Political System* is a readable and far-ranging description of the postwar growth of the major East Asian economies. Japan is the major economic force in the spectacular development of the region, but close behind are the other countries or Asian "tigers" that Fallows calls "the Contenders": Taiwan, Hong Kong, Korea, Singapore, Malaysia, Indonesia, and Thailand. More briefly, Fallows considers countries that are "on the sidelines" for the time being: Vietnam, Myanmar, and the Philippines.

The strength of Fallows' book is that it is unified, presenting a strong case that these Asian countries form a single system. Although the countries have important differences—duly noted by Fallows—they have learned the Japanese model of economic development and largely accepted it. The book profits from the author's familiarity with each country, and this also provides a unifying theme. During four years Fallows lived with his family in the Asian countries he describes, and he enlivens his account with personal anecdotes and colorful details. He also interviewed officials in these countries, and his quotations provide both sharpness and vividness.

The book has two shortcomings. There is almost no discussion of United States trade policy toward Japan. This is probably deliberate: The focus is consistently on what East Asia has done, not what the United States should do about it. The implication is simply that "the Asian system" should be taken seriously; a reader interested in the problems of trade negotiation should look elsewhere. A second shortcoming is Fallows' discussion of Western economic theory. Here he has more to say. Some of his suggestions are interesting but remain on an impressionistic level. They require more space to be convincing; as it is they are fragmentary and sometimes distracting.

Fallows considers the dynamic East Asian economies as a group, with Japan providing a widely copied model for development. All countries in the group employ government direction and policy—"industrial policy"—to foster economic development. They are, however, not state-directed economies like the former Soviet Union, North Korea, or China before 1991. They are a mixture of free markets and competition on the one hand and, on the other, deliberate planning by state agencies and "talented bureaucrats."

What is the Japanese "system"? Most important, it fosters production—and the continued growth of production—over consumption. It also puts a far greater emphasis on market share, and the cumulative growth of this market share, than on immediate profit. In more general terms,

> Japanese spokesmen would emphasize the worth of the collective interest rather than that of the individual; would emphasize administrative institutions insulated from the ups and downs of democracy; would talk about "excessive competition" as something their economy avoided; would say that international trade should be open in only certain ways; and would claim that international order was strongest with a dominant power, rather than some abstract rule of law.

These, Fallows believes, are the underpinnings of the success of the Japanese economy. Coupled with one of the highest personal savings rates in the world (three times that of Americans), a disciplined and well-educated work force, nonadversarial relations between management and labor, highly developed technology, and underconsumption, the results have been dramatic. Many of these qualities have been admired and emulated by Japan's neighbors.

Another aspect of the "system," perhaps less admirable, has been adversarial trade. Fallows approvingly quotes Peter Drucker:

> Competitive trade aims at creating a customer. Adversarial trade aims at dominating an industry. . . . Adversarial trade, however, is unlikely to be beneficial to both sides. . . . The aim in adversarial trade . . . is to drive the competitor out of the market altogether rather than to let the competitor survive.

It would be difficult to pursue adversarial trade on a broad scale without cartels, or the famous interlocking *keiretsu* that have so successfully resisted foreign penetration. The typical *keiretsu* had a bank at its center, with links of cross-ownership with suppliers and both large and small companies. The Korean equivalents are called *chaebol*. In the mid-1970's, Japan's Ministry of International Trade and Industry, MITI, launched its VLSI projects, the acronym standing for "Very-Large-Scale Integration." These involved preferential access to capital, government-sponsored research, strategies for licensing technology from foreign (mainly American) suppliers, and other means to help Japanese producers overcome the foreign lead in high-technology production.

At its most aggressive, this has led to a "win at any cost" spirit. In 1985, American semiconductor officials, who were preparing a dumping complaint against their Japanese rivals, found the following copy of a Hitachi sales presentation:

> *Quote 10% Below Competition.*
> *If they requote . . .*
> *Bid 10% under again.*
> *The bidding stops when Hitachi wins. . . .*
> *Win with the 10% rule. . . .*
> *Find Intel and AMD sockets. . . .*
> *Quote 10% below their price. . . .*
> *If they requote,*
> *Go 10% again.*
> Don't quit until you *win!*

Fallows covers considerable ground in his book, sketching the background of at least eleven countries. He tries to explain, for example, why one of the most Western-style, democratic countries of the Pacific Rim, the Philippines, is the least successful economically. With a project so broad, some details are bound to be incorrect, and they should not pass unchallenged. Fallows describes Japan's military (or fascist?) regime of the 1930's and the war years as "abnormal," outside the country's more general twentieth century development. Yet in *Japan in War and Peace* (1993), the historian John Dower has argued just the opposite: that many institutions responsible for Japan's dominant position in the global economy have roots in the rapid military industrialization of the 1930's. One need not have read Dower to realize that many cultural and social forces of the 1930's still exist: conformity and powerful pressures against individualism, a prevalent "us versus them" mentality, a sense of victimization, an emphasis on purity, Shinto ritual, and the continuity represented by the Yasukuni Shrine. In general, however, Fallows' historical accounts are based on genuine erudition. He goes beyond ephemeral journalism and is well-read in political and economic literature.

When Fallows writes about economic theory, he is on shakier ground. He is vexed by much journalistic reporting—"politicians, newspaper editorials, television talk shows and the other forms of punditry that define reasonable and unreasonable ideas." Fallows is right that there is a prodigious amount of hot air and silliness in current reporting about Japan, not to mention books of fiction. Much of this is on a low level; only occasionally do newspapers publish well-informed articles about the Japanese economy. Fallows has the problem of the serious writer who straddles the borderline between journalism and serious scholarship. Probably he should have been more selective, ignoring much of the highly charged partisan debate and applying critical distinctions with greater care. For example, the editorial page of *The Wall Street Journal* is deliberately intended to be provocative, and its editor does not report to the editor of the rest of the newspaper. It should not be quoted in a book of this kind.

Many of Fallows' ideas about economic theory are plausible. He is correct that American notions about free trade often verge on "religion"; moralistic lectures by American politicians can be absurd, embarrassing, and hypocritical. Frequently they cannot withstand a serious analysis of the realities of trade negotiation or of economic history. Fallows reminds readers that protective tariffs were a major cause of the American Revolution; Britain did not want to protect the weak, fledgling industries of the Colonies but sought instead to bind them permanently to the powerful British economy. Fallows claims that the United States is advising Japan and its Asian neighbors to maintain "open markets" just as Britain advised the Colonies to remain "open"—and prey to the superior manufacturing resources of the British. Some of Fallows' other ideas are suggestive: about economic history, about the German thinker Friedrich List, about "competition" as a cultural concept with more variables than Americans care to admit, and about the special exceptions that Anglo-American economists are willing to make for an economy at war but not for one at peace.

These ideas are usually presented in passing rather than systematically. Probably they should not have been discussed in the same context as emotional journalism, uninformed Japan-bashing, and "punditry." If Fallows had brought his ample knowledge of history, culture, and religion to bear and crossed swords not with George Will but with Paul Samuelson, his discussion would have been even more rewarding.

John Carpenter

Sources for Further Study

The Christian Science Monitor. May 18, 1994, p. 15.
The Economist. CCCXXXI, May 28, 1994, p. 89.
Far Eastern Economic Review. CLVII, September 1, 1994, p. 56.
Foreign Affairs. LXXIII, September, 1994, p. 126.
Issues in Science and Technology. X, Summer, 1994, p. 73.
The New York Times Book Review. XCIX, June 5, 1994, p. 26.
Newsweek. CXXIII, February 7, 1994, p. 34.
Publishers Weekly. CCXLI, February 28, 1994, p. 66.
Time. CXLIII, June 6, 1994, p. 68.
The Washington Post Book World. XXIV, April 17, 1994, p. 4.

LOST PURITAN
A Life of Robert Lowell

Author: Paul Mariani (1943-)
Publisher: W. W. Norton (New York). 527 pp. $27.50
Type of work: Biography
Time: 1917-1977
Locale: Boston and New York

A detailed biography of Robert Lowell, the renowned American poet

Principal personages:
ROBERT LOWELL, a major American poet
CHARLOTTE LOWELL, his dominating mother
ELIZABETH HARDWICK, his second wife, a writer
CAROLINE BLACKWOOD, his third and last wife

The first question to ask about Paul Mariani's biography of Robert Lowell is why there should be a new life of Lowell so soon after Ian Hamilton's biography, *Robert Lowell.* Hamilton's revelations about Lowell's disruptive manic episodes and sexual adventures were startling when published in 1982. What can Mariani add to this scandalous presentation of the great American poet's foibles? As it turns out, he has much to add. Mariani has more interviews with those who had a close relationship with Lowell and more letters to and by him, and he can draw on Lowell's own autobiographical fragments, memoir, and writings. The result is likely to become the definitive biography of Lowell. It sheds important light on Lowell's relationship with such figures as Randall Jarrell, Jean Stafford, Elizabeth Hardwick, and especially Lowell's last wife, Caroline Blackwood. Mariani's *Lost Puritan: A Life of Robert Lowell* is not a critical biography, but it is as full a rendering of Lowell's life as readers are likely to get.

Robert Lowell was born in 1917 into the famous Lowell family of Boston. He was not a member of the main branch of that famous family. His father, Robert Trail Spence Lowell III, was a naval officer rather than a writer or intellectual; he had attended United States Naval Academy at Annapolis rather than Harvard University and rose to the rank of lieutenant commander by the time he left the navy. He was, however, a weak and dilatory man who was dominated by his wife, Charlotte Winslow Lowell. She was a formidable woman who could not bear to be separated from Boston or her father, Arthur Winslow. She forced her husband to retire from the navy so that she could remain in Boston and he could earn a better living at Lever Brothers, a job he soon lost. Her relationship with the future poet was fierce and smothering. Mariani is quite good at describing the conflicts in the family; he brings out fully the oedipal conflict between Robert Lowell and his mother and the struggle he had to free himself from her domination.

The family conflict came to a head when Lowell, in his first year at Harvard, struck his father and knocked him down. The elder Lowell had written some insulting remarks to the father of Robert's fiancée, Anne Dick. Lowell's parents were opposed to the engagement and the marriage, and the incident resulted in Lowell's leaving Harvard. He went to the home of Allen Tate, a poet and critic, in Tennessee. When he was told there was no room in the house and the only way he could stay there was to pitch a tent, Lowell bought a Sears Roebuck tent and camped out on the Tates' front lawn. He then entered Kenyon College to be with the American poet and critic John Crowe Ransom.

Lowell's parents were shocked at his leaving Harvard. Yet it was a successful move for him. Tate and Ransom were accomplished poets and critics, and they served as more useful father-figures for Lowell than his weak father. At Kenyon Lowell also embarked on lifelong friendships with the poet Randall Jarrell and the fiction writer Peter Taylor.

After he was graduated summa cum laude from Kenyon, Lowell met and married the fiction writer Jean Stafford. Mariani provides an excellent overview of their stormy relationship, especially through quotes from letters and interviews with Stafford, whose remarks are always witty and sometimes acute. It was during this period that Lowell became a convert to Roman Catholicism. He was seeking some absolute authority, especially one he could use in his poetry, and also a way to cut himself off from his parents. Charlotte Lowell had once said that Catholicism was a religion for Irish maids, and now her son was a communicant. Stafford also became a convert, although not as zealous a one as Lowell.

Lowell refused to accept induction into the military in World War II. He based his decision on the bombing of civilians in Germany and Franklin Delano Roosevelt's policy of unconditional surrender. Mariani reproduces the manic letter Lowell wrote to the president to justify his actions. As a result of his refusal, he was sentenced to a year in a federal prison in Danbury, Connecticut.

During this period, he began writing his earliest important poems and gathered enough poems for his first volume, *Land of Unlikeness* (1944). The poems were clogged and obscure, as Lowell was following the example of Tate and the dictates of the New Criticism. The book received respectful reviews; the critics noted a new and unpolished voice in American poetry. Mariani does not discuss the poetry at any length, and he fails to cite many of the reviews the books of poetry received. He tends to quote the poems throughout the book as if they exemplified aspects of Lowell's life. Sometimes this works brilliantly, but at other times it can be misleading.

Lowell's next book, *Lord Weary's Castle* (1946), was a far more accomplished work, but the poems were still filled with Catholic imagery and often obscure. The book received the Pulitzer Prize in poetry and adulatory reviews. Lowell had established his reputation as an American poet. His private life was troubled, however, by the earliest signs of the manic-depressive illness that would plague him for the rest of his days, and his marriage to Stafford was dissolved in 1948.

Lowell met Elizabeth Hardwick at Yaddo, a writers' colony. In one of his earliest manic episodes, he thought that the director, Elizabeth Ames, was a Communist and should be driven out. Nothing came of these accusations, but the stance of absolute knowledge and power that Lowell assumed here would be duplicated later with more troublesome results. He married Hardwick in 1949; the relationship was often troubled, but it marked the most secure and fruitful period in Lowell's life.

Lowell's next book of poems, *The Mills of the Kavanaughs* (1951), was a disappointment. It included a narrative told in couplets that was almost impossible to decipher. Lowell needed a new style, a new subject, and, perhaps, a new father-figure. He was to find all of these in William Carlos Williams, a poet who had rejected the principles of the New Critics and the example of T. S. Eliot. Williams' free verse and personal poetry helped Lowell find his new style and subject in *Life Studies* (1959).

Life Studies was written after the death of Lowell's parents. The volume included poems on both his mother and his father, as well as poems on his manic episodes and his experiences in prison and in mental institutions. The book was immediately recognized as setting a new direction for American poetry. Mariani offers helpful insights on the origins of the book; he discusses Lowell's interest in Williams' poetry and W. D. Snodgrass' *Heart's Needle*, as well as his ambiguous attitude toward the Beat poets. He says little, however, about the poems that make up *Life Studies*, although some of the poems are cited as evidence of Lowell's relationships with others.

Lowell had by now received every significant honor that was available to an American poet. One critic called the period "the Age of Lowell." Yet his personal life remained troubled. His relationship with Elizabeth Hardwick was solid, and they now had a daughter, Harriet; however, Lowell was subject to manic attacks, followed by hospitalization, and a recovery marred by depression. These attacks occurred about once a year, and new drugs such as Thorazine and lithium were not able to control them. While he was in a manic state, Lowell would often announce that he was leaving his wife to marry a young woman. Naturally, this threatened his marriage. Mariani quotes from a number of letters and interviews with Hardwick which clearly show her sympathy with Lowell's problem but also her belief that the marriage could not last under these conditions.

Lowell's next book was *For the Union Dead* (1964), but Mariani has almost nothing to say about changes in Lowell's style or the reception of the book. He is better on the new political direction in Lowell's next book, *Near the Ocean* (1967). Lowell was disturbed by the Vietnam War and opposed it vigorously. He joined the March on Washington, although he was not arrested for his participation. Later, he was to support the quixotic candidacy of Senator Eugene McCarthy.

Lowell changed his style once more with *Notebook 1967-68* (1969), which later became *Notebook* (1970) and then *History* (1973). The book is a long sequence of blank-verse sonnets. He believed that the structure of the sonnet would give him the enclosure of a fixed form in which he could roam free with his loose blank verse. Many critics have seen this experiment as a failure, and Lowell did need to revise his first attempt in this form many times.

In 1970, Lowell met and had an affair with Lady Caroline Blackwood. This relationship was not like those he had with many young women while he was in a manic state. His marriage to Hardwick was weakening, and he seems to have felt invigorated by the sexual relationship with Blackwood. This part of Lowell's life is very sketchy in the Hamilton biography, but it is fully rendered by Mariani. The relationship and eventual marriage constituted a disaster for Lowell. He had a series of manic episodes that frightened Blackwood, and he never felt at home in England.

His next book, *The Dolphin* (1973), celebrated Blackwood as the "Dolphin" who had cured Lowell by going "for my body." The book also had a number of poems about Hardwick and the breakup of their marriage. Some of the poems even included parts of letters that Hardwick had written to Lowell. She felt humiliated at the revelations and embarrassed at the printing of her private correspondence. Lowell made it clear that he intended the book as an updated version of George Meredith's *Modern Love* (1862), another book of sonnets about the dissolution of a marriage. Soon after, *For Lizzie and Harriet* (1973) was published and included sonnets that had been taken from *Notebook*. It dealt with the painful break with and separation from Hardwick and Harriet.

As Mariani shows, Lowell remained conflicted even after the marriage to Blackwood and the birth of their son, Sheridan. Lowell remained in touch with Hardwick and seemed to be torn between the two women. Some of this conflict is reflected in Lowell's last book, *Day by Day* (1977). Here Lowell finally dropped the sonnet form and recovered an ease of tone and voice that had been lacking in his work since *Notebook*.

By 1976, it became clear to Lowell that his marriage to Blackwood had been a mistake. He returned to the United States to teach at Harvard and made plans for a reunion and perhaps a reconciliation with Hardwick. In 1977, however, he suffered a heart attack in a taxi outside Hardwick's apartment in New York. He was sixty years old, honored as one of America's finest poets. Though his achievement was marred by an illness he could not control or avoid, he made great poetry out of his struggle with mental illness, his troubled relationship with his family, and his shifting relationships with the women he loved and married.

Paul Mariani's *Lost Puritan* is clearly the best biography that the reading public has had and is likely to have of Robert Lowell. It is clearly written and is filled with observations and assessments of the poet by those who were closest to him. In addition, Mariani's sympathy for Lowell and his problems comes through his narrative of Lowell's life. Many literary biographies, including Hamilton's *Robert Lowell,* do not have that sympathy and affinity with the subject of their research. In a preface, Mariani speaks about his first encounter with Lowell's poetry. He was overwhelmed by the poems, and something of that reverence is evident in this thorough biography. Other biographies of Lowell will probably be written, but it is doubtful that any of them will add much to this scrupulously researched effort by Mariani.

James Sullivan

Sources for Further Study

Booklist. LXII, July 1, 1994, p. 909.
Boston Globe. September 18, 1994, p. 17.
Chicago Tribune. October 9, 1994, XIV, p. 3.
Kirkus Reviews. LXII, July 1, 1994, p. 909.
Library Journal. CXIX, October 1, 1994, p. 81.
The New York Times Book Review. XCIX, November 20, 1994, p. 3.
Publishers Weekly. CCXLI, July 18, 1994, p. 232.
San Francisco Chronicle. October 16, 1994, p. REV1.
The Wall Street Journal. October 12, 1994, p. A13.
The Washington Post Book World. XXIV, October 2, 1994, p. 4.

A MAP OF THE WORLD

Author: Jane Hamilton (1957-   )
Publisher: Doubleday (New York). 390 pp. $22.00
Type of work: Novel
Time: The 1990's
Locale: Prairie Center, Wisconsin

This elegiac and moving novel has all the makings of a latter-day tragedy—a drowned child, an innocent mother jailed, the dissolution of a marriage and a way of life—but author Jane Hamilton manages to transcend her subject matter and weave a story that is as much about rebirth and redemption as it is about death and despair

Principal characters:
ALICE GOODWIN, the principal narrator, a wife and mother
HOWARD GOODWIN, her husband, the secondary narrator
EMMA and CLAIRE GOODWIN, their daughters
THERESA COLLINS, Alice's best friend, the mother of a drowned child
DAN COLLINS, Theresa's husband
LIZZY and AUDREY COLLINS, Theresa and Dan's daughters
PAUL RAFFERTY, Alice's lawyer

Jane Hamilton's elegiac and moving second novel, *A Map of the World*, has all the makings of a latter-day tragedy: a child drowned, an innocent woman jailed, the dissolution of a marriage, the loss of a home and way of life, the unraveling of a family. In less capable hands such material could only read as maudlin, exploitive, even operatic—the storyline for a daytime drama. Yet Jane Hamilton is not merely a capable writer; she is a startlingly gifted one. In *A Map of the World* Hamilton, whose first novel, *The Book of Ruth*, won the 1989 PEN/Hemingway Foundation Award, manages to transform, indeed transcend her subject matter and in the process weave a story that is as much about rebirth as it is about death, as much about forgiveness as it is about despair and as much about love's healing qualities as it is about all of its attendant treacheries. With *A Map of the World* Hamilton has created exactly that: a guide for life in this cruel and beautiful universe—simple, stark, and true.

Like all worthy tragedies, Hamilton's tale charts a fall from grace and innocence that could not have happened to nicer people. The Goodwin family is good. Alice, Howard, and their young daughters, Emma and Claire, are outsiders in the small Wisconsin farming community of Prairie Center, in which they settled six years before to raise dairy cows and live away from the encroaching threat of subdivisions, strip malls, and freeways. Howard, devoted father, husband, and farmer, loves his family and his hard-won (and debt-ridden) piece of land with equal determination. Alice, sensitive and dreamy wife and mother, works as a nurse at Blackwell Elementary School during the school year and does her best to keep her house and daughters together in the summers. That she is not altogether comfortable with farm life and is given over to fits of doubt about their return to the land makes the reader identify with her. Alice is as real as she is realistic, even when wringing truth from "the stink and mess, the frenetic dullness of farming, our marriage, the tedium of work and love." "All of it," she says, "was my savior."

Yet this simple if slightly imperfect way of life is not meant to be. Told from the distance of a year's remove in prose that is magnificently lucid, the tragedies that befall Alice Goodwin and her family unfold with an exquisite and painful certitude. Readers know from the very first page that Alice will suffer: "I opened my eyes on a Monday morning in June last summer and I heard, somewhere far off, a siren belting out calamity. It was the last time I would listen so simply to a sound that could mean both disaster and pursuit." This first disaster, the one that sets off the tragic chain of events that all but destroys Alice and her family, is the sudden accidental drowning of Alice's best friend's daughter, who is entrusted to Alice's care.

It is the very ordinary nature of the circumstances surrounding the tragedy itself that makes Hamilton's story, and Alice's, such a compelling and believable one. Alice is baby-sitting her friend Theresa's two daughters and her own two girls one hot summer morning. Howard is working outside in the barn. While searching through a drawer to find her bathing suit so that she can take the girls swimming in the pond that lies on the farm property, Alice pauses to reminisce for a few short moments with a drawing she made as a child (the title's map of the world), time enough for Theresa's daughter Lizzy to toddle away from the house and into the pond. When Alice comes downstairs a few minutes later and discovers that Lizzy is missing, Hamilton makes the reader inhabit every single second of the subsequent terror and disbelief that Alice must endure. Time moves with the slow-motion pacing of all accidental horrors—the long seconds of understanding and lucidity just before a car crash, before the world breaks open wide.

> I pulled her up and slung her over my shoulder, tripping through the water, screaming then, screaming for help. I didn't know how to make enough noise, to be heard. I was shrieking with so much force I felt as if I might split, and yet all the world was placid, still. The leaves in the trees hung limp like palsied hands. I lay Lizzy on her back, that was right, and then I tilted her chin and put my ear to her cold chest, and tried to listen.

What happens next would test the faith of a saint, but at no time does Hamilton overplay the dark fates awaiting her characters. While still deeply grieving for her unwitting role in Lizzy's drowning, a few days after the accident occurs Alice is arrested and charged with several counts of sexual abuse in a case brought by one of the students in the school where she works as a nurse. Prairie Center and its inhabitants have risen up against Alice Goodwin, and since they cannot punish her for Lizzy's accidental death or the crime of being an outsider in their midst, they will punish her for something else, however unfounded and horrifying. Alice must pay. While this seems almost too much to bear (or for readers to believe), Hamilton's gift for presenting life in a starkly unflinching manner—unadorned and unapologetic—carries the action: "It hurt to stand and it hurt to lie down, and it hurt to open my eyes to the light and it hurt to shut them and see." Alice's guilt, coupled with her inability to forgive herself for Lizzy's death (even though Lizzy's mother, Theresa, has absolved her), forces her to accept whatever punishment life might impose. A singular tragedy spawns another, and yet another, and Alice treats each one not as an aberration but as a natural occurrence, an atonement for her sin of being all too human.

Bad things do happen to good people, and for Alice Goodwin and her family this simple fact of life means surviving "the misfortunes that sometimes seemed to be of biblical proportions and at other times seemed like the sort of thing that could easily happen to anyone, as ordinary and expected as a leaky pipe or a stalled car." So skillful is Hamilton's depiction of these ordinary and devastating events that the reader never doubts that they are possible, indeed probable.

When the police arrive unannounced at the Goodwins' farm to arrest Alice on the sexual abuse charges and remove her to the county jail, the narrative shifts to Howard's perspective. This section, the middle third of the novel, begins as Howard watches, powerless, as his wife is manacled and loaded into a squad car to be driven away. While Howard admits to himself, "I am as guilty as the next person, thinking that hardship comes to others," he does not succumb to the acceptance of unjust punishment with Alice's martyrlike calm. Howard is a fighter, a strong and steady soul, and when Alice is dragged off to jail, he devotes every waking moment to winning back her freedom.

At this point Alice and Howard's real struggles begin, and they are not merely the heroic battles that Hamilton has so gracefully crafted on the surface—Howard's efforts to scrape together the means to retain an attorney and meet the astronomically high bail set; Alice's fight to maintain life and limb while in jail; together, their battle to face the shame and accusations heaped upon them from all sides—but also the more mundane and treacherous struggles lingering just beneath. Howard must decide whether he can salvage a marriage mired in grief. Alice must find the strength to go on living in a world that has lost almost all reason and meaning. They both must let go of a way of life—their simple farm existence—perhaps forever. In this way *A Map of the World* has less to do with tragedy itself than with its aftermath, less to do with random and horrific events than with finding a path through them. As Howard reflects, "We are shaped, time and time again, by luck, the prevailing winds." The trick is to survive one's own best intentions.

Yet surviving is exactly what the Goodwins try to do, and with the help of Paul Rafferty, a lawyer who agrees to take on Alice's case, it looks as if they might have a chance. With Alice awaiting trial in jail, Howard focuses all of his attention on obtaining her freedom, and this means more sacrifice. The passages describing Howard's attempts to care for his two young girls in their quickly disintegrating household—feeding them Marshmallow Fluff sandwiches for breakfast, lunch, and dinner, bribing them with toys when he must leave them with a neighbor while he goes to visit Alice in jail—beautifully convey his frustration and feelings of helplessness. Whereas Alice's strength lies in her ability to accept, even forgive, her small-town accusers, to embrace her fate, Howard's strength lies in strength itself. He possesses the physical and emotional fortitude necessary to be a modern-day farmer in a hard, cold country. When faced with the all but impossible burden of living life day-to-day while all around the world is crumbling, however, he begins to give in to doubt: "I felt very tired. I didn't know if I had ever loved anything. I guess I couldn't have said what it meant to love someone. We had a life together. Alice was my wife." When it becomes clear that the only way Alice might be freed is if Howard sells the farm and uses the proceeds to make her bail, he must choose between a way of life—a place in the world—and the ephemeral love for a woman of whom he feels more and more uncertain. Howard's choices are not so much between winning and losing, between making the right decision and the wrong one, as between the merely devastating and the impossible: "The summer had been a test of some sort. I suppose it was a test of faith. If that was so I had failed. But I also wasn't sure that there would have been any way to win."

The final third of the novel shifts once more to Alice's perspective. Her days in jail and the trial and its aftermath are recounted in a voice that is transformed by hardship, worn smooth by days of blameless grief. Alice emerges in this final section as a sort of messenger from another world, having undergone a spiritual conversion while in prison. She brings back a simple truth: "This was the lesson, perhaps, that I was sent to learn: The old life was worth having at any expense." Life moves imperceptibly in one direction and a child drowns. It moves in another and the day is like any other. In *A Map of the World*, Hamilton shows readers that terror and banality lie side by side.

Liesel Litzenburger

Sources for Further Study

Booklist. XC, June 1, 1994, p. 1771.
The Christian Science Monitor. June 3, 1994, p. 13.
Los Angeles Times Book Review. June 5, 1994, p. 3.
The New York Times Book Review. XCIX, July 17, 1994, p. 26.
The New Yorker. LXX, August 15, 1994, p. 78.
Newsweek. CXXIII, June 13, 1994, p. 55.
Publishers Weekly. CCXLI, April 4, 1994, p. 57.
Time. CXLIII, June 27, 1994, p. 75.
U.S. News and World Report. CXVI, June 13, 1994, p. 82.
The Washington Post Book World. XXIV, May 29, 1994, p. 5.

MARINA TSVETAEVA
The Double Beat of Heaven and Hell

Author: Lily Feiler (1915-   )
Publisher: Duke University Press (Durham, North Carolina). 299 pp. $19.95
Type of work: Literary biography
Time: 1892-1941
Locale: Russia, Italy, Germany, Czechoslovakia, France, and the Soviet Union

A biography of the Russian poet, Marina Tsvetaeva, told against the background of the Russian Revolution and informed by psychological insights

Principal personages:

MARINA TSVETAEVA, a Russian poet, playwright, and essayist
IVAN TSVETAEV, her father, professor of art history at the University of Moscow and founder of the Alexander III Museum of Fine Arts (now the Pushkin Museum)
MARIYA ALEKSANDROVNA, her mother, a pianist
ANASTASIYA (ASYA) TSVETAEVA, her sister
SERGEY EFRON, her husband, member of the White Army, later a collaborator of the NKVD, the Soviet secret service
ARIADNA (ALYA) EFRON, her daughter
GEORGI (MUR) EFRON, her son
MAKSIMILIAN VOLOSHIN, a Russian poet, writer, and critic, her friend and patron
SOFIA PARNOK, a Russian poet, her lover
OSIP MANDELSTAM, a Russian poet, her friend and lover
SONYA (SONECHKA) HOLLIDAY, a Russian actress, her lover
BORIS PASTERNAK, a Russian poet, her friend and correspondent
KONSTANTIN RODZEVICH, Efron's friend and Marina's lover
RAINER MARIA RILKE, a German poet, correspondent of Pasternak and Tsvetaeva
ANNA AKHMATOVA, a Russian poet

Marina Ivanovna Tsvetaeva, born in Moscow on October 9, 1892, committed suicide in Yelabuga, a small village in the Tatar Republic, on August 31, 1941. Her grave lay unmarked for nearly two decades, as did her reputation. In 1955, during Nikita Khrushchev's "thaw," Tsvetaeva's daughter, Ariadna, was released from seventeen years in the Soviet Union's gulag and Siberian exile. She and her aunt, Anastasiya, freed in 1959, devoted the rest of their lives to resurrecting Tsvetaeva's life and poetry. During the 1960's and 1970's, Tsvetaeva became the most popular poet of the *samizdat*, the underground publishing world of the Soviet Union, influencing such young poets of that generation as Yevgeny Yevtushenko and Bella Akhmadulina. In the 1980's and 1990's, she became increasingly known through European and American volumes of her work, both in Russian and in translation. Although it is generally agreed that no definitive English translation of her poetry has appeared—it is fiendishly difficult to translate because of its musicality, elliptical quality, fractured syntax, and dependence on the nuances of Russian speech patterns—she has been restored to a position among the four or five most important Russian poets of the first half of the twentieth century.

Marina Tsvetaeva, Osip Mandelstam, Boris Pasternak, and Anna Akhmatova, all born between 1889 and 1892, are often considered a poetic quartet by critics because of their individual genius, their affinity for and influence upon one another's work, their similar European-Russian educations, and their suffering under the repression of the Soviet government. Vladimir Mayakovsky, born in 1893, shared their genius and suffering, but spoke in a voice more purely Russian and proletarian. In *Marina Tsvetaeva: The Double Beat of Heaven and Hell*, Lily Feiler acknowledges the affinity among the poets, but is most concerned with exploring the individual drama of Tsvetaeva's life. Feiler sees the poet as a romantic loner:

> She was never part of a group; she stood alone in poetry as in life. She was oblivious to politics, but her ethical standards inform all her work; she despised the fat, the greedy, and the bigoted. Victory had no meaning for her; hers was the lost cause and her hero was the outsider—the outlaw and the artist. She had no respect for church or state; only the individual mattered to her.

The loneliness at the core of Tsvetaeva's life was caused, Feiler posits, by the wounded narcissism of a child whose individuality was never accepted by her mother. She contends that the unresolved relationship with her mother hindered Tsvetaeva's ability to leave the fantasized world of childhood narcissism and left her unable to sustain a normal adult relationship: "Tsvetaeva was simply not able to see the Other, to accept the limitations of ordinary, reciprocal love."

Marina Tsvetaeva was the elder of two daughters of the marriage between Ivan Tsvetaev, a professor of art history, and Mariya Aleksandrovna; she had an elder stepsister, Valeriya, and stepbrother, Andrey, from her father's first marriage. The emotional relationships within the household were strained. Tsvetaev, still in love with his dead first wife, was twenty-four years older than Aleksandrovna, an accomplished pianist whose father had refused her a concert career. She married Tsvetaev, who was looking for a companion and mother for his children, after breaking with her first love, a married man. Although the Tsvetaev marriage remained passionless, Mariya proved to be an able partner to her husband in his efforts to raise funds and create a collection for his museum of classical sculpture. Valeriya resented the presence of her stepmother, who doted on Andrey. Marina and her younger sister Anastasiya (Asya) grew up in an atmosphere filled with music and books, taught by European tutors, spending the winters in Moscow and the summers on an estate near Tarusa in Kaluga Province. Although their mother was disappointed that her daughters were not sons, she held her children to the highest expectations of romantic idealism and accomplishment. She was determined that Marina would become a musician, and the child was forced to practice four hours a day at the piano. Despite having her early attempts at poetry ridiculed by the family, especially by her mother, the young Marina knew that all of her " 'unmusicalness' was nothing more than *another* vocation!" In her essay "The Poet on the Critic," written in 1926, Tsvetaeva reveals the enormous influence this early musical training had on her poetry. Describing the source for her poetry she wrote, "I obey something which sounds in me; constantly, but not consistently—sometimes it points, sometimes commands. . . . That which points is an aural path to the poem: I hear a tune, I don't hear the words. I seek the words."

In 1902, Mariya Aleksandrovna contracted tuberculosis, so the family left for Italy to seek a cure. For the next four years Marina and Asya lived abroad—in Nervi, near Genoa, where their mother was recuperating; in Switzerland, at a boarding school where the Tsvetaeva sisters resisted the strong religious indoctrination of the Lacaze nuns; and in Freiburg, at the Brink Pension with its strong German discipline, boredom, and bad food. Despite the sojourn, Mariya's health deteriorated, and the family returned to Russia in 1905 as the workers' protests in St. Petersburg and Moscow were being brutally suppressed by the Czarist regime. Marina's mother died in July, 1906—Marina was fourteen. Feiler contends that her mother's death at this stage in the poet's adolescence prevented her from resolving the relationship with her mother: "Precisely because there was no one to rebel against, Tsvetaeva was exposed to all the storms of adolescence while chained to her mother's immutable values."

Expelled from a boarding school for her rebellious attitudes, Tsvetaeva attended various gymnasiums, grew close to her sister, gave up the piano, and wrote poetry. She came under the influence of the Symbolist poets when she became friends with Ellis (the pseudonym of Lyov Lvovich Kobylinsky), Vladimir Nilender, and, most important, Maksimilian Voloshin. At the turn of the century, the Symbolist poets had revived the Russian poetic tradition, dormant during the great age of Russian prose in the nineteenth century. Ellis and Nilender wooed Tsvetaeva with their intellect and their experience—both proposed to her, but the eighteen-year-old Tsvetaeva was not ready to leave the "innocence" of childhood. Feiler sees in her rejection, especially of Nilender, with whom she had a complex relationship, an emerging pattern of rejection of reciprocal relationships: Tsvetaeva could only accept a romantic relationship that she could control, either as the mother or the child. Voloshin, on the other hand, offered friendship and patronage.

In 1910, while in her last year of school, Tsvetaeva took a collection of her poems to a printer and paid for the publication of five hundred copies of her book, *Vecherny albom* (1910; evening album), which she then took to a bookshop. She sent off a few inscribed copies to important writers, four of whom wrote reviews of the volume. The most admiring was Voloshin, who appeared one day at her door and took her under his wing. He directed her reading, introduced her into Moscow's literary society, and invited her and Asya to spend the summer of 1911 at his country house in Koktebel, where Marina met and fell in love with Sergey Efron.

Tsvetaeva's love affair with Efron carried her into a wider life. The two set up housekeeping together and finally married in January, 1912; their daughter Ariadna (Alya) was born in September. In their first years together, they lived comfortably and participated in Moscow's literary and theatrical societies. The marriage was founded on the ideal of freedom for both partners—it was the elastic that bound them together while they strayed far from each other. Efron would be carried off by the winds of political necessity, first into the White Army opposing the Bolshevik revolutionaries, then into exile in Europe where he was converted to a faith in Stalinism, and finally back to the Soviet Union. Tsvetaeva hurled herself into romantic affairs (some sexual, some not) with poets, actresses, publishers, and Efron's friends. Still, she followed her husband into exile and then back into certain persecution in the Soviet Union.

Feiler contends that the "steely, arrogant" Tsvetaeva endowed Efron with the romantic qualities of her heroic vision, while envisioning him as her "little dark-haired boy." She describes the marriage in terms of disastrous imbalance:

> He became first a "son," later a "brother," always coming from the same "cradle." He was her "duty" in life. In her own fashion, she always remained loyal to him. But more than twenty years later, she would write to a friend: "Marriage and love rather destroy a personality, it's an ordeal.[. . .] And an early marriage (like mine) is a disaster altogether, a blow for all of life."

This kind of out-of-context quotation from Tsvetaeva's published correspondence is typical of Feiler's psychoanalysis. Although there is no denying Tsvetaeva's total dedication to poetry at the expense of personal relationships, there also is no denying her intense connection with her family—her ambivalent and tenuous tie to Efron, and her adoration of her children, which encompassed smothering attention, neediness, and immense pride. It is important to note that, despite her sexual infidelities, Tsvetaeva remained personally loyal to Efron even when he was implicated in an assassination carried out by the Soviet secret police and had to return to the Soviet Union. She was also, in her own way, devoted to Alya and her son Georgi, nicknamed Mur, who was born in 1925 while Tsvetaeva and Efron were in exile in Prague.

Tsvetaeva was caught in Moscow during the Russian Civil War (a period also known as War Communism) from 1918 to 1921, while Efron was fighting with the White Army in the Crimea. At twenty-five, she found herself poverty-stricken with two children, Alya and Irina, born in 1917. During the famine of 1919, Tsvetaeva put the children in an orphanage in an attempt to provide them with food. During a period when she took the ailing Alya home to nurse her, Irina died of malnutrition. Feiler uses Tsvetaeva's letters to indict her with neglect of Irina and further blames her for not taking any mementoes of Irina with her when she left Russia in 1922.

Although Feiler attempts to explain Tsvetaeva's behavior in terms of psychological imperatives, there is, nevertheless, a strongly judgmental tone in her narrative. Feiler leaves the reader with the impression that Tsvetaeva was a disastrous wife, a failed mother, and an impassioned philanderer. Perhaps she was all of these, but Feiler seems to be morally measuring Tsvetaeva's life against some kind of psychological norm. The norm she posits, however, is not reflected in the milieu in which Tsvetaeva lived. The norm of early twentieth century Russian, European, and American intellectuals and artists encompassed heightened enthusiasms and promiscuity—one need only compare Tsvetaeva's experiences with those of her contemporaries to see the similarities. Young, idealistic, and caustically intelligent, they rebelled against the stifling moralism of the nineteenth century and were caught in the global upheavals of revolution and world war. Perhaps the whole generation of poets suffered from neuroses—the Europeans and Americans: T. S. Eliot, Ezra Pound, H. D. (Hilda

Doolittle), E. E. Cummings, and Federico García Lorca; as well as the Russians: Akhmatova, Pasternak, Mandelstam, Mayakovsky, and Tsvetaeva. Feiler claims that her book is "not a case history but an attempt to understand Tsvetaeva's persona through a close reading of her texts . . . [using] psychological theories to lend more substance to my intuitive interpretation." This attempt to encapsulate Tsvetaeva's life, and even her work, in a neurotic reaction ultimately diminishes both the individual and the art.

While Feiler's psychobiography may add some interesting grist for the mills of Tsvetaeva scholars, it is a misleading introduction to the poet. The reader loses sight of the accomplishments of one of the major voices of the early twentieth century. Tsvetaeva wrote more than two thousand poems, numerous essays, a half-dozen or so plays, and carried on a voluminous correspondence with important literary figures of the day, including Boris Pasternak and Rainer Maria Rilke. Although she held no political loyalties, she is an important witness to the cataclysmic events of the Russian Revolution. Yet it is in her craft and her genius that her measure should be taken.

Jane Anderson Jones

Source for Further Study

Library Journal. CXIX, October 15, 1994, p. 58.

THE MASTER OF PETERSBURG

Author: J. M. Coetzee (1940-   )
Publisher: Viking (New York). 250 pp. $21.95
Type of work: Novel
Time: Autumn, 1869
Locale: St. Petersburg, Russia

In autumn, 1869, Fyodor Dostoevsky returns from Dresden to St. Petersburg to contend with the violent death of his stepson Pavel and with the mysteries of literary mastery

Principal characters:
FYODOR MIKHAILOVICH DOSTOEVSKY, a forty-nine-year-old Russian novelist
SERGEI GENNADEVICH NECHAEV, a revolutionary, the founder of the People's Vengeance
ANNA SERGEYEVNA KOLENKINA, the former landlady of Dostoevsky's dead stepson, Pavel Alexandrovich Isaev
MATRYONA, her young daughter
P. P. MAXIMOV, the judicial investigator in Pavel's case
KATRI, a young Finnish woman aligned with Nechaev
PYOTR ALEXANDROVICH IVANOV, a beggar and police spy

Born in Cape Town into an Afrikaans-speaking family, J. M. Coetzee would eventually become one of the leading English-language authors of South Africa. As a graduate student at the University of Texas at Austin in 1969, Coetzee submitted a doctoral dissertation titled "The English Fiction of Samuel Beckett: An Essay in Stylistic Analysis." He was fascinated by how and why Beckett negotiated a transition from English to French as the medium of his fiction and by the way language itself becomes an issue in much of Beckett's work. In his first six books of fiction, usually set in South Africa or in an unspecified landscape that could be African, Coetzee focuses on isolated characters for whom language is not so much a medium as a riddle and a muddle. With his latest novel, however, Coetzee moves to nineteenth century Russia and to an actual historical figure, the author Fyodor Mikhailovich Dostoevsky. The Russian master has replaced Beckett as Coetzee's tutelary muse.

Though he has lived in Germany, Coetzee's Dostoevsky is not adept at code-switching. He grieves in Russian for the death of his stepson Pavel Alexandrovich Isaev, and he ponders the adequacies of any language to assert mastery over the mysteries of life and death. "If he were more confident of his French," Dostoevsky, sexually aroused by his dead son's landlady, assures himself, "he would channel this disturbing excitement into a book of the kind one cannot publish in Russia." Yet Dostoevsky is not confident enough, and he does not commit translingualism. Instead, he begins to write again in his native Russian, and Coetzee confronts the challenge of mustering up the Russian master's words in English, of using the template of his own chosen tongue to suggest what might have been thought 125 years earlier through the Slavic language. The novel's protagonist uses Russian in order to resuscitate his dead stepson Pavel, and Coetzee uses English in order to conceive a life beyond his own.

If, as a wit once quipped, Ford Madox Ford's *The Good Soldier* (1915) is "the finest French novel in the English language," Coetzee's *The Master of Petersburg* is in effect a nineteenth century Slavic book written in twentieth century English, a rival to Joseph Conrad's *Under Western Eyes* (1911) as the finest Russian novel in the English language. Or rather it is the fictional prolegomenon to a novel already written in Russian—Dostoevsky's *Besy* (1871-1872; *The Possessed,* 1913). Coetzee imagines the circumstances leading to the genesis of the Russian master's work.

The Master of Petersburg begins in October, 1869, as Dostoevsky arrives in the Russian capital after extended residence abroad. Summoned back by news that Pavel, age twenty-two, is dead, the forty-nine-year-old Dostoevsky, wracked by grief and guilt, is determined to learn the cause. As if to conjure up the spirit of his dead stepson, he moves into Pavel's room, dons his clothing, and pores over his diary. He becomes sexually involved with Pavel's landlady, Anna Sergeyevna Kolenkina, and attempts to learn from her young daughter, Matryona, exactly how his stepson died, and lived. Dostoevsky discovers the extent of the filial resentment that Pavel, who was seven years old when the author married his mother, felt toward him, especially after that mother died and his stepfather took a young new bride. He also begins to penetrate the febrile underworld of student radicals into which Pavel had been drawn.

In scenes reminiscent of his own *Prestuplenie i nakazanie* (1866; *Crime and Punishment*, 1886), Dostoevsky is interrogated by P. P. Maximov, a wily judicial investigator who insists that Pavel was murdered by his coconspirators in the violent revolutionary movement. Maximov attempts to induce Dostoevsky to help track them down. Sergei Gennadevich Nechaev, the charismatic young leader of a clandestine group called the People's Vengeance, tries to convince Dostoevsky, who himself spent a decade in Siberia for political crimes, that Pavel was murdered by the police and to recruit the author for service in insurgency. He scolds Dostoevsky for having abandoned youthful ideals to the complacency of middle age. The rebel berates the novelist, who is five years younger than Coetzee, for having become a hack—"an old, blinkered horse going round and round in a circle, rolling out the same old story day after day." Nechaev affects the rhetoric of radical egalitarianism, insisting that "the day of ordinary people is arriving." Yet he is an imperious, callous, and manipulative opportunist, for whom everything, including murder and deceit, is permitted. Is the sentimental, epileptic writer any match for such a man?

Beset by the forces of both repression and rebellion and tormented by unresolved antagonisms with his stepson, Dostoevsky visits Pavel's grave and climbs to the top of the tower along Stolyarny Quay from which he jumped, fell, or was pushed to his death. *Fathers and Sons* is the title of his compatriot Ivan Turgenev's most famous novel (*Ottsy i deti,* published 1862, translated in English in 1867), and it is also the theme that haunted Dostoevsky, in the patricidal plot of *Bratya Karamazovy* (1879-1880; *The Brothers Karamazov*, 1912) as well as during the days that led to his writing *The Possessed.* Coetzee's Dostoevsky broods over "the true reason why he is bereft: because the ground of his life, the contest with his son, is gone, and his days are left empty? Not the People's Vengeance but the Vengeance of the Sons," he asks himself:

"is that what underlies revolution—fathers envying their sons their women, sons scheming to rob their fathers' cashboxes?" The novelist's ideal and only interlocutor, the anchor for his every thought and phrase, is his absent son, and, except as a figment of dreams or fiction, Pavel offers nothing in response.

Dostoevsky reads fragments of fiction that his stepson left behind. Asserting his mastery, the professional novelist begins writing his own fiction, the book that is to transform the historical Sergei Gennadevich Nechaev into a character named Pyotr Verkhovensky. It appropriates the late Pavel's imagination and elements from their father-son discord, as well as from Dostoevsky's relationships with Anna Sergeyevna, Maximov, and Nechaev. In his own assertion of literary sovereignty, Coetzee has, in *The Master of Petersburg*, conjured up the genesis to *The Possessed*, the novel of fanatical disaffected politics that Dostoevsky was to publish two years later. Its title has also—and more accurately—been translated as *The Devils* and *Demons*, and Coetzee cannily has his Anna Sergeyevna utter the word "devils" during a moment of orgasm.

What attracts Dostoevsky to Anna Sergeyevna, despite the fact that a young wife awaits his return to Dresden, is a belief that not only does she hold the key to understanding Pavel's life in Petersburg but that she can also in some sense invoke the dead stepson. He dreams of marrying the landlady, whom he calls "a conductress of souls." If the two begot a child, Dostoevsky is convinced, their offspring would be a surrogate for the vanished Pavel, with whom death denied him the possibility of reconciliation. "You have it in your power," he pleads with her. "You can bring him back." Yet Anna Sergeyevna insists that such mastery over others' souls is the province of the novelist: "You are an artist, a master. . . . It is for you, not for me, to bring him back to life." *The Master of Petersburg* is an account of how Dostoevsky begins to assert his artistic mastery, to take up his pen and resume command over his own and others' lives.

The theme of mastery is also explicitly invoked in the tense relationship that develops between Dostoevsky and Nechaev, a wily demagogue who exerts his will over many, including Matryona and a young Finnish woman named Katri. He had apparently succeeded in recruiting Pavel as part of a network spinning a murky scheme to assassinate a roster of prominent local figures. Nechaev's mastery of disguises enables him to elude the grasp of the secret police. His ruthlessness enables him to slay the government spy who, posing as a beggar, is befriended by Dostoevsky.

Conversations between Dostoevsky and Nechaev, like those between Dostoevsky and Maximov, are a complex game of cat-and-mouse, each side vying to position himself for the triumphant purr. Will the magistrate succeed in using Dostoevsky to infiltrate and crush the radical movement with which his son was implicated? Or will Dostoevsky coax Maximov into releasing Pavel's private papers, which the grieving father is anxious to retrieve? Will Nechaev manage to enlist the famous novelist in the cause of revolution? Or will Dostoevsky outwit the insurrectionist Machiavelli who might well have killed his son? The novelist is not deceived by Nechaev's utopian vision. He reviles the man as a charlatan, yet, notes Coetzee, "he no longer knows where the mastery lies—whether he is playing with Nechaev or Nechaev with him." Coetzee's account of the author's rivalry for mastery has precedence in Coetzee's 1987 novel *Foe*, in which another castaway, Susan Barton, competes with Daniel Defoe for authority to frame the story of Robinson Crusoe.

"To believe and to love—the same thing," according to Coetzee's Dostoevsky, for whom either is a struggle. Spare of incident, *The Master of Petersburg* is an intensive exercise in character analysis, and the character that it analyzes is a riven man, driven to overcome the chasm between thought and action. The author of *Dvoynik* (1846; *The Double*, 1917) is portrayed through a series of desperate mental duels—with Maximov, Nechaev, and the ghost of Pavel, but most urgently with himself. Coetzee's 1992 book of essays, on largely literary themes including Beckett and Dostoevsky, was called *Doubling the Point: Essays and Interviews*, and the point of his fictional account of Dostoevsky Agonistes is to examine the human psyche as an arena for warring impulses.

Through acute suffering comes redemption for Raskolnikov, the ax murderer of *Crime and Punishment*. "I am not here in Russia in this time of ours to live a life free of pain," says Coetzee's protagonist, who decides not to take the train that would return him to the familial and familiar comforts he abandoned in Dresden. Coetzee positions his novel in the distant time and place in order to scrutinize the movements of a famous tortured soul. *The Master of Petersburg* concludes with intimations of transcendence, with the possibility of deliverance through literary art. Dostoevsky conceives of the novel that he has begun to compose as "a trap to catch God." Coetzee's brief novel comes to an end before Dostoevsky can determine whether he has caught his prey. Coetzee's own ambitions, however, are a bit more modest, and he deftly snares the reader.

Steven G. Kellman

Sources for Further Study

Chicago Tribune. November 27, 1994, XIV, p. 3.
Library Journal. CXIX, September 1, 1994, p. 213.
Los Angeles Times Book Review. November 20, 1994, p. 3.
New Statesman and Society. VII, February 25, 1994, p. 41.
The New York Review of Books. XLI, November 17, 1994, p. 35.
The New York Times Book Review. XCIX, November 20, 1994, p. 9.
Publishers Weekly. CCXLI, September 5, 1994, p. 88.
The Spectator. CCLXXII, February 26, 1994, p. 31.
Time. CXLIV, November 28, 1994, p. 87.
The Times Literary Supplement. March 4, 1994, p. 19.

MEMOIRS OF THE BLIND
The Self-Portrait and Other Ruins

Author: Jacques Derrida (1930-)
First published: Mémoires d'aveugle: L'autoportrait et autres ruines, 1990, in France
Translated from the French by Pascale-Anne Brault and Michael Naas
Publisher: University of Chicago Press (Chicago). Illustrated. 141 pp. Paperback $24.95
Type of work: Art criticism

An examination of vision, blindness, self-representation, and the process of drawing, with comparisons to the creative production of a text

Memoirs of the Blind: The Self-Portrait and Other Ruins originated from an exhibition held at the Louvre Museum, Paris, during the fall and winter of 1990-1991. This exhibition was the first of a series called Parti Pris (taking sides), for which critics whose disciplines are specifically not those of the pictorial or plastic arts organize and write commentaries to accompany and complement the works chosen. The rationale for this unconventional means of organizing an exhibit of pictures was to introduce original yet arguably justifiable critical perceptions into the context of art criticism. A by-product is the risk, perhaps even the encouragement, of unconventionality.

The original ways in which Jacques Derrida perceives and interprets virtually everything he writes about made him an appropriate choice for organizing the first Parti Pris. Though he has written art criticism, Derrida is primarily a literary critic, and he is best-known to readers of English for *De la grammatologie* (1967; *Of Grammatology*, 1976). This early masterwork, which is alternately brilliant, insightful, and clever, and arcane, abstruse, and playful, springs from the deconstructionist sign theory that swept the European and American literary establishment in the 1970's. In *Of Grammatology* Derrida reduces the writing process to its most basic element, which he identifies as the *grammé*, the "trace." By this he means the strokes of the pen that, taken in conventional arrangements, the *grammai* ("traces," but also "tracings" and "strokes of writing"), carry the outline of the text's meaning. Understood in this way, all writing is *sous rature* (under erasure), and every text carries the constituents of every other text.

Memoirs of the Blind approaches the production and perception of art in a comparable way. Here Derrida identifies the *tracé* ("tracing" or "outline") that the process of drawing requires. The *tracé* is akin to a miner's lamp. Formulated by the eye-fingers of the artist, it picks objects present but otherwise invisible out of blind blankness. On several levels, then—those of the artist, the work itself, and those who perceive the work—Derrida describes the process of creating drawings and identifying their signification. Using blindness as a trope for the ongoing process, sight for direction and critical appreciation, and insight for significance beyond the *tracé* as measure of the artist's (or the critic's) success moves Derrida closer than he had been to the language of his late colleague Paul de Man, yet Derrida also identifies a consciousness of the drawings themselves.

For Derrida, an artist drawing a self-portrait traces all the individuals that the artist ever was and all the artist will become, as well as the individual the artist perceives as the self at the time of the particular drawing. Though one can envision a blind sculptor, it is harder to imagine a blind draftsman; yet it is for Derrida the finger-eye guided by the mind that provides insight. Every self-portrait is a *memoir*, reflecting the "memory," the "story," the "history" that was, is, and will be. Through the *tracé*, every drawing participates in the signification of every other drawing in a remarkable confluence of profound blindness and blazing insight. Every drawing is correspondingly a ruin, signifying that which is not apparent in the *tracé* as well as that which is explicit.

Considered conventionally, the consequences of this argument are devastating, for they deny the contribution of an artist's technical development to the effectiveness of signification. The childhood scribblings of Rembrandt van Rijn hold the same signifiers as his most painstaking self-portraits. Perhaps this is the reason that the artists Derrida chooses to discuss are not those normally identifiable as the first rank. All are competent, most are French, and many are identifiable with the historical period known as the Enlightenment. Is the puckish Derrida underscoring his perception of the inextricable matrix of blindness, inspiration, and insight through such choices? Is he mimetically identifying his self-confessed technical deficiencies in drawing with those of the artists he discusses? Such autobiographical confessions appear at various points in the text, even as he employs an eccentric dialogue technique to carry his discussion. Abandoning the conventional third-person mode, an unnamed critic with definitely unconventional perceptions dominates a diffident interviewer. Derrida effectively uses this latter persona to substitute for the reservations a general reader might well have concerning the master's comprehensive pronouncements. Still, the tone maintained is that of brilliant, facile teacher and serious but too silent student. On another level, both of these anonymous voices are those of Derrida, who initially acknowledges his reluctance to commit his unconventional ideas about drawing to writing.

Is Derrida's confession that he always had considered his own ability to draw inferior to that of his brother in any way related to the fact that many of the artists he chooses to discuss are generally rated below the first rank? Such artists serve Derrida's approach to technique particularly well. His concerns are the relationship between sight and insight, the mind's eye and the theme of blindness, the disjunction between the eye of the artist and the production of the artist's hand. The works, all of which appear in the text, are of several varieties: depiction of blindness, relation of blind individuals to their environment, blindness cured, blindness that brings insight, the self-portrait and self-portrait series and its diachronic relationship to landscape portraiture. As one might expect, mythic and literary themes predominate.

Derrida begins with several of the studies of blind people made by Antoine Coypel (1661-1722). Coypel was an iconoclast, his choice of subjects generally opposed to the taste of the late seventeenth century; yet by the last third of his life, Coypel had won acceptance. His blind subjects, exclusively men, advance to a goal unknown by them. In this sense, they are also self-portraits, the artist's search for his stylistic voice. Even when some definite program underlies the work, as in Christ's healing the blind men of Jericho, it is not specifically a cure for blindness that they seek. As Derrida perceives it, these blind men instinctively grope for truth, which they sense in the person of Christ—the quest of every honest inquiry in whatever medium one expresses it.

Derrida frequently notes the open gestures, the extended arms and open hands of the blind figures of various artists. Jacques-Louis David (1748-1825), most familiar for his representations of mythic and historical subjects from classical antiquity, portrays Homer, blind poet of the *Iliad* and *Odyssey* (c. 800 B.C.), with the same open gesture Coypel employs as he sings his verse to an impromptu audience. Here Derrida identifies the artist's concerns with those of Homer, indeed implies that the search for the true is common to all the arts, whether pictorial, musical, or literary. Mistaken perceptions, at least apparently so, concern Derrida in his discussion of the biblical theme of the blind Isaac's testamentary blessing of his younger son Jacob for the elder Esau. For Derrida, the seeming mistake actually shows the light of vision, a theme captured not only in the biblical text but also in the position of Jacob's head, his countenance, and his hand as they appear in a work by Francesco Primaticcio (1504-1570).

Though he rarely makes specific assertions on the purpose of perceiving the drawn line in this unusual way, Derrida has clearly made certain original and worthwhile observations on the commonality of the arts and the interiority of inspiration. He thereby avoids the subjective aesthetic judgments that often haunt critical writing, though his ways of seeing, fascinatingly seductive as they are, often remain idiosyncratic. For Derrida, the monocular stare of a cyclops represents animal narcissism—relentless, savage, but lacking the insightful gaze of the human being. He quotes Homer's vivid description of Odysseus blinding Polyphemus (*Odyssey* 9.406-414), and he notes that Odysseus claims his right name only after he has blinded the cyclops, when he is no longer *Outis* (Nobody). The double wordplay of the passage appeals to Derrida; *outis* and *mē tis* both mean "nobody," but *mētis* means "trick" or "cunning."

Derrida wonders whether "anyone ever represented the movement of this lever, of this *mochlos*, or fiery-pointed stake, as it draws a piercing spiral into Polyphemus' bleeding eye." This kind of insertion seems an innocent rhetorical question, indeed one bordering on the naïve. On the one hand, it is difficult to believe that Derrida is unaware that the blinding of Polyphemus was a favorite theme of Greek artists from the seventh century B.C. Even so, Derrida's words, here as elsewhere, are protean. His main point is that Odysseus wielding the *mochlos* is akin to the writer with pen and the draftsman-artist with pencil. Yet would Derrida be satisfied that the ancient representations of Polyphemus' blinding concerned themselves sufficiently with the movement of the stylus? The analogy is clever indeed; for Derrida, the production of art is essentially a destructive act, though its purpose is transmission of insight. The ruse by which Odysseus blinds the cyclops corresponds to the strategy by which an artist's skill exerts control on the raw material of the subject and reveals its *tracé*. The blinding of Oedipus, once he has learned his double sin of patricide and incest, thus becomes a parallel literary example, as does the blinded Samson, who recognizes the true source of his strength only after he has fallen prey to the Philistines.

Confessional elements necessarily follow from the sight-blindness-insight matrix that Derrida identifies. This is obvious in the androgynous self-portraits of Jean-Baptiste Siméon Chardin (1699-1779), less so in the *trompe l'oeil* of Jean-Marie Faverjon (1828-1873), in which the eyes, forehead, and hands of a man, presumably the artist, point, emerge from behind, and indicate another painting, a mythic consummation scene of lovers framed by a curtain draped in the form of an eye. The painting within a painting describes the desire, insight, and indeed voyeurism that attend both the production of art and its appreciation.

Derrida also touches on the relationship of the conversion experience to insight and to the violence of the creation process. He notes Caravaggio's use of light in his *The Conversion of Saint Paul* and compares it with drawings on the same theme by Lelio Orsi (1511-1587) and Laurent de La Hyre (1606-1656). All the constituents that Derrida identified before emerge again: blindness, light, insight, creation, and here re-creation of a life. Still, it is noteworthy that Derrida makes no observations on the relative aesthetic worth of the three works. Art criticism written more traditionally would surely have included some commentary on the dramatic superiority Caravaggio achieves through his use of darkness and light.

Saint Augustine's *Confessiones* (c. A.D. 400; *Confessions*) figure prominently as a literary touchstone for the conclusion of Derrida's book. Augustine's conversion in the garden appears in literary terms, his bibliomantic encounter with a text from Saint Paul. Derrida, however, focuses on Augustine's numerous references to weeping and tears, symbolic of clouded vision and acquired insight. He parallels this, quite unconventionally but with great élan, to the Dionysian counter-confessions of Friedrich Nietzsche in *Ecce Homo* (1908; English translation, 1911). For Derrida, as different and philosophically irreconcilable as Nietzsche is to Paul and Augustine, the question that faces all three remains that of blindness and insight, a concern that is subjective in the medium through which it is expressed but universal in its appearance across the disciplines.

Memoirs of the Blind is a handsomely produced soft-covered book that resembles an exhibition catalog, which indeed it is in part. It contains seventy-one reproductions on high-quality paper, all but the pen-and-ink drawings in full color. It is more important, however, as an application of Derrida's aesthetic theories to art criticism. However problematic and subjective they may be, these perceptions remain a welcome complement to the author's masterwork, *Of Grammatology*, and readers of that earlier work will find comparably stimulating analysis here.

Robert J. Forman

Sources for Further Study

Lingua Franca. IV, May/June, 1994, p. 14.

Print Collector's Newsletter. XXV, September/October, 1994, p. 154.

MENCKEN
A Life

Author: Fred Hobson (1943-   )
Publisher: Random House (New York). 650 pp. $35.00
Type of work: Biography
Time: 1880-1956
Locale: Baltimore, Maryland; and New York City

Exploring both H. L. Mencken's literary successes and his personal failures, this biography provides a fascinating account of one of the twentieth century's most influential critics and journalists

Principal personages:

HENRY LOUIS (H. L.) MENCKEN, a newspaperman, author, and editor, whose caustic wit made him a national figure during the 1920's and 1930's
ALFRED A. KNOPF, the founder of a major New York publishing firm who became one of his closest friends
AUGUST MENCKEN, his brother, who cared for him after he was disabled by a massive stroke in 1948
THEODORE DREISER, a novelist, whose early friendship with Mencken grew increasingly estranged
F. SCOTT FITZGERALD, a novelist, whose work Mencken respected but whose life he abhorred
SINCLAIR LEWIS, a novelist, whose admiration for Mencken endured despite the repeated strains in their friendship
MARION BLOOM, the would-be author with whom Mencken had an extended love affair during the 1920's
SARA HAARDT MENCKEN, who married the author in 1930 and died of tubercular meningitis five years later

With the posthumous publication of the famous critic's diary, edited by Charles A. Fecher (*The Diary of H. L. Mencken*, 1989), and recollections of his early friends and acquaintances (*My Life as Author and Editor*, 1993), the reputation of H. L. Mencken suddenly began to decline. The man whom Walter Lippmann had once called "the most powerful influence on a whole generation of educated Americans" appeared in his most private writings to be guilty of flagrant anti-Semitism, racism, and homophobia, as well as unrestrained hostility against Southerners and rural life in general. If the 1920's had one been heralded as "the decade of Mencken," the 1990's seemed to be a low ebb in Mencken's reputation. All at once, the author was accused of embodying all the bigotry and blindness that had led the nation into two world wars, habitual violations of civil rights, and a host of other evils still endemic in modern society.

Fred Hobson's *Mencken: A Life* provides a much-needed corrective to this point of view. Endeavoring to present Mencken as a flawed human being who was nevertheless a great author and a product of his time, Hobson succeeds in developing a balanced and comprehensive portrait of one of the twentieth century's most influential literary figures. Though aware of Mencken's greatness, Hobson never attempts to gloss over his genuine limitations. For example, Hobson provides a particularly devastating account of Mencken's feelings toward homosexuals. Mencken's homophobia, nowhere alluded to in the works that he published during his lifetime, has emerged only through a careful study of his letters and the entries made in his secret diaries. On the other hand, Mencken's feelings of superiority over the Jews were well known even in his lifetime. Though such feelings may have been common among members of his class and profession, in Mencken's case they became increasingly pronounced, and an increasing embarrassment, as World War II continued.

In the end, Mencken's flaws of character proved more costly to himself than offensive to those who read his weekly columns. His homophobia, for example, deprived him of the opportunity to become acquainted with Hugh Walpole, Lord Alfred Douglas, and Somerset Maugham. His pro-German and anti-Jewish sentiments, enunciated in articles throughout the 1930's and early 1940's, led to his increasing isolation and, ultimately, to his being disregarded altogether. During World War II, the society that had lionized Mencken only a decade earlier all but ignored his political commentary and turned its attention instead to his works on American English and his nostalgic sketches of his early life.

More than anything else, Mencken was a curious set of contradictions. Though much of his life was marked by contempt for the Jews, his closest friend was the Jewish publisher Alfred A. Knopf. Though he filled his diaries and personal correspondence with derogatory terms for blacks, he had been more receptive to such black authors as George S. Schuyler, W. E. B. Du Bois, and Langston Hughes than most editors of his time. Though he maintained a lifelong disdain for both marriage and the Deep South, in 1930 he suddenly married a woman who came from Montgomery, Alabama, the very heart of the Confederacy. As Hobson's biography makes clear, much of what Mencken believed he was writing in jest or for rhetorical effect was read, even in his own lifetime, with a seriousness that had never been intended. This practice has continued, even expanded, with the appearance of Mencken's diaries. The hyperbole with which he addressed many of his subjects is no longer considered an appropriate form of humor.

Perhaps the most telling of all the contradictions in the life of H. L. Mencken was his ability to combine religious skepticism with social and political conservatism. Mencken's conservative views were derived from the tradition of Henry St. John, Lord Bolingbroke, rather than Edmund Burke. He distrusted the pious certainties of clerics no less than the social utopianism of New Dealers. For Mencken, the enemies of society included both religious fundamentalists such as William Jennings Bryan (whom Mencken characterized as "ignorant, bigoted, self-seeking, blatant and dishonest") and supports of big government such as Franklin Delano Roosevelt and the members of his "Brain Trust." Roosevelt, Mencken believed, was a traitor to his class, while Bryan represented a crude simplicity that seemed out of place in the twentieth century. Though Bryan and Roosevelt bore no resemblance to each other in either personality or ideas, Mencken viewed them as similar because they posed an equal threat to the secularism, tradition, and social conformity that he held so dear.

Hobson, who had presented an earlier study of Mencken in his highly regarded work *Serpent in Eden: H. L. Mencken and the South* (1974), has taken great care to treat his subject fairly. At times, Hobson's attempts at impartiality must have tried his patience sorely. As the author admits in his preface, he is "a southerner, a professor of literature, a political liberal, and an admirer of Franklin D. Roosevelt," all the things that Mencken hated most in life. Nevertheless, these differences of opinion with his subject are all but imperceptible in the biography. Hobson achieves a delicate balance between the harsh criticism of Mencken that followed publication of his diaries and the strident defenses of the critic that arose in reply. *Mencken* captures its subject both as an author and as a human being, presenting all the foibles, excess, and outrageousness that made Mencken so readable to begin with.

One of the most revealing aspects of Hobson's biography is its discussion of how Mencken's public values had been shaped by incidents in his personal life. Mencken's lifelong distrust of college professors may be traced, at least in part, to his inability to receive more than a high school education. Mencken's letters and the recollections of him preserved by his friends reveal that the author of *The American Language* (1919, rev. 1921, 1923, 1936) never felt entirely at home with the culture and values of his native country. From boyhood on, Mencken believed that he would always remain an outsider to his fellow Americans. He identified more with the Old World values of his eighteenth and nineteenth century European forebears than with those of other German Americans who lived on his own block in Baltimore. Until a massive stroke incapacitated him in 1948, Mencken distanced himself from American films, radio, television, and popular music. For entertainment, he preferred the food, conversation, and classical music that he shared with members of the Saturday Night Club, a group that he helped form in 1904. Gradually, the appeal of European music and culture became so strong for Mencken that he could not even pretend to be objective during the two world wars.

Mencken's lifelong sense of being a stranger to American values proved, in the end, to be well founded. The *Evening Sun* received so many protests against Mencken's pro-German columns during World War I that his contributions were temporarily suspended. His loyalties to the United States were questioned both in print and by a governmental investigation. During World War II, Mencken foresaw that the constraints on his views would become so intolerable that his contributions to the Sun papers dwindled and finally ceased altogether.

While these events gave Mencken a certain degree of notoriety, there were other aspects of the critic's life that were hidden even from his closest friends. In 1930, when Mencken finally decided to marry, many of those who knew him best were astounded by the apparent suddenness of this decision. The anatomical artist Max Brödel, whom Mencken had seen at least weekly during the time that he was dating Sara Haardt, received a note from the critic identifying his bride as one "Sara Haardt, a lovely girl." Mencken had apparently never mentioned even the existence of Haardt despite years of conversation with Brödel. To the other women in Mencken's life, the news of his marriage came with equal surprise—and an even greater sense of betrayal. The actress Aileen Pringle and the opera singer Gretchen Hood, both of whom had reason to believe that they were having serious relationships with Mencken, were completely unaware of his feelings for Haardt until their engagement was announced. Mencken's ability to compartmentalize his life may help explain the apparent inconsistencies between the values that he expressed in his life and work and those that he confided to the secrecy of his diaries.

The ideals that Mencken most respected included honor, competence, and a sense of duty free from complaint or bitterness. To those who failed to live up to his own stringent code Mencken could be harsh, even brutal. Hobson offers repeated proofs that, especially in relationships with his fellow writers, Mencken was a demanding and unforgiving friend. His early enthusiasm for the works of Theodore Dreiser cooled dramatically as his disapproval of Dreiser's promiscuity increased. Though initially one of Ernest Hemingway's harshest critics, he came to appreciate the author's clarity of style and concluded that *Death in the Afternoon* was the finest book of 1932. His friendship with F. Scott Fitzgerald waned when the novelist seemed bent on self-destruction both from alcoholism and in his unstable marriage to Zelda. Mencken similarly wearied of Edgar Lee Masters when the poet took advantage of their friendship by repeatedly cataloging his complaints against his estranged wife. As Mencken himself said on several occasions, "When I am done with a man, I am done with him."

The picture of Mencken that Hobson provides in this biography is thus highly complex. The famous editor of *The Smart Set* and *The American Mercury* emerges in Hobson's work as a more complete, and more puzzling, individual than the character seen in either his books or his diaries. Though Mencken was responsible for coining the terms "Bible Belt" and "Scopes monkey trial," he never felt completely comfortable in the very society that most felt his influence. Though as early as 1922 he predicted the catastrophe that would befall the Jews in Germany, he soon gained a reputation for anti-Semitism that was derived largely from a single paragraph in the first edition of his *Treatise on the Gods* (1930).

The truth of H. L. Mencken may ultimately be found in neither the accolades of the 1920's nor the condemnation of the 1990's. Mencken embodied much of the bigotry shared by others of his period and class. Nevertheless, he did set the literary standards of a generation and eloquently defended the language of a people with whom he never felt completely at home.

Jeffrey L. Buller

Sources for Further Study

Booklist. XC, March 1, 1994, p. 1176.

Kirkus Reviews. LXII, February 1, 1994, p. 114.

Library Journal. CX, February 15, 1994, p. 158.
Los Angeles Times Book Review. April 24, 1994, p. 1.
National Review. XLVI, May 16, 1994, p. 73.
The New Republic. CCX, June 27, 1994, p. 34.
The New York Times Book Review. XCIX, May 8, 1994, p. 10.
Newsweek. CXXIII, May 16, 1994, p. 64.
The Wall Street Journal. April 29, 1994, p. A13.
The Washington Post Book World. XXIV, May 1, 1994, p. 4.

MERCY OF A RUDE STREAM
Volume I: A Star Shines over Mt. Morris Park

Author: Henry Roth (1906-)
Publisher: St. Martin's Press (New York). 290 pp. $23.00
Type of work: Novel
Time: 1914 to the early 1920's
Locale: New York City

This first book of a multivolume novel about a Jewish boy and his immigrant family in New York focuses on economic, personal, and social crises in a culturally and religiously alien society

Principal characters:
IRA STIGMAN, a Jewish boy
CHAIM STIGMAN, his father, an Eastern European immigrant
LEAH STIGMAN, his lonely and isolated mother

A Star Shines over Mt. Morris Park is the first book in a projected multivolume work, *Mercy of a Rude Stream*, about New York Jewish immigrant life. *Call It Sleep*, Henry Roth's only previous novel, received a mixed reception in 1934. Some critics favorably compared it to James T. Farrell's Studs Lonigan novels and James Joyce's *A Portrait of the Artist as a Young Man* (1916), whereas others reacted negatively, deeming it politically and socially incorrect. *Call It Sleep* was soon forgotten, until it was reprinted in 1964 and acclaimed as a memorable narrative of the American immigrant experience and a major twentieth century novel. It became a best-seller and remains in print. Roth's new work has distinct echoes of the earlier novel in setting, period, and subject. A young boy is the central character in each, and both dramatize life in a dysfunctional household within a sometimes violent and usually alien urban world. Unlike *Call It Sleep*, however, the 1994 book has two narrative points of view. Young Ira's realistic saga of his family and early adolescence is interspersed with interludes in which old Ira, writing an autobiographical novel about his early life, talks to his computer (dubbed Ecclesias) about his craft, recollections, and reflections on history, current events, and literary predecessors. The digressions aim to clarify and universalize Ira's narrative, but his story is delineated sharply enough to stand by itself, as convincingly as Albert Schearl's in *Call It Sleep*, and the asides diminish the narrative's epic quality by calling attention to its episodic form and autobiographical realism.

Roth's Stigman story starts in 1914, at the onset of World War I, and continues through the early 1920's. The family conflicts are varied: those who are assimilated versus immigrants tied to European customs; incompatible husbands and wives, enduring dysfunctional marriages of convenience; youth rebelling against their elders; the religiously observant versus the secular; and the politically active (mainly socialists) vainly attempting to encourage the apolitical. Another pervasive and deeply felt conflict, between Jew and non-Jew, reinforces the social alienation that the Stigmans feel, even Ira, who develops close relationships with non-Jews. While attempting to accommodate to the culture and religions of a new country, the Stigmans also confront debilitating economic struggles.

The novel begins with the arrival in New York of Ira's mother's family from Galitzian Austro-Hungary. The patriarch Ben Zion Farb, his wife, and his eight children have come to America in stages, newcomers joining others as money becomes available for passage. Ira's father Chaim, for example, preceded his wife and son and "scrimped . . . saved . . . stinted to the point of alimentary collapse" to accumulate fare money for them. Soon after his maternal grandparents arrive, Ira and his parents move from the East Side, traditional abode of Eastern European Jewish immigrants, to a Jewish neighborhood in Harlem, closer to Leah Stigman's family and a milk shed where Chaim can obtain stock for his delivery route. Within months, however, they move to a non-Jewish neighborhood, since Leah is unhappy with an apartment "in the back" and craves one with windows "in the front." They forsake electricity, hot running water, a private bathroom, and steam heat for a cold-water flat with "a window on the street to lean out of." Chaim is amenable to the move because of the low rent and a nearby stable for his horse and wagon.

The early part of the novel is composed mainly of vignettes and anecdotes about family members, most of whom subsequently fade as Ira's role expands and he becomes increasingly alienated from many of his newly arrived relatives, whose foreignness seems exaggerated because of the glaring contrast with his non-Jewish milieu. Naïvely, Ira had expected them to be "bountifully pre-Americanized"; instead, they are uncouth, speak an incomprehensible Yiddish, and make "lopsided and outlandish gestures." The eight-year-old takes solace in solitude, going outside his ghetto to prosperous Fifth Avenue, with its stores, restaurants, and "self-satisfied strollers." In Mt. Morris Park, whose paths lead to different New York worlds, he explores as a "self-sufficient, resourceful and intrepid" rover in the "visionary land," sealing his covenant by sipping from a rivulet. Immediately after this solitary odyssey, Ira returns to his former neighborhood, telling old friends Heshy and Izzy that his new neighborhood is "full of lousy Irish *goyim* [who] call me Jew bestit all the time, an' they wanna fight." Though happy to see him, the pals treat him with a deference due visitors, and Ira realizes he is "a guest now among his own kind" and "excluded from belonging."

The opening pages thus introduce Ira's extended family, presenting character portrayals that lay the basis for subsequent problems and conflicts, while setting forth an overriding alienation theme: separation from friends, the impossibility of renewing relationships, embarrassment with an Old World family, taunting and threats endured at the hands of non-Jewish boys, and jarring experiences that introduce an adolescent to sex.

Sadly, the courage and "East Side cockiness" that Ira acquires to cope with his Irish tormentors are destroyed by his mother's humiliating intervention and a savage beating by his father in response to an Irish mother's complaint. Nevertheless, the boy gains a sense of belonging through friendship with Eddie Ferry, who "didn't mind that Ira was Jewish." During their explorations, Ira sees strange produce and nonkosher meats and starts questioning "the sanctity of kosher food, . . . custom, . . . observance . . . all impediments to entering Eddie's world." These experiences foreshadow those he has later as stockboy at Park & Tilford, gourmet grocers, a job that increases his awareness of class and ethnic differences, including the inferior status of blacks. Adding to his alienation is the fact that, unlike his Jewish contemporaries, he does not regularly attend Hebrew school, because of his family's moves, the Stigmans' precarious finances, and his own indifference to his heritage.

Chaim's instability and temper lead to business failure, an erratic job record, and even a journey to St. Louis for help from two financially secure and politically connected brothers. His father's departure produces no immediate void for Ira, since Chaim also is ineffectual as parent, and the boy quickly turns to surrogates. One is Uncle Max, who makes a sled for his nephew. Another is personable and generous Uncle Louie, a postman, socialist, and gentleman farmer, who speaks "like a real American, a Yankee," and who courts Leah (without success) while Chaim is away.

When the United States enters the Great War, Chaim returns from the fruitless St. Louis odyssey, facing imprisonment or the draft unless he obtains war-essential employment. He becomes a trolley-car conductor, but the vehicle's lurching makes him ill, and after being beaten by a drunk sailor, he quits, gets work as a waiter, and somehow eludes the draft. In contrast, Leah's brother Moe (another favorite uncle) is drafted, serves overseas, and returns as a family and neighborhood hero.

Surrogate father figures notwithstanding, Ira eventually laments, "If only Pop would talk to him like Uncle Louie, could show him the way, could have been there before, prepared the way." Among all else, then, Ira looks in vain for a father as protector and partner: "Oh, how different it would be if you loved your father: The Irish kids ran to meet theirs when they came home from work."

Of his schooling, from elementary grades onward, Ira recalls little of substance but much about teachers' quirks, prejudices, and perversions. By his early teens, however, he is an avaricious reader, embracing a salmagundi of works, including *Adventures of Huckleberry Finn* (1884), *Das Kapital* (1867-1894), *Les Misérables* (1862), *The Call of the Wild* (1903), *Lorna Doone* (1869), *Riders of the Purple Sage* (1912), and poems by George Gordon, Lord Byron and Samuel Taylor Coleridge. Though a failure as a Boy Scout, he punts well in touch football and therefore is a coveted team member. This also is the time of his bar mitzvah, a thirteen-year-old boy's ceremonial initiation into the Jewish religion and manhood. For Ira, however, the event feeds his alienation, making him realize "he was only a Jew because he *had* to be a Jew; he hated being a Jew . . . saw no virtue in being one, and realized he was caught, imprisoned in an identity from which there was no chance of ever freeing himself."

While in the eighth grade, Ira gets a job with a food, wine, and liquor merchant to the rich. Wearing his blue serge suit, he enters "the richly aromatic, richly subdued mahogany demesne" of the store, is escorted to its cellar, introduced to the Jewish shipping clerk and black porter, and directed to clean the elevator sump. Sullen and disappointed, he persists in the foul job, surmising that "maybe he was being tested." Indeed, having passed the initiation, he becomes a trusted crew member, even being tapped to deliver a basket to a mansion, his introduction to the elite: "Rich, so that was rich? That was being rich, that was—oh, he knew the word: taste. Taste. And manners." This job and its varied opportunities end when the store closes because Prohibition has cut into profits. Ira is regretful, since he "had found such an enjoyable niche" and Mr. Klein, the stockroom chief, had become another surrogate father. For the first time, Ira felt "accepted by outside the Jewish world . . . approval by those not his own."

Because additional volumes of *Mercy of a Rude Stream* are to follow, Roth tells only part of his story in *A Star Shines over Mt. Morris Park*. The volume ends inconclusively, for the lives of Ira and the others have scarcely changed. Though the book is largely prologue, Roth shows, as he ruminates in an Ecclesias aside, "the damned things that happen to innocence, or ignorance, in the slums, . . . in alien slums, in heterogeneous ones." Like *Call It Sleep*, then, *A Star Shines over Mt. Morris Park* is a compelling, though episodic and incomplete, *bildungsroman* or initiation novel, in a tradition encompassing not only Farrell and Joyce but also such works as Mark Twain's *The Adventures of Huckleberry Finn*, J. D. Salinger's *The Catcher in the Rye* (1951), and John Knowles's *A Separate Peace* (1959). It is weakened, however, by the author's determined realism, different from his method in *Call It Sleep*, and reflects his rejection of Joyce, an "erstwhile literary liege," whom he mocks (in Ecclesias comments) as a necromancer with a "hermetic ego" who "couldn't assimilate the great cosmopolitan 'universal' Western culture that surrounded him on the European continent."

Roth suggests in his title and epigraph what subsequent volumes have in store for Ira. The title for the series has its source in William Shakespeare's *King Henry VIII* (1612-1613), in which a boy's "summers in a sea of glory" are contrasted with a "weary and old" man left "to the mercy/ Of a rude stream." Acknowledging the irony of Shakespeare's "mercy," Roth in his epigraph declares that he, on the other hand, uses the word literally, for "the rude stream did show me Mercy." Presumably, then, Ira (Roth's alter ego) also will overcome adversity and ultimately will prevail in later volumes, so in this first book Roth may be setting the stage for a family saga in the manner of John Galsworthy or Thomas Mann. Although in an early Ecclesias conversation Roth criticizes such "generational novels," he presumably believes that his will be different.

Gerald H. Strauss

Sources for Further Study

The Christian Science Monitor. January 31, 1994, p. 17.
The Economist. CCCXXX, February 12, 1994, p. 91.
Los Angeles Times Book Review. January 30, 1994, p. 1.
The New York Review of Books. XLI, March 3, 1994, p. 24.
The New York Times Book Review. XCIX, January 16, 1994, p. 3.
The Times Literary Supplement. February 25, 1994, p. 20.
The Washington Post Book World. XXIV, February 20, 1994, p. 6.

MIDDLEPASSAGES

Author: (Edward) Kamau Brathwaite (1930-)
Publisher: New Directions (New York). 120 pp. Paperback $9.95
Type of work: Poetry

A collection of fourteen poems spanning the length of Brathwaite's career as a poet and highlighting the importance of Caribbean rhythms and music in his poetry

The awarding of the 1992 Nobel Prize in Literature to Derek Walcott helped bring poetry of the Caribbean region to world attention. Readers of Kamau Brathwaite did, however, detect a downside to this news. While Walcott's own achievements in poetry are certainly worthy of recognition, and while the attention given to him may have helped to shine a little more light on other literature of the region, Walcott was a decidedly safer choice for the award than the equally worthy Brathwaite would have been, if only because Walcott generally sticks to the conventions of standard written English. Kamau Brathwaite, who stands with Walcott as the other living giant of Caribbean poetry, writes in a mixture of dialects drawn mostly from the Caribbean region, which are used to create a poetry that is inclusively pan-Africa and pan-Third World. To read through a number of Brathwaite's poems with any degree of understanding is to explore this internationalist, pan-Africanist aesthetic that Brathwaite has charted.

In poetry circles, Brathwaite is best known as the author of two trilogies of poems focused on the Caribbean islands. The first three volumes, *Rights of Passage* (1967), *Masks* (1968), and *Islands* (1969), were republished as a single volume called *The Arrivants: A New World Trilogy* (1973). Taken as a whole, *The Arrivants* constitutes a spiritual journey through the Caribbean, to the English and African sources of Caribbean culture, and back to the Caribbean with a vision transformed. The second trilogy, comprising *Mother Poem* (1977), *Sun Poem* (1982), and *X/Self* (1987), takes a slightly broader view, focusing on the mix of voices in the Caribbean region rather than the growth of an individual consciousness, and adds consideration of the nature and limitations of sex roles to Brathwaite's discussion of race and geography. He is also well known as the author of many nonfiction works about Caribbean society and literature, including *The Development of Creole Society in Jamaica, 1770-1820* (1971) and *History of the Voice: The Development of Nation Language in Anglophone Caribbean Poetry* (1984).

MiddlePassages is a collection of fourteen poems, many of which were included in his earlier trilogies, some of which are more recent. Though the book was published in 1992 by a British publisher, its publication by New Directions marks the first time one of Brathwaite's books of poetry has been published by an American-based publisher. As the title suggests, there is a running theme regarding the effects of slavery on Caribbean culture and indeed on the world, but the title also carries other suggestions. In *The Zea Mexican Diary* (1993), which includes excerpts of Brathwaite's personal diary, recorded around the time of his wife's death in 1986, the entry that reports his wife's death is titled "Middle Passages." This suggests that the title has deep reverberations for Brathwaite, not only of the grief caused by the passage of slaves across the Atlantic but also of the spiritual passages that death entails for both the dead and the living. Journeys, especially the journey to African roots, is a recurring motif in *MiddlePassages*.

Written from the perspective of an inhabitant who watched Christopher Columbus landing, "Colombe" suggests the lyric beauty that this inaugural European visitor to the Caribbean islands must have seen: "yellow pouis/ blazed like pollen & thin/ waterfalls suspended in the green." Did Columbus understand the violence to which his discovery would lead? "But did his vision/ fashion as he watched the shore/ the slaughter that his soldiers// furthered here?" In the final image of the poem, Columbus strides to shore, oblivious to the crabs snapping at his feet. Columbus as Brathwaite envisions him is not an evil man, nor particularly a great man. Instead, he is a dreamer who is oblivious of the effects of his dreams upon others.

"Duke Playing Piano at 70" pictures Duke Ellington's wrinkled hands as alligator skins, swimming easily along a piano keyboard. In the old musician's music, the poet hears echoes of Bessie Smith, the great blues singer who was known as "Empress of the Blues," as well as of Jesse Jackson running for president to "keep hope alive." For Brathwaite, Ellington's "alligator skin" hands are at once artifacts of the past, participants in the present, and harbingers of the future. By the end, a renewal has taken place; the poet urges, "look/ the old man's alligator hands are young."

Music is central to Brathwaite's poetry; he uses any number of devices to bring the sense of music to the printed page. His poems sing and sway and bounce and thunder with all the African-based music that he can squeeze into them. For sheer beauty, no poem in this collection tops "Flutes." Describing the sounds of bamboo flutes, Brathwaite uses a language that almost seems to bounce between notes and to hold notes like the music itself:

> it is the kite ascending chord & croon & screamers
> it is the cloud that curls to hide the eagle
> it is the ripple of the stream from bamboo
>
> it is the ripple of the stream from blue
> it is the gurgle pigeon dream the ground doves coo
> it is the sun approaching midday listening its splendour
>
> it is your voice alight with echo . with the bright of sound

Several poems, especially "Soweto," written about the Soweto massacre and dedicated to Winnie and Nelson Mandela, draw on the rhythm of drums. The coming of Mandela is pictured at the end as the coming of the "bongo man," announced by a drum whose noise, "bruggadung bruggadung," is presented in increasingly larger print to give the sense of drumbeats coming nearer.

One of Brathwaite's great political themes is the history of violence against African peoples and the Third World in general. "The Visibility Trigger," dedicated to "Kwame Nkrumah & the leaders of the third world," surveys the European history of using guns to kill and subdue Third World peoples. Like "Colombe," it is told from the point of view of a man watching the foreigners land on his shore.

i offered you a kola nut
your finger huge & smooth & red
and you took it your dress makola blue

and you broke it into gunfire

With the coming of guns into this land, a way of life of "birth which is child which is hunter which is warrior/ which is breath" disappeared.

One of the most effective and powerful poems in the book is "Stone," dedicated to Mickey Smith, a poet and political activist who was "stoned to death on Stony Hill, Kingston," in 1983. Often Brathwaite uses the visual appearance of lines on the page to great effect (the book is set in a typeface that Brathwaite himself is designing), and in the case of "Stone," the bare page above the poem's first line, "When the stone fall that morning out of the johncrow sky," helps to suggest the openness of the sky and the solidity of a stone falling out of it to kill a human being. The images that follow are a mixture of pain and lyricism, as the dying man tries to convince himself that he is in a dream in which nobody can hear him, "even though/ there were so many poems left & the tape was switched on." A reverie of images follows in which the approaching violent death suggests various images, some of which are startling for their beauty: "& it was like a wave on stony hill caught in a crust of sun/ . . . & it was like the blue of space was filling up the heavens/ wid its thunder." The stones continue to fall, rushing onward, as do the images swirling through the speaker's head, until, in the final transformation of the stone, the speaker and stone merge: "i am the stone that kills me." The ending, like the poem itself, strikes a chord of poignant lyricism remarkable for its lack of fear or bitterness.

Brathwaite consciously manipulates not only the placement of words on a page but virtually every formal visual aspect of language. Punctuation in his hands seldom maintains its standard meaning. Periods may come in the middle of a word and be placed to suggest several possible layers of meaning. For example, the second section of "Letter SycoraX"—a poem that, in part, deals with the need of the colonized to reformulate the language of the colonizer—begins

Why a callin it

X?

a doan write.
ly know

The effect can be disconcerting and even baffling, yet Brathwaite's careful manipulation of many facets of the appearance of his language allows him to suggest in print some of the nuances of human speech. Also, because many of his poems are written in a nonstandard dialect, his idiosyncratic punctuation allows him to suggest meanings and emphases that a nonstandard English speaker might find in the language but a speaker of standard English would usually miss.

"Letter SycoraX" is written from the perspective of a Calibanesque figure who is writing to his mother on a computer with obvious glee. In much Caribbean literature, Caliban is reinterpreted from William Shakespeare's *The Tempest* (c. 1611-1612) to be a figure of the unassimilated Caribbean subject, the antihero who resists the power of the invader, Prospero. Just as Caliban appreciated Prospero's gift of language for the sole reason that it allowed him to curse, the speaker of "Letter SycoraX" is interested in appropriating and subverting the language of the capitalist structure—he compares his use of the computer to those who have "taken we blues and gone." Where did he learn to type? he knows his mother will want to know. He never did, he admits quite proudly, "but I mwangles!"—which seems to imply that he "manages," "mangles," and "wrangles" the language with his typing

The speaker of "Letter SycoraX" wants to learn the use of this computer because it can give him power over the "prospero ling ./ go," which is to say, the language of Prospero. Yet he will not learn language because a Prospero figure forces him; he will learn it to subvert it to his own ends. Making a pun on cursing and computer cursers, he implies that in his hands, the computer will become an electronic wand with which to lay an effective curse on Prospero. The power to sit in front of what he calls an "eeee-lectrical" mallet and chip his words into the face of the computer screen makes him feel at the end "like moses or aaron or one a dem/ dyaaam isra/ light."

The speaker well knows that power over language is related to the power of the law. As the poem implies in a variety of ways, but especially with its image of Richard Nixon (referred to as "Nix") and Adolf Hitler having a discussion with Pol Pot and Idi Amin Dada in the underworld while economists smoke Cuban cigars and talk of "pullin we up by we/ boot/ straps," a crucial part of controlling people is to control discourse. Manipulating his own language in his own poem makes the speaker into a prophet of his own future, at least symbolically, and makes him feel, as he says, "like i is a some. is a some. is a some/ body."

In one of Derek Walcott's best-known poems, "A Far Cry from Africa," he wonders whether he must choose between his African heritage and identity and the English language he loves. Brathwaite's solution to this problem is to love the English language of the African peoples and to make that the language of his poetry. Among other things, the title *MiddlePassages* implies the middle passages of a piece of music, and this collection is a concise guide to the music of Brathwaite's poetry from the years that perhaps he now considers the middle part of his life. If so, the promise is of a transition, perhaps to a music that is only beginning to take shape.

Thomas J. Cassidy

Sources for Further Study

Choice. XXX, May, 1993, p. 1460.
The Observer. November 22, 1992, p. 65.
Stand Magazine. XXXIV, Spring, 1993, p. 83.
The Times Literary Supplement. November 27, 1992, p. 27.
The Village Voice Literary Supplement. April, 1994, p. 15.
World Literature Today. LXVII, Spring, 1993, p. 425.

MILLROY THE MAGICIAN

Author: Paul Theroux (1941-)
Publisher: Random House (New York). 437 pp. $24.00
Type of work: Novel
Time: The 1990's
Locale: Massachusetts, Colorado, Vermont, and Hawaii

A carnival magician becomes a television celebrity by using magic and spirituality to try to change how Americans think about food

Principal characters:
HARRY MILLROY, a magician and television personality
JILLY FARINA, his teenage companion and assistant
ROY "DADA" FARINA, her father
"GAGA," her grandmother
VERA TURTLE, Dada's common-law wife

Paul Theroux has created a rich body of consistently interesting work, including such novels as *The Family Arsenal* (1976) and such travel books as *The Great Railway Bazaar* (1975). *Millroy the Magician*, his thirtieth book, reflects Theroux's continuing concern with what it means to be lonely and unloved in the contemporary world.

Cape Cod may be picturesque and romantic to its visitors, but to many year-round residents it is merely a place to live. Fifteen-year-old Jilly Farina lives there in lower-middle-class squalor, sometimes with her drunken, widowed father, whom she calls Dada, sometimes with her abusive grandmother, known as Gaga. Jilly is without purpose until she meets Millroy the Magician at the Barnstable fairgrounds, and he induces the boyish adolescent to be his companion and assistant.

The large, bald, mustached Millroy is much more than a magician. He restricts himself to a diet of foods mentioned in the Bible, mostly grains, nuts, and fruits. After he proposes a segment mixing magic and nutrition to a Boston children's program, he quickly takes over the show, dumping the obnoxious, effeminate host by exposing the man's hatred for children. Millroy enlists the short, slender Jilly, who he has dressed as a boy and introduces as his son, Alex, to recruit teenagers as cast members for the show. Millroy's program is a big hit until his charges go too far in advocating how the foods favored by the magician will result in healthier bowel movements. (Millroy is as obsessed by excrement as by food.)

Millroy's next venture is to take over a rundown Boston diner and convert it, with the help of a crew of inner-city African American teenagers, into a successful restaurant featuring his Scripture-inspired dishes. The success of the Day One Diner is parallel to that of the Sunday-morning religious program in which Millroy combines magic, spirituality, and healthy recipes.

As the program and the diners spread to other parts of the United States, Millroy becomes a major celebrity, and the news media paint him as a con man resembling the protagonist of Sinclair Lewis' *Elmer Gantry* (1927). These charges are unfair, since Millroy asks for no followers or donations, merely that people change the way they eat. The attacks are also to be expected, since he grows, despite his modest claims, increasingly messianic as the popularity of his movement grows. Like an earlier messiah, Millroy is betrayed by his followers when they turn him in to police for having an unnatural relationship with his supposed "son." The magician and Jilly then flee to the big island of Hawaii, where she reassumes her female identity.

Theroux deliberately keeps the reader off balance in assessing Millroy's character and motivations by using unworldly Jilly as the first-person narrator. Jilly chooses to live with Millroy because his world is cleaner, healthier, and safer than what she has known with Dada and Gaga and because she has yearned to find out what the world offers outside their limited milieu. With him, she is truly alive for the first time. Yet while she approves of his work, admires him, and protects him, she is never quite certain what exactly he is up to and is made especially uneasy by her male pose. *Millroy the Magician* centers around the contrast between Millroy's confidence in his skills and Jilly's bewilderment over a complex world from which the magician is a refuge.

The Millroy-Jilly relationship has uncomfortably sexual overtones from the beginning, when he tells her, "I want to eat you." He feeds on her innocence, yet he also literally feeds her: "I want to fill you up. I want to put it all into you, be responsible for everything inside you." Jilly does not want Millroy to think that while he controls what goes into her body it is "his to use." "It was small and skinny and he was helping it to grow healthier," she says, "but did that give him any rights to touch me? He did not try or even seem interested, but even so the answer was a flat no." Their relationship is also almost like that of a vampire and his victim: As Millroy grows stronger, Jilly grows weaker. "The longer we were together, the less I knew him, the harder it was to predict how he would react; and I had less and less idea of how to please him."

Jilly sympathizes with Millroy's position as a great man destined to do great works but misunderstood by an ignorant society. He wants the public to be less dazzled by his magic than moved by his humanity, but he realizes that many obstacles can intrude. The media broadcast lies about him, nonbelievers make fun of him, and marketing experts attempt to buy his power and influence. Millroy ignores the slanders and resists the monetary temptations until his power eventually seems to be driving him insane. In saying, "Someday this will be a Day One country," is he a prophet leading a nation into health or a burgeoning megalomaniac?

Millroy is more sorcerer than magician. He uses magic not only to amuse and instruct but also to frighten and coerce, pulling large, slimy rats out of the mouths of his enemies, taking off a finger, chopping it into pieces, and feeding them to his apostles. During a period of confusion, Jilly leaves Millroy briefly, and his powers diminish: "He needed my innocence, and as long as we were together, we were both strong in peculiar ways, and if we were separated, we would be weak and destructible." After they leave Boston, however, Millroy begins abusing his powers, calling up a vicious storm during their flight to Hawaii to keep the other passengers from eating the dreadful airline food, dazzling their superstitious Hawaiian neighbors in Hawaii by having a corpse rise from her deathbed and speak. Instead of using magic as a tool for achieving a useful end, Millroy becomes a bully: "The whole time I had known him he had been my hero not for his magic, which often frightened me, but for his kindness."

Jilly is more frightened when Millroy finally professes his love: "I had never stopped seeing him as the man who could turn me into a glass of milk and drink me. He was made of cold metal; he had unpredictable power. Why didn't he know that it was impossible for me to love him, or that his love made me feel unsafe?" Millroy proves his love by disappearing into the sea until Jilly discovers that she now has magical powers and calls him back to life and love. In giving up his powers to her, he proves himself worthy of her affection.

Theroux is clearly influenced here by the relationship between the middle-aged Humbert Humbert and the adolescent Dolores Haze in Vladimir Nabokov's *Lolita* (1955). Nabokov's selfish protagonist is redeemed by his realization that he sincerely loves Lolita. Theroux makes a similar point about the differences between selfish and selfless love that ties in smoothly with the novel's other overt and subtle Christian symbols. Jilly's acceptance of his love and her awareness of her own can be interpreted in a number of non-Christian ways as well, especially the difficulty of love existing when one partner has too much power over the other and the need for sacrifice in a romantic relationship. No such interpretations can assuage the unease created by Jilly's constant fear of sexual advances before this transformation and by a romance between a fifteen-year-old girl and someone old enough to be her grandfather.

Millroy is successful as a spirituality-through-diet guru because of the vulgarity of television evangelists and the emptiness of conventional religion. He disdains the latter: "The trouble with most religions is that they make you feel so miserable on earth that you know you're going to feel equally miserable after you're dead." His message, by contrast, is physically and spiritually healthy. His distrust of conventionality leads him always to refer to the Bible as The Book and God as Good and to ridicule the way people interpret the Bible to suit their superstitions and prejudices. While Millroy is hardly an Elmer Gantry or a Jimmy Swaggart, Theroux uses him to display the corruption implicit in zealotry. He claims to have died and risen from the dead and eats the meal Jesus ate following his resurrection. Despite himself, his ego gets in the way of his message.

Another main target of Theroux's satire is contemporary America's obsession with marketing and media. Once Millroy's program becomes a success, he is inundated by marketeers with offers of merchandising, franchising, and endorsements. They want Millroy's face on food products and T-shirts and to market his ideas "to yuppies who are obsessed with the aging process." They cannot take his rejections seriously, because such marketing enterprises are what everyone in American business strives for. As his power increases and Millroy begins losing touch with his real self, he weakens and begins formulating marketing plans: "Grow, package and sell food from The Book. . . . Company motto—'We know beans.'" Theroux demonstrates how power corrupts even the ideals of those who perceive themselves immune to such influences.

He also shows both the innocuous vapidity of television and its potential for doing harm. Lower-middle-class people such as Vera Turtle, Dada's common-law wife, have their sets always turned on for reasons they make no attempt to understand. Pathetically lonely people such as Hazel DeHart have lives so empty that they imagine those they see on television are their friends; as a result, DeHart erects a shrine to Millroy. Theroux underscores the hypocrisy of the medium when Millroy's first program is canceled after his protégés urge their audience to remove their clothing before excreting and to read The Book during bowel movements. Natural acts are obscene; greed is not.

Millroy the Magician has superficial similarities to other works in the tradition of American literature dealing with confidence tricksters, such as Herman Melville's *The Confidence-Man* (1857) and Mark Twain's *The Mysterious Stranger* (1916). While Theroux presents his protagonist as more realistic and sympathetic, he is as pessimistic about the state of humankind as his predecessors. The novel most resembles Theroux's own *The Mosquito Coast* (1982), which also has an innocent adolescent narrator from Massachusetts torn between love and fear of an authority figure, the mad father who drags his family to Central America to escape the evil influences of civilization.

While *Millroy the Magician* is an intelligent, always interesting novel, it is not all that it might have been. Here Theroux is more realistic than in *The Mosquito Coast* in creating the point-of-view of a naïve teenager, but the result is a too simplistic style. Readers familiar with Theroux's other works will miss the sophistication and density of detail seen in such novels as *Saint Jack* (1973) and *The Black House* (1974). While there is frequent humor in Theroux's travel books, verbal and situational comedy are remarkably absent from his fiction. For a satirical novel, *Millroy the Magician* is surprisingly unfunny. It is much less entertaining than another treatment of the interrelationships between food, health, morality, and business, T. Coraghessan Boyle's witty *The Road to Wellville* (1993).

Michael Adams

Sources for Further Study

The Economist. CCCXXIX, November 20, 1993, p. 111.
Library Journal. CXVIII, October 15, 1993, p. 90.
Los Angeles Times Book Review. March 20, 1994, p. 8.
New Statesman and Society. VI, October 8, 1993, p. 38.
The New York Times Book Review. XCIX, March 6, 1994, p. 9.
The New Yorker. LXX, March 14, 1994, p. 92.
Publishers Weekly. CCXLI, March 7, 1994, p. 48.
Time. CXLIII, March 7, 1994, p. 69.
The Times Literary Supplement. October 8, 1993, p. 26.
The Wall Street Journal. April 11, 1994, p. A12.

MODERN IRISH LITERATURE
Sources and Founders

Author: Vivian Mercier (1919-1989)
Edited by Eilís Dillon
Publisher: Clarendon Press/Oxford University Press (New York). 381 pp. $45.00
Type of work: Literary history and criticism

A posthumous collection of Mercier's source studies of Irish literature, from the Celtic origins to significant modernist writers of the twentieth century, including G. B. Shaw, W. B. Yeats, James Joyce, Samuel Beckett, and others

Edited and "presented" by Eilís Dillon, Vivian Mercier's widow, this volume is both a definitive study of Irish literary sources and a memorial to its author, who died in 1989. For the painstaking efforts of Dillon, readers will be grateful, especially because Mercier had originally intended to publish a two-volume study that he had considered "his most important work." How much of this proposed text has survived in the present tome one can only guess. In reconstructing Mercier's work, Dillon was fortunate to have her husband's first draft and "many relevant footnotes," but much of the research may well have been lost. Dillon concedes that she has brought to press "a part, at least, of [Mercier's] larger plan." To place the reconstructed book in the context of Mercier's wide range of interests, Declan Kiberd's scholarly introduction clearly establishes the direction of the author's research and his lifelong, engagement with Irish literature.

As such, the volume commemorates Mercier's achievements. Included is an appendix of his published works from 1943 to 1982—a massive listing of books, monographs, articles, and reviews treating not only Irish language and literature but also English and Continental topics. A reader needs to understand Mercier's range as a scholar/historian in order to appreciate the depth of his research. Other scholars may have published more titles, but few show Mercier's dedication to the task. As Kiberd points out, Mercier in his mid-thirties "suddenly" decided to study and master the Irish language. Coming to the discipline relatively late in his career, he brought to this study a comprehensive knowledge of literature and sharp critical skills. Other twentieth century philologists have also brought distinction to Celtic studies, but none surpass Mercier in his particular grasp of Irish literature in the larger setting of European cultural traditions.

Finally, as Kiberd demonstrates, Mercier applied to his scholarship a rich understanding of the Anglo-Irish milieu in which he was brought up. As a student in 1928 at Portora Royal School, Enniskillen, he learned by rote many of the Evangelical Protestant traditions that had earlier influenced Oscar Wilde, Samuel Beckett, and other prominent literary figures. Later he attended Trinity College, Dublin, another major educational pathway of his predecessors in literature, most notably James Joyce. From French Huguenot stock on his father's side and Irish on his mother's, Mercier was fortunate in his upbringing to experience the richness of two competing cultures, yet to acquire tolerance for each.

If readers are tempted to skip the first four chapters of the volume, which treat historical and social-background material, to move forward to the inviting chapters on the modernist writers, they should resist that impulse. With patience, good humor, and tact, Mercier explains the necessary (but not at all tedious) background information needed to appreciate the likes of George Bernard Shaw, John Millington Synge, and the others. In "The Rediscovery of the Gaelic Past," he reviews the publications of early scholars (and pseudoscholars, whom he calls charlatans), demonstrating their achievements and failures. Unlike other recent Celtic philologists, who generally skim over the bad writing to hurry ahead to the good, Mercier takes his time to make certain that the reader understands each step, no matter how tentative, in the movement toward rediscovery of Gaelic literature. In fact, Mercier does not skip anything. One has the certainty that the author has reread every scrap of scholarship and has reevaluated every document, every legend, in order to discover for the reader's sake many long-ignored passages and translations that merit attention. For example, in treating Standish Hayes O'Grady's erudite catalog of the Irish manuscripts in the British Museum, Mercier writes: "Having read widely in the work myself, I can testify to the pleasure, even where the manuscripts deal with law or medicine, though of course the poetry is the most attractive."

With the same thorough attention to detail, Mercier reviews in "Irish Writers and English Readers: Literature and Politics, 1798-1845" Anglo-Irish works from a particular point of view: that early nineteenth century Irish literature was truly an amalgam of two political ideologies, one derived from the Catholic Irish, the other from the Protestant Ascendancy. This amalgam, he argues, has created a unique literature, one that has absorbed elements from the competing religious parties. In "Evangelical Revival in the Church of England, 1800-69" Mercier clarifies for the reader the meaning of Irish Evangelicalism, a religious/cultural movement that is not at all similar to twentieth century American (or even twentieth century British) evangelicalism. Unless one understands, as Mercier helps the reader to understand, the history of this revival, one may confuse religious concepts that influenced major writers during the modernist period. Finally, in "The Revival Begins," the author treats the Cú Chulainn saga from Samuel Ferguson through Standish O'Grady and on to William Butler Yeats, whose special vision of the myth altered the sources that he used.

Having treated the "sources" and "founders" of Anglo-Irish literature in Gaelic writings and in the religious and political background of the nineteenth century, Mercier turns next to the chief modern practitioners. By "modern" he means "modernist"; Mercier's study rarely touches on material after 1940. Although the chapters dealing with Shaw, Yeats, Synge, Joyce, and Beckett (in that order) may be read sequentially, as parts of a single work, they may also be read as isolated essays. In nearly every one, he argues a particular point of view: that Shaw was an "Irish international"; that Yeats was a "master craftsman"; that Synge was categorized by his Irish compatriots as either a "devil or saint"; that Beckett was steeped in his Evangelical-based knowledge of the Bible.

Yet with the essay on Joyce—in many ways the best of the lot—Mercier departs from his usual method of connecting the writer to a religio-cultural point of view. Instead, he analyzes in careful detail the structure of *Ulysses* (1922). Remarkable for its author's close reading of the text and his critical acuity, this essay on Joyce could easily be separated from the rest of the material in the volume; it stands apart as a set piece. Although Mercier defines for the reader ways in which Joyce's Irish-Catholic education molded the master's thinking, the essay as a whole is less concerned with Joyce's cultural identity than with his art.

In contrast, when Mercier treats Shaw, Yeats, Synge, and Beckett, he emphasizes their Protestant-Evangelical cultural biases. Even writers who on the surface appear to lack a conventional Christian frame of reference are shown to reflect this bias, no matter (in the case of Shaw) how brief the religious education, no matter (in the case of Yeats's Theosophy) how altered into unconventional directions, no matter (in the case of Beckett's agnosticism) how contradictory. The strength of Mercier's scholarship rests on the educational background he shares with these notable Anglo-Irish writers. Thanks to this background, he can see in Shaw's now-neglected *John Bull's Other Island* (1904) a major statement of the dramatist's philosophy. Unlike many other scholars, Mercier reads Shaw's early novels not as artistic failures or as tentative gropings toward drama, but as consistent moral statements that progress, with greater success of course, toward the themes of the plays.

Also from this background, he reads in Yeats's early works, including *The Countess Cathleen* (1892), no "subtle conflict of 'moral motives'," but a general consistency with the poet's ideology. Mercier believes that Synge's break with Evangelical orthodoxy, one that occurred early in the writer's career, formed the second stage of his break with "suburbia"—that is, the community of upper-middle-class Protestants.

Finally, in his reading of Beckett's plays, Mercier observes a consistent rather than ambiguous (or paradoxical) central bias springing from the artist's youthful involvement with Evangelicalism. Beckett's *En attendant Godot* (1952; *Waiting for Godot*, 1954), Mercier believes, is a complex Christian parable. To him, Vladimir and Estragon (or Didi and Gogo, as they call each other) are waiting for a God who does indeed arrive—although they mistake the meaning of this appearance. Disguised as Pozzo/Lucky, Godot represents both the chastising Deity and the Suffering Servant of the Scriptures. "Didi and Gogo fail to recognize him, just as, Christians believe, the Jews failed to recognize their Messiah." So startling (yet sensible) is this analysis that Mercier appears to lose heart in working out its details:

> I do not expect this interpretation to be accepted; frankly, I do not quite believe in it myself. I am just putting it forward as an example of how the simple yet universal elements and relationships in *Waiting for Godot* can be interpreted as symbols of so many truths, both human and divine.

In spite of the author's disclaimer, his analysis can stand on its merits. Mercier's interpretation is persuasive—a brilliant contribution to Beckett criticism.

The final chapter—in some respects Mercier's most innovative—titled "European-Irish Literary Connections in the Twentieth Century," may have been incomplete at the time of his death. At any rate, the chapter lacks the prose fluidity of most of the other sections of the book. Mercier's point of view is that Irish (or Anglo-Irish) literature of the modernist period must be separated from that of British writing during the same period. Figuratively speaking, to Mercier the tail (Irish) wags the dog (English), rather than the other way around. Although most literary historians include Shaw, Joyce, and Beckett among "English" writers, Mercier makes a sharp distinction: Irish writers represent their own national heritage.

To prove his point, the author details historical "connections" that modernist Irish writers maintained with major (often avant-garde) European literary movements. In addition to Joyce's well-documented links to Continental writers, especially to those in Italy and France, Mercier discusses similar links to the Continent of writers such as George Moore, Beckett, Brendan Behan, and Flann O'Brien. He shows, moreover, that a tradition of Irish-French literary connections had begun as early as the nineteenth century among such Anglo-Irish writers as Thomas Moore, Maria Edgeworth, C. R. Maturin, and Oscar Wilde. Then during the first half of the twentieth century, Anglo-Irish writers influenced French literature, chiefly, and in turn shared technical innovations with writers such as Édouard Dujardin, Valéry Larbaud, J. K. Huysmans, Raymond Queneau, and Claude Simon. For these Continental writers, according to Mercier, their Irish literary counterparts were not "English"; they had their own special national identity.

Thus Mercier insists that modernist Anglo-Irish literature must be hyphenated. By tracing the roots of Evangelical Protestantism through literary figures from Wilde and Shaw to Beckett and others, he makes clear for the reader precisely how Anglo-Irish literature originated and how it flourished.

Leslie B. Mittleman

Sources for Further Study

Choice. XXXII, December, 1994, p. 600.
London Review of Books. XVI, July 7, 1994, p. 8.
The Spectator. CCLXXII, June 4, 1994, p. 35.
The Times Literary Supplement. December 16, 1994, p. 7.

MODERNIST QUARTET

Author: Frank Lentricchia (1940-   )
Publisher: Cambridge University Press (New York). 305 pp. $54.95; paperback $16.95
Type of work: Literary criticism

Frank Lentricchia reexamines the cultural foundations and aesthetic development of four modernist poets

This excellent introductory study of the poetry of Robert Frost, Wallace Stevens, Ezra Pound, and T. S. Eliot began in 1983 with an editor's request for Frank Lentricchia to write an entry on modern American poetry for the *Cambridge History of American Literature* (1994). This beginning helps explain Lentricchia's audacity in trying to encapsulate the careers of these poets whose works have spawned hundreds of critical volumes (he sidesteps this anxiety of influence by largely not citing earlier scholarship). His close juxtaposition of four major poets helps the reader understand the complex movement called modernism, which was able to encompass such a wide variety of aesthetics. While the four poets pursued very different careers, they all grew up in the same cultural milieu of early twentieth century America. Lentricchia shows how their aesthetics formed in reaction to the genteel, ladylike poetry found in the little magazines of the late nineteenth century, the Fireside school of poetry, the commodity culture, and the corrupt publishing interests—all factors that made up the literary status quo of their youth.

Lentricchia comes to this topic fully qualified. He has already written books on Stevens and Frost, which he draws upon for this study. His *After the New Criticism* (1980) discusses poststructuralism, deconstruction, feminism, and other late twentieth century critical movements and their debt to the New Criticism. In *Modernist Quartet*, Lentricchia writes a blend of gender, class, economic, aesthetic, and philosophical criticism that contextualizes each poet's world without diminishing his talents and idiosyncrasies. Unlike other critics, Lentricchia does not try to turn each writer into a creature of his historical scene or class or gender. He adopts critical modes when they are useful and then moves on. His study wavers between an introductory survey of modernist poetry and something more ambitious, a complete reassessment of the place of the moderns in present-day criticism.

Lentricchia brings to the reader's attention some useful and unexplored cultural and historical backgrounds before he evaluates the work of each poet in turn. His preface concerns the poetic regime that the high modernists revolted against, the Fireside poets (William Cullen Bryant, Henry Wadsworth Longfellow, James Russell Lowell), who abruptly died out in the early 1900's, and the genteel poets (R. H. Stoddard, Bayard Taylor, Richard Gilder) who followed them at the turn of the century in America. The Fireside poets left a legacy of safe, iambic, homiletic poetry meant to be read aloud to the whole family. The genteel poets, armed with an immense publishing empire, extended this trend into the twentieth century. Their poetry was moral, vague, full of lofty sentiments, aesthetically at odds with the burgeoning realistic novel, and feminine in the sense that upper-class wives were dictating the poetry's tastes by buying it. In addition, Palgrave's *Golden Treasury* (c. 1861), a bestseller for decades, set the standard for public consumption of poetry intended for people who wanted a bit of culture between work hours. Palgrave's anthology was an immense financial success, and it helped determine the commercial path of poetry of the time: Lyrics should be short, dissociated from contemporary problems or social changes (unlike realistic novels), restricted to accepted poetical topics and forms, and packaged for mass consumption. Thus, as Pound found out to his horror, economics in America determined aesthetics. The lyric had become another impersonal commodity.

By the turn of the century, poetry had deliberately become out of touch, disengaged, antique, a cultural dinosaur. Something needed to be done, or the novel was going to overtake poetry altogether as a viable art form. In a way, one could scarcely think of a more opportune moment in history for the modernists to appear. They had only to call attention to the weakness, irrelevance, and corruption of the prevailing aesthetics in poetry, and the field was wide open for any innovation. As Eliot pointed out, not one living poet writing in English was available for leading a young poet in search of a new idiom. Eliot had to cross languages to the French Symbolists to find his direction as a writer. While Pound researched Italian, Chinese, and other world literatures for hints of a modern voice, Frost looked to the working-class vernacular of his native New England. All four poets had to start from scratch to reinvent poetry and find their own traditions.

Lentricchia then introduces three Harvard philosophers, George Santayana, William James, and Josiah Royce, who supplied the intellectual groundwork for the modernist revolt through their teachings and books. Santayana's theories on aesthetics were a major influence on Wallace Stevens, who was Santayana's student and wrote "To an Old Philosopher in Rome" (1952) in his honor. Royce's search for an ideal intellectual community found its champion in the later T. S. Eliot, who sought both a tradition and a society in such works as *The Idea of a Christian Society* (1939). Frost taught William James to his students and shared many of James's Emersonian views of the individual's autonomy in the face of all forms of tyranny. Santayana's theories about perception paved the way for Pound's declarations on imagism.

Interestingly, Royce and James held radically different views in their works. While James championed the autonomous American individual in opposition to imperialistic tyranny—society, government, or religion—Royce looked for the advantages of community to help foster the individual. James also disagreed with Santayana's idealistic notions of aesthetic value. Thus while Santayana helped codify modernist aesthetics, James helped instill in the modernists an extreme skepticism toward any form of authority. Meanwhile, Royce started the poets thinking about the social goals of their high modernist poetics.

After considering the influential philosophers of the period, Lentricchia explores the economic status of the lyric in the early twentieth century, suggesting more than anything else the unprecedented pressures of money on all these poets. Capitalism and the growing culture of commodity encouraged the systematic repetition of a given commodity: If shoes could be mass-produced, why not poetry? The implications of this economic shift brought multiple challenges to a beginning poet. First of all, how does the poet reconcile aesthetic commitment with economic pressures? Frost uneasily reconciled the two by relentlessly publicizing himself and his poetry as a kind of commodity, but this brought problems for his poetry later, when he began to speak directly as a bard to his populace. Stevens enrolled in law school and worked his way up through the business world in insurance, reserving time on evenings, weekends, and vacations for writing poetry. Pound moved out of America altogether and supported himself by editing and by accepting money from his parents. Eliot moved to England and initially eked out a difficult existence as a banker and editor; financial pressures helped bring on his nervous breakdown, which ultimately enabled him to pen *The Waste Land* (1922). In every case, the simple challenge of supporting himself and his family formed part of the poet's modernist aesthetic. Each had to disconnect radically from the socioeconomic world that produced him (Frost less so than the others) and produce avant-garde poetry without much hope of financial remuneration.

The culture of commodity brought on other tensions as well. Palgrave had found that only dissociated poems of short length sold well in the mass markets, and so in reaction all four modernist poets wanted to write longer poems in the tradition of Homer's *Odyssey* (c. 800 B.C.) or Dante's *Inferno* (c. 1308-1321) to counteract the trivialization of poetry they found in the shorter lyric. Commodity culture wanted to make poetry bite-size, easily digestible in a short sitting, and limited in its subject matter to properly "poetic" sentiments (love, moons, misty valleys). The modernists responded by bringing into this narrow world a new heterogeneity of voices on a broader canvas. Eliot incorporated different languages, dialects, multiple allusions, and grotesque, unpleasant city imagery into his poetry, shocking readers out of the easy complacency of genteel lyrics. Frost brought in a colloquial vocabulary even more rustic than William Wordsworth's and incorporated the voices of poverty-stricken menial workers into a genre usually restricted to the comfortable middle or upper classes. In *The Cantos* (1917 through 1970), Pound inserted into his collage of voices large chunks of history, including actual texts of earlier writers such as John Adams and Thomas Jefferson. After years of the genteel poets' refining elements out of poetry, the moderns brought everything and anything back in. Unlike their predecessors, the modernists did not shrink from the impurities of existence.

After exploring the philosophical and economic background of all four poets, Lentricchia then traces the career of each of them in turn, looking for biographical reasons for shifts in the poetry's aesthetics. Frost, who begins the series, is something of an anomaly, because for years critics did not consider him a modernist at all, certainly not a high modernist. Frost wrote very much in the vein of the Fireside poets before him, and his easy accessibility, his bardic homilies, and his great popularity later in life seemed to disqualify him from serious critical study. Lentricchia counters this judgment by claiming that Frost had to subvert the Fireside style from within because of economic pressures. Determined to make a living as a user-friendly American poet, Frost mastered the art of publicizing himself. Along with Eliot, Frost turned the combination of himself and his poetry into a profitable commodity for a populace that might not have bothered to read the poetry alone. What the public usually failed to recognize, however, was that his poetry often contained an insidious ulterior meaning that would profoundly undercut any easy sentiments. By introducing a new narrative realism into Fireside aesthetics, Frost, in effect, attacked many of its assumptions from within.

Stevens makes an interesting study for Lentricchia's concerns with economics and gender. While Frost resembled a Fireside poet, Stevens resembled a leftover genteel poet building his world of aesthetic pleasures to help cover up the monotonous repetitions of the industrialized world. Stevens centered his aesthetics on the notion of pleasure, which required poems that brought a freshness and purity to life in order to break routines. At the same time, Stevens worried about writing "ladylike poetry" and the necessity of earning an income to support his family and his interests. While Frost turned himself into a showman, Stevens eventually earned a law degree and methodically worked his way up in an insurance agency. He led a double life, balancing a sense of freedom in writing poetry with the obligation of work, affirming a masculine identity in an art form dominated, he thought, by the tastes of women. With Stevens, Lentricchia best discusses the imprisoning effects of modern life, its emotional and perceptual deadening.

Pound and Eliot are the most difficult and most written about of the modernist poets respectively, and Lentricchia attempts to cut through the myths that still surround their works. He gives credit to Pound's seminal influence on modernism through his theories, his critical works, his editing of works such as *The Waste Land,* and his trumpeting and publishing of key poets early in their careers. He acknowledges that some have found *The Cantos* pure gibberish but then points out how the poem creates a kind of culture for writers, a whole curriculum of little-known voices in history that embody Pound's standard of poetry freed from all abstraction, rhetoric, and sentiment. Meanwhile, Eliot comes down to postmodern readers as all reputation. Lentricchia attempts to re-create the surprise people felt when they first encountered his muse of despair, the unsavory urban scenes, and the ironic antiromanticism that directly opposed the genteel lyricism of the day. Like Pound and novelist Henry James, Eliot moved to England to find a literary culture lacking in America. Even as he grew more conservative with age and fame, Eliot still wrote avant-garde poetry that questioned his every critical assumption. Through Lentricchia's lens, Eliot appears as the reluctant modernist whose love of literary tradition, doctrine, and established literary form did not stop him from undermining all of them in his poetry.

Lentricchia's love for these poets shows in every line. What makes this study work is his enthusiasm for the experiment of modernism, which founded its aesthetics on freedom—freedom from habit, conventional thinking, and the robotization of commodity culture. Lentricchia concludes with the apocalyptic vision of Don Delillo, a world where most humans are already equivalent to commodities and the greater repetition of media images makes it that much harder for anyone to escape dehumanizing influences. The economic, philosophical, and aesthetic challenges that the modernists faced are still prevalent, their social goals still unfulfilled. Lentricchia's study finds hints of a direction in the works and lives of this modernist quartet.

Roy C. Flannagan III

Source for Further Study

National Review. XLVI, November 21, 1994, p. 68.

THE MORAL ANIMAL
The New Science of Evolutionary Psychology

Author: Robert Wright (1957-   )
Publisher: Pantheon Books (New York). Illustrated. 467 pp. $27.50
Type of work: Psychology

A combination of scientific history, self-help manual, and historical biography, this work provides an accessible introduction to sociobiology and its attempts to explain behavior through evolutionary theory

Robert Wright's *The Moral Animal: The New Science of Evolutionary Psychology* offers the general audience a survey of research in the field that has come to be known both as sociobiology and as evolutionary psychology. Building upon the studies of Edward O. Wilson, Robert Trivers, George Williams, and William Hamilton, Wright develops an evolutionary model through which he seeks to explain various aspects of modern society. According to Wright, the roots of contemporary behavior should be sought not in modern society itself but in those tendencies and desires that would have enhanced a person's reproductive success during the early history of evolution.

Unlike the Social Darwinists of the late nineteenth and early twentieth centuries, Wright does not regard "the survival of the fittest" as a model for modern behavior. The author carefully distinguishes between tendencies that may have been productive in his hypothetical "ancestral environment" and those that are socially productive today. In addition, he explains how such diverse traits as altruism, marital infidelity, sibling rivalry, and parental love may have evolved through their ability to enhance survival or reproduction in the most primitive of human communities.

Wright's basic premise may be summarized as follows: If any genetically based behavior increases, even marginally, the likelihood that a person will reproduce, then this behavior will be favored by natural selection. Over the course of time, the genes leading to this behavior will spread throughout a population at the expense of genes that have little or no survival value. One illustration of this pattern would occur when genetically based tendencies lead an animal to produce large numbers of offspring, all of which have the same genetic code and the same behavioral tendencies. Something similar would occur in the case of genes encouraging people to protect their families. Since close relatives share a large amount of genetic information, benevolence toward kin causes one's own genetic code to prosper as it is spread by siblings and cousins.

Arguments such as these are unlikely to persuade anyone who views environment, rather than heredity, as the leading factor in determining human personality. Nor do they prove conclusively that human behavior is genetically based as Wright claims or that his hypothetical "ancestral environment" could have existed in the age before a united protohuman species divided to form races, cultures, and societies scattered across the globe. Nevertheless, much of Wright's argument is compelling. For example, his suggestion that sexual infidelity may originate in a form of reproductive strategy seems particularly convincing. In early hunting and gathering communities, successful reproductive strategies must have been distinctly different for the two sexes. For men, frequent relationships with large numbers of women inevitably led to more offspring. For women, sexual relationships with a large number of men did not necessarily result in a larger number of pregnancies. Thus, in Wright's "ancestral environment," it was in a woman's reproductive interest to be highly selective about her partners; by succumbing only to men who were "rich," strong, and healthy, women ensured that their offspring would have the greatest chance to survive and produce children of their own. For men, a successful reproductive strategy relied not so much upon quality as upon quantity. The predisposition to engage in sexual unions indiscriminately would have been favored by natural selection simply because it led to larger numbers of equally promiscuous (male) children.

These differences in reproductive strategy also help explain why men may be more likely than women to leave their partners for younger mates. A man's period of sexual potency is lengthy; by finding a younger partner, a man may extend his reproductive opportunities by ten to twenty years. On the other hand, switching mates does not in most cases increase a woman's reproductive potential. To the contrary, an older, more established male may increase a woman's survivability, as well as that of her children, while a younger partner lacking in social status may not have the capacity to provide adequate support for her family.

This bleak image of male evolutionary progress is not, however, the sole message of *The Moral Animal*. Because human children have a prolonged period of vulnerability, men who are predisposed toward greater "parental investment" increase the likelihood that their offspring will survive. In addition, the greater sexual selectivity of females means that men's willingness to care for children may increase their possibilities of finding willing sexual partners. As a result, in comparison to other species—even other primates—human males show relatively high degrees of loyalty to mate and offspring.

The process of evolution also provides Wright with a theory for understanding such baffling social phenomena as the sexual double standard and what he calls the "Madonna-whore dichotomy." The resources required to nurture children are scarce, making it counterproductive for men to squander parental investment on children who are not their own. For this reason, Wright argues that men tend to divide women into "good girls" and "bad girls." Good girls or "Madonnas" are those who succumb to sex only after a long period of courtship; since they are unlikely to engage in sexual experimentation, men will presume that their children are legitimate and worthy of a high investment of resources. Bad girls or "whores" are those who have been easy sexual conquests; in the ancestral environment, men may have been uncertain about the legitimacy of their children and thus unlikely to invest heavily in relationships with such women.

Wright also suggests that men tend to be angered primarily by a spouse's sexual infidelity: Once again, a woman's sexual disloyalty casts the legitimacy of a man's children into doubt and may render his parental investment meaningless. Women, on the other hand, tend to be more disturbed by a spouse's emotional infidelity: Falling in love with someone else means that a man is unlikely to continue his high degree of investment in the earlier relationship. Thus, for much of human history, the greatest disgrace for a man was to be a cuckold; the greatest disgrace for a woman was to be a whore. For critics who regard the differences between the sexes as resulting from social norms rather than from nature, these aspects of Wright's argument raise several disturbing questions.

A more compelling section of *The Moral Animal* is Wright's discussion of the universality of class distinctions throughout human societies. Even in those cultures that have claimed complete indifference to struggles for rank, Wright demonstrates that class distinctions do exist—even if superiority is achieved in them only through indifference to one's own superiority. Hierarchies, Wright demonstrates, may be found among all the higher primates. It would be extremely unusual, therefore, for human societies to lack these structures. Moreover, since in other species males of high status regularly have increased opportunities for sex, the impulse to attain higher rank was all but certain to have been favored by natural selection.

Competition for resources affects a wide variety of human activities. Wright argues, for example, that sibling rivalry may have had its origin in the competition of infants for parental care and nourishment. Sibling affection, on the other hand, seems to arise from the tendency of all humans to protect members of their own kinship group. While male competition for resources results from a desire for status and its consequent increase in sexual opportunities, female competitiveness may have originated in the struggles of women to secure the attention of those males who command resources that may be shared with their offspring.

The positive aspects of human behavior are attributed by Wright to "reciprocal altruism" or, in his unnecessarily awkward coinage, "non-zero-sumness." Altruism in Wright's model results from the observation that it was in one's own interest to treat others kindly in the ancestral environment. Within the kinship group itself, benevolence enhanced the survivability of close relatives, who, after all, shared a significant portion of one's own genetic material. In the larger community, favors were rendered to others in the hope that these acts of kindness would be returned when assistance was needed by oneself or one's offspring. When expected favors are not offered, however, the selfish individual may be punished with great vehemence. In this way, Wright explains both the ostracism inflicted upon those who commit even minor lapses in small communities and the tendency of human beings to gossip about others who cheat or take advantage of the less fortunate.

One of the weakest sections of *The Moral Animal* is the part that explains the book's title. While sociobiology could be regarded as lending support to ethical systems ranging from ancient Epicureanism to modern existentialism, Wright explores only the foundation that evolution provides to nineteenth century utilitarianism. His efforts to soften what he himself admits is a cynical view of the human condition seem halfhearted at best. He argues that the reciprocal altruism once extended only to the kinship group and the local community can be developed to include an entire nation-state (as it is in many countries today) and ultimately to the whole of humanity.

In the end, Wright's arguments on this point seem labored, unconvincing, and wholly unnecessary. If the evolutionary progress of the human race has resulted in parts of the brain that merely predispose one to certain behaviors, then why regard people as genetically compelled to do anything? Wright's view that individuals may resist innate tendencies for the sake of a greater moral good is, in the end, very little different from what an earlier age would have interpreted as resisting the temptations of one's "animal instincts." Thus Wright's genetic predisposition, like Faust's devil, may urge one to indulge in all manner of (currently) inappropriate behaviors, but it cannot force a person to engage in any particular behavior. People are still free to follow any ethical doctrine that they choose.

A second weakness of *The Moral Animal* is the author's highly conversational style. His frequent use of parenthetical expressions is distracting and makes the text seem disjointed. His reliance on colloquial terms, such as "kids" for "children" and "jibes with" for "corresponds to," seems strangely out of place in a book that claims to be a serious piece of scholarship. Wright's argument would be stronger if he had eliminated the chatty effusions that, all too often, undermine the very points he is attempting to make.

A final weakness of the work is Wright's repeated use of Charles Darwin as an example of both the values represented by the Victorian Age and the reproductive strategies of Everyman. If, as Wright has argued, genetic factors do not determine one's behavior but merely produce certain tendencies, it is highly unlikely that any one individual would embody all the patterns that he discusses. On the contrary, predisposed behaviors should be detectable only statistically, as researchers examine evidence transcending historical periods, cultures, differences in social class, and the unique features that are found in the life of any one human being. By turning repeatedly to Darwin's own life and career for evidence to support his theories, Wright narrows the focus of what could have been an analysis broad enough to include the entire human race.

Nevertheless, the strengths of Wright's argument transcend these flaws. *The Moral Animal* is a highly readable account of evolutionary theory for the general reader who wishes to explore possible explanations for human behavior that seems at times self-destructive, futile, or simply inexplicable.

Jeffrey L. Buller

Sources for Further Study

Booklist. September 15, 1994, p. 86.
Boston Globe. October 23, 1994, p. 17.
The Economist. CCCXXXIII, November 5, 1994, p. 89.
Library Journal. CXIX, August, 1994, p. 109.
Los Angeles Times Book Review. September 4, 1994, p. 4.

The Nation. CCLIX, November 28, 1994, p. 662.
The New York Times Book Review. XCIX, September 25, 1994, p. 3.
The New Yorker. LXX, September 12, 1994, p. 37.
Publishers Weekly. CCXLI, July 25, 1994, p. 38.
The Wall Street Journal. September 22, 1994, p. A8.

MOUNTAIN OF FAME
Portraits in Chinese History

Author: John E. Wills, Jr. (1936-   )
Publisher: Princeton University Press (Princeton, New Jersey). Illustrated. 403 pp. $24.95
Type of work: History
Time: About 2000 B.C. to 1989
Locale: Mainland China

An attempt to show the meaning of Chinese history through the biographies of persons who played influential roles in its stirring drama, especially in the light of their moral character and capability

In *Mountain of Fame: Portraits in Chinese History*, John E. Wills, Jr., professor of history at the University of Southern California, takes a "lives-and-times" approach that was used in China as early as the second century B.C. by the famous "Grand Historian," Sima Qian. Later Chinese dynastic histories followed the same model, using biographies of eminent persons who influenced the historical process for good or ill.

As to historiography in the West, Thomas Carlyle proclaimed, "The history of the world is but the biography of great men." Thus he wrote *Heroes and Hero Worship* (1841). Ralph Waldo Emerson considered the importance of "eminent men," and he meant that in his title *Representative Men* (1850). Finally, Friedrich Nietzsche developed the concept of *die monumental Geschichte* (monumental history), by which he meant the study of past heroes who could show that human beings are capable of greatness despite the general mediocrity of the masses.

That Wills's "slice-of-life" history is not a new technique is not a discredit to him. What counts is how effectively he uses this traditional form to achieve a sense that history and the significant individual constitute a total living organism, which is what is historically significant. The biographic technique particularly appeals to the reader's moral judgment, but the writing of it must have an aesthetic purpose if it is to be part of literature.

Wills begins where most cultural history usually begins—in the "misty mid region" of mythology. Mythology is important, for it is the symbolic code of a people's existence and imagination. In this realm, persons may be few and animals many. In China, the earliest human beings tend to be half animal, yet they may be gods or semidivine. The demigods seem to be the ones who prepare the chaotic earth for human habitation and a name.

Thus Wills presents the mythical "Three Sovereigns": Fu-xi, who has the body of a serpent or dragon; Shen-nong, who has the head of an ox; and Huang-di, the "Yellow Lord," who has a man's body but whose color is that of the China earth. Fu-xi taught human beings how to hunt and fish, to domesticate animals, and to breed silkworms. He invented the trigrams that formed the basis of Chinese script. He also urged official and permanent marriage. His wife, Nu-gua, invented many feminine arts. Huang-di has no animalistic body parts and appears simply as the Earth Father. This mythology shows that the early Chinese imagination was strongly biological, energetic, and animalistic, but it strove to humanize itself as if to contradict some future theory that human beings are nothing but animals.

As a complete human being, Huang-di was third in the line of the first "Five Emperors" of China. He was a strong military leader; having invented the magnetic compass, he used it in a dense fog to locate his enemy. Wills then presents the "Three Rulers" of China's "Golden Age," or the time of the Zhou Dynasty, which began about 1027 B.C.: Yao, Shun, and Yu. Yao regulated the calendar and adopted the "Five Punishments," from branding to beheading. Shun instituted triennial government examinations and allowed banishment to be substituted for some severer punishments. Yu, called "Yu the Great," became the founder and first emperor of the Xia Dynasty and ascended the throne in about 2205 B.C. The Chinese people idealized the reigns of the Three Rulers; their Golden Age became a historical model toward which later regimes were expected to aspire.

The teachings of Confucius (Latin for Kong Fuzi), who flourished 476 B.C., were based on his "idealization of the past" and "rooted in reality and in ideas," as Wills says, that had developed five hundred years previously. In fact, Confucius claimed no originality for himself, declaring that he was merely a transmitter of tradition. His teachings were gradually adopted by the vast majority of Chinese people and were maintained from his time into the first decade of the twentieth century. Wills manages to convey the essence of Confucius the man with a simple story. The disciple Zi Lu told Confucius that the governor had asked him about his master and he had been unsure what to say. Confucius said, "Why didn't you simply say something like this: He is the sort of man who forgets to eat when he tries to solve a problem that has been driving him to distraction, who is so full of joy that he forgets his worries and who does not notice that old age is coming on?"

Shihuang-di, the first emperor of the Qin Dynasty (221-207 B.C.), was a man of fierce energy, iron will, and sharp individuality. He conquered six opposing states and then unified China into a single empire. He abolished the feudal system and centralized the government. He linked together some segments of the Great Wall that had been built earlier. When Confucian scholars resented the emperor's innovations, he burned their books. With the death of Shihuang-di in 210 B.C., however, Qin totalitarianism passed away.

Sima Qian (145-c. 70 B.C.) was the author of the first comprehensive history of China and hence was China's Herodotus. In his *Shi Ji* (c. 90 B.C., records of the historian), he left his autobiography, and in the body of work he included the biographies of many individuals as well as topically organized collective biographies.

Two critical events served to shape Sima Qian's life. He was the son of the regime's grand astrologer, Sima Tan, and inherited his tasks. The most important project was the comprehensive history of China that his father had started just before his last illness. After the three-year filial mourning period had passed, Sima Qian gained access to the official records of the regime. The second critical event occurred as the result of Sima Qian's spirited defense of a military general, Li Ling, who had fiercely angered Emperor Wu by allowing himself to be captured alive by the Hsiung-nu tribesmen. Sima Qian was found guilty of "defaming the emperor" and was subjected to the humiliation of castration, a condition that embittered him the rest of his life. Upon recovery, however, he resumed his historiography.

Wang Mang (33 B.C.-A.D. 23) was the nephew of the consort of an emperor of the Han Dynasty. Although he was in no way a possible successor to the throne, he nevertheless aspired to sit on it. Through the clever and ruthless manipulation of his relatives together with the support of the empress dowager, he managed to proclaim himself emperor. Ever afterward, however, he was known as "the Usurper." According to Wills, however, Wang appeared sincerely committed to Confucian ideals. He sought "to realize his dream of an institutionalized Zhou revival." Yet excesses and conflicts of various kinds occurred in the course of Wang's reign, so that he was killed in a revolt of his own troops.

The individuals mentioned so far are covered in the first five chapters of Wills's book. Despite a reserved style, Wills provokes sufficient interest to get readers involved. He is particularly effective in his pieces on Confucius and Sima Qian because he brings to the surface not only each man's ideals and aspirations but also each one's disappointments and sufferings.

In the body of his book—the next ten chapters—Wills presents portraits of the following: Ban Zhao (A.D. 52?-120?), a distinguished female scholar-poet; Zhuge Liang (A.D. 181-234), a wise and resourceful minister and military adviser to Liu Bei, King of Shu in the Three Kingdoms period; Hui Nêng (d. A.D. 713), Sixth Patriarch of Chan (or Zen) Buddhism and author of the Platform Sutra; Empress Wu Fu (reigned A.D. 690-705), a ruthless ruler and nymphomaniac; Su Dongpo (real name Su Shih; 1036-1102), a great poet, master of the prose *fu*, calligrapher, and modest statesman; Yue Fei (1103-1141), an outstanding military man; Qin Chiji (1148-1227), a wise and pious Daoist (Taoist) monk; Wang Yang-ming (1472-1529), a distinguished prose writer, poet, neo-Confucian philosopher, and scholar-official; Zheng Chenggong (1624-1662), a fierce rebel opposed to the Manchu Qing Dynasty; Qianlong, a majestic Ch'ing emperor (reigned 1736-1795), a great patron of the arts, and a poet in his own right.

The portraits of this middle group range from sparkling to bland. The sketch "Hui Neng" is among the latter. Although this Chan patriarch's calmness and wisdom are described competently, his inner spiritual strength is not captured; in Wills's treatment he is more a demonstrative puppet than a living force. In contrast, the priest Qui Chuji is rendered with great effectiveness—psychologically, religiously, and aesthetically. This superb portrait is biographical history at its best.

Chinese tradition considers Zhuge Liang the perfect prime minister and military adviser. He became attached to the adventurer and scion of the Han ruling family, Liu Bei, whom he made king of Shu and guided in his contentions with other rulers. As a military adviser, he became notable for his use of the Eight Locked Gate Maze. As a consequence of his stellar performance, he was called the "Sleeping Dragon" and "Great Brightness." As long as Liu Bei followed the advice of Zhuge Liang, he was very successful. When his passion for revenge got the better of his judgment, however, he failed to heed his minister's advice, a negligence that brought about his own defeat and death.

Zhuge Liang, Liu Bei, and the latter's sworn brothers, Guan Yu and Zhang Fei, are of special interest because they have fictional counterparts who are idealized and romanticized in perhaps the first Chinese historical romance, the *San-quo zhi yan yi* (*The Romance of the Three Kingdoms*), attributed to Le Guon-chung, who lived 1330-1400. This military romance with its idealized characters or heroes set in the period of the Three Kingdoms is comparable to Alexandre Dumas père's *Les Trois Mousquetaires* (1844; *The Three Musketeers*, 1846). Although the characterizations and events of *The Romance of the Three Kingdoms* do not always conform with the historical sources, the work remains an indispensable source for understanding the traditional Chinese mind. Mao Zedong, Wills says, may have been "more deeply shaped by it than by Marx and Lenin."

Wu Zhao was brought into Emperor Gaozong's harem as a concubine, and soon the emperor had eyes only for her. She bore him a child. Scheming to get rid of Empress Wang, she smothered her own baby and accused the empress of the murder. Gaozong believed her. Then she accused the empress and another concubine of plotting to poison the emperor, and she ordered that their hands and feet be cut off and their bodies thrown into a wine vat. Gaozong made her Empress Wu.

As Empress Wu she dominated the government while Gaozong lived (he died in 683) and later, while first one of her sons and then another held the title of emperor. Finally she declared her own dynasty and exercised full imperial power. After the death of Gaozong, her enormous sexual appetite came to the fore. She took her pharmacist as her lover; he furnished her with aphrodisiacs, and she made him a monk and installed him as an abbot of a Buddhist monastery. Later she took a new lover, a court physician. At the age of seventy, she took two lovers in their twenties, the Zhang brothers, who made the court a place of fun and games. They so threatened the stability of the government that high officials finally took action and deposed Empress Wu in 705.

Wills examines Empress Wu within the framework of history with impressive skill. Yet his effort to be her apologist, especially when making her the victim of "male prejudice against active female participation in government" in seventh century China, is rather off the mark, a reverse anachronism.

Wills concludes his book with five chapters that begin with the Taiping Rebellion (1850-1864) and end with the Tiananmen Square fracas in Beijing in 1989. This section includes portraits of Sun Yat-sen, Chiang Kai-shek, Mao Zedong, Deng Xiaoping, and a number of other figures. Here Wills succeeds best with his treatment of two revolutionary anti-Manchu opponents, the young student Zou Rong and his older scholar companion Zhang Binlin, who were members of the Patriotic School of Shanghai at the turn of the century. The first was the author of a manifesto to inspire revolutionary ardor in China's youth, published in 1903. It urges the Chinese to "sweep away millennia of despotism in all its forms, throw off millennia of slavishness, annihilate the five million and more of the furry and horned Manchu race." The two men's revolutionary fervor, however, was cooled by their arrest and imprisonment. In prison, Zhang Binlin wryly remarked to Zou Rong, "We scholars don't have enough strength to tie up a chicken." Zou Rong died in prison in 1905, but the older Zhang survived.

Unfortunately, what otherwise are mostly fine essays on Liang Qichao, Chiang Kai-shek, and Mao Zedong lack lively details of their speech and relationships; the sketches of the latter two deal entirely with public image and lack any kind of moral judgment. For example, it is known that Chiang Kai-shek had a volatile temperament, that he could be ruthlessly cruel, and that he was a practiced lecher. Wills does succeed in showing the human side of Mao Zedong in public life. The suffering and death Mao caused by the Great Leap Forward, whose disruption of agriculture caused at least twenty million deaths from starvation, and the Cultural Revolution, in which the Red Guards killed many people and imprisoned many more, are recorded by Wills without comment.

On the whole, however, Wills's sweep of five thousand years of Chinese history through biographical sketches of twenty or more eminent persons is done with competence and finesse and reveals the keys to understanding China in terms of Confucian ethics, the emperor-minister relationship, and the idea of the Mandate of Heaven. His fine book is well worth reading and should achieve its intended purpose.

Richard P. Benton

Sources for Further Study

Library Journal. CXIX, September 1, 1994, p. 198.

The New York Times Book Review. XCIX, October 30, 1994, p. 43.

DUE	RETURNED	DUE	RETURNED
1.		13.	
2.		14.	
3.		15.	
4.		16.	
5.		17.	
6.		18.	
7.		19.	
8.		20.	
9.		21.	
10.		22.	
11.		23.	
12.		24.